Welcome **PAUL FERGUSON**

Welcome to the 27th edition of the Weatherbys Cheltenham Festival Betting Guide, which is once again br[ought to] you in association with Hollyw[ood Bets].

WHILST the Guide has been in existence for much longer, this is my eighth year at the helm and the hope is that you find it more of a rounded publication these days. As ever, each and every race at this year's Festival is covered from a statistical and trends perspective, whilst I have attempted to add – with the help of some familiar names – more editorial in recent years.

The ever eloquent Rory Delargy tackles the *Banker Or Bust* section, with daily selections from Sam Turner (Daily Mail & Racing TV) and Jodie Standing, author of the excellent Point-to-Point Recruits. Jess Stafford (Racing TV) is back with her *Breeding Angles* feature, whilst *The Irish View* has once again been penned by Donn McClean (Sunday Times & Racing TV), with the *Foreword* kindly written by leading commentator, Richard Hoiles.

And, for a second year, the duo responsible for Trackside, paddock judges Vicki Gibbins and Dave Massey, provide recent eye-catchers from the prelims. Many thanks go to all of this year's contributors, whilst that gratitude is extended to my colleagues in Weatherbys' head office, in particular Len Peacock, and to those photographers whose images have been used.

Aintree is covered, too. Each Grade 1, as well as the Grand National itself, whilst I have once again tackled

The [...] to r[...] *Spr[...]* E[...] k[...] forward to? A tantalising start, as Old Park Star bids to provide Nicky Henderson with a fourth Supreme since 2016 and a sixth win in the race in all. I am already looking forward to next year's Arkle with him in mind.

Whilst the Irish have dominated in recent years, it is refreshing to see so many British-trained runners prominently positioned in the market for the novice races, which bodes well for the future. Last year's Champion Bumper appears to be a form line which will be strongly tested during the week, with El Cairos and Idaho Sun set to tackle the Supreme, No Drama This End heads the betting for the Baring Bingham and, of course, the winner Bambino Fever looks to be a leading contender to land the Dawn Run.

As always, I hope you find this year's Guide an informative and thought-provoking read, which helps you in finding a winner or two throughout the four day fixture. And, maybe a couple at Aintree, for good measure.

Be lucky,
Paul.

Old Park Star

Contents

Welcome 1
Foreword 4
Cheltenham Festival Running Order 5
The Irish View 6
Breeding Angles 18
Trackside Paddock Notes 25
British Novice Hurdlers 27
Lulamba Out To Defy An Ageing Trend 29
The Bumper Division 110
Spring Horses To Follow 215
Fresh For Aintree 224
Randox Grand National Preview 284

CHELTENHAM - DAY 1

Sky Bet Supreme Novices' Hurdle 30
Singer Arkle Challenge Trophy Novices' Chase 36
Hallgarten And Novum Wines Juvenile
Handicap Hurdle (Fred Winter) 42
Ultima Handicap Chase 46
Unibet Champion Hurdle 50
TrustATrader Plate Handicap Chase 56
Princess Royal National Hunt Challenge
Cup Novices' Handicap Chase 60
Daily Tips (Part I) 62
Banker Or Bust 65
Daily Tips (Part II) 68

CHELTENHAM - DAY 2

Turners (Baring Bingham) Novices' Hurdle 72
Brown Advisory (Broadway) Novices' Chase 78
Coral Cup Handicap Hurdle 86
Glenfarclas Cross-Country Chase 90
betMGM Queen Mother Champion Chase 94
Debenhams Johnny Henderson Grand Annual
Handicap Chase 100
Weatherbys Champion Bumper 104
Daily Tips (Part I) 114
Banker Or Bust 117
Daily Tips (Part II) 120

CHELTENHAM - DAY 3

Ryanair (Dawn Run) Mares' Novices' Hurdle 124
Jack Richards (Golden Miller) Novices' H'cap Chase 128
Close Brothers Mares' Hurdle 132
Paddy Power Stayers' Hurdle 138
Ryanair Chase 144
Pertemps Network Final Handicap Hurdle 150
Rosconn Group Fulke Walwyn
Kim Muir Challenge Cup 154
Daily Tips (Part I) 158
Banker Or Bust 161
Daily Tips (Part II) 164

CHELTENHAM - DAY 4

JCB Triumph Hurdle 168
William Hill County Handicap Hurdle 174
Mrs Paddy Power Mares' Chase 178
Albert Bartlett (Spa) Novices' Hurdle 182
Boodles Cheltenham Gold Cup 188
St James's Place Festival Challenge Cup Hunters' Chase 196
Martin Pipe Conditional Jockeys' Handicap Hurdle 200
Daily Tips (Part I) 206
Banker Or Bust 209
Daily Tips (Part II) 212

AINTREE - DAY 1

William Hill Manifesto Novices' Chase 228
Boodles Anniversary 4-Y-O Juvenile Hurdle 234
Bowl Chase 238
William Hill Aintree Hurdle 242

AINTREE - DAY 2

William Hill Mildmay Novices' Chase 248
Top Novices' Hurdle 252
JCB Melling Chase 256
Oddschecker Sefton Novices' Hurdle 260

AINTREE - DAY 3

Turners Mersey Novices' Hurdle 264
Liverpool Hurdle 268
Hallgarten Maghull Novices' Chase 272
Randox Grand National 276

GRIMTHORPE CHASE
FRI 27 & SAT 28 FEB

THE ULTIMATE ENDURANCE TEST
19 JUMPS | 3 MILES | 2 FURLONGS

18+ Bet Responsibly. GambleAware.org.

Foreword
RICHARD HOILES

IT WAS a pilgrimage every September I would make with my Mum. Dragging her to the Sports Book section of W H Smith every day to see if the one copy each branch got of the National Hunt Superform Annual had arrived. It was a hefty tome covering the jumps season that had just ended and was filled with its own magical language of in running comments, *'al prom k.o well'* along with some basic analytics of a horse's career to date.

The frisson of excitement of spying its arrival and being the first to claim the sole copy is quite possibly the same that others now feel about the arrival of the 27th Cheltenham Festival Betting Guide. Times have changed, whereas once the transferring of the data from the latest Superform edition to my lovingly kept index cards could reveal secrets of a horse's ability to perform to its best, whether it be trip, handicap ceiling, ground or track, nowadays those previously obscure facts are there for all to see at the click of a mouse.

The march of time and technology means there is no longer a Superform annual (and soon no W H Smith on the High Street!). It, along with many of the paper based form books, has not withstood the march of the electronic age yet the Festival Guide continues to set the pace in its field both in physical and now digital form. The reason has been its ability to move with the times. In the early editions a single uncovered fact regarding data trends was revolutionary whereas now in a world where there can be information overload, it is sifting the wheat from the chaff that becomes the challenge.

Statistics are not a silver bullet to success but their logical and considered application can be. The world did not stop turning when the Challow Hurdle winner (The New Lion) finally laid that Cheltenham Preview staple of being incapable of winning at the Festival but the reasoning that that Newbury victory occurred (like this season) on unseasonably fast ground more akin to conditions at Cheltenham in March enhanced the chances of it happening was discussed.

That type of critical analysis can be found in abundance with the comments from the many sharp minded contributors to this year's Guide as well as consideration of some of the less developed areas such as paddock and pedigree analysis which sets this Guide apart from the many that have tried to mimic it's success.

The thoughts and discussions it provokes can help crystallise, both positively and negatively, your own conclusions in trying to solve the 28 puzzles that make up the best four days of National Hunt racing anywhere in the world.

Enjoy this year's Guide. The answers as always are somewhere in its pages.

Richard.

Cheltenham Festival Running Order

DAY 1 – CHAMPIONS DAY
TUESDAY 10TH MARCH (OLD COURSE)

1:20	Sky Bet Supreme Novices' Hurdle (Grade 1)
2:00	Singer Arkle Challenge Trophy Novices' Chase (Grade 1)
2:40	McCoy Contractors (Fred Winter) Juvenile Handicap Hurdle
3:20	Trustmarque Ultima Handicap Chase
4:00	Unibet Champion Hurdle (Grade 1)
4:40	TrustATrader Plate Handicap Chase
5:20	Princess Royal National Hunt Novices' Handicap Chase

DAY 2 – LADIES' DAY
WEDNESDAY 11TH MARCH (OLD COURSE)

1:20	Turners Novices' Hurdle (Grade 1)
2:00	Brown Advisory Novices' Chase (Grade 1)
2:40	Coral Cup Handicap Hurdle *
3:20	Glenfarclas Cross Country Handicap Chase
4:00	BetMGM Queen Mother Champion Chase (Grade 1)
4:40	Debenhams Johnny Henderson Grand Annual Handicap Chase
5:20	Weatherbys Champion Bumper (Grade 1) **

DAY 3 – ST PATRICK'S THURSDAY
THURSDAY 12TH MARCH (NEW COURSE)

1:20	Ryanair Mares' Novices' Hurdle (Grade 2)
2:00	Jack Richards Novices' Limited Handicap Chase
2:40	Close Brothers Mares' Hurdle (Grade 1)
3:20	Paddy Power Stayers' Hurdle (Grade 1)
4:00	Ryanair Chase (Grade 1)
4:40	Pertemps Network Final Handicap Hurdle
5:20	Rosconn Group Fulke Walwyn Kim Muir Amateur Jockeys' Handicap Chase

DAY 4 – GOLD CUP DAY
FRIDAY 13TH MARCH (NEW COURSE)

1:20	JCB Triumph Hurdle (Grade 1)
2:00	William Hill County Handicap Hurdle
2:40	Mrs Paddy Power Mares' Chase (Grade 2)
3:20	Albert Bartlett Novices' Hurdle (Grade 1)
4:00	Boodles Cheltenham Gold Cup (Grade 1)
4:40	St James's Place Festival Hunters' Chase
5:20	Martin Pipe Conditional Jockeys' Handicap Hurdle

---

* It was announced in late January that Coral was to end its 52-year sponsorship of the Coral Cup. At the time of going to print, a replacement sponsor had not been confirmed. Therefore, for the purposes of the race preview and other references to the race throughout the Guide, we have left the title as the Coral Cup.

** The 2026 Weatherbys Champion Bumper will be run in memory of Sir Johnny Weatherby, who sadly passed away in December at the age of 66.

The two races in question will – along with the Jack Richards Novices' Handicap Chase and the County Hurdle – see reduced fields go to post this year, with maximum permitted in all four being reduced by two runners. This will have an impact on those attempting to get in at the foot of the weights in those handicaps.

The other significant change ahead of the 2026 Festival is that the distance of the Broadway (Brown Advisory) Novices' Chase has been increased to 3m1f and will now be run over the same course-and-distance as the Ultima on day one. This has been detailed in the race preview.

The Irish View

BY DONN McCLEAN

Donn is chief racing writer with The Sunday Times (Ireland). A four-time nominee for the HWPA racing writer of the year award, he is a presenter and analyst on Racing TV and writes a weekly column for The Irish Field. He has ghost-written six racing autobiographies and is a regular contributor to Sporting Life.

CHAMPIONSHIP RACES

CHAMPION HURDLE

THERE was a point in the Irish Champion Hurdle at the Dublin Racing Festival at Leopardstown on the first day of February, just after they had raced through the wings of the omitted second last flight – we hadn't seen the sun in a while – when **Brighterdaysahead** moved up on the inside of the wilting El Fabiolo and Lossiemouth moved up on the outside.

This was the match that people had come to see. The re-match. The last time these two mares had met, in the December Hurdle at Leopardstown's Christmas Festival, Lossiemouth had come out on top. But that was Brighterdaysahead's seasonal debut, her first run since she was beaten in the Mares Champion Hurdle at Punchestown in May, her first run since Gordon Elliott and Gigginstown House decided that she would remain over hurdles this season.

The intention had been to go chasing with her, of course, but a slight setback delayed her chasing bow, then delayed it again, which took her into the teeth of the season. Late enough to be shedding your novice chasing status for a mare who was young enough to go novice chasing next season. Then they supplemented her for the December Hurdle. Then she finished second to Lossiemouth.

She only had a length to find on Willie Mullins' mare from Christmas, and the vibe from Cullentra was that she had improved for her seasonal debut, probably by more than the length by which she was beaten. In that instance, it was a question of how much more than that length did Lossiemouth have in hand.

We knew that the answer to that question was forthcoming when the two raced around the home turn in the Irish Champion Hurdle and squared up again. Two top-class mares, both seven years old, born within a couple of weeks of each other, both officially rated 159. They were rated to dead-heat.

They didn't dead-heat though. Not many horses do. From early in the Irish Champion Hurdle, Jack Kennedy on Brighterdaysahead appeared to be happier than Paul Townend on Lossiemouth, who just wasn't travelling or jumping with her habitual verve.

It was different to Christmas too. At Christmas, Lossiemouth sat in behind the leader and kicked for home first as Brighterdaysahead stalked. In the Irish Champion Hurdle, with her seasonal debut under her belt, Brighterdaysahead was ridden more forward by Jack Kennedy, in the leader's slipstream, with Lossiemouth stalking.

Then the run across the top of the track, through the wings of the second last flight, then the pincer movement with El Fabiolo in the middle.

Jack Kennedy got lower in the saddle as they wheeled around the home turn. Paul Townend did too. For a few strides, it was difficult to know which mare was travelling better when they straightened up for home, but Brighterdaysahead still had an advantage of a couple of lengths, and it appeared as if Lossiemouth wasn't getting any closer. As they approached the last, it looked like the Gigginstown House horse was actually extending her advantage. She jumped the last well and that was effectively that. She kept up gallantly up the hill and beat her old rival by just over three lengths. One-all.

That performance catapulted Brighterdaysahead to the top of the Champion Hurdle betting, and that makes sense. Level with The New Lion in most lists. In the back of your mind is the fact that she has been to Cheltenham twice, and she has been beaten twice. But there were excuses on both occasions, it may not have been down to the track. She deserves her place at the top of the market.

It may be that **Lossiemouth** will go for the Mares' Hurdle again now on the back of this defeat, bid to complete her hat-trick in that race. But she would still be a big player in the Champion Hurdle picture, should she finally take her chance in the race. It may be down to happenstance, but she has now won just two of her five races at Leopardstown. There may be nothing in it, but she has been beaten just four times in her life, and three of those four defeats were at Leopardstown. By contrast, she is four for four at Cheltenham.

Poniros stayed on to take third place in the Irish Champion Hurdle. Last year's Triumph Hurdle winner was racing for the first time since he finished down the field in the Ascot Stakes at the height of summer. He should come on for this, and he obviously goes well at Cheltenham, although we know how difficult it is for five-year-olds in the Champion Hurdle.

Anzadam was just caught by Poniros for third. He settled better here than he had in the December Hurdle, which was probably the main objective. He is only six and this was just his seventh race ever, so he retains plenty of scope for further progression. He should do better with this run under his belt, a faster pace and better ground should help him, and he could be a lively outsider.

GOLD CUP

HERE we go again. Maybe. Last year, the Irish Gold Cup produced the Cheltenham Gold Cup winner, a JP McManus horse who wasn't entered in the Cheltenham Gold Cup at the time.

Fact To File was seriously impressive in winning this year's Irish Gold Cup. He was rolling from early, just behind the leaders and popping away under Mark Walsh, who moved him towards the inside after Spindleberry jumped across him at the second fence.

He jumped his way there, joined the leaders at the fourth last fence and made his way from there. He led on the run to the home turn travelling well, and he stayed on strongly over the last and up the run-in.

He stayed too. That was the worry when he wheeled around the home turn, apparently travelling way better than his pursuers. But he was strong all the way to the line. He was faster than all his rivals through the final four furlongs and he was faster than all his rivals through the final furlong, at the end of which he had 5 lengths in hand over his stable companion Gaelic Warrior.

Second behind Galopin des Champs in the Savills Chase last season and third behind him in this race last year, Willie Mullins' horse was imperious in winning the Ryanair Chase last season over the intermediate trip, when he put up one of the most visually impressive performances of last season. He was even tried over 2m at Punchestown last April, he ran in the Champion Chase, not in the Punchestown Gold Cup.

But he is a Point-to-Point winner, and he won the Brown Advisory Chase at Cheltenham as a novice doing handsprings, and he stayed all right in the Irish Gold Cup. This is a performance that is all the way up there with his Ryanair Chase victory.

JP McManus' horse has never been beyond 3m½f, so we don't know for sure if he will get the extra two furlongs of the Cheltenham Gold Cup,

Fact To File was imperious in the Irish Gold Cup

but he wasn't stopping at the end of the Irish Gold Cup, so there is every chance that he will. And his record at Cheltenham reads 211, his only defeat coming in the Champion Bumper – he has never run over hurdles – when he finished second to A Dream To Share.

It would be highly unusual for an Irish Gold Cup winner not to run in the Cheltenham Gold Cup and, if he is supplement to the race, it goes without saying, he will be one of the leading players.

Galopin des Champs has been one of the leading players in the Gold Cup in each of the last three years, as evidenced by form figures in the race of 112. A setback meant that he missed his habitual date with the John Durkan Chase for his seasonal return. He had to make his debut instead in the Savills Chase at Leopardstown at Christmas, in which he put up a wholly admirable performance to finish third behind Affordale Fury.

But the magnitude of his progression from his first run to his second this season did not match the magnitude of his progression from his first run to his second in each of the last two seasons. He had to settle for third place in the Irish Gold Cup, same as in the Savills, his bid for an unprecedented four-in-a-row thwarted by his two younger stable companions.

He is still a player in the Gold Cup picture, of course. It may be that he will be able to improve again from his second run to his third this season, and, remember, he is trained by Willie Mullins. But he is 10 now, and still no 10-year-old has won the Cheltenham Gold Cup since Cool Dawn won it in 1998.

Last year's Gold Cup hero **Inothewayurthinkin** has been a shadow if his Gold Cup-winning self this season. You can easily allow him his run in the John Durkan Chase on his seasonal return, over a trip that was sharper than ideal, but you would have wanted to have seen much more from him in the Savills Chase and again in the Irish Gold Cup. It will be some training performance by Gavin Cromwell if he can get him back at concert pitch again on 13th March.

Spillane's Tower threw his hat back into the Gold Cup ring when he won the Cotswold Chase at Cheltenham in January. Of course, he is going to have to improve on the bare form of that run, beating the admirable 11-year-old L'Homme Presse by three parts of a length, getting 6lb, but he left the impression that he had a fair bit more in hand than that.

More importantly, Jimmy Mangan's horse retains the potential to go higher. He was a top-class novice chaser, a dual Grade 1 winner, and he was only just beaten by Fact To File in the 2024 John Durkan Chase, when he had Galopin des Champs over 2 lengths behind him.

This season's John Durkan Chase winner **Gaelic Warrior** will also be a big player in the Gold Cup picture, if he goes there and not to the Ryanair Chase. Winner of the Arkle as a novice, he won the Aintree Bowl in April and he was beaten a nose and a nose in that thrilling King George. He has 5 lengths to make up on Fact To File on their running in the Irish Gold Cup, but he had his stable companion a neck behind him when they finished first and second respectively – and a veritable distance clear of their rivals – in this season's John Durkan Chase.

Lively big outsiders? Maybe **Lecky Watson**. He will have to leave this season's form behind, and he could be more a Grand National project now than a Gold Cup project, but he does go well at Cheltenham, and he was under-rated when he won the Brown Advisory Chase last year.

QUEEN MOTHER CHAMPION CHASE

MAJBOROUGH was brilliant in winning the Dublin Chase at the eponymous racing festival. Cheekpieces on for the first time and Mark Walsh just let him roll. He did everything. He jumped, he travelled, he put his rivals to the sword early, and he careered away to win by 19 lengths.

The Triumph Hurdle winner from 2024, JP McManus' horse won the Irish Arkle at last year's Dublin Racing Festival, and he was sent off at prohibitive odds for the Arkle at Cheltenham, but his jumping undid him. He made a significant mistake at the fourth last fence, the final ditch, and he made a much worse and more high-profile mistake at the second last, after which, not helped by another mistake at the last, he did remarkably well to get back up again and finish third. It is probable that, had it not been for that mistake, he would have won the Arkle too. Just shows you, the engine that he has.

It has taken him a couple of runs this season. He was beaten by Found A Fifty in the Hilly Way Chase and he was beaten by Solness and Marine Nationale in the Paddy's Rewards Club Chase. But this was the real Majborough. This was all his talent and pace and class. His jumping was straight too, not out to his left, as he had been in the past, and he just came further and further away from his rivals. According RaceiQ, he was 2.4secs faster than his fastest rival through the final four furlongs.

It may be exclusively down to the cheekpieces, or it may be down to a sense of maturity, aided by the cheekpieces. Either way, you can be sure that he will have the cheekpieces on again at Cheltenham. He is only six, and there could be even more to come from him.

The reigning champion **Marine Nationale** stuck to his task well to take second place behind Majborough in the Dublin Chase. Barry Connell's horse was beaten too in the Dublin Chase last year, and he bounced out of that to win the Champion Chase by 18 lengths.

That was just his second run at Cheltenham, and it was his second win. A Supreme Novices' Hurdle and a Champion Chase, check, check.

The soft ground at Leopardstown would not have been in his favour. We know that the chase track dries out quickly at the Foxrock track, but it was unraceable the day before the Dublin Chase was run this year, and the times tell us that the ground was soft, and that is not Marine Nationale at all. It was his class and his determination that took him into second place, just in front of Found A Fifty. He could improve significantly on this at Cheltenham on better ground.

The **Il Etait Temps** bubble was deflated somewhat at Ascot in January. He was a beaten horse in the Clarence House Chase when he came down at the second last fence. But that obviously wasn't his running. Before he ran at Ascot, he was installed as favourite for the Champion Chase as he had beaten Jonbon pointless in the Tingle Creek.

Cheltenham was a worry before Ascot though, and it remains a worry. In three runs there, he has never won and he has never been at his best. As with Brighterdaysahead, it may be that there were extraneous variables at play, but he still has to prove that he is a Cheltenham horse.

Quilixios is the forgotten horse of the piece. He was almost certainly booked for second place in last year's renewal when he came down at the final fence, but he still would have finished closest by far to Marine Nationale.

He hasn't run since then, and he is nine now, but he has raced just nine times over fences. Also, he goes well fresh, his record after a break of 90 days or more reads 111211. The 2021 Triumph Hurdle winner, we know that he can operate at Cheltenham, and we know how well Henry de Bromhead's horses go there.

STAYERS' HURDLE

BOB OLINGER notched up another Stayers' Hurdle for the older brigade last year. That's two of the last three renewals now that have been won by a horse aged in double figures.

Before Sire du Berlais won the Stayers' Hurdle in 2023, you had to go back to 1986, to Crimson Embers, who was recording his second win in the race, to find the last horse aged older than nine to win it, four years after he had won his first.

Bob Olinger was brilliant last year under a superb ride from Rachael Blackmore, who smuggled him into the race and delivered him late, used the turn of foot that he still possessed as a 10-year-old, a horse whose stamina for a strongly-run 3m was still in doubt.

Il Etait Temps has yet to prove himself at Cheltenham

Bob Olinger is 11 now, but Sire du Berlais won it as an 11-year-old, and Henry de Bromhead's horse proved that he retained all his enthusiasm when he finished second behind Teahupoo in the Christmas Hurdle at Leopardstown at, well, Christmas.

It was a 1-2 for Brian Acheson's Robcour operation in the Stayers' Hurdle last year, with **Teahupoo** just giving best to Bob Olinger on the run-in and the pair of them pulling well clear of their rivals. You have to feel for Teahupoo who, if the ball had hopped a little more kindly for him in Stayers' Hurdles past, could be a three-time winner.

As it is, Gordon Elliott's horse has finished placed in two and won one, the 2024 renewal, and he looks as good as ever this year. He just got home by a nose from Ballyburn in the Hatton's Grace Hurdle on his debut this season, his third win in the Hatton's Grace, and he confirmed and extended his superiority over that rival in the Christmas Hurdle, when Bob Olinger split the pair of them. The plan was always for him to go straight to Cheltenham from the Christmas Hurdle and you can be sure that he will be a big player in the race again. And he proved at Leopardstown that he is not as dependent on soft ground as was once thought.

Even outside of Teahupoo, Gordon Elliott has a really strong hand again this year in a race that he has won three times in the last four years. **Honesty Policy** has morphed into a genuine contender. Winner of the Grade 1 Mersey Novices' Hurdle at Aintree in April over 2m4f on just his fourth run over hurdles, he ran a massive race in the Long Walk Hurdle at Ascot on his debut this season.

Sent off as favourite that day, in front of Impose Toi and Strong Leader, he came under a ride at the top of the home straight, but he found lots for pressure to keep on to take a close-up third behind those two rivals. He saw out the 3m trip well and, a six-year-old who has raced just six times over hurdles, he could improve considerably from Ascot to Cheltenham.

The evergreen **Home By The Lee** proved that he retained all his enthusiasm for racing when he won the Galmoy Hurdle at Gowran Park in January, and Joseph O'Brien's horse is another 11-year-old who could have a say, and we know that **Ballyburn** has the talent to run a big race on his day. **The Yellow Clay** has been beaten in each of his two runs this season but, second behind The New Lion and in front of Final Demand in the Turners Hurdle last year, he would be a lively outsider if he could bounce back to his best. He should stay the trip all right. He could improve for it.

RYANAIR CHASE

IT'S the perennial conundrum with the Ryanair Chase: who is going to eschew the Gold Cup and the Champion Chase and line up here?

We thought that **Fact To File** was all set for the Ryanair, he was a banker to line up in Thursday's race, it was his only entry at the meeting, but then he goes and wins the Irish Gold Cup, and there's all this talk about supplementing him for the Gold Cup.

Gaelic Warrior could run in the Ryanair, the Arkle winner, the John Durkan Chase winner, but he is also the Aintree Bowl winner, and he ran a big race in the Irish Gold Cup, so the Gold Cup has to be a big possibility too.

Banbridge could run in the Ryanair, or he could run in the Gold Cup, or he could wait for Aintree. Joseph O'Brien's horse was desperately unlucky not to win his second King George in December, beaten by the bob of The Jukebox Man's head. He was well beaten at the Cheltenham Festival in each of the last two seasons, and this hypothesis that he is not a Cheltenham horse appears to have gained traction. But he was never travelling in the Gold Cup last year, and the ground was too soft for him in the Ryanair Chase in 2024. His two previous runs at Cheltenham were in the Martin Pipe Hurdle in 2022, which he won, and in the Arkle Trial the following November, which he also won. It's difficult to argue that he is not a Cheltenham horse. He just needs decent ground.

Romeo Coolio could run in the Ryanair, or he could run in the Arkle or the Brown Advisory Chase. Unusual. That's an unusual combination of Cheltenham Festival entries, but that's Romeo Coolio for you, a novice whose optimum trip for now anyway is probably two and a half miles.

That said, Gordon Elliott's horse was good in winning the Racing Post Novice Chase at Leopardstown over Christmas, and he just got home by a neck from Kargese in the Irish Arkle, both over an extended two miles. And it looks like connections are inclined to stick to the novice route, so it could be the Arkle for him. More about him anon.

Heart Wood looks set for the Ryanair, and he is a player in the race. Second to Fact To File in last year's renewal, Henry de Bromhead's horse was well beaten in the John Durkan Chase, but then, most horses were well beaten in this season's John Durkan Chase. Heart Wood was much better in the New Year's Day Chase at Tramore, when he made just about all the running and ran out an impressive winner. A stiff two and a half miles suits him well.

NOVICE CHASERS

ARKLE TROPHY

IT IS not ideal that **Kopek des Bordes** missed the Dublin Racing Festival. It now looks like he is going to be lining up in the Arkle with just one run over fences in public under his belt.

Well Chief did it, won the Arkle after just one run over fences. Western Warhorse did it. But Well Chief had been running over hurdles earlier in the 2003/04 season too. Runner-up in the Triumph Hurdle as a juvenile, he won the Elite Hurdle in November 2003 and he won the Gerry Feilden Hurdle later that month, before winning on his chasing debut at Taunton in February. Then he beat Kicking King in the Arkle, as a five-year-old, getting 4lb then.

Western Warhorse was similar in 2013/14, but he was quite different too. He was well beaten in the conditional jockeys' handicap hurdle at Cheltenham's November meeting on his return that season, and he finished sixth in a Pertemps qualifier at Newbury's Hennessy Gold Cup meeting. He actually missed his intended chasing debut, at Kempton on King George day, after he unseated his rider and bolted before the start. Then he went to Doncaster in early January and scraped home on his chasing debut. Then he won the Arkle, in a first-time hood, returned at an SP of 33/1 which could have been twice that.

Kopek des Bordes has plenty of other elements in his favour though as an Arkle candidate. He was a top-class novice hurdler last season, he won the Grade 1 Tattersalls Ireland Novice Hurdle at the Dublin Racing Festival, and he won the Supreme Novices' Hurdle at Cheltenham, beating William Munny and Romeo Coolio, the three of them clear.

He looked really good on his chasing debut at Navan in November too. He warmed to his task nicely, his jumping was good, getting better as the race developed, and he sauntered to victory, 13 lengths clear of the runner-up Lovely Hurling, a 145-rated hurdler and an untried hurler, and all the way through the winning line.

The No Risk At All gelding lacks experience for sure. He ran in just one bumper and in just four hurdle races before he made his debut over fences. He is a serious talent though, and he is trained by Willie Mullins.

Romeo Coolio is also a serious talent. Third in the Supreme Novices' Hurdle at Cheltenham last season and second in the Top Novices' Hurdle at Aintree, he is even better over fences than over hurdles. His jumping makes him so.

Gordon Elliott's horse has raced four times over fences, and he has won four times. Impressive in winning the Grade 1 Drinmore Chase at Fairyhouse in November over 2m4f, he dropped down in trip

There was little between Romeo Coolio (right) and Kargese in the Irish Arkle

and won the Grade 1 Racing Post Novice Chase at Leopardstown's Christmas Festival, when he needed every yard of the 2m1f trip to get up and catch Irish Panther. Then he went to the Dublin Racing Festival and beat Kargese in the Irish Arkle. Just.

A trip just shy of two miles on the Old Course at Cheltenham on good to soft ground presents a test that is almost certainly sharper than ideal for the Kayf Tara gelding. Racing Post standard time for 2m1f at Leopardstown is 4mins 5secs. Standard time for the minimum distance on the Old Course at Cheltenham is 3mins 52secs. He does have the option of stepping right up in trip to an extended three miles for the Brown Advisory Chase, and he also has the option of stepping into open company for the Ryanair Chase over the intermediate trip. None of the three options is ideal, but it may be that he will run in the Arkle before stepping up in trip next season.

Kargese only has a neck to find on Romeo Coolio on their running at the Dublin Racing Festival, and there is every chance that she will find that. A momentum-halting mistake at the final fence didn't help her there, but she showed a lot of grit and tenacity to close to within a neck of the winner by they got to the winning line. Three strides after the line she was up.

Willie Mullins' mare was top-class as a hurdler. Winner of the Grade 1 Spring Juvenile Hurdle at the Dublin Racing Festival, she gave Majborough a real race in the Triumph Hurdle, with the pair of them clear of their rivals, and she won the Champion Four-Year-Old Hurdle at the Punchestown Festival. Last season, she went back to Cheltenham and won the County Hurdle.

She was well beaten by Kala Conti on her debut this season, but she progressed significantly from there, she beat Lovely Hurling at Leopardstown at Christmas with as much authority as that with which Kopek des Bordes beat him at Navan In November. We know that she goes well at Cheltenham too. She could be a big player in the Arkle.

So could **Irish Panther**. He is a little bit of a forgotten horse in the race, possibly because he didn't run at the Dublin Racing Festival. But Eddie and Patrick Harty's horse was only just caught by Romeo Coolio in the Racing Post Novice Chase at Leopardstown over Christmas, and the greater speed test that the Arkle presents should suit him better.

The ground was just softer than ideal for him at the Dublin Racing Festival, so it made sense to skip that and, a progressive 152-rated individual who was impressive in winning his beginners' chase at Naas in November, he could be a little under the radar.

BROWN ADVISORY NOVICES' CHASE

THE market for the Brown Advisory Novices' Chase turned on its head when **Final Demand** was beaten at long odds-on in the Ladbrokes Novice Chase at the Dublin Racing Festival.

Willie Mullins' horse had been so impressive in each of his two previous runs over fences, but it didn't look likely from a long way out at Leopardstown. One of the hallmarks of his first two chases was his jumping. He jumped 14 fences at Navan in November and he jumped 14 more at Limerick at Christmas, and he didn't miss one of them. At Leopardstown, he was good over the first four, but he got in a little tight to the fifth, and he made a mistake at the ninth. That allowed his stable companion Kaid d'Authie up on his inside.

JP McManus' horse moved on from there, jumped the third last in front and was better than his rival over the second last. That was race over. Final Demand weakened, he actually ceded second place to Western Fold, as Kaid d'Authie powered over the final fence and up the run-in to run out an impressive winner.

You can't dismiss a horse after just one run. It clearly wasn't Final Demand's running, for whatever reason. He was such a classy novice hurdler last season – third behind The New Lion in the Turners Novices' Hurdle at Cheltenham, winner of the Grade 1 Alanna Homes Novice Hurdle at Punchestown – and he looked so good in each of his first two chases. He is going to have to bounce back now though.

Kaid d'Authie just has to roll on. He wasn't as classy a hurdler as his stable companion, but he looked good in winning his beginners' chase at Fairyhouse on New Year's Eve, and he obviously took a big step forward at Leopardstown in the re-fitted cheekpieces.

He had worn the headgear once before, in the Louis Fitzgerald Hurdle at the Punchestown Festival in April, which he duly won. It may not be a coincidence that that was his best performance over hurdles by a fair way.

Willie Mullins said after the Leopardstown race that the Choeur du Nord gelding was always a horse who showed him plenty at home, that he had been disappointed with his performances on the racecourse up until that point. Perhaps the cheekpieces are the key, perhaps they have unlocked his latent talent. Either way, similar to Majborough in the Champion Chase, it would be surprising if he isn't wearing the accessories when he turns up at Cheltenham.

Western Fold ran a big race to move into second place behind Kaid d'Authie in the Leopardstown race. In truth, it never really looked like he was going to get to the winner, and he probably beat a below-par rival for the runner-up spot, but it was still a wholly admirable performance from Gordon Elliott's horse on ground that should have been far too soft for him. As well as that, it was his first run since he finished third behind Envoi Allen in the Champion Chase at Down Royal on 1st November. He could come on appreciably for the run.

Western Fold is an unusual novice, in that he has run 11 times over fences. He won the Mayo National at Ballinrobe in May off a mark of 138 – at the meeting at which Doctor Steinberg won his bumper, by the way – then won the Galway Plate off a 10lb higher mark. Then he went to Gowran Park and won the Grade 2 PWC Champion Chase, beating Affordale Fury, again on ground that should have been softer than ideal.

As you will see in the deeper reaches of this book, between three and five runs over fences is the sweet spot for the Brown Advisory Chase winner, but Western Fold should have better ground and he is classy and he stays. He could be the exception that proves the rule, even if it is a phrase that doesn't make lots of sense.

Henry de Bromhead could also have a strong hand in the race. **Koktail Divin** split Oscars Brother and Bossofthebrownies in the Grade 2 Florida Pearl Chase at Punchestown in November, and he was impressive in winning his beginners' chase at Leopardstown at Christmas, dropped down slightly in trip.

Fellow Knockeen resident **The Big Westerner** gave Jasmin de Veaux a real race in the Albert Bartlett Hurdle last year, proving her ability to operate at Cheltenham, and she might have got closer to him had she not been hampered at the second last flight.

She has been good over fences this season too. Second to Jimmy du Seuil in a beginners' chase at Fairyhouse in November on her chasing bow, she stepped forward from that last time when she stayed on well to get the better of the talented subsequent winner Jade de Grugy in the Grade 2 Dawn Run Mares' Novice Chase at Limerick over Christmas. The Westerner mare may be at her best on soft ground, but she proved that she could handle good to soft ground in the Albert Bartlett Hurdle.

Oscars Brother could also be a lively outsider. Acquired by JP McManus following his win in the Florida Pearl, he has since won the Ten Up Novice Chase, and it is interesting that he has been given an entry in the Grand National. He has options.

Koktail Divin seen ahead of last year's Mersey at Aintree

NOVICE / JUVENILE HURDLERS

SUPREME NOVICES' HURDLE

TALK THE TALK is only five, but he should probably be a dual Grade 1 winner by now. Joseph O'Brien's horse looked good when he won the Grade 3 four-year-olds' hurdle at Fairyhouse on Hatton's Grace Hurdle weekend, and he looked even better when he hit the front on the run to the final flight in the Grade 1 Future Champions Novice Hurdle at Leopardstown's Christmas Festival.

He didn't really make a mistake at the final flight either. Wheeled towards the outside by Sam Ewing, he quickened up and moved into a clear lead on the approach to the obstacle, and he soared over it. He didn't actually touch the flight. He over-jumped it, possibly because he had so much energy left. But he landed steeply and his momentum took his centre of gravity beyond his base and took him to the ground.

We will never know for sure whether or not he would have won that day and, such was the strength with which the winner Skylight Hustle finished off his race – more of Skylight Hustle anon – it is probable that Talk The Talk would have had to have found plenty on the run-in in order to prevail. But he traded at 1.04 in-running, and that looks about right.

Simon Munir and Isaac Souede's horse gained the Grade 1 win that he deserved though last time, in the Tattersalls Ireland Novice Hurdle at the Dublin Racing Festival. He only just got up to win by a short head in the end, but that doesn't tell the full story of the race.

It was a race in which the early pace was not strong, and Talk The Talk was back in the field early on, further off the pace than ideal given the moderate early fractions. Tenth of the 12 runners as they left the back straight, he was still no better than eighth when they passed the two-furlong marker with one flight of hurdles to jump. Rider J J Slevin didn't panic on him either, he wound him up gradually, over the last and up the hill and he hit the front on the line. Literally. Hardly an inch before it.

The RaceiQ data from the race backed up what you saw with your eyes too. A finishing speed of over 113% of overall speed, which confirms the sedateness of the early pace, and Ballyfad and King Rasko Grey were up there on it from early. Talk The Talk was fastest of all through the final four furlongs of the race, and through the final furlong, 0.22secs faster than the runner-up Ballyfad, who was, in turn, slightly faster than the third-placed King Rasko Grey.

Two final points about this race. Firstly, it looked like a strong race beforehand, and the 'right' horses came to the fore, which adds ballast to that hypothesis. Runner-up **Ballyfad** had been impressive in winning his maiden hurdle at Leopardstown's Christmas Festival, when he clocked fast finishing splits himself. Also, the runner-up from that race, Leader d'Allier, was really impressive in winning his own maiden hurdle at Punchestown next time.

The third horse from the Tattersalls Ireland Novice Hurdle was **King Rasko Grey**, who ran out a good winner of his maiden hurdle at Limerick over Christmas from Shuttle Diplomacy, who was impressive himself in winning his maiden hurdle at Naas next time.

The form looks rock solid. And there was a nice break between the front three and the fourth and fifth horses, Koktail Brut and Blake, who had finished first and second in the Grade 2 Royal Bond Hurdle at Fairyhouse in November.

Second point about the race: Joseph O'Brien's comments afterwards. The trainer said that the plan was always to hold up Talk The Talk in the race, even though they were aware that there might not be much pace on, even though they realised that, if he was beaten, those tactics might be the reason why. The primary objective was to educate him, allow him settle in behind and pass horses.

If he won, he won. If he didn't win, he didn't win. Either way, the objective was for him to learn, with the future in mind. And not just the future this season, not just Cheltenham, but beyond. He is only five. There is no knowing by how much the Born To Sea gelding could progress, and he is in hands that will facilitate that progression.

There was talk of Talk The Talk perhaps going for the Turners Novices' Hurdle instead of the Supreme shortly after the race, but Joseph O'Brien confirmed a couple of days later that the Supreme was the target. And that makes sense. His five runs to date have all been over the minimum trip, he has the pace for it, he can quicken and he seems highly adaptable in terms of ground conditions. And his jumping was good at the Dublin Racing Festival.

The day before Talk The Talk fell at the final flight in the Future Champions Novice Hurdle, **El Cairos** had done something similar in a maiden hurdle. Same flight of hurdles, just over 25 hours earlier. So, similarly, it was good to see Gordon Elliott's horse get his win over hurdles on the board at Thurles in January.

The No Risk At All gelding is another hugely exciting prospect. An impressive winner of a good Newbury bumper last season when he was trained by Gary and Josh Moore and owned and ridden by David Maxwell, he finished fifth in the Champion Bumper at Cheltenham before going to the Punchestown Festival and finishing a good second to Baron Noir.

He was racing for the first time over hurdles and for the first time for Gordon Elliott in that maiden at Leopardstown at Christmas, but the confidence behind him was reflected in the market. Sent off at 8/15, he travelled easily through his race and he showed a potent turn of foot when Jack Kennedy asked him to pick up, putting a distance of ground between himself and his rivals on the run to the final flight. There is still no knowing how good he could be.

TURNERS NOVICES' HURDLE

THINGS could change in the interim, things have a habit of changing in interims, but, at the time of writing, it looks like Ballyfad and Skylight Hustle could go for the Turners Novices' Hurdle, not the Supreme. Same with Mighty Park.

You can use any one of a whole gamut of words to describe **Mighty Park**'s performance on his debut over hurdles at Fairyhouse in January. Awesome, astonishing, amazing, and that's even before you move onto B.

Willie Mullins' horse only got into the race as a reserve too. When he did, it took the market a little while to adjust but, when it did, it sent him off as clear favourite, usurping erstwhile favourite, his stable companion Roc Dino, who would have been an 18-length winner without him.

Roc Dino was the only rival who could go with the winner for any appreciable part of the race, but he wilted from before the home turn. Then Roc Dino came out and got to within three lengths of El Cairos at Thurles next time. He probably improved considerably from his Fairyhouse run, his first since February last year, but it still adds ballast to Mighty Park's performance. And the fourth horse from the race, Agameoftwohalves, won his maiden hurdle at Punchestown next time.

It was JP McManus' horse's first run for Willie Mullins, his first run since he finished second in a Point-to-Point behind Harry Lowes, who was with Derek O'Connor then, and who has since won a novices' hurdle for Dan Skelton. A supremely well-bred individual, a three-parts brother to Might Bite and a half-brother to Beat That, he is another whose potential upside is sky-high.

Ballyfad is reportedly not overly impressive at home, but he won his only Point-to-Point and he won his two bumpers before Christmas this season, and he was impressive in winning his maiden hurdle at Leopardstown on his hurdling bow. He came 9½ lengths clear of Leader d'Allier, who enhanced the form when he ran out a ready winner of his only maiden hurdle at Thurles next time.

Ballyfad had to give best to Talk The Talk in the Brave Inca Novice Hurdle, just, and time may prove that there was no disgrace in that. Gordon Elliott's horse has the pace for the Supreme, should connections choose to go down that route, but there is plenty of stamina in his pedigree too, and he could be better suited by the test that the Turners presents.

It's a similar story with his stable companion **Skylight Hustle**. Second behind subsequent River Don Hurdle winner Thedeviluno on his hurdling bow at Gowran Park in November, the Robcour gelding cut loose at Fairyhouse next time, making just about all the running and winning by over 20 lengths.

He stepped forward nicely last time at Leopardstown too. It may be that Talk The Talk would have beaten him had he not come down at the final flight, but there was a lot to like about the strength with which Skylight Hustle went to the line. Also, winner of his only Point-to-Point and a half-brother to Sean Says, a winner over an extended 3m, he could improve for stepping up to the intermediate trip.

King Rasko Grey could run here instead of in the Supreme, and the step up in trip could help him too, and Doctor Steinberg could run here instead of in the Albert Bartlett, but, winner of the Nathaniel Lacy Hurdle at the Dublin Racing Festival, you have to think that the Albert Bartlett is the race for him. More about Doctor Steinberg in due course.

Two others worth considering at big prices. **Heads Up** is on a recovery mission now after a wholly abject performance in the Grade 2 Classic Hurdle on trials day at Cheltenham at the end of January.

That wasn't his running though, for whatever reason. He raced too keenly, he didn't jump well, he was a beaten horse long before the race really started. That race was at the end of the card, in the half-light and delayed, and maybe he got upset by the waiting around. You just have to put a line through it.

If you can forgive him that run, there is a case to be made. John McConnell's horse ran a massive race in the Champion Bumper last season to finish second, beaten only by Bambino Fever. He did have the run of the race, Sean Bowen got out in front on him and set a sedate pace, off which he quickened.

Even so, he had No Drama This End behind him that day. He had Idaho Sun behind him, he had El Cairos behind him, he had Sortudo behind him. He jumped well too when he won on his hurdling debut at Listowel in September, and he got to within 3 lengths of No Drama This End in the Grade 2 Hyde Novices' Hurdle at Cheltenham in November. As long as he is back and ready to go again, he could out-run big odds.

Shuttle Diplomacy could also out-run big odds. Third in the Champion Bumper last year at a big price, Tom Cooper's horse kept on well to finish second behind the classy King Rasko Grey at Limerick's Christmas meeting, giving him 8lb, before going to Naas in January and running out an impressive winner of his maiden hurdle. He obviously goes well at the track, and he could be an interesting contender for a trainer who is having a really good season, and who has trained Forpadydeplasterer and Total Enjoyment to win at the Cheltenham Festival in the past.

ALBERT BARTLETT NOVICES' HURDLE

YOU can understand the Turners talk for **Doctor Steinberg** after he won the Nathaniel Lacy Hurdle at the Dublin Racing Festival. He was keen through the early stages of that race, so much so that, when Paul Townend asked him to pick up, you could have expected him to wilt.

On the contrary, the more the race progressed, the stronger he got, so much so that he won by 8 lengths, and he was well over a second faster than his fastest rival through the final furlong of the race.

It was a serious show of strength. He had to have expended more energy than he needed to expend through the early throes, and the fact that he had the reserves to do what he did at the end of the race speaks volumes. If he can settle better, he could take another step forward.

Willie Mullins' horse has been a little bit of a revelation this season over hurdles. He won just one of his four bumpers last season, a Ballinrobe contest at the end of May, and he was well beaten at the Galway Festival on his final run in a bumper. Over hurdles this season, though, he has excelled. He is unbeaten.

He won his maiden at Galway in last October, and he won the Grade 2 Navan Novice Hurdle, where he beat subsequent River Don Hurdle inner Thedeviluno, before he went to Leopardstown and won the Nathaniel Lacy Hurdle, where he beat the Grade 2 Dorans Pride Hurdle winner Kazansky. There is bags of stamina in his pedigree, he is a half-brother to Stay Humble and Smuggler's Blues, both of whom stayed 3m at least, and he could be even better with a stronger test of stamina.

Thedeviluno is a really likeable individual too. Paul Nolan's horse stayed on strongly to win his maiden hurdle at Gowran Park in November, when he had the aforementioned subsequent Grade 1 winner Skylight Hustle back in second place, with the 139-rated The Passing Wife back in third. Then he went to Doncaster and, on a day on which Paul Nolan also won the Grade 2 Yorkshire Rose Mares' Hurdle with Feet Of A Dancer, won the Grade 2 River Don Hurdle.

Thedeviluno stays well, he is proven now over 3m, and he has raced just three times over hurdles, so there should be more to come from him. He is in good hands too.

I'll Sort That is also in good hands. The Sandmason gelding provided Declan Queally with his first Grade 1 winner as a jockey and provided his father with his first Grade 1 winner as a trainer when he won the Ballymore Novice Hurdle at Naas in early January.

The six-year-old gelding is tough. He looked in trouble when he made a mistake at the final flight in the Grade 3 For Auction Hurdle, run over 2m at Navan in November, but he stayed on strongly up the hill to get up and win by three parts of a length.

And he looked in trouble in the Ballymore Novice Hurdle at Naas too when Sortudo loomed up in his wingmirrors. But he found lots for pressure again and, even at the end of a gruelling 2m4f, dug deep on the run up the hill and repelled the challenge of Willie Mullins' horse. He has the Tuners option too, and there is plenty of pace in his pedigree, his dam won over six furlongs, but, such is his attitude and his tenacity, the potency of those attributes may be maximised in the Albert Bartlett.

Kazansky could step forward again too, Gordon Elliott's horse dug deep to beat County Final in the Grade 2 Dorans Pride Hurdle at Limerick, a race that has been a good pointer to the Albert Bartlett Hurdle in the past, and **Sortudo** could out-run his odds if he takes his chance in the race.

TRIUMPH HURDLE

NARCISO HAS was beaten in the Grade 3 juvenile hurdle at the Hatton's Grace Hurdle meeting at Fairyhouse in November, but that was his first run for Willie Mullins, and it was his first run since April. Also, he was beaten by Mange Tout, a talented filly who had race fitness on her side.

JP McManus' horse showed the benefit of that run when he went to Leopardstown at Christmas and won the Grade 2 juvenile hurdle impressively.

They sent him off as favourite for the Grade 1 Spring Juvenile Hurdle at the Dublin Racing Festival, despite the fact that he was meeting his old rival Mange Tout on worse terms compared to the terms on which they met when at Fairyhouse when she beat him by almost 3 lengths. The market didn't care though, they sent him off the even money favourite, and he won like one.

He was utterly dominant in the Spring Hurdle. He got out in front under Mark Walsh, jumped really well and stayed on strongly to win by 4½ lengths. The Spring Hurdle is a really good pointer to the Triumph Hurdle, and he is a worthy favourite for the juveniles' race at the Cheltenham Festival.

But it can pay to look beyond the winner of the Spring Juvenile Hurdle when you are looking for the Triumph Hurdle winner – ref Majborough, Lossiemouth, Farclas, Ivanovich Gorbatov, Tiger Roll, Countrywide Flame – and **Selma de Vary** stayed on nicely to take second place at Leopardstown.

That was the Zarak filly's first run for Willie Mullins too. Winner of a three-year-olds' hurdle At Auteuil in early November for Emmanuel Clayeux, the vibe before the Leopardstown race was that she hadn't done that much at home since her arrival from France, that she would probably improve appreciably for the run. She is a player.

Their stable companion **Proactif** stuck to his task well in winning a four-year-olds' hurdle at Fairyhouse in January, in which he beat another stable companion **Macho Man**, and one or both of those could add to the strength of Willie Mullins' hand in a race that the trainer has won five times in the last six years.

Narciso Has heads a strong bunch of Mullins-trained juveniles

Breeding Angles

BY JESS STAFFORD

Racing TV | Fanduel TV | Thurloe Thoroughbreds | Bred For It

PEDIGREE MEETS PERFORMANCE: FINDING THE 2026 GOLD CUP EDGE

ANALYSING a horse's pedigree to sharpen betting strategy is something I've been fascinated by for many years. When it comes to Cheltenham, it has always felt like the edge I wanted to explore and share - leaving form students and professional tipsters to their own conclusions while I focused on the long-term breeding patterns that might point us towards a Festival winner.

More often than not, that approach has proved valuable. From season to season, the meticulous work done by breeders - producing the next generation of National Hunt talent for agents, owners, trainers and jockeys to capitalise on - continues to inspire this column. Fashionable bloodlines come and go, the latest 'next big thing' is often fawned over, yet traditional, old-fashioned influences have a habit of resurfacing when it matters most.

Pedigree analysis is one of the most compelling aspects of our sport, supported by a wealth of data stretching back more than 15 years thanks to Weatherbys, whose work in compiling sire, dam and damsire details for every Cheltenham Festival runner is invaluable. Their daily celebration of Festival-winning sires and breeders is something I'd love to see pushed even further - after all, breeding success deserves centre stage during Cheltenham week.

Like every industry, racing must continue to modernise. We have already embraced technology - from the early days of sectional timing to far more advanced performance metrics. In National Hunt racing in particular, stride length, jump efficiency, jump index and lengths gained at fences now provide meaningful insight. Platforms such as RaceiQ draw on billions of datapoints and AI-driven modelling to deepen our understanding of race performance. Trainers, too, increasingly rely on heart-rate monitors and biometric data to track a horse's wellbeing and conditioning.

Breeding has not been left behind. Artificial Intelligence and genomic tools are now being used to complement traditional pedigree analysis, helping breeders identify optimal stallion-mare matches based on DNA compatibility. What does this mean for Cheltenham? For now, probably very little. It is highly unlikely that the horses lining up over the four days have been materially influenced by AI-led mating decisions. But the future is coming - and Festival performance data may yet become another key reference point for National Hunt breeders when selecting stallions.

That intersection - where pedigree trends meet modern data - is where things become particularly interesting from a betting perspective.

With that in mind, I've taken a closer look at the pedigrees and performance data of several leading Gold Cup contenders, exploring what their bloodlines and numbers tell us about their prospects at this year's Festival. With the established Gold Cup form already well documented, attention here turns to those yet to line up in the race but whose pedigrees hint at untapped Gold Cup potential.

JANGO BAIE – STAMINA PROMISED, STILL MATURING

JANGO BAIE will be the first son of Tiger Groom to line up in a Cheltenham Gold Cup. Tiger Groom, a useful French hurdler who stayed well, hails from a deep Aga Khan family, with his dam a middle-distance winner whose progeny performed to a high level across both codes. Although Tiger Groom has only one Festival success to his name - Jango Baie's Arkle victory - the line has produced honest, durable types, including Behrajan, fifth in Best Mate's 2003 Gold Cup.

Jango Baie is out of Tennessee, a daughter of the influential Kapgarde. While Kapgarde is yet to establish himself as a Gold Cup-producing damsire, he has already tasted success in the race as the sire of A Plus Tard. Tennessee's family is stacked with staying, cross-country performers, reinforcing the stamina influence.

The wider family further supports that profile: younger brother Kando Baie has excelled over staying trips in France, while half-sister Imany Baie improved markedly with distance later in her career. Stamina, on paper, is not the issue.

Jango Baie already owns a Cheltenham Festival victory, his Arkle success showcasing high cruising speed (36.22mph top speed; 104.91% Finishing Speed Percentage) despite a relatively modest Jump Index (7.8) and a short average stride length (6.24m). This season's step up in trip has brought mixed but encouraging signals: a win in the 1965 Chase at Ascot and a respectable fourth in a high-class King George.

Key data:
1965 Chase: Jump Index 8.2 | Lengths gained jumping 7.17 | Avg stride 6.47m
King George: Jump Index 7.3 | Lengths gained jumping -1.75 | Avg stride 6.46m

The improved stride length suggests growing comfort over longer distances, though inconsistency in jumping efficiency remains a concern. The pedigree screams improvement with age, and while he may still be learning his trade at Gold Cup level, Jango Baie looks a horse whose best days may yet lie ahead.

THE JUKEBOX MAN – STOUT BLOOD, EFFICIENT EXECUTION

LIKE Jango Baie, The Jukebox Man offers us two valuable data points this season. Pedigree-wise, he brings far fewer unanswered questions. A son of Ask - a Coronation Cup and Prix Royal-Oak winner - he represents one of the great value success stories in National Hunt breeding.

Ask proved a prolific sire of stayers, producing the likes of The Wallpark, Ask Dillon and Ask Me Early. Crucially, the Ask–Flemensfirth cross (Flemensfirth being The Jukebox Man's damsire) has already delivered high-class staying chasers, with Flemensfirth's reputation as a broodmare sire beyond question - Noble Yeats and Nick Rockett among his standout descendants.

Add in Ask's Sadler's Wells influence, and the stamina credentials begin to stack up convincingly.

From a data perspective, The Jukebox Man's King George performance paints a fascinating picture: a solid jump index of 8.2, shorter stride length (6.42m) and modest lengths gained jumping (2.86). That profile suggests a horse who jumps smoothly and efficiently, maintaining speed through accuracy rather than raw galloping power. The question for the Gold Cup is whether that blend of speed and jumping precision will translate over a relentlessly run three-and-a-quarter miles.

SPILLANE'S TOWER – PEDIGREE POWER MEETS PERFORMANCE

SPILLANE'S TOWER booked his place in the 2026 Cheltenham Gold Cup with a resolute and thoroughly professional performance in the Cotswold Chase. Carrying the familiar silks of JP McManus, he offers the leading jumps owner a genuine opportunity to land back-to-back victories in the Festival showpiece with yet another son of Walk In The Park, bred by his wife, Noreen McManus.

Until relatively recently, Walk In The Park's relationship with the Gold Cup had been curiously underwhelming. Despite establishing himself as the dominant National Hunt sire of his generation, he had yet to saddle a runner in the race, and his overall Cheltenham Festival record stood at a respectable but unspectacular five winners from 44 runners. That narrative began to shift decisively in 2024, when Inothewayurthinkin delivered a clear-cut success in the Kim Muir. The result was particularly satisfying from a breeding perspective, forming part of a Festival double for the McManus-owned mare Sway, whose daughter Limerick Lace captured the Mares' Chase.

The following season marked a watershed moment. Inothewayurthinkin returned to Cheltenham in 2025 and delivered Walk In The Park his first Gold Cup victory, while another of the sire's representatives, Monty's Star, emerged from the race with immense credit in fourth. In the space of two Festivals, Walk In The Park had gone from Gold Cup absentee to headline act - and it comes as little surprise that his influence is now being felt even more strongly.

This year's Gold Cup entries include no fewer than seven sons of Walk In The Park, five of them drawn from the same 2017 crop - just his second season standing at Grange Stud. From the moment he arrived in Ireland, Coolmore committed wholeheartedly to him, sending an extraordinary 1,121 mares across his first five seasons. Unlike the Flat, National Hunt breeding rewards patience, with results often taking years to crystallise, but it is now abundantly clear that Walk In The Park hit the ground running with his Irish books. From his first crop emerged Nick Rockett, a Grand National winner, and Facile Vega, victorious in the 2022 Champion Bumper. From the second crop - nine years on - we are now looking at a cluster of legitimate Gold Cup contenders.

Spillane's Tower is very much a product of that early faith. His dam, In The Habit, visited Walk In The Park in both his first and second seasons at Grange Stud. On paper, she may not have possessed the same racetrack credentials as Sway, a multiple Listed winner in France who performed with distinction in Britain, but her pedigree was quietly compelling. Unraced herself, In The Habit hails from a deep German family on her dam's side, notably including her half-sister Cherry Danon, producer of the German 10-furlong Group 1 winner, Calif.

Crucially, In The Habit carries Monsun as her damsire - a name that has become almost priceless in modern National Hunt breeding. While Monsun's legacy as an elite German Flat sire is well established, his influence on jumps racing has been profound. He has played a pivotal role in shaping this generation of National Hunt stallions, appearing as sire or broodmare sire of the likes of Network, Shirocco, Getaway and Ocovango. The presence of Monsun in a pedigree is now synonymous with soundness, stamina and durability - traits that breeders actively seek when aiming at the very top staying prizes.

Spillane's Tower therefore benefits from two of the most powerful and proven influences in National Hunt breeding, one on either side of his pedigree - and that genetic promise has translated convincingly to the racetrack. His Cotswold Chase victory was a textbook Gold Cup trial, showcasing both his jumping fluency and his ability to sustain pressure over a demanding trip. The data only reinforces that impression: a jump index of 8.8, 6.34 lengths gained jumping, and an average stride length of 6.22 metres underline his efficiency and balance, with the jump index, in particular, standing out as highly encouraging for a Gold Cup contender.

Spillane's Tower is a horse who blends pedigree power with polished performance - and, perhaps most importantly, one who still appears to have room for improvement. In a division where incremental progress can make all the difference, that combination places him firmly among the leading contenders for the 2026 Gold Cup.

HAITI COULEURS – THE FRENCH ANOMALY THAT KEEPS PROVING US WRONG

WHAT makes this year's Gold Cup picture so compelling is the sheer diversity of pedigrees and profiles converging at the top of the staying chase division. There is no single blueprint, no dominant stallion line or prevailing fashion - and few horses illustrate that better than Haiti Couleurs, the 2025 Irish and Welsh National winner and a striking example of creative, conviction-led French National Hunt breeding.

Haiti Couleurs is by Dragon Dancer, a son of Sadler's Wells whose own racing career was defined more by courage and character than by silverware. His sole victory came in the Listed August Stakes in 2007, but he remains best remembered for his gallant, front-running display in the 2006 Derby, where he was beaten just a short head after wearing his heart firmly on his sleeve from the outset. That willingness to battle - to go forward, to keep finding - has clearly been passed on to his best progeny, none more so than Haiti Couleurs, whose popularity has grown steadily on the back of his relentless galloping style and refusal to yield.

Haiti Couleurs is very much the product of Haras du Saz's belief in Dragon Dancer, whom they stood in Nantes from 2013 to 2016. The Simon family, who own Haras du Saz, are well known for backing their stallions with mares they value, and while Dragon Dancer may not have possessed an especially fashionable race record, his pedigree carried genuine depth and quality. He is, of course, by the great sire of sires Sadler's Wells, while his dam Alakananda is a half-sister to both Alborada, the dual Champion Stakes heroine, and Albanova, a multiple Group 1 winner. That kind of family may not shout instant commercial appeal, but it speaks volumes about latent class and durability.

Where Haiti Couleurs' pedigree truly begins to stand out, however, is on the dam side. He is out of Inchala, who was tried once over hurdles without success but did manage to win on the Flat at Nancy

Spillane's Tower – an improving son of Walk In The Park

in her early career. Inchala hails from an AQPS family, with her dam Betty Royale and granddam Lady Royale bred by the iconic Cypres family, whose influence on French jumping bloodstock is difficult to overstate. The Simon family initially sent Inchala to their stallions Early March and Johann Quatz before electing to try her with Dragon Dancer in the final year he stood at Haras du Saz. At that time, Dragon Dancer was standing for just €1,000, covering small books, and like much of the Haras' produce, Haiti Couleurs was sent to the sales at a young age.

With only Lady Royale and her Listed-winning son Hidalgo Royale carrying black type in the family, it is little surprise that Haiti Couleurs failed to set the sales ring alight. Yet the page contains a crucial and easily overlooked influence - Royal Charter, the damsire of Inchala. A hugely important broodmare sire, Royal Charter has left an indelible mark on staying chasers, appearing in the pedigrees of horses such as Eldorado Allen, Quel Esprit, cross-country stalwart Auvergnat and multiple Cheltenham winner Diesel d'Allier. It is an influence the Simons were clearly right to believe in.

Haiti Couleurs was sold as a two-year-old at the Arqana Mixed Sale for just €7,000 to Luke Cummins through George Mullins, went unsold as a store in 2020, and ultimately found his way to Rebecca Curtis for £68,000 after two runs in Irish point-to-points - the second a far more encouraging effort than the first. His name, I'm told, comes from a French song, which feels fitting for a horse whose story is steeped in French breeding philosophy.

What is most striking about Haiti Couleurs is that his pedigree does not scream greatness, nor does it advertise obvious Gold Cup star quality at first glance. Instead, it exemplifies the traditional French approach - unwavering support of home stallions, patience over fashion, and faith in families built on toughness rather than hype. Haiti Couleurs may yet prove an outlier, but he is equally an embodiment of a breeding system that refuses to follow the crowd.

In that sense, his story is not entirely dissimilar to that of the two-time Gold Cup winner Galopin des Champs, himself by the relatively unfashionable Timos, who later stood in Tunisia and Libya, and out of a modest but winning jumps mare in Manon des Champs. Prior to producing Galopin des Champs and his Listed-winning full sister Flute des Champs, Manon des Champs had enjoyed only limited success as a broodmare. The cross with Timos was simply the one that clicked. It is tempting to wonder whether the Dragon Dancer and Inchala mating represents a similar moment of alignment.

What truly elevates Haiti Couleurs into Gold Cup contention, however, is not sentiment but data. He outperforms many of his principal rivals when it comes to jump index and lengths gained jumping, metrics that are increasingly important in assessing staying chasers at the very highest level. His Welsh National victory, while not achieved in Grade 1 company, was a performance of that calibre, and the numbers demand respect. An average stride length of 6.51 metres, combined with 8.50 lengths gained jumping and a jump index of 7.0, paints the picture of a relentless, efficient galloper - one whose profile closely mirrors that of Galopin des Champs at a similar stage in his Gold Cup journey.

Haiti Couleurs has shown that he can jump, gallop and stay - the three non-negotiables for a Gold Cup contender. The question that now remains is whether he possesses the necessary class, or the ability to shorten his stride when the tempo lifts, to live with faster horses at the very top of the division. If he can, then this French-bred anomaly may yet have more to say on the sport's biggest stage.

GAELIC WARRIOR & FACT TO FILE – WILL THEY OR WON'T THEY?

THE final two horses worthy of serious pedigree consideration ahead of any potential Gold Cup tilt are the two Willie Mullins-trained runners who, at the time of writing, may yet be steered towards the Ryanair. Fact To File and Gaelic Warrior have already produced a compelling mini-rivalry this season, and on form alone, a Gold Cup rematch would feel entirely justified.

Fact To File was breathtaking in the Irish Gold Cup, turning the tables decisively on Gaelic Warrior with a 5-length victory, having previously come off second best in their John Durkan clash in November. Both horses also emerged with credit from the King George, further underlining their class at the highest level. While connections of Gaelic Warrior appear keen to keep the Gold Cup option open, Fact To File was left out at the entry stage - prompting the inevitable question: will he be supplemented, and does his pedigree offer enough reassurance that he will stay?

On breeding, there is every reason for confidence. Fact To File is from the final crop of the outstanding French stallion Poliglote, whose influence at Cheltenham has been profound. He sired a Gold Cup third through Don Poli in 2016, while his most celebrated son, Sire du Berlais, relished the Cheltenham hill when landing two Pertemps Finals and the 2023 Stayers' Hurdle. Fact To File's own family reinforces the stamina message: his half-brother Charlatemps was a multiple chase winner over extended trips in France, and his dam is a half-sister to proven staying chasers Khelkalou and Tempoline.

While there is speed throughout the pedigree - particularly on his dam side, where many relatives were effective at intermediate distances – Fact To File appears to have inherited the ideal blend. His Irish Gold Cup performance produced a finishing speed of 102.48%, a figure that points to stamina with the ability to quicken when required. From a pedigree and performance perspective, he has all the makings of a legitimate Gold Cup contender.

Gaelic Warrior, by contrast, presents more of a puzzle over the full Gold Cup trip. By Maxios, a high-class Flat performer from a mile to 10 furlongs, and out of a Niarchos-bred mare with strong Flat credentials including Italian Classic form in the family, his profile leans more towards speed than stamina. The influence of Monsun, Maxios' sire, may yet assert itself, but Gaelic Warrior's exuberant racing style raises the question of whether he will settle well enough to truly see out the Gold Cup distance.

VERDICT:
FROM blue-blood powerhouses like Spillane's Tower to unconventional success stories like Haiti Couleurs, the 2026 Gold Cup presents a true melting pot of pedigree philosophies. When layered with modern performance data, those bloodlines begin to tell an even richer story.

Pedigree alone will never pick a Gold Cup winner – but when it aligns with the numbers, it can still give us a valuable edge.

Spillane's Tower sets the benchmark for the 2026 Gold Cup on pedigree and data, Haiti Couleurs brings proven stamina and jumping toughness – but Jango Baie is the one to side with for upside, his pedigree suggesting he may still be improving into a peak Gold Cup horse.

KIRSTEN RAUSING'S 'A' FAMILY SHAPES CHELTENHAM CONTENDERS

WE HAVE become increasingly familiar with Flat-bred horses making a successful transition to the National Hunt code, and it remains a constant fascination of mine to study the families of these converts in search of the clues hidden within their pedigrees. More often than not, the ingredients are there in plain sight: size, scope, balance and – perhaps most importantly – the attitude to adapt to hurdling and, in time, chasing. But it is when those Flat-bred crossovers begin to link seemingly unrelated Cheltenham Festival contenders that my bloodstock-focused appetite is truly whetted.

When Minella Study lit up our screens in the Triumph Hurdle Trial at Cheltenham in December, it would never have occurred to me that he hailed from the very same influential family as the sire of Haiti Couleurs. Yet, a deeper dive into the page reveals precisely that – and in doing so, highlights once again the remarkable versatility of one of the most celebrated families in the modern Thoroughbred.

Minella Study was bred by champion Flat breeder Kirsten Rausing of Lanwades Stud, a name more readily associated with Prix de l'Arc de Triomphe and Champion Stakes glory than with Cheltenham Festival contenders. That said, Ms Rausing is no stranger to seeing her homebreds grace the Festival stage. Tritonic's fifth-place finish in the 2021 Triumph Hurdle offered a notable example, while her stallion Sea The Moon has also made his presence felt at Cheltenham through Allmankind's third in the 2020 Triumph.

The Triumph Hurdle, with its emphasis on speed and agility in juvenile hurdlers, has long been the natural home of ex-Flat recruits, and Minella Study fits that mould perfectly. He is by Study Of Man, a stallion who has made a rapid impact on the Flat, highlighted most recently by his exceptional daughter Kalpana, who landed back-to-back Group 1 victories on Champions Day at Ascot. This March will see Study Of Man represented by his first Cheltenham Festival runner in Minella Study – but the dam side of the pedigree is already well acquainted with elite Festival and championship-level success.

Minella Study is out of Albamara, a member of the extraordinary 'A' family that Ms Rausing has cultivated so masterfully over several decades. Albamara is a daughter of Albanova, herself a dual Group 1 winner and a full-sister to the dual Champion Stakes heroine Alborada. Albanova, in turn, has become one of the great matriarchs of the modern era, her influence extending through elite performers such as Alpinista and Eldar Eldarov, the latter now beginning his own chapter as a National Hunt stallion. It is this deep-rooted quality that Minella Study draws upon – a pedigree steeped in class, toughness and adaptability.

So where does this leave Haiti Couleurs? A closer inspection of his pedigree reveals a fascinating connection. His sire, Dragon Dancer, also descends from the same 'A' family through his dam Alakananda, who is a half-sister to Alborada. That relationship makes Dragon Dancer and Minella Study close cousins – an unexpected but compelling link between two very different Cheltenham hopefuls.

Does this bode well for either horse? Perhaps not in isolation, but it certainly reinforces the notion that the 'A' family possesses an innate versatility that transcends codes. The National Hunt success already delivered through Dragon Dancer – most notably via the heroic exploits of Haiti Couleurs – suggests that this blue-blooded Flat family is more than capable of producing elite jumpers. Minella Study may yet add another chapter to that story, further underlining the depth, durability and adaptability of one of the sport's most distinguished breeding dynasties.

TRACKSIDE
CHELTENHAM FESTIVAL

Paddock Analysis Service

GET A UNIQUE BETTING ANGLE THIS FESTIVAL

ALL 28 RACES FOR ONLY £20!

Providing invaluable real time information direct from the paddock straight to your mobile before each race.

Available to buy online at
weatherbysshop.co.uk

Paddock experts, Vicki Gibbins and David Massey, nominate four horses from the prelims at the Dublin Racing Festival.

WESTERN FOLD (GORDON ELLIOTT)
2nd Ladbrokes Novice Chase

THE Ladbrokes Novice Chase threw Cheltenham Festival betting into disarray as Final Demand failed to make any impact as the 30/100 favourite. There was no obvious issue from a paddock perspective, but the much-talked-about ground appeared to be his undoing and the ante-post markets were happy to forgive the misdemeanour, with Willie Mullins' charge remaining near the top of the betting.

It was Gordon Elliott's **Western Fold** who caught the eye in the preliminaries; simply because he needed the run. There was little further to discuss about the gelding, who gave any layers a scare as he made eye-catching progress before the last fence to finish second behind Kaid d'Authie. It was an excellent performance from the experienced chaser, who holds interesting collateral form with subsequent Grade 1 winner Affordale Fury and it's likely he'll enter the Cheltenham Festival picture under the radar.

TALK THE TALK (JOSEPH O'BRIEN)
1st Tattersalls Ireland Novice Hurdle

AS A paddock observer, it is sometimes important not to be *'bogged down'* by the physical stature of horses and their likely suitability for ground conditions. Big horses can move well on fast ground, and light, nimble types can float through sodden conditions – there's plenty of different thought processes about physical conformation versus suitability and horses do have a tendency to make fools of any pre-conceived ideas.

The Tattersalls Ireland Novice Hurdle provided a perfect example. **Talk The Talk**, a flashy chestnut with four white legs, walked into the paddock with the poise and grace of a dancer; a light-framed, athletic gelding with a star quality that captured the attention. King Rasko Grey was his complete opposite. Mullins horses don't tend to stand out, they are workmanlike and solid; muscular powerhouses with a job to do and King Rasko Grey fit the typical profile.

Talk The Talk looked the quality individual, but King Rasko Grey appeared to be the horse for the Leopardstown job and they both ran well with Talk The Talk succeeding in a thrilling finish. It was an eye-catching effort from a horse who should only improve for a sounder surface and as long as he's not left his Cheltenham race in Ireland, it will be hard not to side with Joseph O'Brien's charge come March.

SELMA DE VARY (WILLIE MULLINS)
2nd Spring Juvenile Hurdle

CHELTENHAM wouldn't be Cheltenham without a second or even third-string Willie Mullins horse causing a surprise – think Poniros in the Triumph Hurdle or Lecky Watson in the Brown Advisory last year.

Selma de Vary has the potential to spring a surprise should she head to the Triumph Hurdle, despite her well-beaten second in the Spring Juvenile Hurdle behind strong favourite Narciso Has. Recruited from Emmanuel Clayeux's yard in France, the daughter of Zarak was only transferred to the Willie Mullins stable in early January.

It was a tough ask for the filly to make her Irish debut in a Grade 1 and she presented in the preliminaries with *'new girl at school'* vibes – tentative and veering on tense, given time in the saddling box by the Mullins team rather than being sent straight into the paddock with her stablemates. A fine-limbed, delicate filly, she was undoubtedly fit and ran well to finish 4½ lengths adrift of the winner, despite losing ground at the start and early jumping errors.

Overturning the form with Narciso Has in the Triumph Hurdle could be a tough ask, but this is a filly who should only improve.

MOONVERRIN (MARTIN HASSETT)
1st Irish EBF Mares I.N.H. Flat Race

THE aftermath of the mares' bumper was dominated by discussions of jockey Stephen Connor misjudging the winning post and losing by a short head to Finian Maguire aboard Moonverrin.

Whilst undoubtedly the story of the race, the narrative probably detracts from the performance of Martin Hassett's **Moonverrin**, who was identified in the paddock as a possible alternative to the worthy favourite Brosna Shine. Initially on her toes and skittish, the filly settled well in the preliminaries and kept catching the eye with her athletic, light-framed build and willingness to accept reassurance from handlers. She relaxed in the race too: settling midfield under Maguire before making up steady headway at the three-furlong marker.

Although the daughter of Well Chosen idled when reaching the front, she was attractively galvanised by the presence of Royal Hillsborough on her inside and Tiktok Casey on the outer, displaying a game attitude to secure the win by a short head. Would she have won without the error of Stephen Connor? We don't know, but this is a filly willing to both settle and battle – key attributes for a future star.

RACING BANK

Family-owned.
Racing-led.

A bank built for the racing world

WEATHERBYS

weatherbys.bank/racing-bank

British Novice Hurdlers

WITH the key trials out of the way, British-trained novice hurdlers remain at the top of the ante-post market for both the Supreme Novices' Hurdle and the Baring Bingham the following day.

Nicky Henderson's **Old Park Star** tops the betting for the first race of the meeting, as he looks to provide the trainer with a fourth win in the race since 2016. Irish-trained horses have won nine of the past 13 renewals, including the past three, but whilst the Tattersalls Ireland Novice Hurdle at Leopardstown produced a cracking finish, it didn't establish a standout performer to topple the three-time winning hurdler at the head of the market.

Successful at Kempton, Cheltenham and in Haydock's Rossington Main Novices' Hurdle, Old Park Star looks to be a relentless galloper, who hurdles well and maintains a strong pace. With Irish speedsters El Cairos and Talk The Talk likely to be in stalking positions, it should make for a fascinating opening contest.

Donald McCain's Cinders And Ashes won the same Haydock Grade 2 en route to Supreme success in 2012 – the last time that Britain won both races in the same year, incidentally – and in a season which has been refreshing to see a smart crop of youngsters emerge on this side of the Irish Sea, the son of Well Chosen heads the pack to provide the *'home team'* with the best possible start.

In 2025, The New Lion became just the second British-trained winner of the Baring Bingham Novices' Hurdle in 12 years. Paul Nicholls has yet to taste success in the 2m5f contest, despite having saddled plenty of fancied runners in the race in recent years, but is responsible for the exciting **No Drama This End**, who bids to end a frustrating run in the race for the former champion trainer.

Only ninth in last year's Champion Bumper – a race which was falsely run but has worked out well this season – he is, like former stable-mate Old Park Star, unbeaten in three starts over hurdles. Pitched straight into Grade 2 company, he won the Hyde Novices' Hurdle on debut, before easing to victory in Sandown's Winter and landing a first Grade 1 in Newbury's Challow.

The latter has been a (notoriously) disappointing guide towards this race, although The New Lion showed that the double can be done last year. Even Nicholls' top-class Denman was beaten here after winning the Challow (re-routed to Cheltenham that season) and more recently, Challow winners from his stable such as Bravemansgame, Stage Star and Hermes Allen were all beaten in this very race. With a score to settle, the smooth travelling No Drama This End is Nicholls' leading light heading into the Festival.

No Drama This End bids to provide Paul Nicholls' with a first Baring Bingham success

PLUMPTON RACECOURSE

CHELTENHAM PREVIEW RACEDAY

Preview panel live from the Final Fence Restaurant @ 12:30pm

MONDAY 9TH MARCH

Gates open: 12pm | Preview Panel: 12:30pm | First race: 2pm

u18s Race FREE

Hospitality in our Final Fence Restaurant for just £80 per person!
Overlooking the final fence, this restaurant offers a unique vantage point to witness the exhilarating action up close as you enjoy a wonderful 3 course set lunch.

www.plumptonracecourse.co.uk

Lulamba Out To Defy An Ageing Trend

IN LAST year's Guide, I wrote about the potential of two key trends being broken. As per the previous page, The New Lion was successful in the Baring Bingham, putting to bed the longstanding disappointing run of Challow winners in the race.

The other was not broken; the record of five-year-olds in the Arkle. Majborough was unable to justify odds-on favouritism to become the first five-year-old winner of the Arkle since the age-allowance was removed in 2008. The last successful five-year-old was Voy Por Ustedes (2006), who followed on from Champleve, Flagship Uberalles and Well Chief, with the quartet successful in the space of eight renewals.

Voy Por Ustedes was receiving 5lb when successful 20 years ago, whilst the age-allowance was as big as 8lb when Champleve won and when Flagship Uberalles led home a five-year-old first, second and fourth the following year. Well Chief only received 4lb from Kicking King when winning in 2004 but five-year-olds have, for the past 18 years, had to race off level weights with their elders.

For several years, we saw fewer horses sent chasing at four turning five, but it seems to be *'en vogue'* again at present, and **Lulamba** is set to be the latest to attempt to buck this trend. Five took their chance in 2007 – the final year in which such horses received weight – whilst the record since that removal stands at 0-12, following the defeat of Majborough in 2025. Eight of the dozen were sent off at single figures, with seven of them returning at odds of 6-1 or shorter, so hardly *'no hopers'*. Fakir d'Oudairies was beaten 1½ lengths by Put The Kettle On and Majborough went down by less than a length last year, suggesting that both would likely have won with any sort of weight concession.

So, how about Nicky Henderson's Triumph Hurdle runner-up; can he defy the statistics? Following wins at Exeter and Sandown, and more recently in open company at Newbury, he is the clear standout 2m novice in Britain. The Arkle could end up being a small field and with such a strong contender set to represent the age group (similar comments penned last year, it must be said), this trend remains very much under threat.

Whilst the depth of his earlier form can be questioned, he beat seasoned performers in the Game Spirit and has enjoyed a trouble-free campaign, whereas chief market rival Kopek des Bordes was forced to miss both Christmas and the Irish Arkle. Experience is in his favour, although the sharper test that the Old Course will present is an imponderable. He is, however, a major player on a pivotal opening day for his stable.

Lulamba looks to become the first 5yo Arkle winner in 20 years

SKY BET SUPREME NOVICES' HURDLE

2m 87y (Grade 1) – Old Course

OVERVIEW

WHILST we no longer see the 20+ runner field of years gone by, the Supreme Novices' Hurdle still tends to be run a relatively strong gallop, with tension high among jockeys and the crowd alike. The traditional *'curtain raiser'* of the week, it requires speed to hold a position throughout and stamina to last home, on the back of said strong gallop. Holding your position and being tactically astute are key components to winning races over the minimum trip on the Old Course and this race has been dominated by Irish-trained horses in recent years, with nine of the past 13 winners coming from Ireland. Rather like in the following day's Baring Bingham, Point-to-Point experience is beginning to become a positive, whilst four of the past five winners were unbeaten over hurdles. Respect winning form at Grade 1 level and Willie Mullins and Nicky Henderson both boast a strong record in the race.

A DIFFERENT RACE THESE DAYS

IN 1998, there were no fewer than 30 runners in the Supreme Novices' Hurdle, something that younger racing fans might find staggering and in fact, difficult to believe. 28 went to post in 2002 (the largest field this century) and between 2003 and 2009, we saw between 19 and 22 runners. Since 2013, however, we have only twice seen more than a 16-runner Supreme and nine of those past 13 renewals have produce field sizes of 14 or less, with only eight and nine, respectively, going to post in 2021 and 2022. Covid-19 was blamed in 2021 but only 11 have run in each of the past two renewals and the race is no longer the *'cavalry charge'* that it once was, with much less reliance now on luck in running.

With nowhere near the strength in depth in such races (all top-end novice contests) these days, they are naturally less competitive, which in turn means that results are likely to prove more predictable.

HURDLING EXPERIENCE

IN-KEEPING with the previous subsection, the fact that the past six winners had run just twice (3) or three times (3) over hurdles previously further highlights the issue. Between 2009 and 2019, the minimum amount of runs from a winner of the Supreme was four, with *Klassical Dream* having run seven times in all as a hurdler, with five of those runs coming in France. Four or five runs were ideal during that period but it is no longer the case. The smaller the field, the less chance of things going wrong and indeed three of the past four winners arrived at Cheltenham on the back of just two starts over hurdles. I would now be much less inclined to consider inexperience as a negative.

WINNING EXPERIENCE

24 OF THE past 26 winners had won at least twice previously over hurdles, so although overall experience might be less significant than in years gone by, showing the ability to win races is most certainly still a positive. *Summerville Boy* is the only horse to win the Supreme in the past 18 renewals having yet to win at least twice over hurdles previously.

LAST TIME OUT WINNERS

AS YOU would expect for a Grade 1 novice hurdle, the majority of winners of the race arrived at Cheltenham on the back of a win, with no fewer than 25 of the past 29 winners having won last time out. *Slade Steel* showed just a couple of years ago that the Supreme can be won on the back of a defeat, but he is one of just two winners in the past 15 renewals to prove successful in the Festival opener on the back of having suffered a defeat, the other being the enigmatic *Labaik*.

THE UNBEATEN HURDLER

FOUR of the past five winners of the Supreme arrived at Cheltenham unbeaten, with three of those – namely *Constitution Hill*, *Marine Nationale* and *Kopek des Bordes* – having run (and won) just the twice. *Altior* was also unbeaten (4-4) and in all, eight of the past 12 winners were unbeaten during the current campaign. Those last couple of words are significant when referencing *Vautour*, *Douvan* and *Klassical Dream* who had been beaten in France before moving to Ireland, however all three were unbeaten for Willie Mullins during that current campaign.

Pay healthy respect to those with an unblemished record, especially those who had also won a Grade 1 on their most recent start.

GRADED CLASS PERFORMERS

THE final sentence of the previous subsection leads us on nicely, with no fewer than eight of the past 12 winners having recorded a Grade 1 win on their most recent start. This is a strong statistic and one which should be taken very seriously. *Slade Steel* also hailed from Grade 1 company, having finished runner-up at that level on his most recent start, whilst 13 of the past 14 winners had recorded a Graded win (including Grade 2s and Grade 3s) at some point during the season.

The 2024 winner chased home Baring Bingham winner Ballyburn in the **Tattersalls Ireland Novice Hurdle** – registered as the **Brave Inca Novice Hurdle** – a race which has become the perfect stepping-stone to Supreme glory. No fewer than six of the past 13 winners had contested the Grade 1 at the Dublin Racing Festival, which was previously staged over 2m2f. The other five winners had all won that race, including last year's winner *Kopek des Bordes*, who ran out a hugely impressive 13-length winner at Leopardstown, resulting in him being sent off at very short odds at Cheltenham. All five of those winners were trained by Willie Mullins, whereas this year's race was won by the Joseph O'Brien stable, with Talk The Talk.

Remaining in Ireland, *Marine Nationale* became the first horse since *Like-A-Butterfly* (2001-2002 season) to win the **Royal Bond Novice Hurdle** in the early part of the season, then go on to Supreme glory.

KEY TRENDS

- 25 of the past 29 winners won last time out
- 9 of the past 13 winners were trained by either Willie Mullins (6) or Nicky Henderson (3)
- 8 of the past 12 winners had won a Grade 1 novice hurdle on their most recent start
- Horses rated 153+ are 7-20 during the past 12 years
- 16 of the past 17 winners were aged 5 or 6
- 16 of the 26 winners this century were trained in Ireland (this includes 9 of the past 13)
- 13 of the past 14 winners had won a Graded novice hurdle earlier in the season
- 12 of the past 13 winners were sent off at single figures (11 of those returned at 6-1 or shorter)
- 9 of the past 12 winners were rated 150+
- 8 of the past 12 winners were unbeaten during the current campaign
- 8 of the past 24 winners had contested a Graded bumper the previous spring
- 6 of the past 13 winners had run in the Tattersalls Ireland Novice Hurdle on their most recent start (5 of them had won; all trained by Willie Mullins)
- The past 6 winners had only run 2 or 3 times over hurdles
- 5 of the past 15 winners had won an Irish Point-to-Point at the start of their careers
- Only 3 of the past 21 winners were outright favourite (although 2 have been successful in the past 5 years as well as 1 joint-favourite)
- Only 2 of the past 23 winners were older than 6
- Only 2 of the past 15 winners failed to win last time out
- Only 1 of the past 12 winners was rated below 148
- Only 1 of the past 33 winners wore headgear (last year's winner)
- 4yo's are 0-15 this century
- Genuine ex-Flat horses tend to struggle nowadays
- Be wary of William Hill (ex-Betfair) Hurdle form

In the interim, both *Champagne Fever* and *Labaik* had contested the former Grade 1 contest, which was downgraded prior to last season and is now a Grade 2. This season's race was won by Koktail Brut.

Romeo Coolio finished runner-up in last season's Royal Bond before winning the **Future Champions Novice Hurdle** at Leopardstown's Christmas fixture and ended up hitting the frame in the Supreme. To date, only *Appreciate It* has completed this particular Grade 1 double, although Abacadabras and

Facile Vega won the Festive contest before finishing runner-up at Cheltenham, so winners of that race have been knocking on the Supreme door of late. Skylight Hustle won the race this season, although Talk The Talk was leading when stumbling after the final flight.

Both *Vautour* and *Douvan* won the **Moscow Flyer Novice Hurdle** at Punchestown en route to Cheltenham (the former having time to win the Brave Inca, too). More recently, Impaire et Passe won the Moscow Flyer before winning the Baring Bingham, Mystical Power won the 2024 renewal before going very close in the Supreme and last year's winner Salvator Mundi went on to win the Top Novices' Hurdle at Aintree, after disappointing in the Supreme. This year's Grade 2 was won by another Mullins inmate, Sober.

In the UK, the **Sharp Novices' Hurdle** – run this year as the **Oddschecker Novices' Hurdle** – is the first Graded race over this sort of trip, although having been brought forward to take place at Cheltenham's October (Showcase) meeting, it remains to be seen as to whether it will have much of an impact. It could be that it now features second season novices, or those who won late on in the previous campaign, whilst still holding novice status. Whether a genuine Supreme contender would have the time to get out and win a maiden or novice en route to the October fixture remains to be seen, but the decision behind the switching of the contest was to then allow such horses the option of contesting the Newton Novices' Hurdle at Haydock's Betfair Chase fixture. In recent years, only *Altior* (won) and *Summerville Boy* (2nd) had contested the Sharp, when it was staged at the November (Open) meeting and this season's race was won by Fortune de Mer.

As part of those changes within the division – prior to the 2023-2024 campaign – the Tolworth Novices' Hurdle was moved from Sandown to Aintree's new Boxing Day fixture and was renamed as the **Formby Novices' Hurdle**. It's its former guise, it was won by *Constitution Hill* and *Summerville Boy*, although when staged at Sandown, it was often more of a pointer towards the Baring Bingham. Indeed, last season's winner Potters Charm went on to run in the 2m5f contest, whilst this season's Grade 1 went the way of Idaho Sun, who beat (then Supreme favourite) Mydaddypaddy.

EX-FLAT HORSES TEND TO STRUGGLE

THERE was a time when former Flat horses had to be respected in the Supreme, with *Arcalis* and *Ebaziyan* successful in 2005 and 2007, respectively. *Labaik* is now the only former Flat winner of the race in the past 19 renewals, however, with many such horses now sold to race abroad rather than switching codes. There was no such representation last year and any such runners should be treated with a degree of caution.

BUMPER FORM

IN CONTRAST to the previous subsection, bumper form is becoming increasingly more significant and again, last year's winner *Kopek des Bordes* had won at one of the previous spring festivals, successful in the sales race at Fairyhouse over Easter. A traditional National Hunt background – hailing from bumpers and/or Point-to-Points – is becoming more and more noteworthy in the Supreme, with eight of the past 24 winners having contested a Graded bumper the previous spring.

Four of the past 15 winners had contested the **Weatherbys Champion Bumper** 12 months earlier, again Romeo Coolio hitting the frame in both races. Last year's Champion Bumper saw the mare Bambino Fever beat 16 rivals, who included El Cairos (5th) and Idaho Sun (6th).

SUMMER FORM

THIS is something which I have now highlighted in the past couple of editions of the Guide, with more and more better quality horses appearing in bumpers – and, sometimes over hurdles – during the supposed 'off season' of the summer. A Dream To Share very much fell into this category before winning the Champion Bumper three years ago, whilst *Marine Nationale* won bumpers in late-May and mid-August before developing into a top-class novice, culminating in Supreme success. Mystical Power also won a bumper in late-May before winning on his first start over hurdles at Galway, before finishing runner-up in the Supreme, then winning at Aintree and Punchestown. Therefore, don't be too quick to dismiss 'summer form' these days.

POINT-TO-POINT FORM

WHILST *Kopek des Bordes* missed out on this, four of the previous five winners had contested at least one Irish Point, with three of them successful in that sphere, the outlier being *Constitution Hill*, who made a final fence mistake which cost him victory. A little further back, *Al Ferof* and *Champagne Fever* – winners in 2011 and 2013, respectively – were also ex-Points winners to land the Supreme and although horses from such a background previously had a stronger record in the Baring Bingham, they are very much beginning to come to the fore in the Supreme. Pay healthy respect to winning form in Irish Points, as well as strong/winning bumper form.

OFFICIAL BHA RATINGS (150+)

NINE of the past dozen winners had already obtained an official BHA Rating of 150 or higher, which kind of ties in with the earlier subsection of Graded form being almost essential. Seven of those nine winners were rated 153+ and *Kopek des Bordes* added to this impressive statistic last year, taking the record of such runners to 7-20 during the past 12 years alone. That is a hugely impressive strike-rate and horses with such a lofty rating deserve utmost respect.

During those past 12 years, only one winner – that being *Labaik* – was rated below 147 and really, we should be focusing on those rated 150 or more. Proven form, over potential, often wins the day in the Supreme these days. Indeed, last year saw plenty of relatively inexperienced horses take their chance, with six of the 11 runners yet to have even been handed an official mark. *Tutti Quanti* – the sole British-trained runner in the race – was rated just 125, whilst the only three horses rated in the 140s (between 146-148) finished directly behind the winner, who was a long way clear on ratings.

AGE

ONLY two of the past 23 winners were over the age of six, whilst 16 of the past 17 winners were aged either five (7) or six (9). The six-year-olds hold a slight advantage but by no means as big of an advantage as they do in the Baring Bingham or Albert Bartlett.

There was once again no juvenile representation in 2025, so the record of four-year-olds this century remains at 0-15. With the Triumph no longer the huge field *'lottery'* of old, we see fewer juveniles taking on their elders in the Supreme.

MARKET FORCES

JUSTIFYING odds of 4-6, *Kopek des Bordes* became just the third successful outright favourite in the past 21 renewals, although both *Vautour* and *Constitution Hill* were sent off joint-favourite in recent years. Indeed, thee of the past five winners were either favourite or joint-favourite, whilst the past eight winners hailed from the top four in the betting and seven of them returned at 6/1 or shorter. 12 of the past 13 winners came from the top four in the market, again 11 of them priced at 6/1 or less. With the race less-competitive these days (as per the opening subsection), it seems to have become increasingly more predictable, with the top of the market dominant.

MULLINS & HENDERSON DOMINANCE

DAY one often belongs to this paring, in particular **Willie Mullins**, who has now won the Supreme on eight occasions, spanning back to 1995 when *Tourist Attraction* provided him with his very first Cheltenham Festival winner. More recently, Mullins has won the opener six times since 2013 and although he is often mobhanded in the race, it is his shortest-price runner who invariably prevails. Indeed, of those recent half-dozen winners, all six were *'stable first string'* according to the betting and all returned at 6/1 or shorter (as per the previous subsection). Both A*ppreciate It* and *Kopek des Bordes* have justified odds-on favouritism in the past five years and his runners warrant (obvious) thoughtful consideration.

With Mullins lacking an outstanding candidate this year, it could be that he has several runners.

Between them, Mullins and **Nicky Henderson** have won nine of the past 13 renewals, with the latter responsible for three. Again, his winners were well found in the market and he would be a lot more selective in terms of horses who he would run in the race. Having won it in 1986 and 1992 with *River Ceiriog* and *Flown*, Henderson endured a tough time of it between 2003 and 2017, often hitting the crossbar and seeing some well-fancied and subsequent high-class performers beaten. Binocular, Sprinter Sacre, My Tent Or Yours and Buveur d'Air were among the Henderson-trained *'losers'* during this period, but he got back on track when *Altior* struck 10 years ago and given that he was without representation in 2021, 2023 or 2025, his strike-rate during the past decade stands at an impressive 3-13, with a further four hitting the frame. Therefore, 54% of Henderson's runners during the past 10 years have finished in the first three; a magnificent record for a race of such stature.

Ante-post favourite Old Park Star is the trainer's leading contender this year.

OTHER TRAINERS TO NOTE

RATHER surprisingly, **Paul Nicholls** is the only other trainer to have won the Supreme more than once since the turn of the century. That said, it is now 15 years since the former champion trainer last won the race and despite being responsible for the only British-trained runner last year, Nicholls often targets either the Baring Bingham or Aintree with his leading novice hurdler(s). Indeed, he was without a runner in nine of the renewals since he last won the race.

And, as touched upon previously, despite having won the race just the once, **Gordon Elliott** has gone close with several others and Romeo Coolio was his fourth runner to hit the frame, whilst *Slade Steel* completed the novice hurdle set for **Henry de Bromhead** in 2024. The trainer had earlier won the Baring Bingham, Albert Bartlett and Dawn Run, so is in a select ground of just two (Mullins the other, of course) to have won all four. Workahead proved disappointing for de Bromhead last year but his horses invariably come right during Festival week.

Following the second placing of William Munny, **Barry Connell** deserves a positive mention, given that he won the race in 2023 with *Marine Nationale*. If one is deemed good enough to represent his stable, take note.

IRISH DOMINATION

NINE of the past 13 winners were trained in Ireland and this increases to 16 of the past 26 when looking back a little further. During those past 13 years, Tom George is the only British trainer aside from Nicky Henderson to have won the race, and although this hugely positive trend is massively helped by the impressive record of Willie Mullins, it should be noted that since 1998, 10 different Irish trainers have won the race. Invariably, Irish novice hurdles throughout the season are more strongly contested and that surely has an impact when we reach the Festival.

BE WARY OF THE WILLIAM HILL HURDLE

FORMERLY the Betfair Hurdle – and before that the Tote Gold Trophy and the *'Schweppes'* – the **William Hill Newbury Handicap Hurdle** is a piece of form to be wary of. During the past 16 years, eight novices won the valuable handicap before going on to be beaten in the Supreme and they include Get Me Out Of Here, My Tent Or Yours and Kalashnikov, who all filled the runner-up spot at Cheltenham. New eligibility rules meant that there was zero representation in 2025, whilst the fourth-placed Un Sens A La Vie was one of just two novices in this year's field.

OTHER KEY RACE

BOTH *Klassical Dream* and *Kopek des Bordes* won the **TRI Equestrian Maiden Hurdle** at Leopardstown over Christmas, a four-year-old only contest which kicks off the Christmas Festival. Interestingly, Willie Mullins also used the same race to introduce State Man back in 2021 and having fallen two out, he went on to win the County Hurdle during that novice season. It was won this season by Ballyfad.

HEADGEAR

PRIOR to last year, *Flown* was the last horse to successfully wear headgear in the Supreme Novices' Hurdle, with 42 horses beaten in the interim period. Four of last year's 11-strong field wore a hood – an aid which is becoming increasingly more popular these days – and they included the first and second, with three of the four trained by Willie Mullins (not averse to adding headgear these days). Whilst it was once frowned upon and the statistics very much still suggest it is a negative, it wouldn't be a huge shock if *Kopek des Bordes* was the first in an evolving trend. Indeed, Mystical Power (also, Mullins-trained) went close in 2024 and we have seen Il Etait Temps win multiple Grade 1s for the stable in a hood in recent seasons.

ROLL OF HONOUR

Year	Form	Winner	Age	Weight	OR	SP	Trainer	Runners	Last Race (No. of days)
2025	11	Kopek des Bordes	5	11-7	157	4/6F	W Mullins (IRE)	11	1st Gr.1 Tattersalls Ireland Nov. Hurdle (37)
2024	112	Slade Steel	6	11-7	147	7/2	H de Bromhead (IRE)	11	2nd Gr.1 Tattersalls Ireland Nov. Hurdle (37)
2023	11	Marine Nationale	6	11-7	150	9/2	B Connell (IRE)	14	1st Gr.1 Royal Bond Nov. Hurdle (100)
2022	11	Constitution Hill	5	11-7	148	9/4JF	N Henderson	9	1st Gr.1 Tolworth Nov. Hurdle (66)
2021	111	Appreciate It	7	11-7	153	8/11F	W Mullins (IRE)	8	1st Gr.1 Tattersalls Ireland Nov. Hurdle (37)
2020	F11	Shishkin	6	11-7	153	6/1	N Henderson	15	1st Sidney Banks Nov. Hurdle (40)
2019	11	Klassical Dream	5	11-7	154	6/1	W Mullins (IRE)	16	1st Gr.1 Tattersalls Ireland Nov. Hurdle (37)
2018	12231	Summerville Boy	6	11-7	150	9/1	T George	19	1st Gr.1 Tolworth Nov. Hurdle (66)
2017	11RR6	Labaik	6	11-7	144	25/1	G Elliott (IRE)	14	6th Naas Nov. Hurdle (16)
2016	61111	Altior	6	11-7	155	4/1	N Henderson	14	1st Kempton Nov. Hurdle (80)

LEADING TEN-YEAR GUIDES

Royal Bond Novice Hurdle 2 (*Labaik* ref. to race, *Marine Nationale* 1st)
Tattersalls Ireland Novices' Hurdle 4 (*Klassical Dream* 1st, *Appreciate It* 1st, *Slade Steel* 2nd, *Kopek des Bordes* 1st)
Sky Bet Supreme Trial Novices' Hurdle (Sharp Novices' Hurdle) 2 (*Altior* 1st, *Summerville Boy* 2nd)
Tolworth Novices' Hurdle 2 (*Summerville Boy* 1st, *Constitution Hill* 1st)
Navan Novice Hurdle 2 (*Labaik* ref. to race, *Slade Steel* 1st)
TRI Equestrian Maiden Hurdle 2 (*Klassical Dream* 1st, *Kopek des Bordes* 1st)

Leading Contenders

OLD PARK STAR — Trainer: Nicky Henderson
Failed to win a bumper in three starts last season but is 3-3 over hurdles since moving to Nicky Henderson, recording wins at Kempton, Cheltenham (New Course) and Haydock, where he showed a fine turn of foot to win the Grade 2 Rossington Main by 18 lengths. An exciting prospect, who sees his races out very strongly, he sets a good standard (BHA Rating 151) and bids to provide his trainer with a sixth win in the race (and a fourth since 2016). Looks potentially top-class.

TALK THE TALK — Trainer: Joseph O'Brien
Runner-up in the sales bumper at Newbury last spring, he won a Limerick maiden hurdle before landing a Grade 3 at Fairyhouse and looked desperately unlucky when stumbling after the final flight at Leopardstown over Christmas. Returned to the same course and gained Grade 1 compensation in the Tattersalls Ireland Novice Hurdle, where he showed a fine turn of foot to quicken up off a relatively sedate pace. Shapes like he will improve for contesting a more truly run race and is an obvious contender.

EL CAIROS — Trainer: Gordon Elliott
Fifth in last year's Champion Bumper, he fell when in command at Leopardstown over Christmas and duly got off the mark in a much weaker maiden at Thurles, although it wasn't without a fright at the final flight (again). A horse who possesses plenty of natural pace, better ground and a strongly run race should bring about improvement, but he did show a tendency to wander off a true line in bumpers, so there is a suspicion that he isn't totally straightforward. A very talented novice, nevertheless.

BALLYFAD — Trainer: Gordon Elliott
Lost his unbeaten record when narrowly going down to Talk The Talk at the DRF, he had earlier won a brace of bumpers and impressed when winning on hurdles debut. Shapes like he will appreciate a stiffer test and does have the Baring Bingham as an option, with Gordon Elliott also having both El Cairos and Skylight Hustle to consider. A thoroughly likeable five-year-old with a determined attitude, he looks capable of making an impact in either race, with a more truly run contest likely to bring about further improvement.

MYDADDYPADDY — Trainer: Dan Skelton
Looked a high-class prospect when winning a Huntingdon bumper and his first two starts over hurdles, at Carlisle and Haydock. His hurdling was fast and fluent, and as a result, he was sent off at 8-13 to land the Formby at Aintree. Despite travelling well, he was unable to get to the winner, with the omitted hurdles up the home straight offered as an excuse. Sure to move well for a long way, he will need to find more at the business end of this race but remains with considerable potential.

IDAHO SUN — Trainer: Harry Fry
Winner of the aforementioned Formby, he also would surely have benefited from the hurdles remaining in, but displayed a fine attitude to repel the challenge of Mydaddypaddy. He had earlier won easily at Fontwell and Bangor, whilst his bumper form reads well, with him beating several subsequent winners at Newton Abbot and Windsor, before finishing sixth in last year's Champion Bumper. A strong stayer over the minimum trip, he is rated just 141 but is yet another who is sure to relish a truly run race.

DAY ONE RACE TWO

SINGER ARKLE CHALLENGE TROPHY NOVICES' CHASE
1m7f 199y (Grade 1) – Old Course

OVERVIEW
THE first steeplechase of the week, the Arkle is a novices' chase which is staged over the minimum trip and has a rich history. Past winners include greats like *Remittance Man*, *Travado*, *Klairon Davis* and *Flagship Uberalles*, whilst winners this century include the likes of *Moscow Flyer*, *Azertyuiop*, *Well Chief*, *Voy Por Ustedes*, *Sizing Europe*, *Sprinter Sacre*, *Simonsig*, *Un de Sceaux*, *Altior* and *Shishkin*, with several of those recent winners trained by Nicky Henderson. This is another race in which Henderson and Willie Mullins boast a strong recent record and although field sizes have been down in recent years, it is still the most prestigious race in the novice chase division staged at the Festival.

CHANGES MADE LAST YEAR
AHEAD of last season, it was announced that the Golden Miller Novices' Chase – run under the sponsorship banner of Turners in recent years – was to be removed and replaced by the returning novices' handicap. The thought process behind this – in part at least, I guess – was that it would in turn make the Arkle and Broadway Novices' Chase more competitive, with trainers/owners not having the option of running a Grade 1 novice over an intermediate trip. In one sense, it worked last year as the winner would almost certainly have run over a longer trip had that race still been in place, however, we still only saw five horses go to post, that being the joint lowest field size this century, along with 2018 and 2021.

HENDERSON & MULLINS DOMINANCE
WITH Sir Gino sadly sidelined, at one stage it looked as though **Nicky Henderson** might not be represented but he opted to drop *Jango Baie* in trip – rather than stepping him up to contest the Broadway (as per the previous subsection) – and although it seemed most unlikely for the majority of the race, he got up to win a dramatic renewal. In doing so, he provided Henderson with a record stretching eighth win in the race and a sixth this century. The great *Remittance Man* and *Travado* got the ball rolling for Henderson in the early 90s and after *Tiutchev* made it three wins for the trainer in 2000, he has enjoyed a fine spell since 2012, winning with it *Sprinter Sacre*, *Simonsig*, *Altior*, *Shishkin* and again last year. The trainer specialises with speed horses in the 2m divisions – both over hurdles and fences – and his record in this contest speaks for itself.

The recent record of **Willie Mullins** is equally as impressive. Mullins has won six of the past 11 renewals, successful four times in five years between 2015 and 2019, whilst *El Fabiolo* and *Gaelic Warrior* have provided him with his most recent victories. He saddled hot-favourite Majborough last year and although he was unable to enhance that fine recent record – surely would have done but for the serious error two out – Mullins' leading contender for this race also warrants utmost respect.

Between them, the pair have now been responsible for 11 of the past 14 winners of the race. Lulamba (Henderson) and Kopek des Bordes (Mullins) head the betting for this year's race.

CHASING EXPERIENCE
11 OF THE past 14 winners had raced no more than three times over fences previously, so rather like with

the opening Supreme Novices' Hurdle, experience isn't as important as it once was. Again, the smaller fields and less competitive nature of the races is surely a key factor in this and *Jango Baie* was able to win last year's race on the back of just two chase starts, something which *El Fabiolo* also managed just three years ago. Experience can't be seen as a negative but certainly the lack of greater experience is no longer a real concern.

Indeed, Majborough ran on the back of just two runs last year – perhaps, a little more experience might have helped his jumping (who knows!) – whilst Sir Gino would have done the same, had he not been ruled out of the Festival, so many leading trainers are clearly leaning this way. In contrast, L'Eau du Sud had been kept busy through the early part of the season – winning three times between October and December before returning to win the Kingmaker en route to Cheltenham – and perhaps, this more aggressive approach (which is refreshing to see in this day and age) isn't advantageous by the time we reach the spring. He certainly seemed a bit flat at Aintree, which came on the back of his fourth placing in the Arkle.

THE UNBEATEN CHASER

NINE of the past 16 winners were unbeaten over fences, although only two of the past seven winners have fallen into this category, so again, it wouldn't appear to be as strong of a trend as it was earlier in the century. Between 2010 and 2018, no fewer than seven of the nine winners were unbeaten and it is a division in which a horse can be dominant, so rattling up a sequence of wins can be achieved.

LAST TIME OUT WINNERS

PRIOR to 2024, the previous 14 winners had won on their most recent start, although *Gaelic Warrior* (unseated his rider when well beaten at the time) and *Jango Baie* (runner-up in the Scilly Isles) have proven that the Arkle can be won on the back of a defeat. Crucially, both horses were contesting Grade 1 novice chases on their most recent starts and both over an intermediate trip, so dropped in distance to win this race. It can, however, usually pay to focus on those who are arriving at Cheltenham on the back of a win, something which is common in all Grade 1 novice events.

GRADED CLASS PERFORMERS

ALTHOUGH last year's winner failed to add his name to the list – beaten a short-head the time before in the Grade 1 Scilly Isles at Sandown – 19 of the previous 24 winners had already won either a Grade 1 or Grade 2 over fences earlier in the season, so pay healthy respect to those arriving at Cheltenham with a

KEY TRENDS

- ⭐ 19 of the past 25 winners had won a Grade 1 or Grade 2 over fences
- ⭐ 11 of the past 14 winners were trained by Willie Mullins (6) or Nicky Henderson (5)
- ⭐ 7 of the past 13 winners had won a Grade 1 or Grade 2 over both hurdles and fences
- ⭐ Horses rated 161+ are 7-16 since 2012
- ✓ 27 of the past 34 winners were aged 6 or 7
- ✓ 19 of the past 25 winners won last time out
- ✓ 16 of the past 23 winners had run 3 or 4 times over fences
- ✓ 16 of the past 22 winners spent just one season over hurdles
- ✓ 15 of the past 22 winners had run at the previous year's Cheltenham Festival
- ✓ 15 of the past 20 winners had won at least twice over fences
- ✓ 12 of the past 18 winners were officially top-rated (BHA Ratings)
- ✓ 10 of the past 14 favourites have won
- ✓ 9 of the past 16 winners were unbeaten over fences
- ✓ Alan King-trained runners are 3-5 since 2006
- ✗ 5yo's are 0-17 since 2007
- ✗ Only 2 winners this century were sent off at double figure odds
- ✗ Only 2 of the past 24 winners had failed to win a Grade 1 or Grade 2 (over hurdles or fences)
- ✗ Only 3 winners this century had run more than 4 times over fences
- ✗ Only 3 of the past 34 winners were older than 7
- ✗ Only 4 winners this century had fallen (or UR) earlier in the season
- ✗ Paul Nicholls has struggled in recent years
- ✗ Gordon Elliott-trained runners are 0-7

Graded win on the board. The fact that Leopardstown reintroduced their Grade 1 at the Christmas Festival (staged over 2m1f) after just a one year absence means that there are again more top-level opportunities in this division in Ireland than there are in Britain.

HIGH-CLASS HURDLES FORM

FORM at a similar level – in Graded company – over hurdles is also a positive. In recent years, the likes of *Moscow Flyer*, *Sizing Europe* and *Un de Sceaux* were verging on Champion Hurdle class as hurdlers and translated that level of ability (and then some) to fences over the minimum trip. The likes of *Douvan*, *Altior* and *Shishkin* were high-class novice hurdlers the previous season, whilst the past two winners – *Gaelic Warrior* and *Jango Baie* – were both Grade 1 winners as novice hurdlers the previous season, last year's winner successful in the very first running of the Formby Novices' Hurdle at Aintree.

Seven of the past 13 winners had actually won a Grade 1 or Grade 2 over both hurdles and fences and only two winners this century had failed to win at either level under either discipline. Look towards those with the strongest form in the book.

CHELTENHAM FESTIVAL FORM

LAST year's winner had never run at the Cheltenham Festival previously but 15 of the 20 winners before him had done and it can usually pay to focus on the novice hurdles from 12 months earlier. *El Fabiolo* also showed that the Arkle can be won without any prior Festival experience but it certainly remains a positive, nevertheless.

Sizing Europe and *Footpad* are a couple of fairly recent winners who had contested the Champion Hurdle the previous season, whilst the majority with Festival form to their name came in novice company, with many a recent Arkle winner sent chasing after their novice hurdle campaign (more of that shortly).

Between 2012 and 2021, four of the 10 winners had contested the **Supreme Novices' Hurdle** on the very same card the previous year, with *Douvan*, *Altior* and *Shishkin* all completing the double. *Sprinter Sacre* had finished third in one of the most competitive Supremes in recent years and the main protagonists from last year's race warrant careful consideration if lining up here. Kopek des Bordes and Romeo Coolio have emerged from last year's Supreme and developed into leading contenders for the Arkle.

Since 2008, five horses – including 2024 winner *Gaelic Warrior*, who had also finished runner-up in the Boodles 12 months earlier – had run in the **Baring Bingham Novices' Hurdle** the previous year. Only *Simonsig* completed the double, although the other quartet all finished in the first five, so again, pay healthy respect to any horse dropping back in trip having run well on day two last year.

QUICKLY SENT CHASING

AS TOUCHED upon in the previous subsection, we have seen Champion Hurdle-standard horses win the Arkle and climbing the hurdling ladder doesn't seem as overly detrimental in the two mile division as it does with stayers (see Broadway preview on day two). However, 16 of the past 22 winners were sent chasing after just one season over hurdles, so again, focusing on those who were contesting novice hurdles a year ago is certainly a positive.

Ideally, when it comes to a novice chaser (in my opinion at least and something which I factor in heavily when producing *Jumpers To Follow* each year), switching to the larger obstacles when still relatively unexposed and on the up is often hugely important. Learning how to jump fences – which doesn't always come naturally to all horses – is likely to be much easier when a horse has had less opportunity to learn the art of low, efficient hurdling, or worse, having picked up bad habits and finds change difficult.

AGE

17 OF THE past 19 winners were aged either six (9) or seven (8) which fits in with the previous subsection. Six of the past eight winners were aged six – which is the most popular age in recent years – with *Edwardstone*, the only *'older'* winner during the past 15 years, successful at the age of eight in 2022. Only 3 of the past 34 winners were over the age of seven.

At the other end of the scale, four five-year-olds were successful between 1998 and 2006, when the age-allowance was very much still in play. That was removed in 2008, making it much tougher for such young horses, who would have to compete off level weights with their elders (over 2m) come the spring. Since 2007, five-year-olds boast a dismal record of 0-17 in the Arkle and this, of course, includes last year's beaten favourite Majborough.

Last season was unusual, as we saw a trio of high-class four-year-olds sent chasing in the autumn/winter of 2024, in Sir Gino, Majborough and Kalif du Berlais, who was able to defy the age statistic in Grade 1 company at Aintree. The hope is that this will once again encourage more younger horses (usually French-bred) to be switched to chasing at an early stage, for all that this record remains a little off-putting.

This is a significant negative barrier which Lulamba will need to overcome, whilst Mambonumberfive is another possible runner-up for that age group.

SOLID JUMPERS

WHILST a fall, or unseat, can be put behind an Arkle winner, ideally we should be focusing on a sound jumper. Indeed, despite his inexperience, *Jango Baie* had looked a natural when jumping around the New Course on chase debut earlier in the season. Only four winners this century had fallen or unseated their rider earlier in the campaign, so letters in a horse's form figures must still be seen as a negative.

OFFICAL BHA RATINGS

SINCE 2008 – when the BHA first published official ratings for all runners (including those trained in Ireland) – 11 of the 18 winners were top-rated and prior to last year, included the previous four and eight of the previous 10. Despite his inexperience, *Jango Baie* was still third best in this regard, with an official mark of 153, and looking at those in the 150s is a good starting point at the very least, with *Put The Kettle On* the only winner rated below 151 in the past 11 years. You usually need a horse rated in the mid-150s to win an Arkle.

We have seen some high-class winners of the Arkle and the likes of *Sprinter Sacre* (169) and *Altior* (170) had already obtained ridiculously high ratings for novices prior to their wins. Since 2012, only 16 horses rated 161 or higher have run in the Arkle and seven of them were successful. Despite the fact that Majborough couldn't add to that impressive strike rate last year, such high-class horses have to be given utmost respect in a race in which the cream often rises to the top.

MARKET FORCES

MAJBOROUGH was a costly blow, early in the week, for punters, with the five-year-old sent off the 1-2 favourite. However, in general, the Arkle has been a 'punter friendly' contest in recent years, with only two winners this century being sent off at double figure odds. 10 of the previous 13 favourites had proven successful, with six of the seven winners between 2012 and 2018 returning at odds-on. This isn't really a race in which we see too many 'shock' results, with *Western Warhorse* the biggest priced winner this century, when scoring at 33-1. *Put The Kettle On* (16-1) was the other winner to return at double figures.

OTHER KEY RACES

THERE is only one Grade 1 novice chase over this sort of trip in Britain prior to the Arkle, with both *Altior* and *Edgestone* winning Sandown's **Henry VIII Novices' Chase** en route to Cheltenham. It is possibly a little early in the campaign and as last season's winner *L'Eau du Sud* showed, it can be difficult to maintain that level of peak form for a whole season. This season's race was won by Lulamba.

Taking place a few weeks later, the **Wayward Lad Novices' Chase** – a Grade 2 staged at Kempton's Christmas fixture – seems to be better placed in the calendar and has thrown up five Arkle winners since the 2011-2012 season. Four of those were trained by Nicky Henderson, who took last year's race with *Sir Gino*, who would certainly have gone off favourite for the Arkle had he not missed the race through injury. This season's renewal went to Ben Pauling and Mambonumberfive.

The Grade 2 closest the Festival, in the calendar, is the **Kingmaker Novices' Chase** from Warwick. That race has been won by three Arkle winners since 1999 but actually often now acts as a better platform to the Maghull Novices' Chase at Aintree. Having taken place shortly before the Guide was sent to print, it was won this year by Steel Ally.

At a lower level, both *Altior* and *Shishkin* started their chasing careers by winning the same 2m2f Kempton **Beginners' Chase** and that race was won this season by Lucy Wadham's Jax Junior.

Similarly, over in Ireland, beginners' chases at Navan are invariably strong early-season contests and both *Douvan* and *Footpad* won the **Irish Stallion Farms EBF Beginners Chase** on their first start over fences. *Vautour* also won that contest before winning at the Festival the following spring, whilst the corresponding race was won by Kopek des Bordes in November.

Without doubt, however, the most significant race in this division in Ireland is (rather unsurprisingly) the **Irish Arkle**, which takes place at Leopardstown's Dublin Racing Festival. Majborough was unable to enhance the fine recent record of horses hailing from that contest in recent years, with *Un de Sceaux*, *Douvan*, *Footpad* and *El Fabiolo* all completing the double in the past 11 years. All four were trained by Willie Mullins, who saddled the second this year, with Kargese narrowly denied by Romeo Coolio.

Following a one year break, the **Racing Post Novice Chase** returned to the Christmas fixture and is staged over the same course-and-distance. *Douvan* and *Footpad* also landed that Grade 1 contest, which was won this season by Romeo Coolio as well.

OTHER TRAINERS TO NOTE

ASIDE from the dominant forces of Nicky Henderson and Willie Mullins (covered in an earlier subsection), **Alan King** boasts the best recent record, with three wins to his name since 2006. Successful with *Voy Por Ustedes* and *My Way de Solzen* in 2006 and 2007, respectively, King struck again with *Edgestone* in 2022 and is very much more selective in terms of his runners in the Arkle. In fact, since 2006 he has only saddled five runners in the race, so boasts an incredible strike rate in it.

Paul Nicholls won a brace of Arkles in the space of four years between 1999 and 2003, with *Flagship Uberalles* and *Azertyuiop*, although his last 13 runners in the race have finished unplaced. Without a runner again in 2025, he often tends to target Aintree with his leading novice chasers these days and indeed took the Maghull (again) with Kalif du Berlais last year.

DAY ONE RACE TWO

In terms of *'other'* Irish trainers, **Henry de Bromhead** does well with 2m chasers in general and has won two Arkles since 2010, with *Sizing Europe* and *Put The Kettle On*, who remains the only mare to have won the race. He has also been responsible for a further three horses to have finished second or third in recent years and his runner(s) should always be given plenty of respect.

Found A Fifty was the first placed horse of **Gordon Elliott** in the Arkle in 2024, with his previous five runners – which included beaten favourites Hardline and Riviere d'Etel – all finishing unplaced. Touch Me Not finished last of five last year and this remains a Grade 1 contest which the leading trainer has yet to master. He looks set to saddle Romeo Coolio this year, although he does have the option of stepping him up in trip for the Broadway on day two.

Lulamba wins the Henry VIII at Sandown

ROLL OF HONOUR

Year	Form	Winner	Age	Weight	OR	SP	Trainer	Runners	Last Race (No. of days)
2025	12	Jango Baie	6	11-7	153	5/1	N Henderson	5	2nd Gr.1 Scilly Isles Nov. Chase (38)
2024	11U	Gaelic Warrior	6	11-7	157	2/1F	W Mullins (IRE)	10	U.R. Gr.1 Ladbrokes Nov. Chase (37)
2023	11	El Fabiolo	6	11-7	162	11/10F	W Mullins (IRE)	9	1st Gr.1 Irish Arkle (38)
2022	B1111	Edwardstone	8	11-4	159	5/2F	A King	11	1st Gr.2 Kingmaker Nov. Chase (31)
2021	111	Shishkin	7	11-4	164	4/9F	N Henderson	5	1st Gr.2 Lightning Nov. Chase (44)
2020	111121	Put The Kettle On	7	10-11	144	16/1	H de Bromhead (IRE)	11	1st Gr.2. Arkle Trophy Trial (114)
2019	231	Duc des Genievres	6	11-4	151	5/1	W Mullins (IRE)	12	1st Gowran Beginners' Chase (24)
2018	111	Footpad	6	11-4	162	5/6F	W Mullins (IRE)	5	1st Gr.1 Irish Arkle (38)
2017	1111	Altior	7	11-4	170	1/4F	N Henderson	9	1st Gr.2 Game Spirit Chase (31)
2016	111	Douvan	6	11-4	161	1/4F	W Mullins (IRE)	7	1st Gr.1 Irish Arkle (51)

LEADING TEN-YEAR GUIDES

Kempton Beginners' Chase 2 (*Altior* 1st, *Shishkin* 1st)
Irish Arkle 3 (*Douvan* 1st, *Footpad* 1st, *El Fabiolo* 1st)
Wayward Lad Novices' Chase 3 (*Altior* 1st, *Shishkin* 1st, *Edwardstone* 1st)
*Supreme Novices' Hurdle 3 (*Douvan* 1st, *Altior* 1st, *Shishkin* 1st)
Racing Post Novice Chase 2 (*Douvan* 1st, *Footpad* 1st)
Irish Stallion Farms EBF Beginners Chase 2 (*Douvan* 1st, *Footpad* 1st)
Henry VIII Novices' Chase 2 (*Altior* 1st, *Edwardstone* 1st)

* denotes previous season

Leading Contenders

LULAMBA   Trainer: Nicky Henderson
Runner-up in last year's Triumph Hurdle, he gained Grade 1 honours at Punchestown and matched that feat on just his second start over fences, in Sandown's Henry VIII Novices' Chase. He bettered that when winning the Game Spirit, where he followed in the footsteps of Sprinter Sacre and Altior, who both won that Grade 2 as a novice before landing the Arkle. That is the strongest piece of chase form on offer and he has already attained a BHA Rating of 163 Bids to become the first winning five-year-old in 20 years.

KOPEK DES BORDES   Trainer: Willie Mullins
Successful in last year's Supreme Novices' Hurdle, he ran out a comfortable winner on his first start over fences at Navan but was then forced to miss Christmas and still wasn't deemed fit enough to contest the Irish Arkle. Will head to Cheltenham on the back of just one chase start, meaning he will bid to emulate the likes of Well Chief and Western Warhorse, who were able to win this on just their second start over fences. Clearly a huge talent, but his preparation can hardly be viewed upon as a positive.

ROMEO COOLIO   Trainer: Gordon Elliott
Third in last year's Supreme, he has developed into a better chaser and is 4-4 over fences, winning three Grade 1s in the process. More impressive over 2m4f on his first two starts, he has since won twice over 2m1f at Leopardstown, staying on strongly on each occasion, to beat Irish Panther and Kargese, respectively. Possibly caught between two stones (distance wise) at Cheltenham, he looked to have a tough race when winning the Irish Arkle and it is hoped that his busy first half of the season doesn't catch up with him.

KARGESE   Trainer: Willie Mullins
Just a neck behind Romeo Coolio in the Irish Arkle, she had him in trouble two out and this sharper test ought to suit. Winner of last year's County Hurdle and runner-up in the 2024 Triumph, she boasts excellent Festival form and has progressed steadily in three chase starts. An easy and wide-margin winner at Leopardstown, she is likely to be ridden positively and boasts plenty of form on better ground. The six-year-old will receive 7lb from the geldings and provided that Irish Arkle hasn't left a mark, she looks capable of a big run.

IRISH PANTHER   Trainer: Eddie & Patrick Harty
Only 10th in last year's County Hurdle, he shed his maiden tag at the ninth attempt, before winning on chase debut at Naas. Quite keen (wears a hood), he put up a career best when beaten by Romeo Coolio at Leopardstown's Christmas fixture. He looked the most likely winner approaching the last and this sharper test should suit. Missed the Irish Arkle due to the ground, he lacks a bit of chasing experience and although he hasn't looked like falling, has got in tight once or twice, which would be a worry at Cheltenham.

STEEL ALLY   Trainer: Sam Thomas
A smart hurdler – winner of a handicap at Haydock and runner-up in the National Sprit Hurdle – he has improved for going chasing and is 3-3, with the hat-trick brought up in the Kingmaker at Warwick. Winner of a graduation chase at Carlisle and a Grade 2 at Ascot, he does shape like an intermediate trip might suit ideally (Aintree could be an option), but he could easily run well if we get soft ground and stamina becomes a factor. Slightly older than your standard Arkle winner, he is a likeable sort.

DAY ONE RACE THREE

McCOY CONTRACTORS JUVENILE HANDICAP HURDLE (Fred Winter)
2m 87y (Premier Handicap) – Old Course

OVERVIEW
THE first handicap hurdle is the *'Fred Winter'* - a race for four-year-olds only which was first run in 2005. Rather like with the Triumph, French-imported juveniles (those who ran in France at the beginning of their careers) boast a strong record a race which has been dominated by the Irish of late. Gordon Elliott has won it on four occasions and Joseph O'Brien has won three of the past seven renewals, including both 2024 and 2025. This is a race which the all-conquering Willie Mullins has yet to master, however.

O'BRIEN ON A HAT-TRICK
WHILST his yard is very much leaning more towards the Flat these days, trainer **Joseph O'Brien** first won this race in 2019 with *Band Of Outlaws* and has followed up with back-to-back wins in the past two renewals, courtesy of *Lark In The Mornin* and *Puturhandstogether*. All three were well found in the market (all sent off at single figures) and it is clearly a race which his team like to target. All three horses had run just three times – the minimum required to get into the race – so it would appear to be a long term plan from an early stage. Two of O'Brien's winners actually contested the same early season race at Cork (more of that later) so a pattern is emerging and in those past seven years, he has saddled 10 runners, including Harsh, who finished fourth at 40-1 two years ago.

ELLIOTT WITH FOUR UP
LEADING Irish trainer **Gordon Elliott** also boasts a magnificent record in the race, having won it four times in the past 13 years. *Flaxen Flare* got the ball rolling for Elliott, who has since saddled *Veneer Of Charm, Aramax* and *Jazzy Matty* to strike in the past eight years. Often very well represented, his winners have returned at odds of 25-1, 33-1, 15-2 and 18-1, so don't let market position put you off in relation to his runners. Campeador might have further enhanced that record some 10 years ago, but for falling at the final hurdle, and any runner(s) from his County Meath base require careful consideration.

IRISH DOMINATION
THE records of O'Brien and Elliott clearly helps but Irish-trained horses have now won the past eight renewals. Noel Meade and Padraig Roche have got in on the act of late and whilst the British-trained runners dominated between 2006 and 2017, the Irish are very much on top nowadays.

MULLINS MISERY CONTINUES
ONE Irish trainer who has yet to get his name on the scoreboard is **Willie Mullins**, who ran another two to no avail last year, Murcia (who won a Grade 1 next time) finishing only eighth and Sony Bill in 14th. Mullins was responsible for three beaten favourites in succession between 2021 and 2023, with both Saint Sam and Gaelic Warrior – still a mystery how he was beaten off a mark of 129 – filling the runners-up spot. The record of runners from Closutton now stands at 0-24 and for the time being at least, runners from that stable – given that they are invariably well found in the market – should be treated with caution.

THE FRENCH INFLUENCE

WE HAVE actually only seen one French-bred winner of this race in the past nine years but previously, such runners really were the dominant force and as we have seen in the Triumph Hurdle, it can be a division in which French-breds flourish. Of more significance when it comes to the *'Fred Winter'* are horses who began their racing careers in France (irrespective of breeding), with 10 of the 21 winners ticking this box. Again, this was slightly more noticeable between 2006 and 2017, but both *Aramax* and *Jazzy Matty* raced in France before joining Gordon Elliott and whilst it might not be the strong positive that it was a few years ago, such runners are still worth noting.

GERMAN-BRED SUCCESS

DESPITE running in France, *Aramax* was a German-bred and *Lark In The Mornin* became the second German-bred winner in the space of five years, when successful in 2024. During this period, Gaelic Warrior (also started off in France) went very close in 2022 and with no horse carrying the *'(GER)'* suffix last year, there have only been five such runners in the past six renewals. Two winners and a second is a hugely noteworthy strike rate and any German-bred juveniles should, therefore, be noted.

AVOID BRITISH-BRED RUNNERS

IN CONTRAST, British-bred horses continue to struggle. The only such winner to date was *Crack Away Jack* in 2008, although he was another who came from France, so wasn't your typical *'Brit'*. Since then, the record of British-bred runners in this race (during the past 17 renewals) stands at 0-73, following the five more reversals last year. They included beaten-favourite Stencil (trained in France but British-bred) and although we have seen such runners hit the frame in the past two years – Robbies Rock finishing runner-up at 50-1 last year being one example – British-bred juveniles should still be treated with caution.

OFFICIAL BHA RATINGS AND WEIGHTS

BETWEEN 2019 and 2022, three of the four winners were rated between 137 and 139, suggesting that the classier horses were starting to come to the fore. We then saw a couple of winners rated 125 and 122 before *Puturhandstogether* scored off 130 in 2025. There isn't too much consistency in terms of official BHA Ratings, although only three of the 21 winners were rated higher than 134, those being the aforementioned trio.

In terms of weight carried, 13 of the 21 winners carried 11-0 or more, including last year's winner

KEY TRENDS

- ⭐ The past 8 winners were trained in Ireland
- ⭐ 4 of the past 13 winners were trained by Gordon Elliott
- ⭐ 3 of the past 7 winners were trained by Joseph O'Brien
- ⭐ German-bred horses are 2-5 during the past 6 years
- ✓ 13 of the 21 winners carried 11-0 or more
- ✓ 13 of the 21 winners had run exactly 3 times over hurdles
- ✓ 12 of the 21 winners had won just once over hurdles
- ✓ 10 of the 21 winners started their careers in France
- ✓ 9 of the 21 winners won last time out
- ✓ 8 of the 21 winners had run against older horses
- ✓ 7 of the past 14 winners returned at odds of 25-1+
- ✓ 6 of the past 15 winners had run in a Grade 1 or Grade 2 earlier in the season
- ✓ Paul Nicholls has trained 3 winners
- ✓ Respect French-bred juveniles (although this trend is fading)
- ✗ Only 3 of the 21 winners were rated higher than 134
- ✗ Only 2 of the 21 winners had won more than twice over hurdles
- ✗ Only 2 of the past 12 winners carried less than 11-0
- ✗ Only 1 of the past 15 winners was sent off favourite
- ✗ British-bred horses are 0-73 during the past 17 years
- ✗ Willie Mullins-trained runners are 0-24

who shouldered 11-6. As with all handicaps, the table below illustrates the rating of the winner, as well as both top- and bottom-weight and as you can see, in recent years, low 120s is now getting in:

	Winner OR	Top Weight OR	Lowest OR
2025	130	136	121
2024	122	134	120
2023	125	142	120
2022	137	138	122
2021	125	141	123
2020	138	140	129
2019	139	141	129
2018	129	139	126
2017	134	139	124
2016	133	142	128

THREE IS THE MAGIC NUMBER

AS ALREADY briefly touched upon, in the opening subsection, Joseph O'Brien's three winners had all run just three times, which is the minimum requirement to make a horse eligible. Whilst the rules changed for open handicaps, this all juvenile affair still requires participants to have run just three times and keeping hurdle runs down to a minimum means that there is less chance of the handicapper getting a true handle on the ability of a horse. Last year's winner became the 13th to have run exactly three times prior to Cheltenham and in most circumstances (certainly with O'Brien, I believe), this is not a coincidence.

WINNING EXPERIENCE

ONLY two of the 21 winners to date had won more than twice over hurdles, whilst 16 of the 21 winners had won either once or never at all. 12 of those 16 had won just one race over hurdles and four of the past five winners fell into this category.

Interestingly, only nine of 21 winners won on their most recent start, so don't let a last-time-out defeat put you off. Indeed, the past three winners arrived at Cheltenham on the back of finishing second, third or fourth.

GRADED RACE FORM

OF THOSE who were beaten last time, five were contesting a Graded race, so were effectively dropping in class. Whilst none of the past four winners had run in a Graded race, six of the previous 11 had done so earlier in the campaign. Again, this is a trend which could be on the decline, so I suggest keeping an open mind in this regard, with recent winners campaigned at a lower level and perhaps, enabling them to get in off lower marks.

Certainly not so long back it seemed to be a positive to have run in a Graded juvenile hurdle earlier in the season, with both *Aramax* and *Jeff Kidder* having run in the **Changing Times Brewery Juvenile Hurdle** at Leopardstown's Christmas Festival. Going back even further, *What A Charm* actually made her debut in the same Grade 2, which was formerly known as the Knight Frank Juvenile Hurdle. She went on to contest the **Spring Juvenile Hurdle** – the Grade 1 staged at the Dublin Racing Festival – a race in which *Flaxen Flare* also finished down the field.

FORM AGAINST ELDERS

THIS is something which we saw a lot more of in the early days of this race, although *Puturhandstogether* took on older horses in his final race ahead of Cheltenham last year and in doing so, became the eighth winner to have run outside of juvenile company. Perhaps, this stands such runners in good stead for the big field scenario which they will be faced with at the Festival.

OTHER KEY RACES

FOUR winners in the space of five years arrived at Cheltenham having run in the same **Naas 4YO Rated Hurdle** on their previous start, with *Band Of Outlaws*, *Aramax* and *Brazil* all successful. *Jazzy Matty* finished fourth in the same race in 2023 and although last year's Naas second Murcia could finish only eighth here, she did go on to win the Grade 1 Anniversary Juvenile Hurdle at Aintree on her next start. This year's race was won by the filly Highland Crystal, who beat Saratoga (immediately installed as joint-favourite) and Munsif.

Last year's winner won a **Cork 3YO Maiden Hurdle** on his second start and the same early December race was where Joseph O'Brien introduced *Band Of Outlaws*. Sponsored by BAR 1 Betting, it was again won by O'Brien, this time by Glen To Glen, successful on his third start.

MARKET FORCES

LOOKING at past results, this race would appear to be one of the more difficult puzzles to solve throughout the whole week. We have seen winners priced at 33-1 (twice) and 80-1 during the past nine years alone and half of the past 14 winners returned at odds of 25-1 or greater. Therefore, don't let a big price put you off.

Band Of Outlaws is the only successful favourite since *Sanctuaire* in 2010 and there is certainly no market dominance in this contest. Although as stated earlier, all three Joseph O'Brien-trained winners returned at single figure odds, so maybe treat things a little differently when it comes to runners from that particular stable.

OTHER TRAINERS TO NOTE

THE case for the leading Irish trainers has already been well made, whilst not so long back it was **Paul Nicholls** who was the man to follow here. The former champion trainer won the *'Fred Winter'* three times in the space of seven years thanks to *Sanctuaire*, *Qualando* and *Diego du Charmil*, the last-named successful on his British debut. Interestingly, the other pair had won a small novice hurdle in the West Country during February, teeing them up nicely for this race. Without a runner last year, Nicholls boasts by far the best record of any British trainer in the race and as a result, runners from his Ditcheat base still need to be monitored closely.

DAY ONE **RACE THREE**

Puturhandstogether provides Joseph O'Brien with a third win since 2019

ROLL OF HONOUR

Year	Form	Winner	Age	Weight	OR	SP	Trainer	Runners	Last Race (No. of days)
2025	312	Puturhandstogether	4	11-6	130	17/2	J P O'Brien (IRE)	22	2nd Fairyhouse Nov. Hurdle (34)
2024	263	Lark In The Mornin	4	11-0	122	9/1	J P O'Brien (IRE)	22	3rd Punchestown maiden Hurdle (57)
2023	2154	Jazzy Matty	4	10-6	125	18/1	G Elliott (IRE)	21	4th Naas Nov. Hurdle (31)
2022	6541	Brazil	4	11-9	137	10/1	P Roche (IRE)	21	1st Naas Nov. Hurdle (31)
2021	2217	Jeff Kidder	4	10-8	125	80/1	N Meade (IRE)	22	7th Gr.2 Mercedes-Benz South Dublin Juv. H'dle (80)
2020	31F31	Aramax	4	11-8	138	15/2	G Elliott (IRE)	22	1st Naas Nov. Hurdle (32)
2019	311	Band of Outlaws	4	11-8	139	7/2F	J P O'Brien (IRE)	21	1st Naas Nov. Hurdle (24)
2018	127	Veneer of Charm	4	11-0	129	33/1	G Elliott (IRE)	22	7th Navan Nov. Hurdle (54)
2017	2P614	Flying Tiger	4	11-5	134	33/1	N Williams	22	4th Gr.2 Adonis Hurdle (18)
2016	322	Diego du Charmil	4	11-1	133	13/2	P Nicholls	22	2nd Prix Verdi (133)

LEADING TEN-YEAR GUIDES

Changing Times Brewery Juvenile Hurdle 2 (*Aramax* Fell, *Jeff Kidder* 7th)
Naas 4YO Novice Hurdle 4 (*Band Of Outlaws* 1st, *Aramax* 1st, *Brazil* 1st, *Jazzy Matty* 4th)
Cork 3yo Maiden Hurdle 2 (*Band Of Outlaws* 3rd, *Puturhandstogether* 1st)

TRUSTMARQUE ULTIMA HANDICAP CHASE
3m1f (Premier Handicap) – Old Course

OVERVIEW
THE first handicap chase of the week, the Ultima is staged over 3m1f and with a large field often assembled, it tends to be run at a strong pace so stamina is essential. Novices have won the past two renewals and boast a strong record in this race, whilst course form is often another positive. If looking at a more experienced chaser, look towards horses who have run in this race previously, whilst three of the past four renewals have gone the way of Lucinda Russell.

TARGET FOR RUSSELL
FOLLOWING the back-to-back wins of *Corach Rambler* and last year's runaway success of *Myretown*, trainer **Lucinda Russell** (now joint trainer alongside **Michael Scudamore**, of course) has won three of the past four renewals of the Ultima. A stable which tends to excel with their staying chasers, this is clearly a race which they like to target and runners from their Kinross base warrant utmost respect, as she has also saddled a couple of placed horses in recent years. Russell saddled two last year, her other runner being Whistle Stop Tour who couldn't overcome being hampered at the very first fence.

NOVICES
SEVEN of the past 12 winners were novices and first season chasers boast a tremendous record in the race. The past two winners had run the bare minimum required for them to be eligible, *Chianti Classico* having run just the three times and with the rules slightly amended prior to last season, *Myretown*, had run in four chases prior to his impressive success. All of those seven recent novice winners had run no more than five times over fences previously, with *Wichita Lineman* – the last novice winner before those seven, in 2009 – another who had run just the three times to qualify. In the past two years alone, there have only been 10 novices among the 45 runners, so the strike rate of such horses is an impressive one.

REPEAT OFFENDERS
TWICE in the past 10 years we have seen back-to-back winners of the Ultima, with both *Un Temps Pour Tout* and *Corach Rambler* winning in successive renewals. In addition to this, *Beware The Bear* and *Vintage Clouds* had run well in the race previously, the former having finished fourth 12 months before his win, whilst the latter had had twice hit the frame in the contest. 2011 winner *Bensalem* is another example of this, as he was in the process of running a huge race as a novice in 2010, when falling late on. That is, therefore, five of the past 15 winners to have run (and run well) in the race previously, so if looking away from the lightly-raced novices, looking towards those who ran well last year is another positive.

COURSE FORM
ALTHOUGH *Myretown* showed last year that this race can be won without any prior Cheltenham experience, form at the track is an obvious positive, as it is in all races at the fixture. Four of the past 10 winners were course-winning novices, so pay healthy respect to those lightly-raced types who have been in action at Cheltenham, either earlier

that same season or even earlier. *Chianto Classico* had run in the previous year's Albert Bartlett, but several recent winners had run at Cheltenham earlier in the campaign. Pay particular attention to the early season staying novice chases.

Looking strictly at previous Festival form, *Myretown* was just the fourth winner in the past 18 to have not run at this fixture the previous year. As per the previous subsection, *Beware The Bear* had run well 12 months earlier but also arrived at the Festival on the back of a course win on New Year's Day.

OFFICIAL BHA RATINGS AND WEIGHTS

12 OF THE past 18 winners were rated between 142 and 148, which is the starting point when looking at official BHA Ratings. *Myretown* was rated much lower than an average recent Ultima winner (127) with only three of the past 18 winners even rated in the 130s. 140 and above is usually where we should be focused and the aforementioned bracket narrows things down further. *Un Temps Pour Tout* (second win) and *Beware The Bear* were successful from marks in the 150s but eight of the past 12 winners won from a mark in the 140s.

In terms of weight carried, prior to last year, 11 of the previous 15 winners had carried 10-10 or more. Again, *Myretown* was an outlier here, successful from joint bottom-weight, whereas it can normally pay to focus on those in the top half of the weights. Often (not in 2025, obviously), the lower weighted/rated runners can be outclassed in this event, as with in many of the handicaps throughout the week, so look towards the middle, or even the top-end of the weights.

As with previous years and for all handicaps throughout the week, the table below illustrates the lowest rated runner – in order to help give you a feel of what kind of figure is required to get in (can be useful from an ante-post perspective) – as well as the top-rated official mark and that of the winner.

	Lowest-rated	Winner OR	Top-rated
2025	127	127	152
2024	139	143	153
2023	129	146	155
2022	138	140	164
2021	132	143	158
2020	133	139	159
2019	140	151	155
2018	137	142	155
2017	134	155	155
2016	131	148	153

KEY TRENDS

- ⭐ 10 of the past 16 winners had run at Cheltenham earlier in the season
- ⭐ 9 of the past 14 winners wore headgear
- ⭐ 7 of the past 12 winners were novices
- ⭐ 3 of the past 4 winners were trained by Lucinda Russell
- ✓ 14 of the past 18 winners finished in the first 4 on their previous start (7 of them won)
- ✓ 11 of the past 12 winners returned at 11-1 or shorter
- ✓ 11 of the past 16 winners carried 10-10+
- ✓ 11 of the past 18 winners were rated between 142-148
- ✓ 5 of the past 11 winners had contested the Coral Gold Cup
- ✓ 5 of the past 15 winners had run in the Ultima the previous year
- ✓ 4 of the past 10 winners were course-winning novices
- ✓ Grade 1-winning hurdlers boasted a good record not so long back
- ✓ Respect form over 3m+
- ✓ Respect David Pipe-trained runners
- ✓ Respect Jonjo & A J O'Neill-trained runners
- ✓ Respect runners trained in the North & Scotland
- ✗ Irish-trained horses are 0-51 during the past 19 years
- ✗ Only 2 Irish-trained winners in the past 57 renewals (since 1967)
- ✗ Only 2 of the past 18 winners were rated in the 130s (although last year's winner was rated just 127)
- ✗ Be wary of those stepping up in distance

CORAL GOLD CUP

FIVE of the past 11 winners had contested Newbury's **Coral Gold Cup**, very much a similar type of race which takes place in the opening part of the season. This is, therefore, the most informative pointer towards the Ultima, besides the previous year's renewal. *Beware The Bear, The Conditional* and *Corach Rambler* (second win) all finished in the first four at Newbury, so pay healthy respect to any horse who ran well this season.

Panic Attack won this season's race, with The Changing Man (runner-up in this race last year) back in third.

PROVEN STAMINA

HORSES who step up from an intermediate trip tend to struggle in the Ultima – perhaps, due to the strong gallop, which could be down to it being the first real *'big field'* contest of the week (over fences)– and having won over a minimum of 3m previously seems to be just about a pre-requisite. Last year's winner set a brisk pace and was able to keep up the gallop throughout, having won over 2m7½f the time before at Kelso, with such a bold front-running performance exposing any stamina doubts of the opposition.

HEADGEAR IS NOT A NEGATIVE

THE past four winners were successful without any, but prior to that, nine of the previous 10 winners wore some sort of headgear. During the past 14 years, 127 of the 309 runners (41%) in the Ultima wore headgear, so the winning ratio remains well above average and such runners are still overperforming, despite the recent change in results. As with any staying handicap chase, you tend to find that trainers of the slightly more exposed runners will reach for some sort of headgear to spark either some improvement or a revival in form. Either way, it certainly shouldn't be seen as a negative.

GRADE 1 HURDLE FORM

THIS is certainly something which he fallen away in recent years, too, but four of the nine winners between 2009 and 2017 were Grade 1 winners over the smaller obstacles, yet found themselves to be well-handicapped over fences. 2014 winner *Holywell* was another very smart hurdler, him being a Pertemps Final winner and having also finished runner-up in Grade 1 company, a month later in the Liverpool Hurdle at Aintree. The same stable's *Wichita Lineman* was one of those four winners and he is a fine case-in-point, with him being rated 156 over hurdles (won the Albert Bartlett) yet got in here off 142 after just three chase starts. Look out for any similar discrepancies between hurdles and chase ratings.

MARKET FORCES

WITH 11 of the past 12 winners returning at 11-1 or shorter, the Ultima has very much become a *'punter friendly'* contest, despite the apparent competitive nature of the race. The past three winners have returned at 6/1JF, 6/1 and 13/2F respectively, so were very much to the fore of the market, with last year's winner landing somewhat of a gamble in the hours leading up to the race. Available at 33/1 just days before the race, *Myretown* was heavily supported into outright favouritism and justified that market confidence with a stellar performance. *Vintage Clouds* produced the only *'shock'* result of late, in terms of the market, and as things stand, those at the top of the betting have been dominant. Indeed, last year saw the favourite beat the joint second-favourite, with the Exacta paying a tidy £65.40 for a £1 stake.

CURRENT FORM

WHEN you get to the previews for other handicaps throughout the week, you will see that supposedly *'out of form'* horses are able to bounce back to form after *'disappointing'* seasons but that isn't the case in the Ultima. Recent winners tend to arrive at Cheltenham on the back of a positive run, with 14 of the past 18 winners having recorded a top-four finish on their most recent start and half of those winners – including *Myretown* last year – were last-time-out winners. *Coo Star Sivola* and *Beware The Bear* also arrived at Cheltenham on the back of a win, so that is three of the past eight winners. Certainly when looking towards a novice in this race, you want to see a horse on the up and the form figures of the past two winners alone (earlier that season) read 112 and 51F1.

NOT A RACE FOR THE IRISH

THE poor run of the Irish in the Ultima continued last year, with another five taking their chance and failing, taking the recent record of Irish-trained runners in the race to 0-51 during the past 19 years. Incredibly, there have only been two Irish-trained winners in the past 57 renewals, those being *Youlneverwalkalone* in 2003 and *Dun Doire* some 20 years ago. Whilst **Willie Mullins** has achieved most things in National Hunt racing, he has still to win a handicap chase at the fixture and in general, this is a race where the statistics tell us to avoid the Irish; not something we can say very often at all.

McMANUS' HOT SPELL

LEADING owner **JP McManus** likes to be well represented in as many of the handicaps throughout the week as possible and between 2003 and 2012, he won this race on three occasions. When it comes to the staying chases, McManus often targets the Kim Muir over this race and we have actually only seen seven runners carry the green and gold in the past decade. However, runners in his silks warrant a second look in all of the handicaps throughout the week.

NORTHERN SOUL

THIS is something which I have highlighted in recent years and it isn't easy to explain why, but the positive run of Northern and Scottish-trained horses continued last year. The excellent strike rate of Lucinda Russell in the race helps, but Sue Smith got in on the act in 2021, making it six winners since 2007 (and seven since 1998) to have won for the *'North'*. We have seen other northern-trained runners hit the frame in recent years, too, and all from a relatively small representation. Perhaps, winning races at the likes of Haydock and Ayr isn't as damaging on a handicap mark as those who have won at Ascot or Newbury, for example, but those travelling South deserve plenty of respect, whatever the reason. Last year's winner went up 4lb for his win at Kelso en route to Cheltenham.

OTHER KEY RACES

ASIDE from the Coral Gold Cup, which has already been covered, the **Classic Chase** from Warwick is another fine line to note, with both *The Conditional* and *Corach Rambler* (ahead of his first win) having run in the 3m5f race. Both horses finished fourth before winning the Ultima, although this year's race was (again, like last year) lost to the weather.

OTHER TRAINERS TO NOTE

THE case for Lucinda Russell and Michael Scudamore has already been made elsewhere, whilst **Kim Bailey** – who now trains alongside long-time assistant, **Mat Nicholls** – won the 2024 renewal with *Chianti Classico*, some 25 years after saddling *Betty's Boy* to win the same race. That stable went close in 2021 with Happygolucky (returned to run well again in 2025 for Mel Rowley), so it would appear to be a race which they now like to target, particularly with a novice.

David Pipe won the race three times between 2008 and 2017 and all from just 17 runners. Again, the Pipe family are renowned for targeting big Cheltenham handicaps throughout the season and David has a fine record in the Ultima, most recently successful with two-time winner *Un Temps Pour Tout*.

Jonjo O'Neill – who now trains alongside son, **A J** – is another to have recorded three Ultima wins, his victories coming between 2009 and 2014. Monbeg Genius, Carbury Cross and Keen Leader have also all gone close for the O'Neill team in the not so distant past, so respect any runners from Jackdaws Castle. Although Crebilly could finish only ninth last year, he had finished runner-up in the *'Plate'* in 2024, whilst Johnnywho filled the same spot (both for McManus, incidentally) in the Kim Muir last year and Hasthing was still in contention when coming down in the National Hunt Chase. Either could have run here and the O'Neill runners warrant a second look in all handicap chases during the meeting.

Both **Alan King** and **Nicky Henderson** have also recorded two wins in the Ultima this century.

Kim Bailey

ROLL OF HONOUR

Year	Form	Winner	Age	Weight	OR	SP	Trainer	Runners	Last Race (No. of days)
2025	51F1	Myretown	8	10-3	127	13/2F	L Russell	24	1st Kelso Nov. H'cap Chase (25)
2024	112	Chianti Classico	7	11-4	143	6/1	K Bailey	21	2nd Kempton H'cap Chase (59)
2023	54	Corach Rambler	9	11-5	146	6/1JF	L Russell	23	4th Coral Gold Cup (108)
2022	3114U	Corach Rambler	8	10-2	140	10/1	L Russell	24	UR Gr.2 Reynoldstown Nov. Chase (24)
2021	753	Vintage Clouds	11	10-11	143	28/1	S Smith	16	3rd Kelso H'cap Chase (25)
2020	3124	The Conditional	8	10-6	139	15/2	D Bridgwater	23	4th Classic Chase (59)
2019	41	Beware The Bear	9	11-8	151	10/1	N Henderson	24	1st Cheltenham H'cap Chase (70)
2018	53241	Coo Star Sivola	6	10-10	142	5/1F	N Williams	18	1st Exeter H'cap Nov. Chase (38)
2017	1036	Un Temps Pour Tout	8	11-12	155	9/1	D Pipe	23	6th Gr.2 Cleeve Hurdle (45)
2016	1224	Un Temps Pour Tout	7	11-7	148	11/1	D Pipe	23	4th Cheltenham Nov. H'cap Chase (45)

LEADING TEN-YEAR GUIDES

*****Ultima Handicap Chase 4** (*Un Temps Pour Tout* 1st, *Beware The Bear* 4th, *Vintage Clouds* 8th, *Corach Rambler* 1st)

Coral Gold Cup 4 (*Un Temps Pour Tout* 10th, *Beware The Bear* 4th, *The Conditional* 2nd, *Corach Rambler* 4th)

Classic Chase 2 (*The Conditional* 4th, *Corach Rambler* 4th)

* denotes previous season

UNIBET CHAMPION HURDLE

DAY ONE RACE FIVE

2m 87y (Grade 1) – Old Course

OVERVIEW

THE feature race on the opening day of the Festival and the feature of the whole season in terms of the 2m hurdling division. During the *'Golden Era'* for hurdling, the Champion Hurdle was won by some greats during the 70s and 80s, after which the great *Istabraq* won three successive runnings of the race and four more horses have won the race twice this century. A strong-traveller, who is able to hold their position and jump quickly is what is required in a Champion Hurdle winner and that last point was pivotal in an incident-packed renewal in 2025. Mares boast a fantastic recent record in the race.

MULTIPLE WINNERS

AS TOUCHED upon in the *Overview*, since the brilliant *Istabraq* won three successive Champion Hurdles around the turn of the century, *Hardy Eustace*, *Hurricane Fly*, *Buveur d'Air* and *Honeysuckle* have all won two Champion Hurdles, with three of the four winning back-to-back renewals. Both *Constitution Hill* and *State Man* came to grief in last year's race when looking to win the race for a second time and this year, with *State Man* sadly on the sidelines, it will be *Golden Ace* who bids to add her name to the tally. *Constitution Hill* could be back for another crack at the race, too.

REGAINING THE CROWN

OF THOSE horses mentioned in the previous subsection, only *Hurricane Fly* was able to wrest back his title, having finished third in 2012. In doing so, he is the only horse in the past 49 renewals, to regain their crown, with the last to do so before him being *Comedy Of Errors* way back in 1975. *Constitution Hill* was unable to improve this dismal trend last year.

HENDERSON & MULLINS DOMINATION

SPOT the theme in the Grade 1s on day one? In the Supreme Novices' Hurdle, Arkle and the feature contest, both **Nicky Henderson** and Willie Mullins are unquestionably the dominant forces. Tuesday is all about speed and both trainers are adept at handling top-class two-milers. Henderson has won the Champion Hurdle nine times and between the pair, they have won 11 of the past 16 renewals, a stat that would have been enhanced last year, had *State Man* stood up at the final flight.

See You Then – another three-time winner – provided Henderson with his first three wins in the race and since 2009, he has won it on six further occasions, thanks to *Punjabi*, *Binocular*, *Buveur d'Air* (twice), *Epatante* and *Constitution Hill*. With Sir Gino suffering a serious injury on trials day, Henderson looks set to rely on his 2023 winner.

Willie Mullins first landed the illustrious prize with *Hurricane Fly* and actually won it four times in the space of six years between 2011 and 2016, with *Faugheen* and *Annie Power* winning back-to-back renewals for the trainer. His latest success came in 2024 when *State Man* justified odds-on favouritism and interestingly, all five of Mullins' Champion Hurdle winners were sent off at the head of the betting. With *State Man* injured, Lossiemouth looks to be his best option this year, but after defeat in the Irish Champion Hurdle, the Mares' Hurdle (again) is the likelier destination for her.

UNBEATEN THIS SEASON

THE 2025 renewal brought an end to the sequence of winners who had gone unbeaten during that season. The previous 10 winners – and 12 of the previous 14 – all arrived at Cheltenham with a string 1s next to their name and as is often the case, there can be a dominant performer in this division. Prior to the victory of *Golden Ace* last year, 2014 winner *Jezki* was the last to have suffered a defeat earlier in the campaign.

LAST TIME OUT WINNERS

GIVEN the results reflected within the previous subsection, it should come as little surprise that last time out winners also boast a strong record in the Champion Hurdle. 31 of the past 36 winners won on their most recent start, so arriving at Cheltenham in form is clearly important. The past 11 winners won on their most recent start and only one winner this century – again, *Jezki* – won this race on the back of failing to record a top-three finish last time (4th in the Irish Champion Hurdle). Although *Golden Ace* had been beaten in her earlier races, she won last year's Kingwell Hurdle en route to Cheltenham.

LIGHTLY-RACED HURDLERS

GOLDEN ACE also enhanced the record of lightly-raced hurdlers in the Champion Hurdle. 11 of the past 16 winners had raced no more than 10 times over hurdles, so looking towards those open to further progress is very much the way to go, especially if looking away from a previous winner of the race. We will get to the *Age* of recent winners shortly, but those up-and-coming hurdlers often shine here.

Indeed, last year's winner became the eighth second-season hurdler to win the Champion Hurdle since 2012, so focusing on last year's crop of novices is always a good starting point. The New Lion is the pick of last year's novices who remained over hurdles, and to date, he has had just the six runs.

CHELTENHAM FESTIVAL FORM

REMARKABLY, *Constitution Hill* is the only horse in 53 years to win this race having won the **Supreme Novices' Hurdle** 12 months earlier. Both *Hors La Loi III* and *Brave Inca* had won a Supreme, but not the previous season, whilst *Jezki* and *Buveur d'Air* had run well in the race in defeat, a year before becoming Champion Hurdle winners.

Istabraq won the **Baring Bingham Novices' Hurdle** – run last year as the **Turners Novices' Hurdle** – prior to his first Champion Hurdle success, a comment which also applies to *Hardy Eustace*. *Faugheen* also dropped back from winning the 2m5f contest to win the Champion Hurdle the

KEY TRENDS

- ⭐ 12 of the past 15 winners were unbeaten during the current season
- ⭐ 11 of the past 16 winners were trained by with Nicky Henderson (6) or Willie Mullins (5)
- ⭐ Mares are 5-12 during the past decade
- ✓ 31 of the past 36 winners won last time out
- ✓ 31 of the past 43 winners were aged 6 or 7
- ✓ 17 of the past 27 winners had won at the Festival previously
- ✓ 11 of the past 16 winners had run no more than 10 times over hurdles previously
- ✓ 10 of the past 15 favourites have won
- ✓ 8 of the past 14 winners were second-season hurdlers
- ✓ 7 of the past 17 winners had contested the Christmas Hurdle at Kempton
- ✓ 6 of the past 16 winners were owned by JP McManus (9 winners in total)
- ✓ 5 of the past 14 winners finished in the first 3 of the previous year's Supreme Novices' Hurdle or Baring Bingham Novices' Hurdle
- ✓ There have been 5 multiple winners this century
- ✗ 5yo's are 2-114 during the past 39 years
- ✗ 10yo's (and older) are 0-32 during the past 41 years
- ✗ Only 3 of the past 15 winners had run more than 12 times over hurdles previously
- ✗ Only 2 of the past 27 winners had not run at the Cheltenham Festival previously
- ✗ Only 1 of the past 49 winners regained their crown
- ✗ Only 1 of the past 22 winners was aged 9
- ✗ Only 1 of the past 55 winners had won the Supreme Novices' Hurdle the previous year
- ✗ International (Unibet) Hurdle winners are 0-14 during the past 22 years
- ✗ Gordon Elliott-trained runners are 0-8

following year and that is something which The New Lion will be looking to emulate.

Both *Annie Power* (infamous last flight fall) and *Honeysuckle* had contested the **David Nicholson Mares' Hurdle** prior to winning this, whilst last year's winner had won the Dawn Run Mares' Novices' Hurdle in 2024. The first winner of that race to break through as a Champion Hurdle winner, it is now 17 of the past 27 winners to have won at the Festival previously.

Obviously, the dual winners (covered in the opening subsection) help towards this trend but previous Cheltenham Festival form is clearly a huge plus. Reverting back to the David Nicholson again briefly and Lossiemouth has won that race in each of the past two years. As already touched upon, following her defeat at Leopardstown, the Mares' Hurdle again seems her most likely destination.

AGE

IN-KEEPING with the earlier *Lightly-Raced Hurdlers* subsection, younger horses tend to come to the fore in this race, with age often catching up with two-mile hurdlers. When winning the race for a second time, *Hurricane Fly* is the only nine-year-old winner in the past 22 years, whilst those aged 10 or older are now 0-32 during the past 42 years, with *Sea Pigeon* the last double-digit aged winner, successful in both 1980 and 1981.

31 of the past 43 winners were aged either six or seven, which is clearly the prime age group, whilst five-year-olds also hold a very disappointing record in the race. Two have proven successful this century – those being *Katchit* and *Espoir d'Allen* – but during the past 39 years, the record of that age group now stands at 2-114, following the second place finish of Burdett Road last year.

MARES' ALLOWANCE

AS HAS been highlighted in previous editions of the *Cheltenham Festival Betting Guide*, the 7lb sex-allowance is a huge positive when it comes to a top-class mare. Admittedly, last year's winner was fortunate in the end but still became the fifth winning mare in the past decade and all from just 12 runners. The Mares' Hurdle allows connections of a high-class mare an easier option (see Lossiemouth), which in fact, probably means any such runners here are even more selective. *Annie Power*, *Epatante* and *Honeysuckle* (twice) were all successful prior to *Golden Ace* and that record is outstanding, in terms of strike rate. Pay utmost respect to a high-class mare in this race.

OTHER TRAINERS TO NOTE

ASIDE from Messrs Henderson and Mullins (covered in an earlier subsection), the only current trainer to have won more than one Champion Hurdle this century is **Henry de Bromhead**, although, of course, his two wins came courtesy of *Honeysuckle*.

The disappointing run of **Gordon Elliott** in the Champion Hurdle continued last year, with Brighterdaysahead – sent off as the 5-2 second favourite – running below par and trailing in almost 20 lengths behind the winner. Apple's Jade was a beaten favourite for Elliott in 2019 and his record in the race now stands at 0-8. Many of his brighter young prospects are sent chasing straight after their novice hurdle campaign.

GREEN AND GOLD GLORY

WITHOUT a runner last year, leading owner **JP McManus** has won the race nine times since 1998. Responsible for three-time winner *Istabraq*, he has since seen *Binocular*, *Jezki*, *Buveur d'Air* (twice), *Espoir d'Allen* and *Epatante* successful in his famous green and gold silks. Since 1998, McManus has had 36 runners in the Champion Hurdle, so boasts a staggering 25% win strike rate, whilst 42% of his runners have finished in the first three. That is a tremendous record for a race of this magnitude and it is clearly a race – and a division – in which he likes to be strongly represented.

McManus' sole entry this year is 2025 Baring Bingham winner, The New Lion, who will bid to provide him with a 10th Champion Hurdle.

MARKET FORCES

PRIOR to last year, we had five winning favourites in a row and in fact, eight of the previous 10 winners were sent off favourite. *Espoir d'Allen* and *Golden Ace* have now produced a couple of *'shock'* results in the past seven years but in general, the Champion Hurdle has gone to form and tends to be won by a horse at the top of the betting. During the past 15 years, only three winners returned at odds greater than 5-1 which further enhances this trend.

OTHER KEY RACES

THE first Grade 1 of the season in this division in Britain is the **Fighting Fifth Hurdle** from Newcastle, a race which Nicky Henderson likes to use as a starting point for his Champion Hurdle contender, whenever possible. Last season's race went the way of Sir Gino (for Henderson) before he went chasing and this season's rather dramatic contest was won by *Golden Ace*.

Seven of the past 17 winners of the Champion Hurdle had contested Kempton's **Christmas Hurdle** on Boxing Day, so it is the most significant Key Race on this side of the Irish Sea. *Faugheen*, *Buveur d'Air* (ahead of his second Champion Hurdle success), *Epatante* and *Constitution Hill* all won the Festive Grade 1 before winning the Champion and this season's contest was won by Sir Gino.

Golden Ace became the first winner since *Punjabi* in 2009 to run in Wincanton's **Kingwell Hurdle** a month before Cheltenham, whilst the race registered as the **International Hurdle** – formerly the *'Bula'* and now rebranded as the **Unibet Hurdle** – is usually a piece of form to be wary of. Switched from the December meeting to trials day a couple of years ago, it still takes place over 2m1f on the New Course, so is often more about stamina than the Champion Hurdle itself. The fall of Constitution

Hill in last year's Champion took the tally of International winners to 0-14 during the past 22 years, so tread carefully with that form line. This year's race was won by The New Lion, but it was marred by the injury sustained by Sir Gino.

The **Irish Champion Hurdle** – staged at the Dublin Racing Festival in February – is the most significant (no shock!) pointer towards Irish success in this race. *Honeysuckle* (twice) and *State Man* won the Irish Champion en route to Cheltenham, so that is three of the past five winners. Going back further, *Istabraq* won the Irish Champion ahead of all three of his wins, as did *Brave Inca* and *Hurricane Fly* ahead of his brace of Champion Hurdles. *Jezki* is the only winner this century to be successful having been beaten in the Irish equivalent on their most recent start, so we really ought to focus on the winner, who this year was Gordon Elliott's Brighterdaysahead.

Ahead of his first Champion Hurdle success, *Hurricane Fly* started his season in the 2m4f **Hatton's Grace Hurdle** at Fairyhouse, a race which *Honeysuckle* (twice) won before completing the Irish-Cheltenham Champion Hurdle double. Lossiemouth won last season's Hatton's Grace before winning the Mares' Hurdle at the Festival and this season's contest went the way of Teahupoo, who will contest the Stayers'.

During his winning season, *State Man* won the **Morgiana Hurdle** at Punchestown and the **December Festival Hurdle** at Leopardstown's Christmas fixture, but both races haven't really featured among Champion Hurdle winners since *Hurricane Fly*. Lossiemouth won both of those Grade 1s this season.

Lossiemouth wins the Morgiana Hurdle

The New Lion wins on trials day

ROLL OF HONOUR

Year	Form	Winner	Age	Weight	OR	SP	Trainer	Runners	Last Race (No. of days)
2025	431	Golden Ace	7	11-3	144	25/1	J Scott	7	1st Gr.2 Kingwell Hurdle (24)
2024	111	State Man	7	11-10	169	2/5F	W Mullins (IRE)	8	1st Gr.1 Irish Champion Hurdle (37)
2023	11	Constitution Hill	6	11-10	173	4/11F	N Henderson	7	1st Gr.1 Christmas Hurdle (78)
2022	11	Honeysuckle	8	11-3	165	8/11F	H de Bromhead (IRE)	10	1st Gr.1 Irish Champion Hurdle (37)
2021	11	Honeysuckle	7	11-3	165	11/10F	H de Bromhead (IRE)	10	1st Gr.1 Irish Champion Hurdle (38)
2020	11	Epatante	6	11-3	159	2/1F	N Henderson	17	1st Gr 1 Christmas Hurdle (75)
2019	111	Espoir d'Allen	5	11-10	162	16/1	G Cromwell (IRE)	10	1st Gr.3 Limestone Lad Hurdle (44)
2018	111	Buveur d'Air	7	11-10	169	4/6F	N Henderson	11	1st Listed Contenders Hurdle (38)
2017	111	Buveur d'Air	6	11-10	157	5/1	N Henderson	11	1st Listed Contenders Hurdle (38)
2016	11	Annie Power	8	11-3	162	5/2F	W Mullins (IRE)	12	1st Punchestown Mares' Hurdle (27)

LEADING TEN-YEAR GUIDES

Hatton's Grace Hurdle 2 (Honeysuckle 1st & 1st)
***David Nicholson Mares' Hurdle** 2 (Annie Power Fell, Honeysuckle 1st)
***Supreme Novices' Hurdle** 2 (Buveur d'Air 3rd, Constitution Hill 1st)
Christmas Hurdle 3 (Buveur d'Air 1st, Epatante 1st, Constitution Hill 1st)
***Champion Hurdle** 3 (Buveur d'Air 1st, Honeysuckle 1st, State Man 2nd)
Irish Champion Hurdle 3 (Honeysuckle 1st & 1st, State Man 1st)
***Punchestown Champion Hurdle** 2 (Honeysuckle 1st, State Man 1st)
Fighting Fifth Hurdle 2 (Buveur d'Air 1st, Constitution Hill 1st)

* denotes previous season

Leading Contenders

THE NEW LION — Trainer: Dan Skelton
Unbeaten in two starts at Cheltenham, he won last year's Baring Bingham and the Unibet Hurdle on trials day on his latest start. That race was run at a crawl and marred by the injury suffered by Sir Gino, but it was pleasing to see him settle better than he had when a faller in the Fighting Fifth and he is clearly very talented. Still lightly-raced, he is a second-season hurdler on an upward curve and in what looks to be a substandard Champion Hurdle, holds strong claims.

BRIGHTERDAYSAHEAD — Trainer: Gordon Elliott
Runner-up to Golden Ace in the 2024 Dawn Run, she disappointed in last year's Champion Hurdle and gained her first win since Christmas 2024 when beating Lossiemouth in the Irish Champion Hurdle, reversing earlier form. The course at Cheltenham remains a query, but she has enjoyed a lighter campaign this year and is building towards a peak performance, whereas last year, she was returning from a short break, following a blistering display at Leopardstown. A high-class mare who is versatile in terms of ground.

CONSTITUTION HILL — Trainer: Nicky Henderson
Winner of the race in 2023, he has now fallen in three of his past four starts. Prior to last year's race, he was unbeaten in 10 starts over hurdles (3 wins recorded at Cheltenham) and was widely regarded as one of the modern greats. However, the wheels have fallen off and he came down at the second flight in Newcastle's Fighting Fifth. Expected to run in a maiden on the Flat at Southwell (Friday 20th February), he has plenty to prove but is also the most naturally talented horse in this field.

LOSSIEMOUTH — Trainer: Willie Mullins
Winner of the Triumph Hurdle in 2023, she has won the Mares' Hurdle for the past two years and is unbeaten at Cheltenham in four starts overall. Having started the season with wins in the Morgiana at Punchestown and Leopardstown's December Hurdle, she headed the ante-post market for the Champion and looked set to finally run in this race. However, her defeat to Brighterdaysahead in the Irish equivalent likely means that she will step back up in trip in an attempt to win the Mares' for a third successive year.

GOLDEN ACE — Trainer: Jeremy Scott
Last year's winner, she is 2-2 at the Festival, having won the Dawn Run in 2024. Following a lifeless return at Wetherby (later transpired that she had scoped dirty), she won the Fighting Fifth before finishing 6 lengths off Sir Gino in the Christmas Hurdle. A high-class mare who is at her best on a sound surface, she possesses plenty of speed and will likely follow last year's path back to Cheltenham, via Wincanton's Kingwell Hurdle (Saturday 14th February). Often underestimated, it wouldn't be a huge shock if she were to go close again.

PONIROS — Trainer: Willie Mullins
Last year's (surprise) winner of the Triumph, he has only had three runs over hurdles and can be expected to improve for his recent return in the Irish Champion. Given a patient ride, he passed tired horses to take third and although he has plenty of ground to make up with Brighterdaysahead, has the scope to improve further. Runner-up to Lulamba at Punchestown last May, he has raced exclusively in Grade 1 company as a hurdler and whilst he had Flat form on soft, he will probably appreciate nicer ground at Cheltenham.

TRUSTATRADER PLATE HANDICAP CHASE
2m4f 44y (Premier Handicap) – Old Course

OVERVIEW
WITH the Mares' Hurdle now being staged on day three, the *'Plate'* has been moved to the opening day and as a result, the race switches from the New Course to the Old Course and the distance is reduced slightly. In theory, this now represents a sharper test, but strong form from the track remains a huge positive, with the past seven winners now having won at Cheltenham earlier in the season. There are a number of handicaps staged on both courses throughout the season, starting with the Paddy Power Gold Cup (the *'Plate'* is now staged over the exact same course-and-distance as the November feature). The December Gold Cup, New Year's Day Handicap Chase and a brace of similar races staged on trials day, which have been particularly informative in recent years. Novices and lightly-raced chasers tend to do well in this event and although the Jack Richards Novices' Handicap Chase was reintroduced in 2025, the novice *Jagwar* landed this prize for Oliver Greenall & Josh Guerriero.

THE RETURN OF THE NOVICES' HANDICAP
AS TOUCHED upon in the *Overview*, the returning Jack Richards didn't prevent a novice from winning the race last year, although the crucial point here being that a novice only requires three runs to be eligible for the novices' handicap, but requires four in order to be eligible for the *'Plate'*. Last year's winner had obtained those four runs by trials day, so despite remaining favourite for the novices' handicap during February and early March, the late switch (which materialised at declaration stage) was always a possibility. Five of the past nine winners were novices (one a second-season novice) and although we are likely to see fewer take their chance here now, such runners still warrant careful consideration.

If eligible, this race might actually be a slightly easier target, in that they won't face so many unexposed and potential improvers, nor would they face a Grade 1 horse of the calibre of Caldwell Potter. Keep this in mind when looking at how much experience a novice has gained; Haiti Couleurs was a good example last year, as he had run in three chases before prepping for Cheltenham over hurdles. This confirmed the National Hunt Chase as his target, as he hadn't gained the relevant experience for either the Ultima or Kim Muir, for example.

LIGHTLY-RACED CHASERS
WE DID see slightly older and more experienced winners of this race between 2022 and 2024, before *Jagwar* turned things around, and prior to 2022, we had seen second-season chasers perform well here also. 13 of the past 21 winners had run nine times or less over fences, so very much still look towards those potential improvers as a starting point. Overall, seven of the past 10 winners were in their first or second season over fences.

Only two of the past 21 winners had run in 12 chases or more, so those *'more exposed'* handicappers tend to struggle to cope with the improving types.

AGE
IN-KEEPING with the previous two subsections, 19 of the past 25 winners were aged nine or younger

and given that those three recent winners (2022-2024) were aged either 10 or 11, this is a relatively strong statistic and one which was extremely noteworthy between 1999 and 2021. There hasn't been a five-year-old winner since *Majadou* in 1999, but *Jagwar* became the fifth six-year-old to win since *Liberthine* in 2005. I would expect this trend to revert to type and the *'younger'* horses might well begin to dominate once again, following on from last year's winner.

A TOUCH OF CLASS

PRIOR to last year, the previous nine winners had all contested a Graded race, either in the novice hurdle division or as a novice chaser. *Jagwar* had climbed the ranks as a chaser, rather than having shown Graded form earlier in his (short) career, but clearly having that level of ability is a positive here. It also shows that a trainer believes the horse to have that *Touch Of Class*, by virtue of allowing them the opportunity to run in a Graded race.

Three recent novice winners also went on to contest a Grade 1 on their very next start, so rather like the Coral Cup (when you get to day two), if you like a young and improving horse, give some thought as to whether or not you believe that they could cope with a rise in class. Invariably these days, Festival handicaps are won by Graded, or future Graded, performers, on the way up.

WEIGHTS AND OFFICIAL BHA RATINGS

AGAIN, prior to last year, the previous 11 winners were all rated in the 140s. *Jagwar* missed out on this stat by just 1lb, meaning that the past dozen winners were now rated between 139 and 149, so this is very much the bracket to focus your attention on. Prior to the last 12 years, six of the previous seven winners were rated in the 130s, so it would appear as though the calibre of winner has increased over this latest period. Horses rated in the 150s seemingly find this too much of an ask.

In terms of weight carried, only two winners this century have shouldered more than 11-4 to success, which again emphasises the fact that it is often difficult for those towards the head of the weights.

KEY TRENDS

- ⭐ The past 12 winners were rated between 139-149
- ⭐ 9 of the past 10 winners had contested a Graded novice hurdle or novice chase
- ⭐ The past 7 winners had won at Cheltenham earlier in the season
- ✓ 19 of the past 25 winners were aged 9 or younger
- ✓ 15 of the past 20 winners ran on or after 25th January
- ✓ 13 of the past 21 winners had run 9 times or less over fences
- ✓ 7 of the past 10 winners were in their first or second season over fences
- ✓ 7 of the past 10 winners won last time out
- ✓ 6 of the past 8 winners returned at 8-1 or shorter (4 justified favouritism)
- ✓ Respect course form
- ✓ Respect David Pipe-trained runners
- ✓ Respect Gigginstown House Stud-owned runners
- ✗ Only 2 winners this century carried more than 11-4
- ✗ Only 2 of the past 21 winners had run in more than 12 chases
- ✗ Only 2 of the past 10 winners returned at odds greater than 16-1
- ✗ Only 3 of the past 22 winners had failed to run during the calendar year

We are, however, seeing slightly bigger weights carried to success than previously was the case, with nine of the past 11 winners shouldering 10-10 or more, so paying close attention to those in the bracket between 10-10 and 11-4 is advisable.

COURSE/FESTIVAL FORM

FORM at Cheltenham is always a positive ahead of the Festival, but in this race in particular it seems especially significant, certainly in recent years. The past seven winners had won at the track earlier that same season, with two of those recent winners – The

	Top Weight (OR)	Bottom OR	Winner OR		Top Weight (OR)	Bottom OR	Winner OR
2025	157	*131	139	2020	157	140	147
2024	152	130	143	2019	156	135	141
2023	157	133	143	2018	155	137	147
2022	155	132	145	2017	158	133	145
2021	154	130	140	2016	157	135	142

* 131 (oh4)

Shunter and *Seddon* – having won handicap hurdles (rather than chases) in the early part of the season.

Four of the past seven winners had run at Cheltenham on trials day, with three of the four successful. The **Timeform Novices' Handicap Chase** is often a deep race and one which works out well during the spring, indeed it has had a big impact on the returning novices' handicap at the Festival in recent years. It has also produced two winners of this race, with both *Simply The Betts* (who beat Imperial Aura, who won the novices' handicap next time) and *Jagwar* successful in this race on their more recent start. Bet365 Gold Cup winner Resplendent Grey was back in fourth, so it was another strong renewal, and this year's race went the way of Jordans Cross, who stayed on strongly to beat Quebecois by a nose.

Over the same course-and-distance, *Siruh du Lac* won the **Betfair Exchange Handicap Chase** and *Coole Cody* finished seventh in that same race before winning this. Obviously, those two races are staged on the New Course (formerly the same course-and-distance as the *'Plate'*) but I still expect them to have an impact, given the ideal timing between fixtures. This year's open handicap was won by Donnacha, who had a head to spare over last year's *'Plate'* winner *Jagwar*.

From earlier in the season, be sure to pay close attention to the form of the **Paddy Power Gold Cup** (November) and the **December Gold Cup**, whilst Shakem Up'arry won the **Betfair Exchange Handicap Chase** (formerly the **New Year's Day Handicap Chase**) on his most recent start. Matata won this year's race, in which December Gold Cup winner Glengouly was pulled-up.

Two of the past four winners had run well in the previous year's **TrustATrader Plate Handicap Chase** – those being *Coole Cody* (somewhat of a course specialist) and *Shakem Up'arry* – so respect the placed horses from last year's renewal, if returning for another crack at it.

RECENT FORM

A POSITIVE recent run seems important, with now seven of the past 10 winners – and this includes six of the past seven winners – having won on their most recent start. During this period, *Road To Respect* also recorded a second place finish on his latest start, so very much look towards those who appear to be in form, something which isn't always the case with all of the Festival handicaps.

In terms of the timing of a recent run, only three of the past 22 winners failed to run during the calendar year, with *Shakem Up'arry* just scraping in here, by virtue of his New Year's Day success. 15 of the past 20 winners ran on or after 25th January, which obviously captures those recent winners who were in action in late January, at Cheltenham's trials day fixture.

TACTICS

THIS is a subsection which will likely need to be reviewed. This held its position for this race, as prominently ridden chasers had a fine record in this race whilst it was staged on the New Course. Over this sort of trip, racing up with the pace on the more expansive track is very much advantageous. However, with the switch to day one and the Old Course, this could well change, so the positive trend has been removed from the *Key Trends* table. Keep an open mind for now, as we could see the race evolve a little in terms of required tactics.

MARKET FORCES

WE HAVE seen plenty of big-priced winners of this race over the years, with *Mister McGoldrick* (66-1), *Something Wells* (33-1), *Carrickboy* (50-1) and *Darna* (also 33s) a quartet of obvious examples between 2008 and 2015. Since then, however, things appear to have become more stable, with only two winners returning at odds greater than 16-1 and six of the past eight winners returned at single figures. Four of those justified outright favouritism and five returned at odds ranging from 9-4 and 5-1, with *The Shunter* (9-4F) the shortest priced winner this century. *Jagwar* returned at 3-1 last year and these seemingly *'easier to find'* winners appear to have coincided with the younger, less exposed victors.

TRAINERS TO NOTE

AS TOUCHED upon previously, **Nicky Henderson** has recorded the most wins of the current crop of trainers (4), although his record is a historical one, with his last winner coming back in 2006 with *Non So*. Without a runner in each of the past four renewals, his record during the previous 10 years stood at 0-15, so it doesn't appear to be a race which he targets with a great degree of conviction these days.

David Pipe last won the *'Plate'* in 2014, but that was his third win in a five-year spell, plus like Henderson, his dad Martin won the race on four occasions. The Pipes often like to target the handicaps at the various Cheltenham meetings throughout the season and this is one of the Festival races in which they have enjoyed most success down the years. Pipe was also without a runner last year, but take note if he deems one good enough to represent his Pond House stables.

Another trainer to record three quick victories in this race was **Venetia Williams**, successful three times between 2007 and 2013. Responsible for a couple of placed horses (first five) shortly after, she saddled two without success last year, but her runners certainly deserve a second look, in a race which she clearly likes to target. Two of her winners returned at long odds, so don't let a big price put you off from this stable.

And, although they won the race for the first time last year, Jagwar provided **Oliver Greenall & Josh Guerriero** with a second Festival success in three years, following on from Iroko's win in the Martin Pipe (2023). Last year's Grand National fourth finished fifth in the Grade 1 Golden Miller Novices' Chase two years ago (on the back of an interrupted campaign) and the training duo have only saddled those three runners at the Festival. Therefore, their record in handicaps at the meeting – since joining forces on the license – reads an impressive 2-2 (100%) so take note of any handicappers that they aim at this race, or any other contest, throughout the week. Of course, both horses also carried the silks of JP McManus.

GIGGINSTOWN HOUSE STUD

40-1 shot Conflated represented owners **Gigginstown House Stud** last year, following on from 80-1 outsider Embittered the year before. They have had just eight runners during the past decade, but managed to record back-to-back wins with *Empire Of Dirt* and *Road To Respect*, and have since had a second and a fifth for good measure. From a relatively small sample of runners, this is a respectable return and their runners are to be noted going forward.

IRISH SUCCESS

FOR years, this was one race in which Irish-trained horses struggled. An Irish win in the *'Plate'* was almost unheard of, but they won five of eight renewals fairly recently (between 2016 and 2023) and such runners were responsible for the second, fourth, fifth and sixth last year. Whilst this was once a race – rather like the Ultima – in which Irish horses could be overlooked with a degree of confidence, that is no longer the case.

Matata

ROLL OF HONOUR

Year	Form	Winner	Age	Weight	OR	SP	Trainer	Runners	Last Race (No. of days)
2025	1131	Jagwar	6	10-10	139	3/1F	O Greenall & J Guerriero	20	1st Timeform Nov H'cap Chase (47)
2024	P61	Shakem Up'arry	10	11-5	143	8/1	B Pauling	21	1st Cheltenham H'cap Chase (73)
2023	328F231	Seddon	10	10-9 (5)	143	20/1	J McConnell (IRE)	23	1st Leopardstown H'cap Chase (77)
2022	2F187	Coole Cody	11	11-2	145	22/1	E Williams	15	7th Gr.3 Cheltenham H'cap Chase (47)
2021	4114131	The Shunter	8	10-5	140	9/4F	E Mullins (IRE)	21	1st Morebattle Hurdle (12)
2020	1121	Simply The Betts	7	11-4	149	10/3F	H Whittington	23	1st Timeform Nov H'cap Chase (47)
2019	111	Siruh du Lac	6	10-8	141	9/2	N Williams	22	1st Gr.3 Cheltenham H'cap Chase (47)
2018	2137	The Storyteller	7	11-4	147	5/1F	G Elliott (IRE)	22	7th Gr.1 Ladbrokes Nov. Chase (40)
2017	14322	Road To Respect	6	10-13	145	14/1	N Meade (IRE)	24	2nd Gr.2 Ten Up Nov. Chase (25)
2016	F2P1	Empire of Dirt	9	10-11	142	16/1	C Murphy (IRE)	22	1st Gr.3 Leopardstown H'cap Chase (60)

LEADING TEN-YEAR GUIDES

Betfair Exchange Handicap Chase 2 (*Siruh du Lac* 1st, *Coole Cody* 7th)
Betfair Exchange Handicap Chase (New Year's Day) 3 (*Darna* 7th, *Coole Cody* 8th, *Shakem Up'arry* 1st)
* TrustATrader Plate Handicap Chase 2 (*Coole Cody* 4th, *Shakem Up'arry* 3rd)
Timeform Novices' Handicap Chase 2 (*Simply The Betts* 1st, *Jagwar* 1st)

PRINCESS ROYAL NATIONAL HUNT CHALLENGE CUP NOVICES' HANDICAP CHASE

3m5f 201y (0-145 Handicap) – Old Course

OVERVIEW

THE *'National Hunt Chase'* was reshaped ahead of last year's Festival and saw 18 horses go to post for the inaugural running of the race as a novices' handicap chase. As such, the previous *Key Trends* were left largely irrelevant/redundant, so at this stage we are without any trends to work from and need to allow the race to bed in before we can look at it from a statistical perspective.

A COMPLETELY NEW RACE

FORMERLY a Graded novice chase for amateur riders (and before that, the original *'National Hunt Chase'* had even more restrictions attached to it), it was converted into a novices' handicap for the first time in 2025 and although I was, personally, a little sceptical about the move, Cheltenham and race-goers alike were rewarded with a strong field of 18 horses going to post. Although the Kim Muir (day three) offers up a similar test (0-145 over 3m2f and also a race for amateur riders), there was clearly more of a suitable pool of horses to contest this race than I had initially thought.

As touched upon in the *Overview*, we will need to see at least a few more renewals before we can begin to form any *Key Trends* for the newly formatted race and as a result, we have also (for now) removed the *Leading Ten-Year Guides*, with the races previously illustrated no longer meaningful.

THE FIRST WINNER

LAST year's winner *Haiti Couleurs* had been targeted at the contest from some way out and by prepping him for Cheltenham over hurdles at Newbury, Rebecca Curtis was clear that this would be the target for her rapidly-improving young chaser (deemed him ineligible for the aforementioned Kim Muir, for example, having had just the three chase starts (minimum requirement for this race, but not enough for open handicaps)).

WEIGHTS AND OFFICIAL BHA RATINGS

LAST year's winner carried 11-4 and was successful from a mark of 135, with the top-weight being Duffle Coat, who carried 12-0 from a mark of 145 (maximum rating allowed to run). Two horses rated 124 were the last two to make the cut, with a field size limit of 18 now in place.

COURSE FORM

ONE thing that was previously a positive and remained key last year was form at Cheltenham. Although the winner had no Festival form to call upon, he had won a 3m1½f novices' handicap at the December meeting – on his third start over fences – and a couple of other fairly recent winners (namely *Tiger Roll* and *Galvin*) had been in action at the October meeting that same season. It can, therefore, still pay to give plenty of respect to those with winning or placed form at the track from earlier in the season.

TARGET FOR CURTIS

ALTHOUGH she first won the race when it was still a Class 2 event some 14 years ago, **Rebecca Curtis** has now won the race on two occasions and her first winner *Teaforthree* wouldn't have been too dissimilar to the type of horse now required to win the race, albeit rated 146 and therefore 1lb too high. A trainer who excels with staying chasers, the switch from Grade 2 to novices' handicap is likely ideal for a yard of Curtis' size and gives such stables a greater chance of Festival success. Given last year's result and the subsequent exploits of *Haiti Couleurs*, who of course then headed to Fairyhouse and won the Irish National, it is likely that the Welsh trainer will continue to target this contest where possible.

The improving Newton Tornado looks to be a likely runner for the trainer this year.

Newton Tornado could represent Rebecca Curtis

ROLL OF HONOUR

Year	Form	Winner	Age	Weight	OR	SP	Trainer	Runners	Last Race (No. of days)
2025	2113	Haiti Couleurs	8	11-4	135	7/2J	R Curtis	18	3rd Newbury H'cap Hurdle (31)
2024	312F	Corbetts Cross	7	11-7	150	15/8	E Mullins (IRE)	7	Fell Fairyhouse Chase (34)
2023	213	Gaillard du Mesnil	7	11-7	155	10/11F	W Mullins (IRE)	10	3rd Gr.1 Ladbrokes Nov. Chase (37)
2022	11	Stattler	7	11-6	153	2/1	W Mullins (IRE)	6	1st Gr.3 Naas Racecourse Nov. Chase (44)
2021	1111	Galvin	7	11-6	152	7/2	I Ferguson (IRE)	12	1st Cheltenham Nov. Chase (144)
2020	12152F	Ravenhill	10	11-6	142	12/1	G Elliott (IRE)	14	Fell Troytown Handicap Chase (107)
2019	12324	Le Breuil	7	11-6	145	14/1	B Pauling	18	4th Gr.2 Haydock Nov. Chase (52)
2018	112BU	Rathvinden	10	11-6	150	9/2	W Mullins (IRE)	16	u.r. Gr.1 Ladbrokes Nov. Chase (37)
2017	22133	Tiger Roll	7	11-6	152	16/1	G Elliott (IRE)	18	3rd Listed Wexford Chase (134)
2016	3P62	Minella Rocco	6	11-6	143	8/1	J O'Neill	20	2nd Gr.2 Reynoldstown Chase (24)

CHELTENHAM FESTIVAL 2026 – DAY 1

Daily Tips

BY SAM TURNER

Formerly Robin Goodfellow of the Daily Mail, Sam has been a regular on Racing TV for more than two decades and now writes a daily column for Betfair.

Supreme Novices' Hurdle
TALK THE TALK

IF ANYONE was in any doubt that **Talk The Talk** can actually 'walk the walk' those questions were answered in style at the Dublin Racing Festival.

An unlucky loser with the race at his mercy when over jumping at the final flight and crumpling on landing in the Paddy Power Future Champions Novice Hurdle over Christmas at Leopardstown, the flashy chestnut made amends in style in the Grade 1 Tattersalls Ireland Novice Hurdle.

In a race run in a dawdle early on, Talk The Talk was settled in rear by J J Slevin as Ballyfad and King Rasko Grey took the field along at a swinging 25-26mph gallop for much of the first circuit, with the respective riders clearly mindful of the demanding conditions.

The steady early pace meant it was likely any horse attempting to make ground from the rear was required to quicken into a gallop which was strengthening from the back straight and that was exactly the scenario which faced Talk The Talk when the front-runners wound up the pace from two out.

Surely those ridden chilly would be totally compromised by the sluggish early tempo, leaving them facing a near impossible task to reel in the pacesetters in an event which incredibly was run 14 seconds slower overall than the Irish Champion Hurdle and nearly six seconds slower than the concluding bumper.

For most of the field that was indeed the case, but Talk The Talk overcame the hindrance, displaying the same change of gear he showcased at Christmas to overhaul the well-placed front-runners and snatch an unlikely Grade 1 victory on the line.

Connections were at pains to teach the Born To Sea gelding how to race and educate him for the future, hence the patient ride, and it was noticeable how well he jumped among horses compared to his previous outing where he ballooned a couple of hurdles, appearing a little novicey.

As trainer Joseph O'Brien told the waiting press corps afterwards, connections were willing to pass up short term gain for the long term good.

"I said to J J (Slevin) that we might get beat because of that (being dropped out), but we were thinking of the horse's long-term career. I thought at halfway there was no chance he was going to make up any ground because they hacked around.

"The second and third sat first and second the whole way and we came from third or fourth last. It's a testament to the horse's ability and also J J made a key move to go from in to out to get a clear smooth, passage home.

"He's a reactive, sensitive horse so we've been conscious to do that in his career so far. In Grade 1 company the last day, people said it wasn't all over, but we were very happy with him on that day, he showed a lot.

"A few people mentioned that he wasn't a great jumper, but he actually is a very good jumper. He just made a few silly mistakes.

"I think his jumping was good today and he's learned from every race. The last day was frustrating but you always learn more from those experiences than when you win."

When questioned if Talk The Talk can go on to win the Supreme, O'Brien added: *"He's probably going to be favourite after that, and he'd certainly have a favourite's chance."*

Those were interesting comments given the layers were happy to leave Old Park Star as a clear market leader, while some even preferred a maiden hurdle winner El Cairos in their lists to O'Brien's Grade 1 hero, content to cut him to 7/1 third favourite, despite the manner of his victory (shortened into 5/1 shortly after the meeting).

Comparing sectional times when one race is so obviously slowly-run can be a perilous exercise, but it's worth looking at the final four furlongs of the hurdle races on the Sunday of the DRF as they really do illustrate the change of gear Talk The Talk possesses.

Final four furlongs sectionals according to RaceiQ data:

Cousin Kate	60.04 sec
Talk The Talk	57.03 sec
Brighterdaysahead	64.86 sec
Moonverrin	63.20 sec

In most cases, I would be wary of Talk The Talk's data as most thoroughbreds can quicken when they have hacked round for a significant portion of any race, but the figures shown on the previous page tell us he was 35-40 lengths quicker through the sectional than Brighterdaysahead.

His burst of acceleration will be a huge asset in the Supreme Novices' Hurdle especially as he also travels so strongly and, if he copes with the preliminaries and hurdles as well as he did at Leopardstown, he could be tough to resist on the run to the line.

Champion Hurdle
ALEXEI

SADLY, robbed of a potential equine superstar in Sir Gino, the Unibet Champion Hurdle is struggling to find a headline act at the time of writing.

The likeable Brighterdaysahead advanced her claims with a commendable victory in the Irish Champion Hurdle, comfortably accounting for main market rival Lossiemouth and reversing the form of the December Hurdle in handsome style.

Whether that level is good enough to win a Champion Hurdle in what appears a less than vintage year, only time will tell, with the data suggesting the DRF hurdling feature suited the grinders rather than the quickeners.

A finishing speed percentage for the first two across the line of just over 94 per cent illustrates just how slowly Brighterdaysahead and Lossiemouth were completing an attritional test and the winner's overall time of 4m4.20s was a full eight seconds slower than it took to run last year's Champion Hurdle.

For a mare that clearly stays very well, Brighterdaysahead is ideally going to need proper soft ground or a very aggressive ride to be fully effective in a Champion Hurdle, while she has also been previously beaten twice at the Festival, albeit she sustained a knee issue in last year's renewal of this race.

This was another sluggish display from Lossiemouth who never really travelled with any fluency throughout.

My immediate thought post-race was that this run may give connections the perfect excuse to switch to the Mares' Hurdle as I have never been convinced they truly believe she is a potential Champion Hurdle winner.

Of the home challenge, The New Lion warmed up for his tilt with a jog and sprint in the Unibet International Hurdle on trials day, hurdling better than he did in the Fighting Fifth to account for Nemean Lion and the 138-rated Brentford Hope who, a week earlier, had won a handicap at Haydock by a neck off 134.

Clearly, The New Lion is a good bit better than that bare form, but the question is how much?

His career best effort came in the Turners Novices' Hurdle where he beat The Yellow Clay and Final Demand, both of whom have been campaigned over staying trips subsequently with varying degrees of success, so was it any surprise that he managed to out speed them after jumping the last?

In truth, I'm left wholly uninspired and unconvinced by those that head the market (there isn't enough space to cover Constitution Hill!), the admirable Golden Ace aside, so one or two at bigger prices like **Alexei** appeal as a more enticing proposition.

At first glance, it was a little disappointing that the selection was beaten in handicap company at Ascot over Christmas and there can't be many prospective Champion hurdlers that have suffered such a reverse prior to claiming success in this race.

It has happened previously though, and those of a certain vintage may remember the wonderful Flakey Dove being beaten in a Tote Gold Trophy at Newbury off 149 just a month before she lifted the 1994 renewal of this event. Connections of Alexei will be hoping history can repeat itself more than 30 years later.

The selection was originally bought by bloodstock agent Tom Malone for the Irishman to ride in a Wincanton charity race, an event which the former jump jockey unsurprisingly turned into a rout!

Connections wasted little time maximising their gelding's fitness following that low-key introduction to UK racing, winning a couple of novice hurdles at Taunton with the tongue tie equipped before his form tailed off a little post-Christmas.

It has been a different story this season though as trainer Joe Tizzard was quick to capitalise on a lenient mark following an encouraging comeback effort in the Welsh Champion Hurdle where, but for a slight error two hurdles from home, Alexei may have beaten the well-backed good-ground lover Celtic Dino.

That race has already thrown up valuable handicap victories for the likes of Wilful (3rd), Listentoyourheart (4th) and Tutti Quanti (6th) with the latter bolting up in a competitive renewal of Newbury's Gerry Feilden Hurdle to further endorse a strong piece of form.

Alexei clearly stepped forward for his comeback as he made short work of a talented bunch of Ascot handicappers prior to bolting up in the Unibet Greatwood Hurdle at the Paddy Power meeting, displaying a sharp change of gear after the final flight to quicken clear of Helnwein and put 6 lengths between himself and his closest rival.

The Greatwood victory not only stamped Tizzard's star hurdler as a viable Champion Hurdle outlier, but it was the third time in succession that he recorded the fastest finishing speed percentage in a race according to the RaceIQ metric.

That data demonstrated that he boasts the ability to quicken at the end of a truly run race, while also confirming Cheltenham is a course which can bring out the best in him.

I was fortunate to speak to the selection's trainer on trials day at Cheltenham where he confirmed that Wincanton's Kingwell Hurdle (takes place whilst the Guide is at print stage) would probably be Alexei's pre-Festival assignment.

When asked if he was keen to roll the big dice in March, Tizzard felt that they might as well have a tilt in an open year rather than try and concede loads of weight to a lightly raced rival in a County Hurdle so, with his effectiveness at the track confirmed and his versatility on most ground assured, Alexei makes some each-way appeal at the sizeable prices on offer at the time of writing.

National Hunt Novices' Handicap Chase
ZERTAKT / HOLOKEA

AT THE time of writing, entries for the longest race at the Festival are unknown, but Zertakt and Holokea are two that appeal at big prices in the ante-post markets, especially as they fought out a terrific finish in a staying handicap chase at the pre-Christmas Cheltenham meeting.

The duo looked to have slipped under the radar somewhat for this marathon test but, given their respective marks, they could prove a threat to all if finding their way into this event at the foot of the handicap.

While their participation is not as yet assured – a mark of 124 was enough to make the final field in this race 12 months ago – Zertakt (122) and Holokea (124) both have valuable experience of the track courtesy of their duel in a Class 3 affair last December, a race which has seen fourth-home The Jukebox Kid uphold the form with an impressive victory at Ascot.

Zertakt finished strongly from well off the pace under Charlie Deutsch that day to claim the rather unfortunate Holokea courtesy of a finishing speed percentage of 106.33%, earning a 6lb rise for his first win over fences at the seventh attempt.

Connections revealed afterwards that they were encouraged to preserve his novice status last term so that he could have a crack at this race and this test of stamina should be ideal for a horse that jumps and gallops so strongly, with the only negative being the quiet season endured by his stable.

Holokea has subsequently posted a fine effort in defeat in an open handicap at Windsor off top-weight, again moving through that event like the best horse at the head of affairs, only to be picked off close home by Neo King.

The first and third were both ridden patiently that day, whereas Holokea was in the van throughout and arguably paid for a forceful ride close home.

He is just the type of horse which should enjoy the rigours and demands of this race and could arguably be rated 130-plus had he converted this opportunity or indeed the one before Christmas at Cheltenham.

Both are worth seriously considering, from an each-way perspective, for this race under the NRNB concession.

Alexei (right) wins the Greatwood Hurdle in November

CHELTENHAM FESTIVAL 2026 – DAY 1
Banker or Bust
BY RORY DELARGY

Rory is a contributor to The Irish Field and Irish Daily Star, whilst he can be seen on Paddy Power's 'The Cheltenham Countdown' show. He also co-writes the 'Punting Pointers' feature for Sporting Life.

Supreme Novices' Hurdle
OLD PARK STAR

THE picture for a number of the Grade 1 contests at Cheltenham should have moved into sharper focus after the Dublin Racing Festival and while that has largely been the case, some of the big events at Leopardstown have served to muddy the waters further.

One horse who had made his case strongly for his Cheltenham target in advance of the DRF is **Old Park Star**, who has won all three starts in novice hurdles, including a victory on Cheltenham's New Course and culminating in a high-class performance to land the Rossington Main Hurdle at Haydock in January. That win earned him a Timeform rating of 155+ (now shown as 155p), which would translate to 169p on the weight-adjusted ratings appearing on the racecard. Just a note here to point out that I'll be using Timeform's ratings throughout for the sake of clarity and uniformity, but that doesn't imply that these ratings are always a reliable measure, and the figures themselves are an expression of what an individual has achieved without context and not a prediction of future performance.

In short, ratings are a significant point of reference, but there are times when we should place less confidence in ratings alone, especially where the context in which they are gained differs significantly from the scenario faced next. Some horses need to dominate to produce their best form while others do only what's required and run to a higher level when given a stiffer task. There's also the matter of distance, ground and track preference to discuss, but ratings represent the simplest way of sorting the wheat from the chaff in racing, and they have a crucial part to play in race analysis.

As it stands, Old Park Star sits atop the adjusted ratings for the Supreme on 155p, with the leading contenders listed below with their unadjusted ratings:

Old Park Star 155p, Talk The Talk 148p, Skylight Hustle 146p, Ballyfad 144p, King Rasko Grey 143

The quartet beneath Old Park Star are all Irish and have met in either the Grade 1 Tattersalls Ireland Novice Hurdle over 2m at the DRF or in the Future Champions. It's possible that the Irish cohort are rated either too high or too low on the whole, but the form intertwines well and the individual ratings make sense based on what's happened in the Grade 1 races already run there, with the form of the Royal Bond at Fairyhouse (now a Grade 2) having taken a couple of knocks subsequently. I'll discuss the individuals under *"Threats"*.

STRENGTHS: Purely on ratings, Old Park Star is the one to beat here, and the market reflects that, so the first thing to do is to dig into the way he's achieved his rating and ask how robust it is.

The son of Well Chosen arrives at the Supreme with a flawless novice record, having won all three starts over hurdles in increasingly impressive fashion. His latest success in the Rossington Main at Haydock showed not only his class but his ability to quicken decisively when asked, demonstrating a strong turn of foot in pattern company despite concerns about the relative sharpness of the track. He has already demonstrated he handles Cheltenham's New Course, a significant advantage for a Festival novice, and his jumping has been efficient and assured throughout the season. Taken together, his profile points to a progressive, battlehardened novice, but one with untapped potential. He looked a little wayward on one occasion in bumpers for Paul Nicholls, but he has looked thoroughly straightforward since joining Nicky Henderson and has coped with his rise through the ranks without turning a hair, suggesting that the atmosphere of the Cheltenham Festival will pose him no issues.

Wins at Kempton, Cheltenham and Haydock show his ability to cope with courses of different characteristics, and while it's clearly a positive to have won so impressively at Cheltenham, that was on the New Course, and it was at Haydock that he proved he had the gears to cope with the sharper Old Course. His jumping has been typically assured for one from a stable whose novices tend to stand out as athletes, and he is not reliant on others to set a race up for him.

WEAKNESSES: The only negative trait demonstrated by Old Park Star to date is that he hung right when runner-up in a Kempton bumper last season. He failed to win in bumpers for Paul Nicholls, and he will be meeting Cheltenham rivals who were superior to him in that field, while the biggest field he's faced over hurdles was when beating nine rivals at Cheltenham in December. A big-field scenario in the Supreme would be an unknown and could require an adjustment in tactics.

His win at Cheltenham is largely deemed a positive, but the stamina requirements of the Old and New Course are surprisingly different with the stiff finish still playing its part on the former, but the relatively sharp run into the home straight requires a nimble horse who can race handily. This is particularly the case on good or quicker ground, and the only time he's looked uncomfortable in a race was on lively ground at Chepstow on his final bumper start for Nicholls. My view is that he answered the question of his ability to maintain his position at Haydock, but the question needs posing all the same.

OPPORTUNITIES: There is little doubt that a well-run race where Old Park Star doesn't have to make the running presents an opportunity for him to improve further and the return to a stiffer track will also help him express his ability more fully. His trainer is a master at bringing his charges to a peak at Cheltenham and while the big meeting is a concern in itself for many horses, it would be a surprise if Old Park Star, whose preparation has been picture-perfect, didn't do himself justice.

THREATS: Ground outside of the usual parameters (yielding – soft) would be an unknown and therefore a factor which could produce an unexpected result, while the DRF was run on heavy ground on the hurdles track, so those who came to the fore in the Tattersalls Ireland Novice Hurdle might be seen as advantaged if the ground turns very testing. The main threats on paper are the horses who filled the first three positions at Leopardstown, namely Talk The Talk, Ballyfad and King Rasko Grey.

Talk The Talk, who would have won the Future Champions at Christmas but for falling at the last was more assured in his jumping this time and did well to win having come from off the pace in a slowly run race. He looks the most talented of the Irish novices, but it's worth remembering that he struggled to jump at speed on quicker ground on his previous start, missing the penultimate flight before overjumping and falling at the last. **Ballyfad** had the run of things but to his credit kept going well from the last and many observers felt he had held on. He appeals as the one who will improve more of the pair having made his racecourse bow in November, and he was coming straight off a maiden hurdle win (on good ground) which is never easy. **King Rasko Grey** was also coming off a maiden win and improved markedly, but he will stay further and is much more likely to run in the Turners over 2m5f. That may also be true of **Skylight Hustle**, winner of the Future Champions, although he remains in both races.

El Cairos is a stablemate of Skylight Hustle but is surely going for the Supreme and is an exciting prospect who was fifth in the bumper last year. He would have won on hurdles debut at Leopardstown but for falling at the last and made amends at Thurles in January, although not before making an almost identical blunder at the last. He has the ability to win a Supreme but lacks a run in competitive company and his jumping is a big concern at this stage.

VERDICT: Extremes of ground are an unknown for a horse raced exclusively on a yielding surface to date but he's a more assured jumper than either Talk The Talk or El Cairos, who look the most talented of his likely rivals, and his form looks a little better in any case. There's no such thing as a certainty, but he ticks all the right boxes to be called an opening-day banker.
BANKER

Champion Hurdle
THE NEW LION

STRENGTHS: The New Lion has put together an exceptional profile, winning all his completed races over hurdles to date. As a novice, he became the first horse to land the Challow Hurdle at Newbury and the Baring Bingham (Turners Novices' Hurdle) at the Cheltenham Festival in the same season, something that had become a "hoodoo" for many classy horses, including Denman.

He suffered his first reverse when falling in the Fighting Fifth at Newcastle where he looked like beating Golden Ace, albeit with the cards not fully played at the time of his exit, and he recovered from that to win the Unibet Hurdle (International/Bula) on Trials' Day at Cheltenham, winning in workmanlike fashion, but doing so by design with the primary aim to fix any jumping frailties that had crept in. As such he was asked to go in tight to his hurdles and did as his rider bade him, before producing a fine turn of foot to win a relative sprint up the straight.

Dan Skelton has always felt that The New Lion was exceptional, saying at an open day before last season's festival: *"I love him; I love everything about him."* Skelton went on to praise the horse as much for his easy-going demeanour and tractability as he did his class, and the horse's temperament appears to be what sets him apart for his trainer. Ability is nothing without the temperament to go with it and The New Lion showed that he was out of the ordinary when beating The Yellow Clay and Final Demand 12 months ago. His win in the Unibet was made straightforward by the injury sustained by Sir Gino in that race, but he was not asked to show all he had and a cosy win was a case of mission accomplished for team Skelton.

WEAKNESSES: Despite his class, The New Lion lacks experience outside novice company and has not felt the white-heat of battle against specialist two-milers. His clearround performance in the Unibet Hurdle was important for confidence-building rather than evidence of being fully battlehardened at the highest level, and it's hard to take that as a performance worthy of Champion standard. His jumping was better at Cheltenham, but he was travelling slower than he would in a Champion Hurdle, and he hadn't entirely impressed with his concentration before taking a heavy fall in the Fighting Fifth.

He showed a useful turn of foot to win off a slow pace at Cheltenham, but he was being asked to quicken against proven stayer Nemean Lion and the 138-rated Brentford Hope, so any credit he gets for being able to quicken from the last needs to accept the size of the task he will face in a similar race in March where his rivals will be better equipped to fend off his late thrust.

Prior to falling, he almost ran out at Newcastle and again dived to his left when coming down. Had he stood up, he would not have had much, if anything, to spare over Golden Ace, with Anzadam and Nemean Lion close up. Nemean Lion is consistent 151-rated hurdler (160 Timeform) and consistently falls just short at the top level. Golden Ace was coming off her only poor run to date and wasn't in quite the same form as when winning the Champion Hurdle despite again inheriting victory, and the much-touted Anzadam has since finished fourth behind Lossiemouth and Brighterdaysahead at Leopardstown before being beaten further by the latter in the Irish Champion Hurdle. With most of those performers reliable types, it's hard to reach the conclusion that the British challenge for the Champion Hurdle – headed by The New Lion – is as strong as the Irish, although the prospect of more improvement is a redeeming feature.

Finally, The New Lion also lags behind on the clock, with his best Timefigure of 150 coming from the Turners and his only figure this season a positively glacial 45 in the *"Bula"*. To contrast, Brighterdaysahead clocked a figure of 166 last Christmas, Lossiemouth's pick is 160 from last spring and Constitution Hill did a freakish 178 at his peak and a best of 160 last season. Again, fast Timefigures aren't only about class, but also opportunity, and it's impossible to gain a big figure in a slowly run race. Or when you're lying on the floor.

OPPORTUNITIES: Not only is there the prospect of improvement from The New Lion for a well-run race at Cheltenham, but the loss of key rivals also counts in the "opportunity" column. The Champion Hurdle picture has been impacted by injuries and absences, with State Man ruled out for the season before his intended return and Sir Gino sustained a significant pelvic injury on trials day, removing the division's strongest British challenge. Those absences, and the fact that few other challengers have emerged from last season's novices, makes the task of winning the Champion easier on paper.

The New Lion has been unsuited by having to make his own pace or sitting off an unusually slow tempo in both his starts, and his detractors need to admit that a solid gallop at Cheltenham could see him in a much better light.

THREATS: With State Man and Sir Gino absent, the equine threats to The New Lion are the mares Brighterdaysahead, Golden Ace and Lossiemouth. Constitution Hill is the elephant in the room but has gone from the best jumper of a hurdle I've ever seen to a disaster. A Flat outing at Southwell will be no help in regard to his jumping issues, so I won't include him in analysis.

Brighterdaysahead is hard to judge but has the best two pieces of form since the start of last season. Her effort to beat Winter Fog and State Man by 30 lengths and more in the December Hurdle last term was exceptional, but she probably left her season behind in running that race in a scarcely believable 3min 45.2sec, looking a shadow of that in two subsequent runs. She's been nursed back to herself since, shaping very well when second to Lossiemouth in the corresponding race and then beating that rival in the Irish Champion Hurdle. Her poor record at Cheltenham is often cited, but her previous run saw her a slightly unlucky second to Golden Ace in the Mares' Novice in 2024 and few remember that she was trying to concede 5lb to the current Champion Hurdler that day. Crabbing her for that run is madness, and pinning a dislike for Cheltenham on last year's disappointing Champion Hurdle effort ignores not only that, but also that she was well below form at Punchestown the following month. Her Irish Champion run would make her favourite but for those persistent doubts, while **Lossiemouth** wasn't far below her best despite seeming to hate the conditions on the day. Lossiemouth sometimes looks like she isn't enjoying herself, as when running behind Constitution Hill in the Christmas Hurdle in 2024, but the figures show that she always runs her race, whether she likes it or not. Her figure for winning at Punchestown last term is arguably a few pounds too high, but she has produced a large number of top-class performances whether judged on the clock or collateral form.

Golden Ace could also run in the Mares' Hurdle, but that would look odd as she is the defending Champion. She's had luck on her side but would have closed the gap on State Man if he hadn't fallen and, Wetherby aside, she's been a model of consistency.

VERDICT: Of course, The New Lion is capable of winning the Champion Hurdle and the fact that he's rated below several others on Timeform's figures is not a definitive view of his standing. In winning a falsely run race on his only completed start out of novice company, he's not had the opportunity to post a big number, and this will be his chance to do so. He is favourite, however, and if Lossiemouth was committed here rather than the Mares' Hurdle, I believe that both she and her Leopardstown conqueror Brighterdaysahead have more compelling claims, and that's not factoring in the current champion Golden Ace, who mustn't be underestimated.

BUST

CHELTENHAM FESTIVAL 2026 – DAY 1

Daily Tips

BY JODIE STANDING

Author of Point-to-Point Recruits, Jodie excels in spotting talent at an early stage in a horse's career.

Supreme Novices' Hurdle
OLD PARK STAR

THE Supreme Novices' Hurdle has always carried a sense of ceremony, the race that cracks open the Festival and sets the tone for everything that follows. It has launched stars of every mould, from the raw brilliance of Constitution Hill to the relentless accuracy of Vautour. Reputations are made in a heartbeat and shattered just as quickly, the race rewarding balance as much as brilliance, demanding fluency at speed and the temperament to handle an occasion that can swallow a novice whole.

Willie Mullins and Nicky Henderson have dominated the modern era, and this year's renewal is building up to be another thriller, but one horse has steadily shaped as though he belongs at the top table and that is **Old Park Star**.

The imposing six-year-old failed to get off the mark in three bumpers for Paul Nicholls but the switch to hurdles for Nicky Henderson has been transformative. He first hinted at what was to come when winning at Kempton in November where he beat a strong field of previous winners by upwards of 3 lengths. The form has substance, with Un Sens A La Vie winning next time at Ludlow and Fortune Timmy bolting up by 24 lengths on Boxing Day before finishing third in a Grade 2 at Cheltenham on Trials day.

Old Park Star travelled with the assurance of a horse who knew exactly what was required, sitting on the heels of the leaders before sweeping to the front between the final couple of flights. Once given a shake of the reins, he asserted with authority and crossed the line with plenty up his sleeve.

Cheltenham posed a different question in December, but he answered it with a performance that made viewers sit up straight. He routed the field by 12 lengths, head in chest, his cruising speed and cleverness at his hurdles combining to produce a display of rare polish.

The Grade 2 Rossington Main presented his sternest assignment, yet again he was flawless. Nico de Boinville kept things simple on the front end and never moved a muscle as Old Park Star turned the screw exiting the back straight. His unyielding nature was once more on show as he forged clear and won on the bridle by 18 lengths.

Although yet to dine at the top table, he has answered every question so far. The main concern going into Haydock was whether he would possess the pace for what is usually more a test of speed than stamina, but he showcased the same naturally high cruising speed he had displayed at Cheltenham. He also wastes no time in the air, measuring his hurdles with the eye of a seasoned campaigner.

He looks the complete package and is one of the most exciting two-mile novice hurdlers we have seen for some time. It is too early for comparisons, but his stature, intelligent head and unrelenting nature bring to mind echoes of Sprinter Sacre.

We should not be dismissive of the opposition. Before Old Park Star tore the Rossington Main apart, this looked a wide-open renewal with El Cairos at the forefront. Gordon Elliott's chestnut has class and gears, his Champion Bumper fifth reading well, while his second to Baron Noir at Punchestown suggested he might have won had he been more straightforward late on.

He was making a smooth transition to hurdles at Leopardstown over Christmas when moving a couple of lengths clear at the last before stumbling and coming down. He made amends at Thurles in January, though again clattered the final flight before scooting clear. Clearly, he has speed to burn, but his uncertainty over the flights could leave him vulnerable.

Joseph O'Brien's Talk The Talk must also come into the reckoning, having already struck at Grade 1 level. The five-year-old has reportedly been described as the trainer's best jumps horse he has ever handled, and he was in the midst of vindicating those comments at Leopardstown over Christmas, holding the Grade 1 Future Champions Novice Hurdle at his mercy before coming down at the last.

He made amends for that mishap in the Tattersalls Ireland Novice Hurdle at the Dublin Racing Festival, a performance that can be marked up given the ground he had to make up off the home turn before staying on strongly to deny the rallying

Ballyfad by a short head, with King Rasko Grey one paced in third. Although clearly not short of speed, he also has the stamina to see him home, while his form on varying ground surfaces is another tick in the box. He looks the main threat to Old Park Star and if Joseph O'Brien is on the money with his assessment, he is going to make it a compelling battle to the line.

Others to note include Mydaddypaddy, who blotted his copybook in the Formby, and Idaho Sun, whose current odds of 16/1 underestimate him. Baron Noir at 33/1 is progressing, though whether that is enough to mix it with the best is another matter.

There is depth everywhere you look, but Old Park Star has shaped like a superstar waiting for his big moment. It will take something special to topple him.

Arkle Novices' Chase
MAMBONUMBERFIVE (NRNB)

THE Arkle still has the feel of a division lacking depth behind Lulamba, who has won all three of his chase starts in emphatic style, including the Grade 1 Henry VIII at Sandown and the Grade 2 Game Spirit at Newbury. However you frame it, he is the worthy favourite, but the picture behind Nicky Henderson's star novice remains muddy.

Mambonumberfive ran on the same early February Saturday as Lulamba but suffered his first defeat over fences in the Kingmaker at Warwick, where a shoddy round of jumping ended his chance before the race began in earnest. Prior to that, he had shaped like a lively Arkle contender, and while the Kingmaker was a bitterly disappointing effort and far from the ideal preparation for the stiffest test of his career, it is worth stressing that both of his poor runs for the yard — the Kingmaker and his stable/British debut at Cheltenham last season — came on soft ground. Those are the only two times he has encountered such conditions in Britain, pulling up the first time and looking to hate it the second.

By contrast, all three of his earlier chase runs this season on a sounder surface showed him to be a rapidly progressive novice, including a strong-staying performance in a deep Aintree handicap from 128, another authoritative win at Newbury from 133, and a deeply impressive step into Graded company in the Wayward Lad, where he overcame mid-race errors to surge clear of Hansard by 7 lengths.

Although the case for Mambonumberfive has been tempered, the broader shape of the race remains largely unchanged. Kopek des Bordes has had a less-than-ideal preparation, Kargese and Romeo Coolio had a hard race at the Dublin Racing Festival — with the latter not looking a natural two-miler — and beyond Lulamba there is still no obvious standout. What has changed is the price, with Mambonumberfive once around the 14/1 mark and now out to 50/1, which could be an overreaction.

There is a real possibility that Ben Pauling may skip the Festival and head to Aintree over 2m4f, but if they do roll the dice and the ground at Cheltenham is good/good to soft, it could bring Mambonumberfive back to the level he showed earlier in the campaign. At 50/1, he is still worth chancing, with the Non-Runner-No-Bet concession the safest option.

Mambonumberfive wins the Wayward Lad at Kempton

National Hunt Novices' Handicap Chase
ONE BIG BANG / BLAZE THE WAY

AT THE time of writing, there are a whole host of horses near the top of the ante-post betting that are unlikely to qualify for the National Hunt Chase, but **One Big Bang**, who sits around the 20/1 mark, makes plenty of appeal.

The James Owen-trained six-year-old looks as though he has been campaigned with this race firmly in mind and his form doesn't look too shabby having finished a solid runner-up to Wade Out in a Listed Novices' Chase in November, only giving way on the run-in when the winner came with a wet sail under a never-say-die ride from Sean Bowen.

Despite that being the grey gelding's chasing debut, he travelled and jumped like a horse with experience under his belt and pulled over 9 lengths clear of Paul Nicholls' Isaac des Obeaux, who went on to win his next start by 5 lengths. And while the winner let the form down next time when only fourth to Salver on Winter Million Weekend at Windsor, he did have the ability to beat Wendigo on his chasing debut at Worcester in October.

One Big Bang then went to Southwell in December where he won a match race against Kamsinas over an extended 3m, asserting after the last and winning with plenty in hand by 5 lengths. Dropped back in trip to 2m3f at Doncaster in January for a run which qualified him for this race, he unsurprisingly found the distance shy of his optimum but stuck on at the one pace without ever threatening to get involved, eventually finishing just over 5 lengths behind Western Knight.

With solid handicap form over hurdles in the bank, he won a Pertemps qualifier at Haydock off a mark of 126, beating Doddiethegreat by just over 2 lengths. That form was reversed in the Final at last year's Festival, where One Big Bang finished fifth, 6¾ lengths behind Nicky Henderson's winner, who led home Jeriko du Reponet. The form stood up again at Punchestown, with Jeriko du Reponet reversing placings with his stable companion, while One Big Bang was a further 5½ lengths back in third.

Although One Big Bang is yet to race beyond an extended 3m, he has plenty of staying blood in his family and his relaxed style of racing should lend itself perfectly for when stamina is at a premium. Poised on a mark of 139, I hope to see him go well for a trainer who has quickly made a name for himself.

The other horse that I had in mind for this test is **Blaze The Way**, who despite disappointing when beaten 25 lengths by Argento Boy at Naas in January, relished every yard of an extended 3m2f at Cheltenham in December where he cruised to a comfortable 5-length success over L'Homme Presse from a mark of 138 (should have been 136 but he was 2lb out of the weights).

A rise to 140 doesn't appear at all harsh and with his dam a close relation of Weird Al, stamina ought not to be an issue. He could, though, head to the Kim Muir, although his regular pilot, Danny Mullins, would not be able to take the ride in that race.

Blaze The Way – a course winner earlier this season

RACE & STAY
EST: 2012
OUR HEART IS RACING

Great Value Racing Packages in Ireland
With all you need included

raceandstay.com
+353 59 8623998

TURNERS NOVICES' HURDLE (Baring Bingham)

2m5f (Grade 1) – Old Course

OVERVIEW
THE modern day Baring Bingham winner requires a turn of foot and we have seen in recent years alone, the likes of *Sir Gerhard, Impaire et Passe, Ballyburn* and *The New Lion* win the race for speed late on. Indeed, horses stepping up in distance boast a good record here, as do previous Grade 1 winners, with the classier – and higher-rated – novices often coming to the fore. Class often shines through and the top-end of the market is also often dominant. *Istabraq* won this race prior to his three Champion Hurdle wins, although ex-Flat horses have struggled of late, whilst *Hardy Eustace* and *Faugheen* also won it before landing the Champion. Ex-Pointers, who went on to win a bumper and then a Graded novice hurdle have a strong record and prior to last year, it is a race which the Irish have dominated in recent years. Willie Mullins alone has won seven of the past 17 renewals.

CHALLOW TREND BUSTER
FOR years, the fact that no winner of the **Challow Novices' Hurdle** had gone on to win the Baring Bingham has been a discussion point in the build-up to the Festival. Prior to last year, 21 winners of the Newbury contest unsuccessfully attempted to win this race but *The New Lion* put that to bed last year when quickening to beat The Yellow Clay and Final Demand. A record of 1-22 is still poor, however, and often the reason is that much more stamina is required to win a Challow, with that Grade 1 often run on gruelling, winter ground. That wasn't the case last season and *The New Lion* was a smooth winner, so factor in conditions. With the changing climate, we do at times now see the Challow run on better ground and when that is the case, it is more of a positive towards the winner come the spring.

The ground was again described as good this season and the race was won by Paul Nicholls' No Drama This End.

SEVEN ON THE BOARD FOR MULLINS
THE once-raced hurdler *Fiveforthree* provided trainer **Willie Mullins** with a first win in the Baring Bingham and he has won it a further six times since. Seven wins in the past 17 renewals is a hugely impressive return, with subsequent Champion Hurdle winner *Faugheen* his third winner of the race, some 12 years ago. More recently, Mullins saddled *Sir Gerhard, Impaire et Passe* and *Ballyburn* to win three successive renewals and although Final Demand could finish only third when stable *'first string'* (Mullins ran another five, all priced between 33-1 and 100-1) last year, runners from this stable must be given utmost respect.

Since 2009 when *Mikael d'Haguenet* was successful, all six of Mullins' winners were sent off either favourite or second-favourite, so focus on his shortest-priced runner. Also, his past four winners were stepping up in trip having won a Graded race over 2m on their most recent start, so respect any with a similar profile (more in relation to that trend anon).

IRISH DOMINATION
BRITISH-TRAINED runners were successful in both 2012 and 2013, with *Simonsig* and *The New One* winning, respectively, although between 2014 and 2024 (inclusive), only the Ben Pauling-trained

Willoughby Court prevented an Irish whitewash. Irish-trained horses won 10 of those 11 renewals and although the aforementioned Willie Mullins was responsible for five of the 10, it is a hugely significant trend. **Gordon Elliott** won the race twice during this period – successful with *Samcro* and *Envoi Allen* – and this race would appear to be where he likes to send his leading novice. Responsible for last year's runner-up, his runner(s) should also be given careful consideration.

The New Lion was able to break the stranglehold in 2025, but 10 winners out of the past 12 still suggests that the Irish-trained novices are at an advantage, often their domestic Graded novice hurdles stronger than those staged in Britain. Although there isn't one outstanding candidate, there are a lot of Irish-trained horses just behind this year's ante-post favourite.

THE UNBEATEN HURDLER

AGAIN, since 2014 when *Faugheen* was successful, eight of the 12 winners were unbeaten over hurdles, including *The New Lion* who had won all three starts prior to last year's victory. Recent winners *Bob Olinger* and *Ballyburn* were beaten on debut before winning their next two starts, whereas the other five winners between 2018 and 2024 were also all unbeaten, *City Island* was (effectively) unbeaten as he had been disqualified on debut having passed the post in front. Last year's front three were all unbeaten over hurdles – and dominated the race from a trends perspective in many ways – and horses with a string of 1s next to their name are to be taken seriously. We simply don't know their ceiling at this early stage in their careers.

HURDLING EXPERIENCE

INTERESTINGLY, last year's front three had a varying degree of experience, with the winner having a record of 3-3 ahead of the Festival, whereas The Yellow Clay had won four times and Final Demand just the twice. In recent years, *Sir Gerhard* and *Impaire et Passe* had won two from two before winning this race and rather like in the Supreme (explained on day one), perhaps experience is becoming less significant as the field size reduces and we become used to less competitive novice races at the Festival. The last winner to have run four times earlier in the season was *The New One* some 13 years ago and we saw Potters Charm disappoint last year on the back of a busy campaign and indeed The Yellow Clay definitely appeared to be below par before falling in his re-match with Final Demand at Punchestown. Recent results suggest that we should very much focus on those horses who have run just twice or three times over hurdles.

Earlier this century, *Galileo* and *Fiveforthree* struck on the back of just one run over hurdles, but those victories came in 2002 and 2008, respectively, and it is a huge ask to be expected to win a race of this nature on the back of having won a maiden or an ordinary novice.

KEY TRENDS

- ★ Horses who have won a P2P, bumper and a Graded novice hurdle are 8-15 during the past 16 years
- ★ 13 of the past 17 winners were in the top 2 according to official BHA Ratings
- ★ 10 of the past 12 winners were trained in Ireland
- ★ 7 of the past 17 winners were trained by Willie Mullins
- ★ The past 16 winners had won at least 1 bumper
- ✓ 25 of the past 31 winners (including the past 10) won last time out
- ✓ 19 of the past 26 winners were aged 6
- ✓ 15 of the past 27 winners were unbeaten during the current season
- ✓ 14 of the past 17 winners had already won a Graded novice hurdle (9 had won a Grade 1)
- ✓ 13 of the past 14 winners hailed from the top 3 in the betting
- ✓ The past 12 winners had run no more than 3 times over hurdles
- ✓ 10 of the past 16 winners had won an Irish Point-to-Point
- ✓ 10 of the past 17 winners won over 2m-2m2f on their previous start
- ✓ 7 of the past 14 favourites have won
- ✓ Nigel Twiston-Davies has won the race 3 times
- ✓ Respect horses rated 150+
- ✓ Respect strong bumper form
- ✗ Only 2 of the past 14 winners retuned at odds greater than 9-2
- ✗ Only 1 of the past 35 winners failed to finish 1st or 2nd last time out
- ✗ Only 1 of the past 20 winners had not won a bumper
- ✗ Only 1 of the past 17 winners had not won at least twice over hurdles
- ✗ Nicky Henderson-trained runners are 1-22 this century
- ✗ Challow Novices' Hurdle winners are 1-22
- ✗ Ex-Flat horses are 0-31 during the past 20 years
- ✗ Paul Nicholls-trained runners are 0-10 since 2000

ARRIVING IN FORM

GIVEN the number of unbeaten winners in recent years, unsurprisingly, plenty of last-time-out winners have been successful here. In fact, 25 of the past 31 winners won on their most recent start and this includes the past 10. Only one of the past 35 winners failed to finish either first or second last time – that being *Massini's Maguire*, who finished third on trials day – so focus solely on those with a 1 or 2 next to their name. In-form horses dominate this race, rather than those looking to bounce back to form.

GRADED NOVICE HURDLE FORM

OF THOSE 10 most recent winners (all won last time out), only one failed to win a Graded race on their most recent start, that being *City Island* who had been disqualified on debut, so was able to run in a second maiden hurdle before winning a winners-of-one novice at Naas, rather than dipping his toe into Graded company. *Willoughby Court* and *Impaire et Passe* were successful at Grade 2 level, whilst the other seven winners had all won a Grade 1 on their most recent start, again suggesting the class rises to the top. Again, last year's dominant front three had all won a Grade 1 contest the time before and any such runner this year should be noted.

Looking at the season as a whole and not just the most recent start, 14 of the past 17 winners had won a Graded race at some stage, so such strong form is clearly hugely significant.

KEY IRISH RACES

BOTH *Sir Gerhard* and *Ballyburn* had won the **Tattersalls Ireland Novice Hurdle** at the Dublin Racing Festival on their most recent start, a race which *Samcro* also won en route to landing the Baring Bingham. Since the introduction of the DRF, the race formerly known as the Deloitte Novice Hurdle (and still registered as the **Brave Inca Novice Hurdle**) has been staged over 2m, having earlier been run over the slightly uncommon distance of 2m2f. *Windsor Park* finished runner-up in that race before winning here and going back even further, both *Istabraq* – way back in 1997 – and *Hardy Eustace* had run in the Deloitte en route to the Festival, the former successful. They went on to win five Champion Hurdles between them, so the requirement for natural pace is evident.

With four of the past 11 winners hailing from the Tattersalls Ireland – and four of the past 12 Supreme winners, too – it is clearly the key race in the division from earlier in the season. This year's race was won by Talk The Talk, who beat Ballyfad and King Rasko Grey.

Both *Envoi Allen* and *Bob Olinger* had won the **Ballymore Novice Hurdle** (registered as the **Slaney Novice Hurdle** and previously staged as the Lawlor's Of Naas) which takes place in early January and over a similar 2m4f trip. Last year's Lawlor's Of Naas was won by The Yellow Clay, who finished runner-up here, whilst Albert Bartlett winner Jasmin de Vaux finished back in fourth, so again, it is often a strong form line. This year's race was won by I'll Sort That, who beat Sortudo.

Willie Mullins has used the Grade 2 **Moscow Flyer Novice Hurdle** as a springboard to Supreme success in recent years but he also won that Punchestown contest with both *Mikael d'Haguenet* and *Impaire et Passe* before they won the Baring Bingham. Staged over a sharp 2m, it was won last year by subsequent Aintree Grade 1 winner Salvator Mundi (also Mullins-trained) and this year's renewal went the way of Mullins' Sober.

Both *Sir Gerhard* and *City Island* won the **Thornton Recycling Maiden Hurdle** at Leopardstown's Christmas fixture, a race which was won this season by Murat, although El Cairos was all set to win before coming down after the last. Interestingly, *Ballyburn* also won his maiden at the same fixture, a meeting which often throws up high-class winners of the maiden hurdles and bumpers.

Looking back at bumper form and *Samcro, Envoi Allen* and *Sir Gerhard* had all won the **"Future Champions" Bumper** at Navan, some 15 months before winning this race. Now a Listed race, it was won last season by Gordon Elliott's Kalypso'chance, who beat Champion Bumper second, Heads Up, before himself finishing down the field at Cheltenham and last of six at Punchestown.

And, the 2m2f **Point-to-Point Bumper** from Gowran Park (now run as the **"Doc's Bumper"**) – which takes place on the Saturday before the Festival – has produced a trio of winners of this race 12 months later. *First Lieutenant, Yorkhill* and *Bob Olinger* all won that race and it was won in 2025 by Ksar Fatal for Willie Mullins, although he is now in training with Barry Connell.

NATIONAL HUNT BACKGROUND

THERE was no ex-Flat representation in last year's race, so the record of such runners remains at 0-31 during the past 20 renewals. *Istabraq, Galileo* and *No Refuge* were three ex-Flat winners between 1997 and 2005, but since then, such runners have struggled and a more traditional National Hunt background is much more of a positive.

The past 16 winners had all won at least one bumper, with *The New Lion* adding to the tally, by virtue of his impressive victory at Market Rasen and plenty had shown strong form in that sphere, at the previous year's spring festivals.

Both *Envoi Allen* and *Sir Gerhard* had won the **Weatherbys Champion Bumper** 12 months earlier, with *Monsignor* – back in 2000 – the last horse before those to complete the Festival double. Between 1998 and 2013, *French Holly, Fiveforthree* and *The New One* had all run well in the same race and the 2024 Champion Bumper winner, Jasmin de Vaux, obviously returned to Cheltenham last year to win the Albert Bartlett. Last year's race was won by Bambino Fever, whilst El Cairos, Idaho Sun, Sortudo and No Drama This End all finished between fifth and ninth.

The New One went on to win the **Weatherbys nhstallions.co.uk Bumper** at Aintree, a Grade 2 in which *Willoughby Court* – prior to last year, the last British-trained winner of this race – had finished fifth. Last year's race on Grand National day was won by Green Splendour.

POINT-TO-POINT WINNERS

10 OF THE past 16 winners had won an Irish Point-to-Point at the beginning of their careers, once again highlighting that *National Hunt Background*, as per the previous subsection. Such horses (Point-to-Point winners) are starting to have an influence in the Supreme, too, but they have been dominant for a longer period of time in the Baring Bingham.

As highlighted in previous editions of the Guide, former winning Pointers who then go on to win a bumper and a Graded novice hurdle boast a particularly strong record in this race. *Ballyburn* was the only horse to match up against this profile in 2024 and there was no such qualifier last year, leaving the record at 8-15 during the past 16 years. No Drama This End is one who ticks all of the boxes this year.

STEPPING UP IN DISTANCE

ALTHOUGH *The New Lion* had been winning over an intermediate trip earlier in the season, it was evident that he wasn't short of speed and had won races through pace. 10 of the previous 16 winners had won over a trip of 2m-2m2f on their previous start, again highlighting the fact that natural pace is a positive here. In recent years, *Sir Gerhard, Impaire et Passe* and *Ballyburn* all won Graded races over 2m on their latest start and having a turn of foot at the business end of this race is important. We saw last year, the winner was quicker than two future stayers and it is very much something that we should focus on. Having won a Graded novice hurdle over the minimum trip is a huge positive.

OFFICIAL BHA RATINGS

13 OF THE past 17 winners were officially top-rated according to the official BHA Ratings. *Ballyburn* was rated 157 ahead of his win in the race two years ago, whilst *Yorkhill* (albeit only second-highest), *Samcro* and *Envoi Allen* were also rated between 155-156, so such a lofty rating has to be greatly respected. Despite the fact that *The New Lion* was rated only 147 before last year's race, we should really lean towards those who have already obtained a mark in the 150s. 12 of the past 14 winners hailed from the top three on ratings, so those with the proven form very much tend to come to the fore. The other pair were fourth-best, incidentally.

AGE

WHEN successful in 2022, *Sir Gerhard* became the first seven-year-old winner since *French Holly* back in 1998. And, in fact, since the race was established in 1971, there have only ever been three winners over the age of six. There were a clutch of four-year-old winners in the early days of the race but none since *Crystal Spirit* in 1991, with juvenile runners a rarity these days.

Since 1999, 19 of the past 26 winners were aged six and that is clearly the optimum age. *Impaire et Passe* is the only five-year-old winner in the past dozen years, with the two before him being *Peddlers Cross* and *The New One*, who weren't far off Champion Hurdle class subsequently. You need a genuine high-class performer to win this race at five, with six being the prime age.

MARKET FORCES

SEVEN of the past 14 favourites have won and again, with class often coming to the fore, 13 of the past 14 winners hailed from the top three in the market, so those towards the head of the betting (and from the top of the ratings bracket) are largely dominant. Only twice in those past 14 years has the winner returned at odds greater than 9-2, further highlighting the fact that the top of the market is usually the place to look. Last year's 1-2-3 were the top three in the betting (and on ratings). Their prices ranged from 6-4 to 3-1, surprisingly resulting in a Trifecta return of £25.30, with the field being priced at 12-1 bar the trio.

BRITISH TRAINERS TO NOTE

ALTHOUGH Potters Charm failed to shine in 2025, **Nigel Twiston-Davies** has the best record of the British trainers. Now training alongside son **Willy**, he has won the race three times, although those wins have been spread out, successful in 1993, 2004 and latterly with *The New One* in 2013. Potters Charm was actually only the third runner from the stable since that latest success, so the Twiston-Davies team are clearly selective about who they run here and any horse deemed good enough should be respected.

Nicky Henderson was without a runner last year but his record remains a poor one, despite winning the race with *Simonsig* some 14 years ago. Finian's Rainbow, Aigle d'Or and Champ were all beaten in the race when relatively well fancied and this century, Henderson's record stands at 1-22. He tends to target the Supreme with his leading novice and boasts a much stronger record in the Festival opener as a result. Tread carefully with runners from Seven Barrows.

Fellow leading trainer **Paul Nicholls** is another with a disappointing record in the race to date and considering that he is responsible for this year's ante-post favourite, No Drama This End, it is worth exploring a little. Nicholls has only saddled three runners in the past 14 renewals, but Bravemansgame, Stage Star and Hermes Allen were all beaten in this race on the back of having won the Challow Novices' Hurdle, a race which No Drama This End won when last seen. Between 2002 and 2011, Nicholls had a further seven horses beaten in this race, including Denman (also won the Challow) and Rock On Ruby, who both finished second.

A record of 0-10 this century suggests it is something to consider, especially as seven of the 10 were sent off at single figures (five sent off at 7-1 or shorter), with Denman (11-10) and Hermes Allen (9-4) both beaten favourites.

OTHER KEY RACES IN ENGLAND

THE Challow Novices' Hurdle and the leading bumper races from the previous season have been covered already, so what about some of the other earlier season contests from this side of the Irish Sea. In-keeping with the earlier (Irish) theme with regards to stepping up in distance, both *French Holly* and *Monsignor* won the **Tolworth Novices' Hurdle** at Sandown en route to victory here, as did (more recently) *Yorkhill*. That 2m Grade 1 is now staged at Aintree on Boxing Day – and run as the **Formby Novices' Hurdle** – and was won this season by the Harry Fry-trained Idaho Sun

Prior to *The New Lion*, the previous two British-trained winners had won the Leamington Novices' Hurdle at Warwick, so I found it a little strange that this was a race chosen to be dropped from the programme a couple of years ago. The removal of that Grade 2 leaves the **Classic Novices' Hurdle** on trials day as the obvious stepping stone over an intermediate trip, a race in which both *The New One* and *Massini's Maguire* hit the frame. Kripticjim narrowly beat Taurus Bay in this year's renewal.

Earlier in the campaign, the **Winter Novices' Hurdle** is another Grade 2 over a similar distance and both *No Refuge* and *Simonsig* finished runner-up at Sandown mid-season. This is another race which went the way of No Drama This End.

ROLL OF HONOUR

Year	Form	Winner	Age	Weight	OR	SP	Trainer	Runners	Last Race (No. of days)
2025	111	The New Lion	6	11-7	147	3/1	D Skelton	11	1st Gr.1 Challow Nov. Hurdle (74)
2024	211	Ballyburn	6	11-7	157	1/2F	W Mullins (IRE)	7	1st Gr.1 Tattersalls Ireland Nov. Hurdle (38)
2023	11	Impaire Et Passe	5	11-7	148	5/2	W Mullins (IRE)	10	1st Gr.2 Moscow Flyer Nov. Hurdle (59)
2022	11	Sir Gerhard	7	11-7	151	8/11F	W Mullins (IRE)	9	1st Gr.1 Tattersalls Ireland Nov. Hurdle (38)
2021	211	Bob Olinger	6	11-7	150	6/4F	H de Bromhead (IRE)	7	1st Gr.1 Lawlor's of Naas Nov. Hurdle (63)
2020	111	Envoi Allen	6	11-7	156	4/7F	G Elliott (IRE)	12	1st Gr1 Lawlor's of Naas Nov. Hurdle (66)
2019	1D11	City Island	6	11-7	147	8/1	M Brassil (IRE)	16	1st Naas Nov. Hurdle (32)
2018	111	Samcro	6	11-7	155	8/11F	G Elliott (IRE)	14	Gr.1 Tattersalls Ireland Nov. Hurdle (39)
2017	211	Willoughby Court	6	11-7	147	14/1	B Pauling	15	1st Gr.2 Leamington Nov. Hurdle (60)
2016	11	Yorkhill	6	11-7	156	3/1	W Mullins (IRE)	11	1st Gr.1 Tolworth Nov. Hurdle (74)

LEADING TEN-YEAR GUIDES

Ballymore Novice Hurdle 2 (*Envoi Allen* 1st, *Bob Olinger* 1st)
*Point-to-Point Bumper 2 (*Yorkhill* 1st, *Bob Olinger* 1st)
Tattersalls Ireland Novice Hurdle 3 (*Samcro* 1st, *Sir Gerhard* 1st, *Ballyburn* 1st)
*Weatherbys Champion Bumper 2 (*Envoi Allen* 1st, *Sir Gerhard* 1st)
*"Future Champions" Flat Race 3 (*Samcro* 1st, *Envoi Allen* 1st, *Sir Gerhard* 1st)
Leopardstown Maiden Hurdle 2 (*City Island* 1st, *Sir Gerhard* 1st)

* denotes previous season

Leading Contenders

NO DRAMA THIS END Trainer: Paul Nicholls

Unbeaten in three starts over hurdles, he has raced exclusively in Graded company, winning the Hyde on the New Course, Sandown's Winter Novices' Hurdle and the Challow at Newbury. Prior to last year, the latter had proven to be a poor guide towards this race and indeed Paul Nicholls won it with Denman, Bravemansgame, Stage Star and Hermes Allen before all were beaten here. A good-looking son of Walk In The Park, he stays this distance strongly and is an exciting prospect with obvious claims.

DOCTOR STEINBERG Trainer: Willie Mullins

An impressive winner over 2m6f at the Dublin Racing Festival, he heads the betting for the Albert Bartlett and given how well he stayed, despite racing keenly, this is only likely to become his target on testing ground, as the further he went, the better he looked at Leopardstown. He had earlier beaten Thedeviluno (form ties in with Skylight Hustle) in the Grade 2 Navan Novice Hurdle and looks to be thoroughly progressive. Tactical pace would be a worry over this trip on better ground.

MIGHTY PARK Trainer: Willie Mullins

Fairly prominent in the market for both this and the Supreme, he only made his belated reappearance on 15th January, when winning a Fairyhouse maiden by 38 lengths. Allowed an uncontested lead, he lacks experience and will find life a lot tougher here. Nevertheless, looks a very smart prospect – having also caught the eye when runner-up in an Irish Point – and Willie Mullins did win this race with the once-raced Fiveforthree in 2008. There is still a chance that he could run once more before Cheltenham.

SKYLIGHT HUSTLE Trainer: Gordon Elliott

Winner of a Point on decent ground, he finished only fourth in his only bumper last season but has left that form a long way behind over hurdles. Beaten by subsequent River Don winner Thedeviluno on heavy ground at Gowran Park, he won in a canter at Fairyhouse before winning the Grade 1 Future Champions at Leopardstown. Although a shade fortunate, that form was advertised by Talk The Talk and he looks to be a big player for a stable who won this race in 2018 and 2020.

BALLYFAD Trainer: Gordon Elliott

Another from the Elliott stable who could step up in distance, he won two bumpers during November and beat a subsequent winner by 9½ lengths on his hurdles debut. Returning to Leopardstown, he ran a big race to finish just a short-head off Talk The Talk at the DRF, so his form ties in with his stable-mate and he, too, shapes like stepping up in distance will suit. Another Points winner, he has a fine attitude and with form on better ground in the book, is another with plenty going for him.

ACT OF INNOCENCE Trainer: Nicky Henderson

Ran well in competitive bumpers at Punchestown and Newbury before winning on his final start for Paul Nicholls, he justified strong support when winning a Newbury maiden hurdle on his first start for Nicky Henderson and after only just failing to concede 20lb to Minella Yoga (Grade 2 placed next time), returned to winning ways in the Listed Sidney Banks. Enjoying the longer trip, he won comfortably without having a tough race and that should have set him up ideally for this test. Versatile in terms of ground, he looks to be a contender.

DAY TWO RACE TWO

BROWN ADVISORY NOVICES' CHASE (Broadway)

3m1f (Grade 1) – Old Course

OVERVIEW

THE Broadway Novices' Chase – sponsored in recent years by Brown Advisory – is another contest with a rich history, the lengthy *Roll Of Honour* including the likes of *Arkle, Tied Cottage, Florida Pearl, Looks Like Trouble, Denman, Bobs Worth, Lord Windermere* and more recently, *Fact To File*. Willie Mullins has trained the past two winners and seven in total, whilst the previous year's Albert Bartlett can often be a good pointer towards success. Whilst proven stamina was once seen as a necessity, we seem to be seeing speedier types win the race nowadays, with several recent winner having shown strong form over shorter distances.

A SHARPER TEST NOWADAYS?

PRIOR to recent years, having proven form over 3m seemed to be a pre-requisite ahead of the Broadway, although the past six winners had won over 2m3½f-2m5f on their latest start, suggesting that slightly speedier types were winning the race. Reduced field sizes and, therefore, less of an end-to-end gallop possibly contributed towards this, and with the removal of the Golden Miller as a Grade 1, this is now more likely to become an option (again) for those who could have run on day three.

However, and this is quite significant, the distance of the race has been increased this year from 3m 80y to 3m1f, so is staged over the exact same course-and-distance as the Ultima on day one. This makes the race a slightly stiffer test and one extra fence will be jumped as a result, meaning that the first fence comes up quite quickly, as opposed to the field swerving – slalom like – around what is now the opening obstacle. It will be interesting to see if this change has an impact to results moving forward, but it is certainly something to consider, especially with those runners who are stepping up in trip.

CHASING EXPERIENCE

AS TOUCHED upon in the second paragraph of the previous subsection, *Lecky Watson* had run just twice over fences prior to the Festival, something which *The Real Whacker* had achieved just two years earlier. Previously, this was seen as somewhat of a negative, with *Don Poli* the only other horse to be successful (earlier) this century on the back of two chase starts, with 1998 winner *Florida Pearl* the last before him. Interestingly, three of the four were trained by Willie Mullins.

In general terms, again, the smaller fields likely play a part here. In a race which was once a real test of stamina and often run at an end-to-end gallop, we have seen fields of just six and seven in the past two renewals. Six also went to post in 2021 when *Monkfish* was successful and this certainly places less pressure on jumping and, therefore, experience can be deemed less significant. Interestingly, only one of the past seven winners had run more than three times over fences.

GRADED FORM IS ESSENTIAL

ONE thing that is still essential is form in Graded company. 18 of the past 19 winners had already recorded a first or second in either a Grade 1 or Grade 2 novice chase, whilst each and every one of the past 24 winners had at least contested a Graded event. Whilst that seems rather obvious, the 2020 renewal is worth remembering, when

Champ ran down both Minella Indo and Allaho, both of whom arrived at the Festival having won just a beginners' chase and lacked any Graded race experience. Quai de Bourbon – a more-fancied (according to the market) stable-mate of the winner – fell into this category last year and unseated his rider down the far side. Be wary of those who don't have any Graded-race experience over fences to their name.

And, of those past 19 winners, *Might Bite* was the one who missed out on a first or second placing, although he would have won the Kauto Star but for taking a heavy fall, so we really ought to be focusing on those who have already performed well at a high level in novice chase company.

OUT NICE AND EARLY

LAST year's winner didn't actually make his chasing debut until 16th December, although in doing so, became the 28th winner in succession to have had that first chase start prior to the turn of the year. 2014 winner *O'Faolains Boy* won on 21st December, whilst the other 19 of the winners since 2005 had run over fences during October or November. Getting out early and having the time to gain the required experience (less so now, I guess) is still important, especially with inclement weather often putting paid to races mid-season. Debuting by mid-November is ideal really, thus allowing a second run over fences over the busy Festive period at the latest.

A DEFEAT ISN'T THE END OF THE WORLD

FOLLOWING the three successive victories of *Monkfish*, *L'Homme Presse* and *The Real Whacker*, *Lecky Watson* made it four wins in five years for unbeaten chasers. However, prior to 2021, *Denman* and *Don Poli* were the only unbeaten winners this century (since *Florida Pearl*). It will be interesting to see if this pattern continues but it certainly wasn't too much of a negative to have been beaten over fences – usually early season – ahead of the Broadway. Half of the past 16 winners were actually beaten on chase debut, with *Fact To File* falling into this category, with stayers often starting over shorter before gradually stepping up in distance. A defeat on debut at least gives a horse another chance to gain some further experience in a second beginners' chase (or a novice without a penalty) before being forced up in grade, but, this is kind of in-keeping with the earlier subsection, *Chasing Experience*. Don't be put off by an early season reversal, especially if there were positives to take from the race and the horse in question continued to improve throughout the season, although

KEY TRENDS

- ★ The past 24 winners had contested a Graded novice chase
- ★ 18 of the past 19 winners had finished 1st or 2nd in a Grade 1 or Grade 2 novice chase
- ★ 7 of the past 16 winners had contested the Albert Bartlett the previous year
- ★ The past 6 winners won over 2m4f-2m5f last time out
- ★ 3 of the past 5 winners were trained by Willie Mullins (7 winners in total since 1998)
- ✓ The past 28 winners made their chase debut before the turn of the year
- ✓ 25 of the past 30 winners spent just one season over hurdles
- ✓ 21 of the past 25 winners had between 3-5 chase starts (although 2 recent winners ran just twice)
- ✓ 16 of the past 19 winners were aged 7
- ✓ 15 of the past 23 winners won last time out
- ✓ 13 of the past 22 winners were trained by Mullins, Henderson or Nicholls
- ✓ 11 of the past 19 winners had won a bumper and/or a Point-to-Point
- ✓ The past 11 winners were rated 150+
- ✓ 10 of the past 11 winners returned at 8-1 or shorter
- ✓ 8 of the past 16 winners were beaten on chase debut
- ✓ 6 of the past 11 favourites have won
- ✓ 4 of the past 10 winners had fallen over fences
- ✓ Second-season chasers are 4-14 this century
- ✓ 2 of the past 10 winners were British-bred (low representation)
- ✗ Only 2 winners this century failed to finish 1st or 2nd last time out
- ✗ Only 3 of the past 16 winners failed to run at the previous year's Festival
- ✗ Only 3 of the past 31 winners were younger than 7
- ✗ Only 2 winning French-breds in the past 19 years
- ✗ Only 1 of the past 7 winners had run more than 3 times over fences
- ✗ Mares are 0-12 during the past 28 renewals
- ✗ Gordon Elliott-trained runners are 0-11 since 2011
- ✗ Henry de Bromhead-trained runners 0-7 during the past 11 years
- ✗ Be wary of top-class staying hurdlers
- ✗ Drinmore Novice Chase winners are 0-10
- ✗ No Kauto Star winner has ever won the race (form can often be reversed)

that recent pattern of unbeaten chase winners certainly could be signalling a moving landscape. Again, perhaps with those speedier types winning, such horses are able to win over an intermediate trip, whereas genuine stayers might find such races a tad sharp before improving once upped to 3m. Keep an open mind here.

DON'T WORRY ABOUT A FALL

AGAIN, a horse failing to complete seems to be less significant in this division, as it does ahead of the Arkle, for example. Four of the past 10 winners had taken a tumble (fall or unseat) earlier in the season, but only *Champ* did this on his last run before winning the Broadway. Ideally, a horse needs to have had another run and restored their confidence before being pitched into a Festival novice chase. *Might Bite* took a horrid fall in the Kauto Star but had time to win a small race at Doncaster next time, whilst *Topofthegame* had fallen the previous season (chase debut) before reverting to hurdles and starting a fresh during the 2018-2019 campaign.

QUICKLY SENT CHASING

NO HORSE matched this profile more so than *Fact To File* – or before him, *Florida Pearl* – by skipping a hurdling campaign and going chasing straight after the Champion Bumper. However, in general terms, you want to look towards those who were contesting novice hurdles this time last year, as opposed to those who spent longer over the smaller obstacles. As touched upon in the Arkle preview, bad habits can creep in with those who have two or three years hurdling and it is much more significant with stayers than with those two-milers. We have seen some notable reversals in this race of horses who had reached a high level as staying hurdlers, with Punchestowns, Grands Crus, Time For Rupert, Smad Place, More Of That and Thyme Hill all beaten at relatively short odds.

25 of the past 30 winners were sent chasing after one season over hurdles. Of the other four (disregarding *Fact To File* briefly), *Champ* and *L'Homme Presse* were sent chasing after their novice hurdle campaigns, just that they were second-season novices over hurdles, whilst *Might Bite* and *Topofthegame* were both sent chasing immediately after their novice hurdle seasons but following early season disappointments, were switched back to hurdles before starting again the following season. So, as you can see, the intent was there initially and getting a horse over fences as soon as is possible is very important in helping to develop a future staying chaser.

When putting together *Jumpers To Follow* each year, the novice chasers I tend to include will invariably be the leading novice hurdlers (for Grade 1 purposes) from the previous season. I am very much of the belief that if you have a potentially smart chaser on your hands, get them jumping fences at the earliest possible stage.

ALBERT BARTLETT A KEY POINTER

SEVEN of the past 16 winners had run in the previous year's **Albert Bartlett Novices' Hurdle**, which is clearly an important piece of form. *Weapon's Amnesty*, *Bobs Worth* and *Monkfish* all completed the double, whilst *The Real Whacker* was also set to contest the Albert Bartlett 12 months before his Broadway success, only to be declared a non-runner on the day. Last year's winner – who had finished fourth in the Champion Bumper two years earlier – finished fifth behind Stellar Story in the 2024 Albert Bartlett and the runner-up chased him home in this race. The Big Westerner and Wendigo are a couple who ran well last year and have since developed into smart novice chasers.

OTHER FESTIVAL FORM

ONLY three of the past 15 winners had failed to run at the Cheltenham Festival the previous year and these included fairly recent winners *L'Homme Presse* and *The Real Whacker*, although as per the previous subsection, the latter was due to take his chance in the Albert Bartlett until the very last minute. It was a case of normal service being resumed last year, with *Lecky Watson* having run well at the previous two Festivals and strong form at Cheltenham previously is an obvious plus. Interestingly, the past two winners had run well in the **Weatherbys Champion Bumper** of 2023, *Fact To File* finishing second and *Lecky Watson* fourth. Respect any horse coming from that contest, with the 2024 renewal seeing the aforementioned Jasmin de Vaux successful.

OTHER KEY RACES

THE Albert Bartlett has already been covered but there are a couple more significant staying novice hurdles from the spring festivals to note, starting with the **Sefton Novices' Hurdle** from Aintree. *Blaklion* finished fourth in that Grade 1, which was won by *Champ* prior to him going chasing the following autumn. Last year's Sefton went the way of Julius des Pictons, who has missed this season through injury.

Having run in the last three races mentioned (followed a good path), Argento went on to contest the **Channor Real Estate Group Novice Hurdle** at

Punchestown (finished 5th) and *Lecky Watson* had filled the same position 12 months earlier. *Presenting Percy* finished sixth in the same race – which for many years was run as the Irish Mirror Novice Hurdle – and the 2025 renewal saw Jasmin de Vaux beat Honesty Policy, with the pair nicely clear.

In terms of novice chases from the current campaign, the **Kauto Star Novices' Chase** at Kempton on Boxing Day is now the only Grade 1 over 3m in this division from earlier in the season. Remarkably, no horse has ever completed the double. We have seen horses turn the form around – on what is a completely different track (this being undulating and left-handed vs the flat, right-handed track at Kempton) – and *Might Bite* was unlucky not to do so in the 2016-2017 season, but as things stand, winners of the Kauto Star (formerly known as the 'Feltham') are to be treated with caution. Last season's winner The Jukebox Man sadly didn't run again through injury, whilst this season's race was won by Kitzbuhel.

Over in Ireland, the early season **Drinmore Novice Chase** is another with a disappointing record here, with winners of that 2m4f Grade 1 currently 0-10 in the Broadway. Last season's winner Croke Park missed Cheltenham to wait for Aintree as he was believed to have wanted an intermediate trip (decision didn't pay off), whilst I Am Maximus won the previous year's Drinmore, immediately after which he lost his novice status. This season's race was won by a more traditional novice, Romeo Coolio.

The Fort Leney Novice Chase has been won by *Don Poli* and *Monkfish* in recent years en route to Broadway success, but that Grade 1 was removed from the calendar this season and as a result, the distance of the **Faugheen Novice Chase** at Limerick was increased, to offer the Irish staying novices a Festive option. Staged over 2m5f, it was won in December by Final Demand.

Like Croke Park, he placed in the **Ladbrokes Novice Chase** (formerly the **Dr PJ Moriarty**) behind Ballyburn at the Dublin Racing Festival, a race which was won by *Fact To File* ahead of his Broadway win. *Monkfish* also landed the 2m5f Grade 1, which can often go the way of a stayer, with four winners in the space of five years (2009-2013) either winning it or finishing placed en route to Cheltenham. This year's race was won by Kaid d'Authie.

MULLINS ON A HAT-TRICK

FOLLOWING the back-to-back wins of *Fact To File* and *Lecky Watson*, trainer **Willie Mullins** will be bidding to win a third successive Broadway Novices' Chase. Also successful in 2021 with *Monkfish*, he has now trained three of the past five winners, having won it back in 1998 with *Florida Pearl*, in 2004 with *Rule Supreme*, in 2009 with *Cooldine* and 11 years ago with the strong stayer *Don Poli*. With seven wins on the board, Mullins is the most successful trainer in this race and during the past decade alone, he also saddled Shaneshill to finish runner-up and has been responsible for the third-placed horse in 2017, 2020, 2022 and 2023.

With less options now available to a Grade 1 novice chaser, he is sure to be well-represented once again, having run no fewer than four of last year's seven strong field. He appears to hold a strong hand this year, with Final Demand, Kaid d'Authie and Kitzbuhel all possible runners.

OTHER TRAINERS TO NOTE

WITH four wins on the board since 2005, **Nicky Henderson** is the most successful British trainer, with his three latest victories coming since 2012. His first three winners all ran in the Kauto Star at Kempton on Boxing Day (all beaten, of course).

Star de Mohaison and *Denman* provided **Paul Nicholls** with successive wins in the race back in 2006 and 2007, and he won the race for a third time in 2019 with the giant *Topofthegame*. A lot more selective in terms of his runners in all novice races at Cheltenham these days, Nicholls' runners still warrant plenty of consideration and between them, Messrs Mullins, Henderson and Nicholls have now won 13 of the past 22 renewals of this race.

Gordon Elliott has struggled to find the key to this race and his *'losers'* include subsequent Gold Cup winner Don Cossack, whilst both No More Heroes and Delta Work (all three owned by Gigginstown House Stud, incidentally) were beaten when sent off favourite. Gerri Colombe was another beaten favourite for the stable in recent years, whilst he ran two last year, Stellar Story finishing runner-up and Better Days Ahead in third. Stellar Story was another to carry the famous silks of Gigginstown (who have won the race twice, with the non-Elliott-trained pairing of *Weapon's Amnesty* and *Don Poli*) and Elliott's record in the race now stands at a disappointing 0-11 since 2011.

Another leading Irish trainer who has yet to win this prize is **Henry de Bromhead**, who has also seen a future Gold Cup winner (Minella Indo) beaten in this race. Along with Monalee and Monty's Star, he finished runner-up and all three carried the colours of owner Barry Maloney. Gorgeous Tom represented the stable last year, taking de Bromhead's tally to 0-7, and in fact, last year's seven runners were all trained by Mullins, Elliott or de Bromhead (a little concerning to say the least).

AGE

THE aforementioned *Star de Mohaison* was the sole five-year-old winner this century, although since then (2005), the age-allowance has reduced dramatically (he received a whopping 10lb when successful 21 years ago) and it is a stiff test for such young horses over this sort of trip, for all that they have a better record in Aintree's Mildmay Novices' Chase. In fact, *Don Poli* is the only six-year-old winner this century, too, with the last before him being *Florida Pearl*. Interestingly, both were trained by Willie Mullins and he opted to run Galopin des Champs in the Golden Miller due to him being the same age during his novice campaign. That would obviously no longer be an option and it is also worth noting that Mullins' two six-year-old winners had run just twice earlier in the campaign (similar to Galopin des Champs) and I doubt that was simply by coincidence. A slight digression but worth noting all the same.

Back to matters in hand and 16 of the past 19 winners (this includes the past five winners) were aged seven, which seems to be the optimum age. As stated earlier, sending a horse chasing at an early stage is important and six-turning-seven seems to be ideal when it comes to the staying division. *Rule Supreme* was successful at eight in 2004, after which only *Might Bite* and *Champ* (both Henderson trained) were successful for that age group.

NATIONAL HUNT BACKGROUND

ALTHOUGH *Lecky Watson* didn't match up against either, 11 of the past 19 winners had won a Point-to-Point and/or bumper at the start of their careers. Last year's winner actually ran in five bumpers and after finishing runner-up on three occasions, finished a creditable fourth in the Champion Bumper (as already covered) so did at least have relatively strong form to call upon from that sphere. 2024 winner *Fact To File* was a Point-to-Point winner, who developed into a high-class bumper performer, winning at Leopardstown on debut before finishing runner-up in the Grade 2 at the DRF and in the Champion Bumper. Be sure to look back at early form in both divisions, with a win in either (or both) a positive.

SECOND-SEASON CHASERS

THERE were again no qualifiers last year and *Topofthegame* is the last second-season chaser to prove successful, but from a relatively small pool of horses, such runners boast a good record (4-14 this century). Both him and *Might Bite* had run just once the previous season – falling (in the case of the former) and reverting to hurdling before being given a fresh start the following year – with 2000 winner *Lord Noelie* boasting a similar profile. *Rule Supreme* was much more experienced and could be classed as a genuine 'second-season chaser'. It will be interesting to see if this trend makes a comeback, with experience a little less important than once was the case.

BREEDING

THERE was also once again no British-bred representation last year, so the record of such runners remains at a highly respectable 2-10 during the past decade, with *Blaklion* and *Presenting Percy* successful. Often British-bred horses require a test of stamina (boast a good record in staying novice races) and that is the case here.

As you would expect, given that it is a staying chase and they are usually by far and away the most represented, Irish-bred horses are the dominant force and *Lecky Watson* was another such winner 12 months ago. However, after a real desperate spell between 2007 and 2021, when French-bred horses had a dismal record of 0-36, *L'Homme Presse* and *Fact To File* struck and with the removal of the Golden Miller – a race in which French-bred horses excelled (over an intermediate trip, which can often be ideal) – I suspect that this recent upturn in results can continue. Last year's pair to carry the '(FR)' suffix were, admittedly, disappointing, but their representation should grow here in coming years and positive results ought to continue also.

NOT A RACE FOR MARES

SINCE 1996, mares have a record of 0-12 in this race and within that dozen, the likes of Fiddling The Facts, Lady Cricket, Like-A-Butterfly and Pomme Tiepy were all sent off at relatively short odds (single figures). The last mare to be successful was *Brief Gale* some 31 years ago and following the introduction of the Mares' Chase, it could be that we see even less take their chance moving forward. If one does line up, however, treat them with caution.

The Big Westerner, runner-up in last year's Albert Bartlett, is a likely contender this year, with the longer trip sure to play to her strengths (stamina). The Mares' Chase remains an option but this would appear more suitable.

MARKET FORCES

LECKY WATSON struck at 20-1 last year, although six of the previous 10 winners were sent off as outright favourite and they included odds-on shots *Monkfish* and *Fact To File*. Last year's result aside, this race was beginning to have a more predictable feel to it of late (since the field sizes reduced), although Ballyburn was obviously an expensive failure for favourite backers in 2025. Prior to last year, O'Faolains Boy – successful at 12-1 in 2014 – was the last winner to return at odds greater than 8-1, so *'shock'* results aren't too common here.

OFFICIAL BHA RATINGS

THE past 11 winners were all rated 150 or higher going into the race and even allowing for the fact that he had run just twice, *Lecky Watson* matched this trend in 2025. Despite his long odds (available at much bigger just a week before the meeting, too), he was actually the joint second top-rated horse in last year's race, on a mark of 152, with only Ballyburn rated higher. *Presenting Percy* was top-rated with 158, whilst *Monkfish* (164), *L'Homme Presse* (159) and *Fact To File* (159) all had lofty ratings ahead of winning the race in recent years. Focus on those rated in the 150s, paying particular attention to those Graded winners who have already reached a mark in the high 150s.

Kitzbuhel wins the Kauto Star at Kempton

ROLL OF HONOUR

Year	Form	Winner	Age	Weight	OR	SP	Trainer	Runners	Last Race (No. of days)
2025	11	Lecky Watson	7	11-7	152	20/1	W Mullins (IRE)	7	1st Gr.3 Kildare Nov. Chase (59)
2024	211	Fact To File	7	11-7	159	8/13F	W Mullins (IRE)	6	1st Gr.1 Ladbrokes Nov. Chase (38)
2023	011	The Real Whacker	7	11-7	153	8/1	P Neville	10	1st Gr.2 Dipper Nov. Chase (73)
2022	1111	L'Homme Presse	7	11-4	159	9/4F	V Williams	9	1st Gr.1 Scilly Isles Nov. Chase (38)
2021	111	Monkfish	7	11-4	164	1/4F	W Mullins (IRE)	6	1st Gr.1 Ladbrokes Nov. Chase (38)
2020	11F	Champ	8	11-4	153	4/1	N Henderson	10	Fell Gr.2 Dipper Nov. Chase (70)
2019	22	Topofthegame	7	11-4	155	4/1	P Nicholls	12	2nd Gr.1 Kauto Star Nov. Chase (77)
2018	13112	Presenting Percy	7	11-4	158	5/2F	P Kelly (IRE)	10	2nd Gr.2 Red Mills Chase (26)
2017	21F1	Might Bite	8	11-4	154	7/2F	N Henderson	12	1st Doncaster Nov. Chase (34)
2016	4F121	Blaklion	7	11-4	150	8/1	N Twiston-Davies	8	1st Gr.2 Towton Nov. Chase (39)

LEADING TEN-YEAR GUIDES

*Albert Bartlett Novices' Hurdle 4 (*O'Faolain's Boy* 4th, Blaklion p.u., *Monkfish* 1st, *Lecky Watson* 5th)
Kauto Star Novices' Chase 2 (*Might Bite* fell, *Topofthegame* 2nd)
*Sefton Novices' Hurdle 2 (*Blaklion* 4th, *Champ* 1st)
Dipper Novices' Chase 4 (*Blaklion* 2nd, *Champ* Fell, *L'Homme Presse* 1st, The *Real Whacker* 1st)
Ladbrokes Novice Chase 2 (*Monkfish* 1st, Fact *To File* 1st)
*Channor Real Estate Group Novice Hurdle 2 (*Presenting Percy* 6th, *Lecky Watson* 5th)

* denotes previous season

Leading Contenders

FINAL DEMAND — Trainer: Willie Mullins
Third in last year's Baring Bingham, he won two Grade 1s over hurdles and the seven-year-old made a perfect start over fences, jumping for fun en route to winning at Navan. Winner of the Faugheen at Limerick, he didn't jump with the same fluency at the DRF, where he was well beaten into third by Kaid d'Authie. Needs to leave that form behind and to date, 2m6f is as far as he has gone under Rules. Had earlier looked a top-class chasing prospect and if forgiven that latest effort, remains a leading contender.

KAID D'AUTHIE — Trainer: Willie Mullins
Took down his stable-mate in the Ladbrokes Novice Chase at Leopardstown, showing much improved form for the re-application of cheekpieces. Beat Wingmen (as Final Demand had done in his beginners) at Fairyhouse, after chasing home Kitzbuhel at Punchestown, and seems to be heading in the right direction with every run. The longer trip looks sure to suit and he has plenty of form on better ground. Made a serious error at the first when pulled-up in last year's Baring Bingham (sent off 40-1 that day).

THE BIG WESTERNER — Trainer: Henry de Bromhead
A gallant second in last year's Albert Bartlett, she ran well on chase debut against Jimmy du Seuil (admittedly, been disappointing since) before winning the Grade 2 Dawn Run at Limerick over Christmas, where she beat Jade de Grugy (herself an 18l Grade 2 winner next time). Whilst the Mares' Chase is an option, the trip of this contest is likely to be much more suitable and she would appear to be a solid jumper. Soft ground would enhance her claims, although having had just the two starts is a minor concern.

WENDIGO — Trainer: Jamie Snowden
Fifth in last year's Albert Bartlett, he travelled well when runner-up on chase debut and got off the mark in a Grade 2 at Newbury, again staying on strongly over 2m4f. The runner-up franked that form in the Lightning Novices' Chase at Windsor, after Wendigo had finished third in the Kauto Star at Kempton. Whilst the longer trip was in his favour, the sharp track didn't appear to suit and he warmed up for Cheltenham with a facile success against weaker opposition at Ayr. The new increased distance of this race is a positive.

WESTERN FOLD — Trainer: Gordon Elliott
An experienced second-season novice, who won the Mayo National and Galway Plate. His Grade 2 defeat of Savills Chase winner Affordale Fury is very strong and the seven-year-old stayed on well, on unsuitably soft ground, to split Kaid d'Authie and Final Demand at the DRF. Back on a sounder surface and up in trip, he could well play a leading role, despite the fact that he looks to have a less 'sexy' profile than some of those above him in the market. Second-season novices have a decent record in this race.

OSCARS BROTHER — Trainer: Connor King
A strong stayer, he has improved markedly for going chasing. Beaten 8 lengths by Western Fold on debut (winner had run 5 times) he won at Galway before outstaying Koktail Divin in the Florida Pearl. Following a break and having changed ownership, he put up a tremendous performance to win the Ten Up and is now 2-2 over 3m on testing ground. A horse with lots of options – the Irish and Aintree Nationals (would need one more run) being two – he would warrant serious consideration if the ground were soft.

geegeez.co.uk

CHELTENHAM & AINTREE FESTIVALS

YOUR ULTIMATE BETTING GUIDE COMPANION

Scan QR to get your first month free, with code 'CFBG'

INTUITIVE RACECARDS | **IN-DEPTH ANALYSIS** | **EXCLUSIVE TOOLS**

DAY TWO — RACE THREE

CORAL CUP HANDICAP HURDLE
2m5f (Premier Handicap) – Old Course

OVERVIEW
THE first open-aged handicap hurdle of the week, the Coral Cup often requires a lightly-raced hurdler, who has the potential to scale greater heights in time. *Jimmy du Seuil* was extremely lightly-raced and in many ways, was a typical winner of the race. French-bred horses have done well over the years, as have those rated in the 140s (in the top 8 of the handicap) and he was the sixth Irish-trained winner in the past decade. Whilst novices don't boast the strong record here which they do it he County and Martin Pipe, second-season hurdlers tend to fare well in the Coral Cup and form over the minimum trip is another positive, with this often developing into a speed test at the finish. Certainly speed trumps stamina in this (often) strongly-run event, with hold-up horses who travel strongly often doing well.

LIGHTLY-RACED HURDLERS
WHILST (as touched upon in the *Overview*) novices don't have a particularly strong record here – as opposed to in both the Martin Pipe and County and day four – lightly-raced hurdlers and those in their second season very much do. Indeed, last year's winner *Jimmy du Seuil* is very much a case-in-point, with him having only had five previous runs over hurdles, all coming the previous season as a novice. With the new rules introduced last year – firstly, that a novice must have run five times over hurdles to be eligible for Festival handicap hurdles, then it was later extended to non-novices – he was reportedly saved for the race during the second half of the season and became the 19th winner this century (from 25) to have won the Coral Cup on the back of nine starts or less over hurdles. Between 2022 and 2024, the three winners were more exposed, but it was a case of reverting to type last year and those with the greater scope to improve are very much the starting point. In particular, take a close look at last season's novices, with second-season hurdlers often coming to the fore.

AGE
YOUNGER horses tend to perform well here, which is in-keeping with the previous subsection. Since the race was introduced in 1993, there has only ever been one double-digit aged winner – that being *Chance Coffey* in 1995 – and there have actually only been two successful nine-year-olds during the past 28 renewals, so *'older'* contenders should really be readily overlooked. 13 of the past 18 winners were aged seven or younger and that record was much stronger before *Commander Of Fleet* and *Langer Dan* (second win) broke a couple of these standout trends.

Given that five-year-olds tend to struggle in open age races, those of that age group have a decent record here, with *Sky's The Limit, Spirit River, Carlito Brigante* and *Aux Ptits Soins* striking in a 10-year period between 2006 and 2015. Last year's winner was only six, whilst five of the past nine winners were aged seven. Focus firmly on those in the bracket between five and seven.

OFFICIAL BHA RATINGS AND WEIGHTS
11 OF THE past 16 winners were rated in the 140s, including the last three. *Langer Dan* was twice

successful off a mark of 141, whilst *Jimmy du Seuil* won off 146 in 2025. That is the area to focus on mainly, although we have seen *'classier'* types strike in this race in the past dozen years, with *Whisper*, *William Henry* and *Commander Of Fleet* winning from marks in the low 150s. Only three of the past 17 winners scored off marks in the 130s, so statistically speaking, it can pay to look towards the better quality – and higher-rated – runners.

11 of the past 17 winners came from the top eight horses in the handicap, reiterating the final sentence of the opening paragraph. Last year's winner fell into this category, too (very much ticked plenty of boxes), whilst Ballyadam has finished placed in each of the past two renewals from marks of 147 and 151, respectively, carrying 12-0 then 11-12. This goes to show that those classier performers can go well, whilst we have seen another clutch of horses rated in the low 150s go close in recent years, so it wouldn't be a shock to see another win before long.

	Winner OR	Lowest OR	Top-rated
2025	146	131	153
2024	141	128	147
2023	141	134	151
2022	152	137	154
2021	138	130	155
2020	140	138	154
2019	151	133	153
2018	143	135	153
2017	148	136	156
2016	149	139	158

CLASS OFTEN SHINES THROUGH

AS SOMEWHAT of a continuation to the previous subsection, those higher-rated and *'classier'* types do tend to fare well in the Coral Cup and when adding in the potential for further improvement (see *Lightly-Raced Hurdlers*) you often get the key ingredients to an archetypal winner of the race. Whilst it is difficult to predict the future, many a recent winner has gone on to compete in Graded company before long, so if looking towards a younger, lightly-raced type, ask yourself the question as to whether or not you could see the horse breaking out of handicaps and into Graded races.

Ballyadam is a good example of a horse coming the other way, running well under a big weight, having been contesting Graded contests and often, quality will shine through in this event (hence those rated in the 130s often struggle to land a blow). With

KEY TRENDS

- 19 of the 25 winners this century had run 9 times or less over hurdles
- 13 of the past 16 winners had run at Cheltenham previously (11 of them had recorded a top-4 finish at the very least)
- 13 of the past 18 winners were aged 7 or younger
- 11 of the past 24 winners were French-bred
- 11 of the past 18 winners could be found in the top-8 of the handicap
- 11 of the past 17 winners were rated in the 140s
- 4 of the past 7 winners wore headgear
- 4 of the past 16 winners were trained by Nicky Henderson
- 4 of the past 11 winners had run no more than once that season
- 3 of the past 14 winners were trained by Gordon Elliott (albeit from a lot of runners)
- Respect form over 2m
- Respect a strong-travelling hold-up performer
- Respect first-time cheekpieces (or blinkers)
- Only 1 of the past 22 favourites has won
- Only 1 winner was aged 10
- Only 2 of the past 28 winners were aged 9
- Only 4 of the past 17 winners returned at odds shorter than 12-1

no middle-distance Graded race at Cheltenham over hurdles, horses are often forced to run here – or wait for the Aintree Hurdle – which means that this is usually the best quality (in terms of depth) of the handicap hurdles throughout the week.

COURSE FORM

13 OF THE past 16 winners had run at Cheltenham previously, with 11 of them having recorded a top-four finish at the very least. Last year's winner had run in the Baring Bingham Novices' Hurdle 12 months earlier, where he had finished runner-up to stable-mate Ballyburn, form which was seemingly overlooked by many, by virtue of disappointing runs at Aintree and Punchestown and his subsequent 313-day absence.

Langer Dan had finished second in the 2021 **Martin Pipe Conditional Jockeys' Handicap Hurdle** before winning his brace of Coral Cups, whilst *Son Of Flicka* did the same, filled the runners-up spot in the day four contest prior to winning this race. *William Henry* had finished fourth in the **Coral Cup** 12 months before winning this race and like *Langer Dan*, returned off the exact same mark.

Two fairly recent winners had finished seventh in the **Supreme Novices' Hurdle** the previous March, whilst another couple of not-so-distant winners had run in the **Greatwood Hurdle** earlier in the season. Having form over 2m is also a decent weapon to have, as pace at the business end of the race – rather like in the Baring Bingham – can be significant.

TACTICS

THAT final sentence leads us on nicely to what is required, tactically, to win a Coral Cup. They tend to go a strong gallop here, so having the requisite natural pace to hold a position and travel efficiently is a huge plus. Whilst we have seen horses go well from the front, it isn't overly common and being held-up (off said strong gallop) is often the best approach. Look for a smooth traveller, with a turn of foot, which is where the 2m hurdles form comes into play.

FRENCH-BRED SUCCESS

BETWEEN 2002 and 2017, nine of the 17 winners were French-bred and although we have seen much less of this trend in more recent years, *Jimmy du Seuil* added his name to the list, alongside *Dame de Compagnie* as the latest French-bred victors. Last year's winner was very much out of the mould of winners from earlier in the century; a second-season, French-bred, highly-rated, lightly-raced hurdler and it was during the period when those younger winners were successful, that the French-bred horses shone. Invariably, they will be more forward than the Irish- and British-bred jumpers, so it goes without saying that they are likely more ready to perform at a high level from a younger age.

Interestingly, and more of his overall record shortly, the two winners trained by Willie Mullins were lightly-raced, French-bred hurdlers and *Jimmy du Seuil* led home a French-bred one-two last year, beating Impose Toi by 3 lengths.

MARKET FORCES

LAST year's winner returned at 16-1 and that is kind of indicative of the run of results which we see in the Coral Cup, which is – according to the market, at least – one of the most difficult races of the whole week to predict. Since 2018 alone, we have seen winners priced at 20-1, 28-1, 33-1 and 50-1, and although *Langer Dan* was twice relatively well found in the market, only four of the past 17 winners returned at odds shorter than 12-1. Certainly don't let a big price put you off a horse in this race.

In terms of successful favourites, we have seen just one outright favourite win the race in the past 22 renewals and Be Aware was another disappointing market leader in 2025.

HEADGEAR WORTH NOTING

THE four winners between 2019 and 2022 all wore headgear of some sort and although we have had three years without such a winner, others have run well. In 2023, the second and fifth were both sporting first-time cheekpieces and Impose Toi was doing the same when filling the runners-up spot in 2025. Franciscan Rock – fifth at 50-1 in 2024 – is another, so take note of any horse who has *'p1'* illustrated alongside their name in the race card.

Commander Of Fleet was wearing first-time blinkers when successful in 2022 and his trainer, Gordon Elliott, has a fine record in the Pertemps Final with horses wearing headgear.

OTHER RACES TO NOTE

BOTH *Supasundae* and *Heaven Help Us* had run in the **Boyne Hurdle** at Navan (again, the *'drop in class'* angle coming into play here) shortly before winning the Coral Cup and interestingly, Tiger Roll (twice) and Delta Work ran in the same Grade 2 race before winning the Cross County Chase. Pay close attention to the *'also-rans'* from that contest with the spring festivals in mind.

Son Of Flicka and *Langer Dan* (ahead of his second win) had finished unplaced in the **Lanzarote Hurdle** at Kempton in January, a competitive handicap over a similar distance. *William Henry* also won the Lanzarote, albeit 14 months before landing this prize, and this year's race went the way of Nicky Henderson's Iberico Lord.

And, Willie Mullins' two winners – *Bleu Berry* and *Jimmy du Seuil* – had both finished fifth in the Grade 1 **Champion Novice Hurdle** over 2m4½f at the Punchestown Festival the previous spring, a race which was won in emphatic fashion in 2025 by the Mullins-trained Final Demand.

TRAINERS TO NOTE

THE brace of *Langer Dan* means the **Dan Skelton** has won two of the past three renewals and as was highlighted in last year's edition, his record in handicap hurdles in general is an exceptional one. As well as winning this race twice, Skelton has won two Greatwoods since 2016, two Betfair Exchange Trophies since 2013, the 2023 and 2024 renewals of the Lanzarote Hurdle (no race in 2025) and, of course, three County Hurdles since 2016. His runners in such valuable handicaps warrant utmost respect, despite the fact that he was responsible for last year's beaten favourite, Be Aware.

The record of **Willie Mullins** was highlighted as being a negative in recent editions of the Cheltenham Festival Betting Guide. Despite having won it with Bleu Berry in 2018, his record between 2010 and 2024 (inclusive) stood at 1-50, but he added to his tally last year and having now won the race twice in the past eight years, it is hard to be too critical, for all that he again ran three, including Bunting, who was pulled-up having been prominent in the ante-post market. Interestingly, and as touched on briefly in an earlier subsection, his two winners boasted a very similar profile. Both second-season hurdlers, both French-bred and both were almost forgotten by virtue of quiet campaigns. Jimmy du Seuil hadn't been seen all season and Bleu Berry had run just once, when returning to action at the Dublin Racing Festival. Keep a close eye on any runner with a similar profile.

Remaining in Ireland and **Gordon Elliott** has won the race three times since 2011 but is another who is often well-represented and again saddled five runners last year. Three winners in the past 15 renewals sounds a very positive record on the face of it, but given the number of runners from the stable, it again wouldn't be the strongest of strike rates.

Nicky Henderson is the most successful trainer in the Coral Cup, with four wins on the board since 2010. All four winners from Seven Barrows had won at Cheltenham previously and his record with such horses (course winners) stands at a hugely respectable 4-17, with his two runners last year being previous Cheltenham scorers. 100-1 shot Captain Morgs failed to land a blow but Impose Toi ran a sound race to finish runner-up and was more in-keeping with his earlier winners, profile wise.

HITTING THE CROSSBAR

WITHOUT a runner last year, trainer **Martin Brassil** and owners **Sean & Bernadine Mulryan** were responsible for the beaten favourite in 2024, when Built By Ballymore was heavily-supported but could finish only 14th. However, in the two previous renewals, these connections went extremely close, with subsequent top-class chaser Fastorslow beaten a short-head into second in 2022 and An Epic Song a head second the following year. In a race that they clearly like to target, any runners representing this shrewd operation should be noted. Of course, Fastorslow returned to Cheltenham the following year when just touched off in the Ultima and the owners enjoyed Festival success a couple of years ago when Lark In The Mornin won the 'Fred Winter'. Dancing On My Own provided the owners with Aintree (Red Rum Handicap Chase) success in 2023 and their runners – which are relatively few and far between, in fairness – in feature handicaps deserve plenty of respect.

LIGHT CAMPAIGN IS NO NEGATIVE

BOTH Bleu Berry and William Henry won this race on the back of just one start earlier in the season and last year's winner, of course, landed the prize on his belated seasonal reappearance. Going back a little further and Aux Ptits Soins was having his first start since the previous September and was making his British debut, so don't think that a light campaign is a negative. That is four of the past 11 winners to have run no more than once earlier in the season, and as a result, Bleu Berry, William Henry and Jimmy du Seuil were all somewhat overlooked in the market. Take note of any such runner this year.

ROLL OF HONOUR

Year	Form	Winner	Age	Weight	OR	SP	Trainer	Runners	Last Race (No. of days)
2025		Jimmy du Seuil	6	11-7	146	16/1	W Mullins (IRE)	26	5th Gr.1 Champion Nov. Hurdle (313)
2024	6P90	Langer Dan	8	11-8	141	13/2	D Skelton	21	14th Lanzarote Hurdle (60)
2023	378	Langer Dan	7	11-4	141	9/1	D Skelton	26	8th Gr.2 Relkeel Hurdle (73)
2022	5F1PU83	Commander Of Fleet	8	11-5 (5)	152	50/1	G Elliott (IRE)	23	3rd Gr.2 Boyne Hurdle (22)
2021	211	Heaven Help Us	7	10-2 (7)	138	33/1	P Hennessy (IRE)	26	1st Leopardstown H'cap Hurdle (38)
2020	51	Dame de Compagnie	7	10-12	140	5/1F	N Henderson	25	1st Cheltenham H'cap Hurdle (88)
2019	P	William Henry	9	11-10	151	28/1	N Henderson	25	p.u. Wincanton Hurdle (77)
2018	0	Bleu Berry	7	11-2	143	20/1	W Mullins (IRE)	26	17th Listed Leopardstown Hurdle (40)
2017	8124	Supasundae	7	11-4	148	16/1	J Harrington (IRE)	25	4th Gr.2 Boyne Hurdle (24)
2016	421	Diamond King	8	11-3	149	12/1	G Elliott (IRE)	26	1st Punchestown Hurdle (67)

LEADING TEN-YEAR GUIDES

*Supreme Novices' Hurdle 2 (Supasundae 7th, Heaven Help Us 7th)
Boyne Hurdle 2 (Supasundae 4th, Commander Of Fleet 3rd)
*Coral Cup 2 (William Henry 4th, Langer Dan 1st)

* denotes previous season

GLENFARCLAS CHASE
3m6f 37y (Premier Handicap) – Cross Country Course

OVERVIEW
ONE of the changes ahead of the 2025 Cheltenham Festival was to revert that *'Cross Country Chase'* back to being a handicap, after eight renewals of the race as a conditions event. In truth, the race was becoming more predictable (and some would say a little unfair) as we were starting to see former Grade 1 chasers head down this route towards the end of their careers. The move to re-introduce the handicap format should ensure a more level playing field for all. With this in mind, some of the *Key Trends* will be more geared towards the race in its former format, so it could take another few years for new patterns to form. Regardless of the format of the race, it has been dominated by Irish-trained horses over the years and in particular, trainer Gordon Elliott is one who likes to target the contest in large numbers.

2025 – BACK TO A HANDICAP
ALTHOUGH last year saw the first renewal of the race as a handicap since 2015, it was the class horse in the field who came out on top, with *Stumptown* defying top-weight and a mark of 157 (more of the weights and measures shortly). Theoretically, the decision to switch the contest back to being a handicap should make it a more balanced contest, rather than the one which saw former Grade 1-winning chasers starting to dominate.

OFFICIAL BHA RATINGS AND WEIGHTS
DESPITE the fact that he didn't have that Grade 1 background, last year's winner found himself burdened with top-weight and from a lofty mark of 157. He had earned his rating by climbing the cross country ranks, winning at Punchestown on reappearance and at Cheltenham in December. Whilst that would likely have hindered him in a *'standard handicap chase'* around a parkland course (pulled-up in the Grand National on his very next start), ratings possibly don't matter quite as much in this event. If a horse takes to this unique track, it can be a huge positive and with so many twists and turns, carrying a big weight doesn't seem to be as detrimental as it would be in many other feature handicaps.

In terms of Official BHA Ratings, the past seven winners were all rated 150+, although six of those obviously came during the period when the race was a conditions event. Looking solely at the times when the race has been a handicap, *Stumptown* became the third winner to score off a mark in the 150s.

IRISH DOMINANCE
17 OF THE 20 winners were trained in Ireland and it doesn't seem to matter as to whether it is/was a handicap or a conditions event in this regard, the Irish are very much the dominant force in this division. Following the (later) disqualification of *Any Currency* some 10 years ago, Philip Hobbs (now trains alongside former assistant, Johnson White) is the only British trainer to have, officially, won this race, striking twice with *Balthazar King*. *Easysland* won for France in 2020, whilst every other winner was trained in Ireland. Many of the leading British trainers don't take this race, or discipline as a whole, seriously, whereas many of their Irish counterparts are happy to target a good horse at it. Focus on the Irish-trained runners.

ELLIOTT'S EXCELLENCE

ONE trainer in particular who likes to target this race is **Gordon Elliott**, successful five times in the past eight renewals, whilst three-time winner *Tiger Roll* was also trained out of Cullentra House when winning his third Glenfarclas Chase for Denise Foster. Elliott was, of course, serving his infamous suspension at the time. Elliott was out of luck with his six, yes six, runners last year and it has to be pointed out that all six winners to come out of his stable came during the time when the race was a conditions event. However, given his record in top staying handicap chases, I suspect that he will continue to target the race now it is a handicap (again) and this was evidenced last year. We might not see a *Delta Work* standard of horse represent the yard but expect Elliott to be well-represented and give due respect to runners from that stable.

OWNERS TO NOTE

AS TOUCHED upon briefly in the previous subsection, **Gigginstown House Stud** were responsible for five wins in the space of six years (between 2008 and 2013) thanks to the trio of wins from *Tiger Roll* and the brace from *Delta Work*. The leading owners had earlier won the race with *Rivage d'Or* in 2015, so they have actually been responsible for six of the past 10 winners of the race (no race in 2024, of course). Prior to last year's changes, Michael O'Leary seemed unimpressed but still allowed Coko Beach to take his chance, so I suspect that they will continue to support the race.

Fellow leading owner **JP McManus** also has a fine record in the race and has won it on seven occasions. Successful in four of the first five renewals, he has more recently won it with *Josies Orders* (after the disqualification of *Any Currency*), *Cause Of Causes* and *Easysland*. Surprisingly without a runner last year, McManus' representatives also warrant careful consideration.

COURSE FORM

LAST year's winner had won the corresponding race at the December meeting and with that being his first start on this course, made him the seventh winner to have run just once on this unique course previously. He did, of course, have experience of the Banks Course at Punchestown, too, but the stat relating to just the one run is significant, as often a set of connections will allow their horse just that one visit to get a sight of the obstacles and see if they take to the track.

The corresponding races at both the November and December meetings are significant form guides (14 of the 20 winners had run in at least one)

KEY TRENDS

- 17 of the 20 winners were trained in Ireland
- 14 of the 20 winners had run in the Cross Country race at either the November or December meetings
- 7 of the 20 winners were owned by JP McManus
- 6 of the past 10 winners were owned by Gigginstown House Stud
- 5 of the past 7 winners were ridden by Keith Donoghue
- Gordon Elliott boasts a fantastic record in the race
- 17 of the 20 winners returned at 7-1 or shorter
- 10 of the past 15 winners finished unplaced last time out
- 9 of the 20 winners ran in the National Hunt Chase as a novice
- 9 of the past 14 winners were aged 8 or 9
- 9 of the past 12 winners wore a tongue-tie
- 7 of the past 9 winners wore headgear
- 7 of the 20 winners had run just once at this unique track
- The past 7 winners were rated 150+
- 6 of the past 13 winners had a break of 89+ days
- Enda Bolger has trained the winner 5 times
- Only 1 of the 20 winners was younger than 8
- Only 2 of the 20 winners had no Cross Country chase experience
- Only 3 of the past 18 winners had won more than once earlier in the season
- Only 4 of the past 15 winners won last time out
- Only 4 of the 20 winners hadn't run on this track
- Paul Nicholls-trained runners are 0-13
- Willie Mullins-trained runners are 0-17

and as such, both feature prominently in the *Leading Ten-Year Guides* element of the *Roll Of Honour*. Final Orders won the December race before finishing fifth to Favori de Champdou on trials day, in a race which was rescheduled from November. J'Arrive de L'Est finished runner-up in both races.

There have only ever been two winners of this race to arrive at Cheltenham with zero cross-country experience, be it here at Cheltenham or on the aforementioned track at Punchestown, with *Easysland* gaining his experience on home soil in France. Respect form from Punchestown, too, with last year's winner boasting a record of U11 on that particular course before switching his attention to Cheltenham.

THE DONOGHUE EFFECT

JOCKEY **Keith Donoghue** has now won five of the past seven renewals and his ability to ride horses around this track is an incredible asset. Having partnered *Tiger Roll* to all three victories, he was aboard *Delta Work* when he won his second Glenfarclas Chase and was again sublime aboard last year's winner. A master of his trade when it comes to this discipline, his chosen mount should be duly noted.

This season, Donoghue has excelled aboard *Stumptown* in the Velka Pardubicka, before riding Final Orders to win at this track in December.

MARKET FORCES

NO FEWER than 17 of the 20 winners returned at 7-1 or shorter and this included the past eight winners, with seven of those returning at 9-2 or shorter. The past three favourites have obliged and during the period whilst the race was a conditions event, the race was seemingly becoming much easier to work out, with those classier horses towards the head of the betting very much dominating. The race being reverted to a handicap could/should mean it becomes more competitive moving forward and as a result, it might not necessarily be as easy to find the winner, although four of the first five home last year were priced between 5/2F and 15/2.

MULTIPLE WINNERS

WE HAVE seen four multiple winners during the first 19 runnings of this race, with *Garde Champetre* and *Balthazar King* the first pair to double up. *Delta Work* is the other two-time winner, whilst stable-mate and dual Grand National winner *Tiger Roll* is the only horse to have won the race on three occasions. It is a specialist discipline and as a result, there is a smaller pool of horses to contest this race, which in turn means that there is a greater probability of a repeat victor. *Stumptown* is likely to be back in a bid to defend his crown

AGE

IN THE early days of the race, we saw three 12-year-olds successful during the first five renewals. *Any Currency* was 13 when passing the post in front (although was later disqualified and the race awarded to the eight-year-old, *Josies Orders*) but *'officially'* the only winner over the age of 10 during the past 14 renewals was *Tiger Roll* when winning the race for a third time. Nine of those past 14 winners were aged either eight (5) or nine (4) and we are certainly seeing *'younger'* horses winning it. Not too young, however, with *Easysland* the sole winner under the age of eight, the 2020 scorer winning at the tender age of six.

HEADGEAR AND TONGUE-TIE

AS HIGHLIGHTED last year, plenty of previous winners of this race had sported headgear of some sort and *Stumptown* continued the trend, with first-time cheekpieces applied by Gavin Cromwell. Headgear on staying handicappers is nothing new, so this is/was one particular trend that I expect to continue. He was without a tongue-tie, but nine of the previous 11 winners wore one of those breathing aids, so again, certainly don't see it as a negative if one is applied.

OTHER TRAINERS TO NOTE

WITH four wins during the first five renewals and another when *Josies Orders* was awarded the race 10 years ago, **Enda Bolger** was the man to follow in this sphere for many years and perhaps, with the race reverting to being a handicap, it will see him get involved once again, as he didn't really have the ammunition to compete with those former Grade 1 horses when the race was a conditions event. The County Limerick trainer has always been well-supported by leading owner JP McManus, indeed all five of his winners carried the famous green and gold hoops.

Both without a runner (again) last year, **Paul Nicholls** and **Willie Mullins** each has a disappointing record in this race, standing at 0-13 and 0-17, respectively.

OTHER KEY RACES

AHEAD of last year, I removed a couple of races from the *Leading Ten-Year Guides*, feeling they were less relevant now the race is a handicap once again. One which has featured heavily over the years – and with that also switching to a novices' handicap last year, could still have a big impact – is the **National Hunt Chase**, with nine of the 20 winners having run in that race during their novice season. Last year's race was won by subsequent Irish Grand National winner, Haiti Couleurs, but pay attention if any of the beaten horses switch to the cross country scene at some stage.

CURRENT FORM

STUMPTOWN became just the fourth winner of this race to have won on their most recent start. Not just that, 10 of the past 15 winners finished unplaced, so don't be too disheartened by a seemingly *'poor'* run last time out, often that final race will have been used as a stepping stone to this race rather than anything else. *Stumptown* also became just the third winner to have won more than one race earlier in the campaign, so his profile was slightly out of kilter in terms of a more standard winner.

Also, six of the past 13 winners enjoyed a short break of 89 days or more, so being freshened up (slightly) ahead of the Festival certainly wouldn't appear to be a negative.

Keith Donoghue has made this race his own in recent years

ROLL OF HONOUR

Year	Form	Winner	Age	Weight	OR	SP	Trainer	Runners	Last Race (No. of days)
2025	11	Stumptown	8	11-10	157	5/2F	G Cromwell (IRE)	16	1st Cheltenham X-C Chase (89)
2024	RACE ABANDONED								
2023	136	Delta Work	10	11-7	159	11/10F	G Elliott (IRE)	16	6th Gr.2 Boyne Hurdle (31)
2022	466	Delta Work	9	11-4	160	5/2F	G Elliott (IRE)	16	6th Gr.1 Irish Gold Cup (39)
2021	P6	Tiger Roll	11	11-4	166	9/2	D Foster (IRE)	13	6th Gr.2 Boyne Hurdle (24)
2020	1111	Easysland	6	11-4	152	3/1	D Cottin (FR)	14	1st Pau (Listed) X-C Chase (38)
2019	41	Tiger Roll	9	11-4	159	5/4F	G Elliott (IRE)	15	1st Gr.2 Boyne Hurdle (24)
2018	2P5	Tiger Roll	8	11-4	150	7/1	G Elliott (IRE)	16	5th Glenfarclas H'cap XC Chase (90)
2017	5P05	Cause of Causes	9	11-4	–	4/1	G Elliott (IRE)	16	5th Glenfarclas H'cap XC Chase (46)
2016	3428	Any Currency *	13	11-4	–	11/1	M Keighley	17	8th Glenfarclas Cond. XC Chase (96)

* Any Currency passed the post first but was disqualified on 25 August 2016 following a positive post-race test for a prohibited substance. Josies Orders, originally the runner-up, was subsequently promoted to first.

LEADING TEN-YEAR GUIDES

Boyne Hurdle 3 (*Tiger Roll* 1st & 6th, *Delta Work* 6th)
Cheltenham Cross Country Handicap (Nov. meeting) 4 (*Any Currency* 2nd (*Josies Orders* 1st), Cause of Causes 5th**, *Tiger Roll* 4th & P.U)
Cheltenham Cross Country Handicap (Dec. meeting) 3 (*Any Currency* 8th (*Josies Orders* 1st), *Tiger Roll* 6th, *Easysland* 1st)
***Glenfarclas Cross County Chase** 4 (*Any Currency* 2nd, *Tiger Roll* 1st & 2nd, *Delta Work* 1st)

* denotes previous season
** rescheduled and run on trials day in January

BetMGM QUEEN MOTHER CHAMPION CHASE
1m7f 199y (Grade 1) – Old Course

OVERVIEW
THE feature contest on day two and the highlight of the season in this division, the Queen Mother Champion Chase requires a slick jumper to win it, with mistakes at this level – over this (minimum) trip – extremely costly (see Jonbon last year). Successful between 1983 and 1985, *Badsworth Boy* is the only three-time winner of the race, although we have seen a further eight horses since win it on two occasions. Nicky Henderson and Paul Nicholls have each won the race six times, whilst Henry de Bromhead won it for the fourth time in 2024. Previous Festival form is a huge positive here, with last year's winner successful in the Supreme Novices' Hurdle in 2023.

UP AND DOWN FOR MULLINS
ALTHOUGH *Energumene* provided him with back-to-back wins in the race in 2022 and 2023, the record of **Willie Mullins** in the Queen Mother isn't an overly strong one at this stage. Prior to those successive wins, he suffered some noticeable reversals, with Un de Sceaux, Douvan, Chacun Pour Soi and El Fabiolo all beaten, when sent off at odds-on, since 2016 alone. His dual winner was pulled-up last year, so his record in the race can be described as *'mixed'* at best at this stage.

Majborough and Il Etait Temps head Mullins' entries and provide the trainer with a strong hand.

IRISH TAKEOVER
ALTHOUGH Mullins has chipped in with the brace of wins courtesy of *Energumene*, Irish-trained horses have been dominant of late and have now won the past five renewals. **Henry de Bromhead**, who has now won the race on four occasions in total, is also responsible for two of those past five winners, whilst Barry Connell struck last year, with his stable star and former Supreme winner, *Marine Nationale*. The record of de Bromhead is particularly noticeable and whilst *Sizing Europe* was his first winner back in 2011, he has now won three of the past nine renewals, with *Special Tiara* successful in 2017. He is a trainer who excels with 2m chasers, in general.

Between 2012 and 2020 (inclusive), *Special Tiara* was the sole Irish-trained winner of the race during that nine-year period. However, the Irish have taken over of late.

MULTIPLE WINNERS
AS TOUCHED upon in the *Overview*, there have been eight two-time winners of this race since 1987, with *Pearlyman, Barnbrook Again* and *Viking Flagship* all completing the double up to the mid-90s. Since the turn of the century, *Moscow Flyer, Master Minded, Sprinter Sacre, Altior* and *Energumene* have all won the race twice and *Marine Nationale* will bid to add his name to this illustrious list. Looking back even further, a total of 14 horses have won the race more than once since 1960.

Back-to-back winners are much more common than horses attempting to regain their crown, with the statistics similar to that of the Champion Hurdle. Only three previous winners have managed to do this, which is an obvious negative to the chance of 2024 winner *Captain Guinness*.

SECOND-SEASON CHASERS

IF LOOKING for a new/first-time winner of the race, the starting point should be with last season's novices, as since 2003, 14 of the past 23 winners were indeed second-season chasers. Such horses clearly have the greater scope for improvement and it seems the leap into open company is achievable in this division, with *Marine Nationale* adding his name to the tally in 2025.

Unfortunately, last year's winner was forced to miss the **Arkle Trophy** in 2024 through injury. However, winners of that Grade 1 fare well in this race the following year, with seven of the past 14 winners (from the previous season) to have run in the Champion Chase proving successful. Gaelic Warrior didn't run in the race last year, having won the Arkle in 2024, whilst last year's Arkle winner Jango Baie has been campaigned over longer trips this season.

Between 2012 and 2014, three successive winners had contested Aintree's **Maghull Novices' Chase** the previous April and that Grade 1 was won in 2025 by the sadly ill-fated Kalif du Berlais.

LIGHT CAMPAIGN IS A POSITIVE

NOT since 2014, when *Sire de Grugy* was successful, has the winner of the Champion Chase run more than three times earlier in the season and he is in fact the only such winner in the past 21 renewals. Between 2020 and 2023, the four winners had all run just twice earlier in the season, whilst *Captain Guinness* and *Marine Nationale* had each run three times, following a similar path for the most part. Last year's winner had to be built up in terms of overall chasing experience, having had his novice campaign curtailed and restricted to just two runs.

Since 1999, only eight horses have run in the Champion Chase on the back of just one chase run and remarkably, four of them have proven successful, so arriving at Cheltenham still seemingly 'fresh' can be a positive.

A DEFEAT IS COMMON THESE DAYS

SINCE 2003, there have only been six winners of this race who were unbeaten earlier in the season. Given that we do tend to see dominant performers in this division, it is a little surprising, although the reversal of several high-profile performers in recent years (more of that shortly) has clearly contributed to this. During the past 16 years, *Sprinter Sacre* and *Altior* (both twice) are the only pair to do this, so a defeat earlier in the campaign certainly shouldn't be off-putting. Indeed, last year's winner became the second horse in six years to win the Champion Chase having failed to win earlier in the season.

KEY TRENDS

- ⭐ 7 of the past 14 Arkle winners (from the previous season) to have run have won
- ⭐ 5 of the past 14 winners were trained by Nicky Henderson
- ⭐ 4 of the past 15 winners were trained by Henry de Bromhead
- ⭐ 15 of the past 25 winners had won at the Festival previously
- ✓ 31 of the past 39 winners were aged 7-9
- ✓ 19 of the past 21 winners had run 2-3 times earlier in the season
- ✓ 14 of the past 23 winners won last time out
- ✓ 14 of the past 23 winners were second-season chasers
- ✓ 14 horses have won this race more than once since 1960
- ✓ 12 of the past 26 winners were trained by Nicky Henderson or Paul Nicholls
- ✓ 11 of the past 14 winners returned at 6-1 or shorter
- ✓ 9 of the past 17 winners had run no more than twice earlier in the season
- ✓ 8 of the past 14 winners contested the Clarence House Chase (6 finished 1st or 2nd)
- ✓ 6 of the past 12 winners contested the Shloer Chase
- ✓ The past 5 winners were trained in Ireland
- ✓ Horses who are 1-1 over fences during the current season are 4-8 since 1999
- ✓ 3 of the past 10 winners hadn't run since Christmas (or even earlier)
- ✓ Respect the winner of the Tingle Creek Chase
- ✗ Only 1 of the past 21 winners had run more than 3 times that season
- ✗ Only 1 of the past 14 winners returned at double-figure odds
- ✗ Only 1 mare has ever won the race
- ✗ Only 3 of the past 27 winners hadn't won a race earlier in the season
- ✗ Only 3 of the past 51 winners were aged 6 or younger
- ✗ Only 3 previous winners regained their crown
- ✗ Only 5 of the past 39 winners were aged 10 or older
- ✗ 7 odds-on favourites have been beaten in the past 10 years
- ✗ Fall / UR from earlier in the season is a negative
- ✗ The record of Dublin Chase winners is 0-6 (although the past 2 winners were beaten in that race)

Altior (ahead of his second win in 2019) is the only winner in the past nine to have won more than one race earlier that same season, so peaking at the right time and coming to the boil seems more important these days, than putting a string of wins together throughout the season.

ARRIVING IN FORM

BETWEEN 2002 and 2019, no fewer than 14 of the 18 winners arrived at Cheltenham on the back of a win, but this is now another trend which has come to a rather abrupt halt. The past six winners were all beaten on their most recent start and the first two of those, *Politlogue* and *Put The Kettle On*, were beaten during December and were subsequently freshened up ahead of the spring. The past five winners finished either second or third on their most recent outing.

COMPLETED STARTS

YOU have to go back to *Master Minded* in 2008 to find the last winner of the Queen Mother Champion Chase who had either fallen or unseated their rider earlier that season. *Moscow Flyer* (first win in 2003), *Azertyuiop* and *Voy Por Ustedes* did the same (unseated) in the early part of the century, so actually no winner this century has fallen. A serious mistake can be costly enough at this level in a 2m chase, so look for a sound jumper and one without letters next to their name in their form figures.

AGE

19 OF THE past 25 winners were aged between seven and nine, which is the ideal age bracket. Going back even further, this figure increases to 31 of the past 39 winners, further emphasising the dominance of such horses.

The past eight winners fell into that bracket, although we saw back-to-back 10-year-old winners before that, in the shape of *Sprinter Sacre* and *Special Tiara*. However, the only other *'older'* (double-digit aged) winner this century was *Moscow Flyer*, when he regained his crown as an 11-year-old in 2005.

At the other end of the scale, *Master Minded* (twice) and *Voy Por Ustedes* are the only winners under the age of seven during the past 51 renewals. It should be remembered that *Master Minded* won this race as a five-year-old, in what I still believe to be the single best performance – given his age – at the Festival during my lifetime. It really was an incredible display and one which we are unlikely to ever see repeated.

MEASURED AND ASSURED

I TOUCHED briefly in the Overview what is required to win a Champion Chase and having touched upon the brilliance of *Master Minded* in the previous subsection, I had to give another mention to the performance of *Sprinter Sacre* when winning the race for the first time in 2013. Seven at the time, it was a sublime performance of class, power and precision and was all that you could wish to see from a top-class 2m chaser. He was right at the top of his game at that stage, indeed putting in another scintillating performance in the Melling Chase the following month. From a purists point of view, the 2013 winner was just about perfection, I merely referenced *Master Minded* given his ridiculously young age.

CHELTENHAM FESTIVAL FORM

BACK to matters in hand and last year's winner may have missed the Arkle the year before, but he was a Festival winner in 2023 when landing the Supreme Novices' Hurdle, making him the 15th winner in the past 25 to have already recorded a win at this fixture. Clearly, the dual winners of the race help that recent statistic, but Festival form – and winning form at that – is clearly hugely significant here and should always be viewed upon in a positive manner.

MARKET FORCES

IT HAS been well documented in recent years – and will be again in the build-up to this year's meeting – that the Champion Chase has become somewhat of a graveyard for short-priced favourites in recent years. In the past decade alone, we have seen seven odds-on shots turned over, including *El Fabiolo* in 2024 and *Jonbon* in 2025. For whatever reason (jumping issues can be one), it seems to be the one big race during the week in which leading contenders regularly appear to *'fluff their lines'*. The other three favourites during this period have won, but nevertheless, it is hugely noticeable.

Despite this, we still don't see many bigger priced winner of this race, with *Special Tiara* the only winner to return at double figures during the past 14 years. The majority of recent winners could have been found just behind the market leader(s), with 11 of those past 14 winners returning at 6-1 or shorter.

BRITISH TRAINERS TO NOTE

THE leading Irish trainers have been covered in earlier subsections, whilst the leading British trainers in the Champion Chase are **Paul Nicholls** and Nicky Henderson, who have each won the race six times and between them, they have won 12 of the past 26 renewals. Nicholls' wins span back to *Call Equiname* in 1999, before *Azertyuiop* and *Master Minded* (twice) struck for the Ditcheat operation. More recently, *Dodging Bullets* and *Politologue* have added to his tally, and he has been light on representation in the past five years.

Nicky Henderson first won the Champion Chase in 1992 with *Remittance Man*, then won his next five in the space of 10 years, thanks to *Finian's Rainbow*, *Sprinter Sacre* (twice) and *Altior* (twice). His only two runners since his last win in the race were Shishkin (pulled-up when sent off at odds-on in 2022) and last year's runner-up Jonbon (also odds-on favourite).

CLARENCE HOUSE OFTEN THE KEY FORM

NO FEWER than eight of the past 14 winners had contested Ascot's **Clarence House Chase** (occasionally, rescheduled to Cheltenham on trials day) on their most recent start, with the timing seemingly ideal between mid-January and the Cheltenham Festival. Six of the eight finished either first or second, with *Energumene* twice beaten in it before winning the Queen Mother. Last year's Clarence House was won by Jonbon, who finished a well-beaten second here, and he stayed on strongly to defend his crown in January.

OTHER KEY RACES

STAGED at Cheltenham in November, the **Shloer Chase** is often the first opportunity for horses in this division to run in Britain and six of the past 12 winners of the Champion Chase ran in the early-season Grade 2. Surprisingly, only two of the half-dozen were successful and this season's race went the way of L'Eau du Sud.

The first Grade 1 in the division in England is the **Tingle Creek Chase** at Sandown in early-December, which five of the past 13 Champion Chase winners had contested. Four of those were successful, whilst a little further back, *Moscow Flyer* twice headed over to Sandown, unseating Barry Geraghty on the first occasion, before winning a memorable race during the 2004/2005 season. This season's Tingle Creek was won by Il Etait Temps.

Over in Ireland, *Energumene* won the **Hilly Way Chase** at Cork on reappearance in each of his Champion Chase-winning seasons. This season's race was won by Found A Fifty.

Over the Festive period, Leopardstown's **Paddy's Rewards Club Chase** is the obvious target for a top-class two-miler and *Put The Kettle On*, *Captain Guinness* and *Marine Nationale* were all actually beaten in it mid-season. Solness won the race for a second time in December, although *Marine Nationale* was an '*unlucky*' loser, having made a serious error early in the race.

The past two winners were also beaten at the same track's Dublin Racing Festival on their final outing, in the **Dublin Chase**. Solness had won that contest before finishing only fourth in this race and in contrast, winners of the Dublin Chase have a very poor record here, which now stands at 0-6. The Tied Cottage was formerly the ideal race for Irish horses en route to the Champion Chase, but that contest was replaced by the Dublin Chase once the DRF was introduced and prior to last year, we saw Min (twice), Chacun Pour Soi (twice) and El Fabiolo all beaten having won that February contest. Majborough won this year's race in emphatic fashion.

Paul Nicholls

DAY TWO RACE FIVE

Il Etait Temps wins the Tingle Creek

ROLL OF HONOUR

Year	Form	Winner	Age	Weight	OR	SP	Trainer	Runners	Last Race (No. of days)
2025	232	Marine Nationale	8	11-10	159	5/1	B Connell (IRE)	8	2nd Gr.1 Dublin Chase (38)
2024	1P3	Captain Guinness	9	11-10	162	17/2	H de Bromhead (IRE)	6	3rd Gr.1 Dublin Chase (39)
2023	13	Energumene	9	11-10	175	6/5F	W Mullins (IRE)	7	3rd Gr.1 Clarence House Chase (46)
2022	12	Energumene	8	11-10	175	5/2	W Mullins (IRE)	7	2nd Gr.1 Clarence House Chase (53)
2021	13	Put The Kettle On	7	11-3	156	17/2	H de Bromhead (IRE)	9	3rd Gr.1 Paddy's Rewards Chase (80)
2020	25	Politologue	9	11-10	165	6/1	P Nicholls	5	5th Gr.1 Tingle Creek Chase (95)
2019	111	Altior	9	11-10	175	4/11F	N Henderson	9	1st Gr.1 Clarence House Chase (53)
2018	1	Altior	8	11-10	170	Evs F	N Henderson	9	1st Gr.2 Game Spirit Chase (33)
2017	315	Special Tiara	10	11-10	159	11/1	H de Bromhead (IRE)	10	5th Gr.1 Clarence House Chase (46)
2016	11	Sprinter Sacre	10	11-10	170	5/1	N Henderson	10	1st Gr.2 Desert Orchid Chase (80)

LEADING TEN-YEAR GUIDES

Clarence House Chase 4 (*Special Tiara* 5th, *Altior* 1st, *Energumene* 2nd & 3rd)
Tingle Creek Chase 2 (*Altior* 1st, *Politologue* 5th)
***Arkle Chase 2** (*Altior* 1st, *Put The Kettle On* 1st)
***Champion Chase 6** (*Sprinter Sacre* p.u., *Special Tiara* 3rd, *Altior* 1st, *Politologue* 2nd, *Energumene* 1st, *Captain Guinness* 2nd)
Desert Orchid Chase 2 (*Special Tiara* 1st, *Altior* 1st)
Shloer Chase 4 (*Sprinter Sacre* 1st, *Special Tiara* 3rd, *Politologue* 2nd, *Put The Kettle On* 1st)
Hilly Way Chase 2 (*Energumene* 1st & 1st)
Paddy's Rewards Club Chase 3 (*Put The Kettle On* 3rd, *Captain Guinness* p.u., *Marine Nationale* 3rd)
Dublin Chase 2 (*Captain Guinness* 3rd, *Marine Nationale* 2nd)

* denotes previous season

Leading Contenders

MAJBOROUGH   Trainer: Willie Mullins
Beaten less than a length after serious mistakes in last year's Arkle, he was far from fluent in the Hilly Way Chase, nor at Leopardstown over Christmas, but bounced back to form in first-time cheekpieces in the Dublin Chase, making all to beat Marine Nationale by 19 lengths. Jumping much better ridden positively, expect similar tactics to be deployed at Cheltenham and he did, of course, win the Triumph Hurdle in 2024, so his Festival form is strong. If his jumping stands the test, he looks sure to run another huge race.

MARINE NATIONALE   Trainer: Barry Connell
Last year's winner, he also won the 2023 Supreme Novices' Hurdle, so is 2-2 at the Festival. Became unbalanced by jinking at an early fence at Leopardstown over Christmas, where he did remarkably well to finish as close as he did (still finished 2¾l in front of Majborough) before seemingly missing the start a fraction in the Dublin Chase. He could never erode the deficit from off the pace and lost ante-post favouritism for this as a result. Better ground would enhance his claims and he clearly loves Cheltenham. Remains a big player.

IL ETAIT TEMPS   Trainer: Willie Mullins
Was developing into a top-class two-miler, with victories in the Celebration Chase and Tingle Creek at Sandown coming either side of his reappearance win over 2m5f in the Clonmel Oil Chase. Never really travelled and was beaten when falling in the Clarence House, so needs to bounce back and his Cheltenham record isn't inspiring, having been beaten in the Triumph (5th), Supreme Novices' (5th) and Arkle (3rd). Clearly very talented but arrives at Cheltenham on the back of a disappointing run and with course form to prove.

L'EAU DU SUD   Trainer: Dan Skelton
Fourth in last year's Arkle, he returned with an impressive victory in the Shloer Chase (beat Jonbon by 15l) before being beaten a long way by Il Etait Temps in the Tingle Creek. His form seemed to tail off last spring, so it is likely that a lighter campaign has been a deliberate ploy and it isn't hard to envisage him travelling strongly around a track that suits. Runner-up in the 2024 County Hurdle, he is 2-3 over fences at Cheltenham and has a good record when fresh.

QUILIXIOS   Trainer: Henry de Bromhead
Not seen since falling at the final fence last year, he was still in contention at the time and is another previous winner of the Triumph, his success coming back in 2021. Whilst it is a big ask after such a lay-off, it wouldn't be a huge shock to see him run well, given his record at the track and also on the back of a break. Despite seemingly versatile, his better form has come on nicer ground, as it was when he gave Marine Nationale 4lb and a beating at Naas in November 2024. Not to be forgotten.

JONBON   Trainer: Nicky Henderson
Runner-up at three Festivals, including when beaten 18 lengths in this race last year. A serious error put paid to his chance that day and although he has twice won the Shloer, the track at Cheltenham doesn't seem to bring out the best in him. Twice successful over 2m4f at Aintree, the Ryanair seems a likely option, especially with JP McManus responsible for Majborough at the top of this market. A gutsy winner of the Clarence House when last seen, he is now 10 and probably past his best, certainly over the minimum trip.

DAY TWO RACE SIX

DEBENHAMS JOHNNY HENDERSON GRAND ANNUAL HANDICAP CHASE
1m7f199y (Premier Handicap) – Old Course

OVERVIEW
WE HAVE now had five runnings of the Grand Annual on day two, with it previously having been staged as the very last race on the final day of the fixture. As a result of the change in running order, the race was also forced to change tracks – from the New Course to the Old Course – and the distance reduced, too. Naturally, the race is a sharper test now, on the tighter track over the bare minimum trip, so a speedy two-miler is required to succeed. This is a race in which novices and second-season chasers tend to do well and last year's winner was winning at the Cheltenham Festival for a second time in three years.

NOVICES
EIGHT of the past 17 winners were novices, including *Jazzy Matty*, although he had gained plenty of experience through the summer, running eight times in all during the current campaign, with six of those runs coming over fences. *Unexpected Party*, successful in 2024, was also an experienced novice, with Dan Skelton's grey failing to record a win during the previous campaign, therefore successful in this race as a second-season novice on the back of 11 chase starts. Plenty of novices were successful earlier this century, whilst *Chosen Mate* – successful on the back of just three chase starts in 2020 – would no longer be eligible to run. One of the rule changes ahead of last year's Festival was that novices would need to have run a minimum of four times in order to qualify to run in open (non-novice) handicaps at the fixture. That ruling was later extended to include all horses, not just novices.

LIGHTLY-RACED CHASERS
WITH 13 of the past 17 winners being in their first couple of seasons over fences, it is not just novices who do well in the Grand Annual but lightly-raced chasers in general, with second-season chasers also providing plenty of recent winners. Nine of those winners had run nine times or less over fences, so focusing on those with the greater scope to improve is a good starting point.

Only two of the past 17 winners had run more than 13 times over fences previously, again emphasising how difficult it can be for the more *'exposed'* runners to compete in these Festival handicaps.

REPEAT OFFENDERS
IF LOOKING for another angle – away from those novices and likely improvers – looking towards horses who have run well in this race previously is another good option. Eight of the past 20 winners had run in the **Johnny Henderson Grand Annual Handicap Chase** before, many the previous year. In fact, three of the past 19 winners were sent off favourite 12 months earlier, with the record of such horses standing at 3-10 during that period. Last year's beaten favourite was *Unexpected Party*, successful in 2024, of course, and last year found only one too good.

Another couple of good examples of form in this race previously would be *Croco Bay* and *Oiseau du Nuit*. The former had finished third and fifth in previous editions of the race before scoring at 66-1, whilst the latter – also successful at big odds (scored at 40-1 in 2011) – had been sent off as short as 8-1 in 2010. If a horse was relatively *'well-fancied'* one year and returns somewhat overlooked the following year, take note.

CURRENT FORM
UNLIKE with most races at the Festival, *Current Form* seems less significant when it comes to the Grand Annual. As you can see from the previous subsection, horses are often overlooked when coming back for another crack at the race and often this has been a long-term aim, with races earlier in the campaign somewhat of a *'means to an end'*, the end goal being that the horse should peak in March. Eight of the past 12 winners either finished unplaced or failed to complete on their most recent start, whilst seven of those had failed to record a win of any sort, earlier in the season. Recording a victory in handicap company seems to be detrimental to the chances of winning this contest, whilst only two of the past 22 winners won last time out, both of those being novices who landed a beginners' chase.

Generally speaking, if looking towards horses who have been in winning form throughout the campaign, they should really only have been doing so in novice company. Last year's winner had won twice, but was successful in a beginners chase at Wexford and a conditions event in early October.

COURSE FORM
JAZZY MATTY had, of course, won the *'Fred Winter'* as a juvenile – just two years earlier – at the Cheltenham Festival and gained some valuable chase experience at the track when runner-up at the October meeting. Clearly, his connections had a plan to return to the Festival as he was given a lengthy break, only returning with a prep-run over hurdles at Thurles in January. His head second at the October meeting came in a novices' chase, whilst the following handicaps are worth noting from earlier in the season:

Three of the past eight winners had contested the **Paddy Power Gold Cup** in November, with *Le Prezien*, *Sky Pirate* and *Unexpected Party* all finishing between third and fifth in the middle-distance contest. This season's race was won by the mare *Panic Attack*.

The 2m handicap staged at the same fixture – run this year as the **Hine Solicitors Talking Sense Handicap Chase** – is also worth noting and it was won this season by *Triple Trade*.

And, from the October meeting, the **squareintheair.com Handicap Chase** is another race to be staged over the same course-and-distance as the Grand Annual and has thrown up a couple of recent winners. This season's race was won by Dan Skelton's *Calico*.

As with all of the handicaps throughout the week, pay attention to course form.

WEIGHTS AND OFFICIAL BHA RATINGS
EIGHT of the past 12 winners carried 11-0 or more, with *Jazzy Matty* and *Unexpected Party* breaking this trend. In fact, only one of the past four winners has matched up against this profile, so it could be an evolving trend. Seven of those eight winners carried between 11-0 and 11-6, which was until recently at least, the area of the weights to pay most attention to.

KEY TRENDS
- 13 of the past 17 winners were novices or second-season chasers
- 12 of the past 14 winners were rated between 135-147 (10 of them rated between 138-147)
- JP McManus has won 4 of the past 21 renewals (also responsible for 9 runners-up since 2003)
- 4 of the past 9 winners had run over hurdles earlier in the season
- Last year's favourite is 3-10 during the past 19 years
- 13 of the past 20 winners were aged between 6-8
- 9 of the past 17 winners had run 9 times or less over fences previously
- 9 of the past 12 winners carried 11-0 or more
- 8 of the past 20 winners had run in this race previously
- 8 of the past 12 winners enjoyed a break of 50+ days
- 8 of the past 12 winners were unplaced or failed to complete last time out (7 of them hadn't won a race that season)
- 4 of the past 22 winners were trained by Paul Nicholls
- 4 of the past 9 winners had run during the summer
- Respect course form
- Only 2 of the past 17 winners were older than 9
- Only 2 of the past 17 winners had run in more than 13 chases
- Only 2 of the past 21 winners were favourite
- Only 2 of the past 22 winners won last time out
- Winning a handicap earlier in the season is generally a negative
- Willie Mullins-trained runners are 0-9 this century

In terms of BHA Ratings, 12 of the past 14 winners were rated between 135 and 147, with 10 of those hailing from the slightly narrower bracket of 138-147. Only two horses have proven to be successful from marks in the 150s in recent years, whilst since 2011, mid 130s has been a minimum requirement. *Oh Crick* (130) and *Pigeon Island* (129) were back-to-back, lower-rated winners in 2009 and 2010, but such horses don't always get in nowadays (Primoz scraped in off 130 in 2025).

	Top Weight OR	Bottom OR	Winner OR
2025	156	130	135
2024	156	132	138
2023	155	139	141
2022	156	136	136
2021	158	136	152
2020	155	140	147
2019	153	134	139
2018	154	139	150
2017	154	135	147
2016	152	137	140

HURDLES FORM
FOUR of the past nine winners have now been in action over hurdles earlier in the season, with *Jazzy Matty* – a hurdles winner at this meeting – enjoying a prep run at Thurles in a handicap hurdle. Two fairly recent winners had contested the **Galway Hurdle** the previous summer before switching to fences, whilst *Global Citizen* had raced exclusively over hurdles throughout the season, before reverting to fences in this very race. It was common in the Grand National for many a year, to protect a chase mark by running over hurdles and it is certainly becoming increasingly noticeable among recent winners of the Grand Annual. If this really is a long-term plan, often a trainer will look to use hurdles at some stage.

FRESHENED UP
AS ALREADY touched upon in an earlier subsection, last year's winner only ran once between Cheltenham's October meeting and the Festival, that coming in said hurdle race at Thurles. Clearly, freshened up with a spring campaign in mind, he became the eighth winner in the past 12 years to have been given a break of 50+ days ahead of the Festival, so again, if this has indeed been a long-term objective, a horse is likely to have been given a short break. Three of those winners had between 104 and 277 days off, so

don't be put off by a lack of recent match practice, it has likely been part of a formulated plan.

SUMMER FORM
INTERESTINGLY, last year's winner became the fourth winner in the past nine to have been running during the summer months before being given a relatively light campaign, during the season proper. This is something we should monitor in the coming years, as there could be a pattern emerging here. Certainly, don't overlook summer form, thinking it is not as strong as form during the core jumps season, as again, it could well have been part of a long-term plan (similar to the previous two subsections).

AGE
THE prime age bracket appears to be between seven and nine, although *Jazzy Matty* struck for the *'younger'* horses last year, successful at the age of six, something which *Oh Crick* and *Solar Impulse* have also achieved since 2009. Those aged nine and younger very much dominate, with only three double-digit aged winners in the past 27 renewals. With *Global Citizen* aged 10, we have only seen two winners over the age of nine in the past 17 renewals, so very much focus most of your attention of those younger runners. 13 of the past 20 winners were aged between six and eight.

MARKET FORCES
ANOTHER of the more difficult races to predict throughout the week according to the market, with only two winning favourites in the past 21 renewals. Since 2016 alone, we have seen two winners return at odds of 28-1, *Maskada* won at 22-1 and *Croco Bay* struck at a whopping 66-1 just seven years ago. Those two successful favourites were very lightly-raced novices – *Alderwood* and *Chosen Mate* – so don't let a big price put you off here, especially if looking towards one of the slightly more exposed runners, perhaps one who has run well previously and has seemingly been *'out of form'* during the current campaign.

TARGET FOR McMANUS
THE Emmet Mullins-trained So Scottish was only a mid-division finisher in the green and gold last year and it has actually now been eight years since his last win in the race, but owner **JP McManus** has still been responsible for four winners in the past 21 renewals. *Fota Island*, *Bellvano* and *Alderwood* were all novice winners for McManus between 2005 and 2013, before *Le Prezien* struck as a second-season chaser; he had been sent off favourite as a novice 12 months earlier. Responsible for a further nine runners-up since 2003, focus more on any lightly-raced novices who McManus' team target at the race.

TRAINERS TO NOTE

LE PREZIEN was also the last winner in the race for trainer **Paul Nicholls**, who has won the race four times since 2004 when *St Pirran* was successful. Again, his last three winners were all aged seven, so respect any *'younger'* runners from Ditcheat, although he has been without a runner in each of the past two renewals. His last runner, Thyme White, was still travelling well (at big odds) when falling in 2023.

Nicky Henderson has been without representation for the past five years, which is a little surprising as he once targeted the race in great numbers, after it was renamed in honour of his late father. Since 2005 – when the race was renamed – Henderson has saddled no fewer than 39 runners in the race, so although he has won it twice during this time, with *Greenhope* (another who had run well in the race the previous year) and *Bellvano*, his strike rate wouldn't be very good. It will be interesting to see if he starts to target the race again, going forward.

And, with **Willie Mullins** still yet to win a handicap chase at the Cheltenham Festival, his record here (this century) stands at 0-9. It wouldn't be a race that he pays too much attention to – in comparison to other handicaps throughout the week – but it remains a record to be wary of, nevertheless.

Jazzy Matty wins in 2025

ROLL OF HONOUR

Year	Form	Winner	Age	Weight	OR	SP	Trainer	Runners	Last Race (No. of days)
2025	0F13P122	Jazzy Matty	6	10-7	135	15/2	C Collins (IRE)	20	2nd Thurles h'cap hurdle (52)
2024	15549	Unexpected Party	9	10-10	138	12/1	D Skelton	16	9th Cheltenham Nov. H'cap Chase (46)
2023	F10	Maskada	7	11-1	142	22/1	H de Bromhead (IRE)	19	11th Leopardstown H'cap Chase (38)
2022	92023	Global Citizen	10	10-6	136	28/1	B Pauling	16	3rd Contenders Hurdle (39)
2021	25112	Sky Pirate	8	11-6	152	14/1	J O'Neill	19	2nd Gr.2 Kingmaker Nov. Chase (31)
2020	P60341	Chosen Mate	7	11-4	147	7/2F	G Elliott (IRE)	18	1st Gowran Beginners Chase (50)
2019	2	Croco Bay	12	10-12	139	66/1	B Case	19	2nd Worcester H'cap Chase (277)
2018	238	Le Prezien	7	11-8	150	15/2	P Nicholls	22	8th Gr.3 Caspian Caviar Gold Cup (91)
2017	22080	Rock The World	9	11-5	147	10/1	J Harrington (IRE)	24	11th Cheltenham H'cap Chase (146)
2016	33P	Solar Impulse	6	11-0	140	28/1	P Nicholls	24	p.u. Exeter Graduation Chase (92)

LEADING TEN-YEAR GUIDES

Paddy Power Gold Cup 3 (*Le Prezien* 3rd, *Sky Pirate* 5th, *Unexpected Party* 5th)
*Grand Annual Chase 3 (*Rock The World* 3rd, *Le Prezien* 8th, *Croco Bay* 5th)
squareintheair.com Handicap Chase 2 (*Rock The World* 11th, *Le Prezien* 2nd)
Guinness Galway Hurdle 2 (*Rock The World* 17th, *Chosen Mate* PU)

* denotes previous season

DAY TWO — RACE SEVEN

WEATHERBYS CHAMPION BUMPER
(In Memory of Sir Johnny Weatherby)
2m 87y (Grade 1) – Old Course

OVERVIEW
INTRODUCED as the *'Festival Bumper'* back in 1992, the Champion Bumper was handed Grade 1 status in 1996 and Weatherbys' sponsorship began the following year, when the high-class *Florida Pearl* was the second consecutive winner of Willie Mullins, who has dominated the race ever since. Having won five of the past six renewals, Mullins has now won the race 14 times in total and when he isn't in charge of matters, Irish-trained horses usually still prevail. In recent years, those with the stronger form – winners of Graded races, in particular – and those with the higher BHA Ratings have come out on top. Mares also have a particularly strong record in the race, from a relatively small pool of runners. Indeed, *Bambino Fever* became the third mare to win in the past nine years.

MULLINS – 14 NOT OUT
HAVING first won the race with *Wither Or Which* – who he also rode – in 1996, **Willie Mullins** has now won the Weatherbys Champion Bumper on a staggering 14 occasions and this includes five of the past six renewals. As we know, the strength in depth within his stable continues to grow with each passing year and as a result, he is often mobhanded when it comes to this race. Since 1994, Mullins has saddled 112 horses in the Champion Bumper and this includes the quintet that went to post in 2025. The most he has saddled in one renewal was 10 in 2023 – when he didn't actually win the race (*Fact To File* finishing runner-up) – and this century alone, he has had no fewer than 106 runners in the race, which is quite incredible really.

Although it wasn't always the case, in recent years we have seen his shortest-priced runner come out on top and again, that was (just about) the case last year, with him responsible for the second, third and fourth favourites, with the winner sent off at 4-1.

Expect Mullins to (once again) be very well represented this year.

IRISH DOMINATION
IF MULLINS fails then it is usually another Irish trainer who succeeds here, with *Moon Racer* and *Ballyandy* – successful in 2015 and 2016, respectively – the only British-trained winners during the past 14 years. The past nine winners were Irish-trained and overall, 26 of the 33 winners were trained in Ireland. Plus, of the seven British-trained winners, three actually made their racecourse debuts in an Irish bumper before being sold and moved to the UK. Therefore, only four of the 33 winners actually started their careers in a bumper in England.

Gordon Elliott was out of luck last year, with his two runners including beaten favourite *Kalypso'chance*, but he has won the Champion Bumper twice in the past nine years, plus he had prepared *Sir Gerhard* ahead of his win in 2021 renewal, only for Cheveley Park to move him to Mullins ahead of the Festival, shortly before Elliott's infamous ban was announced. Also responsible for two seconds and two thirds in the past six years, Elliott also likes to target this race with intent and will likely continue to do so.

RACECOURSE EXPERIENCE
BETWEEN 1996 and 2013, seven of the 17 winners had run in just one bumper, with several not even having any previous Point-to-Point experience and it was widely accepted that the *'lesser exposed'* runners

were those to focus on. Since then, however, only *Jasmin de Vaux* has been able to score on the back of just one bumper winner, during the past dozen years, and you have to go all the way back to *Cue Card* in 2010 to find the last winner who had run just the once under Rules, with no prior Pointing experience.

Racecourse experience is becoming more significant, with *Ballyandy* the busiest winner in recent years, him having run four times ahead of the Cheltenham Festival. Four of the past nine winners had run three times, but a minimum of two runs – with that second run often coming in a stronger race – now becoming par for the course.

GRADED/LISTED FORM

THAT final sentence leads us on nicely to this subsection. It has become increasingly noticeable that recent winners had contested (and won) bumpers at a good level prior to Cheltenham. Eight of the past 10 winners had won a Graded or Listed bumper on their most recent start, with five of the past eight winners having won one of two Grade 2 races staged at the Dublin Racing Festival. Whilst in years gone by it paid to look towards the potential improvers, it now seems to be a race which favours those with winning experience at a good level and having the proven form already in the book.

KEY RACES

THREE recent winners – namely *Envoi Allen, Facile Vega* and *A Dream To Share* – all won the Grade 2 **Paddy Power Cheltenham Countdown Podcast I.N.H. Flat Race** at the Dublin Racing Festival, a race which was won last year by Colcannon, who was ineligible for the Champion Bumper due to his vast experience. It again worked out well in the spring, however, with runner-up Sortudo (finished 7th at Cheltenham) winning at Fairyhouse and Green Splendour (5th) won the Grade 2 at Aintree. Usually a strong piece of form, it was won this year by Broadway Ted.

At the same two-day fixture, both *Relegate* and *Bambino Fever* won the Grade 2 for mares, the **Coolmore N.H. Sires Irish EBF Mares I.N.H. Flat Race**, a race that was won this year by Moonverrin, albeit in dramatic circumstances.

Considering that the Dublin Racing Festival was only introduced in 2018, five winners to hail from that fixture in eight years is a very strong return. Plus, Appreciate It and Kilcruit both won the geldings' race prior to finishing runner-up in the Champion Bumper, so pay close attention to both pieces of form.

Envoi Allen had earlier won the **Future Champions INH Flat Race** at Navan the previous December. Formerly a Grade 2 contest, it now holds Listed status

KEY TRENDS

⭐ Willie Mullins has trained the winner 14 times (including 5 of the past 6 winners)
⭐ 26 of the 33 winners were trained in Ireland
⭐ The past 22 winners won last time out
⭐ 5 of the past 8 winners won a Grade 2 at the DRF
⭐ Horses rated 132+ are 7-19 during the past 17 years
⭐ 3 of the past 9 winners were mares (from 15 runners)
✓ 21 of the past 29 winners (including 7 of the past 8) were aged 5
✓ 10 of the past 24 winners won during the previous spring or summer
✓ 10 of the past 17 winners were in the top 2 according to official BHA Ratings
✓ 9 of the past 11 winners returned at 7-1 or shorter (8 of them 5-1 or shorter and in the top 2 of the betting)
✓ 8 of the past 10 winners had won a Graded or Listed bumper
✓ 8 of the past 10 winners had run during February
✓ 8 of the past 28 winners finished 1st or 2nd at Leopardstown over Christmas
✓ 7 of the past 8 winners were unbeaten
✓ 6 of the past 12 winners had run in 3 or more bumpers
✓ 5 of the past 7 winners had won a 4yo Irish Point-to-Point before racing under Rules
✓ 3 of the past 7 winners were owned by Cheveley Park Stud
✓ In 2021, 2022 & 2023 the top 2 on BHA Ratings (and in the betting) finished 1st & 2nd
✓ Respect Gordon Elliott-trained runners
✓ Respect course form
✓ Respect horses rated 130+
✗ 4yo's are 1-93 during the past 29 renewals
✗ Only 2 of the past 15 winners had run in just 1 bumper
✗ Only 2 of the 33 winners were beaten last time out
✗ Only 4 of the 33 winners made their racecourse debut in a UK bumper

and it was also won by *Sir Gerhard* and before him, *Dunguib* en route to the Festival. Last season's winner Kalypso'chance failed to justify favouritism at Cheltenham, whilst this season's race went the way of Oh My Word.

COURSE FORM

GIVEN the relative lack of success of the *'home'* contingent, there aren't any specific *Key Races* in Britain so to speak (not recently anyway), although the past two UK-trained winners had both won at Cheltenham earlier in the season, as had the Irish-trained *Cork All Star*. Both he and *Ballyandy* had won the Listed **Prestbury NH Flat Race** from the November meeting, a race in which *Liberman* finished runner-up to the classy Rhinestone Cowboy before winning the Champion Bumper in 2003. *Moon Racer* had won at the October meeting before being given a lengthy break (similar to *Liberman*) ahead of the Festival.

Fergal O'Brien's Chicker was successful at the October meeting, before finishing sixth behind Saint Clovis in the Listed race in November.

OFFICIAL BHA RATINGS

IN 2008, the BHA began to publish an official rating for horses contesting the Champion Bumper and in recent years, as those with the stronger form have started to come to the fore, the higher-rated horses have very much been the dominant force. 10 of the past 17 winners were either top- or second-top on official BHA Ratings and these include *Bambino Fever*, who was joint top-rated with a lofty rating of 130 last year.

Horses rated 130+ warrant utmost respect and if you focus solely on those rated 132 or higher (no representation last year), you would have found seven winners during those past 17 years and all from just 19 runners. Pay close attention to any horse(s) with such a high rating once again this year

In 2021, 2022 and 2023, the top-rated pairing actually finished first and second in the Champion Bumper, so these ratings are to be taken seriously, as the BHA handicapper is clearly adept at handing out worthy figures to the leading contenders.

LAST TIME OUT/UNBEATEN WINNERS

THE past five winners were all unbeaten prior to Cheltenham, as were *Relegate* and *Envoi Allen*, so that is seven of the past eight winners, with only *Ferny Hollow* able to win during this period, having suffered a reversal earlier in the season.

The past 22 winners arrived at Cheltenham on the back of a win and whilst the record of *Unbeaten Winners* clearly helps, that is quite significant. The aforementioned *Liberman*, whose form looked strong in light of what Rhinestone Cowboy had done as a novice hurdler, was the last horse to win the Champion Bumper on the back of a defeat. In fact, only two horses have ever won this race on the back of a defeat, so focus on those who won last time.

RECENT RUN

ALTHOUGH I touched upon winners arriving on the back of a break in an earlier subsection, it has very much changed tact in recent years, with no fewer than eight of the past 10 winners having run (and won) during February. In fairness to *Jasmin de Vaux*, he only made his Rules and bumper debut on 28th January, so was never likely to run again before Cheltenham, which leaves only *Sir Gerhard* to have lacked a recent run in the past decade.

As well as the two Grade 2s at Leopardstown taking place, Newbury stages a Listed event on William Hill Hurdle day and that contest was won by *Ballyandy* before he became the last British-trained winner of the Champion Bumper. That was another former Grade 2 which has been dropped to Listed status in recent years.

EARLY STARTERS

BETWEEN 2002 and 2017, nine of the 16 winners had run either the previous spring or during the summer and *A Dream To Share* added his name to the list in 2023, him having been successful in bumpers during May and June before returning from a break to win at the DRF. *'Summer form'* shouldn't be overlooked these days and we have seen the likes of Marine Nationale and Mystical Power develop into smart novice hurdlers on the back of a summer campaign in recent years. Windbeneathmywings would have been near enough favourite for last year's Champion Bumper had he not met with a setback and he, too, started out during the summer, so don't be too quick to dismiss form from that time of year.

MARKET FORCES

WE SAW several big-priced winners of the Champion Bumper not so long back, with *Monsignor* scoring at 50-1 in 1999, whilst *Hairy Molly* struck at 33s in 2006 and *Cue Card* returned at 40-1 in 2010. However, more recently, results have become more predictable, with only two winners returning at odds greater than 7-1 in the past 11 years. Eight of those nine shorter-priced winners returned at 5-1 or less, with all eight hailing from the top two in the betting.

In 2021, 2022 and 2023, as well as the top two on BHA Ratings filling the first two places, the top two in the market did the same. The race, therefore, seems to be more predictable all around, as the horses with the better form continue to shine.

AGE

AS WELL as defying the inexperience statistic, *Cue Card* remains the only four-year-old winner of the Champion Bumper in the past 29 renewals. With two more four-year-olds beaten last year, the record of such runners during that period now stands at 1-93, so they are clearly up against it somewhat, despite the age allowance. Considering that *Cue Card* ended up developing into a top-class performer over many years, it shows what kind of horse must be required to win at such a tender age. Indeed, he is the only four-year-old winner of the race as a Grade 1 and in its current format, with the two previous four-year-old winners coming in the first four renewals of the race. The last before *Cue Card* was 1995 winner *Dato Star*, another high-class performer who was verging on Champion Hurdle class. With that in mind, the percentage call is very much to overlook such young runners.

At the other end of the scale, we have seen seven six-year-olds win the race this century but crucially, only one in the past eight years. Five certainly seems to be the popular age at present.

MARES' ALLOWANCE
WITH three mares successful in the past nine years, the 7lb sex-allowance is clearly hugely significant when it comes to a high-class performer. As already touched upon, last year's winner was officially joint top-rated and that was before the 7lb allowance was factored into proceedings. *Mucklemeg* and *Total Enjoyment* were earlier winners of this race – successful in 1994 and 2004, respectively – but we see more and more better quality mares in training these days and Willie Mullins certainly isn't afraid to run a good one here against the boys, evidenced by the wins of *Relegate* and *Bambino Fever*. During those past nine years, only 17 mares have run and two of those were four-year-old fillies, so a record of 3-15 is hugely noteworthy.

LEOPARDSTOWN CHRISTMAS FORM
GOING back to the 1996 and 1997 winners, both *Wither Or Which* and *Florida Pearl* had won at Leopardstown's Christmas fixture and were subsequently kept fresh for this race. The mare *Total Enjoyment* did likewise, whilst *Hairy Molly* was beaten at the Christmas meeting on debut. More recently, *Champagne Fever* and *Ferny Hollow* were beaten at the same fixture, whilst *Silver Concorde* and *Facile Vega* were victorious at Leopardstown's four-day Festive bonanza.

The bumpers (and maiden hurdles for novice hurdle purposes) often tend to be strong contests across the four days and as a result, we see plenty of future stars on show. Pay healthy respect to the results of the bumpers at this meeting, with this race in mind.

POINT-TO-POINT FORM
PRIOR to switching to this sphere, *Bambino Fever* had won a maiden Point at Stowlin the previous May and became the fifth winner of the Champion Bumper in the past seven years to have started off life between the flags. *Envoi Allen*, *Ferny Hollow*, *Sir Gerhard* and *Jasmin de Vaux* had also all won an Irish Point before running in bumpers, so pay healthy respect to any such contenders this year. The strength of Irish Point-to-Point form continues to grow and as such, it is having a big impact on this race as a result. Interestingly, all five had won a four-year-old maiden before winning this race at the age of five.

OWNERS TO NOTE
HAVING been responsible for three consecutive winners between 2019 and 2021, **Cheveley Park Stud** haven't had a runner in the race since and boast an incredible 100% record in it. The decision for the stud to step back from National Hunt runners for the time being is a disappointing one from the sport's perspective and it is very much hoped that they return before too long. They were clearly very shrewd in terms of the horses which they bought with this race in mind and certainly in terms of those they entered and in the end, decided to run.

JP McManus was responsible for the first and second in 2023, with *A Dream To Share* providing him with a second Champion Bumper, some 29 years after *Mucklemeg* won. He has, however, gone close on a number of occasions, with Joe Mac, Regal Encore and Blue Sari all finishing runner-up between 1998 and 2019. The mare Aqua Force disappointed for McManus last year.

And, **Miss M A Masterson** has yet to win the race but was responsible for the runner-up in 2018 (Carefully Selected), 2020 (Appreciate It) and 2021 (Kilcruit). Margaret Masterson could be represented this year by the four-year-old Quiryn

BRITISH TRAINERS TO NOTE
NOMINATING a British trainer to note isn't easy, given the record of the Irish in the race, but the Pipes have won the Champion Bumper twice, with Martin successful with *Liberman* and son **David Pipe** saddling *Moon Racer* to win some 11 years ago. As highlighted earlier, Pipe would have had a strong contender last year in the shape of Windbeneathmywings, had injury not ruled him out, and he looks to be building a nice team of young horses at Pond House once again.

And, although **Nigel Twiston-Davies** has only won the race once, he is the last British trainer to do so, plus he has a fine record in Aintree's Grade 2, winning that four times between 1998 and 2014. Interestingly, King's Road (6th in 1998) and The New One (6th as a 4yo in 2012) had both run well in the Champion Bumper prior to winning at Aintree. Now training alongside son **Willy**, the Twiston-Davies stable would be selective in terms of the runners they have in the Champion Bumper, so take note if one is deemed good enough. And, if they run well, keep them in mind for Grand National day.

Listed winner Bass Hunter is a possible runner in the Champion Bumper

ROLL OF HONOUR

Year	Form	Winner	Age	Weight	OR	SP	Trainer	Runners	Last Race (No. of days)
2025	11	Bambino Fever	5	11-0	130	4/1	W Mullins (IRE)	17	1st Gr.2 Leopardstown Mares' Bumper (38)
2024	1	Jasmin de Vaux	5	11-7	126	9/2	W Mullins (IRE)	19	1st Naas Bumper (45)
2023	111	A Dream To Share	5	11-7	135	7/2	J Kiely (IRE)	21	1st Gr.2 Leopardstown Bumper (39)
2022	11	Facile Vega	5	11-5	138	15/8F	W Mullins (IRE)	20	1st Gr.2 Leopardstown Bumper (39)
2021	11	Sir Gerhard	6	11-5	132	85/40	W Mullins (IRE)	14	1st Listed Navan Bumper (89)
2020	221	Ferny Hollow	5	11-5	124	11/1	W Mullins (IRE)	23	1st Fairyhouse Bumper (18)
2019	111	Envoi Allen	5	11-5	127	2/1F	G Elliott (IRE)	14	1st Gr.2 Leopardstown Bumper (39)
2018	11	Relegate	5	10-12	120	25/1	W Mullins (IRE)	23	1st Gr.2 Leopardstown Mares' Bumper (39)
2017	811	Fayonagh	6	10-12	129	7/1	G Elliott (IRE)	22	1st Listed Fairyhouse Mares' Bumper (39)
2016	1121	Ballyandy	5	11-5	134	5/1	N Twiston-Davies	23	1st Listed Newbury Bumper (32)

LEADING TEN-YEAR GUIDES

Future Champions Bumper 2 (*Envoi Allen* 1st, *Sir Gerhard* 1st)
Paddy Power Cheltenham Countdown Bumper 3 (*Envoi Allen* 1st, *Facile Vega* 1st, *A Dream To Share* 1st)
Coolmore NH Stallions Bumper 2 (*Relegate* 1st, *Bambino Fever* 1st)

CHESTER RACECOURSE

2026 FIXTURES

MAY

6th, 7th & 8th	Boodles May Festival
Saturday 30th	Roman Day

JUNE

Friday 12th	The Allington Hughes Law Friday Social
Saturday 13th	The Saturday Social
Saturday 27th	Summer Saturday in Partnership with Matthew Clark

JULY

Friday 10th (Eve)	Ibiza Classics Evening
Saturday 11th	Music Weekend Saturday
Saturday 25th	Midsummer Meeting

AUGUST

Sunday 2nd	Family Fun Day
Saturday 22nd	Powells Jewellery Ladies Day

SEPTEMBER

11th & 12th	Virgin Bet Autumn Festival
Saturday 19th	The Season Finale

BOOK NOW AT CHESTER-RACES.COM

The Bumper Division

BY PAUL FERGUSON

BAMBINO FEVER provided Willie Mullins with an incredible 14th win in the Weatherbys Champion Bumper last year and having saddled a clutch of promising winners since the turn of the year, it seems likely that he will once again be well represented.

First to strike was **Quiryn**, successful in the first four-year-old bumper of 2026. A four-year-old by French Flat stallion Sottsass, he was in training in France as a three-year-old but didn't make it to the track (twice declared a non-runner) and was successful at Naas on soft ground. Ridden patiently by Patrick Mullins, he eased into contention between horses and was still on the bridle when hitting the front.

The runner-up gives the form a little substance, as he had earlier finished 5 lengths off Minella Yoga in an academy hurdle, after which the winner moved to Paul Nicholls, for whom he won an introductory hurdle and finished third in the Grade 2 Finesse Juvenile Hurdle at Cheltenham on trials day.

Bred to be smart, Quiryn is a half-brother to Prix du Cadran winner Mille et Mille, whilst also being a half-brother to Trapista, a winner over hurdles and fences for Jonjo & A J O'Neill and JP McManus. Light on experience, another concern would be the fact that he is just four, with Cue Card the sole four-year-old winner – from 93 to have tried – during the past 29 renewals. Whilst he might be more forward than most horses of his age (given that he was in training in France), it is a negative.

He carries the green and blue silks of owner Margaret Masterson, who was responsible for the Champion Bumper runner-up three times in the space of four years recently; Carefully Selected, Appreciate It and Kilcruit.

A full-brother to Gaelic Warrior, **Our Trigger** was another winning four-year-old for the Mullins camp, successful in a four-runner race at Gowran Park on Thyestes Chase day. Despite having been given a bump on the home bend, he readily accounted for his three opponents on heavy ground and whilst it is difficult to get carried away by the result, it is worth noting that the third-placed Ballygorey Ruby had finished a similar distance behind Quiryn at Naas.

As well as having the age statistic to overcome, it is worth noting that Cue Card is also the only winner in the past 17 years to have won the Champion Bumper on the back of one run and with no prior Point-to-Point experience.

Runner-up in a four-year-old maiden at Dromahane last spring, **The Irish Avatar** made a striking winning start under Rules at Navan. Sporting the silks of Gigginstown House Stud, he made all and travelled with purpose throughout. Racing alone down the centre of the course, the son of Poet's Word wasn't hard pressed to pull 9 lengths clear of Low Kick, who Gigginstown had paid £170,000 to secure, on the back of a third-place finish in a Point-to-Point Bumper at Aintree last May.

Again, it is difficult to get too excited about the level of form achieved, but he moved like a nice horse and visually at least, it was a really pleasing start. Out of the smart mare Dinaria des Obeaux (winner of a Grade 3 over hurdles and a Grade 2 over fences), he is bred to be nice and I would expect him to form part of the Mullins battalion for Cheltenham.

Another to prove successful at Naas, **Love Sign d'Aunou** shot to the head of the ante-post market for the Champion Bumper with a 24-length success over 2m2½f on heavy ground. Like The Irish Avatar, he made all under Patrick Mullins and one by one, his rivals fell away as he kept up the gallop. A five-year-old by Goliath du Berlais – a Grade 1-winning chaser who enjoyed success as a sire in this sphere towards the back end of last season – he clearly stays very well and drew effortlessly clear of the runner-up. Whilst the second is a seven-year-old, he did win a brace of Points in November and the third had finished much closer the time before.

Stamina seems to be a strong suit of his, as he stayed on powerfully when winning his maiden Point – albeit on better ground – at Loughanmore last April, where he beat Gin Tonic, a maiden hurdle winner who is now rated 124 (I.H.R.B. Rating). He might appreciate soft ground and a strong gallop to bring out the best in him at the Festival and he follows a similar path to that of 2024 winner Jasmin de Vaux, who won the same Naas contest.

Prior to the victory of Love Sign d'Aunou, **Bentragghill** had headed the ante-post market, following his win at Leopardstown over Christmas. Only third in a four-year-old maiden Point at Fairyhouse when trained by Cormac Abernethy (front two have both won over hurdles, in fairness), the son of Getaway made a successful start under Rules, despite racing keenly in the hands of Jody Townend. Sweeping around the outer to lead on the home bend, he picked up well on decent ground, to score by a comfortable 4¼ lengths, with Lemmy Caution (3ʳᵈ) providing a bit of substance to the form.

A half-brother to several winners – including Gordon Elliott's useful mare, Party Central – the five-year-old was Mullins' sole entry in the bumper on day one of the Dublin Racing Festival (took place on the rescheduled Monday card this year), but was taken out at the final forfeit stage.

In recent years, the two Grade 2s which take place at Leopardstown's Dublin Racing Festival have proven to be key pointers towards Champion Bumper success. Envoi Allen, Facile Vega and A Dream To Share all won the DRF Future Stars I.N.H. Flat Race – run this year under the banner of the Paddy Power Cheltenham Countdown Podcast – en route to Cheltenham, whilst Appreciate It and Kilcruit both finished runner-up at the Festival, having won the Grade 2 on their latest start.

This year's race didn't appear to be the strongest renewal on paper and in a slowly run affair, it was won by **Broadway Ted**, who got the better of a couple of stable-mates (all trained by Gordon Elliott) in a tight three-way finish. The winner had been successful at Ayr in December and clearly enjoys testing conditions. Out of a Grade 3-winning mare, who was 3-3 in bumpers, he is bred to cope with quicker conditions, although he will need to improve to figure at the spring festivals.

Both Relegate and Bambino Fever won the mares' only contest, which takes place at the same fixture, before gaining Grade 1 honours at Cheltenham. This year's race didn't have a standout performer, but did produce one of the more bizarre finishes of the season to date. Having travelled well, **Moonverrin** looked set to win easily when hitting the front, but hung to her right and looked like pulling herself up. Passed by **Royal Hillsborough**, her rider then eased up, mistaking the 50 yard marker for the winning post, allowing Moonverrin to get back up and win. In truth, the finish didn't give the feel of Champion Bumper form, but the pair could be interesting if kept to races against their own sex, at Fairyhouse, Aintree or Punchestown.

Gordon Elliott opted to bypass the DRF with **Keep Him Company**, following his victory over Passenger at Leopardstown's Christmas meeting. The six-year-old finished strongly on that occasion, so looks to be another with plenty of stamina in the locker, having earlier beaten a couple of stable companions at Fairyhouse. Versatile in terms of ground, he ran out a comfortable winner of a soft-ground maiden at Kildorrey last March and is another who might appreciate an ease underfoot on day two of the Festival.

Out of a Dom Alco mare, there is plenty of stamina in his pedigree and like The Irish Avatar, the son of Walzertakt represents owners Gigginstown House Stud and will bid to become just the second six-year-old winner of the race in nine renewals. Whilst we saw Silver Concorde, Moon Racer and Fayonagh successful for that age group between 2014 and 2017, Sir Gerhard is the sole six-year-old winner since.

Leopardstown's Christmas fixture often produces significant bumper winners and another to note from the meeting is **The Mourne Rambler**, who carried the silks of Savills Chase winner Affordale Fury, ensuring that it was a Festive period to remember for longstanding owner, Philip Polly. Runner-up in a Portrush maiden in October, the son of Well Chosen – sire of exciting novice hurdler Old Park Star – travelled well and hit the front between the final two fences, only to be outstayed by the winner, with the pair nicely clear.

At Leopardstown, the five-year-old came wide into the home straight and picked up well to win on yielding ground and the third-placed Premier Division gives the form some reliability, with him having finished a little closer to Keep Him Company the time before. The fifth placed horse, Outofafrika (beaten 10 lengths), has already given the form a boost by winning at Fairyhouse, so it could be a piece of form which works out well, and The Mourne Rambler is bred to do well in this sphere.

From a family which trainer Noel Meade knows very well, he is a full-brother to Sixshooter and She's A Star (dam of last season's smart bumper performer, Colcannon) and a half-brother to Blue Mosque, all of whom were successful in this division and were precocious types for the stable. His trainer hinted after that Leopardstown success that he could head straight to Cheltenham and it would not be a surprise to see him put up a bold show.

Whilst several of his rivals will be hoping for soft ground, his pedigree suggests that he will be quite versatile in that regard and although Meade has yet to taste victory in the Champion Bumper, Corskeagh Royale finished runner-up in 2008, and he also saddled the second in the very first running of the then 'Festival Bumper' in 1992, when Tiananmen Square chased home Montelado. He reversed that form at Punchestown and Meade has since won that Grade 1 with Leading Run and Mick The Man. That would appeal as another likely spring target for this promising five-year-old, who could represent a bit of value at current odds of 20-1.

Runner-up to The Mourne Rambler, **Cityofblindinlites** probably isn't one for Cheltenham, but is certainly a name to note throughout the closing months of the season. Representing Martin Brassil and owners Sean & Bernadine Mulryan, he ran a huge race considering that he didn't have any previous racecourse experience. Reluctant to line up beforehand, he wore a hood and a tongue strap and was reported, by his rider Finian Maguire, to have hung right throughout. With that in mind, perhaps we will see him on a right-handed track next time and these connections do have a tendency to run their brighter prospects at the Punchestown Festival.

Two-time Navan winner **Oh My Word** was last seen winning a Listed event in December, when beating Panjandrum by 11 lengths. He had travelled strongly and was far too good for the opposition, with Passenger (went on to finish much closer to Keep Him Company and probably found the ground too testing here) back in third. That appeared to be a much more polished performance than when winning an ordinary race at 33-1 on debut, so the Poet's Word five-year-old is clearly heading in the right direction. Whether he will be able to cope with quicker conditions is an unknown, but he certainly looks to be a promising sort for Westmeath trainer Thomas Cleary.

Domestically, the Listed bumper (formerly a Grade 2) which Newbury stages in early February is often a strong race and it was won this year by **A Likeable Rogue**, for Cleveland-based trainer John Dawson. Pitched in at Listed level on debut, he finished fourth at Cheltenham in November and had won on soft ground at Wetherby but showed considerable improvement here. It did appear that several in behind failed to handle the deteriorating conditions, whereas the grey son of Kingston Hill stayed on strongly under Brian Hughes, who was riding a rare winner at the Berkshire venue. Bred to cope with better ground, it will be interesting to see if that is the case, as he went through the heavy terrain with ease at Newbury.

No Walkover and Half Hoping, who had finished first and second at Chepstow before both winning on Boxing Day, were among those in behind who disappointed and it is hard to see youngsters coming back from having such a hard race on heavy ground in the spring. With that in mind, it is unlikely that we will see either return to the fray.

Risky Obsession eventually finished sixth, beaten 113 lengths (yes, you did read that correctly), but moved well to the three furlong pole and is certainly one who can be forgiven the run on the basis of the ground. A half-brother to Ask Paddington, he is bred for better ground and won both his Point on good-to-yielding and beat Smile John Boy (had impressed at Hereford the time before) on good-to-soft at Warwick, despite showing distinct signs of greenness. Dan Skelton's five-year-old, who was initially bought by David Maxwell before being sold on at his dispersal, could be given another chance on a sounder surface, although again, this must have taken plenty out of him so his season might well be over.

One who wasn't declared for the Newbury race was **Bass Hunter**, who looked a smart prospect when winning at the Berkshire venue back in November. The second and fourth have come out of that bumper and won, whilst Chris Gordon's enthusiastic son of Authorized then won a Listed race at Ascot. Drawing clear off the home bend, it had looked like he would run out an impressive winner, but having tired in the closing stages, was hanging on near the line. He clearly has a huge engine, but will need to race more professionally if he is to enter calculations in Graded races in the spring.

Better ground might help and I wonder if his trainer might think about some sort of headgear – most likely a hood – if he does head to Cheltenham. Aintree is another option and he is clearly a talented six-year-old. Hopefully, he has the mental constitution for such a test.

Fourth behind Bass Hunter at Newbury, Harry Derham's **Lover Desbois** travelled noticeably well en route to winning at Kempton. Never too far from the pace under Finian Maguire, he eased upsides early in the home straight and showed a good turn of foot to win at the second attempt. A five-year-old by Beaumec de Houelle, he could find the track at Aintree to his liking.

Bass Hunter had been due to contest the bumper staged on day three of the Winter Million fixture at Windsor. A non-runner due to having been cast in his box, the race went the way of Dan Skelton's **St James's Finest**, who had earlier finished fourth behind No Walkover in a good race at Chepstow. A five-year-old grey by Jukebox Jury, he wasn't beaten too far on debut and showed plenty of improvement to lower the colours of a previous Listed winner. It will be interesting to see if he is asked to run again come the spring, as both earlier pieces of form came on soft ground. If we do get to see him again, he has the ability to carry a penalty to success, if being kept to a lower level than Graded company.

Diamond Street was another recent bumper winner for the Skelton operation, on soft ground at

Doncaster, under Tristan Durrell, who is enjoying a momentous season. Ridden patiently and confidently, the chestnut son of Diamond Boy travelled kindly and once hitting the front, cleared away to win by 10 lengths, with a further 24 back to the third. Whilst it is difficult to get carried away by the level of form achieved, the second had won an Irish Point, the third had experience and had finished much closer in two previous bumpers, and the fourth (beaten 38 lengths) had finished 13½ lengths behind No Walkover at Aintree. There is, therefore, reason to believe that it was a reasonable race at the very least and the manner of success was taking.

Fellow Warwickshire-based trainer Olly Murphy introduced a nice type at Southwell in early-December, **Old Habits**. Another partnered by a young jockey to note, Lewis Saunders, the son of Malinas, who finished only third in an Irish Point (beaten 18½ lengths), came from off the pace, which isn't always easy around the Nottinghamshire venue, and victory looked unlikely as he was pushed along turning for home. However, he picked up well and despite looking quite green, was in the lead by the furlong pole. Pulling clear, he finished the best part of 5 lengths in front of Cool Customer (beaten a neck by Risky Obsession in a maiden Point) and the form was franked when the third-placed That'll Be Oxo beat the runner-up at Hereford.

The McNeill Family and the Stone Family co-own Old Habits – alongside longstanding supporters of the game Grahame & Diana Whateley – and the first named pairing look to have another bright young prospect on their hands, in the shape of Jamie Snowden's **Milpat**. Runner-up on his sole start in France (winner was all set to win on debut for Gordon Elliott and Gigginstown when falling at Cork in December), the four-year-old made a winning British debut at Huntingdon shortly before Christmas. In receipt of plenty of weight, the son of Cokoriko enjoyed a dream run, up the inside rail. Pushed along, he cornered well and scampered clear to win with plenty in hand. Given both his age and physique, it will be interesting to see if he is asked to run again, but it wouldn't be a huge shock to see him turn up at Aintree, given the pace he clearly possesses and the regard in which he appears to be held.

Another winning four-year-old to catch the eye was Nicky Henderson's Kapgarde filly **Stars Align**, who struck in a 'junior' bumper at Ludlow under Freddie Gordon. Due to heavy fog, visibility was greatly reduced, but the winner appeared to be moving well at the top of the home straight and nudged out under hands and heels, seemed to win with a bit in hand. Both the time and the fact that they finished in a bit of a heap in behind suggests that it was a slowly run race and whilst that form has yet to be tested, the sixth had won at Doncaster on debut. Clearly, much more will be required if she is asked to contest a better quality race.

In terms of British-trained mares, **Ti'manzel** and Malina Road possibly set the standard by virtue of their respective Listed wins. The former – trained by Gary & Josh Moore – was successful at Huntingdon on debut and went on to run well under a penalty behind the aforementioned St James's Finest at Windsor. A five-year-old by No Risk At All, she finished strongly each time and could be one for the Nickel Coin at Aintree, given that she ran well against geldings last time. Both runs have come on soft ground, so the Listed race at Sandown on Imperial Cup day (Saturday 7th March) is another option.

Both races are also likely to come under consideration for Fergal O'Brien's **Malina Road**, who beat a stable-mate at Ludlow before winning the Alan Swinbank at Market Rasen. O'Brien won that Listed event with Dysart Enos before she landed the Nickel Coin and last year's winner Kingston Queen finished third in the Aintree Grade 2. She stayed on well to beat Ben Clarke's **The Flaggy Shore**, who had earlier impressed in winning at Warwick. Both former Points winners who look capable of taking a step up in class, they pulled nicely clear at the Lincolnshire track. Both mares held an entry at Ascot on Saturday 14th February.

Finally, a couple of maidens to monitor before the season concludes are **Ma Wang de Bois** and Bande Organisee. The former finished 5½ lengths off the aforementioned Smile John Boy (went on to finish second to Risky Obsession) at Hereford, where he travelled noticeably well in the hands of Harry Cobden. Emma Lavelle was enduring a quiet spell at the time and the son of Beaumec de Houelle showed more than enough to suggest that he can win a bumper towards the end of the campaign.

Of even more interest is Rebecca Curtis' **Bande Organisee**, who finished third in a Chepstow bumper which has worked out well since and has already been highlighted. A horse who caught the eye when falling in a couple of Irish Points – latterly when challenging Minella Machine (finished fourth behind The Mourne Rambler at Leopardstown) – he played up in the prelims ahead of his Rules debut, but it didn't prevent him from finishing third behind No Walkover and Half Hoping (both won on Boxing Day), whilst in fourth was St James's Finest. The imposing five-year-old has held entries since but has yet to reappear and ought to be difficult to beat in an average bumper when he does.

CHELTENHAM FESTIVAL 2026 – DAY 2

Daily Tips

BY SAM TURNER

Formerly Robin Goodfellow of the Daily Mail, Sam has been a regular on Racing TV for more than two decades and now writes a daily column for Betfair.

Brown Advisory Novices' Chase
WENDIGO

FINAL DEMAND went into the Dublin Racing Festival one of, if not the, shortest ante-post favourite heading to Cheltenham in March.

Punters were willing to overlook a functional, workmanlike Christmas win at Limerick, making last season's Turners Novices' Hurdle third a red-hot favourite for a test which in theory really ought to suit a horse that announced himself at last season's DRF.

Unfortunately for connections, a sluggish and laborious round of jumping in the Ladbrokes Novice Chase saw Final Demand and Paul Townend unable to keep tabs on stablemate Kaid d'Authie who gained 3 lengths on his field courtesy of his polished technique to run a smooth winner and record a win which saw his odds crash from 25/1 into 3/1 in a place for this event.

Purchased from the same French hurdle as Majborough back in the spring of 2023, the six-year-old was the second JP McManus chaser on day one of the DRF to relish the use of cheekpieces as he emulated his fellow French recruit to score readily and advance his claims for Grade 1 glory at the Festival.

Given his dam is a half-sister to French cross-country chase winner (3m7f) in Disco d'Authie, a step up in trip should be within the remit of Kaid d'Authie, but it's worth noting that the distance for this race has stretched out another 110 yards this year which should really play to the strengths of the dour stayers.

Talking of which, step forward **Wendigo**. Unfortunate not to finish closer in last year's Albert Bartlett Novices' Hurdle when hampered and stumbling two out, Jamie Snowden's seven-year-old has impressed on his transition to fences, acquitting himself well in the autumn before coming into his own upped to three miles in Grade 1 company at Kempton on Boxing Day and in a small-field Ayr novices' chase last time.

Although decisively beaten by Kitzbuhel in the Kauto Star at Christmas, I thought Wendigo ran a blinder to take third, especially as he found the track and unseasonably quick ground all against him on such a speed track.

While the winner found a great rhythm at the head of affairs, Gavin Sheehan was always out of his comfort zone on the son of Great Pretender until stamina became more of a requirement late in the day.

Last of the six runners turning for home, the seven-year-old charged home in the straight to record a finishing speed percentage according to the RaceiQ data of 109.91% as the tempo slackened off a little, while his closing four-furlong sectional was only just over a second slower than The Jukebox Man in the day's feature King George VI Chase, and that form hasn't worked out too badly.

That was clearly a superb effort from Wendigo in conditions that were far from his optimum and, with this race often won by a grinder rather than a flashy traveller, he should find this test to his liking, especially as he also edged to his left a little at his fences on Boxing Day.

Given that he now has four chase starts on his C.V. and has been allotted a mark of 147, the Festival handicaps could also be a route to Cheltenham glory for Snowden's grand chaser.

With that in mind, it is worth bearing in mind that the National Hunt Handicap Chase is a 0-145 and Wendigo would have to go into open company for the first time if connections chose the handicap path.

However, the eclipse of Final Diamond at the DRF surely opens up the novice staying chase division and, with the Kauto Star throwing up subsequent winners like Salver as an endorsement to the form, surely connections would be silly to pass up a chance of Grade 1 glory at the Festival.

Coral Cup
KOPECK DE MEE

TRYING to predict what might run in the Coral Cup at the time of writing without entries is nearly as tough as trying to find the winner, but I would be very interested in **Kopeck de Mee** if he makes the line up.

Those with a decent memory will recall the son of Masterstroke being the subject of an almighty plunge to win last year's Martin Pipe Conditional Jockeys' Handicap Hurdle on his stable debut for trainer Willie Mullins.

That sizeable market move came to nothing as the six-year-old trailed in 20th of the 24 runners, fully 52 lengths behind impressive winner Wodhooh, after an ambitious plan to try and make all in such a competitive heat flopped badly.

However, the Mullins and JP McManus think tank clearly learned from that chastening experience as the selection reappeared at Aintree three weeks later looking much more the horse that won four times in his native France and had clearly shown plenty on the Closutton gallops.

The aggressive riding tactics employed at Cheltenham were consigned to the bin with rider Mark Walsh at pains to settle his mount in rear as Wellington Arch coasted along at the head of affairs.

Unfortunately for Walsh, as well as his mount travelled through that two-and-a-half mile handicap, a slight error at the second last hurdle left him with a tough task in trying to reel in the all-the-way winner who clung on close home to register victory by a swiftly diminishing margin.

It was still a brilliant effort from Kopeck de Mee who recorded a vastly superior finishing speed percentage compared to his 19 rivals and it is worth bearing in mind that he left horses like Impose Toi (now rated a stone higher) in his vapours as Walsh sent him in pursuit of a talented winner.

His Aintree performance was clearly more representative of the horse connections had purchased and unfortunately we haven't seen much of him this season other than an ill-fated return to action at Navan before Christmas when he fell at the final fence on a rather mixed chasing debut.

Mullins appears to have shelved that project as we haven't seen Kopeck de Mee since and it would be a surprise if his maiden status over fences was threatened at this late stage of the season.

The sensible play, if trying to win a Coral Cup can be described as that, would be to target some of the spring's major handicap hurdles as a mark of 143 – he was raised 7lb for Aintree – could see him very competitive in strongly-run races if ridden the same way as he was on Merseyside.

The selection was entered in a Punchestown charity race scheduled to be held in early February so is clearly ready to see a racecourse again and, as we know, his connections are always more than happy to play the long game when it comes to executing a plan.

In some respects, his profile has similarities to last year's winner and stablemate Jimmy du Seuil, who himself had undergone an interrupted and unorthodox preparation prior to turning one of the season's most competitive handicaps into a rout from a mark of 146.

Hopefully, history might repeat itself in this year's renewal.

Queen Mother Champion Chase
MARINE NATIONALE

IT IS fair to say Barry Connell's belief in **Marine Nationale** is absolute.

Even after his gelding's reverse at the Dublin Racing Festival in the Ladbrokes Champion Chase, Connell remained defiant, saying: *"It'll hopefully be a different state of play at Cheltenham on nicer ground.*

"He's never run on heavy before, but I thought he might get away with it. He just didn't seem to enjoy it at any stage of the race.

Wendigo wins at Ayr in late January

"I'm disappointed not to win but we gave it a go. He's not a hard horse to get fit, so I could have skipped today but I wanted to support the race. I think we'll see a different horse on spring ground."

Myself and Connell might be in the minority, but I also thought he ran a blinder, despite being beaten 19 lengths by a resurgent Majborough, who turned in to peak Moscow Flyer in the first-time cheekpieces.

Admittedly, 19 lengths is a large margin to make up when the duo are set to next do battle on the second day of the Festival.

But for those of us fashioning a case for Marine Nationale to retain his title, there are a couple of reasons for believing that bookmakers who pushed him out to as big as 7/2 off the back of this defeat were overreacting.

The obvious excuse was the ground at the DRF which, although not quite as bad on the chase course as was feared, still proved deeper than the selection would have liked as was apparent from an early stage.

Historically a smooth traveller, the French Navy gelding looked laboured from flag fall and, in stark contrast to the winner, could never find the required fluency at his fences.

While Majborough gained more than 16 lengths on his field courtesy of his electric jumping, Marine Nationale lost nearly five in registering a RaceiQ jump index of just 6.6 compared to the winner's lofty 9.5 rating.

Quite simply, that was where the race was won and lost as Majborough revelled in the conditions to produce a clear career best, while his main market rival was stuck in the mud, toiling in rear.

In the circumstances, it was Marine Nationale's class which carried him into second past confirmed heavy ground lover Found A Fifty and that silver medal left the Leopardstown record of Connell's nine-year-old at just one win from six starts.

Contrast those statistics with a Cheltenham C.V. which boasts impressive victories in the Supreme Novices' Hurdle and last year's Queen Mother Champion Chase and the chances of Marine Nationale start to look a little more compelling.

Providing conditions aren't desperate at Cheltenham on day two, Marine Nationale must surely have a great chance of eroding the Leopardstown deficit and, although Majborough shot to the head of Timeform's National Hunt ratings (figure of 179) for this success, will the cheekpieces work quite so well a second time?

As a fan of Majborough, I was delighted to see him silence one or two critics with such a bold round of jumping and, once he'd flown the first couple in a great rhythm, he was never truly in danger of being caught.

It will be fascinating to see if those tactics work quite so well in a Champion Chase as he may not enjoy the freebie in front that he relished here and the prospect of better ground in the spring is sure to play to the strengths of a speed horse like Marine Nationale.

It promises to be a fascinating clash providing conditions aren't extreme and, if that is the case, Connell's Cheltenham hero is taken to wreak his revenge.

Marine Nationale looks to defend his crown on day two

CHELTENHAM FESTIVAL 2026 – DAY 2
Banker or Bust
BY RORY DELARGY

Rory is a contributor to The Irish Field and Irish Daily Star, whilst he can be seen on Paddy Power's 'The Cheltenham Countdown' show. He also co-writes the 'Punting Pointers' feature for Sporting Life.

Brown Advisory Novices' Chase
FINAL DEMAND

STRENGTHS: An exiting novice hurdler in 2024/25, **Final Demand** was a Grade 1 winner at the DRF in 2025, beating Wingmen by 12 lengths and starting out over fences by beating the same rival by 13 lengths at Navan in November, at which point he was made a warm favourite for the Brown Advisory, which had been publicly stated as his Cheltenham target. He built on that chase debut success by winning the Grade 1 Faugheen Novice Chase at Limerick, where his chief rival and stablemate Jimmy du Seuil disappointed.

Final Demand was able to win a Grade 1 on just his second start under Rules, and ended the season with another at Punchestown, albeit finishing only third in the Turners at Cheltenham behind The New Lion when considered a banker by many. He has always been regarded as a chaser by Willie Mullins and the 17.2hh bay switched to fences at the earliest opportunity.

His chase debut win was summarized by Timeform thus: *"Final Demand is as exciting a prospect as any going chasing this time around and made a faultless transition to fences after seven months off; close up, jumped accurately, travelled well, jumped on fourth, drew clear between last two, impressive."*

The Halifax firm were even more glowing at Limerick, describing his jumping as *"a sight to behold"* as he won *"without breaking sweat"*; they went on to call him *"a top-class prospect... sure to prove as effective as 3m+... rightly already a short-priced favourite for the Broadway at Cheltenham."*

WEAKNESSES: For a novice described as *"flawless"*, he did not impress with his jumping in the Grade 1 Ladbrokes Novice Chase at the DRF, where he had a soft lead until joined by Kaid d'Authie after a circuit and was outjumped by that rival in the final mile, not making any blunders as such, but not taking a cut at his fences and losing ground to the eventual winner at most. That was disappointing enough but Paul Townend's comment the *"the bubble's burst"* was disheartening, as jockeys tend to be much more forgiving. Trip and ground were no concern at Leopardstown and with two stablemates in the race, no-one tried to make things awkward for Final Demand, and although his jumping was adequate on the first circuit, there was no joy to behold in it.

It's been assumed that Final Demand is a top-class performer, but he's looked best when thrashing the likeable but limited Wingmen and he came up short at Cheltenham last season when as short as 6/4 for the Turners. Connections didn't think that Kaid d'Authie would be able to live with him in the Ladbrokes, but the winner had no trouble keeping tabs and gradually gained control in the second half of the race. Perhaps we've allowed style to trump substance with a horse who looks the perfect specimen but is beginning to display signs of being mortal.

OPPORTUNITIES: There had been no sign that making his own running might be an issue for Final Demand, but he did shape as if he would have preferred a lead at Leopardstown, and that could potentially sharpen his performance. Five weeks also allows him to regain his rhythm on the schooling grounds, and it's possible that a pair of cheekpieces would be beneficial given how he lacked focus at a few fences.

THREATS: In retrospect, the expectations were so high for Final Demand that fairly workmanlike performances on his first two chase starts came in for praise that was too fulsome in the circumstances. His Grade 1 at Limerick saw Jimmy du Seuil run poorly, as he did again before falling at Leopardstown, and he was left with just Gold Dancer and a 100/1 shot to beat. Gold Dancer is a very useful novice but was probably inconvenienced by heavy ground at Limerick having shown improved form on yielding when winning a pair of Graded races prior to that. **Kaid d'Authie** didn't have the profile of Final Demand going into the Ladbrokes at Leopardstown, but the pair were closely matched having both handed a thrashing to Wingmen on earlier chase starts and Kaid d'Authie had faced a stiffer test when second to

Kitzbuhel at Punchestown. In the circumstances it appeared that he was simply more progressive over fences than the odds-on favourite and he should do better still. That comment applies in spades to **Western Fold** who was an eyecatcher in second in that Leopardstown contest.

Giving the first two a head start, Western Fold made ground from off the pace under a considerate ride and needed just one flick of the whip from Jack Kennedy to move into a menacing second at the last fence. The winner rallied again, but Western Fold did well to close the gap as he did, especially as this was his first run since chasing home Envoi Allen and Affordale Fury at Down Royal in November. Best on good or yielding ground, Western Fold needed to get his eye in after a break and will be better with a run behind him. You can talk all you like about facile winners and jumping a joy to behold, but form with high-class horses carries more weight than easy wins against inferiors, and Western Fold's stacks up with the best. Winner of the Galway Plate, he beat Affordale Fury at Gowran before finishing on his tail at Down Royal and has thoroughly earned a lofty HRI rating of 157 (Timeform a miserly 154). Unlike many with lofty ratings, Western Fold has run to his on multiple occasions. After 11 runs, he's unlikely to progress much further, but is a dangerous opponent.

VERDICT: Final Demand has picked the wrong time to display feet of clay and both his jumping and his previous achievements are looking less solid than when he made his chasing bow. With those mentioned above, plus **The Big Westerner** and **Wendigo** also pressing their claims, there appears to be strength in depth to the Brown Advisory, while the likes of **Kitzbuhel** and **Romeo Coolio** arguably have stronger claims than the current favourite if they ended up running here.

BUST

Queen Mother Champion Chase
MAJBOROUGH

STRENGTHS: An impressive winner of the Triumph Hurdle in 2024 on just his second start for Willie Mullins, **Majborough** was the leading two-mile novice chaser in Britain and Ireland last season, losing out narrowly in the Arkle after making several serious errors, but still rallying gamely to lead briefly on the run-in. He then slammed the Arkle runner-up by 14 lengths on the same terms at Punchestown to demonstrate his superiority in the division.

A creditable third to Solness in Grade 1 company at Leopardstown over Christmas, he showed his liking for soft ground when running out a dominant winner of the Dublin Chase there in early February, his near 20-length mauling of current champion

Final Demand in the build up to last year's Festival

Marine Nationale the outstanding performance of the Dublin Racing Festival.

WEAKNESSES: Jumping let him down on his only previous visit to Cheltenham and he has adjusted to his left when running on right-handed tracks, notably when beaten by Found A Fifty in the Hilly Way Chase at Cork in December.

OPPORTUNITIES: Majborough is characterised in places as a chancy jumper and he certainly let fly with abandon in the Arkle, to his eventual demise, for all he did not fall. He wasn't perfect at Leopardstown on his previous outing as a novice but even the best jumpers can go through sticky patches, and it is encouraging that he was largely error free at Leopardstown at Christmas on ground that was quick enough for him. If he was better there, then his jumping was back to being a big asset in the Dublin Chase, where an aggressive ride seemed to bring out the best of him, and he produced a career-best on soft ground, posting a Timeform rating of 179 which was matched by an identical Timefigure, which was at odds with the testing ground. The Champion Chase gives him the chance to exorcise the demons of the Arkle, and it's worth remembering that his defeat there still saw him run very well in the circumstances.

THREATS: I'd say that good or faster ground might be the biggest threat to Majborough, while the memory of his mixed round of jumping in the Arkle raises a concern that the fences at Cheltenham don't suit him as much as Leopardstown, where the fences are stiff, but more kindly sited. Soft ground would also make the fences less of a concern, so continued rain takes two big worries out of the equation.

In terms of equine threats, **Marine Nationale** will be a much bigger threat than he was in the Dublin Chase where he ran despite his owner/trainer's misgivings about the surface. He won the Supreme and the Champion Chase on a yielding surface and clearly saves his very best for Cheltenham. I thought he showed real guts to stay on for second last time despite looking well beaten between the final two obstacles and he is undoubtedly the one that can give Majborough most to worry about.

VERDICT: The assumption was that Majborough impressive progress to Triumph glory would be mirrored last year over fences, and I think he was judged too harshly for a single defeat that still saw him run well enough to win an average Arkle. Since then, there are plenty who want to suggest that he's reached his limit, but we need to allow for the fact that Majborough is still just a six-year-old and the fact is that he's entitled to progress in an uneven manner given his age and inexperience.

He looked much closer to the finished article in the Dublin Chase and while I would expect Marine Nationale to get much closer to him on less testing ground at Cheltenham, a 19-length beating of that rival last time sets a very high standard for others to match.

BANKER

Majborough sets a high standard based on his Dublin Chase success

CHELTENHAM FESTIVAL 2026 – DAY 2

Daily Tips

BY JODIE STANDING

Author of Point-to-Point Recruits, Jodie excels in spotting talent at an early stage in a horse's career.

Turners Novices' Hurdle
NO DRAMA THIS END

I HAVE turned this race over from every angle, searching for a chink in **No Drama This End**'s armour, imagining different scenarios and potential dangers, but whichever path I follow, I keep arriving at the same conclusion. Paul Nicholls' undefeated hurdler remains the one they all have to beat, and he is a worthy favourite as we stand in early February.

His bumper win on soft ground at Warwick on New Year's Eve 2024 earned him a place in last season's Champion Bumper, where he ran with credit to finish ninth. He held every chance heading down the hill before a bump knocked him off balance, and he plugged on at the one pace up the climb to finish 9 lengths behind Bambino Fever. That form has aged well with the race continuing to churn out winners, most notably Idaho Sun, who finished sixth that day before going on to land the Grade 1 Formby Novices' Hurdle, while El Cairos is in the mix for this year's Supreme.

Switched to hurdles this season, No Drama This End was thrown in the deep end on his debut in the Grade 2 novices' hurdle at the Paddy Power meeting in November. Sent off at 5/1 behind the 7/4 favourite Heads Up – a horse with solid winning form, having beaten the subsequent dual scorer L'Evangeliste at Listowel – he travelled with the poise of a horse who belonged at this level. Sitting just behind the pace, he flicked through the tops of his hurdles like an old hand, his only blemish coming at the second last when lining up the long-time leader. Still full of running, he eased into contention approaching the final flight, touched down with purpose, and sauntered clear up the hill to win by 3 lengths from Heads Up, with King's Bucks a head further back in third.

He followed that with another polished display in the Winter Novices' Hurdle at Sandown, where he conceded a 5lb Grade 2 penalty yet still came home in a canter, putting 5 lengths between himself and The Blue Room. Once more he moved through the race with a sense of inevitability, Cobden only needing to squeeze him turning for home before he shifted up a gear and settled the matter.

The natural next step was the Grade 1 Challow Novices' Hurdle, where he encountered good ground for the first time. Aware that he did not want the race to develop into a sprint, his rider adopted different tactics, sending him forward and turning the screw from the home turn. The gelding responded generously after the penultimate flight and quickened again on the run-in to hold off Klimt Madrik and Tiptoptim. It was not as visually striking as his previous two wins, but it revealed his versatility in adapting to different ground, different tempos, and the responsibility of setting his own fractions.

He is a horse with more natural stamina than outright speed, yet he is far from slow, as he demonstrated when finding that extra gear after the last at Newbury. And while there will be improvers in the line-up, No Drama This End has already proved himself at the highest level and, crucially, has been up the hill at Cheltenham twice, which is a factor I always consider one of the most important when assessing the credentials of a young horse.

All things considered, No Drama This End brings the most complete and battle-hardened profile into the race. He has already shown he can operate at Grade 1 level, adapt to different ground and race shapes, and crucially, finish his races with purpose up the Cheltenham hill. In a division where many still have questions to answer, he arrives with fewer unknowns than most and a depth of experience that should stand him in good stead. For those reasons, he remains the one I want on my side in the Turners.

Brown Advisory Novices' Chase
WESTERN FOLD

THE Brown Advisory market shifted notably after Final Demand's defeat at the hands of Kaid d'Authie at the Dublin Racing Festival, his stable companion putting 12¼ lengths between them, with Gordon Elliott's Western Fold splitting the pair. Final Demand had been the even-money favourite to lift the trophy in March, but bookmakers have eased him to around 4/1. If the run proves too bad to be true and something later comes to light, that may yet look a fair price, but the Brown Advisory is a race that exposes any frailty, and it may be wiser to look further afield.

Kaid d'Authie would be the obvious alternative. He shapes as though the step up to 3m1f would be no inconvenience, and he may even improve for it, given his dam is a half-sister to a winner over 3m7f. He was a little novicey at Punchestown when second to Kitzbuhel and again when beating Wingmen at Fairyhouse, but he was much sharper in cheekpieces at Leopardstown. Even so, those earlier jumping lapses could resurface on quicker ground, and he was disappointing at the Festival last year when pulling up in the Turners Novices' Hurdle. Another point to factor in is that the last six-year-old to win this race was Don Poli in 2015.

Of the trio who completed the Grade 1 Novice Chase at the Dublin Racing Festival, the one I am keen to keep onside at Cheltenham is Western Fold. The Brown Advisory has long been a race that rewards the dour stayer over the flashy traveller, and **Western Fold** fits the mould of a scrapper rather than a bridle horse.

With 11 chase starts behind him, he has gathered a wealth of experience and has really come into his own since the spring. He won a beginners chase at Tipperary in May and followed up in a Listed contest at Ballinrobe less than three weeks later. Those victories lifted his mark from 138 to 148, but that did not stop him winning the Galway Plate by 4½ lengths from Jesse Evans, and he then beat the subsequent Savills Chase winner, Affordale Fury, in a Grade 2 at Gowran Park in October.

Handicaps now behind him, he stepped into Grade 1 company for the Champion Chase over 3m at Down Royal in November and ran a bold race from the front, eventually finishing third, 5¼ lengths behind Envoi Allen, with Affordale Fury reversing the form by splitting them. Freshened up, he returned to the Dublin Racing Festival on ground that was far from ideal, and although he looked in danger of being tailed off, he stayed on powerfully off the home turn and was finishing as strongly as anything at the line.

With an uncomplicated way of racing, a sound jumping technique and a depth of experience that many of his rivals lack, he makes considerable appeal in a race where several have questions to answer. Good ground would only enhance his prospects.

Against him, I hold plenty of respect for Jamie Snowden's Wendigo, who finished fifth in last year's Albert Bartlett behind Jasmin de Vaux. He was narrowly denied on his chasing debut at Worcester, then produced a polished round of jumping to beat No Questions Asked in the Grade 2 John Francome Novices' Chase at Newbury, staying on strongly to the line. Kempton proved a shade sharp for him on Boxing Day, yet he still finished his race off well to be 3¾ lengths behind Kitzbuhel. A spin around Ayr over 3m should have tightened him up for Cheltenham, and he arrives with a solid each-way chance.

No Drama This End wins at Cheltenham in November

Grand Annual Handicap Chase
HIGHLANDS LEGACY

BY THE time the Grand Annual comes around on Wednesday, we will hopefully have already seen Mambonumberfive produce a career-best effort to win the Racing Post Arkle Novices' Chase on the opening day, and should that prove the case it would only reinforce the appeal of **Highlands Legacy**, whose form ties in so closely with Ben Pauling's gelding and who looks a compelling candidate for what is always a fiercely competitive 2m handicap chase.

Jonjo and A J O'Neill's seven-year-old never really cut the mustard as a hurdler, winning only once in maiden company in April 2024 before being overturned at short odds in a run-of-the-mill novices' hurdle at Worcester a couple of months later. After that run he was not seen again until January 2025, with connections evidently feeling there was little point in launching a chasing campaign in the second half of the season, so he remained over hurdles, running four more times but failing to add to his tally before signing off on a mark of 115.

A chaser on looks, the switch to fences at the start of this term has been the making of him, and he struck at the first time of asking at Worcester in early October. There he beat Escapeandevade by 2 lengths, which has worked out to be a strong piece of form with the runner-up since finishing a decent second to David's Well at Haydock before returning to that venue to beat the subsequent winner Sunnyvilla.

Seventeen days later, Highlands Legacy headed to Aintree from a 6lb higher mark but despite finishing second, he ran a career-best behind the then 128-rated Mambonumberfive, who was receiving the 7lb age allowance as a four-year-old. Highlands Legacy was beaten only three parts of a length, but I was taken with how powerfully he travelled before keeping on strongly to pass the subsequent December Gold Cup winner Gengouly in the shadows of the post, while the subsequent three-time winner Jour d'Evasion was just shy of 9 lengths further behind in fifth.

Raised another 3lb to a rating of 124, Highlands Legacy then contested a strong novices' handicap chase at Newbury in December and again emerged with plenty of credit when finishing second to the then 129-rated Mighty Bandit, whose form also ties in closely with Mambonumberfive, having finished second to him at the Coral Gold Cup meeting. Highlands Legacy travelled strongly throughout but was a little sticky over the fourth last and then landed awkwardly over the penultimate fence, a minor error that cost him momentum at a crucial stage. Even so, he stuck to his task and closed the deficit on the run-in without ever quite looking likely to reel in the winner, eventually crossing the line 1¾ lengths adrift.

Again, that form has since been emphatically boosted, with Mighty Bandit winning by 8 lengths at Doncaster. His rating has been elevated to 142, while Lookaway (third in that race) has since won an incident-packed race at Kempton by 24 lengths and is now rated 139.

Another 3lb rise to 127 followed, and Highlands Legacy headed to Windsor on Berkshire Winter Million weekend, where he confirmed the Newbury form with Torneo, who had finished 2¾ lengths behind him when fourth. Despite Torneo enjoying a 4lb pull in the weights this time, Highlands Legacy still found enough to beat him a head, again showing a willing attitude off the bridle to pull out extra in the dying strides, having travelled powerfully throughout.

Form cannot always be taken literally, but all four of Highlands Legacy's chase starts stand up to close scrutiny, and his new mark of 133 still looks well within his scope. A strong traveller with tactical pace to hold his position, he is also a sound jumper and should be able to sit just off the pace before plotting a passage coming down the hill.

Confident that he not only has the speed for the 2m trip but will also stay further in time, the gelding appeals as a horse who can finish powerfully up the hill. Being a novice with only the four starts over fences, he's still relatively unexposed and I am confident that there is still more to come. At around 20/1 at the time of writing, he makes plenty of appeal.

Jonjo & A J O'Neill

RYANAIR MARES' NOVICES' HURDLE (Dawn Run)

2m 179y (Grade 2) – New Course

OVERVIEW

WE HAVE now had 10 runnings of the Dawn Run Mares' Novices' Hurdle, which for the first time last year, was moved to open the card on day three. Yet another race which has been dominated by Willie Mullins (to begin with, at least), he won the first five renewals, whilst Henry de Bromhead has won two of the past five. Given that the race takes place over a trip just shy of 2m1f on the New Course, stamina is important and form over slightly further appears to be a positive. Prior to the past couple of years, winning form at Graded level seemed hugely important, whilst unbeaten mares have won three of the past four renewals, although last year's winner was very inexperienced, successful on just her second hurdles start.

MULLINS WAS THE MAN

DURING the first five renewals of the race, trainer **Willie Mullins** was very much the man to follow here, winning each and every running between 2016 and 2020. Usually well represented, his seven runners failed to hit the frame last year, taking his tally in the race to 5-34. Surprisingly, after saddling the first and second in both 2019 and 2020, Mullins has only had one mare hit the frame in the past five years, that being Grangee, who finished third in 2022. Both Mullins and his sources (usually in France) know exactly what is required when it comes to recruiting a high-class mare and as a result, I would expect him to return to the winners' enclosure in this event before too long.

Bambino Fever looks to be the leading contender from the Mullins stable, with last year's Champion Bumper winner heading the ante-post market at the time of writing.

IRISH DOMINATION

AFTER three successive British-trained winning mares, it was a case of normal service being resumed in 2025 as *Air Of Entitlement* scored for the Irish, providing **Henry de Bromhead** with a second win in the race in the space of five years, following on from *Telmesomethinggirl* in 2021. Another trainer who excels with mares, in general – Honeysuckle being a prime example – de Bromhead has also been responsible for the runner-up in 2021 (saddled the one-two that year) and 2023, and the third in 2024. During the past five years, he has saddled 12 mares, so two winners and three placed efforts is a fine return. His record could have been greater, had the aforementioned dual Champion Hurdle winner not been ruled out through injury in 2019 and runners from his stable warrant careful consideration.

One leading Irish trainer who has yet to strike here is **Gordon Elliott**, who was actually without a runner last year. His record, therefore, remains at 0-9 and although he has had a second, third and fourth over the years, he saw Brighterdaysahead beaten at short odds just two years ago.

EXPERIENCE IS OFTEN KEY

THE word *'often'* is important in this subheading, as it certainly wasn't important last year, *Air Of Entitlement* successful on the back of just one previous run over hurdles. We have, however, seen experience to be a positive in earlier years, with six of the previous nine winners having run four times or more over hurdles, with *Let's Dance* (9 runs) and

Telmesomethinggirl (8) the most experienced of all. Four of the five winners between 2017 and 2021 were second-season novices, so don't see experience as a barrier to success, often it can be advantageous.

PREVIOUS FESTIVAL FORM
TWO of those second-season novice winners had actually run at the Festival over hurdles the previous year. *Let's Dance* had finished fourth in the Triumph Hurdle and remained a maiden into the following campaign, whilst *Concertista* actually finished runner-up in this race on her hurdling debut the year before she landed the prize.

Fifth in last year's Triumph Hurdle, Place de La Nation had looked like being a contender for this until being beaten at Fairyhouse recently. The aforementioned Bambino Fever looks to win at back-to-back Festivals (heads the ante-post market at the time of going to print) and both mares - like the two mentioned in the previous paragraph - are trained by Willie Mullins.

BRITISH-BRED SUCCESS
PRIOR to 2023, British-bred mares had a poor record in this race. However, the back-to-back wins of *You Wear It Well* and *Golden Ace* means that such runners now have a much more respectable record, with it standing at 2-31 after the 2024 renewal. There wasn't one single British-bred runner last year and although the negative trend still appears in the *Key Trends* table, it is by no means such the negative as it was between 2016 and 2022.

THE FRENCH CONNECTION
THIS coincided with the period of Willie Mullins dominance and as we have seen over the years, Mullins (and his French sources) are highly capable of finding top-class mares over in France. Four of the first five winners were French-bred and all five had run in France before moving to Ireland. We see this kind of dominance among the juvenile hurdlers but it is clearly evident with Mullins-trained mares, too. Pay healthy respect to any of his runners with this profile/background.

GRADED FORM
FIVE of the first eight winners had won a Graded race earlier in the season, in fact all five had won a Grade 2 or Grade 3 on their most recent start. Prior to last year, the record of mares having won a Graded race last time out stood at a highly respectable 5-15, although Aurora Vega and Hollygrove Cha Cha failed to enhance this, taking the tally to 5-17.

KEY TRENDS
- ★ Mares unbeaten during the current season and won a Graded race last time boast a record of 4-8
- ★ 7 of the 10 winners were trained in Ireland
- ★ The first 5 winners were trained by Willie Mullins
- ✓ All 10 winners were aged 5 or 6
- ✓ 8 of the 10 winners had won over 2m2f or further
- ✓ 6 of the 10 winners returned at 15-2 or shorter
- ✓ 6 of the 10 winners had run at least 4 times over hurdles
- ✓ 6 of the 10 winners were unbeaten during the season
- ✓ 5 of the 10 winners started their careers in France
- ✓ 5 of the 10 winners won a Graded race last time out (record 5-17)
- ✓ 4 of the 10 winners were French-bred
- ✓ 4 of the 10 winners were second-season novices (2 had run at the previous season's Festival)
- ✓ The past 4 winners won a bumper
- ✓ 2 of the past 5 winners were trained by Henry de Bromhead
- ✗ 7yo's are 0-26
- ✗ Nicky Henderson-trained mares are 0-13
- ✗ JP McManus-owned mares are 0-12
- ✗ Gordon Elliott-trained mares are 0-9
- ✗ 4yo fillies are 0-9
- ✗ Alan King-trained mares are 0-6
- ✗ Gigginstown House Stud-owned mares are 0-5
- ✗ British-bred mares are 2-31
- ✗ Only 2 of the 10 winners were ex-Pointers
- ✗ Only 1 of the 10 winners had failed to at least place over at least 2m2f (or further)

It is worth remembering that the penalty structure was removed from this race in 2025, so moving forward, Grade 2 winners will no longer have to carry a penalty and all mares – except for any four-year-old fillies (age allowance) – will carry the same weight.

KEY GRADED RACES
THE aforementioned pairing of Aurora Vega and Hollygrove Cha Cha had actually won two of the more notable races earlier in the calendar. The last named had won Sandown's Grade 2 **Jane Seymour Mares' Novices' Hurdle**, a race sponsored by the *Cheltenham Betting Festival Guide*, incidentally, and one that was also won by both *Love Envoi* and *You Wear It Well* the month before Festival glory. This year's race, which had been brought forward, was re-routed to Warwick and won by Kingston Queen.

Aurora Vega had won the **Solerina Mares Novice Hurdle**, a Grade 3 contest which has been won by both *Limini* and *Laurina* en route to Cheltenham. Staged over 2m2f at Fairyhouse, this year's rearranged contest was won in impressive fashion by Oldschool Outlaw, who had earlier beaten Bambino Fever on debut. Both the 2023 and 2024 winner of the Solerina went on to win the Grade 1 Honeysuckle Mares Novice Hurdle, back at Fairyhouse, at their Easter Festival, as did Honeysuckle herself. It is clearly a piece of form to note with the spring in mind.

OTHER KEY RACE

AWAY from the Graded action and the other race to feature in the *Leading Ten-Year Guides* section of the *Roll Of Honour* is the **Irish Stallion Farms EBF Paddy Mullins Mares Handicap Hurdle**, which takes place at the Dublin Racing Festival. *Concertista* and *Telmesomethinggirl* both finished third in that hotly-contested handicap and perhaps, the hustle and bustle of that kind of race stands a mare in good stead (experience wise) ahead of this big field novice event. Any This year's race was won by the improving novice Cousin Kate, who is now rated 131 and could be aimed at the Dawn Run.

FORM OVER FURTHER

THE New Course at Cheltenham can often result in a demanding finish and indeed, last year's winner appeared to outstay the runner-up on the long climb to the line. *Air Of Entitlement* had won her maiden hurdle over 2m4f at Down Royal and in doing so, became the eighth winner (of the 10) to have won over a trip of 2m2f or further. Significantly, those three *Key Races* highlighted in the previous two subsections are run over 2m2f-2m4f and having that kind of proven stamina is clearly important. Only one winner to date hadn't at least placed over a trip of 2m2f+ so pay close attention to those with form over an intermediate trip.

UNBEATEN THIS SEASON

SIX of the 10 winners to date were unbeaten during the current season, with three of the past four winners unbeaten over hurdles. *Air Of Entitlement* had run just the once, but the others had run a minimum of twice over hurdles and *Love Envoi* boasted a tremendous 4-4 record ahead of her win, four years ago. Both *Let's Dance* and *Laurina* had been beaten either the previous season or in their native France, but during the current campaign, were both also unbeaten.

When combining an unbeaten mare with one who had won a Graded race on their most recent start, the record stands at a hugely noteworthy 4-8 and there were no such qualifiers last year. Respect any such runners this time around.

NATIONAL HUNT BACKGROUND

ALTHOUGH it still remains a negative on the *Key Trends* table, *Air Of Entitlement* became the second Point-to-Point winner to win this race and given that *Love Envoi* had won a Point-to-Point Bumper (during Covid-19 when restrictions were in place), it is possible that this trend will continue to improve, especially as we see more and more high-class mares appear from the Pointing ranks.

You Wear It Well was a dual bumper winner, *Golden Ace* had won on debut before finishing runner-up in the Grade 2 Nickel Coin at Aintree and last year's winner was successful in a Cork bumper on Rules debut, so a traditional *National Hunt Background* is very much favourable.

AGE

ALL 10 winners were aged either five or six, with the first four being aged five, possibly due to those French imports being slightly more precocious types. Galileo Dame became the ninth four-year-old filly to take her chance last year (finished 6th when sent off at just 9-2), whilst there were a couple of seven-year-olds in the field, taking the record of that age group to 0-26. Aurora Vega was one of the seven-year-olds to run last year and she was sent off at 9-1, so two of the top four in the market appeared to be up against it from an *Age* perspective. Focus on those aged five and six.

MARKET FORCES

DURING the first six renewals, only *Eglantine du Seuil* won at odds greater than 5-1, with her returning at the huge price of 50-1. The first three winners were sent off as favourite, two of those returning at odds-on, whilst we have seen three double-figure priced winners of late. Considering her lack of experience, it wasn't a shock to see *Air Of Entitlement* return at 16-1, and the race, in general, seems to be increasing in terms of strength in depth from a quality perspective, whilst those early renewals were probably weaker contests.

NOTABLE OWNERS

HAVING won the first two renewals, with *Limini* and *Let's Dance*, **Mrs Susannah Ricci** is an owner to respect, especially as she has only had two runners in the eight renewals since, so boasts a fine strike rate of 50% (2-4).

We no longer see the colours of Sullivan Bloodstock Limited – responsible for the next two winners

– in National Hunt racing. Whilst **Kenneth Alexander** has only managed to win one renewal to date, he has seen his Halka du Tabert finish third and has had a plethora of runners in recent years. Given his breeding operation, this is only likely to continue and his runners in this race should be respected as a result.

And, as highlighted in the past couple of editions, both **JP McManus** and **Gigginstown House Stud** are leading owners who have yet to land this prize. McManus had two runners last year, taking his tally to 0-12 – with the dozen including subsequent Champion Hurdle winner Epatante – and Gigginstown had the one runner, taking their tally to the slightly less disappointing 0-6.

BRITISH TRAINERS TO NOTE

ALL three British trainers to have won this race have been selective in terms of runners thus far and given that **Jamie Snowden** has won the aforementioned *Key Race*, the Jane Seymour Mares' Novices' Hurdle, on three occasions since 2021, it is obvious that he knows how to handle a high-class young mare. A winner in Listed company in November, La Conquiere is a likely contender for the Snowden stable this year.

Both Snowden and **Harry Fry** have only had two runners apiece in the race to date, with the latter also having won the Grade 1 Honeysuckle Mares Novice Hurdle at Fairyhouse some 11 years ago with Bitofapuzzle, who had run in the Mares' Hurdle as a novice on her previous start (would likely have run here had the race been in place a year earlier).

Golden Ace was the very first runner for **Jeremy Scott** and as he was unrepresented last year, he boasts a 100% strike rate in the race to date.

Nicky Henderson was again without representation in 2025, so his dismal record stands at 0-13, whilst **Alan King** is another trainer who does well (in general) with mares, but is 0-6 here, despite saddling Dusky Legend to twice hit the frame (in each of the first two renewals). Henderson's *'losers'* include Luccia (sent off 6-4 in 2023) and the aforementioned future Champion Hurdler, Epatante.

Paul Nicholls saddled two last year and has actually only had four runners in the race in total, so it is difficult to be too critical of his record at this stage, but none of the four have gone close and the quartet does include Posh Trish (sent off 3-1 in 2019) and Jubilee Alpha, who was a 15-2 chance in 2025. Both mares finished only eighth.

Jamie Snowden

ROLL OF HONOUR

Year	Form	Winner	Age	Weight	OR	SP	Trainer	Runners	Last Race (No. of days)
2025	1	Air Of Entitlement	6	11-4	-	16/1	H de Bromhead (IRE)	23	1st Down Royal Maiden Hurdle (77)
2024	11	Golden Ace	6	11-2	124	10/1	J Scott	8	1st Taunton Mares' Nov. Hurdle (37)
2023	1121	You Wear It Well	6	11-7	135	16/1	J Snowden	21	1st Gr.2 Sandown Nov. Hurdle (28)
2022	1111	Love Envoi	6	11-7	135	15/2	H Fry	19	1st Gr.2 Sandown Nov. Hurdle (28)
2021	13113	Telmesomethinggirl	6	11-2	136	5/1	H de Bromhead (IRE)	15	3rd Leopardstown h'cap hurdle (39)
2020	433	Concertista	6	11-2	141	9/2	W Mullins (IRE)	22	3rd Leopardstown h'cap hurdle (39)
2019	13	Eglantine du Seuil	5	11-2	-	50/1	W Mullins (IRE)	22	3rd Listowel Nov. Hurdle (180)
2018	11	Laurina	5	11-7	144	4/7F	W Mullins (IRE)	14	1st Gr.3 Fairyhouse Nov. Hurdle (48)
2017	21111	Let's Dance	5	11-7	147	11/8F	W Mullins (IRE)	16	1st Gr.2 Nathaniel Lacy Nov. Hurdle (46)
2016	11	Limini	5	11-7	145	8/11F	W Mullins (IRE)	16	1st Gr.3 Fairyhouse Nov. Hurdle (47)

LEADING TEN-YEAR GUIDES

Paddy Mullins Mares Handicap Hurdle 2 (*Concertista* 3rd, *Telmesomethinggirl* 3rd)
Jane Seymour Mares' Novices' Hurdle 2 (*Love Envoi* 1st, *You Wear It Well* 1st)

JACK RICHARDS NOVICES' LIMITED HANDICAP CHASE (Golden Miller)

2m4f 127y (Grade 2 Limited Handicap) – New Course

OVERVIEW

ARGUABLY the most significant – and, perhaps importantly, the best received – change ahead of the 2025 Cheltenham Festival was the return of the novices' handicap chase. The Grade 1 Golden Miller Novices' Chase (run latterly as the *Turners*') was removed and the former *'Centenary'* Novices' Handicap Chase reinstated after just a four-year hiatus. Previously a 0-140 contest, the upper ceiling was increased in 2018 and the revamped race now has no upper ceiling (as was the case briefly when the race was originally introduced), which meant the ill-fated Springwell Bay was able to shoulder top-weight from a lofty mark of 154 last year.

A NEWLY SHAPED HANDICAP

GIVEN that there is no upper ceiling, we could continue to see horses rated in the 150s aimed at this, should their connections believe this to be the right trip for them. With no Graded option over an intermediate distance, connections of such horses would either need to step up to 3m to contest the Broadway, or alternatively, wait for Aintree, where there are Grade 1 novice chases over a variety of distances, including the 2m4f Manifesto. In theory, this should increase the quality across the board and this race was certainly full of quality last year. Long may that continue.

CENTENARY IS NO MORE

BETWEEN 2021 and 2024, the *'Centenary'* actually took place at Sandown on Imperial Cup day, just three days before the Festival would get underway. However, it was never as hotly-contested as the original Festival race and in truth, the race bared little resemblance. As a consequence, these results have not been included in either the Roll Of Honour or used towards the Key Trends, which focus solely on the runnings of the race at the Cheltenham Festival.

SWAPPING OLD FOR NEW

WITH the race now taking place on day three, the novices' handicap is now staged on the more expansive New Course, having previously been staged on day one and on the Old Course. You would, therefore, imagine that it should now favour those with a little more stamina, and this should be a consideration when looking at past results (prior to last year) and the Key Trends table. It is unlikely to have a huge impact, however, on the trends.

OFFICIAL BHA RATINGS AND WEIGHTS

AS WITH all of the handicaps throughout the week, the table illustrates the highest-rated runner, as well as the official BHA Rating of the bottom weight (gives you an idea of what will be required to get into the race) and that of the winner. As already touched upon, with the upper ceiling once again removed – there was actually no upper ceiling in the very early days of the race (Big Buck's actually ran here off 148 with a young Nick Scholfield taking off 7lb) before the 140, then 145 bracket came in – this is one trend that will likely be changeable. Caldwell Potter proved successful from a mark of 147 last year, making him the highest-rated winner of the race, but that view is skewered somewhat, in that a horse of his class would previously have been ineligible for many years.

In terms of weight carried, last year's winner carried 11-4, due to the presence of the high-class Springwell Bay at the top of the handicap. Prior to last year, seven of the previous nine winners carried 11-7 or more and were clearly found towards the top end of the handicap, but if horses rated in the 150s continue to take their chance, we could see the average weight carried drop, despite the classier horses contesting the race. This will likely take a few years to form a more balanced set of results.

Back to official ratings briefly and 11 of the past 12 winners were rated 137 or higher, with the past three winners now rated 143 or higher. The classier horses were beginning to dominate the race as a 0-145 contest and I suspect that might continue with the race in the new format.

	Top Weight (OR)	Bottom OR	Winner OR
2025	154	134	147
This race was not contested between 2021 and 2024			
2020	145	139	143
2019	145	138	144
2018	145	137	137
2017	142	137	138
2016	140	136	140
2015	140	135	137
2014	140	132	137
2013	140	132	140
2012	142	132	142

TIMEFORM NOVICES' HANDICAP CHASE

PRIOR to the race being reintroduced in 2025, four of the previous eight winners had contested the **Timeform Novices' Handicap Chase** on trials day. Now staged over the same course-and-distance (New Course), *Mister Whitaker* completed the double in 2018, whilst *Irish Cavalier* and *Imperial Aura* both hit the frame. *Imperial Aura* finished runner-up in a really strong renewal in 2020, with him winning this race and the winner, Simply The Betts, going on to win the 'Plate'.

Stage Star won the 2023 Timeform-sponsored race before winning the now defunct Grade 1 Golden Miller and last year's winner, Jagwar, is another who returned to win with the 'Plate' having been ante-post favourite for this race for long parts of the season. More on that race choice shortly, but as you can see, the trials day event is a hugely significant piece of form and should be taken very seriously. Last year's

KEY TRENDS

- 4 of the past 9 winners ran in the Timeform Novices' Handicap Chase on trials day
- 9 of the past 15 winners had won a P2P and/or a bumper
- The past 3 winners were rated 143+
- 14 of the 17 winners finished 1st or 2nd last time out
- 13 of the 17 winners were aged 6 or 7
- 13 of the past 14 winners had run 3 or 4 times over fences
- 12 of the past 13 winners were trained in Britain
- 11 of the 17 winners returned at 9-1 or shorter
- 11 of the past 12 winners were rated 137+
- 10 of the 17 winners had won just once over fences
- 7 of the past 10 winners carried 11-7+
- 7 of the past 11 winners had run at the track earlier in the season
- 6 of the 17 winners had run at the previous year's Festival over hurdles
- 4 of the past 6 winners ran in a Graded novice chase last time out
- Brian Hughes has ridden the winner twice (and a 2nd) from just 5 rides
- Paul Nicholls has won the race twice
- Only 1 of the 17 winners had won more than twice over fences
- Only 2 of the 17 winners were older than 7
- Only 2 of the 17 winners were aged 5
- Only 2 of the 17 winners returned at odds greater than 12-1
- Only 2 of the 17 winners failed to record a top-3 finish last time out
- Only 2 of the 17 winners were Irish-trained

race also featured the subsequent bet365 Gold Cup winner, Resplendent Grey (4th), and Masaccio (3rd) also won a valuable spring prize, at Ayr's Scottish Grand National fixture.

This year's race was won by Jordans Cross, who came from off the pace to run down Quebecois. The pair could re-oppose at the Festival.

CHASING EXPERIENCE

13 OF THE past 14 winners had run three (7) or four (6) times over fences previously, with the past three all having run the minimum three times in order to be eligible. The important thing here is that the minimum requirement remained at three runs for this race but should a novice wish to run in an open handicap, a fourth run is required. The aforemen-

tioned Jagwar had gained that fourth run on trials day, which allowed his connections the option of making the late switch to the *'Plate'* and whilst many would think running in an open handicap to be a more difficult assignment for a lightly-raced novice, it has to be remembered that you are much less likely to run into an equally progressive and well-handicapped performer. Indeed, last year's winner won a Grade 1 on his next start at Aintree, whereas you are highly unlikely to come across such a smart and improving performer in the *'Plate'*. Take this into account when looking at this race in advance.

WINNING EXPERIENCE
10 OF THE 17 winners – including the past three – had won just once over fences previously. Three maiden chasers have also won this race, so again, this goes some way towards protecting a handicap mark ahead of the Festival. *Hunt Ball* was very much an exception to the rule (many rules, in fact), with him having won four of his six chase starts, making him the one and only winner of this race to have won more than twice over fences previously.

NOT REALLY A RACE FOR THE IRISH (SO FAR)
THE Tom Taaffe-trained *Finger Onthe Pulse* struck for the Irish in 2008, but during the past 13 renewals, Alan Flemming's *Tully East* is the only Irish-trained winner. Irish-trained horses finished second, third and fourth behind *Caldwell Potter* in 2025 and with there no longer an upper ceiling on the race, this suspect record could be in danger, with better quality horses now able to take their chance. For now, however, it remains a race in which the Irish have struggled.

TWO UP FOR NICHOLLS
WITH *Caldwell Potter* providing **Paul Nicholls** with a second win in the race – his first coming courtesy of another grey, *Chapoturgeon*, back in 2009 – the former champion trainer became just the second trainer to record more than one victory in the race to date, the other being the late-Ferdy Murphy.

The original novices' handicap chase was actually renowned for providing a widespread of various winners, with several trainers breaking their Cheltenham Festival maiden tag in this race. It has certainly been a much more open race than many throughout the week in this regard.

AGE
ONLY two of the 17 winners were over the age of seven, those being *Copper Bleu* and *Ballyalton*, successful at ages eight and nine, respectively. 13 of the 17 winners were aged either six (4) or seven (9) with the latter clearly the prime average age. As for *'younger'* winners of the race, *Chapoturgeon* was successful as a five-year-old in 2009 and more recently, subsequent Gold Cup winner *A Plus Tard* also won this race at the age of five.

10 of last year's 19 runners were aged eight or older, whilst the fourth-placed Nurburgring (received a 2lb age allowance) was the sole five-year-old in the field. At this stage, it can pay to focus on those aged six and even more so, seven.

MARKET FORCES
PRIOR to last year, the previous two winners justified favouritism, although there had only been two earlier successful favourites, those being *Reveillez* in 2006 and *Hunt Ball* in 2012. Plenty of other winners could have been found just behind the market leader, however, with 11 of the 17 winners returning at single figure odds. We have only seen two winners return at odds greater than 12-1, so for a competitive handicap, it does tend to go to a horse towards the top of the market and does appear to be quite a *'punter friendly'* contest, despite its nature.

DROPPING IN CLASS
WE SAW a couple of winners during the first four renewals win this race on the back of having run in Grade 2 novice chases and it has become more common place again in the past six renewals. Four of those past six winners had contested a Graded novice chase on their most recent start, with *Caldwell Potter* having finished runner-up to Gidleigh Park in the Lightning Novices' Chase at Windsor. In fact, five of those six winners had finished second in a Grade 2 or Grade 3, with *Ballyalton* a faller in the Reynoldstown at Ascot. Given that I expect the quality to continue to rise, or certainly repeat last year and remain of a high standard, this could be an important trend moving forward.

OTHER KEY RACES
PRIOR to running in the Timeform Novices' Handicap Chase on trials day, both *Rajdhani Express* (1st) and *Mister Whitaker* (2nd) had run in Kempton's **Ladbrokes Novices' Handicap Chase**, a similar contest which can also often be quite informative. The Boxing Day contest was reduced to a 0-130 this season, so might have less of an impact moving forward, but it was won in good style by Olly Murphy's Barlovento.

Remaining at Kempton, both *Hunt Ball* and *Present View* won on Adonis Hurdle day (after the

Guide was sent to print) in a race staged last year as the **Ladbrokes 'Get Rewarded With Ladbrokes' Handicap Chase** and was won by Bad, who bypassed Cheltenham but returned to the Sunbury venue the day after the Gold Cup to win what was once the consolation race. Take note of this year's winner, especially – if like *Present View* – a win was required in order for them to be rated high enough to get into this race.

CURRENT FORM

ARRIVING at Cheltenham on the back of a positive run seems to be important, with only two of the 17 winners having failed to record a top-three finish last time. *Ballyalton* was a faller, so only *Rajdhani Express* finished out of the frame (7th in the Timeform Novices' Handicap on trials day), whilst 14 of the 17 winners actually finished either first (7) or second (7) on their latest start. Four of the past five winners headed to Cheltenham having finished runner-up last time out.

HUGHES THE MAN

AS HAS been highlighted in previous editions of the Guide, **Brian Hughes** has won this race twice from just five rides. Successful aboard both *Ballyalton* and *Mister Whitaker*, he was narrowly denied in 2014 aboard Attaglance, whilst his 2017 mount, Double W's, appeared to be a non-stayer and duly dropped in distance to win the Red Rum at Aintree next time. Hughes was again without a ride last year and clearly boasts a tremendous strike rate in it, with his quiet and patient style clearly well suited to the hurly burly of a truly-run Festival handicap.

OTHER TRAINERS TO NOTE

ASIDE from Paul Nicholls (covered in an earlier subsection), there is no current trainer with a noteworthy record in this race. However, I suspect that with there being no upper ceiling, the leading trainers will start to target the race more regularly, with it noticeable that both Willie Mullins and Gordon Elliott each ran three horses last year. Time will tell in this regard, but I suspect the new format will allow the more powerful yards to have a say, as they look to split up their novice chasers.

COURSE FORM

OBVIOUSLY, the impressive record of runners from the Timeform-sponsored race on trials day helps this statistic but nevertheless, seven of the past 11 winners had run at Cheltenham earlier in the season. *Imperial Aura* actually twice finished runner-up at the track before his win in the race in 2020, whilst *Caldwell Potter* finished third on his second start over fences, beaten at short odds by the subsequent Arkle winner, Jango Baie. Respect form from the track from earlier in the season, especially those who have run well and possibly, hit the frame at least.

In terms of Festival form, six of the 17 winners had run over hurdles at the previous year's fixture. Again, course form is never a negative in any race at Cheltenham, especially in these competitive handicaps.

		ROLL OF HONOUR						
Year	Form	Winner	Age	Weight	OR	SP	Trainer	Runners	Last Race (No. of days)
2025	132	Caldwell Potter	7	11-4	146	7/1	P Nicholls	19	2nd Gr.2 Lightning Nov. Chase (55)
This race was not contested between 2021 and 2024									
2020	3122	Imperial Aura	7	11 5	143	4/1F	K Bailey	20	2nd Timeform Nov. H'cap Chase (45)
2019	212	A Plus Tard	5	11 7	144	5/1F	H de Bromhead (IRE)	20	2nd Gr.3 Punchestown Nov. Chase (58)
2018	3121	Mister Whitaker	6	11 2	137	13/2	M Channon	19	1st Timeform Nov. H'cap Chase (45)
2017	162	Tully East	7	11 8	138	8/1	A Fleming (IRE)	20	2nd Gr.3 Flyingbold Nov. Chase (23)
2016	U62F	Ballyalton	9	11 10	140	12/1	I Williams	20	Fell Gr.2 Reynoldstown Nov. Chase (24)
2015	323	Irish Cavalier	6	11 7	137	11/1	R Curtis	20	3rd Timeform Nov. H'cap Chase (45)
2014	32121	Present View	6	11 7	137	8/1	J Snowden	19	1st Kempton H'cap Chase (17)
2013	2F17	Rajdhani Express	6	11 12	140	16/1	N Henderson	20	7th Timeform Nov. H'cap Chase (45)
2012	1112111	Hunt Ball	7	12 0	142	13/2F	K Burke	20	1st Kempton H'cap Chase (17)

LEADING TEN-YEAR GUIDES

Timeform Novices' Handicap Chase 4 (*Radjhani Express* 7th, *Irish Cavalier* 3rd, *Mister Whitaker* 1st, *Imperial Aura* 2nd)

Ladbrokes Novices' Handicap Chase 2 (*Rajdhani Express* 1st, *Mister Whitaker* 2nd)

Ladbrokes Handicap Chase 2 (*Hunt Ball* 1st, *Present View* 1st)

DAY THREE RACE THREE

CLOSE BROTHERS MARES' HURDLE (David Nicholson)
2m3f 200y (Grade 1) – Old Course

OVERVIEW
INTRODUCED in 2008, the Mares' Hurdle has been an Irish benefit, with no fewer than 15 of the 18 winners having been Irish trained. 11 of those were trained by Willie Mullins, who won it on six occasions with the brilliant *Quevega* and more recently, the grey *Lossiemouth* has won each of the past two renewals. Form in open Graded company against geldings is a huge positive, with the higher-rated and classier mares often able to stamp their authority on the race. Dual Champion Hurdle winner *Honeysuckle* is the biggest example of this, successful in both 2020 and 2023.

ANOTHER MULTIPLE WINNER
FOLLOWING the six straight victories of *Quevega* between 2009 and 2014, *Honeysuckle* became the second mare to win this race twice, successful in 2020 and 2023, and *Lossiemouth* became the third multiple winner last year. As you will see from the next couple of subsections, a standout performer in this division isn't a rarity and class often rises to the top. Dominant against her own sex, it is still to be confirmed if *Lossiemouth* bids for three in a row, or takes her chance in the Champion, but her participation seems likely.

IS IT A FAIR MATCH?
I OPENED with this subsection last year and following her second successive victory in the race, even the participation of *Lossiemouth* raises more than a few eyebrows. This time last year, it was unclear as to whether she would line up here in an attempt to defend her crown, or take on the boys in the Champion Hurdle. To the annoyance of many, she ran here. And, despite winning easily, left a bitter taste, with many believing that there should now be some sort of ceiling on this race, forcing mares of her ability into the Champion. That debate will, no doubt, roll on, but as things stand, a mare of her class is eligible to run and by the rules of the game, her connections did nothing wrong. When we look at the next subsection, you will see that is clear that a high-class mare can dominate this race (and division) and this is the reason why people call for a possible 150-rated ceiling. Or a ruling which states if you have won an open Grade 1, you are no longer eligible for the race. Breeders will disagree and the debate will wrangle on.

OFFICIAL BHA RATINGS
12 OF THE 18 winners to date were rated 153 or higher prior to the race, which again shows a class advantage. *Lossiemouth* was top-rated on 155 ahead of her win in 2024 and had reached an official BHA Rating of 160 prior to last year's win. *Honeysuckle* was top-rated on 159 in 2023, so the past three winners were clear in this regard. *Lossiemouth* was 9lb clear of the field last year and duly beat stablemate and second-best (rated 151) Jade de Grugy by 7 lengths. Overall, nine of the 18 winners were clear top-rated.

At the other end of the scale, we have seen just three winners rated below 147 (and only two in the past 17 years) and we really should be leaning towards those rated in the 150s and above.

MULLINS' DREAM 11

HIS record with mares in general is a fantastic one, but **Willie Mullins** really has dominated this race almost since inception. Without a runner in the very first renewal (2008), he won nine of the next 10 runnings of the Mares' Hurdle, with only *Apple's Jade* breaking his stranglehold. And, as we all know, he trained that mare the previous season (and sourced her from France) before the split – which has since been resolved – between himself and Gigginstown House Stud. He would almost certainly have won the 2019 renewal, too, had *Benie des Dieux* (who would have been Another Multiple Winner) not fallen at the final flight and after five years without a win in the race, *Lossiemouth* has provided wins number 10 and 11, respectively.

Mullins, aided by bloodstock supremo Harold Kirk and others over in France, knows exactly the type of mare required to win these top-level races and his record in the Dawn Run also speaks volumes (won the first five renewals of that novices' contest). He saddled three last year, with 66-1 shot Gala Marceau falling, and was responsible for the one-two, with the Exacta paying £5.10. Pay utmost respect to his chosen runner(s) again this year.

MORE RICHES FOR RICCI

LOSSIEMOUTH (last year) became owner **Mrs Susannah Ricci's** fourth winner of the Mares' Hurdle since 2016 and she has only had 10 runners in the race, during the past 11 years. A further three hit the frame, whilst 2018 winner *Benie des Dieux* would almost certainly have gone back-to-back but for falling 12 months later, suffering a similar fate to that of subsequent Champion Hurdle winner, Annie Power, who was clear when famously coming down in 2015. Ricci's impressive record of 4-10 could easily have read 6-10 and her silks are synonymous with high-class mares.

IRISH DOMINATION

THE record of Willie Mullins clearly plays a massive role but in general, the Irish have dominated this race since 2009. The very first renewal went the way of Donald McCain's novice *Whiteoak* and there was actually only one Irish-trained mare in the field. Since then, however, only *Roksana* (Dan Skelton) and *Marie's Rock* (Nicky Henderson) have struck for British trainers and the former was somewhat fortunate by virtue of the fall of *Benie des Dieux*.

Henry de Bromhead has won the race twice – albeit with *Honeysuckle* on each occasion – and was also responsible for the runner-up in 2024. He has also twice won the Dawn Run in the past five years so is another trainer who does well with mares, in general.

KEY TRENDS

- ★ 16 of the 18 winners had won against geldings (13 of which had won in Grade 1 or Grade 2 company)
- ★ 15 of the 18 winners were trained in Ireland
- ★ 11 of the 18 winners were trained by Willie Mullins
- ★ Susannah Ricci-owned runners are 4-10 during the past 11 years (another 3 placed)
- ✓ 14 of the 18 winners were aged 5-7
- ✓ 13 of the 18 winners won last time out
- ✓ 12 of the 18 winners were rated 153+
- ✓ 11 of the 18 winners were French-bred
- ✓ 11 of the 18 winners had won or placed at the Cheltenham Festival previously
- ✓ Respect form over further
- ✓ Respect Kenneth Alexander-owned mares
- ✗ Only 2 of the 18 winners had failed to win over a minimum of 2m4f
- ✗ Only 3 of the 18 winners were rated below 147
- ✗ Only 4 of the 18 winners returned at odds greater than 6-1
- ✗ Quevega & Honeysuckle are the only winners over the age of 7
- ✗ Winners of the previous year's Dawn Run Novices' Hurdle are 0-5
- ✗ Be wary of ex-Flat performers

And, although **Gordon Elliott** has (officially) only won the race once, *Black Tears* was also trained out of Cullentra House whilst he was serving his enforced suspension in 2021. Queens Brook has twice hit the frame since for the Elliott team and runners from either stable should also be respected.

In total, 15 of the 18 winners were trained in Ireland and all 15 were trained by Mullins or de Bromhead, or trained out of Cullentra House.

BREEDING

NINE of the 11 winners between 2009 and 2020 were French-bred and although *Quevega* winning the race on six occasions might not help give a true reflection, such mares still won three of the five renewals between 2016 and 2020. And, of course, *Lossiemouth* is French-bred, so that is now 11 of the 18 winners in total, so such runners should be given serious consideration, for all that their representation, last year at least, was significant (6/10 were French-bred).

British-bred mares once struggled here but thanks to the victories of *Honeysuckle* (twice) and *Black Tears*, it is no longer the negative trend that it once was. Interestingly, You Wear It Well and Golden Ace were recent back-to-back British-bred winners of the Dawn Run, so it might be something worth monitoring, particularly given that they would have nowhere near the representation (numerically) of the Irish- or French-bred mares.

STAMINA REQUIRED

YOU could argue against this trend now, with both *Honeysuckle* and *Lossiemouth* fully effective over the minimum trip. However, that pairing are/were clearly a class above the opposition and would likely have won this race over any distance ranging from 2m-2m5f. Those dual winners aside, plenty of previous winners of this race had shown form over further and prior to the first win of *Lossiemouth* – who at the time hadn't raced beyond 2m1f – having won over a minimum distance of 2m4f was almost a pre-requisite. *Whiteoak* was the only other winner of the race who had yet to win over this sort of trip and being a speedy novice, she would likely have been aimed at the Dawn Run if that race was in existence at the time.

Perhaps, therefore, the stamina angle is more significant when there isn't a clear standout performer in the division. *Quevega* was a multiple winner over 3m (after her first success) and *Roksana* was a stayer, so don't be put off by form over 3m.

NATIONAL HUNT BACKGROUND

ALTHOUGH she was sent hurdling at the age of three, *Benie des Dieux* had raced on the Flat in France and is the sole ex-Flat winner of this race to date. Such runners – certainly genuine ex-Flat horses (not French imports) – should be overlooked, in favour of a more traditional *National Hunt Background*.

Glens Melody, *Black Tears* and *Marie's Rock* were all bumper winners before going hurdling, so if looking away from a French recruit, form in that division is an obvious positive. Interestingly, *Honeysuckle* is the only winner of the race to have started life as a Point-to-Pointer, something which I suspect will change in the future but for now at least, it certainly isn't a positive.

FORM AGAINST GELDINGS

NO FEWER than 16 of the 18 winners had won a race of some sort against the boys, with 13 of those having recorded a victory in at least one open Grade 1 or Grade 2. This is a very strong statistic and one which needs to be paid close attention to. Invariably, open races – in particular Graded races – will be much stronger than mares' only contests. If a mare is up to holding her own, or in fact beating, decent geldings, it will stand them in very good stead in this race. *Lossiemouth* and *Honeysuckle* were prime examples of this and any such runner, who has been competing against the best in open company, should be shown due respect.

GRADED FORM

FOLLOWING on from the previous subsection, whilst Graded form against geldings is a huge positive, a minimum requirement here is Graded form in mares' only events. Only one of the 18 winners had failed to at least record a top-four finish of some sort in a Grade 1 or Grade 2 and that was *Benie des Dieux*, who was a Grade 3 winner in France before being kept relatively low-key throughout her early days with Willie Mullins.

PREVIOUS FESTIVAL FORM

GIVEN the number of multiple winners, the previous year's renewal of this race is an obvious starting point. Aside from that, both *Apple's Jade* and *Lossiemouth* contested the **Triumph Hurdle** the year before winning this, in the first instance for the last-named.

One race which, surprisingly, has yet to prove to be a good breeding ground for this race is the **Dawn Run Mares' Novices' Hurdle**, with winners of that contest having a disappointing record of 0-5 in the Mares' Hurdle. Obviously, 2024 winner Golden Ace didn't enjoy a bad 2025 Festival when landing the Champion Hurdle, but Limini, Concertista (both sent off favourite) and Love Envoi are among those to have failed. Last year's Dawn Run was won by Air Of Entitlement, who disappointed in handicap company at Leopardstown over Christmas.

OTHER KEY RACES

BOTH *Apple's Jade* and *Lossiemouth* (ahead of her first win) were high-class juveniles from the previous season. As well as running in – and winning in the latter's case – the Triumph (as per the previous subsection) the pair had earlier won the **Changing Times Brewery Juvenile Hurdle** at Leopardstown's Christmas fixture and after Cheltenham, went on to win the Grade 1 **Champion Four Year Old Hurdle** at the Punchestown Festival. Murcia finished fourth at Punchestown, having won the Grade 1 Anniversary Hurdle at Aintree, and is one who could head down this route.

In terms of the current season, no fewer than four of the past nine winners started the campaign in the **Hatton's Grace Hurdle** at Fairyhouse, again highlighting that form in open Grade 1 company against the boys is hugely significant. *Apple's Jade*, *Honeysuckle* (twice) and *Lossiemouth* all started their campaigns in the 2m4f race and three of the quartet proved successful.

Lossiemouth was a faller in the **Irish Champion Hurdle** on her final start before Cheltenham last year, which was reportedly factored into the reasoning for her running here rather than in the Champion itself, whilst *Honeysuckle* also contested the same race ahead of her two wins in the Mares' Hurdle, winning it once and finishing runner-up on the other occasion. Brighterdaysahead beat Lossiemouth this year, recording a one-two for mares.

Remaining in Ireland, the **Quevega Mares Hurdle** has also proven to be a stepping stone to success in recent years, with *Apple's Jade* and *Black Tears* taking in the Punchestown event during February. The race took place after the Guide was sent to print but is clearly a piece of form worth noting.

And, domestically, the **Warwick Mares' Hurdle** was won by both *Glens Melody* and *Marie's Rock* on their latest start before winning this. The Listed race also takes place in February and was won this year by the game Hollygrove Cha Cha, who made all under a fine ride.

LAST TIME OUT WINNERS

13 OF THE 18 winners had recorded a victory on their most recent start and of the five who were beaten, four had raced in pattern company against geldings, the last two in the aforementioned Irish Champion Hurdle. Clearly, performing well in defeat at a higher level is of equal significance but if you are looking towards a mare who has been racing against her own sex, ideally you want a last-time-out winner on side. *Black Tears* is the only winner of this race to have been beaten in a mares' only event on her last start.

AGE

AS TOUCHED upon in the *Other Key Races* subsection, both *Apple's Jade* and *Lossiemouth* were high-class juveniles the season before winning this race and they are the only pair of five-year-old winners since the first two runnings. *Quevega* was also coming out of juvenile company – although she actually disappointed in the Champion Four Year Old Hurdle at Punchestown – and it would seem that you need a very smart mare to be successful at that age.

Youthfulness is a positive, however, with only *Quevega* (on three occasions) and *Honeysuckle* (second time around in 2023) winning the race over the age of seven. Eight of the past 11 winners were aged six or seven, which appears to be the optimum age bracket, unless you are looking at a (potentially) very good five-year-old.

Despite having won the race twice already, *Lossiemouth* is still only seven and clearly somewhere near her prime at present.

ALEXANDER'S RUNNERS NOTED

OWNER **Kenneth Alexander** has twice enjoyed success in this race – thanks to the double of *Honeysuckle* – but he has also seen Elfile finish third (in 2020 when chasing home *Honeysuckle*) and both Telmesomethinggirl and Jade de Grugy have filled the runners-up spot in each of the past two renewals. He has had nine runners carry his pale blue and white spotted silks during those past six years and Telmesomethinggirl, who had won the Dawn Run as a novice, was also in the process of running a big race when being brought-down in 2022. Alexander's runners should be noted.

Jade de Grugy could represent Alexander

MARKET FORCES

BETWEEN 2014 and 2023 (inclusive), the only mare to justify outright favouritism was *Vroum Vroum Mag* but *Lossiemouth* has now done so (twice), whilst *Honeysuckle* was also joint-favourite in 2023. *Quevega* was favourite for all six of her wins – sent off at odds-on four times – and plenty of other winners could have been found just behind the market leader, with only four of the 18 winners returning at odds greater than 6-1. Those towards the top-end of the market tend to dominate.

Last year's Martin Pipe winner Wodhooh wins the Ascot Hurdle

ROLL OF HONOUR

Year	Form	Winner	Age	Weight	OR	SP	Trainer	Runners	Last Race (No. of days)
2025	12F	Lossiemouth	6	11-5	160	4/6F	W Mullins (IRE)	10	Fell Gr.1 Irish Champion Hurdle (37)
2024	1	Lossiemouth	5	11-5	155	8/13F	W Mullins (IRE)	11	1st Gr.2 International Hurdle (45)
2023	32	Honeysuckle	9	11-5	159	9/4JF	H de Bromhead (IRE)	9	2nd Gr.1 Irish Champion Hurdle (37)
2022	371P1	Marie's Rock	7	11-5	140	18/1	N Henderson	12	1st Listed Warwick Mares Hurdle (31)
2021	331	Black Tears	7	11-5	148	11/1	D Foster (IRE)	10	1st Gr.3 Quevega Mares Hurdle (15)
2020	111	Honeysuckle	6	11-5	158	9/4	H de Bromhead (IRE)	9	1st Gr.1 Irish Champion Hurdle (38)
2019	3	Roksana	7	11-5	142	10/1	D Skelton	14	3rd Listed Contenders Hurdle (38)
2018	11	Benie des Dieux	7	11-5	147	9/2	W Mullins (IRE)	9	1st Listed Opera Hat Chase (31)
2017	12212	Apple's Jade	5	11-5	153	7/2	G Elliott (IRE)	17	2nd Listed Quevega Mares' Hurdle (20)
2016	111	Vroum Vroum Mag	7	11-5	154	4/6F	W Mullins (IRE)	19	1st Gr.2 Warfield Mares' Hurdle (52)

LEADING TEN-YEAR GUIDES

Quevega Mares Hurdle 2 (*Apple's Jade* 2nd, *Black Tears* 1st)
Hatton's Grade Hurdle 4 (*Apple's Jade* 1st, *Honeysuckle* 1st & 3rd, *Lossiemouth* 1st)
Irish Champion Hurdle 3 (*Honeysuckle* 1st & 2nd, *Lossiemouth* Fell)
*****Changing Times Brewery Juvenile Hurdle** 2 (*Apple's Jade* 1st, *Lossiemouth* 1st)
*****Champion Four Year Old Hurdle** 2 (*Apple's Jade* 1st, *Lossiemouth* 1st)
*****Triumph Hurdle** 2 (*Apple's Jade* 2nd, *Lossiemouth* 1st)

* denotes previous season

Leading Contenders

LOSSIEMOUTH — Trainer: Willie Mullins

Winner of this race in 2024 and 2025, she won the Triumph in 2023 and is 4-4 at Cheltenham overall. A top-class mare, who has won 13 times from 17 starts, she is a nine-time Grade 1 winner and after being beaten in the Irish Champion Hurdle, is likely to bid to retain her crown. Stepping back up to 2m4f is a positive and having beaten Wodhooh at Aintree last spring, already has winning form over her main market rival. If she does turn up here, she will likely be hard to beat.

WODHOOH — Trainer: Gordon Elliott

Unbeaten in two starts over course-and-distance, she won last year's Martin Pipe and has continued to progress since. Beaten by Lossiemouth at Aintree (her one and only defeat over hurdles), she won the Ascot Hurdle on reappearance before carrying a penalty to a gritty success at Leopardstown. Freshened up, she arrives at Cheltenham on the back of a break and looks sure to go well. Should Lossiemouth run in the Champion, Gordon Elliott's mare would assume favouritism and she is at her best on decent ground.

BRIGHTERDAYSAHEAD — Trainer: Gordon Elliott

Runner-up to Golden Ace in the Dawn Run in 2024, she disappointed in last year's Champion Hurdle, following a busy first half of the season. Beaten 9 lengths by Jade de Grugy at Punchestown, she didn't reappear until Christmas, when just a length off Lossiemouth, and turned that form around in the Irish Champion. Expected to take her chance in the feature on day one, she would be another to warrant serious consideration, should she be rerouted here. It does, however, seem as though Wodhooh is the stable number one for this race.

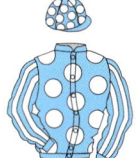

JADE DE GRUGY — Trainer: Willie Mullins

Runner-up last year, she gained Grade 1 honours at Punchestown and the switch of track (New Course) would be in her favour, as she is more about stamina than speed. That said, her participation has to be in some doubt, with her having spent this season in the novice chase division. Having needed the run on debut, she gave The Big Westerner a race at Limerick, before winning a Grade 2 by 18 lengths. A high-class mare who shouldn't be dismissed lightly if rerouted to this race.

FEET OF A DANCER — Trainer: Paul Nolan

Has the option of the Stayers' Hurdle and saw out the 3m trip well at Doncaster when last seen, but this would appear to be an easier option and she isn't short of speed. Runner-up to Wodhooh over Christmas, she had earlier won a Listed race over 2m2f on reappearance and ran well at last year's Festival when fourth in the Pertemps Final. A seven-year-old who appreciates soft ground, this likeable daughter of Authorized would be one of the *'livelier outsiders'* to consider in a race which could cut up.

TAKE NO CHANCES — Trainer: Dan Skelton

Hasn't won since beating subsequent County Hurdle winner Kargese at Ascot in January of last year, she has faced some stiff tasks this season, but was only a neck behind Strong Leader in the West Yorkshire Hurdle and finished third in the Long Distance Hurdle at Newbury. Third behind Potters Charm at Windsor, she stays this trip well and will appreciate reverting to mares' only company. A consistent performer, it wouldn't be a shock to see her go well at big odds.

DAY THREE RACE FOUR

PADDY POWER STAYERS' HURDLE
2m7f 213y (Grade 1) – New Course

OVERVIEW
FOR the first time this year, the Stayers' Hurdle will be overshadowed – according to the running order (race five is the feature race nowadays) – by the Ryanair Chase as the day three feature, although this race still forms part of the original 'Big Four' contests during the week and is the highlight in the staying hurdle division. Although we have seen more experienced hurdlers come out on top in recent years, between 2014 and 2021 it was second-season hurdlers who were dominant. Prior to that, we saw three horses dominate both this race and the division as a whole, during an 11-year spell (2002-2012), with *Baracouda* (2), *Inglis Drever* (3) and *Big Buck's* (4) winning nine renewals between them. The past two winners have carried the silks of Robcour and both had shown high-class form over shorter distances earlier in their careers, something else which is very much a positive.

MULTIPLE WINNERS
AS TOUCHED upon in the *Overview*, we saw a trio of multiple winners during the early part of this century and *Flooring Porter* added his name to the tally, when going back-to-back in 2021 and 2022. Looking back a little further, *Galmoy* was another back-to-back winner during the 80s, so respect previous winners of the race returning to have another crack at it.

With *Bob Olinger* now 11 years of age, perhaps *Teahupoo* is the more likely, should he bid to regain his crown. Still only nine, he finished third in 2023 and runner-up last year, having been sent off favourite for the past three renewals. A horse who we don't usually see too often, he has won both starts this season, looking as good as ever at Leopardstown over Christmas.

SECOND-SEASON HURDLERS
WHEN looking away from a previous winner of the race, looking towards last year's novices is a good option, with seven second-season hurdlers winning the race in the space of eight years, between 2014 and 2021. *Bacchanal*, *Iris's Gift*, *Inglis Drever* (first win) and *My Way de Solzen* all won the Stayers' in their second season over hurdles, too, between 2000 and 2006.

With Jasmin de Vaux (Albert Bartlett winner) out injured, Honesty Policy is the pick of last season's novices to have made an impact in this division.

STRONG NOVICE HURDLE FORM
IT GOES without saying really, but if focusing on novices from the previous season, looking at those with strong novice hurdle form would make sense. *Penhill*, *Paisley Park* and *Lisnagar Oscar* had all contested the **Albert Bartlett Novices' Hurdle** the year prior to winning the Stayers' Hurdle, so take note of any horse graduating from that contest. Three recent winners also contested the **Sefton Novices' Hurdle** at Aintree the previous spring.

Inglis Drever and *Cole Harden* had both contested the **Baring Bingham Novices' Hurdle** the previous year, with the former initially campaigned as a Champion Hurdle horse, before stepping up in distance (more of that anon) for the first time in this race. He went on to become one of the modern greats, in terms of the staying hurdling division.

Whilst Honesty Policy missed Cheltenham, he won the Grade 1 Mersey Novices' Hurdle at Aintree and went on to finish runner-up to Jasmin de Vaux at Punchestown.

RESPECT EX-FLAT HORSES

GIVEN that the hurdles track on the New Course lends itself to a hold-up performer and, of course, there is also less emphasis on jumping – the aforementioned Jasmin de Vaux winning the Albert Bartlett last year being another good example – this can be a race in which ex-Flat horses perform well. The likes of *Inglis Drever*, *Nichols Canyon* and *Penhill* are all examples of this, with the trio all having reached a good level in handicaps on the Flat before developing into high-class staying hurdlers. Another former top-class stayer, the brilliant *Baracouda*, also came off the Flat originally, so pay healthy respect to any such runner this year. If looking towards an ex-Flat performer, we should be looking towards a horse who had obtained a rating of at least 90 under that code.

PATIENT TACTICS WORK WELL

AS TOUCHED upon in the previous subsection and often in contrast to the chase track on the New Course (certainly over an intermediate trip over fences), patient tactics are often rewarded over hurdles. Again, with less emphasis on jumping – with only two hurdles jumped in the final seven furlongs of this race – it gives those who come from behind ample time to make their move later in a race. Last year's winner *Bob Olinger* was a good example of this, Rachael Blackmore still sitting last of the main pack at the top of the hill and as the leaders committed for home, she left her challenge until approaching the final flight. Pay healthy respect to those who like to come from behind.

FORM OVER SHORTER

INGLIS DREVER, *Nichols Canyon* and going back a little further, *Solwhit* (another who had smart Flat form, incidentally) had all shown high-class hurdles form over shorter, before being upped in distance to contest this race. Often, if a horse doesn't quite look up to Champion Hurdle standard, the next option will be to try them over further, with this race then entering calculations. *Teahupoo* and *Bob Olinger* also both shown good form shorter earlier in their careers, so also pay healthy respect to any horse who has shown strong form over 2m or even an intermediate trip.

COURSE FORM

GIVEN the amount of multiple winners of the race, it is hardly surprising that strong form at the track is a positive. 17 of the past 29 winners had won or placed at the Festival previously and last year's winner was somewhat of a Cheltenham specialist. Winner of the Baring Bingham in 2021, he was a fortunate winner of the Golden Miller Novices' Chase the following year, but had made it 3-3 at the track when winning the Relkeel Hurdle in 2024.

KEY TRENDS

- ✓ 7 of the past 12 winners were second-season hurdlers
- ✓ 8 of the past 19 winners had contested the Cleeve Hurdle on trials day
- ✓ 19 winners this century were sent off at single figure odds
- ✓ 17 of the past 29 winners had won or placed at the Festival previously
- ✓ 13 of the past 21 winners won last time out (although only 2 of the past 8)
- ✓ 13 of the past 19 winners were rated 160+
- ✓ 8 of the past 22 winners were British-bred
- ✓ 6 of the past 12 winners arrived at Cheltenham on the back of a break (since Christmas or longer)
- ✓ 3 of the past 13 winners were ex-Flat horses
- ✓ Respect strong form over shorter
- ✓ Respect those who like to be ridden patiently
- ✓ Respect last year's winner
- ✓ Respect any horse rated 168+
- ✗ Only 3 of the past 52 winners were older than 9
- ✗ Only 3 of the past 36 winners were aged 9
- ✗ Only 4 of the 25 winners this century failed to finish 1st or 2nd last time out
- ✗ Be wary of those beaten in the race previously
- ✗ No 5yo has ever won the race

Teahupoo had placed in the 2023 renewal of the **Stayers' Hurdle** before winning it 12 months later and again, given the record of past winners, looking at last year's race is essential. The 2024 winner proved it can be done, but often it can be difficult for horses who have been beaten in this race previously. Last year's front two look on course to renew rivalry.

The **Cleeve Hurdle**, which takes place on trials day, has been a key guide towards the Stayers' in recent years, with eight of the past 19 winners having contested the Grade 2, which is now staged over the exact same course-and-distance as this race (previously run over 2m5f). It is an obvious stepping-stone to the Stayers' and this year's race was won by the improving Ma Shantou, who boasts a fine record at the track.

OTHER KEY RACES

THE first real option for staying hurdlers in England is Wetherby's West Yorkshire Hurdle, although that hasn't had much of an impact in recent years, with Newbury's **Long Distance Hurdle** (staged at the Coral Gold Cup meeting) and Ascot's **Long Walk Hurdle** – which is the first and only Grade 1 of the season in this division (in the UK) ahead of the Stayers' itself –

being the two more obvious races for likely Stayers' Hurdle contenders. Only two of the past 11 winners ran at Newbury, however, and just two of the past 10 ran in the Long Walk, with *Thistlecrack* winning both. Impose Toi won both races this season, graduating from handicap company.

Both *Paisley Park* and *Lisnagar Oscar* had run in the **Betfair Stayers' Handicap Hurdle** at Haydock on Betfair Chase day, with the former successful from a mark of 147. Crambo finished third in the 2023 contest before winning the Long Walk on his next start (as did *Paisley Park*) so it is a race which can throw up a future Grade 1 performer.

Over in Ireland, both *Flooring Porter* (ahead of his second win) and *Bob Olinger* started their season in the **Lismullen Hurdle** at Navan in mid-November, with the former a faller and last year's winner finishing runner-up in the 2m4f contest. He then went on to finish runner-up in the **Christmas Hurdle** at Leopardstown, a race which has now produced four winners in the past five years. It is the obvious mid-season target for an Irish staying hurdler (again, the sole Irish Grade 1 at this trip prior to Cheltenham), although interestingly, of those four recent winners, only *Flooring Porter* (ahead of his first win) actually won the Leopardstown race.

This season's Lismullen Hurdle was won by Colonel Mustard, whilst *Teahupoo* ran out a thoroughly dominant 7-length winner of the Christmas Hurdle, with *Bob Olinger* chasing him home.

AGE

PRIOR to 2023, the last double-digit aged winner was *Crimson Embers* way back in 1986. Since then, *Sire du Berlais* (11yo) and *Bob Olinger* (10yo) have struck for the *'older'* generation, with earlier results very much suggesting that we should be leaning towards those aged between six and eight. Between 2000 and 2022, all bar three winners fell into this age bracket, with the other trio being nine-year-olds (two of which were winning the race for a third and fourth time, respectively). Since the race was reformed, no five-year-old has ever proven successful, with it likely being too much of a test for a horse just out of juvenile company. Despite recent results, I would still suggest focusing on those aged between six and eight, with just the three winners over the age of nine in the past 52 renewals.

BRITISH-BRED SUCCESS

WE HAVE seen seven British-bred winners of the Stayers' Hurdle in the past 22 renewals and all from just 50 runners, with Crambo, who also ran in 2024, the sole representative last year. Often strong stayers, Strong Leader has been another good example of this in recent seasons, with him winning several Graded races – including the Liverpool Hurdle at Aintree – and such runners warrant careful consideration. *Thistlecrack*, *Nichols Canyon* and *Penhill* were three successive British-bred winners not so long back.

OFFICIAL BHA RATINGS

13 OF THE past 19 winners were rated 160 or higher, whilst two more – *Cole Harden* in 2015 and *Bob Olinger* in 2025 – fell just shy of that, officially rated 158 ahead of their respective wins in the race. *Lisnagar Oscar* was the lowest-rated winner this century, with every other winner rated 152 or higher and we really should be focusing on those rated in the 160s when possible. Five successive winners, between 2008 and 2012 – *Inglis Drever* (third win) and *Big Buck's* (x4) – were all rated in the 170s and it is rare to see a horse in this division with such a lofty official BHA Rating, with *Paisley Park* and *Thistlecrack* only reaching 168 ahead of their respective wins. It isn't easy for a stayer to obtain such a high rating and when they do, they are usually hard to beat.

RECENT FORM

SIX of the past dozen winners – again, including *Bob Olinger* – arrived at Cheltenham on the back of a short break, having been off the track since the Festive period, or earlier. *Penhill* was winning this on his belated reappearance (fantastic training performance), *More Of That* had been absent since Cheltenham's December meeting, *Teahupoo* had been off since the Hatton's Grace at the start of the season, whilst the other three to fall into this bracket had all last run in the aforementioned Christmas Hurdle at Leopardstown.

In terms of recent performance, 13 of the past 21 winners won last time out, whilst only four winners this century failed to record a top-two finish on their most recent start. A positive performance is very much a plus ahead of the Stayers'.

MARKET FORCES

WE HAVE seen a mixed bag of results in recent years, with *Thistlecrack*, *Paisley Park* and *Teahupoo* justifying favouritism during the past decade, whilst we have also seen much bigger-priced and somewhat *'shock'* winners in the shape of *Lisnagar Oscar* and *Sire du Berlais*. Between 2000 and 2014, the first 14 winners this century were all priced at 8-1 or shorter, with five outright favourites proving successful during this period.

When there is a dominant force in this division, often they will standout above the opposition and the market responds accordingly. However, when that isn't the case, horses enter the Stayers' Hurdle picture from leftfield at times (failed chasers, for example) and as a result, the ante-post market for this race can be a little volatile throughout the season. It is the one *'big race'* throughout the week which is often most open to change during the months building up to the Festival.

TRAINERS TO NOTE

FOLLOWING his wins in the race in both 2023 and 2024, as well as saddling a placed horse in both 2023 and 2025 (responsible for both placed horses last year), **Gordon Elliott** is very much the most recent successful trainer in this race. Elliott also won three successive renewals of the Pertemps Final between 2018 and 2020, so clearly knows how to handle a high-class 3m hurdler. Elliott looks to hold an extremely strong hand this year, with *Teahupoo* and *Honesty Policy* at the top of the ante-post market at the time of going to print.

Thanks to the four victories of *Big Buck's*, **Paul Nicholls** remains the most successful trainer in the race to date, although he tends to send his better young prospects chasing at the earliest opportunity and the four-time winner only ended up in this division by default, due to his jumping during the early part of his second season over fences.

Likewise, **Nicky Henderson** tends to send his better young horses over fences after their novice hurdle campaign and his two wins in this race came some time ago now, *Rustle* successful back in 1989 and *Bacchanal* winning the 2000 renewal.

More recently, **Jonjo O'Neill** – now training alongside son **A J**, of course – won it twice, with *Iris's Gift* (2004) and *More Of That* (2014) and as we saw with Black Jack Ketchum in between (sent off favourite in 2007), he doesn't mind leaving a high-class performer over hurdles with this race/division in mind.

Willie Mullins went back-to-back in 2017 and 2018, but was dealt a pre-season blow when Jasmin de Vaux was ruled out through injury, whilst Ballyburn didn't build on a promising return in the Hatton's Grace over Christmas.

And, **Gavin Cromwell** is the latest trainer to strike twice, although his two wins were, of course, provided by the same horse, *Flooring Porter*.

LEADING OWNERS TO NOTE

THE STEWART FAMILY again stand out here but by virtue of their one winning horse *Big Buck's*, whilst leading owner **JP McManus** has won the race four times since 2002, with three different horses. French-raider *Baracouda* provided McManus with his first two wins in the race, which were followed by *More Of That* and *Sire du Berlais*.

Andrea and Graham Wylie also had four winners (*Inglis Drever* x3 and *Nichols Canyon*) but are no longer active National Hunt owners (unfortunately), whilst **Robcour** has now won each of the past two renewals and saw *Teahupoo* and *Bob Olinger* fight out the finish in 2025. Brian Acheson appears to have an ever-growing presence in the National Hunt game and this race has been kind to him of late.

ROLL OF HONOUR

Year	Form	Winner	Age	Weight	OR	SP	Trainer	Runners	Last Race (No. of days)
2025	22	Bob Olinger	10	11-10	158	8/1	H de Bromhead (IRE)	13	2nd Gr.1 Christmas Hurdle (75)
2024	1	Teahupoo	7	11-10	162	5/4F	G Elliott (IRE)	12	1st Gr.1 Hatton's Grace Hurdle (102)
2023	55P4	Sire du Berlais	11	11-10	152	33/1	G Elliott (IRE)	11	4th Gr.2 Boyne Hurdle (32)
2022	F2	Flooring Porter	7	11-10	164	4/1	G Cromwell (IRE)	10	2nd Gr.1 Christmas Hurdle (79)
2021	13211	Flooring Porter	6	11-10	160	12/1	G Cromwell (IRE)	15	1st Gr.1 Christmas Hurdle (80)
2020	239F3	Lisnagar Oscar	7	11-10	146	50/1	R Curtis	15	3rd Gr.2 Cleeve Hurdle (47)
2019	1111	Paisley Park	7	11-10	168	11/8F	E Lavelle	18	1st Gr.2 Cleeve Hurdle (47)
2018	-	Penhill	7	11-10	153	12/1	W Mullins (IRE)	15	2nd Gr.2 Punchestown Nov. Hurdle (324)
2017	312F	Nichols Canyon	7	11-10	161	10/1	W Mullins (IRE)	12	fell Gr.1 Irish Champion Hurdle (46)
2016	111	Thistlecrack	8	11-10	168	EvensF	C Tizzard	12	1st Gr.2 Cleeve Hurdle (47)

LEADING TEN-YEAR GUIDES

Long Walk Hurdle 2 (*Thistlecrack* 1st, *Paisley Park* 1st)
Cleeve Hurdle 3 (*Thistlecrack* 1st, *Paisley Park* 1st, *Lisnagar Oscar* 3rd)
*****Sefton Novices' Hurdle** 2 (*Thistlecrack* 1st, *Lisnagar Oscar* 3rd)
*****Albert Bartlett Novices' Hurdle** 3 (*Penhill* 1st, *Paisley Park* 13th, *Lisnagar Oscar* 5th)
Betfair Stayers' Handicap Hurdle 2 (*Paisley Park* 1st, *Lisnagar Oscar* 9th)
Christmas Hurdle 4 (*Flooring Porter* 1st & 2nd, *Sire du Berlais* P.U., *Bob Olinger* 2nd)
*****Stayers' Hurdle** 2 (*Flooring Porter* 1st, *Teahupoo* 3rd)
Lismullen Hurdle 2 (*Flooring Porter* Fell, *Bob Olinger* 2nd)

* denotes previous season

Leading Contenders

TEAHUPOO   Trainer: Gordon Elliott
Winner of the race in 2024 and twice placed, including when runner-up last year, he looked as good as ever when winning a strongly run Christmas Hurdle at Leopardstown. Freshened up since, he had earlier won a third Hatton's Grace Hurdle and is now a seven-time Grade 1 winner. Sets the standard in this division, is versatile in terms of ground (despite having a preference for soft) and although this looks to be a stronger renewal than last year and the fact that he is now nine, he remains the one they all have to beat.

HONESTY POLICY   Trainer: Gordon Elliott
Only made his debut under Rules in January 2025 and won the Grade 1 Mersey Novices' Hurdle just three months later. Stepped up to 3m, he got to within a ½-length of Jasmin de Vaux at Punchestown and ran well when third in the Long Walk on his sole start this term. That form was let down in the Cleeve, but he has only had the six starts and is open to considerable improvement. Although a little more experience would have been preferable, he is likely to be suited by this test.

BOB OLINGER   Trainer: Henry de Bromhead
Last year's winner, he boasts a perfect record (4-4) at Cheltenham and although he was fortunate in 2023, has now recorded three victories at the Festival. Given a fine ride last year, he had too much speed for Teahupoo in a slowly run race and a similar scenario would again enhance his claims. Beaten 7 lengths by Teahupoo in the Christmas Hurdle, on his only start since last year's win, he is now 11 but remains a high-class performer who has been a credit to his connections.

MA SHANTOU   Trainer: Emma Lavelle
Only seventh in last year's Albert Bartlett, he is 3-3 at Cheltenham this season, successful in handicaps off marks of 129 and 138, before comfortably winning the Cleeve Hurdle on trials day. His Haydock blip aside, he seems to be on a sharp upward curve and showed his ability to handle softer conditions when winning the Cleeve. Emma Lavelle took the Stayers' with Paisley Park in 2019 and this seven-year-old boasts a similar profile. Now rated 154, he has to be taken very seriously.

IMPOSE TOI   Trainer: Nicky Henderson
Another who progressed from handicaps, he finished runner-up in last year's Coral Cup and won off 148 at Aintree on reappearance. He then won Newbury's Long Distance Hurdle and confirmed the form (on worse terms) with Strong Leader in the Long Walk at Ascot. Unable to cope with Ma Shantou in the Cleeve (did concede 6lb), a real thorough test at the trip might just expose any stamina limitations as he isn't short of speed. The Liverpool Hurdle should suit ideally after he runs in the Stayers'.

KABRAL DU MATHAN   Trainer: Dan Skelton
Rapid improver over intermediate trips this season, he was expected to bypass Cheltenham in favour of Aintree, but held an entry in Haydock's Rendlesham Hurdle (Saturday 14th February) whilst the Guide was at print stage and if he were to win there, his connections might find the Stayers' too hard to resist. Impressive in the Relkeel at Cheltenham on New Year's Day, he has bags of pace and whilst the trip is an unknown (at the time of writing), he is on a sharp upward curve. Would be a fascinating runner.

Unparalleled style and comfort at one of the world's premier racecourses

With an interest in up to six meticulously chosen racehorses, the Royal Ascot Racing Club, Ascot's premium year-round Membership, is more than just a racing club.

MEMBERSHIP BENEFITS INCLUDE:

- Entry to Ascot on all racedays for Member plus a guest including the Royal Meeting
- An interest in up to 6 horses in training with top-class trainers
- Horses chosen meticulously by The Hon Harry Herbert & John Warren, Racing & Bloodstock Advisor to His Majesty The King
- Access to convivial yet relaxed Clubrooms overlooking the winning line and the unsaddling enclosure
- Fully inclusive dining by the renowned Rhubarb Food & Design
- Opportunity to bring additional guests to enjoy the Clubrooms
- Regular stable visits and Member-only events

To register your interest or for more information please contact
RARC@ascot.com or 0344 346 3624

DAY THREE RACE FIVE

RYANAIR CHASE (Festival Trophy)
2m4f 127y (Grade 1) – New Course

OVERVIEW
WE HAVE now had 21 runnings of the Ryanair Chase – 18 of which as a Grade 1 – and the middle-distance contest is now firmly established as part of the Festival roster. Another race in which Willie Mullins boasts a fantastic record, he has long been prepared to target a top-class horse at it, whilst many others have seen the race as an unwanted distraction, with it diluting both the Queen Mother Champion Chase and Gold Cup. Form over at least 2m4f is essential and many a winner of the race will have strong form over 3m in the book, so stamina is an obvious positive.

SIX UP FOR MULLINS
AS TOUCHED upon in the *Overview*, trainer **Willie Mullins** has long been prepared to target this race with a top-class performer and his list of winners – all six coming in the past 10 years, incidentally – pay testament to this. *Vautour, Un de Sceaux, Min, Allaho* (twice) and *Fact To File* were genuine top-class performers and during the past decade, Mullins has saddled 20 horses in the race, although he relied solely on the winner last year. Given the strength-in-depth in his stable at present, it is always likely to be a race which he continues to target.

Last year's winner heads Mullins' entries, although after his Irish Gold Cup success, his target may change.

FRENCH-BRED SUCCESS
AS WELL as providing his trainer with a sixth win in the race, *Fact To File* became the 12th successive French-bred winner of the Ryanair Chase. Such horses appear to relish an intermediate trip, with their blend of speed and stamina seemingly a perfect fit for this race (it wasn't too dissimilar with the now defunct Golden Miller Novices' Chase). More and more French-bred runners take their chance in top-level contests these days – indeed six of last year's nine runners ticked this box – but their record stands out and it clearly isn't coincidental.

AGE
TARANIS is the sole six-year-old winner of this race but it was still a Grade 2 back in 2007 and in truth, the quality of field was nowhere near what it tends to be today. Between 2006 and 2011, three 10-year-olds were successful, although *Albertas Run* is the last double-digit aged winner, when winning the race for a second time, 15 years ago. Since then, all 14 winners were aged between seven and nine, which is very much the age bracket to focus on. This race tends to go the way of an up-and-coming chaser (more of that shortly) and seems to favour the *'younger'* contenders, which also ties in with the previous subsection, as French-bred horses tend to be much more forward in the early part of their career.

LIGHTLY-RACED CHASERS
BETWEEN 2013 and 2018, five of the six winners were second-season chasers and although there hasn't been as many of late, *Allaho* (ahead of his first win) and *Fact To File* very much fell into this category, ticking several boxes of an archetypal Ryanair winner. Overall, 14 of the 21 winners had run 12 times or less over fences, so it can usually pay to look away from the more exposed runners and focus on those younger contenders, who are still on the up, certainly

when looking for a new winner of the race. *Envoi Allen* was one of a couple of recent nine-year-old winners of the race, but he had still only run in a dozen chases before landing this prize. Other *'older'* / *'more experienced'* winners, *Un de Sceuax* and *Min*, were formerly high-class two-milers, trying something different a little later in their careers.

GRADE 1 CLASS

HAVING won at the top level is almost essential. Since the race was upgraded, 14 of the 18 winners had already secured at least one Grade 1 success and *Fact To File* added to this tally, by virtue of his two Grade 1 wins as a novice and victory in the John Durkan on reappearance. In terms of a recent run, 12 of those past 18 winners had finished first or second in a Grade 1 or Grade 2 on their most recent start, whilst another pair (the past two winners actually) finished third. Therefore, as well as looking for strong Grade 1 form, look for a horse who performed well in strong company last time out.

CHELTENHAM FESTIVAL FORM

SINCE the race was upgraded, all 18 winners had run at the Cheltenham Festival the previous year. And, plenty had strong form down the years, with *Envoi Allen* having won a Champion Bumper and a Baring Bingham Novices' Hurdle in his early days, whilst *Vautour* was another dual winner, having won the Supreme Novices' Hurdle and the now-defunct Golden Miller Novices' Chase. That contest was the obvious stepping stone to the Ryanair – with four of the past 12 winners having contested it – but as it no longer exists, I have removed it from the *Leading Ten-Year Guides* section of the *Roll Of Honour*.

Last year's winner had finished second in the 2023 Champion Bumper and having bypassed a hurdling campaign, won the 2024 Broadway Novices' Chase. That kind of strong Festival form is (obviously) a huge positive.

Three of the past nine winners had been beaten in the **Queen Mother Champion Chase** the previous year, before stepping up in trip. This race looks to be an option for last year's QMCC runner-up, Jonbon, who finished strongly at Ascot recently.

Overall, 15 of the 21 winners had won or placed at the Festival previously, with a couple more just missing out with fourth and fifth places, respectively.

COURSE FORM

LOOKING at form at Cheltenham in general – not just at the Festival – is another positive, with 17 of the 21 winners having recorded a victory at this

KEY TRENDS

- 6 of the past 10 winners were trained by Willie Mullins
- The past 12 winners were French-bred
- All 18 winners (since the race became a Grade 1) had won over a minimum of 2m4f
- Horses rated 170+ are 4-6
- Since the race was upgraded, all 18 winners had run at the Festival the previous year
- 18 of the 21 winners were in the top-3 of the betting
- 17 of the 21 winners had won at Cheltenham previously
- 16 of the past 17 winners were aged 7-9
- 15 of the 21 winners had won or placed at the Cheltenham Festival previously
- 14 of the past 18 winners had already won at least one Grade 1 race
- 14 of the 21 winners had run 12 times or less over fences
- 11 of the past 18 winners finished 1st or 2nd in a Grade 1 or Grade 2 last time out (2 more finished 3rd)
- 8 of the past 18 winners were beaten in the King George at Kempton
- 8 of the past 12 winners had a break of 47+ days
- 8 of the past 12 winners were top- or second-top rated (BHA Ratings)
- 7 of the past 13 winners were second-season chasers
- 7 of the past 14 favourites have won (the past 5 trained by Willie Mullins)
- 6 of the past 17 winners hadn't run since the Christmas period
- 3 of the past 5 winners were owned by Cheveley Park Stud
- Respect strong form over 3m
- ✗ Only 1 of the past 17 winners was aged 10
- ✗ Only 2 of the 21 winners returned at odds greater than 17-2
- ✗ Yet to win over 2m4f (or further)
- ✗ No previous course form
- ✗ No winner over the age of 10
- ✗ Gordon Elliott-trained runners are 0-8

venue. Therefore, pay healthy respect to those with winning form from other fixtures at the track, as well as those who have strong Festival form to their names. As this race takes place on the New Course, even greater emphasis should be taken with winning form on this more expansive track.

PROVEN STAMINA

LAST year's winner was another good case-in-point here. He had strong form over 3m – indeed, he had won the Broadway 12 months earlier – but didn't look Gold Cup material (trip would have been questionable) and plenty of recent winners boasted strong 3m form. Having won over a minimum of 2m4f is a necessity, with all 18 winners since the race was upgraded matching this profile (even those who had contested the QMCC the previous year). *Fact To File* was very much cut from a similar cloth to dual winner *Allaho*, in that they liked to get on with things and had the stamina in reserve to keep up the strong gallop. Both horses were beaten in the **Savills Chase** at Leopardstown over Christmas – as was *Balko des Flos* – whilst last year's winner was also beaten in the Irish Gold Cup over 3m.

Dropping in trip, having run in Grade 1 company over 3m, is quite significant, with no fewer than eight of the past 18 winners (since the race became a Grade 1) having been beaten in the **King George VI Chase** at Kempton on Boxing Day. Again, if a horse just fails there, the Ryanair likely becomes a more realistic target than the Gold Cup.

Fact To File finished only sixth in the King George, after which he was only entered in the Ryanair. However, having since won the Irish Gold Cup, his target had yet to be confirmed, at the time of going to print.

OTHER KEY RACES

ALTHOUGH it is an early-season handicap, Aintree's **Old Roan Chase** has produced a couple of Ryanair winners in the past 11 years, with *Uxiandre* and *Frodon* contesting it, the latter proving successful. This season's race was won by Hitman, running in the race for a fourth time, with Master Chewy (5th in this race last year) 2 lengths away in second.

Over in Ireland, the obvious starting point for Grade 1 chasers over an intermediate trip (plenty of stayers start off there, too) is the **John Durkan Memorial Chase** and it was won last season by *Fact To File*, on what was his first start out of novice company. *Min* and *Allaho* (twice) also began their seasons in the Punchestown contest, which was brought forward in the calendar slightly a couple of years ago, in order to allow the main protagonists enough recovery time to run again at Christmas. This move has proven to be a positive one and with four Ryanair winners in the past six years to have emerged from it, the race is clearly hugely significant. This season's race was won by Gaelic Warrior, who beat stable-mate *Fact To File* by a neck, with the pair well clear of the remainder.

Prior to both of his wins, *Allaho* was successful in the **Horse & Jockey Hotel Chase** – formerly the **Kinloch Brae**) at Thurles in January. With that track (thankfully) avoiding what seemed like certain closure at one stage, this year's contest went the way of Appreciate It.

ARRIVING FRESH

EIGHT of the past dozen winners arrived at Cheltenham on the back of a 47-day break or longer and interestingly, Henry de Bromhead's two winners – namely *Balko des Flos* and *Envoi Allen* – had both been side-lined since being beaten at Christmas time. Take note if the trainer takes a similar approach moving forward, as A Plus Tard was given a similar break ahead of winning the Gold Cup for the same stable (and when 3rd in this race when sent off favourite in 2020). Likewise, *Dynaste* and *Vautour* were last seen in action in the King George on Boxing Day, similar to *Imperial Commander* and *Albertas Run* (ahead of his second win in 2011) when going back a little further. Certainly, don't let a short break put you off, it doesn't seem to be a negative at all here.

OFFICIAL BHA RATINGS

EIGHT of the past 12 winners were either top- or second best in terms of *Official BHA Ratings*, with last year's winner actually one of four horses to share a top mark of 166. The other seven came from the top two in that regard, whilst four the eight were rated in the 170s and only six horses rated 170 or higher have ever contested the Ryanair Chase. Four winners is obviously a hugely positive return, with all four – *Vautour*, *Un de Sceaux*, *Min* and *Allaho* (second win in 2022) – all being trained by Willie Mullins. As stated earlier, Mullins is more than happy to run a top-class chaser here and doesn't see the race as being 'inferior' to the longer-standing Grade 1s.

Having started the season rated 173, *Fact To File* has an I.H.R.B. Rating of 171, following his sixth at Kempton.

MARKET FORCES

FACT TO FILE became the seventh outright winning favourite last year, with the other six all coming between 2012 and 2022. The last five winning favourites were also all trained by Willie Mullins. In general, the majority of winners could have been found in the top three or four in the market, with only two of the 21 winners returning at odds greater than 17-2. When winning the race for the first time, *Albertas Run* scored at 14-1, whilst 11 years ago we saw *Uxizandre* return at 16s, for what was AP McCoy's final ever Festival winner.

OTHER TRAINERS TO NOTE

THE imperious record of Willie Mullins has been covered elsewhere, whilst **Paul Nicholls** comes next, with three wins to his name, albeit two of his three came before the race was a Grade 1. *Frodon* is Nicholls' sole winner during the past 18 years and he was again without a runner in 2025.

More recently, **Henry de Bromhead** has won the race twice since 2018 and he has since been responsible for the runner-up in 2024 (2023 winner *Envoi Allen*) and last year, saddled the second and third, with Heart Wood chasing home *Fact To File* at the rewarding odds of 18-1. As touched upon in an earlier subsection, pay particular attention to any runner from this stable who has had a break since the Festive period. Heart Wood was yet another example of this last year, this being his first start since the aforementioned Savills Chase, in which he finished a non-staying fourth.

Gordon Elliott was without a runner last year, so his record in the race remains at 0-8, with just two of the eight hitting the frame. They include subsequent Gold Cup winner, Don Cossack.

CONNECTIONS TO NOTE

HAVING won the race for three successive years between 2021 and 2023, **Cheveley Park Stud** clearly (like Willie Mullins) don't mind running a top-class chaser in the Ryanair and their 2023 winner *Envoi Allen* has twice hit the frame since. A Plus Tard also finished third back in 2020 (before returning to win the Gold Cup) so it is a race in which their famous red, white (sash) and blue (cap) silks have become associated with.

Fact To File wins eased down last year

ROLL OF HONOUR

Year	Form	Winner	Age	Weight	OR	SP	Trainer	Runners	Last Race (No. of days)
2025	123	Fact To File	8	11-10	166	6/4F	W Mullins (IRE)	9	3rd Gr.1 Irish Gold Cup (40)
2024	4323	Protektorat	9	11-10	165	17/2	D Skelton	11	3rd Gr.2 Denman Chase (33)
2023	17	Envoi Allen	9	11-10	163	13/2	H de Bromhead (IRE)	9	7th Gr.1 King George VI Chase (80)
2022	11	Allaho	8	11-10	174	4/7F	W Mullins (IRE)	7	1st Gr.2 Horse & Jockey Hotel Chase (53)
2021	641	Allaho	7	11-10	162	3/1F	W Mullins (IRE)	11	1st Gr.2 Horse & Jockey Hotel Chase (50)
2020	12	Min	9	11-10	170	2/1	W Mullins (IRE)	8	2nd Gr.1 Dublin Chase (40)
2019	1211	Frodon	7	11-10	169	9/2	P Nicholls	12	1st Gr.2 Cotswold Chase (47)
2018	1232	Balko des Flos	7	11-10	166	8/1	H de Bromhead (IRE)	6	2nd Gr.1 Leopardstown Chase (78)
2017	1611	Un de Sceaux	9	11-10	171	7/4F	W Mullins (IRE)	8	1st Gr.1 Clarence House Chase (47)
2016	12	Vautour	7	11-10	176	EvensF	W Mullins (IRE)	15	2nd Gr.1 King George VI Chase (82)

LEADING TEN-YEAR GUIDES

King George VI Chase 2 (*Vautour* 2nd, *Envoi Allen* 7th)
*Queen Mother Champion Chase 3 (*Un de Sceaux* 2nd, *Min* 5th, *Envoi Allen* 3rd)
John Durkan Memorial Chase 4 (*Min* 1st, *Allaho* 6th & 1st, *Fact To File* 1st)
Savills Chase 3 (*Balko des Flos* 2nd, *Allaho* 4th, *Fact To File* 2nd)
Horse & Jockey Hotel Chase 2 (*Allaho* 1st & 1st)

* denotes previous season

Leading Contenders

FACT TO FILE — Trainer: Willie Mullins
Last year's brilliant winner, he was beaten a neck in the John Durkan before disappointing in the King George at Kempton. Bounced right back to his best in the Irish Gold Cup, proving he thoroughly sees out 3m in a strongly run race and that could well result in him being supplemented for the Gold Cup. If he returns for this race, he will take the world of beating if in the same form, with the New Course ideal for his style of racing. A top-class performer, his Festival form figures read 211.

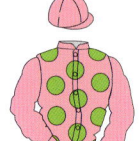

GAELIC WARRIOR — Trainer: Willie Mullins
Beat Fact To File in the John Durkan and again finished in front of him in the King George, before chasing him home (beaten 5l) in the Irish Gold Cup. Again, the Gold Cup looks the more likely option at this stage, but if he were to drop in distance, he could be allowed to stride on. In Fact To File's absence, he would be clear favourite and is another with a fine Festival record, having finished runner-up in both the Fred Winter and Baring Bingham, before winning the Arkle in 2024.

JONBON — Trainer: Nicky Henderson
Runner-up in the Supreme, Arkle and Champion Chase, he hadn't quite looked the force of old in the Celebration Chase, nor on his first two starts this season, when well beaten in both the Shloer and Tingle Creek. Bounced back to form with a gutsy display in the Clarence House, where his finishing effort strongly suggested that going back up in distance would suit. He has twice won the Melling Chase at Aintree (2m4f) and an Ascot Chase entry (Saturday 14th February) suggests that this could be his target.

HEART WOOD — Trainer: Henry de Bromhead
Runner-up last year, he has 9 lengths to find with Fact To File, who also finished a long way ahead of him in this season's John Durkan. He had earlier won over 2m7f at Punchestown and repeated the feat at Tramore on New Year's Day. Whilst the Gold Cup remains an option, this seems the more realistic target, given how well he ran in the race last year. Somewhere in between (2m6f-2m7f) might actually be his optimum, so perhaps Sandown's Oaksey Chase would be an ideal spring target later on.

IMPAIRE ET PASSE — Trainer: Willie Mullins
Winner of the Baring Bingham in 2023, he has bypassed the Festival in each of the past two seasons, instead waiting for Aintree where he won the Aintree Hurdle and Manifesto Novices' Chase. Whilst he holds an entry in the Gold Cup, this would likely be his target if heading to Cheltenham, although we have yet to see him this season, so perhaps he will take in a less demanding race en route back to Liverpool. Still only eight, he has only had five chase starts and has won three of them.

PANIC ATTACK — Trainer: Dan Skelton
A rapidly-improving mare, who won the Paddy Power Gold Cup and the Coral Gold Cup during the early part of the season. Returning to Newbury, she destroyed inferior opposition in a Listed race, where her jumping was a joy to behold. An attacking ride from the front around the New Course could see her go well wherever she turns up and whilst the Mares' Chase would seem the more obvious target, she would receive 7lb from the geldings here and the race does feel as though it could cut up quite significantly from entry stage.

Sandown Park
RACECOURSE

IMPERIAL CUP DAY
The Ultimate Pre-Cheltenham Party
SATURDAY 7 MARCH

BOOK NOW

SCAN TO BOOK

DAY THREE RACE SIX

PERTEMPS NETWORK FINAL HANDICAP HURDLE
2m7f 213y (Premier Handicap) – New Course

OVERVIEW
THE longest distance of the handicap hurdles staged throughout the week, the Pertemps Final is the culmination of an ongoing series of qualifiers, which take place at various tracks – in Britain and Ireland – throughout the season. A top-six finish was once enough to secure eligibility into the Final (provided the horse was rated high enough) but that has more recently been changed to a top-four finish in one of said qualifiers, whilst the latest change – brought in ahead of the 2025 Festival – was that winners of any qualifiers would be guaranteed a run, provided their handicap mark permits it. In recent years, lightly-raced hurdlers who were less-exposed over staying trips have started to shine, as they tend to do in the other feature handicaps throughout the week. The most significant *'trial'* so to speak, in recent years, has been the Leopardstown Qualifier which takes place at the Christmas fixture.

IRISH DOMINATION
FOLLOWING three wins in the past four years for British-trained horses, this subsection might need revisiting next year, but the Irish won six successive renewals between 2016 and 2021, then *Good Time Jonny* made it seven wins in eight years in 2023. The past two winners were trained in the UK, but overall in recent years, this has been one of the handicaps which Irish-trained horses have dominated and from a relatively small representation. Certainly, they have outperformed the number of runners, with the fields during those eight years (2016-2023) made up of just 24% Irish runners (37/157). Feet Of A Dancer was the only Irish-trained runner to finish in the first five last year and it will be interesting to see if this *'British revival'* can be sustained.

Gordon Elliott has the best record of the Irish during this period, winning the race three times in a row between 2018 and 2020, courtesy of *Delta Work* and *Sire du Berlais* (twice). He has also been responsible for another five horses to finish in the first four, three of which finished runner-up, as did The Bosses Oscar in 2021, when officially trained by Denise Foster. This is clearly a race which the Cullentra House team like to target and he ran another two in it last year. Elliott's record with horses sporting both headgear and a tongue-tie stands at a noteworthy 3-4 (75%) so take note when both aids are added to one from his stable.

LEOPARDSTOWN QUALIFIER
PRIOR to 2024, six of the previous eight winners (during the period of *Irish Domination*) had run in the **Leopardstown Qualifier** at the Christmas fixture. Admittedly, there are fewer opportunities for Irish horses to qualify on home soil (more qualifiers in Britain than in Ireland) but this race clearly fits in well, time wise, in the build-up to the Final. Five of the six qualified in this race, whilst *Sire du Berlais* (ahead of his second win) could only finish ninth and was forced to travel over to England (Warwick) the following month, again due to fewer domestic opportunities.

This season's race was won by Joseph O'Brien's Duke Silver, with Yeah Man, Small Town Hero and Intent Approach filling the frame. All four were quite lowly-rated at the time, however.

OTHER KEY RACES

REMAINING in Ireland and the **Punchestown Qualifier** – which takes place in January – is another race to note, with three recent winners having run here. Two of those had also taken in the Leopardstown race beforehand, whilst *Delta Work* qualified by finishing third at Punchestown, having been campaigned in Graded novice events before that.

In England, the first major race in the staying handicap division is Haydock's **Betfair Stayers' Handicap Hurdle**, formerly the *'Fixed Brush Hurdle'*. It is a while since it had an impact here but it remains a valuable contest and this season's race was won by Electric Mason, who was earlier beaten by Ma Shantou in a Cheltenham Qualifier.

In terms of qualifiers, the aforementioned **Warwick Qualifier** has proven to be the best indicator, with two Final winners coming out of the January race in the past six years. Unfortunately, this year's race was lost due to bad weather.

WEIGHTS AND OFFICIAL BHA RATINGS

LAST year's winner was rated below the current average, successful off a mark of 132, with 12 of the previous 14 winners having found themselves in the bracket between 138 and 148. *Doddiethegreat* actually became the lowest-rated winner of the race since *Kayf Aramis* back in 2009, whilst overall, last year's race was a below par affair, with Thomas Mor carrying top-weight from a mark of just 143, the lowest-rated top-weight in recent history. He was, in fact, the only horse in the race rated in the 140s, which is hugely surprising, given that we often see horses rated in the 150s contesting it. This century, only *Sire du Berlais* (second win) has won from a mark in the 150s, so such highly-rated performers can usually be overlooked. Interestingly, the first six home in 2025 were rated between 129 and 136, which is indicative of the quality of the renewal.

In terms of weight carried, *Sire du Berlais* shouldered top-weight that second year, whilst *Fingal Bay* did the same in 2014 (from a mark of 148). Every winner since 2012 has carried a minimum of 10-9 and 12 of the 14 carried 10-11 or more, even including *Doddiethegreat*. Despite his lower rating, he still shouldered 11-2, due to the lower top-weight and it being a weaker than usual renewal.

KEY TRENDS

- ★ Gordon Elliott boasts a fantastic recent record in the race
- ★ 9 of the past 10 winners wore a tongue-tie (from 23% representation)
- ★ 6 of the past 10 winners ran in the Leopardstown Qualifier (Christmas fixture)
- ✓ The past 14 winners carried 10-9+ (12 of them carried 10-11+)
- ✓ 13 of the past 14 winners were aged 8 or younger
- ✓ 12 of the past 15 winners were rated between 138-148
- ✓ 11 of the past 14 winners had run 10 times or less over hurdles
- ✓ 10 of the past 16 winners failed to win earlier in the season
- ✓ 10 of the past 13 winners were unexposed over a staying trip
- ✓ 9 of the past 12 winners returned at 14-1 or shorter
- ✓ 9 winners this century wore headgear (respect first time headgear being applied)
- ✓ 7 of the past 10 winners were trained in Ireland
- ✓ Respect JP McManus-owned runners
- ✓ Respect horses who have been chasing earlier in the season
- ✗ Only 1 winner this century was rated 150+
- ✗ Only 1 winner this century hadn't run during the calendar year
- ✗ Only 1 of the past 42 winners was older than 9
- ✗ Only 1 of the past 36 winners was aged 5
- ✗ Only 1 of the past 16 winners won more than once earlier in the season

LIGHLY-RACED/UNEXPOSED STAYERS

ONCE a race for seasoned/battle-hardened handicappers, the Pertemps is now more akin to the other handicap hurdles staged throughout the week, in that the less exposed now tend to come to the fore,

	Top Weight (OR)	Bottom OR	Winner OR		Top Weight (OR)	Bottom OR	Winner OR
2025	143	124	132	2020	152	131	152
2024	154	129	138	2019	148	134	145
2023	147	121	142	2018	155	136	139
2022	156	134	141	2017	147	137	146
2021	151	126	134	2016	154	135	139

Cheltenham Festival Betting Guide 2026

those unexposed over a staying trip, in particular. 11 of the past 14 winners had run 10 times or less over hurdles and despite him being older than some of the other recent winners (more of that shortly), *Doddiethegreat* was still very much *'lightly-raced'* having had just the nine starts. Many of these winners – including last year's winner, who had run over 3m for the first time on his previous start in a qualifier at Haydock – had run just once or twice over this sort of trip. Therefore, look for a horse who still has the scope to improve and even more importantly, one who hasn't had many tries at this distance.

AGE

IN-KEEPING with the previous subsection and *'younger'* horses have started to come to the fore. As touched upon, due to injury and time on the sidelines, *Doddiethegreat* was nine (despite being so lightly-raced) but every winner between 2012 and 2024 was aged eight or younger. During this period, *Delta Work* struck at the age of just five, making him the only winner of that age group in the past 36 renewals. We should, therefore, be focusing our attention on those aged between six and eight, and with only one of the past 42 winners over the age of nine, those in double digits should also be readily overlooked.

TONGUE-TIED

THIS trend is becoming increasingly significant. Nine of the past 10 winners have now worn a tongue strap and from a relatively small representation, certainly in relation to that extremely healthy return. As highlighted last year, *Monmiral* was just one of six runners to wear such an aid in 2024 and *Good Time Jonny* was one of only four in 2023, whilst *Doddiethegreat* was one of just three runners last year. Overall during the past decade, only 23% of runners (53/232) wore a tongue strap, so that is a massive return. In the past three years alone, only 19% (13/69) fell into this category and in 2022, *Alaphilippe* was only a neck away from making this a clean sweep for the decade. Pay huge respect to such runners this year.

HEADGEAR

NINE of the past 10 winners also wore headgear, with *Monmiral* wearing blinkers for the first time when successful two years ago. Pay particular attention to those who are sporting any form of headgear for the very first time (incidentally, it was a first time tongue-tie for *Doddiethegreat* last year), with a trainer often attempting to keep something up their sleeve for the big day. Last year's winner wore cheekpieces for just the second time.

RECENT FORM

OFTEN a horse will still need to qualify – as was the case with the past two winners, who ran just 19 days and 26 days earlier, respectively – so a run will be required during February in one of the later qualifiers. However, if a horse has qualified much earlier in the season, don't be put off by a seemingly *'poor'* run on their most recent start, as it will likely be no more than a stepping-stone to this race, should their ticket to the Final already be booked. Five of the past 16 winners finished unplaced on their latest start, further highlighting this.

During those past 16 years, only three last-time-out winners have won the Pertemps Final and 10 horses during this period – including six of the past seven – failed to win a race earlier in the season, so don't let that put you off. In fact, it seems to be a positive, so look beyond just the set of a form figures. During those past 16 years, only one winner had won more than once earlier in the campaign, so don't expect to see the winner arrive with a string of 1s alongside their name.

Only one winner this century failed to run during the calendar year, that being *Sire du Berlais* ahead of his first win, with him kept fresh having qualified at Leopardstown over Christmas.

MARKET FORCES

WITH three of the past four winners returning at 25-1, the Pertemps Final is invariably one of the more difficult puzzles to solve throughout the whole week. There was a spell – between 2014 and 2021 – when all eight winners were priced at 14-1 or shorter, with four of them returning at single figures and three of those being priced between 9-2 and 6-1. *Fingal Bay* and *Sire du Berlais* (first win) justified favouritism, so it was starting to have a more predictable feel to it, but things have reverted to type somewhat of late and a big price shouldn't put you off here.

REVERTING TO HURDLES

INTERESTINGLY, the past three winners had run over fences earlier in the season, before reverting to hurdles and having their attention turned to a Pertemps Qualifier. Clearly not the original plan, this is something we see regularly in the Lanzarote Hurdle (a race I cover from a trends perspective in *Jumpers To Follow*) and perhaps, it is the same here – when chasing doesn't look like working out, a new plan is formulated. Going back a little further, both *Buena Vista* and *Cape Tribulation* (back-to-back winners in 2011 and 2012, respectively) boasted a similar profile, so respect those who had been chasing to begin with this season and were switched back to hurdles at a more recent date.

TRAINERS TO NOTE
DODDIETHEGREAT provided **Nicky Henderson** with a second win in the space of 11 years, following on from *Call The Cops* in 2015. He actually saddled last year's runner-up, too, whilst Mill Green twice finished third (at big odds) for the Seven Barrows stable, both in 2022 and 2023.

Jonjo O'Neill – who now trains alongside son, **A J** – remains the most successful trainer in the race, with four wins on the board. However, those wins were recorded between 1991 and 2013, so it is more of a historical record at this stage. The Jackdaws Castle team were again without a runner in 2025.

And, whilst **Fergal O'Brien** has yet to win the race – or any at the Festival thus far – he has twice gone very close, courtesy of Barney Dwan and Alaphilippe, whilst Imperial Alcazar was strongly-fancied in 2021, so it does appear to be a race, and series, which O'Brien likes to target. It wouldn't, therefore, be a shock if his maiden Festival success did come in this race.

McMANUS WITH FIVE ON THE BOARD
JONJO O'NEILL'S very first winner, *Danny Connors*, carried the green and gold hoops of **JP McManus**, as did his third winner *Creon*. *Kadoun* was successful for the owner in 2006 before the double of *Sire du Berlais* took his tally to five wins in the race, shortly after Glencoe had finished runner-up. In fact, McManus was responsible for four horses to finish either second or third between 2012 and 2018, and he again saw his silks fill the runners-up spot last year, when Jeriko du Reponet chased home his stable-mate.

Nicky Henderson

Year	Form	Winner	Age	Weight	OR	SP	Trainer	Runners	Last Race (No. of days)
2025	5PP2	Doddiethegreat	9	11-2	131	25/1	N Henderson	24	2nd Haydock Qualifier (26)
2024	744	Monmiral	7	10-12	138	25/1	P Nicholls	22	4th Chepstow Qualifier (19)
2023	4030	Good Time Jonny	8	11-4	142	9/1	A J Martin (IRE)	23	12th Leopardstown H'cap Hurdle (39)
2022	733	Third Wind	8	10-11	141	25/1	H Morrison	22	3rd Gr.2 Rendlesham Hurdle (26)
2021	1324F	Mrs Milner	6	10-9	134	12/1	P Nolan (IRE)	22	Fell Leopardstown H'cap Hurdle (39)
2020	494	Sire du Berlais	8	11-12	152	10/1	G Elliott (IRE)	24	4th Warwick Qualifier (61)
2019	86	Sire du Berlais	7	11-9	145	4/1F	G Elliott (IRE)	24	6th Leopardstown Qualifier (76)
2018	33243	Delta Work	5	10-10	139	6/1	G Elliott (IRE)	23	3rd Punchestown Qualifier (23)
2017	11541	Presenting Percy	6	11-11	146	11/1	P Kelly (IRE)	24	1st Fairyhouse H'cap Hurdle (19)
2016	31433	Mall Dini	6	10-11	139	14/1	P Kelly (IRE)	24	3rd Fairyhouse H'cap Hurdle (26)

LEADING TEN-YEAR GUIDES
Punchestown Qualifier 3 (*Mall Dini* 3rd, *Presenting Percy* 4th, *Delta Work* 3rd)
Tommy Carberry Handicap Hurdle 2 (*Mall Dini* 3rd, *Presenting Percy* 1st)
Leopardstown Qualifier 6 (*Mall Dini* 4th, *Presenting Percy* 5th, *Sire du Berlais* 6th & 9th, *Mrs Milner* 4th, *Good Time Jonny* 3rd)
Warwick Qualifier 2 (*Sire du Berlais* 4th, *Third Wind* 3rd)

ROSCONN GROUP FULKE WALWYN KIM MUIR CHALLENGE CUP AMATEUR RIDERS' HANDICAP CHASE

3m2f (0-145 Handicap) – New Course

OVERVIEW

PRIOR to 2009, the Kim Muir was staged on the Old Course and run over a distance of 3m½f. However, once it was switched to day three and, therefore, the New Course in 2010, the distance increased to 3m2f and it is very much now more a test of stamina. With that in mind, having proven form over trips in excess of 3m is a positive, for all that we have seen several recent winners who possessed decent form over slightly shorter. Prior to last year, the previous six winners were novices and it is a race which the Irish have bossed in recent years, winning six of the past seven renewals. In 2012, the upper ceiling was increased from 140 to 145 and with it being an amateur riders' race, jockey bookings are important.

CHANGES TO THE NATIONAL HUNT CHASE

I STARTED with this subsection last year and with that contest now becoming a handicap (and, now open to professional jockeys), I did wonder if it would have an impact on this race. Despite this, we still saw novices finish second, third and fourth in 2025 and Johnnywho was only a neck away from justifying favouritism and continuing the impressive recent record of novices (more of that shortly). Whilst we can't judge this solely on the back of just one run (since the *Changes To The National Hunt Chase*), it is something to monitor in the coming years.

NOVICES

AS TOUCHED upon in the *Overview*, prior to last year we saw six successive novice winners of the Kim Muir and Johnnywho went agonisingly close to increasing that run to seven. Prior to last season, changes were introduced to the handicaps at the Festival, meaning that novices would require four runs over fences in order to be eligible for non-novice (only) handicaps. This would have had an impact in 2021, with the mare *Mount Ida* successful on the back of just three previous starts over fences. Last year's Gold Cup winner *Inothewayurthinkin* was successful on the back of just four runs in 2025 and despite the changes to the National Hunt Chase (see previous subsection), which now means that novices have a similar option on day one, such runners should still be given careful consideration.

Three of the past dozen winners were second-season novices, as was last year's fourth *Weveallbeencaught*, so don't dismiss any such runner lightly, whilst we should pay healthy respect to a novice dropping in class, having contested a Graded race earlier in the season. *Any Second Now* and *Mount Ida* had run in a Grade 2 novice chase on their most recent start, whilst *Inothewayurthinkin* had run in a Grade 1 on his penultimate start. Again, last year's runner-up boasted a similar profile, having contested three Grade 2s – he really would have been a stereotypical recent winner of the race.

TACTICS

LAST year's winner was ridden in midfield from an early stage, whereas *Inothewayurthinkin* came from a long way back, after a series of slow jumps ensured than he sat in last place early on. A patient ride works well here, however. Perhaps, it is partly to do with the fact that it is an amateur riders' race, but they seem to go hard and plenty get racing quite early, whereas we have seen plenty of recent winners creep into the race late on and be delivered with a well-timed run. Therefore, give plenty of respect to genuine hold-up performers.

CURRENT FORM
ONLY two of the past 23 winners won last time out, but plenty of recent winners recorded a top-three finish on their most recent start, including *Daily Present* last year. In truth, there isn't any sort of real pattern here, although between 2017 and 2022, all six winners finished first, second or third on their most recent start. The key point here being that it is uncommon for a last time out winner to land the Kim Muir.

WINLESS CAMPAIGN
SINCE 2015, eight of the past 11 winners had failed to record a win earlier in the season and going back to the period of 2009-2012, *Character Building*, *Junior* and *Sunnyhillboy* also fell into the same bracket. During the past 15 years, only *Chambard* has managed to win more than once earlier in the season, too, so this isn't a race where we can expect to see a horse racking up a sequence of wins en route to the Festival. Rather like with the Grand Annual (which has a similar trend), novices can be the exception – in terms of recording a win earlier in the campaign – whereas proven handicappers seem to want to peak on the day. Don't be put off by the fact a horse hasn't won this season and having won a handicap earlier in the campaign certainly isn't a positive.

WEIGHTS AND OFFICIAL BHA RATINGS
LAST year's winner was slightly below the average in terms of official BHA Ratings, *Daily Present* rated just 130, with 10 of the previous 13 winners rated in the narrow bracket between 137 and 143. 2024 winner *Inothewayurthinkin* won off 145 and shouldered top-weight, but given he returned to Cheltenham in 2025 to win the Gold Cup, he certainly wasn't badly handicapped.

Since the race switched to the New Course (2009), only *Daily Present* has carried less than 11-0 (again, he was a slightly below par winner in recent terms) and during the past 17 years, only one winner has carried less than 10-12, prior to the jockey's claim. Therefore, both weights and ratings now suggest that we should really be focusing on the upper end of the handicap, with the better quality horses (generally) coming to the fore since the upper ceiling was increased to 145 (2012).

KEY TRENDS

- ⭐ 10 of the past 14 winners were rated between 137-143
- ⭐ 6 of the past 7 winners were novices
- ⭐ Gordon Elliott boasts a very strong record in the race
- ✓ 14 of the past 17 winners carried 11-4+ (prior to jockey's claims)
- ✓ 10 of the past 16 winners retuned at single figure odds
- ✓ 10 of the past 13 winners were aged 7 or 8
- ✓ 10 of the past 15 winners had failed to win earlier in the season
- ✓ 9 of the past 15 winners wore headgear
- ✓ 9 of the past 16 winners recorded a top-3 finish last time out
- ✓ 5 of the past 7 winners had shown good form over shorter
- ✓ 5 of the past 11 winners wore a tongue strap
- ✓ 4 of the past 14 winners were owned by JP McManus
- ✓ 3 of the past 12 winners were second-season novices
- ✓ Respect hold-up performers
- ✓ Respect novices dropping in class (from Graded company)
- ✓ Focus on those aged 9 and younger
- ✗ Only 1 of the past 17 winners carried less than 10-12 (prior to jockey's claim)
- ✗ Only 1 of the past 15 winners had won more than once earlier that season
- ✗ Only 1 6yo winner since 1971
- ✗ Only 2 of the past 21 winners were older than 9
- ✗ Only 2 of the past 23 winners won last time out
- ✗ Patrick Mullins has yet to ride the winner

	Top Weight (OR)	Bottom OR	Winner OR
2025	144	127	130
2024	145	127	145
2023	145	129	131
2022	145	127	134
2021	145	132	142
2020	145	135	141
2019	144	133	143
2018	145	119 (oh 6)	138
2017	145	133	137
2016	145	134	142

AGE

WE SAW plenty of 'older' horses win the Kim Muir during the 80s and 90s, but since 2005, only two of the past 21 winners were over the age of nine. Since 2013, 11 of the 13 winners were aged eight or younger, so we are seeing a different type of horse win the race these days. *Inothewayurthinkin* was the first six-year-old winner since 1981, so focus more on those aged between seven and nine, with more attention to the seven and eight-year-olds. Last year's first four home were all aged seven or eight and they have been the dominant age groups of late.

MARKET FORCES

BOTH *Junior* and *Sunnyhillboy* justified favouritism in 2011 and 2012, respectively, whilst more recently, *Mount Ida* and *Inothewayurhinkin* did the same, the latter attracting heavy support and returning at odds of 13-8, despite his tender age and the fact that he had never won a race over fences. Five of the six winners between 2015 and 2020 also returned at single figure odds, so the race was beginning to have a more predictable feel to it, but either side of that *Domesday Book* and *Chambard* struck at 40-1. There is no real pattern here, although the race feels a little more 'punter friendly' these days, with last year's front three priced between 9-2F and 12-1.

FORM OVER SHORTER

FIVE of the past seven winners had shown decent form over shorter trips, so whilst you would assume that stamina would be a necessity over 3m2f, clearly a bit of tactical speed can help. As touched upon in the *Tactics* subsection, a patient approach and the pace to make a late move can help here, so form over an intermediate trip seems to have become a positive. Stepping up in distance clearly brought about significant improvement in both *Mount Ida* and *Inothewayurhinkin*, so take note (especially with a lightly-raced novice), if a horse takes a marked rise in distance for this contest.

As touched upon in the *Overview*, the race distance was increased when it switched from the Old Course to the New Course and as a result – certainly in the early days – stamina was seen as being more important. Form over 3m+, therefore, isn't a negative, it just seems that in recent years, we have seen slightly quicker horses come to the fore, coinciding with a better quality of winner of the race.

IRISH DOMINATION

IN A race which was once dominated by British-trained horses, the Kim Muir has become an Irish benefit of late, with Irish-trained horses now winning six of the past seven renewals. All six horses were winning for different trainers, although **Gordon Elliott** also won the race in 2016, so boasts a fine recent record in it. He struck again with *Milan Native* in 2020 and *Mount Ida* came out of his Cullentra House Stables when successful for Denise Foster (when Elliott was serving his suspension) the following year. **Willie Mullins** saddled the third last year, but is still to win a handicap chase at the Cheltenham Festival, a record which he is likely to be keen to rectify at some stage (given that he has broken almost every other record in the game).

JOCKEY BOOKINGS ARE KEY

AS WITH all amateur riders' races, jockey bookings are hugely important and the leading Irish amateurs are often first to be snapped up. **Derek O'Connor** was sublime aboard *Inothewayurthinkin*, who provided the veteran rider with a second Kim Muir success in the space of six years, following on from *Any Second Now*, both of course carrying the silks of JP McManus (more of his record shortly). Pay close attention to who the leading Irish riders partner.

The exception would be **Patrick Mullins**, who has yet to ride the winner of this race. He rode the third for his dad last year and given team Mullins' record in this race, perhaps it shouldn't be too surprising that he has yet to tick this race off his illustrious C.V. Since 2011, Patrick Mullins' record in the Kim Muir stands at 0-12.

HEADGEAR CAN BE A HELP

WITH nine of the past 15 winners wearing headgear of sorts, it certainly isn't a negative. Often headgear can help in staying handicaps and that seems to be the case here, with *Daily Present* adding to the tally, by virtue of his blinkers. Last year's winner had worn blinkers just once previously (on his latest start) so pay particular attention to similar types, maybe wearing headgear for just the first or second time.

TONGUE-TIED

DAILY PRESENT also wore a tongue-strap, as did the three recent winners to hail from Gordon Elliott's stable, something we have seen with his runners in other staying races. It seems significant when it comes to runners from Cullentra House, whilst *The Package* also wore a tongue strap when successful some 11 years ago. Such aids wouldn't be as popular as headgear, so five winners in 11 years is a strong return and such runners continue to outperform their representation (certainly not as popular as headgear in terms of number of runners).

ANOTHER McMANUS TARGET

LEADING owner **JP McManus** likes to have runners in as many of the Festival handicaps as possible, but the Kim Muir is a race in which he has a fine recent record, winning four of the past 14 renewals. Last year's Gold Cup winner *Inothewayurthinkin* was the latest of those in 2024 and like his previous winner before him, he was ridden by Derek O'Connor, who has long been part of *'Team McManus'*. O'Connor now trains and rides McManus' Point-to-Point horses, so pay particular attention to any horse who he rides in the famous green and gold. The pair were very close to going back-to-back last year, with *Johnnywho* beaten a neck, whilst McManus was also responsible for the third-placed *Sa Majeste*. McManus also owned the runner-up in both 2014 and 2017, so pay healthy respect to his runners this year, especially any lightly-raced novices.

UK TRAINERS TO NOTE

WITHOUT a runner in any of the past eight renewals, **David Pipe** won the Kim Muir in both 2011 and 2015, with *Junior* and *The Package*. His father Martin won this race in 1991, 2003 and 2004, so it is clearly another handicap which the Pond House operation have enjoyed great success in. Selective in terms of runners in the race these days, respect any horse deemed good enough to represent the Pipe team this year.

Nicky Henderson has won the race three times, but his latest win came back in 2005, whilst **Donald McCain** won it twice earlier in the century, with *Cloudy Lane* in 2007 and *Ballabriggs* three years later.

KEY RACES

TWO of the past 10 winners had run in the **National Hunt Chase** the previous year, *Cause Of Causes* successful and *Missed Approach* having finished runner-up, with the former having run in this race (finished runner-up) two years prior to winning it.

Back-to-back winners *Spring Heeled* and *The Package* had contested the **Oddschecker Handicap Chase**, staged over 3m3½f at the November meeting. This season's race was won by *Marble Sands*, for the David Killahena & Graeme McPherson stable.

And, three of the past dozen winners had contested the **Paddy Power Chase** at Leopardstown over Christmas. This season's race was won by 66-1 shot *Favori de Champdou*, who led home a Gordon Elliott/Gigginstown one-two.

JP McManus

ROLL OF HONOUR

Year	Form	Winner	Age	Weight	OR	SP	Trainer	Runners	Last Race (No. of days)
2025	33	Daily Present	8	10-7	130	12/1	P Nolan (IRE)	23	3rd Punchestown H'cap Chase (60)
2024	2239	Inothewayurthinkin	6	12-0	145	13/8F	G Cromwell (IRE)	22	9th Gr3. Leopardstown H'cap Chase (39)
2023	8421U	Angels Dawn	8	11-0	131	10/1	S Curling (IRE)	23	U.R. Punchestown H'cap Chase (25)
2022	12211	Chambard	10	10-12	134	40/1	V Williams	20	1st Huntingdon Nov. H'cap Chase (11)
2021	312	Mount Ida	7	11-9	142	3/1F	D Foster (IRE)	21	2nd Gr.2 Mares Nov. Chase (50)
2020	452422	Milan Native	7	11-1 (7)	141	9/1	G Elliott (IRE)	23	2nd Gowran Park beginners chase (26)
2019	5253	Any Second Now	7	11-11	143	6/1	T Walsh (IRE)	23	3rd Navan Nov. Chase (25)
2018	P632	Missed Approach	8	11-5	138	8/1	W Greatrex	20	2nd Musselburgh H'cap Chase (41)
2017	5683	Domesday Book	7	11-4	137	40/1	S Edmunds	24	3rd Leicester H'cap Chase (28)
2016	005	Cause of Causes	8	11-9	142	9/2	G Elliott (IRE)	22	5th Gr.2 Naas Chase (25)

LEADING TEN-YEAR GUIDES

*National Hunt Chase 2 (*Cause of Causes* 1st, *Missed Approach* 2nd)
Paddy Power Chase 2 (*Cause of Causes* 12th, *Any Second Now* 5th)

* denotes previous season

CHELTENHAM FESTIVAL 2026 – DAY 3

Daily Tips

BY SAM TURNER

Formerly Robin Goodfellow of the Daily Mail, Sam has been a regular on Racing TV for more than two decades and now writes a daily column for Betfair.

Dawn Run Mares' Novices Hurdle
OLDSCHOOL OUTLAW

HAVING tipped Sixandahalf in this space to win last year's running of this race, revisiting the day three curtain raiser for this year's guide took some resolve.

Memories of Gavin Cromwell's mare easing to the front at the final hurdle, pulling the proverbial cart under a confident Keith Donoghue, live vividly rent free in your correspondent's head, unfortunately so does the image of Air Of Entitlement flying past the selection on the run to the line.

However, that was then and this is now and I'm hoping for a shot at redemption with **Oldschool Outlaw** who looks yet another shrewd purchase by J P McManus.

The Walk In The Park mare was useful in bumpers for former handler Garry Caldwell, winding up last season with a commendable effort in the Aintree Grade 2 bumper behind Seo Linn.

However, her career has reached loftier levels since being switched to Gordon Elliott.

She wasted little time winning for her new handler when stamping her authority on a Listed bumper at Navan last November where her victims included Royal Hillsborough, herself the moral victor of the final race at the Dublin Racing Festival.

That 6-length triumph for her new stable was achieved in routine fashion and the likeable six-year-old made a similarly straightforward transition to hurdling by snugly beating long-term ante-post fancy for this race, Bambino Fever, at Naas a month later.

Although last year's Cheltenham bumper winner closed in after the final flight that day to narrow the margin of victory, Oldschool Outlaw was always well in command and earned a healthy RaceIQ jump index of 8.0 which represented a highly commendable debut, especially in the face of stiff competition from a quality mare like the runner-up.

Indeed, Bambino Fever went on to win her next start to leap to the head of the ante-post market for this event, while there were also victories for third-home Radiator Springs and I'll Raise A Glass (eighth) to give the form some substance.

Elliott gave Oldschool Outlaw a break over Christmas, preferring to prepare her for the Grade 3 Solerina Mares Novice Hurdle (2m2f) at Fairyhouse in early February, a race which has been dominated by archrival Willie Mullins in recent seasons and captured by the likes of Laurina and Honeysuckle in the past.

In turn, Mullins relied on last year's Triumph Hurdle-fifth Place De La Nation to try and complete a fifth successive win in the hurdling feature, but a lively pre-race market suggested the half-sister to Quai de Bourbon faced an uphill task trying to register a third win of the season.

Quite simply, punters only wanted one horse, and their judgement was swiftly vindicated as Oldschool Outlaw toyed with her rivals under a resurgent Mark Walsh before quickening clear of the toiling Place de La Nation heading to the final flight.

A finishing speed percentage in excess of 115% illustrated just how strongly Elliott's mare hit the line and her ability to change gear, whatever the ground, stamps her as a class act in this sphere.

Layers understandably cut her for the victory (into a general 7/2), and the subsequent delight of the owner's racing manager Frank Berry was palpable.

He said: "She jumped great and Mark (Walsh) said Oldschool Outlaw felt good and quickened up lovely after the last.

"She seemingly handles that ground very well and he was very impressed with the way she picked up – you couldn't be happier with her."

Oldschool Outlaw clearly has a tough task trying to repeat her Naas defeat of Bambino Fever as that race came at a time when the Mullins crew weren't firing on all cylinders so last year's bumper heroine can be expected to step forward herself for that facile Fairyhouse success in January.

However, Elliott's half-sister to Castle Carrock from the same family as Annie Angel and Dun Doire, looks a class act in her own right and her temperament and attitude should ensure she doesn't go down without a fight here.

Stayers' Hurdle
MA SHANTOU

CAN it really be seven years since Paisley Park completed a famous and emotive victory in the Stayers' Hurdle?

Quite where the years have gone is open to question, but history could well repeat itself with **Ma Shantou** bidding to give his trainer a second victory in the staying feature.

In some respects, there are parallels that can be drawn between the careers of Paisley Park and the selection as both were well beaten in the Albert Bartlett Novices' Hurdle before starting their first season out of novice company in handicap hurdles.

While Paisley Park shrugged off a mark of 140 to score at Aintree on his 2018 comeback, Ma Shantou was extremely well treated on 129 prior to landing a sizeable gamble in a Pertemps Qualifier at the Cheltenham October meeting.

The son of Shantou made short work of Electric Mason that day and the market expected him to repeat the dose when the old adversaries met up at Haydock in the Betfair Stayers' Handicap Hurdle, an event won in gritty fashion in 2018 by, yes you guessed it, Paisley Park.

There was no joy for Ma Shantou though as he ran poorly, perhaps in keeping with a number of his stablemates who went through a few weeks in the doldrums following their stable's blistering start to the campaign.

Thankfully, the malaise was short lived, and Lavelle's progressive stayer bounced back to form with an impressive defeat of an equally talented and upwardly mobile hurdler in the form of Ace Of Spades at Cheltenham on New Year's Day.

Ma Shantou displayed too many gears for his rivals that day which was encouraging considering the ground was unseasonably good before he then proved his versatility under softer conditions on trials day back at the Cotswold venue, where he smoothly graduated to Graded level with a very taking victory at the expense of Impose Toi.

There were plenty of folk looking to excuse the effort of the runner-up that day with the ground blamed for his seemingly below-par effort.

However, a genuine pace produced a speed figure on a par with Ma Shantou's previous performances at Cheltenham and the data I liked most was the 53.6secs it took for the Cleeve winner to cover the final four furlongs, a figure achieved off the back of that strong gallop.

Given that the International Hurdle, run earlier on the card, was run at a crawl with the three remaining participants, following Sir Gino's sad demise, sprinting for the final quarter of the race, The New Lion was only around seven to eight lengths quicker than Ma Shantou despite covering a mile less.

That confirms that the seven-year-old has both gears and stamina in abundance and, although he

Ma Shantou impresses in winning the Cleeve Hurdle

isn't the biggest, he has both a touch of class and a great attitude.

The long-term market for this year's Stayers' Hurdle has been completely dominated by horses owned either by Robcour or J P McManus with the last two winners, Teahupoo and Bob Olinger, representing the former and the green and gold looking set to be carried by Honesty Policy and the aforementioned Impose Toi.

Teahupoo looked as good as ever at Leopardstown over Christmas, benefitting from a rich seam of form enjoyed by his handler to turn the tables in style on March's Festival conqueror Bob Olinger, but it is worth recalling as impressive as he was over the festive period, that he has also been beaten twice in this race.

His fellow Robcour representative is 4-4 around Presbury Park and unbeaten in three hurdles starts at the track so must surely have frame claims at the minimum once more, even if he is now 11-years-old and only Sire du Berlais since Crimson Embers forty years ago has lifted this prize at that age.

Honesty Policy is the new kid on the block and is still unexposed over hurdles having had just six starts over obstacles, the last of which came when a big eyecatcher in the Long Walk on his seasonal bow.

However, Ma Shantou is blessed with loads of track experience courtesy of his three victories there this term and looks capable of breaking the stranglehold of the Irish superpowers.

Pertemps Network Final Handicap Hurdle
SUPREMELY WEST / ELECTRIC MASON

THE Pertemps Final is one of few Cheltenham handicap hurdles to have so far eluded Dan Skelton, but it is surely a matter of time before the Alcester handler puts the record straight.

At the time of writing, the Champion trainer-elect has a number of qualifiers with Supremely West and Ace Of Spades looking two of the more interesting contenders.

Both have seen the backend of Stayers' Hurdle contender Ma Shantou and, whereas Ace Of Spades has actually won a qualifier to spring to a mark of 139, Supremely West has been fighting all winter to retain a mark in the mid 130s having earned qualification for the final as early as October.

There have probably been nearly as many column inches written about **Supremely West** as former stablemate Langer Dan this term, with his run when a well-beaten 5/4 favourite at the Paddy Power meeting back in November, firmly in the spotlight.

For whatever reason he didn't fire that day as jockey Harry Skelton chose to follow the front-running Gowel Road on the inside part of the track while those that fought out the finish ploughed a furrow towards the outside rail in search of better ground.

Two subsequent outings at Sandown and Aintree, when weak in the market, have seen the eight-year-old slip to an enticing rating of 135 and it will be interesting to see if connections tinker with his wind again before he lines up for this event.

Electric Mason finished 2½ lengths and a place in front of Supremely West in that October qualifier won by Ma Shantou before he headed to the north west to gamely land the Betfair Stayers' Handicap, a race which has worked out superbly since.

Subsequent winners like the aforementioned Ace Of Spades (4th), Nab Wood (6th), Titan Discovery (10th), Red Risk (11th) and Ma Shantou (12th) who has won his next two, including in Graded company, have stamped that race as the warmest staying handicap run to date this season.

Trainer Chris Gordon has resisted the temptation to run his seven-year-old again, preferring to preserve his mark of 139 and it really has been little surprise that he has come into his own over extreme distances this year given his dam is out of a sister to Grand National winner Ballabriggs.

As game and genuine as they come, Electric Mason is just the type to find the rigours of this race to his liking and it's worth noting that his sole defeat this year came at the hands of a horse who is as short at 6/1 for the Stayers' Hurdle at the time of writing.

It would be remiss not to consider Ace Of Spades either given he had the pace to win a four-runner race over two miles at Cheltenham last term and his cosy Huntingdon success was deemed a career best by the ratings boys.

He is a difficult horse to dismiss, but he has some ground to make up on Electric Mason and there is every chance Gordon's grand stayer is also progressing, so he gains the nod.

Electric Mason

CHELTENHAM FESTIVAL 2026 – DAY 3

Banker or Bust
BY RORY DELARGY

Rory is a contributor to The Irish Field and Irish Daily Star, whilst he can be seen on Paddy Power's 'The Cheltenham Countdown' show. He also co-writes the 'Punting Pointers' feature for Sporting Life.

Mares' Hurdle
WODHOOH

STRENGTHS: Wodhooh has won 9 of her 10 starts over hurdles, her only defeat coming in Grade 1 company behind Lossiemouth at Aintree last April, and she has continued to progress with racing, overcoming the moderate form of her stable to run out an authoritative winner of the Martin Pipe over course-and-distance last season. She was suited by the strong pace there but doesn't always get races run to suit, showing a likeable ability to adapt to different tactics in her wins, and finding plenty for pressure.

She has already won twice on the Cheltenham New Course – an important note since the David Nicholson will be run there for the first time this year and the extra emphasis it places on stamina is clearly not an issue for her as it could be for others who have shown their form on the sharper Old Course.

In terms of tactics, she is adaptable because she has the ability to quicken off either a slow or fast gallop and that takes away much of the worry as to how the race will be run. She's also adaptable on the ground, winning on ground ranging from good to soft, although untried on extremes.

She seems to have a perfect temperament and has shown no signs of waywardness in her career, including in her jumping, which tends to be straight and true. She is, in short, the model of what a racehorse ought to be.

WEAKNESSES: She has done all that has been asked of her, except beat the best in her division in Grade 1 company and while that is largely about opportunity, she would look vulnerable pitched in against Lossiemouth, who beat her comfortably at Aintree last season. There are a couple of others with higher ratings in the entries, but there is a fair chance that they will go for the Champion Hurdle. It seems hard to crab Wodhooh but she has been carefully placed to maximise her ability to date and the only time she has raced at the top level resulted in defeat, albeit a career best.

The only other concern for Wodhooh is that her stable has underperformed at the Festival in recent seasons and getting the right preparation for his horses is something that Gordon Elliott has been wresting with for a while. Of course, you could point out that she won last year when the stable had a barren week otherwise, and that's a fair comeback.

She can look workmanlike and tends to do no more than necessary to win. That can make her look vulnerable when assessing collateral form lines, but is easy to characterise as a positive, in that she is likely to find more when required, but it's fair to say she (so far) lacks the wow-factor that punters tend to look for at the top level.

OPPORTUNITIES: The Mares' Hurdle has been run on the sharper Old Course until now, but moving it to Thursday on the New Course asks a different question of the runners, placing the emphasis on stamina. That switch of tracks gives Wodhooh an opportunity to race to her strengths having won competitive handicaps over C&D, beating Joyeuse the first time and then improving further to take the Martin Pipe 12 months ago. She certainly appeals more here than she would have on the Old Course.

Lossiemouth has been the standout mare in the division but Wodhooh's only defeat to her was far from a disappointment, and the division behind the very top seems fluid. Stablemate Brighterdaysahead will surely head to the Champion Hurdle and I have a nagging suspicion that Lossiemouth's connections will still look to take her on again with the score 1-1 this season. If that happens, it would be extremely hard to look beyond Wodhooh in that scenario.

Wodhooh's run style also presents her with an opportunity. While many horses either need to dominate or are best produced from off a solid pace, Wodhooh has demonstrated the tools to cope with either scenario. She can lead and she can come from off the pace with her races showing no real preference, meaning her rider doesn't need to take any tactical gambles.

THREATS: If the field includes **Lossiemouth** or **Brighterdaysahead**, who recently dominated the Irish Champion Hurdle, Wodhooh would probably need to produce a clear career best. She has something to find with either of that pair, and her chance depends to a large degree on neither showing up. The same can be said for **Golden Ace**, although few envisage her switching from the Champion Hurdle having won that race last year.

VERDICT: Wodhooh heads to the Mares' Hurdle with the reputation as a winning machine; a strong traveller, ground versatile, and crucially already proven over the course and distance. Her main question mark is how she measures up against the very best mares at level weights in open Grade 1 company, but it may be that all those rated higher than her will take on the geldings over 2m on Tuesday.

If the big guns show up, she will need to take another step forward, but she may well be able to do so given how she's risen to every challenge she's faced to date. Her consistency, professionalism, and Cheltenham course affinity makes her a major player with legitimate winning claims, which you can amend to "outstanding" should Lossiemouth and Brighterdaysahead clash again in the Champion.

BANKER

Stayers' Hurdle
TEÁHUPOO

HERE we go again – Teahupoo now making a fourth consecutive appearance in this section and it's 2-1 to the author, who is well aware that slightly different circumstances might have seen Gordon Elliott's star a three-time winner of the Stayers' Hurdle. Here are the current standings of those entered in the Stayers' according to Timeform.

Teahupoo	161
Bob Olinger	159
Ballyburn	157
Ma Shantou	155p
Honesty Policy	154
Impose Toi	154

So what has changed since last year, when Teahupoo was outsprinted up the hill by Bob Olinger when favourite to win? The most obvious change is that while he's tended to miss Christmas in the past, Teahupoo won the Christmas Hurdle this year, beating Bob Olinger and Ballyburn, and thereby gaining revenge on the former, who beat him here 12 months ago. What was more remarkable about that win was that it broke a couple of trends. Until now, it's been easy to characterise Teahupoo as best off a lengthy break and on soft or heavy ground and in previous guides I've produced the figures to back this up.

Teahupoo should have been vulnerable in the Christmas Hurdle having reappeared in the Hatton's Grace just four weeks earlier, while the going at Leopardstown was good, which should also have been a negative. Not only did he win that race, but he did so in such style that Timeform raised his rating to 161, having only once bettered 157 prior to that. Everything we know about him is now in flux, but the bottom line is that he's now better than ever, can take a fairly quick turnaround and is no longer reliant on soft or heavy ground to show his best form. Let's do that SWOT analysis.

STRENGTHS: A proven Grade 1 performer at 2½m+ (ran poorly in the Champion Hurdle as a 5-y-o), his record at the highest level in open company reads 1341112211, and his win over last year's Stayers' winner Bob Olinger in December is the best piece of form on offer.

He's a previous Stayers' winner, taking the race comfortably from another previous winner, Flooring Porter in 2024, and he's been placed in 2023 and 2025, looking slightly unlucky when hampered at the last on the first occasion. He travelled best of all last year, but couldn't quite match the finishing speed of Bob Olinger, who has won all four starts at Cheltenham, but lost little by way of reputation.

He retains the speed to win at the top level over 2m4f, taking a third Hatton's Grace at Fairyhouse on his return, but his stamina for 3m is copper-bottomed as he has shown here.

He's very consistent, winning the majority of his races and finishing first or second on nine of his last 11 runs stretching back well over two years and while he's having his fourth attempt at the Stayers', he's still in his physical prime, with no sign at all of any deterioration in form on recent starts. Quite the reverse, in fact.

WEAKNESSES: In the past I've cited the need for soft ground as a weakness for Teahupoo, but I will have to remove that after Leopardstown, but he is certainly vulnerable in tactical races, lacking the turn of foot of Bob Olinger in this last year when the pace was modest and almost caught out by Ballyburn in the Hatton's Grace. That has been his Achilles heel in the past and if the race ends up favouring those who can quicken from the last, he will be at a disadvantage.

OPPORTUNITIES: Not much has been made of the weather of late, but while Teahupoo doesn't need the mud any more, the combination of 3m on soft ground would maximise his chances, whereas a small field race on good or faster is more likely to be tactical. I think soft ground and a good pace is a much more likely scenario, and Teahupoo may do even better with something to set the race up for him on testing ground.

THREATS: As mentioned above, a warm, dry spell and a small field could count against a horse who prefers to pounce off a fast pace and relishes soft ground, but his main threats, as is always the case, are those who will line up against him.

Bob Olinger beat Teahupo fair and square last March and ran with credit behind him at Christmas. His best efforts have come at Cheltenham, and he has won all four races here despite sometimes showing an awkward head carriage.

Impose Toi won the Grade 1 Long Walk in December and was giving the winner 6lb when second to Ma Shantou in the Cleeve last time. He's improved markedly this season, although he has hinted that a stiff 3m may just stretch his stamina, weakening late on over the Stayers' course-and-distance last time.

Honesty Policy was closing in on Impose Toi in the Long Walk and looked a progressive young stayer when scoring at Aintree last April. He's lightly raced and yet to run at Cheltenham, but has the right blend of tactical speed and stamina required for this.

Ma Shantou won the Cleeve over course-and-distance last time and represents the same trainer as previous winner Paisley Park. He's improving but is unproven in Grade 1 company and was getting weight from most of his rivals last time.

VERDICT: I've actually backed Honesty Policy each-way here some time ago (full disclosure and all that) but this column is meant to be about objective assessment not a list of my long-range fancies, and there is no doubt that Teahupoo comes here with stronger credentials than he has in past seasons; I've been keen to oppose him before, but some of the logic for doing so no longer fits, as he demonstrated at Leopardstown at Christmas. He's more likely to get an honest pace than last year and appears to be at the peak of his powers, so...

BANKER

Teahupoo

CHELTENHAM FESTIVAL 2026 – DAY 3
Daily Tips
BY JODIE STANDING

Author of Point-to-Point Recruits, Jodie excels in spotting talent at an early stage in a horse's career.

Dawn Run Mares' Novices Hurdle
ECHOING SILENCE

HENRY DE BROMHEAD is synonymous with mares in the Kenny Alexander colours, largely thanks to the Champion Hurdle heroine Honeysuckle. However, it was Telmesomethinggirl who won this race in 2021, and the trainer looks to have another strong chance of landing the spoils with **Echoing Silence**, a mare who has steadily built a compelling profile and now looks one of the more intriguing contenders in the division.

The six-year-old cost an eye-watering £410,000 at the Cheltenham Sale that followed racing at the 2024 Festival, a price tag that immediately placed her under a brighter spotlight than most. Despite that, she failed to land a blow on her hurdling debut, finishing fifth in a maiden at Navan last December, where she was sent off the 9/4 favourite. That initial disappointment, though, has proved little more than a footnote, as she has been pretty flawless since.

Connections opted to revert her to bumper company in March following that debut hurdling flop, and the decision paid off handsomely. She beat the subsequent two-time winner Kenisa Sport from the Gordon Elliott yard by an easy 2½ lengths, making all and kicking on in good style to cross the line unchallenged.

Put away for the summer, she has returned this season better than ever and won her maiden over 2m4f at Cork in November on yielding ground, beating a tough race-mare in Divaboriva by 6 lengths. Echoing Silence travelled strongly on the heels of the leaders and moved to the front on the bridle over the penultimate flight before quickening clear approaching the last, keeping up the revs all the way to the line. It was a polished, authoritative display that suggested she had taken a significant step forward.

Confirming that promise, she then went to Punchestown in December for a Listed mares' contest over 2m3f on heavy ground. Once again she travelled with purpose behind the pace-setter, wasting little time in the air over her hurdles before quickening to the lead passing the two-furlong marker. From there she stamped her authority and stayed on strongly to hold off the challenge from Switch From Diesel, eventually winning by just shy of 3 lengths, with Carry On Heidi a further 2½ lengths away in third.

Although the bare form of either of her hurdle successes falls short of the level set by the likes of recent Solerina winner Oldschool Outlaw, whose Listed bumper victory and maiden hurdle success have both been significantly boosted since, the manner in which she has dispatched her opposition has been impressive. Lining up against her we could also have Carrigmoornaspruce, who not only beat Switch From Diesel by 6 lengths in a bumper but also overturned the Grade 2 bumper winner Seo Linn at Punchestown. Her runs in defeat at both Down Royal and Leopardstown also read particularly well.

With Echoing Silence, we are dealing with a mare who has steadily progressed in every assignment she has been tasked with. Not only that, but she is also such an imposing physical specimen that there is every reason to believe she will continue to improve with racing and experience. The mares' novices' hurdle run on the New Course presents a stamina test over the 2m1f that will play perfectly into her clear reserves of staying power. Yet it would be a mistake to pigeonhole her as merely a stayer. Despite her winning over 2m4f and 2m3f, she is not short of boot, as shown in her bumper success on good ground last spring, where she showed a sharp turn of foot to settle matters quickly.

All told, Echoing Silence has the profile of a mare on the rise. She is a strong traveller, a good, neat hurdler and looks primed to give Henry de Bromhead another Festival success in these famous colours. The trainer also won the race last year, of course, albeit for a different (powerful) owner.

Pertemps Final Handicap Hurdle
KIKIJO

THE Pertemps Final presents a minefield at the best of times, with three of the last 10 winners returning an SP of 25/1, while only three have returned a single-figure price; the shortest was Sire du Berlais's second success in 2019 at 4/1. Horses tend to come here still unexposed, having qualified without showing their full hand but one candidate who has poked their head above the parapet by winning his last two starts is **Kikijo**.

Philip Hobbs & Johnson White's six-year-old didn't cut much ice on his first couple of starts over obstacles last season, beating only one home at Huntingdon when trailing home 16 lengths behind Bluegrass, and then he finished 25 lengths adrift of Don Hollow when fourth at Uttoxeter on New Year's Eve.

A switch to fences in February saw a change in fortune as he won a novices' handicap chase at Newbury from a mark of 117 by nearly 5 lengths, pulling away at the finish, and that was followed with a decent second to The Boola Boss at the same course when stepped up to 2m6½f from a mark of 121, again staying on strongly without quite getting to the winner.

Sold in the Doncaster Spring Sale to Richard Johnson, the gelding reverted to hurdles at Aintree in October where he relished the step up in trip to 3m½f, keeping on bravely despite making a mistake at the penultimate flight and being crowded over the last. He eventually finished fourth, beaten 3 lengths, but proved willing all the way to the line and challenging for third in the dying strides.

He then built on that effort next time at Cheltenham over 3m from a mark of 120, again adopting a handy position and travelling kindly before upping the tempo off the home bend and finding plenty off the bridle to stay on strongly up the hill to win by 2¾ lengths pulling away.

Raised 7lb, he reappeared just three weeks later at Sandown over 2m7½f and again produced a polished performance to win by ¾ lengths from Turnthelightsdownlow, making the best of his way home from the fourth last and keeping his head bowed low to fend off the challenge from the runner-up from the penultimate flight.

Although Kikijo is now rated on a mark of 135, he's clearly a horse thriving for the step up to 3m and there could well be plenty more to come. A strong traveller and a smooth hurdler, he also gives generously off the bridle with a head carriage of a horse you'd want on your side in the heat of battle.

Kikijo wins at Cheltenham in December

Fulke Walwyn Kim Muir Handicap Chase
WILL THE WISE

EARMARKING a horse for one of the Festival handicaps before we have the weights and entries to hand is always a tricky exercise, and several candidates came under close inspection for this test but the one who keeps drawing me back is **Will The Wise**, representing Gavin Cromwell.

The seven-year-old has built up a solid strike-rate by finishing in the top three on eight occasions and winning four times from just 13 starts, comprising a bumper, a maiden hurdle over 2m6f, a handicap hurdle off 123 over 2m7f, and a novice chase at Galway over 2m2f at the start of this season.

Will The Wise has yet to race beyond an extended 3m, but everything about his racing style suggests a proper stamina test will unlock more. He has repeatedly shaped as a horse who keeps finding at the one pace late on, including when winning at Naas over 2m7f last February and again when finishing sixth in the Pertemps Final at last year's Cheltenham Festival, beaten just under 8 lengths by Doddiethegreat.

Ridden patiently that day, he was anchored towards the rear of mid-division for much of the race before making notable progress approaching the second last. He latched onto the leaders by sneaking up the inner turning for home, and although only able to maintain the one pace up the hill, he stuck on resolutely – more so than the Racing Post comment might imply – to hold sixth on the climb to the line.

That could prove to be a crucial piece of form, as the runner-up was Jeriko du Reponet, who went off as the well-supported favourite and looks like being a fancied runner in this year's Kim Muir. However, Nicky Henderson's gelding was getting 1lb from Will The Wise 12 months ago but looks sure to be conceding weight to him this time around, as Gavin Cromwell's runner is poised on an Irish mark of 138. The form has also worked out well with the fourth, Feet Of A Dancer, and the fifth, One Big Bang.

Following that effort, connections switched Will The Wise to fences in April, clearly believing there was little point lingering over hurdles when his future lay in staying chases. Two educational spins followed before a summer break.

He returned at Galway in October over 2m2f, travelling strongly and making the best of his way home before being edged out late by the now 145-rated Ol Man Dingle, but that experience was put to excellent use a fortnight later over the same course and distance, when he kicked on early and stayed on powerfully to beat the subsequent winner Prends Garde A Toi by just under 3 lengths.

A step back up in trip to 3m for the Troytown at Navan in November from a mark of 136, represented a significant test for a lightly raced chaser in a deep handicap, yet he acquitted himself admirably, keeping on at the one pace to finish fourth behind Answer To Kayf, stablemate Yeah Man, and Dumboyne – all proven stayers.

He then backed that up with another honest effort in the Listed handicap chase at Leopardstown over Christmas, finishing tenth behind Favori de Champdou off 138, making ground over the third last but failing to quicken with the principals off the home bend. Even so, the fact he was sent off 15/2 co-favourite in such a deep field at a time when the yard was notably out of form speaks volumes about how he is regarded. And nothing in that Leopardstown run suggested he wouldn't relish a stronger test over further.

While his siblings and wider family were generally at their best around 2m4f, he is by Well Chosen – a profound influence for stamina – and his one-paced finishing efforts are entirely in keeping with that profile. Still unexposed, particularly at extreme distances, he remains open to improvement from his current mark. Perhaps most crucially, he has already shown he can hold a position and make inroads as a race develops, as he did in last year's Pertemps, and that trait only strengthens the case for a bold bid in the Kim Muir.

Gavin Cromwell

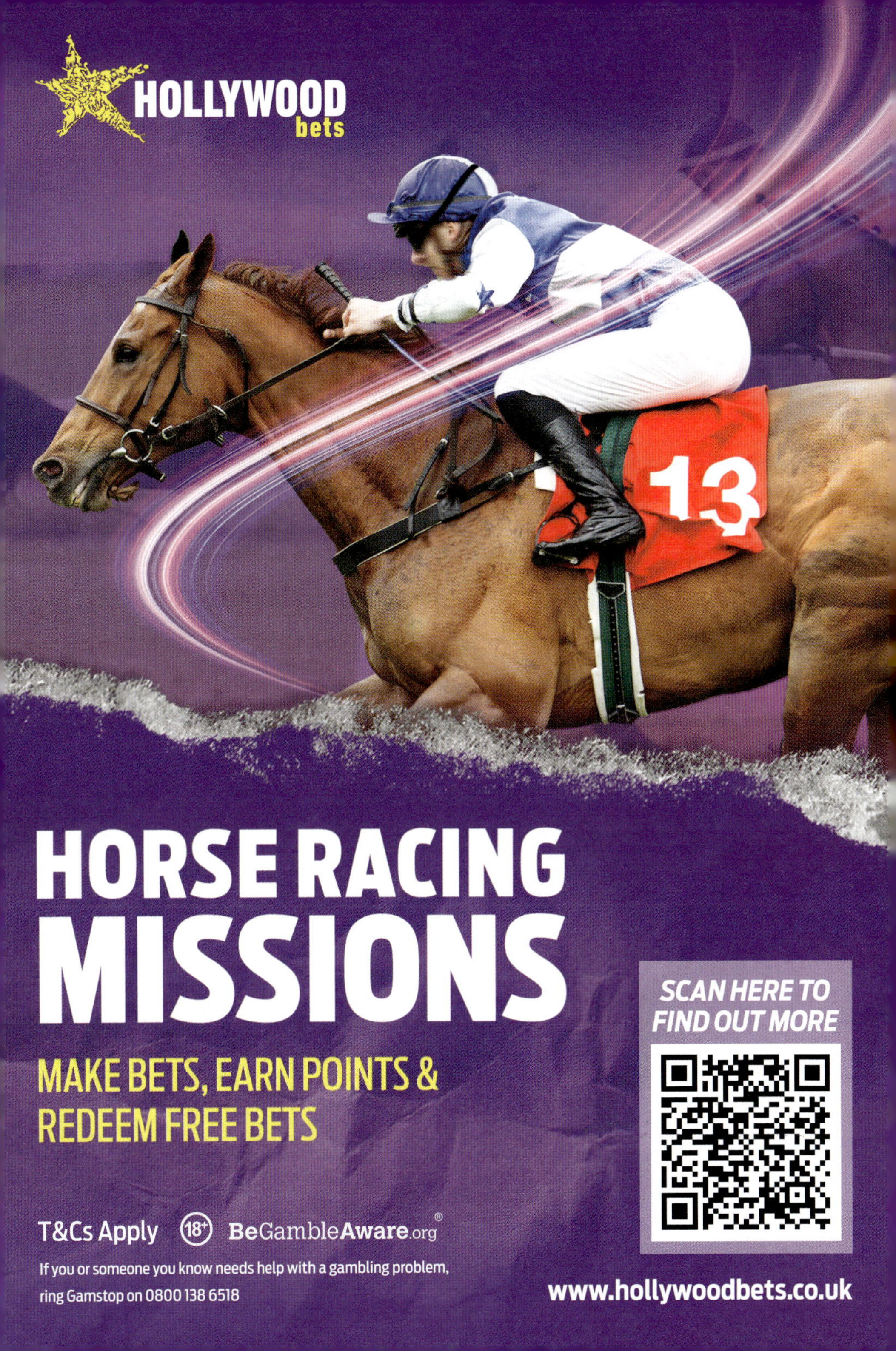

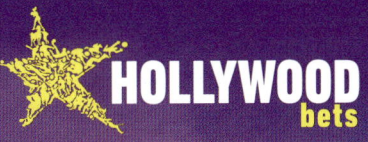

HORSE RACING MISSIONS

MAKE BETS, EARN POINTS & REDEEM FREE BETS

SCAN HERE TO FIND OUT MORE

T&Cs Apply BeGambleAware.org

If you or someone you know needs help with a gambling problem, ring Gamstop on 0800 138 6518

www.hollywoodbets.co.uk

JCB TRIUMPH HURDLE
2m 179y (Grade 1) – New Course

OVERVIEW
GOLD CUP DAY gets underway with the Triumph Hurdle, the four-year-old championship. What was once formerly a cavalry charge, the Triumph Hurdle is now a classier affair with many of the lower rated juveniles now contesting the *'Fred Winter'* earlier in the week. As a result, the Triumph has become a little easier to predict in recent years, although last year saw 100-1 shot *Poniros* cause a huge shock, successful on what was his first ever start over hurdles. That will never happen again (more of that shortly) but he provided trainer Willie Mullins with a fifth win in the past six renewals and Irish-trained horses have now won 10 of the past 13 Triumphs. Respect those coming out of Graded races on their most recent start, in particular the Spring Juvenile Hurdle from Leopardstown.

NEW RULING
MANY chose to call this the *'Poniros Rule'* as it was announced in the summer that hurdling debutants will no longer be able to take their chance in the Triumph Hurdle, or any Grade 1 novice. Many also believed that the ruling was brought in as a deterrent to the powers of trainer Willie Mullins, who actually ran three debutants in the race last year and another pair who had run just once in France and were making their first start for his stable. This isn't the first time Mullins has done this either, with him often liking to throw juveniles into spring Grade 1s, which hands them experience before running as second-season novices the following campaign (Salvator Mundi another good recent examples). The ruling is unlikely to have a huge impact on the race in truth, although it obviously prevents a scenario which we were faced with in 2025.

THE FRENCH CONNECTION
PRIOR to last year, eight of the previous 10 winners had started their careers in France, with seven of those eight winners being French-bred juveniles. Such horses are often more forward than their British and Irish counterparts and as such, will have been jumping from a much earlier age. Again, prior to last year, the previous four winners had won in France before moving to Ireland, with *Vauban* successful on the level and the other trio having already won a race over hurdles in their native country. Last year's runner-up and subsequent Grade 1 winner (reversed form with *Poniros* at the Punchestown Festival) was close to adding to the tally, as he was a winner at Auteuil before moving to Nicky Henderson.

In terms of breeding, of those eight recent winners, only *Quilixios* wasn't French-bred. Although British-bred, he still had that French background, having won over hurdles for Francois Nicolle before being purchased by Cheveley Park Stud.

Pay healthy respect to both French-bred contenders and in particular, any horse who won in France before moving to one of the top yards in Britain or Ireland.

WHEN IS THE RIGHT TIME TO DEBUT?
OBVIOUSLY, an irrelevant question last year, but when is usually the best/right time to make your hurdling debut. Gaining early-season experience certainly doesn't seem to be as important these days as once was the case, although as per the previous subsection, those ex-French winners appear now to be given time to adjust to life in Ireland/Britain before being

unleashed during the second half of the campaign. *Majborough*, for example, had won the previous April but only made his first start for Willie Mullins and JP McManus in the Spring Juvenile on 3rd February, whilst *Lossiemouth* appeared on 4th December, having also won in France the previous spring. *Vauban* only made his hurdles debut on New Year's Eve (again, given time to acclimatise after his move from France), whilst *Pentland Hills* and *Burning Victory* were very late on the scene, only appearing in late February; therefore, don't always assume that all cards have been played after the key trials have taken place.

FIVE FROM SIX FOR DOMINANT MULLINS

PRIOR to 2020, *Scolardy* – way back in 2002 – was the sole Triumph Hurdle winner for trainer **Willie Mullins**, but he has now won five of the past six renewals, including the past four. As we well know, Mullins is the dominant force in National Hunt racing these days and sourcing the right type of juvenile appears to now come naturally to him and his operation. We have seen with the mares' division how Mullins' bloodstock team know exactly where to find a high-class performer and it seems to be heading in the same direction with juveniles, with many of his leading owners allowing him to purchase high-class prospects from France. The earlier *The French Connection* subsection very much ties in with the time that Mullins has taken a stranglehold of the Triumph and given the strength-of-depth in his stable at present, there certainly seems to be no sign of this stopping. Last year, he saddled 11 of the 17 runners, which did suggest that he didn't have an outstanding candidate. He still won the race, of course.

He once again looks to hold a very strong hand, with his team headed by Narciso Has.

SPRING JUVENILE HURDLE

AS TOUCHED upon in the *Overview*, the most significant pointer towards Triumph success in recent years has come in Leopardstown's Grade 1 **Spring Juvenile Hurdle** (staged for the past two years as the **Gannon's City Recovery & Recycling Services Juvenile Hurdle**), which takes place at the Dublin Racing Festival in early February. Prior to last year, the previous four winners of the Triumph had run in the Spring on their most recent start, whilst a further five winners between 2012 and 2018 had taken the same route. Rather surprisingly, of those nine recent winners, only three were successful at Leopardstown, so don't necessarily just focus on the winner, with *Majborough* possibly the best recent example, him finishing third on what was his first start in 307 days. *Quilixios* and *Vauban* recently completed the double and *Lossiemouth* almost certainly would have done, but for meeting trouble in running at Leopardstown.

KEY TRENDS

- ★ 8 of the past 11 winners started their careers in France (7 of which were French-bred)
- ★ 9 of the past 14 winners had contested the Spring Juvenile Hurdle (only 3 were successful)
- ★ 5 of the past 6 winners were trained by Willie Mullins
- ✓ 19 of the past 28 winners won last time out
- ✓ 10 of the past 13 winners were trained in Ireland
- ✓ 9 of the past 17 winners were unbeaten
- ✓ 9 of the past 17 winners were either top- or second-top on official BHA Ratings
- ✓ 6 of the past 8 winners had run no more than twice over hurdles
- ✓ 3 of the past 10 winners were owned by JP McManus
- ✓ 2 of the past 6 winners were fillies
- ✓ Nicky Henderson has trained the winner 7 times
- ✓ Respect Gordon Elliott-trained runners
- ✓ Respect runners from the Hobbs & White stable
- ✓ Respect horses rated 150+
- ✓ Respect winning French form from the previous spring
- ✗ Only 2 of the past 16 winners didn't contest a Graded race last time out
- ✗ Only 3 of the past 21 winners were sent off at odds greater than 12-1
- ✗ The past 8 Adonis winners to have run have all been beaten (all 8 finished unplaced)

Last year's Spring Juvenile was won by Hello Neighbour, who then finished only sixth at Cheltenham, again the third-placed Lady Vega Allen reversing the form and faring best in fourth place. This year's race went the way of Narciso Has, who forged clear to beat the fillies Selma de Vary and Mange Tout.

IRISH IN CONTROL

WHILST the incredible recent record of Willie Mullins clearly helps, Irish-trained juveniles have now won 10 of the past 13 Triumph Hurdles, going back to the brilliant *Our Conor* in 2013. He is the other recent winner to complete the Spring-Triumph double and only two of those 10 recent Irish winners failed to contest the Spring Juvenile, again emphasising the importance of that Grade 1 in its own right, as being a hugely significant race in the calendar for the leading Irish four-year-olds.

In terms of other trainers (aside from Mullins), **Gordon Elliott** won the race in 2014 with subsequent two-time Grand National winner *Tiger Roll* and again in 2018 with *Farclas*, and he also prepared *Quilixios* throughout the majority of his juvenile campaign before he was moved to Henry de Bromhead in the build-up to Cheltenham, following Elliott's infamous suspension. Elliott, who was surprisingly without a runner in 2025, also boasts a fine record in the *'Fred Winter'* so is very much another trainer to respect in this division.

His two winners carried the silks of **Gigginstown House Stud**, whilst another owner to have struck twice recently is **Mrs Susannah Ricci**, successful with both *Vauban* and *Lossiemouth*, whilst *Bapaume* finished third in her pink and vivid green spotted silks in 2017. Both were represented (Gigginstown twice) last year but without success.

GRADED FORM

PRIOR to last year's somewhat freakish result, *Pentland Hills* was the only winner in the previous 15 to be successful without having run in a Graded race on their most recent start. Even *Zarkandar* and *Burning Victory*, who were also winning the race on just their second start over hurdles, boasted winning form at Graded level, the former debuting in the Adonis Juvenile Hurdle and the latter successful in a Grade 3 at Fairyhouse. Given the impact that the Spring Juvenile Hurdle has on the Triumph – and other races (detailed in the next subsection) – in a usual year at least, Graded form is almost essential.

OTHER KEY RACES

PRIOR to the Spring Juvenile, Leopardstown stages the Grade 2 **Changing Times Brewery Juvenile Hurdle** at their Christmas fixture and both *Farclas* (2nd) and *Lossiemouth* (1st) contested that race en route to the Grade 1 at the DRF. This season's race was won in impressive fashion by *Narciso Has*.

Domestically, there is no longer a Grade 1 prior to the Triumph, with Chepstow's **Coral Finale Juvenile Hurdle** downgraded three years ago and that is one fixture change which isn't too difficult to argue with. The Finale rarely has an impact on the spring festivals these days and is often a weaker race now, with *Defi du Seuil* the only winner since *Countrywide Flame* in the 2011-2012 season to have run (and won) at Chepstow on his way to Cheltenham. And, he took in almost every big race throughout the campaign so wasn't your average juvenile in that respect. *Tenter Le Tout* won this season's race for Chester Williams.

As ever, course form is important when it comes to British-trained contenders and the key form guide in the division prior to the Festival is often the **Finesse Juvenile Hurdle**, staged over the exact same course-and-distance as the Triumph on trials day. *Peace And Co* and *Defi du Seuil* (the two latest British-trained winners prior to the once-raced *Pentland Hills*) both won the Finesse on their latest start, as did the diminutive *Katchit* some 19 years ago. Sir Gino was a hugely impressive winner of the 2024 Finesse, before being forced to miss the Triumph and gaining Grade 1 honours at Aintree, whilst this year's contest went the way of Maestro Conti for Dan and Harry Skelton.

Earlier in the season, Cheltenham stages the **Prestbury Juvenile Hurdle** at the November meeting, a race which takes place on the Old Course. Again, this was won by *Defi du Seuil* and *Katchit*, whilst going back to the 1998-1999 season, *Katarino* was another prolific winner who landed this prize for Nicky Henderson. This season's Prestbury was won by One Horse Town, who saw off the strong-travelling Precious Man, and provided trainer Harry Derham with a first Graded race success. The three-year-old hurdle at the December meeting, which was won by Minella Study, seems to have less of an impact on the Triumph.

Katarino went on to win the **Adonis Juvenile Hurdle** before winning the Triumph, as did *Snow Drop* the following year. In fact, five winners between 1999 and 2011 won the Adonis on their most recent start, at which point the Kempton Grade 2 really was the *'key trial'* domestically. However, since then the fortunes of Adonis winners has declined dramatically and the past eight winners of that race to have run in the Triumph have all been beaten and in fact, have all finished unplaced. The Adonis is now a better guide towards Aintree, although last year's winner Mambonumberfive also failed to shine in the Anniversary, having bypassed Cheltenham. Tread carefully should the winner of the Adonis head to Cheltenham, with the race taking place shortly after the Guide was sent to print.

LAST TIME OUT WINNERS

AGAIN, obviously last year was an anomaly, but 19 of the previous 27 winners of the Triumph had won on their most recent start, whilst seven of those eight winners who were beaten last time out came out of the Spring Juvenile Hurdle. So, unless you are looking towards a horse who ran well in defeat in the Leopardstown Grade 1, you very much want to focus on a recent winner. During this lengthy period, *Celestial Halo* – successful in 2008 on the back of a novices' hurdle defeat at Doncaster – is the only winner of the Triumph to be beaten in a race aside from the Spring on their most recent start.

THE UNBEATEN HURDLER

BETWEEN 2009 and 2021, nine of the 13 winners were unbeaten over hurdles and it was very much commonplace to see the likes of *Defi du Seuil* and before him *Our Conor* and *Peace And Co* dominate the division. Whilst it has become less common of late, *Lossiemouth* was hugely unfortunate (badly hampered in the Spring Juvenile) not to add her name to the list in 2023, leaving *Quilixios* as the last 'unbeaten' winner of the race. We should still pay utmost respect to those with a string of 1s next to their name, particularly if they have been winning races at Graded level along the way.

HURDLING EXPERIENCE

THE aforementioned pairing of *Defi du Seuil* (5/5) and *Quilixios* (4/4) were experienced unbeaten hurdlers, although so much experience has become less noticeable in recent years. Since the former won, only *Quilixios* and *Lossiemouth* have run more than twice over hurdles, meaning that six of the past eight winners arrived at Cheltenham on the back of two or less runs. As touched upon in the *Overview*, the introduction of the *'Fred Winter'* means that we see smaller, but more select, fields line up in the Triumph these days and as a result – rather like in the novice hurdles/chases – perhaps experience is less significant than was the case a couple of decades ago. I certainly wouldn't be as put off by just a couple of previous runs now as once would have been the case.

OFFICIAL BHA RATINGS

OF COURSE, last year's winner was without an official handicap rating but nine of the previous 16 winners were either top-rated or second in that respect. Again, those with the stronger (Graded) form tend to come to the fore and as a result, such horses will have been rated higher by the BHA handicapper. *Our Conor* was rated 150 ahead of his win in 2013, whilst more recently both *Peace And Co* and *Defi du Seuil* had obtained a lofty mark of 155 ahead of their respective victories. Any juvenile reaching a mark in the 150s has to be taken very seriously indeed, with only 13 such runners during the past 17 renewals and *Goshen* would have further enhanced this record but for his last flight dramatics in 2020.

MARKET FORCES

THIS trend was again blown out of the water by the 100-1 shot *Poniros* last year, most people simply overlooking a horse without any prior hurdling experience in a Grade 1 championship event. 16 of the previous 20 winners had returned at single figure odds, however, with the race very much having a more predictable (prior to last year!) feel to it these days. Personally, it was a race and a division which I paid less attention to than many others a couple of decades ago, but that has changed in recent years and the winner of the Triumph now appears to be a classier type and easier to identify. As a result, we have seen plenty of recent winners well found in the market, with three successive winning favourites between 2015 and 2017, whilst the three winners between 2021 and 2023 returned at 2-1, 6-4 and 11-8.

FLOURISHING FILLIES

BACK in 2000, the French-trained *Snow Drop* was successful in the Triumph, whilst the two more recent winning fillies were both trained by Willie Mullins, *Burning Victory* and *Lossiemouth*, with the latter leading home a 1-2-3 for Mullins-trained fillies. This is certainly a growing trend and looking towards French-imported fillies who are trained in Closutton is a pattern worth noting. Mullins actually saddled four fillies last year (James Owen ran another) without success, but given the buying power of the stable and their prowess in the French market, it is only likely to continue. The 7lb sex-allowance is clearly significant here, as it is in many other Grade 1 contest.

SEVEN WINS FOR SEVEN BARROWS

FOLLOWING the recent run of Willie Mullins, **Nicky Henderson** only just maintains his position as the overall most successful trainer in the Triumph Hurdle, the Master of Seven Barrows with seven wins to his name to date. *First Bout* and *Alone Success* were winners during the 80s for Henderson, after which *Katarino* struck in 1999. More recently, *Zaynar, Soldatino, Peace And Co* and *Pentland Hills* have all won since 2009 and he has been a shade unlucky in the past two years, Sir Gino forced to miss the 2024 renewal and Lulamba beaten into second having endured an interrupted preparation last year. He remains a trainer who warrants utmost respect with a juvenile and it is interesting that both Sir Gino and Lulamba – like winners *Soldatino* and *Peace And Co* (led home a Henderson 1-2-3) – were French imports, so perhaps he is starting to head back down that route as he goes in search of an eighth Triumph winner.

OTHER BRITISH TRAINERS TO NOTE

NOW training alongside former assistant **Johnson White**, **Philip Hobbs** won the Triumph three times between 2004 and 2017, with *Made In Japan, Detroit City* and *Defi du Seuil*. Without a runner since that last winner some nine years ago, the Hobbs operation boasts a magnificent strike-rate in the Triumph, having had just seven runners during that period from 2004. The stable does not have an entry in this year's race, however.

Alan King won the race twice in three years between 2005 and 2007, and although he hasn't struck again since, has won the Anniversary at Aintree on four occasions, so the dual purpose trainer's runners in top-level juvenile events still warrant careful consideration.

Another with two wins to his name is **Paul Nicholls**, who has also won the Anniversary four times more recently and Aintree has become somewhat more of a target for Nicholls in recent years.

And, although he has yet to win this race, **James Owen** has enjoyed plenty of success in the division as a whole and saw East India Dock hit the frame last year. Given his clear M.O., plus the fact that the Gredley Family seem happy to send a good Flat horse hurdling, it is likely only a matter of time before he has another legitimate contender for the race.

OTHER OWNERS TO NOTE

THE fortunes of both Gigginstown House Stud and Mrs Susannah Ricci have been covered in an earlier subsection, whilst **The Gredley Family** (as per the previous subsection) are likely to continue to target the race, as they go in search of a first Triumph. They saw Allmankind finish third in 2020 and East India Dock filled the same position last year.

Mrs Joe Donnelly saw Haut en Couleurs finish third in 2021 and has been out of luck more recently, with Sir Gino forced to miss the 2024 renewal (when a hot favourite) and Lulamba was beaten into second last year. Subsequent Grade 1 winning novice Salvator Mundi contested the race for the owner in 2024, who continues to spend big money on French recruits and appear to buy a high quality individual from France.

Macho Man and Feel Gut are her possible runners this year.

And, one owner who has had success in the race – and plenty of it – is **JP McManus**, most recently successful with *Majborough* in 2024. *Ivanovich Gorbatov* and *Defi du Seuil* went back-to-back for McManus, who has now won three of the past 10 renewals. He has also been responsible for a further three thirds since 2015 and looks to hold a very strong hand this year, courtesy of the aforementioned Narciso Has and the less exposed Proactif.

Marie Donnelly

ROLL OF HONOUR

Year	Form	Winner	Age	Weight	OR	SP	Trainer	Runners	Last Race (No. of days)
2025		Poniros	4	11-2	-	100/1	W Mullins (IRE)	17	-
2024	3	Majborough	4	11-2	139	6/1	W Mullins (IRE)	12	3rd Gr.1 Spring Juvenile Hurdle (41)
2023	112	Lossiemouth	4	10-9	142	11/8F	W Mullins (IRE)	15	2nd Gr.1 Spring Juvenile Hurdle (41)
2022	21	Vauban	4	11-0	146	6/4F	W Mullins (IRE)	12	1st Gr.1 Spring Juvenile Hurdle (41)
2021	111	Quilixios	4	11-0	147	2/1	H de Bromhead (IRE)	8	1st Gr.1 Spring Juvenile Hurdle (40)
2020	1	Burning Victory	4	10-7	-	12/1	W Mullins (IRE)	13	1st Gr3. Fairyhouse Juvenile Hurdle (20)
2019	1	Pentland Hills	4	11-0	-	20/1	N Henderson	14	1st Plumpton Maiden Hurdle (18)
2018	4122	Farclas	4	11-0	140	9/1	G Elliott (IRE)	9	2nd Gr.1 Spring Juvenile Hurdle (41)
2017	11111	Defi du Seuil	4	11-0	155	5/2F	P Hobbs	15	1st Gr.2 Finesse Juvenile Hurdle (48)
2016	1114	Ivanovich Gorbatov	4	11-0	142	9/2F	A O'Brien (IRE)	15	4th Gr.1 Spring Juvenile Hurdle (41)

LEADING TEN-YEAR GUIDES

Spring Juvenile Hurdle 6 (*Ivanovich Gorbatov* 4th, *Farclas* 2nd, *Quilixios* 1st, *Vauban* 1st, *Lossiemouth* 2nd, *Majborough* 3rd)

Changing Times Brewery Juvenile Hurdle 2 (*Farclas* 2nd, *Lossiemouth* 1st)

Leading Contenders

NARCISO HAS   Trainer: Willie Mullins
Looked an exciting prospect when winning at Auteuil in the spring and built on his first start in Ireland when winning at Leopardstown's Christmas meeting and even more so, when reversing earlier form with Mange Tout in the Grade 1 Spring Juvenile Hurdle at the same venue. A strong stayer, he hurdles well and looks very uncomplicated, and looks to be Willie Mullins' first string. Given his running style, he looks sure to be ideally suited to 2m1f on the New Course and could be very hard to beat.

PROACTIF   Trainer: Willie Mullins
Winner of his sole start in France for Daniela Mele, he made a winning Irish debut at Fairyhouse in mid-January, readily accounting for new stable-mate Macho Man. A big, powerful looking son of Masked Marvel (progeny tend to stay well), he lacks Graded race experience but looked an exciting prospect on his first start for current connections and should they wish to keep him and Narciso Has apart, he has the Supreme Novices' Hurdle as an option, with his win in France coming in September.

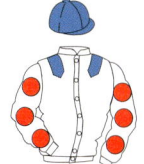

MAESTRO CONTI   Trainer: Dan Skelton
A winner at Moulins for Noel George & Amanda Zetterholm, he has now won both starts for Dan Skelton, latterly in the Grade 2 Finesse on trials day. Looks to have a fine blend of speed and stamina, finishing strongly over the Triumph course-and-distance, despite again racing enthusiastically. Handed a BHA Rating of 136, he will likely need to improve again to fend off a strong-looking Irish challenge, but is a worthy contender who warrants careful consideration. Has won on heavy, good and soft, so isn't ground dependant.

SELMA DE VARY   Trainer: Willie Mullins
Split Narciso Has and Mange Tout on her first start for Willie Mullins in the Spring Juvenile, having won at Auteuil in November and had earlier shown a good level of ability in defeat. A keen going filly by Zarak (sire of several smart juveniles in recent years), she came from off the pace to record an encouraging second and can be expected to improve, although she does look more of a speed filly, so Aintree could be suitable. Wears a hood and represents the winning connections of 2022 and 2023.

FANTASY WORLD   Trainer: Nicky Henderson
Bought for 600,000gns after he won Ascot's Noel Murless Stakes, where he stayed on strongly over 1m6f and earned a rating of 103. A non-runner at Newbury recently, he was handed entries at Haydock and Musselburgh shortly after, so may have made his debut by the time you read this. By French Guineas winner Make Believe, he could be a fascinating recruit to the hurdling ranks, but will need to make an impressive start if he is to book his place in the Triumph field and justify his lofty market position.

MINELLA STUDY   Trainer: Adam Nicol
Won a three-year-old maiden hurdle last summer for John Nallen, he has since joined Adam Nicol and after finishing runner-up in a 2m handicap on the Flat, won the Listed Wensleydale at Wetherby before winning over the Triumph course-and-distance in December. That form reads well, with the second winning easily at Ascot and One Horse Town running well against Maestro Conti on trials day, and although he missed a possible prep-run at Musselburgh, isn't one to underestimate. Clearly on an upward curve.

Cheltenham Festival Betting Guide 2026

WILLIAM HILL COUNTY HANDICAP HURDLE
2m 179y (Premier Handicap) – New Course

OVERVIEW
THE shortest distance handicap hurdle of the week, the County was formerly the final race of the fixture when the meeting was staged over just three days, whilst now it holds a position much earlier on the day four card. Staged over the same course-and-distance as the opening Triumph Hurdle, it is often well-contested and hold-up performers tend to do well, coming off a strong pace. In recent years, Willie Mullins has been the dominant force, winning eight of the past 16 renewals. Dan Skelton is next best in terms of recent results, saddling four winners in the past 10 renewals. Both novices and second-season hurdlers have a fine record here, so focus on those *'younger'* contenders with the greater scope to show further improvement.

MULLINS IS THE MASTER
HAVING first won the race in 2010 with *Thousand Stars*, trainer **Willie Mullins** has now won 50% of the past 16 renewals, with *Absurde* and *Kargese* his two latest winners. Given the competitiveness of the handicap, it is an incredible record, even by Mullins' ridiculously high standards. All bar one of his winners – that being the classy *Arctic Fire* who was having his first run in over a year – were aged five or six, and several of his winners went on to scale greater heights, none more so than *State Man*, who won the race as a novice before winning the Champion Hurdle two years later. *Arctic Fire* won from a mark of 158 and carried top-weight, and Mullins isn't averse to running a high-class horse in this race, although in the main, it has paid to focus on his improving types, those on the way up. *Saint Roi* was another novice winner for the stable, whilst the two latest winners – like several before them – were in their first season outside of novice/juvenile company.

NOVICES
BETWEEN 2006 and 2013 there were three novice winners of the race and although we have seen fewer strike in recent years, three novices in a row landed the prize between 2020 and 2022, with *Belfast Banter* (a second-season novice) sandwiched between the Mullins-trained pairing of *Saint Roi* and *State Man*. Obviously, it is slightly harder to get a novice into the race these days, with the recent rule change meaning that the last named pairing – who had each run three times previously – would no longer be eligible. After the victory of *State Man*, that requirement was increased to four previous hurdles starts and prior to last season, it increased yet further to five runs. It was also extended to non-novices, which meant Joyeuse (winner of the William Hill Handicap Hurdle at Newbury) was not eligible to run. There weren't many novices in the field last year either, but take note when one does line up, particularly one with a progressive profile.

LIGHTLY-RACED HURDLERS
THIS subsection is really a continuation of the previous one. As touched upon, all runners now must have had a minimum of five runs to be eligible to run here (and in other handicap hurdles throughout the week, with the exception being the *'Fred Winter'* of course) but second-season hurdlers boast a tremendous record here and *Kargese* was indeed

having just her second start outside of juvenile company when scoring last year. That now means that 20 of the past 25 winners were either novices or second-season hurdlers and siding with those progressive types, who have the greater scope to improve, is certainly the way to go.

AGE

RATHER in-keeping with those last two subsections, focusing on the *'younger'* contenders is very much a strong positive. 20 of the past 27 winners were aged either five or six – with that clearly the prime age range – whilst only one of those past 27 winners was aged nine. Those in double digits tend to struggle, with the last such winner coming in 1959, and it is 19 years since a nine-year-old won the race. During those past 18 renewals, horses aged nine or older have a record of 0-40, so should really be quickly overlooked.

HIGH-CLASS HURDLERS

ALTHOUGH only the aforementioned *Arctic Fire* has managed to win from a *'high mark'* in recent years, we have since seen plenty run well in defeat and Willie Mullins again saddled the top two in the handicap (Daddy Long Legs carried top-weight off a mark of 152) last year. He certainly isn't afraid to run a good horse here, whilst the likes of Petit Mouchoir, Aramon, We Have A Dream and Pied Piper have all finished runner-up off lofty marks of late, the latter beaten a head off 154 in 2023 before returning to finish third off 156 the following year. Pay healthy respect to these high-class (150+ rated) hurdlers from an each-way perspective and given the recent run of results, it wouldn't be a shock to see another prove successful before too long.

WEIGHTS AND OFFICIAL BHA RATINGS

ONLY two horses have won from a rating in the 150s this century – the other being *Sporazene* back in 2004 – with every other winner this century rated 146 or below. 15 of the past 20 winners were rated in the 130s, with 13 of those rated 134 or higher, whilst *State Man* and *Kargese* were recent winners from a mark of 141. Interestingly, Willie Mullins' four winners since 2020 were all rated between 137 and 141, which gives you a ballpark figure of the type of horse he looks to target the race with.

Subsequent Champion Hurdle winner *State Man* carried 11-1 some four years ago and stable-mate *Kargese* became just the fourth winner this century to carry more than that, when successful from the same rating (slightly lesser renewal) last year. Statistically, and historically at least, it can pay to look at those in the 130s carrying 11-1 or less, but as we have seen of late, slightly classier performers are beginning to make an impact.

KEY TRENDS

- ⭐ 8 of the past 16 winners were trained by Willie Mullins
- ⭐ 20 of the past 25 winners were either novices or second-season hurdlers
- ⭐ 20 of the past 27 winners were aged 5 or 6
- ⭐ 4 of the past 10 winners were trained by Dan Skelton
- ✓ 15 of the past 20 winners were rated in the 130s
- ✓ 14 of the past 22 winners were ex-Flat horses
- ✓ 13 of the past 19 winners were trained in Ireland
- ✓ 12 of the past 22 winners had run in France
- ✓ 9 of the past 18 winners returned at odds of 20-1 or greater
- ✓ 8 of the past 12 winners had run at Cheltenham previously
- ✓ 5 of the past 10 winners had a 72+ day break
- ✓ Paul Nicholls won the race 4 times between 2004-2014
- ✓ Respect hold-up performers
- ✗ Only 1 of the past 26 winners was aged 9
- ✗ Only 2 winners this century were rated higher than 146
- ✗ Only 2 English trainers have won the race in the past 20 years
- ✗ Only 3 of the past 24 winners were outright favourite
- ✗ Only 4 of the past 22 winners carried more than 11-1
- ✗ Horses aged 9+ are 0-40 during the past 18 years
- ✗ Nicky Henderson-trained runners are 0-35 this century
- ✗ Gordon Elliott-trained runners are 0-27 since 2011

	Top Weight (OR)	Bottom OR	Winner OR
2025	152	136	141
2024	156	130	138
2023	155	133	134
2022	152	134	141
2021	155	129	129
2020	150	133	137
2019	153	127 (oh4)	146
2018	154	133	139
2017	158	134	158
2016	152	138	138

EX-FLAT PERFORMERS / TACTICS

WHILST last year's winner had a jumping background, 14 of the previous 21 winners were ex-Flat horses and given that we see less high-quality horses switch codes these days, that is an extremely healthy return. Such horses have a poor record in the novice hurdles at the Festival nowadays but continue to do well in this race, perhaps with the 2m1f on the New Course playing to their strengths.

Again, tactically, this track is set up to help those who like to come from off the pace and there is certainly less emphasis on hurdling than there is on the Old Course. The configuration and lay out of the hurdles means that horses have ample time to make their move from the back of the field and with a strong pace always likely in the County, those who force the pace tend to come back and set things up for the finishers.

Last year's second, third and fourth were all ex-Flat performers and the fourth-placed Ethical Diamond went on to win the Duke Of Edinburgh at Royal Ascot, the Ebor at York and the Breeders' Cup Turf at Del Mar. When I included an image of him on these pages last year, highlighting him as a likely contender for the race, I certainly didn't envisage seeing him winning in America some seven-and-a-half months later.

THE FRENCH CONNECTION

A LARGE number of those ex-Flat winners are included in this figure – as is last year's winner, who had run over hurdles before joining her current connections – with 12 of the past 22 winners having started their careers by running in France, before moving to the UK or Ireland. This is a trend which is popular with juveniles but it is also the case here, so pay significant attention to any French imports who line up this year.

COURSE FORM

PREVIOUS form at Cheltenham seems more significant with British-trained winners of the County Hurdle, although last year's winner also boasted fine form at the track, having finished runner-up in the 2024 Triumph Hurdle. *Faivoir* had good form at Cheltenham as a novice (won at the track), whilst his stable-mates *Superb Story* and *Mohaayed* had both run in the **Greatwood Hurdle** earlier in the season, the former having finished runner-up in the November contest. L'Eau du Sud ran in the Greatwood for Dan Skelton before finishing runner-up in the 2024 County, whilst the stable was represented in this season's contest by *Faivoir* (finished 3rd under Heidi Palin) and the well-backed Mirabad (Knickerbockerglory was a non-runner also). The race was, of course, won in emphatic fashion by Joe Tizzard's Alexei.

SUPER SKELTON

AS TOUCHED upon in the previous subsection, trainer **Dan Skelton** is another with a decent record in the County. In fact, ordinarily and without the incredible record of Willie Mullins, his would look outstanding in the context of a race of this magnitude. Skelton won this race in 2016, 2018, 2019 and 2023, and although Valgrand disappointed last year, runners from his stable have to be given utmost respect here, as they do in all of the leading handicap hurdles throughout the season. Described by many as a magnificent 'target trainer' Skelton excels in handicap hurdles and he has also had a fourth and second in this race in recent years. Since 2016, 44% of his runners have finished in the first six and a winning strike rate of 22% is most noteworthy. With two of his winners returning at 33-1, backing his horses blindly in the County (during this period) would have yielded a profit of £72 to a level stake of £1, so give huge consideration to any horse he aims at this year's contest.

ARRIVING FRESH

LAST year's winner had been given a very light campaign, only reappearing in January and having had just that one run outside of juvenile company (something which Willie Mullins seems keen on these days, with juveniles from the previous season – Lossiemouth a good example at a higher grade). He showed his magnificent training ability when readying *Arctic Fire* to win on the back of a 418-day absence, whilst many a recent winner arrived on the back of a short, mid-season break, with five of the past 10 winners having had a 72+ day break. That run began with *Superb Story*, who wasn't seen after finishing runner-up in the Greatwood some 124 days earlier.

AN IRISH STRANGLEHOLD

PLENTY of Irish-trained horses have won the County Hurdle, with 13 of the past 19 winners now falling into that bracket. However, of late, and partly due to the impressive run of Willie Mullins, the Irish appear to be taking over somewhat, with five of the past six winners hailing from the Emerald Isle. During this period, Peter Fahey has also hit the target with *Belfast Banter*, whilst Tony Mullins, Tom Hogan, Thomas Mullins and Tony Martin have also all struck since 2007.

One leading Irish trainer who has yet to taste success in the County is **Gordon Elliott**, who has run plenty of well fancied horses in recent years and saddled the runner-up (again) last year, Ndaawi. Pied Piper has twice hit the frame for the Elliott stable and not including the trio that were sent out by Denise Foster in his absence, his record since 2011 now stands at 0-27. Tread carefully with runners from Cullentra House.

OTHER BRITISH TRAINERS TO NOTE

ASIDE from his former assistant Dan Skelton (covered in an earlier subsection of his own), **Paul Nicholls** is 'next best' in terms of British trainers and in fact, is the only other British trainer to have won the County Hurdle since 2006, which is quite remarkable. Nicholls won the race three times in the space of nine years – between 2006 and 2014 – having struck in 2004, too, with *Sporazene*, so four wins in the space of 11 renewals was a huge return at that time. More recently, Nicholls' runners have been thin on the ground. Without representation in 2025, he has saddled just six runners during the past decade and interestingly, all four of his winners were aged five or six, so pay close attention to his 'younger' contenders. Three of his winners were also novices.

Successful in both 1993 and 1997, **Nicky Henderson** has a poor record in the County Hurdle this century and was also, again, without a runner last year. Despite being responsible for three runners-up since 2017, the record of Seven Barrows' runners since the turn of the century stands at 0-35.

RESPECT McMANUS' RUNNERS

ALTHOUGH he wouldn't have the best of strike rates in the race, owner **JP McManus** has won three County Hurdles this century, starting with *Master Tern* in 2000. More recently, the Irish-trained pairing of *Alderwood* and *Saint Roi* have added to his tally and like in all handicaps throughout the week, McManus' runners are to be respected. His sole representative, McLaurey, finished a disappointing last of 16 last year, whilst it is worth noting that all three of his winners were novices, that despite *Alderwood* winning at the age of eight (he was a second-season novice). McManus has also been responsible for the runner-up in 2009, 2011 and 2015, and is likely to be well represented again this year.

MARKET FORCES

WE HAVE seen three winning outright favourites in the past six years (all three being Willie Mullins-trained five-year-olds, incidentally) but, overall, there is no real consistent pattern when it comes to where the winner can be found in the market. During the past eight years, we have also seen three winners return at 33-1, so this is another handicap in which you should not be put off by a big price. Whilst *Sporazene* and *Desert Quest* were sent off joint favourites in 2004 and 2006 respectively, the last outright favourite to win before 2020 was *Master Tern* in 2000. So, perhaps, recent results suggest that the race is (potentially) becoming a little more predictable and easier to solve.

NEWBURY HANDICAP HURDLE

ALTHOUGH this race has been removed from the *Leading Ten-Year Guides* section of the *Roll Of Honour*, the race formerly known as the *'Betfair'* and before that the *'Schweppes'* then the *'Tote Gold Trophy'* has still produced two winners in the past 11 years. Now run as the **William Hill Handicap Hurdle**, it takes place shortly before the Guide goes to print and is a similar contest in many ways, in that it is a competitive and valuable 2m handicap hurdle. It is a race in which novices also boasted a fine record in for many years, although the new rules mean that it is more difficult for a novice to gain enough experience (prior to the weights being announced) in order to be eligible. Back in 2010, Spirit River also contested the Newbury race en route to winning the Coral Cup. This year's race was won by Tutti Quanti, with Wellington Arch and *Faivoir* filling the places.

ROLL OF HONOUR

Year	Form	Winner	Age	Weight	OR	SP	Trainer	Runners	Last Race (No. of days)
2025	2	Kargese	5	11-5	141	3/1F	W Mullins (IRE)	16	2nd Gr.2 Ascot Mares' Hurdle (55)
2024	16P4	Absurde	6	10-10	138	12/1	W Mullins (IRE)	17	4th Gr.1 Tattersalls Ire Nov. Hurdle (40)
2023	4P	Faivoir	8	10-7	134	33/1	D Skelton	24	P.U. William Hill Hurdle (34)
2022	F1	State Man	5	11-1	141	11/4F	W Mullins (IRE)	26	1st Limerick maiden hurdle (45)
2021	312562	Belfast Banter	6	10-0	129	33/1	P Fahey (IRE)	25	2nd Gr.2 Novice Hurdle (19)
2020	51	Saint Roi	5	10-13	137	11/2F	W Mullins (IRE)	24	1st Tramore maiden hurdle (72)
2019	5692	Ch'tibello	8	11-5	146	12/1	D Skelton	24	2nd Aintree Handicap Hurdle (97)
2018	1023	Mohaayed	6	10-8	139	33/1	D Skelton	24	3rd Gr.1 Christmas Hurdle (81)
2017		Arctic Fire	8	11-12	158	20/1	W Mullins (IRE)	25	2nd Gr.1 Irish Champion Hurdle (418)
2016	12	Superb Story	5	10-12	138	8/1	D Skelton	26	2nd Gr.3 Greatwood Handicap Hurdle (124)

LEADING TEN-YEAR GUIDES

Greatwood Handicap Hurdle 2 (*Superb Story* 2nd, *Mohaayed* 11th)

MRS PADDY POWER MARES' CHASE (Liberthine)

2m4f 127y (Grade 2) – New Course

OVERVIEW

WE HAVE now had five renewals of the Mares' Chase and all five have gone for export, with Irish-trained mares successful each year to date. Willie Mullins has trained the winner three times, whilst the past four winners all carried the silks of leading owner, JP McManus. Two of the five winners had finished runner-up in the race 12 months earlier, whilst form at the Festival (in general) is another positive. However, as with most mares' only races, form in open Graded company against geldings is arguably the biggest positive. All five winners won last time out.

IRISH DOMINANCE

WE ONCE again saw an Irish dominated finish of the Mares' Chase in 2025, with *Dinoblue* leading home a 1-2-3 for Irish-trained mares, who have now won all five renewals of the Grade 2 contest. Admittedly, more Irish trainers appear to target the race, or have mares of suitable quality at their disposal, but it is still a noteworthy positive trend. Three British-trained mares took their chance last year (all sent off at big odds, it has to be said), taking the tally of such runners to 0-16 to date, with only three managing to record a top-three finish across the five renewals. As things stand, very much favour those trained in Ireland.

MULLINS MAKES IT THREE FROM FIVE

HAVING saddled both *Colreevy* and *Elimay* to win the first two renewals of the race, **Willie Mullins** made it three wins in five years when *Dinoblue* struck in 2025. Mullins was doubly-represented last year, taking his tally of runners in the race to 14 (almost as many as the combined total of UK-trained mares) but we know from the Dawn Run and the Mares' Hurdle that this is a division in which he excels and the new enhanced programme for mares is only likely to benefit a powerful stable such as his. Prior to last year, his earlier winners were second best in terms of market position within his yard, so don't always assume that his apparent 'first string' is the most likely winner, although *Dinoblue* justified strong support and favouritism last year (more of that anon).

FOUR IN A ROW FOR JP

WHILST Mullins' record of three winners in five years is impressive, even more impressive is that leading owner **JP McManus** has now won the past four renewals. 2022 winner *Elimay* was beaten just ½ a length in the inaugural running of the race, so we could easily have been looking at five from five for McManus. Over the five years, McManus has had eight runners in the race and *Limerick Lace* led home a 1-2 in 2024, so he has recorded four wins and two seconds from those eight runners. A remarkable return.

Dinoblue looks set to defend her crown and would appear to be McManus' standout candidate.

ARRIVING IN FORM

ALL five winners to date arrived at Cheltenham on the back of a victory, so heading across the Irish Sea in good form seems to be essential. All four were successful in either Listed or Graded company and in each of the past two years, only three of the nine runners matched up against this profile.

PROVEN STAMINA

PRIOR to last year, the previous four winners had all won over a minimum of 2m3½f and having *Proven Stamina* in the form book is an obvious positive. I must admit, I still had slight reservations about last year's winner in this regard, as she appeared to be outstayed in 2024 by *Limerick Lace*, although on slightly better ground, saw the race out really well to win 12 months later. *Dinoblue* had been campaigned over the minimum trip earlier in the campaign, but it can usually pay to look at those with strong form over a mid-range distance.

Look for a mare who finishes well, too. *Allegorie de Vassy* is a good example of one to be cautious of. Her form would show that she had won over further (2m6½f) but she isn't the strongest of finishers and the hill on the New Course can find such weakness out.

FORM AGAINST THE BOYS

THIS is a drum which I bang constantly when it comes to mares' only events, form against geldings is a huge positive. Such races – especially Graded company – will invariably be much stronger than mares' only races, so if a mare has the ability to mix it in open company against the boys, it will usually stand her in good stead when reverting to racing against her own sex. All five winners to date boasted Graded form against geldings, with last year's winner having been campaigned in the Hilly Way Chase at Cork and the Paddy's Rewards Club Chase at Leopardstown, races which are primarily in the calendar for Queen Mother Champion Chase level horses. That kind of form will always offer a mare a potential class edge in a race of this nature.

CLASS ANGLE

THE first three winners had won on multiple occasions in Graded company, with the very first winner *Colreevy* successful at Grade 1 level in bumpers and as a novice chaser (both against the boys). *Dinoblue* didn't quite fall into this category, but she had won an open Grade 1 (against the geldings) over 2m1f the previous season and as touched upon in the previous subsection, had run in open company twice earlier last season. Look for any standout pieces of form, but consistent form – especially winning form – at Graded level is a huge plus here.

PENALTY STRUCTURE

SUCH was her 'class edge' over the field, *Dinoblue* was the only one of last year's nine runners to run under a maximum penalty of 11-7, which she incurred for that aforementioned Grade 1 success. To date, we have seen only three mares contest this race under that maximum penalty and two have won, the other being *Colreevy*. So, rather in-keeping with the previous two subsections, in particular *Class Angle*, respect any mare who carries this weight as she has clearly earned the right to do so.

In this race, mares will carry a base weight of 11-2, with a 5lb Grade 1 penalty (as above), whilst winners of Grade 2 races will carry a 3lb penalty. *Elimay* managed to avoid such penalties, with her wins at that level achieved in novice company and far enough in advance of her win in this race for them to count against her.

UNBEATEN NOVICES

TWO of the five winners to date – *Colreevy* and *Impervious* – were unbeaten novices, both with a record of 3-3 over fences prior to winning this race. Interestingly, both had beaten the boys in a Graded race so looked to have rock solid credentials and as there is no novice chase for mares at the Cheltenham Festival, this is always likely to prove an attractive option to owners/breeders (and, trainers alike) as it will (again) invariably be weaker than races such as the Arkle or Broadway. As a result,

KEY TRENDS

- All 5 winners were trained in Ireland
- All 5 winners won last time out
- All 5 winners had Graded form against geldings
- All 5 winners had run 3 times that season
- All 5 winners returned at odds of 3-1 or shorter
- All 5 winners were aged 7 or 8
- The past 4 winners were owned by JP McManus
- 4 of the 5 winners were rated 150+ (all 5 were rated 147+)
- 4 of the 5 winners had run at the Cheltenham Festival previously
- 3 of the 5 winners were multiple Graded winners previously
- 3 of the 5 winners were trained by Willie Mullins
- 2 of the 5 winners were unbeaten novices
- Mares carrying the maximum penalty of 11-7 are 2-3
- Respect proven stamina
- UK-trained runners are 0-16
- Mares aged 9+ are 0-12
- Mares aged 6 are 0-3
- Be wary of twice raced mares
- The first 4 favourites were beaten
- Gordon Elliott-trained mares are 0-6 (3 of those were sent off at single figures)

'older' and more exposed mares might always be vulnerable to a high-class novice.

CHASING EXPERIENCE

THE fact that those two winning novices had run three times is significant. We have seen several times already (in the brief history of the race) that novices with only two runs behind them tend to struggle here. Both Concertista (2022) and Allegorie de Vassy (2023) were also *'unbeaten novices'* and sent off favourite for their respective race but crucially, both had run just twice and both were subsequently beaten. There were no such runners in last year's field, but tread carefully if one with such limited experience turns up, especially if they are trading short in the market.

THREE RUNS SEEMS PERFECT

NOT only did the two novice winners run three times earlier in the campaign, all five winners to date were having their fourth run of the season in this race, so three previous outings is clearly perfect in terms of number of runs. Three of the five winners had won at least twice earlier in the season.

AGE

ALL five winners were aged either seven or eight, which is clearly the ideal age range. Only three six-year-olds have taken their chance in the Mares' Chase (currently 0-3), whilst mares aged nine or older have a record of 0-12, following the disappointing effort of 10-year-old Fontaine Collonges last year. Tread carefully with *'younger'* contenders – although that is a very small pool of runners to date – whilst *'older'* runners can be overlooked a little more readily. Focus on those aged seven and eight.

CHELTENHAM FESTIVAL FORM

LAST year's winner became the second mare to win this race having finished runner-up the previous year. *Elimay* did the same, so pay attention to last year's **Mrs Paddy Power Mares' Chase** result, with Brides Hill the one who chased home *Dinoblue*. Last year's winner also finished runner-up in the Grand Annual as a novice in 2023, whilst she finished a disappointing ninth when sent off favourite for the Dawn Run in 2022. She was actually beaten favourite at three successive Festivals, before winning this race in 2025.

The **Dawn Run Mares' Novices' Hurdle** is now a good breeding ground for future Mares' Chase winners, with *Dinoblue* the third to have run in that. Both *Colreevy* and *Impervious* – the two novice winners of this race – had run in that contest 12 months earlier, finishing fifth and sixth, respectively.

Diva Luna finished third in that race last year and has developed into a smart novice chaser, who it seems will be aimed at this race.

Limerick Lace is the only winner of the Mares' Chase to arrive at Cheltenham without any previous Festival (or course) experience.

OTHER KEY RACE

BOTH *Elimay* and *Dinoblue* won the Listed **Opera Hat Chase** at Naas on their most recent start. That 2m race was won again this year by *Dinoblue*, who had little trouble in justifying very short odds.

OFFICIAL BHA RATINGS

FOUR of the five winners were rated in the 150s, with *Dinoblue* top rated on a mark of 157. She beat the next best (Brides Hill rated 154) and we have actually only seen 16 mares rated in the 150s (or higher) take their chance, so any such runner should be given considerable respect. There were only two such runners in 2024 (*Dinoblue* was rated 160 ahead of that renewal), when *Limerick Lace* was successful as a 147-rated mare. Certainly look no lower than the high 140s when using ratings to narrow down the contenders.

MARKET FORCES

PRIOR to last year, all four favourites had been beaten, although the first three winners were second in the market and *Limerick Lace* was third. *Dinoblue* landed a blow for favourite backers last year and all five winners started at odds ranging from 6-4 to 3-1. Given that the classier mares often come to the fore here (holding a class edge over many a rival), don't expect to see a *'shock'* result in the Mares' Chase. Focus on the top two or three in the betting.

OTHER TRAINERS TO NOTE

ONLY three trainers have won the race to date, with **Gavin Cromwell** and Colm Murphy the other duo aside from three time-winner Willie Mullins. The former was without a runner in 2021 or 2022, and was responsible for the runner-up last year, although he did run three. A winner and a second from five runners is still a decent return and his leading contender for the race this year would appear to be Only By Night, runner-up in last year's Arkle.

One trainer who has yet to land this prize is **Gordon Elliott**, who is 0-6 to date, following the third placing of Shecouldbeanything last year. Three of the six were sent off at odds of 7-1 or shorter (Mount Ida the shortest at 5-2 in 2022), so tread carefully with runners from Cullentra House. Kala Conti, like Only By Night owned by Robcour, is a possible runner for Elliott this year.

Diva Luna has developed into a smart novice chaser for Ben Pauling

ROLL OF HONOUR

Year	Form	Winner	Age	Weight	OR	SP	Trainer	Runners	Last Race (No. of days)
2025	221	Dinoblue	8	11-7	157	6/4F	W Mullins (IRE)	9	1st Listed Opera Hat Chase (34)
2024	121	Limerick Lace	7	11-2	147	3/1	G Cromwell (IRE)	9	1st Listed Doncaster Chase (77)
2023	111	Impervious	7	11-5	151	15/8	C Murphy (IRE)	9	1st Gr.3 Punchestown Nov. Chase (61)
2022	321	Elimay	8	11-2	155	9/4	W Mullins (IRE)	8	1st Listed Opera Hat Chase (34)
2021	111	Colreevy	8	11-7	150	9/4	W Mullins (IRE)	11	1st Gr.2 Thurles Mares Nov. Chase (51)

LEADING TEN-YEAR GUIDES

*Dawn Run Mares' Novices' Hurdle 2 (*Colreevy* 5th, *Impervious* 6th)
Opera Hat Chase 2 (*Elimay* 1st, *Dinoblue* 1st)
*Liberthine Mares' Chase 2 (*Elimay* 2nd, *Dinoblue* 2nd)

* denotes previous season

ALBERT BARTLETT NOVICES' HURDLE (Spa)
2m7f 213y (Grade 1) – New Course

OVERVIEW

REGISTERED as the Spa Novices' Hurdle, we have now had 21 renewals of the Albert Bartlett-sponsored contest, which is the longest distance of the novice hurdles staged at the Festival. Introduced in 2005, it was handed Grade 1 status just three years later and the *Roll Of Honour* includes subsequent Gold Cup winners, *Bobs Worth* and *Minella Indo*. Respect Irish Point-to-Point winners and horses who performed well in bumpers and whilst it was once a huge positive to have plenty of hurdling experience, classier types tend to come to the fore nowadays, although this is the one race in this division which can produce a *'shock'* result according to the betting.

MULLINS STRIKES AGAIN

BETWEEN 2005 and 2016, trainer **Willie Mullins** failed to add the Albert Bartlett to his Festival C.V., but since then, the trainer has now won four of the past nine renewals, with subsequent Stayers' Hurdle winner *Penhill* getting the ball rolling. *Monkfish* and *The Nice Guy* followed, whilst 2024 Champion Bumper winner *Jasmin de Vaux* provided Mullins with a fourth win in the race, when successful last year. Whilst it once seemed to be an afterthought, or the target for those not deemed good enough to contest the Baring Bingham on day two, it now seems that Mullins is more intent on targeting horses at the Albert Bartlett in their own right and given the strength in depth in his stable, that is only likely to continue. It goes without saying, but respect runners from Closutton.

IRISH DOMINATION

WHILST the recent record of Willie Mullins clearly helps, Irish-trained horses have dominated this race since 2014. Prior to that, there were only two Irish-trained winners – those being *Weapon's Amnesty* and *Berties Dream* – during the first nine renewals of the race, but things have very much swayed in their favour since. Nine of the past 12 winners were trained in Ireland, although Mullins is the only Irish trainer to have won it more than once.

Both **Noel Meade** and **Gavin Cromwell** have had one winner and one placed horse from very few runners, so any horse either runs warrants respect, whilst **Henry de Bromhead** was successful in 2019 with *Minella Indo* and saw the mare The Big Westerner run a huge race to finish runner-up last year.

For years, **Gordon Elliott** struggled to land a race which he was happy to target with a leading novice, his record prior to 2024 standing at 0-12, with many of the dozen sent off at relatively short odds. The likes of No More Heroes, Death Duty, Commander Of Fleet and Fury Road were all beaten in the Albert Bartlett, before Elliott finally struck with *Stellar Story* two years ago. Wingmen finished only mid-division last year, in the silks of Bective Stud, who suffered dreadful luck in the race in 2022, when Ginto suffered a fatal injury when travelling very strongly.

The first five horses mentioned in the previous paragraph, including winner *Stellar Story*, carried the silks of **Gigginstown House Stud**, who have won the race on three occasions, with *Weapon's Amnesty* and *Very Wood* earlier winners for the leading owner. Again, they don't mind running a high-class novice here and given their buying process – looking for future long-distance chasers – they tend to have the right kind of horse for the race.

DORANS PRIDE IS FORM TO RESPECT

NO FEWER than five of the past 17 winners had contested the **Dorans Pride Novice Hurdle**, run this season as the **Defender Novice Hurdle**. In 2024, *Stellar Story* became the second Dorans Pride runner-up to win the Albert Bartlett, following on from *Vanillier*, whilst the other trio were all successful in it, interestingly whilst it was still a Grade 3 (now a Grade 2). The Big Westerner won last season's Dorans Pride before finishing runner-up in this race, whilst Delta Work won the Pertemps Final on the back of having finished second at Limerick and Faugheen won it before dropping in trip to win the Baring Bingham.

This season's race was won by Gordon Elliott's Kazansky, who had just a head to spare over County Final.

GRADED FORM ALMOST ESSENTIAL

A COUPLE of recent winners – the Willie Mullins-trained pairing of *Monkfish* and *The Nice Guy* – were able to win the Albert Bartlett without having contested a Graded novice hurdle, but that is unusual, with such form usually a pre-requisite. Whilst the latter proved that experience is no longer as significant as once was the case (more of than anon), it does pay to focus on those with previous Graded experience in the form book. Only three of the 21 winners hadn't contested a Graded race on their most recent start and the other of those, Harry Fry's *Unowhatimeanharry*, had won a Grade 2 on his penultimate start, before winning a Pertemps Qualifier at Exeter.

18 of the 21 winners had won or placed at Graded level and although last year's winner just missed out here, he had twice finished fourth in Grade 1s and was a Grade 1 bumper winner, so wasn't lacking for overall class. In fact, the past two winners both won a maiden hurdle on debut before running exclusively in Graded company thereafter (both failed to win again between debut and Cheltenham).

COURSE FORM

WHEN it comes to British-trained winners – which have, of course, been thin on the ground of late – course form at Cheltenham seems important. Seven of the 21 winners to date had won one of three Grade 2s which take place at the track earlier in the campaign (and all from 26 runners).

KEY TRENDS

- 18 of the 21 winners had won or placed in a Graded novice hurdle
- Horses rated 152+ are 3-5
- 4 of the past 9 winners were trained by Willie Mullins
- 10 of the past 14 winners had won an Irish Point-to-Point
- 18 of the 21 winners had contested a Graded novice hurdle on their previous start
- 18 of the past 20 winners were aged 6 (11) or 7 (7)
- 15 of the 21 winners finished 1st or 2nd last time out
- 12 of the 21 winners had won at least twice over hurdles (although the past 5 winners had won just once)
- 12 of the 21 winners had run 4 times or more over hurdles (although this is also becoming less significant)
- 11 of the past 15 winners had won or placed in at least one bumper
- 10 of the 21 winners had won over 2m7f+ (a further 4 had finished placed in a Graded race over that distance)
- 9 of the past 12 winners were trained in Ireland
- 7 of the 21 winners had won the Hyde, Bristol or Classic earlier in the season (from 26 runners)
- 5 of the past 17 winners had run in the Dorans Pride Novice Hurdle at Limerick
- 5 of the past 7 winners had run 3 times or less over hurdles
- 4 of the past 12 winners had run in a bumper at the Punchestown Festival
- 3 of the past 17 winners were owned by Gigginstown House Stud
- 3 of the past 5 winners had run in the Golden Cygnet Novice Hurdle (Nathaniel Lacy) at the DRF
- Respect horses rated 150+
- Jonjo & A J O'Neill-trained runners are 2-3
- Only 1 of the 21 winners was an ex-Flat horse
- Only 1 of the past 20 winners was aged 5
- Only 2 of the past 12 winners returned at odds shorter than 11-1
- Only 2 of the past 16 winners were rated below 140
- Only 2 of the 21 winners failed to contest a Graded race
- Only 4 of the past 18 winners had yet to race over 2m7f+
- Gordon Elliott-trained runners are 1-16
- Nicky Henderson-trained runners are 0-15 since 2012

First up and the least important pointer towards Albert Bartlett success in the **Hyde Novices' Hurdle**, which takes place on the Old Course over 2m5f and is staged at the November meeting. Won by *Black Jack Ketchum* way back in the 2005-2006 season, it is often more of a pointer towards the Baring Bingham but was won this season, on debut, by the Paul Nicholls-trained No Drama This End.

Black Jack Ketchum returned to Cheltenham the following month and won the **Bristol Novices' Hurdle**, a race which takes place on the New Course and over the exact same course-and-distance as this race. *Nenuphar Collonges*, *Unowhatimeanharry* and *Kilbricken Storm* all won the Bristol, too, and this season's race was won by Carlenrig, from the fast finishing They Call Me Hugo.

Staged over 2m4½f (also on the New Course) on trials day, the **Classic Novices' Hurdle** often sees contenders for both the Baring Bingham and this race clash, and *Wichita Lineman*, *Bobs Worth* and *At Fishers Cross* all won that contest on their most recent start. In 2013, *At Fishers Cross* actually beat The New One, whilst in 2007 Massini's Maguire finished third to *Wichita Lineman*, so twice the race has thrown up the winner of both the Baring Bingham and Spa. This year's Classic was won by Kripticjim, who narrowly denied Taurus Bay.

OTHER KEY RACES

IN THE early years of this race, Haydock's Grade 2 **Prestige Novices' Hurdle** certainly had more of an impact, with both *Moulin Riche* and *Brindisi Breeze* running in Merseyside during February. I think that it comes a little close in the calendar ahead of the Festival these days, with a hard race over almost 3m on (often) testing ground, not exactly the ideal prep just a month before Cheltenham. Interestingly, last year's third Derryhassen Paddy was due to contest the Prestige until being declared a non-runner (surprisingly, the ground being too quick) so it is a race that remains on the radar of some trainers, certainly those in the North.

More recently, the **Golden Cygnet Novice Hurdle** – staged as the **Nathaniel Lacy & Partners Solicitors Novice Hurdle** at the Dublin Racing Festival – has been a key pointer towards Spa success. Three of the past five winners had run at Leopardstown on their most recent start, with all three finishing out of the frame. The past two winners finished fourth in the Grade 1 over 2m6f, a race which prior to the introduction of the DRF was run over 2m4f. In its old format, both *Weapon's Amnesty* and *Martello Tower* finished runner-up in the former Grade 2 contest. This year's race was won in impressive fashion by Doctor Steinberg.

Last year's winner *Jasmin de Vaux* had earlier finished fourth in the Grade 1 **Ballymore Novice Hurdle**, a race registered as the **Slaney Novice Hurdle**. Handed Grade 1 status in 2015, it is now a hugely important race in the Irish novice hurdle calendar, shortly after the turn of the year. *Very Wood* finished third in the 2014 renewal and last year's race actually also threw up the Baring Bingham second, with The Yellow Clay successful. Envoi Allen and Bob Olinger also won that race en route to victory in the 2m5f contest, whilst the aforementioned Ginto won it in 2022, before he would surely have gone very close in this race, but for meeting with that (heartbreaking) fatal injury. This year's race was won by I'll Sort That.

NATIONAL HUNT BACKGROUND

DESPITE the fact that ex-Flat horses boast a good record in the Stayers' Hurdle, to date *Penhill* is the only such winner of the Albert Bartlett. Often such horses will step up in distance as they get older or come out of novice company, so past results certainly suggest that we should focus on those with a more traditional *National Hunt Background*.

10 of the past 14 winners had won an Irish Point-to-Point at the beginning of their careers and this includes the past three winners, whilst 11 of the past 15 winners had won at least once in the bumper division. Prior to last year, non-Graded bumper form was what to look out for, but *Jasmin de Vaux* had, of course, won the Weatherbys Champion Bumper the previous year. He became just the second winner to have contested a Graded bumper from the previous season, whilst four of the past 12 winners had run in a bumper at the Punchestown Festival, the other three in non-Graded events.

PROVEN STAMINA

WHILST just 10 of the 21 winners had run over a distance of 2m7f+ under Rules, a further five – including the past two winners – had won a Point-to-Point over 3m, which admittedly, isn't always a guarantee of a horse developing into a stayer. Certainly in the early days of this race, when experience was key, proven stamina was more important and as the classier horses have started to feature, it has become (seemingly) less significant. For example, none of the past five winners had won over a staying trip over hurdles, so I would be less hung up on this nowadays, rather like with the Broadway Novices' Chase on day two.

OFFICIAL BHA RATINGS

SUBSEQUENT Gold Cup winner *Bobs Worth* was one of the classier earlier winners of the race, him top-rated with an official mark of 150 going into the 2011 renewal. Campaigned over shorter, he was fairly prominent in the Baring Bingham market until the late switch, whilst since then, three more winners were rated in the 150s, all three rated 152. Respect any runners rated so high, as we have actually only seen five horses rated 152+ contest the race, so a record of 3-5 is most noteworthy.

At the other end of the scale, only two of the past 16 winners were rated below 140, so that is the minimum requirement really, in terms of Official BHA Ratings.

A NEW TYPE OF WINNER / EXPERIENCE

AS TOUCHED upon several times already, there was a time – not so long back – when focusing on horses with the most experience was a positive ahead of the Spa. The likes of *Berties Dream* and *Unowhatimeanharry* had run 14 and 15 times, respectively, before winning this race, for example. The very first winner *Moulin Riche* had run in eight hurdle races, but the race appears to have evolved of late and since 2019, we have seen five horses win on the back of three starts or less. Therefore, hurdling experience is much less significant these days, with *The Nice Guy* successful on just his second ever start over hurdles and both *Minella Indo* and *Stay Away Fay* won it after two previous outings.

The race has a classier feel to it now than in the early years, with leading trainers now seemingly happier to target it with a better quality of horse, last year's winner being a Champion Bumper winner highlighting this. Therefore, look for genuine Grade 1 form where possible and pay less emphasis on those with less room to improve.

In terms of winning experience, 12 of the 21 winners had won at least twice over hurdles, but again, this is also now changing, with only one of the past seven winners ticking this box. The past five winners had all won just once over hurdles.

CURRENT FORM

NO FEWER than 20 of the 21 winners to date recorded a top-four finish on their most recent start, with 2021 winner *Vanillier* the only outlier. He was found to have been *'sick'* after his 10th place finish in the Nathaniel Lacy, but we really ought to be looking towards those who have performed well on their most recent start. The past two winners also hailed from the same Grade 1 (both finished 4th), whereas 15 of the 20 finished either first (9) or second (6) last time out.

MARKET FORCES

OF ALL the Grade 1 novice races throughout the week, the Spa is the one where we are most likely to see a *'big priced'* or *'shock'* winner. Since 2010, four 33-1 shots have prevailed, whilst the maiden *Minella Indo* struck at a massive 50-1 in 2019. Since *At Fishers Cross* justified favouritism (11-8) in 2013 for Rebecca Curtis, only two of the past 12 winners returned at single figure odds, with *Jasmin de Vaux* the subject of strong support on the day last year. Do not let the market influence you in this race; many a recent winner would have boasted a similar profile as those much shorter in the betting, so don't be put off by big odds.

AGE

FRENCH-RAIDER *Moulin Riche* won the inaugural running of the race as a five-year-old, although *Very Wood* is the only horse to repeat the trick since. Winning the Baring Bingham is difficult enough for a five-year-old, so the longer distance of the Spa is certainly a real test and such youngsters can be readily overlooked. *Unowhatimeanharry* is the sole eight-year-old winner of the race (old for a novice hurdler) so 18 of the 21 winners were aged either six (11) or seven (7), which is clearly the perfect age group. Six of the past nine winners were aged six, with that age group starting to become the dominant one. Back to the younger horses briefly and Allaho – a subsequent top-class chaser – is a good example of a five-year-old who found this test a little too much, so tread carefully with any such runner.

TONGUE-TIED

FOUR of the past 10 winners wore a tongue strap, with that aid often helping stayers breathe over a long distance. Whilst it wouldn't be an outstanding trend, we don't see too many applied to novice hurdlers, indeed just two wore one last year, including the third-placed Derryhassen Paddy. Certainly, don't see it as a negative.

BRITISH TRAINERS TO NOTE

SUCCESSFUL back in 2006 and 2007 with *Black Jack Ketchum* and *Wichita Lineman*, **Jonjo O'Neill** – who now trains alongside son **A J O'Neill** – is the only trainer, aside from Willie Mullins, to have won this race more than once. Without a runner in each renewal between 2008 and 2023, Johnnywho ended the stable's 100% record in the race, but 2-3 is still extremely noteworthy. If the O'Neill team see fit to have a runner in the Spa, take note.

Although **Lucinda Russell** – now training alongside **Michael Scudamore** – has won the race just the once, with the ill-fated *Brindisi Breeze*, she saw the aforementioned Derryhassen Paddy hit the frame last year and the stable does well with staying novice hurdlers, having won Aintree's Sefton in 2021 and 2023. They tend to buy embryonic staying chasing types, rather like Gigginstown House Stud.

Nicky Henderson saddled the first and second in 2011, but has a record of 0-15 since. The 66-1 shot Nativehill failed to complete last year and runners from Seven Barrows should be treated with a degree of caution. In contrast to the Russell-Scudamore stable, Henderson tends to train a speedier type and his better, high-quality novices tend to be aimed at the Supreme (hence his record in the race, then also moving forward into the Arkle and Champion Hurdle).

Doctor Steinberg completes the hat-trick at Leopardstown

ROLL OF HONOUR

Year	Form	Winner	Age	Weight	OR	SP	Trainer	Runners	Last Race (No. of days)
2025	144	Jasmin de Vaux	6	11-7	141	6/1	W Mullins (IRE)	20	4th Gr.1 Golden Cygnet Nov. H'dle (41)
2024	1324	Stellar Story	7	11-7	141	33/1	G Elliott (IRE)	13	4th Gr.1 Golden Cygnet Nov. H'dle (41)
2023	12	Stay Away Fay	6	11-7	136	18/1	P Nicholls	24	2nd Gr.2 River Don Nov. H'dle (48)
2022	111	The Nice Guy	7	11-8	-	18/1	W Mullins (IRE)	16	1st Naas maiden H'dle (47)
2021	2120	Vanillier	6	11-5	144	14/1	G Cromwell (IRE)	16	10th Gr.1 Golden Cygnet Nov. H'dle (41)
2020	211	Monkfish	6	11-5	152	5/1	W Mullins (IRE)	19	1st Thurles Nov. H'dle (54)
2019	32	Minella Indo	6	11-5	-	50/1	H de Bromhead (IRE)	20	2nd Gr.3 Clonmel Nov. H'dle (28)
2018	3113	Kilbricken Storm	7	11-5	143	33/1	C Tizzard	20	3rd Gr.1 Challow Nov. H'dle (77)
2017	11141	Penhill	6	11-5	143	16/1	W Mullins (IRE)	15	1st Gr.2 Limerick Nov. H'dle (78)
2016	1111	Unowhatimeanharry	8	11-5	152	11/1	H Fry	19	1st Exeter Pertemps Qualifier (33)

LEADING TEN-YEAR GUIDES

Golden Cygnet Novice Hurdle 3 (*Vanillier* 10th, *Stellar Story* 4th, *Jasmin de Vaux* 4th)
Dorans Pride Novice Hurdle 3 (*Penhill* 1st, *Vanillier* 2nd, *Stellar Story* 2nd)
Bristol Novices' Hurdle 2 (*Unowhatimeanharry* 1st, *Kilbricken Storm* 1st)
Royal Bond Novice Hurdle 2 (*Very Wood* 5th, *Penhill* 4th)

Leading Contenders

DOCTOR STEINBERG — Trainer: Willie Mullins
Only 1-4 in bumpers, he has been a revelation since sent hurdling, winning all three starts on ground ranging from good-to-yielding to heavy. Having won at Galway, he beat Thedeviluno in the Grade 2 Navan Novice Hurdle before putting up a career-best in the Nathaniel Lacy at Leopardstown. Despite racing keenly, he saw out the 2m6f trip strongly and whilst the Baring Bingham remains an option, this race would look to be the obvious target. The more expansive New Course also appeals as being more suitable.

THEDEVILUNO — Trainer: Paul Nolan
Ran four times in bumpers without winning, but has won twice from three starts over hurdles, successful at Gowran, where he beat Skylight Hustle (Grade 1 winner since) and The Passing Wife (won next time). Runner-up to Doctor Steinburg in the Navan Novice Hurdle, he improved for stepping up to 3m when running out an impressive winner of the Grade 2 River Don at Doncaster. Already seven, he is versatile in terms of ground and looks sure to run a big race for Paul Nolan, responsible for the runner-up in 2020.

ESPRESSO MILAN — Trainer: Willie Mullins
Another who failed to win in bumpers (0-3 for Fergal O'Brien), he has since moved to Willie Mullins and has won both starts over hurdles. Successful on heavy ground over 2m at Punchestown (runner-up won next time), he stayed on strongly to win over 2m6f at Thurles, in a race which was won by 2020 winner Monkfish. Lacks Graded race experience but is an improver and looks sure to stay the trip. Another interesting contender for a stable who holds a strong hand in a race which they have won four times since 2017.

I'LL SORT THAT — Trainer: Declan Queally
A smart bumper performer who boasts plenty of experience, he is 4-4 over hurdles this season (did run once in a maiden hurdle in December 2024), with his last two wins coming in Graded company. Successful in the Grade 1 Ballymore Novice Hurdle at Naas last time, he once again displayed a fine attitude to see off Sortudo, in a race which was ruined somewhat by the lack of hurdles. Also entered in the Baring Bingham, this would seem a more logical target, especially on better ground. Should stay 3m.

SORTUDO — Trainer: Willie Mullins
Looked a stayer in bumpers and boasts plenty of experience from that sphere, including a seventh in the Champion Bumper and a 12-length defeat of I'll Sort That at Fairyhouse. Runner-up to the same rival at Naas in Grade 1 company, he had earlier won a 2m maiden at Cork in impressive fashion. Keener in his races over hurdles, the trip is an unknown and has limited hurdling experience, but is clearly talented and again, he is a shorter price for this than he is for the other novice hurdles.

KAZANSKY — Trainer: Gordon Elliott
Found Doctor Steinberg 8 lengths too good at the DRF but had earlier won a Cork maiden over 2m1f and Limerick's Grade 2 Dorans Pride Novice Hurdle (often a good guide to this race). That wasn't an overly strong event this season and he probably achieved more when runner-up in the Grade 1 last time. No match for the winner, he finished clear of the remainder and looks sure to appreciate stepping back up in distance. Given that latest defeat, is likely to be overlooked in the market but could still run well at rewarding odds.

DAY FOUR
RACE FIVE

BOODLES CHELTENHAM GOLD CUP
3m2f 70y (Grade 1) - New Course

OVERVIEW
NOT only is the Gold Cup the feature contest on day four, but it is also the feature of the whole fixture and in many ways, it is the blue-riband event of the whole National Hunt season. As such, the race needs little introduction and the extended 3m2f trip – against top-class opposition – usually results in one of the sternest test a staying chaser will ever face. With that in mind, those who are still improving – in particular, second-season chasers – have done well in recent years, whilst there have been four multiple winners this century, latterly *Al Boum Photo* and *Galopin des Champs*, who both went back-to-back. Irish-trained horses have dominated the race of late – winning 10 of the past 12 renewals – and a relatively light campaign, building towards a peak performance, is often beneficial.

ANOTHER MULTIPLE WINNER?
AS TOUCHED upon in the *Overview*, four horses this century have won the Gold Cup more than once, the other pairing being *Best Mate* – successful in three consecutive years between 2002 and 2004 – and *Kauto Star*, winner in 2007 and 2009. *Cottage Rake* (1948-1950) and *Arkle* (1964-1966) are another pair of three-time winners, whilst *Golden Miller* (1932-1936) remains the most successful horse in the history of the race, winning it five times in a row.

This year, *Galopin des Champs* will look to regain his crown and join those all time greats on three wins, whilst last year's winner *Inothewayurthinkin* could bid to become the fifth horse this century to win the race more than once. The former has finished placed on both starts this season, whilst the latter has looked a shadow of himself in three runs.

SECOND-SEASON CHASERS
IF LOOKING away from a previous winner, focusing on the previous season's novices is a good starting point, as second-season chasers boast a fine record in the Gold Cup of late. Since *Long Run* was successful in 2011, eight of the past 15 winners were second-season chasers, whilst going back even further, the record stretches to 13 of the past 25 winners. Statistically speaking at least, every other year sees a second-season chaser win the Gold Cup, so pay close attention to those who performed well as a novice last term.

BROADWAY NOVICES' CHASE
NO FEWER than six of the past 18 winners had contested the **Broadway Novices' Chase** – run at present as the **Brown Advisory Novices' Chase** – the previous season. Both *Bobs Worth* and *Lord Windermere* completed the double, as did *Denman* and also *Looks Like Trouble*, who was even earlier (and, therefore, not included in that 6-18 stat). *Long Run* and *Minella Indo* were both placed in the Broadway, whilst *Al Boum Photo* looked set to hit the frame when taking a heavy fall two out.

2024 Broadway winner *Fact To File* returned last year to win the Ryanair, whilst the 2025 renewal went the way of *Lecky Watson*, who beat *Stella Story*. Whilst that pair are available at huge odds, the last named boasts a fine Festival record so would be an *'outsider'* to note.

LIGHTLY-RACED CHASERS

IN-KEEPING with the past couple of subsections, focusing on those with fewer miles on the clock and, therefore, more scope to improve and put up a peak performance on the second Friday in March are often key pointers. 23 of the past 26 winners had run in 12 chases or less prior to winning the Gold Cup, with only *A Plus Tard* outside of his first three seasons over fences among the past 15 winners. *Coneygree* struck as a novice some 11 years ago, but (again) statistically speaking, focusing on those in either their second or third seasons over fences is a positive. Since 2010, 11 of the 16 winners had run nine times or less over fences, so pay healthy respect to those who are far from being fully exposed. It is difficult for a more experienced chaser to win this race, unless they have done so previously, with a career-defining performance often being produced in a first Gold Cup.

QUICKLY SENT CHASING

THIS is something which we look at ahead of the novice chase division and certainly horses being aimed at the aforementioned Broadway Novices' Chase have a better chance of winning if sent chasing immediately after their novice hurdle campaign. That carries forward into open company and the Gold Cup, with every single winner this century having spent just one season over hurdles. We often hear or read about the prospect of horses dominating the hurdling division before embarking on a chasing career, but that is extremely rare and difficult to do, so pay most attention to those who had just one year over the smaller obstacles. If you believe you have a potential future Gold Cup horse on your hands, get them chasing at the earliest possible opportunity.

P2P FORM NOT ALWAYS A POSITIVE

GIVEN the record of former Point-to-Point winners in both the Supreme and Baring Bingham, as well as in the aforementioned Broadway Novices' Chase, you could easily be forgiven for looking towards such runners in the Gold Cup. However, it isn't necessarily the case, with only three of the past 21 winners winning in the Point-to-Point sphere. Prior to that, three-time winner *Best Mate* was a former winning Irish Pointer, but since then, only *Denman*, *Imperial Commander* and *Minella Indo* had won between the flags. *War Of Attrition* and *Native River* both failed to complete in their Point, but overall, such horses don't have the success rate at this level as you might expect.

One theory is that by the time they have been in training to win a Point, often spent a season in

KEY TRENDS

- 25 of the past 26 winners were aged 7-9 (12 of the past 13 winners were aged 7 or 8)
- 23 of the past 26 winners had run in 12 chases or less
- 21 of the 25 winners this century had won or placed at the Cheltenham Festival previously
- Every winner this century had spent just one season over hurdles
- 4 of the past 7 winners were trained by Willie Mullins
- 18 of the 25 winners this century won last time out
- 20 of the 25 winners this century returned at odds of 9-1 or shorter (17 of them at 7-1 or shorter)
- 14 of the past 21 winners had not won beyond 3m½f
- 13 of the 25 winners this century were second-season chasers
- 13 of the past 24 winners had won a Graded novice hurdle over 2m-2m4f
- 12 of the past 23 outright favourites have won (this includes 4 of the past 6 winners)
- 10 of the past 12 winners were trained in Ireland
- 8 of the past 19 winners were French-bred (this includes 5 of the past 7 winners)
- 6 of the past 18 winners had run in the previous year's Broadway (Brown Advisory) Novices' Chase
- 4 of the past 13 winners were 1-1 that season
- 4 multiple winners of the race this century
- Placed horses from the Supreme Novices' Hurdle are 6-7 this century
- No winner this century over the age of 9
- No winner since 2000 had contested the Cotswold Chase on trials day
- Only 1 winning 6yo since 1964
- Only 1 winning 10yo since 1993
- Only 1 of the past 15 winners ran in the Betfair Chase
- Only 1 of the past 14 winners ran in the King George
- Only 2 of the 25 winners this century had won over a distance further than 3m2f
- Only 2 of the 25 winners this century returned at double figure odds
- Only 2 of the past 18 winners had run more than 3 times earlier that season
- Only 3 of the 25 winners this century had placed in the race previously
- Only 3 of the past 21 winners had won a Point-to-Point earlier in their career
- Only 4 of the 25 winners this century failed to finish 1st or 2nd last time out
- Be wary of heavy ground form from earlier in the season

bumpers, then had a couple of years as a novice (over both hurdles and fences), the progression simply isn't there by the time the horse reaches open company and this can be one of the reasons why some prefer to see horses sent straight over hurdles and bypass a bumper campaign.

AGE FOR CONCERN

AGE certainly does catch up with horses when it comes to the top-level races at the Cheltenham Festival and there hasn't been a 10-year-old Gold Cup winner since *Cool Dawn* in 1998. Since 2005, there have actually only been four nine-year-old winners of the race and only one of them has come in the last 13 years, with the other dozen most recent winners being aged seven (4) or eight (8), the latter seemingly the prime age for success.

At the other end of the scale, *Long Run* is the only six-year-old winner of the race since 1964 and runners of that age group are quite few and far between.

IRISH DOMINANCE

GOING back to the 90s and *Imperial Call* was a very rare Gold Cup winner for the Irish. Between 1997 and 2013 inclusive, only *Kicking King* and *War Of Attrition* – successful in successive years in 2005 and 2006 – were the only Irish-trained winners of the race, but since then the tide has very much turned in favour of those who have travelled across the Irish Sea. 10 of the past 12 winners were trained in Ireland and this includes the past seven, with *Native River* the sole UK-trained winner during the past decade. Irish-trained horses have dominated many a feature race in the British calendar, particularly at Cheltenham, and the Gold Cup is (now) certainly no different. Pay healthy respect to the leading Irish challengers.

PROVEN STAMINA IS NOT ESSENTIAL

DON'T be misled by the subheading, having form over 3m in the book is important, but form over this extended 3m2f less so. In fact, having won over marathon distances – trips that exceed that of the Gold Cup – is a huge negative, with only two of the past 25 winners having won over further than 3m2f. That pairing were *Synchronised* and *Native River*, the latter successful in the National Hunt Chase, a race won last year by subsequent Irish Grand National winner Haiti Couleurs. He for one would be up against it here, based on this trend alone.

Many a modern-day Gold Cup winner will have built up in trip over a period of time. *A Plus Tard* was successful over much shorter distances in his earlier days, whilst *Galopin des Champs* was campaigned over an intermediate trip as a novice, before having his stamina stretched out during his second season over fences (at one point, his stamina was questioned by many). Whilst last year's winner had won the Kim Muir over 3m2f at the 2024 Festival, his earlier form all came over shorter, so when looking back at novice form, having contested good races over 2m4f-2m5f can be viewed upon as a positive these days.

Most of the Grade 1 staying chases staged earlier in the season – both in Britain and in Ireland – are around the 3m/3m½f mark, with one exception being the **Betfair Chase** at Haydock, which is now staged over 3m1½f and often on gruelling ground. Some see that as a difficult starting point towards a long season. Grey Dawning won the race this season, but crucially, perhaps, the ground wasn't as testing as it can often be, as the race appeared to leave a mark on him during the last campaign. Only one of the past 15 winners contested the Betfair Chase, which was once (soon after introduction) the obvious early-season target for the UK-trained staying chasers.

The **Cotswold Chase** is another race which appears to have a negative impact on the chances of Gold Cup success. You have to go back to 2000 and *Looks Like Trouble* to find the last Gold Cup winner to have contested the Grade 2 on trials day, another race often staged on testing ground which is also over a distance of 3m1½f on the New Course. Grey Dawning could finish only third here, in a race which was won by Spillane's Tower, who returned to form for Jimmy Mangan and JP McManus.

BLESSED WITH NATURAL SPEED

AS TOUCHED upon in the previous subsection, having the pace to be competitive over an intermediate trip is important. Whilst stamina is often spoken about more fondly when it comes to finding a Gold Cup winner, they must have the natural speed to be able to hold a position and travel kindly throughout; out and out stayers don't tend to win modern day Gold Cups.

Looking back at even earlier form of recent Gold Cup winners will show you that performing at a high level over much shorter in novice hurdles can be important. In fact, 13 of the past 24 had won a Graded novice hurdle over 2m-2m4f, whilst others like *Native River* and even *Inowthewayurhinkin* had run in such races. Last year's winner had no Point-to-Point of bumper experience and was sent hurdling at four, winning his first two before running in Grade 1s at Naas and the Punchestown Festival.

As has been highlighted in previous editions of the *Cheltenham Festival Betting Guide*, horses with placed form in the **Supreme Novices' Hurdle** (surprisingly) have an excellent record in the Gold Cup. *Best Mate* probably ought to have won his Supreme, whilst *Kicking King* and *War Of Attrition* (both ran in the Arkle the following year, with *Kicking King* finishing 2nd) were both placed in the Festival curtain-raiser.

Placed horses from the Supreme boast a record of 6-7 this century and whilst he didn't contest that race, last year's Arkle winner Jango Baie was a Grade 1 winner over 2m as a novice hurdler (Formby Novices' Hurdle) and Nicky Henderson's second-season chaser has seen his stamina being stretched out during the current campaign. He is very much an interesting contender from a trends perspective.

LIGHT CAMPAIGN
WHILST a *Light Campaign* is often frowned upon, they are common place for horses in National Hunt racing these days, but it certainly isn't a negative when it comes to the Gold Cup. Four of the past 13 winners had run just once earlier in the season – and won – whilst the likes of *Best Mate* and *Al Boum Photo* were carefully handled by their respective trainers, which probably contributed towards their longevity. Obviously, we would love to see these Grade 1 horses on a regular basis throughout the season – something which we became more accustomed to with the likes of *Kauto Star* – however, the fact that only two of the past 18 winners had run more than three times earlier in the season suggests that a quieter build up to the big day is the best approach.

HEAVY GROUND FLOPS
ENDURING tough races on deep winter ground can certainly be a negative, see the points raised against both the Betfair and Cotswold Chase in an earlier subsection. Horses who have run on heavy ground earlier in the season boast a poor record in the Gold Cup and in some ways, this is in line to the previous *Light Campaign* subsection. Whilst some horses are at home on deep ground and races are there to be won during the winter months, those who are more focused on winning the Gold Cup in March should probably look to avoid such conditions, which can leave a mark. Tread carefully with those who have run on heavy going.

BEATEN IN THE RACE PREVIOUSLY
HAVING finished runner-up to his stable-mate *Denman* in 2008, the great *Kauto Star* was able to wrest back his title the following year and until recently, having been beaten in the race previously

was another negative trend. However, since 2018, both *Native River* and *A Plus Tard* have shown that you can win a Gold Cup at the second attempt. It is still clearly a difficult thing to achieve and something which *Galopin des Champs* will need to overcome, if he is to join that illustrious list of three-time winners.

OTHER FESTIVAL FORM
I HAVE touched upon a couple of Festival races in earlier subsections, but overall, form at previous Cheltenham Festivals is important. 21 of the 25 winners this century had won or placed at the meeting previously, with *Inothewayurthinkin* adding to the tally last year, by virtue of his victory in the Kim Muir in 2024. *Coneygree* was the last winner to arrive at Cheltenham having not run at the Festival previously, although he had won two Grade 2 novice hurdles at the course, so wasn't devoid of Cheltenham experience.

Imperial Commander won the **Ryanair Chase** during his second season over fences, a race in which both *Don Cossack* and *A Plus Tard* were placed, prior to winning the Gold Cup the following year.

Strong novice hurdle form over shorter distances has been highlighted earlier, but several recent winners of the Gold Cup had run in the **Albert Bartlett Novices' Hurdle** during the early part of their careers. *Bobs Worth* and *Minella Indo* both won the Spa, whilst *Imperial Commander* and *Native River* finished down the field in the Grade 1 race. The Jukebox Man was beaten by Stellar Story (runner-up in last year's Broadway) in the 2024 Albert Bartlett.

PROVEN FORM AT GRADE 1 LEVEL
EACH and every winner this century had already recorded at least one win at Grade 1 level, so it is essential ahead of the Gold Cup, whilst many recent winners were serial scorers in Grade 1 company. Whilst you might think this sounds rather obvious, it ruled out seven horses in 2023 and four in 2024, whilst Monty's Star was flagged up in this very subsection last year, yet he still went off at just 8-1, despite having a record (at the time) of 0-4 in Grade 1s.

CURRENT FORM
LAST year's winner was a bit of an anomaly, in that he hadn't really been in great form throughout the season, for all that he caught many an eye when running on to finish fourth in the Irish Gold Cup, which prompted his connections to supplement him for the race. Prior to last year, 18 of the

previous 24 winners this century had won on their most recent start, so arriving in form is often imperative. Only three of those 24 failed to finish first (18) or second (3) last time out, so we really should be focusing on those who performed well on their most recent start and are heading to Cheltenham in good form.

MARKET FORCES

JUST two of the 25 winners this century – namely *Lord Windermere* and *Al Boum Photo* (ahead of his first win) – were sent off at double figure odds, so 'shock' results are a rarity in the Gold Cup these days. The latter was outright favourite when defending his crown and four of the five favourites between 2020 and 2024 proved successful, including *Galopin des Champs*, who twice justified favouritism. He was last year's beaten favourite, whilst since 2003, we have seen 12 winning favourites from 23 renewals. Focus on those towards the top of the market, the winner can usually be found in the first three or four of the betting.

TRAINERS TO NOTE

THE recent form of Irish-trained horses has already been covered in the *Irish Dominance* subsection and a lot of their overall success comes down to the fact that **Willie Mullins** has now won four of the past seven renewals. Responsible for last year's runner-up, Mullins had previously found it difficult to capture the most prestigious prize of all, but like London buses, four arrived in quick succession, thanks to the doubles of both *Al Boum Photo* and *Galopin des Champs*. As with many of the Grade 1s throughout the week, Mullins is an obvious candidate to provide the winner, given the sheer strength and talent within his group these days. *Galopin des Champs* looks set to form part of Mullins' team for the race once again, although there has to be a strong possibility that Fact To File will be supplemented for the race on March 7th.

Henry de Bromhead saddled back-to-back winners in 2021 and 2022, on each occasion saddling the one-two for good measure. His three entries this year are Envoi Allen, Monty's Star and last year's Ryanair runner-up, Heart Wood.

In the UK, *Long Run* and *Bobs Worth* provided **Nicky Henderson** with two wins in the race in the space of three years, and he has since seen Might Bite and Santini finish runner-up. He hasn't had a genuine contender for a few years, but Jango Baie looks set to represent the Seven Barrows team this year.

And, going back a little further, **Paul Nicholls** obviously enjoyed a fantastic spell between 1999 and 2009, winning four of the 10 renewals (no race in 2001, of course), with *See More Business*, *Kauto Star* (twice) and *Denman*. Nicholls saddled the 1-2-3 in 2008, at a time when he was dominant in the staying chase division.

FRENCH-BRED WINNERS

HAVING earlier seen French-bred success thanks to *Kauto Star* and *Long Run*, such runners have enjoyed even greater results of late, being responsible for five of the past seven winners. *Al Boum Photo*, *A Plus Tard* and *Galopin des Champs* were all French-bred and possibly, indicative of a more modern day Gold Cup winner, a horse blessed with more natural pace and one who was capable of showing high-quality form over shorter, earlier in their careers.

Aside from the two-time winner, other candidates for this year include Nicky Henderson's Jango Baie, whilst last year's Ryanair Chase winner Fact To File would be another French-bred contender, if (as expected) he is supplemented.

OTHER KEY RACES

SEVERAL big races in the calendar have already been covered, but here are a few more – from both a positive and a negative standpoint – that can have a bearing on the Gold Cup.

In Britian, Kempton's **King George VI Chase** is the mid-season showpiece, although the Boxing Day contest has only produced one Gold Cup winner in the past 14 years. Perhaps, that is in part down to the recent Irish dominance (coincidentally, that one winner was the Irish-trained *Don Cossack*), but it was the obvious route to take for British-trained Gold Cup contenders, in the early part of the century. This season's King George was won by The Jukebox Man.

The past two British-trained winners of the race – *Coneygree* and *Native River* – both won the **Denman Chase** at Newbury en route to Cheltenham. *Kauto Star* (ahead of his first win) and *Denman* also won the Grade 2 on their most recent start, so it appears to be a good stepping-stone to Gold Cup success for any 'home challengers'. This year's Denman Chase was won by Haiti Couleurs.

Over in Ireland, the first Grade 1 of the season in this division is Down Royal's **Champion Chase**, which comes a little earlier in the calendar than ideal for some trainers, notably Willie Mullins. The last Gold Cup winner to begin his season in Northern Ireland was *Kauto Star* back in the 2008-2009 season, so again, it seems to have little impact at the top end of this division these days. This season's race was won by Envoi Allen, who landed the prize for a third time.

Often nowadays, Gold Cup contenders in Ireland will begin their campaign over an intermediate trip, in the **John Durkan Memorial Chase** at Punchestown. This race was brought slightly forward in the calendar a couple of years ago, which now means runners have enough time to recover ahead of a Festive target. A hugely beneficial decision, both for this race itself and for the division as a whole, the past three winners of the Gold Cup started their season in it. Back in November, last year's winner *Inothewayurthinkin* was well beaten in a race which was dominated by Gaelic Warrior and Fact To File.

Inothewayurthinkin went on to follow a tried and tested path to Cheltenham, running in the **Savills Chase** at Leopardstown over Christmas, before returning to the same venue to contest the Irish Gold Cup, steadily improving with each run. Six of the past 14 Gold Cup winners contested the Savills, with only two – *Synchronised* and *Galopin des Champs* (ahead of his second win) – completing the double. Four of the past five Gold Cup winners ran in a race which was won this season by Affordale Fury, who beat I Am Maximus and a returning *Galopin des Champs*.

The **Irish Gold Cup** is also hugely significant, both in its own right and also in the campaign of a likely Gold Cup winner. It is the obvious target after the turn of the year for most Irish-trained Gold Cup contenders and *Sizing John* and *Galopin des Champs* (twice) have completed the double in the past nine years. *Minella Indo* and *Inothewayurthinkin* also ran in the Irish Gold Cup on their most recent start, so that is now five of the past nine winners of the Gold Cup to have emerged from the DRF. This year's Irish Gold Cup was won in impressive fashion by Fact To File, who went some way to removing any doubt surrounding his stamina for a staying trip. He beat stable-mate and old adversary Gaelic Warrior by 5 lengths, with *Galopin des Champs* (a further 8½l away in 3rd) completing a Willie Mullins-trained 1-2-3.

Another Festive period race to note, but to a lesser degree, is the **O'Driscoll's Irish Whiskey New Year's Day Chase** from Tramore, a race which Willie Mullins used (twice) with *Al Boum Photo*, who didn't run again after winning it. This year's race was won by Heart Wood, who is more likely to run in the Ryanair Chase..

And, finally in Ireland, looking back to the previous spring and the previous season's **Punchestown Gold Cup** will have found three Gold Cup winners in the past decade. *Don Cossack* was successful some 10 and a half months earlier, whilst both *Al Boum Photo* and *Galopin des Champs* were beaten in that race after winning their first Gold Cups at Cheltenham. The latter bounced back to form last year, rounding off his campaign with a facile victory in the Punchestown Grade 1.

ROLL OF HONOUR

Year	Form	Winner	Age	Weight	OR	SP	Trainer	Runners	Last Race (No. of days)
2025	754	Inothewayurthinkin	7	11-10	160	15/2	G Cromwell (IRE)	9	4th Gr.1 Irish Gold Cup (41)
2024	311	Galopin des Champs	8	11-10	179	10/11F	W Mullins (IRE)	11	1st Gr.1 Irish Gold Cup (41)
2023	11	Galopin des Champs	7	11-10	173	7/5F	W Mullins (IRE)	13	1st Gr.1 Irish Gold Cup (41)
2022	12	A Plus Tard	8	11-10	172	3/1F	H de Bromhead (IRE)	11	2nd Gr.1 Savills Chase (80)
2021	11F4	Minella Indo	8	11-10	164	9/1	H de Bromhead (IRE)	12	4th Gr.1 Irish Gold Cup (40)
2020	1	Al Boum Photo	8	11-10	175	10/3F	W Mullins (IRE)	12	1st Gr.3 Savills New Year's Day Chase (72)
2019	1	Al Boum Photo	7	11-10	164	12/1	W Mullins (IRE)	16	1st Listed Savills Chase (73)
2018	1	Native River	8	11-10	166	5/1	C Tizzard	15	1st Gr.2 Denman Chase (34)
2017	3211	Sizing John	7	11-10	167	7/1	J Harrington (IRE)	13	1st Gr.1 Irish Gold Cup (33)
2016	111F1	Don Cossack	9	11-10	175	9/4F	G Elliott (IRE)	9	1st Gr.2 Kinloch Brae Chase (64)

LEADING TEN-YEAR GUIDES

***Brown Advisory Novices' Chase** 2 (*Al Boum Photo* fell, *Minella Indo* 2nd)
Savills Chase 4 (*Minella Indo* fell, *A Plus Tard* 2nd, *Galopin des Champs* 1st, *Inothewayurthinkin* 5th)
Horse & Jockey Hotel Chase 2 (*Don Cossack* 1st, *Sizing John* 1st)
Irish Gold Cup 5 (*Sizing John* 1st, *Minella Indo* 4th, *Galopin des Champs* 1st & 1st, *Inothewayurthinkin* 4th)
O'Driscoll's Irish Whiskey New Year's Day Chase 2 (*Al Boum Photo* 1st, 1st)
***Cheltenham Gold Cup** 4 (*Native River* 3rd, *Al Boum Photo* 1st, *A Plus Tard* 2nd, *Galopin des Champs* 1st)
John Durkan Memorial Chase 4 (*Don Cossack* 1st, *Galopin des Champs* 1st & 3rd, *Inothewayurthinkin* 7th)
***Punchestown Gold Cup** 3 (*Don Cossack* 1st, *Al Boum Photo* 2nd, *Galopin des Champs* 2nd)

denotes previous season

Leading Contenders

FACT TO FILE — Trainer: Willie Mullins
Needs to be supplemented but given the performance he put in when winning the Irish Gold Cup by 5 lengths, that seems highly likely. Stayed on strongly on that occasion, suggesting that he could indeed last home over the Gold Cup distance and has long been held in the highest regard by his powerful connections. A brilliant winner of last year's Ryanair Chase, he won the Broadway in 2024 and finished runner-up in the 2023 Champion Bumper, so excels at the track and looks to be the one to beat, if getting the trip.

JANGO BAIE — Trainer: Nicky Henderson
Last year's Arkle winner finished a close-up fourth in the King George, having earlier impressed when making a sparkling return over 2m5f at Ascot. Kempton was his first attempt at 3m and he certainly shapes like the Gold Cup trip is within range. An improving and lightly-raced second-season chaser, he ticks plenty of trends boxes and is 2-2 at Cheltenham, having impressed with his accurate jumping on chase debut over 2m4½f. Bypassed the Denman Chase (ground) but is likely to play a leading role.

THE JUKEBOX MAN — Trainer: Ben Pauling
Unbeaten in four starts over fences (his novice season was curtailed through injury last term), he returned to action with a smooth success at Haydock, which teed him up perfectly for the King George. Admittedly, the Boxing Day showpiece was falsely run, but he showed a fine attitude to rally and prevail, following a slightly slow jump at the last. Beaten a head on his sole start at Cheltenham, when runner-up in the 2024 Albert Bartlett, he should stay this trip and is clearly another second-season chaser on the up.

GAELIC WARRIOR — Trainer: Willie Mullins
Runner-up in the Fred Winter and the Baring Bingham, he gained Festival honours in the 2024 Arkle and has improved again since going up to staying trips. Successful at Aintree, he beat Fact To File in the John Durkan and was again in front of his stable-mate when narrowly beaten by The Jukebox Man at Kempton. Runner-up in the Irish Gold Cup, he can race a little freely, which would be a worry over this distance, but he has the talent to play a leading role. The Ryanair remains an option.

GALOPIN DES CHAMPS — Trainer: Willie Mullins
Winner of the race in 2023 and 2024, he didn't perform to the same level last year, although he returned to form when winning in style at Punchestown. Held up in the early part of this season, he only reappeared in the Savills Chase, where he ran well to finish third. Having filled the same position behind Fact To File and Gaelic Warrior in the Irish Gold Cup, he needs to step forward if he is to join the illustrious list of three-time winners of the race. Greatly respected but won't find it easy aged 10.

HAITI COULEURS — Trainer: Rebecca Curtis
Last year's National Hunt Chase winner, he has made incredible progress since going chasing and has already collected an Irish National, a Welsh National and more recently, a Denman Chase. A strong stayer (won three times beyond 3m5½f), he might need soft ground to enhance his claims; not that he requires it but to enable him to hold his position in the early part of the race. A thoroughly likeable and progressive nine-year-old, he is unbeaten in two starts at Cheltenham, but is 0-1 in Grade 1 company.

Leading Contenders

SPILLANE'S TOWER Trainer: James Joseph Mangan
Returned to form with victory in the Cotswold Chase on trials day, on what was his first start over fences since Punchestown last spring, when the ground might have been on the quick side for him. Although he received weight from L'Homme Presse and Grey Dawning, he ran out a convincing winner and is still unexposed as a staying chaser. Threatens to stay the trip and should be given consideration, should we get a soft ground Gold Cup. With Mark Walsh likely to ride Fact To File, maybe Jack Kennedy will retain the partnership.

GREY DAWNING Trainer: Dan Skelton
Winner of the now defunct Golden Miller Novices' Chase in 2024, he was an easy winner of Haydock's Betfair Chase on reappearance but could finish only third behind Spillane's Tower, when a mistake two out didn't help in the Cotswold Chase. Whilst his course form reads well, there is a suspicion that the Gold Cup trip could really stretch his stamina, especially in a strongly run race. Likely to travel well for a long way, the question is what he will have in reserve in the closing stages.

INOTHEWAYURTHINKIN Trainer: Gavin Cromwell
Last year's winner, he is 2-2 at the Festival, having won the 2024 Kim Muir, but he has actually only won three times from 13 starts over fences and doesn't have the profile of your standard Gold Cup winner. Beaten 53 lengths in the John Durkan and 41 lengths in the Savills Chase, he was staying on when taking a tired (and nasty) looking fall in the Irish Gold Cup. Despite his excellent course record, it is difficult to see him bouncing back at this stage and repeating last year's impressive performance.

I AM MAXIMUS Trainer: Willie Mullins
Winner of the Grand National in 2024, he won a bumper at Cheltenham on his racecourse debut (when trained by Nicky Henderson) and finished fourth in the 2022 Baring Bingham. Fourth the following year, he ran a stormer to finish runner-up in the Savills Chase over Christmas and although beaten into fifth in the Irish Gold Cup, could improve on that for meeting better ground. Runner-up in last year's Grand National, Aintree is once again likely to be on his agenda, but he could run here en route back to Liverpool.

NICK ROCKETT Trainer: Willie Mullins
Last year's Grand National winner, he is still very lightly-raced over fences, having won four times from nine starts, including his last three. Not been seen since Aintree, he will need to run once in order to be eligible for the National and it could be that his connections opt to let him take his chance. On an upward curve when last seen, he now has an official I.H.R.B. Rating of 169 and he clearly stays very well. Whilst he could run well at big odds, it would be a huge ask after 11 months off.

AFFORDALE FURY Trainer: Noel Meade
Winner of the Savills Chase on his penultimate start, he couldn't replicate that form on heavy ground in the Irish Gold Cup (pulled-up lame) and is better judged on earlier form. Another who is lightly-raced over fences, he has won three times from eight chase starts, with the pick of his form coming on slightly better ground. Runner-up in the 2023 Albert Bartlett on his sole visit to Cheltenham, the eight-year-old needs to bounce back from a disappointing run but was earlier beginning to look quite progressive.

Cheltenham Festival Betting Guide 2026

ST JAMES'S PLACE FESTIVAL CHALLENGE CUP OPEN HUNTERS' CHASE

3m2f 70y (Class 2) – New Course

OVERVIEW

STAGED over the exact same course-and-distance as the Gold Cup, this is the feature race in the calendar for both the Hunters' Chase division and indeed for amateur jockeys. Still often referred to as the *'Foxhunters'* jockey bookings can be key, with it being an amateur riders' race, with a familiar name in the saddle a definite positive. Often, those with the higher official BHA Ratings and/or those who have run well in the race previously perform well here, whilst we should also pay healthy respect to form in the equivalent contests at Aintree and/or Punchestown from the previous spring. Experience can often play an important role, too.

OFFICIAL BHA RATINGS

ALTHOUGH it wasn't the case last year, with *Wonderwall* rated just 118, those with the higher BHA Ratings often come to the fore. 11 of the past 16 winners were rated 134 or higher, although the past three winners had official marks of just 122, 124 and 118 respectively, so perhaps, this is an evolving trend and we are starting to see lesser quality horses shine. I think part of the reason for those lower ratings was to do with how those three winners were campaigned, two of them raced exclusively in Point-to-Point company, as opposed to running in Hunters' Chases under Rules.

Between 2010 and 2022, we saw plenty of winners rated between 134 and 141, with *On The Fringe* the highest, the 11-year-old rated 147 ahead of his second win some 10 years ago. Despite recent results, still pay healthy respect to those with the higher ratings. As for *Wonderwall*, it is worth remembering that he was only nine and just two years earlier, ran off 134 (coincidence) in the County Hurdle, so it wasn't as if he was devoid of that level of ability at one stage.

NATIONAL HUNT BACKGROUND

LOCAL trainers Jonjo O'Neill – now trains alongside son A J, of course – and Nigel Twiston-Davies have each won one renewal this century, as has Willie Mullins, who struck with *Billaway* in 2022. Paul Nicholls has won the race four times (more of his record later) and is the most successful licenced trainer in this race, but it often goes the way of an *'amateur'* stable, one which is more accustomed to producing winners in Point-to-Points and/or Hunters' Chases.

Recent British-trained winners such as *Hazel Hill* (Philip Rowley), *Porlock Bay* (Willi Biddick), *Premier Magic* (Bradley Gibbs) and *Sine Nominee* (Fiona Needham) all hailed from such stables and those *'permit holder'* trainers deserve plenty of respect, as this will likely have been a long-term aim for their chosen runner(s). Last year's race went to Ireland and Sam Curling, himself a successful Point-to-Point trainer who sells plenty of horses to professional stables, so again, he had the right background. Curling was also responsible for last year's beaten favourite, Angels Dawn.

Although Wonderwall didn't tick the box, 29 of the past 37 winners started their careers by racing in either Point-to-Points or in Hunters' Chases, rather than racing under Rules. Often an ex-Rules horse will enter this division in order to rejuvenate their career – see last year's winner as a case in point – whilst many an ex-Pointer/Hunters' Chase performer will be prepared for a peak performance in this very race.

A FRENCH INFLUENCE

IN TERMS of looking towards horses who had raced under Rules, those with a French background often do well. Focusing on French-bred horses or those who ran under Rules in France, before moving to the UK or Ireland, is another good angle into the *'Foxhunters'* with *Porlock Bay* a good example of this. Dual winner *Pacha du Polder* also ran in France before joining Paul Nicholls, whilst *Sleeping Night* was a high-class performer with a similar background for Nicholls some 21 years ago, and *Baby Run* was another French-bred winner from 2010. Representation for such horses would be much lower here, so their record is more than respectable.

BREEDING

IRISH-BRED winners are the dominant force and given the nature of the race (a steeplechase over a staying trip), you might expect as much. They are often very well represented and are usually responsible for a large proportion of the field each year, so they are entitled to come out on top. As a result, only two of the past 23 winners were not either Irish- or French-bred, with the German-bred *Amicelli* striking in 2008.

Prior to 2024, British-bred runners struggled here, but *Sine Nominee* was able to break that negative trend when scoring for Fiona Needham, clerk of the course and general manager at Catterick racecourse. Four more were beaten last year, taking the tally of British-bred horses to 1-96 during the past 23 years. Therefore, despite that one recent winner, results suggest that such horses still tend to struggle, so tread carefully with those carrying the (GB) suffix.

DUAL WINNERS

NINE horses have won this race twice, with six of those winning successive renewals. The three most recent have come since 2012 and 2013 when *Salsify* doubled up, with *On The Fringe* and *Pacha du Polder* soon adding their names to the tally. *Wonderwall* looks to add his name to this list and has followed a similar prep, freshened up after bolting up at Dromahane in November.

REPEAT OFFENDERS

THOSE recent dual winners clearly help this statistic, but overall seven of the past 16 winners had finished in the first five the previous year. Therefore, pay close attention to the 2025 renewal of the **St James's Place Festival Challenge Cup Open Hunters' Chase**, in which Its On The Line (also 2nd in 2023 & 2024) finished runner-up, with the seven-year-old Willitgoahead back in third.

KEY TRENDS

- 29 of the past 37 winners started their careers in Point-to-Points or Hunters' Chases
- 11 of the past 16 winners had official BHA Ratings of 134+
- 16 of the past 18 winners won or placed last time out
- 15 of the past 18 winners ran during February
- 14 of the past 19 winners had yet to win over this distance
- 9 of the past 11 winners were aged 10 or 11
- 7 of the past 16 winners had finished in the first 5 the previous year
- 4 of the past 19 winners were owned by JP McManus
- Respect French-bred horses who ran under Rules
- Respect genuine Point-to-Point / Hunters' Chase stables (permit holders)
- There have been 3 back-to-back winners during the past 14 years
- Paul Nicholls has won the race 4 times
- Only 1 of the past 38 winners was aged 6
- Only 1 of the past 36 winners was older than 11
- British-bred horses are 1-96 during the past 23 years
- Only 2 of the past 23 winners were not Irish- or French-bred
- Only 2 7yo winners this century
- Only 3 of the past 16 winners ran in a P2P (as opposed to a Hunters' Chase) last time out (although 2 in the past 3 years)

2022 winner *Billaway* had twice finished runner-up before getting his head in front, whilst *On The Fringe* had finished third in 2014 – when looking a suspect stayer – before returning to win the next two renewals. Respect horses who have run well in the race previously.

UNPROVEN STAMINA IS NOT A WORRY

RATHER like in the Gold Cup, looking at horses who have been running over trips short of this distance can be a positive (if looking away from those with prior experience in the race). Building towards a peak performance can include running over slightly shorter and no fewer than 14 of the past 19 winners had yet to win over a distance as far as this. Like *Pacha du Polder*, *Wonderwall* was campaigned over much shorter under Rules, whilst (as touched upon in the previous subsection) *On The Fringe* didn't exactly looked to be blessed with stamina when beaten in 2014, before returning as a stronger horse at the age of 10 and 11. Many a Point-to-Point race will be in or around 3m, as opposed to this extended 3m2f trip.

AGE

SUBSEQUENT high-class chaser *Kingscliff*, who won this race at the start of his career, remains the sole six-year-old winner in the past 38 renewals, with the 2005 Betfair Chase winner successful in 2003. We rarely see *'younger'* horses trained for this race in truth, although both *Cappa Bleu* and *Salsify* won as seven-year-olds between 2009 and 2012 (the only two this century). The latter obviously then won again at the age of eight, but since then *Sine Nominee* is the only other eight-year-old winner, so focusing on those aged nine to 11 is – statistically, at least – the way to go. That can be narrowed down further, too, with nine of the past 11 winners (the nine winners prior to 2024) being aged either 10 or 11. It will be interesting to see if this pattern of slightly *'younger'* winners continues, but for now at least, 10 and 11 seems to be the ideal age.

At the other end of the scale, there has only been one winner over the age of 11 during the past 36 years, so those *'older'* contenders should be readily overlooked.

CURRENT FORM

ARRIVING on the back of a positive run seems to be important, with no fewer than 16 of the past 18 winners heading to Cheltenham after a win or placed effort. Last-time-out winners have now won in each of the past four years, whilst prior to last year, 15 of the previous 17 winners had been in action during February, so respect those with a recent (winning or placed) run under their belts. The Hunters' Chase programme does lend itself to a campaign quite close together but nevertheless, respect a good recent run in that sphere.

In terms of where that last run came – or under which code – it was previously much more common for a winner of the *'Foxhunters'* to have warmed up for Cheltenham by running in a Hunters' Chase, as opposed to a Point-to-Point. Only 3 of the past 16 winners ran *'between the flags'* on their most recent start, but two of those have come in the past three years, so perhaps this is another evolving trend. Both *Premier Magic* and *Wonderwall* had run twice earlier in the campaign – both successful in a couple of Open Points – whilst *Sine Nominee* won a Point in December, before prepping for Cheltenham at Wetherby in February. A horse capable of winning at Cheltenham would more than likely be a class apart from the opposition in Point-to-Point company, so if a horse has taken that route, you should really be looking for a comfortable success. Last year's winner, for example, won by 10 lengths on his latest start, and *Premier Magic* was a 14-length winner on his final start before winning this race.

MARKET FORCES

A DOZEN of the 25 winners this century returned at single figure odds, although we have seen just four winning outright favourites in the past 20 years (*Baby Run* was joint-favourite) and just two in the past nine years. There is certainly no real pattern in terms of market position of recent winners, as we have also witnessed winners priced at 25/1, 66/1 (twice) and 28/1 during the past eight years alone. Don't let a big price put you off here, this is one of the races during the week when *'shock'* results – according to the betting – can happen.

KEY IRISH RACES

THE programme for the Hunter Chase division in Ireland has changed over the years. This has been covered in recent editions of the *Cheltenham Festival Betting Guide*, but in case you are a first time reader, the www.punchestown.com Hunters Chase was once the *Key Irish Race* and although it has moved tracks on several occasions since, remains a race of some interest and takes place in February. *On The Fringe* was twice beaten in that race – when it was staged at Leopardstown – after which it moved (again) to Naas and was run as the **Naas Hunters Chase**, where *Billaway* won en route to Cheltenham. It has been staged for the past couple of years as the **QuinnBet Hunters Chase** – which is easier to now follow, given the number of courses which have hosted the race – and it was won this year by Panda Boy, who appeared to outstay Hunters Yarn from the front.

Over the Christmas period, Down Royal stages the **Bar 1 Betting Hunters Chase**, a race formerly sponsored by Bluegrass Horse Feeds and was previously run over 2m5f. The distance was increased to 3m a few years ago and again, it has thrown up two of the past 11 winners, both of which were beaten in Northern Ireland. Perhaps, at that stage, it is a case of building up fitness towards the spring and Its On The Line won the race for a second time in three years this season. Willitgoahead and Con's Roc filled the places in what appeared to be a strong renewal.

Looking back at the previous spring, and the **Champion Hunter Chase** from the Punchestown Festival can also be a key piece of form. *On The Fringe* twice won that race 10 and a half months before being successful at Cheltenham, whilst last April's contest was won for a third successive year by Its On The Line, who had been beaten just a neck in this race. He is certainly getting closer, as he went down by 1¾ lengths in 2023 and ¾ of a length in 2024.

CONNECTIONS TO NOTE

AS TOUCHED upon in an earlier subsection, **Paul Nicholls** is the only fully licenced trainer to have taken this race – and the division as a whole – seriously in recent years, winning it on four occasions since 2004, when *Earthmover* won the race for a second time, at the grand old age of 13. Nicholls saddled Shearer to finish fifth under daughter Olive last year.

Once the man to follow in the cross-country division, **Enda Bolger** first struck in 1996 with *Elegant Lord* – who he also rode to victory – and has since won it twice more, as a trainer, with *On The Fringe*.

All three of Bolger's winners carried the green and gold hoops of **JP McManus,** who also won the 2007 renewal with Jonjo O'Neill's *Drombeag*. McManus has gone close in each of the past two years with Its On The Line (he didn't own him in 2023) and the leading owner will be hoping that he can finally go one place better this year and provide him with a sixth *'Foxhunters'* win.

Wonderwall was the latest horse to deny Its On The Line

ROLL OF HONOUR

Year	Form	Winner	Age	Weight	OR	SP	Trainer	Runners	Last Race (No. of days)
2025	11	Wonderwall	8	12-0	118	28/1	S Curling (IRE)	24	1st Dromahane Open Point (131)
2024	2121	Sine Nomine	8	11-7	124	8/1	F Needham	12	1st Wetherby Hunter Chase (41)
2023	11	Premier Magic	10	12-0	122	66/1	B Gibbs	23	1st Garthorpe Open Point (40)
2022	21	Billaway	10	12-0	140	13/8F	W Mullins (IRE)	19	1st Naas Hunter Chase (34)
2021	12	Porlock Bay	10	12-0	135	16/1	W Biddick	18	2nd Wincanton Hunter Chase (43)
2020	U17P	It Came To Pass	10	12-0	126	66/1	E O'Sullivan (IRE)	21	P.U. Kilfeacle Open Point (47)
2019	11211	Hazel Hill	11	12-0	139	7/2F	P Rowley	24	1st Warwick Hunter Chase (53)
2018	3	Pacha du Polder	11	12-0	138	25/1	P Nicholls	24	3rd Doncaster Hunter Chase (24)
2017	3341	Pacha du Polder	10	12-0	138	16/1	P Nicholls	23	1st Bangor Hunter Chase (35)
2016	17	On The Fringe	11	12-0	147	13/8F	E Bolger (IRE)	24	7th Leopardstown Inn Hunter (41)

LEADING TEN-YEAR GUIDES

*St James's Place Foxhunters 5 (*On The Fringe* 1st, *Pacha du Polder* 5th & 1st, *Billaway* 2nd, *Premier Magic* P.U.)
QuinnBet Hunters Chase 2 (*On The Fringe* 7th, *Billaway* 1st)
Bar 1 Betting Hunters Chase 2 (*On The Fringe* 2nd, *It Came To Pass* 7th)
*Aintree Foxhunters' 4 (*On The Fringe* 1st, *Pacha du Polder* 6th & 4th, *Billaway* 5th)

* denotes previous season

MARTIN PIPE CONDITIONAL JOCKEYS' HANDICAP HURDLE
2m4f 56y (0-145 Handicap) – New Course

OVERVIEW
INTRODUCED in 2009, the Martin Pipe was initially a 0-140 handicap but after just three renewals, the upper ceiling was increased to 145 and in recent years, the quality of horses contesting it has risen considerably. It has been a good race for novices – particularly those trained in Ireland – and younger horses in general, those with fewer runs over hurdles (less exposed), with no winner being over the age of seven. The *Roll Of Honour* includes several subsequent high-class chasers, none more so that 2021 winner *Galopin des Champs*, who went on to win back-to-back Gold Cups for Willie Mullins, a trainer with an excellent record here. This is a conditional jockeys' event, so with the *'Foxhunters'* for amateurs, professionals' Festival concludes with the Gold Cup itself.

NOVICES
EIGHT of the past 12 winners were novices and this includes the previous four, prior to last year. Seven of those eight winning novices were trained in Ireland, the exception being *Iroko* who was a second-season novice who had run five times over hurdles prior to the Festival. Four of the Irish-trained winning novices had raced just three or four times prior to winning the Martin Pipe and that would no longer be enough to make a horse eligible. Ahead of the 2025 Cheltenham Festival, it was announced that all novices would be required to have run at least five times in order to be eligible for open handicaps throughout the week and this was later extended to all horses, not just novices. The initial ruling was that novices required three runs for Class 1 and Class 2 handicap hurdles – as was the case throughout the whole season – but that was increased to four runs not so long back and now with the Festival in mind (and Aintree), five runs are required.

Be careful if you are playing in the ante-post markets (for all handicaps) as the required runs must be acquired prior to the weights being announced in February. I'm sure that novices will still be aimed at the race and should any line up, in particular those trained in Ireland, be sure to give them utmost respect.

LIGHTLY-RACED HURDLERS
WHILST last year's winner wasn't a novice, she very much fell into this category, with *Wodhooh* unbeaten in six starts over hurdles prior to her success. Including the novices touched upon in the previous subsection, no fewer than 15 of the 17 winners to date had run eight times or less over hurdles, which goes to show that this race really does tend to lend itself to the unexposed and those who are capable of showing further improvement on the day that matters. If looking away from a novice, focusing on a second-season hurdler with that scope to progress is very much par for the course.

AGE
IN-KEEPING with the previous subsection and the *'younger'* horses really do come to the fore. All 17 winners were aged between five and seven, with 15 of them aged either five (6) or six (9), which is clearly the preferred age bracket. We have seen three five-year-olds successful in the past five years, whilst horses aged eight or older have a dismal record

of 0-77 in the Martin Pipe. Those *'older'* and more exposed runners can be readily overlooked.

THE FRENCH CONNECTION

WHILST looking at those *'younger'* contenders, it is no coincidence that five of the six winning five-year-olds were French-bred, including those three most recent winners, during the past five years. As has been highlighted in many a race thus far, French-bred horses are often more precocious, meaning that they are capable of performing at a higher level from an earlier stage in their careers than later maturing types. Last year's winner came off the Flat in Ireland, whereas five of the past 14 winners had run in France before joining their winning connections. We see similarly impressive records in juvenile company, so pay healthy respect to any French imports, as well as those with a French-bred pedigree.

FOUR UP FOR MULLINS

WHILST he still hasn't managed to win a handicap chase at the fixture, leading trainer **Willie Mullins** has a fine record in the two handicap hurdles on Gold Cup day and has won the Martin Pipe on four occasions since 2011. *Sir des Champs* was his first winner, followed by *Don Poli, Killultagh Vic* and most recently, *Galopin des Champs*, although that last win was recorded five years ago. Four winners in a 10-year spell was some going from Mullins, who clearly likes to target this race with a progressive youngster, as all four of his winners were very lightly-raced and aged either five or six. His last three winners were novices and this offers him the ideal opportunity to split up his pack, with him invariably very strong in the novice hurdle department.

FOUR UP FOR ELLIOTT

FOLLOWING the back-to-back wins of *Better Days Ahead* and *Wodhooh*, **Gordon Elliott** has now also recorded four wins in the Martin Pipe, with his victories all achieved in the past nine years. Again, three of Elliott's four winners (his first three) were novices, whilst *Wodhooh* was in her first season outside of juvenile company. Elliott does tend to run plenty of horses in the race – he spent a lot of time earlier in his career working for Martin Pipe and the race clearly means a lot to him – with last year's quintet taking his tally to 46, not including the three sent out by Denise Foster in the year in which he was suspended. If including that trio, there have been no fewer than 44 runners from Cullentra House in the past decade alone, which again highlights that Elliott is prepared to target the race in large numbers. All four of his winners were priced at 12-1 or shorter, with the last two

KEY TRENDS

- ⭐ 15 of the 17 winners had run 8 times or less over hurdles
- ⭐ 8 of the past 12 winners were novices (7 of them were Irish-trained novices)
- ⭐ 4 of the past 9 winners were trained by Gordon Elliott (including the past 2)
- ⭐ 4 of the past 15 winners were trained by Willie Mullins
- ✓ All 17 winners were aged between 5-7 (14 of them were aged either 5 or 6)
- ✓ All 17 winners carried 11-1 or more
- ✓ 12 of the past 15 winners recorded a top-3 finish last time out (9 of them won)
- ✓ 8 of the past 13 winners were rated in the 140s
- ✓ 8 of the past 12 winners had won over further
- ✓ 7 of the past 16 winners ran in a Graded race last time out
- ✓ 7 of the past 10 winners carried between 11-7 and 11-10
- ✓ 5 of the 7 British-trained winners had course form (last year's winner was also a CD winner)
- ✓ 5 of the past 7 winners returned at 8-1 or shorter (the past 3 winners returned at odds ranging from 9-2 to 6-1)
- ✓ 5 of the past 15 winners had run in France earlier in their careers
- ✓ 4 of the past 15 winners were owned by Gigginstown House Stud
- ✓ 2 of the past 7 winners were owned by JP McManus
- ✓ 2 of the past 7 winners were trained by Joseph O'Brien
- ✓ 2 of the past 6 winners were mares
- ✗ Horses aged 8+ are 0-77
- ✗ Horses carrying 11-0 or less are 0-121
- ✗ David Pipe-trained runners are 0-23
- ✗ Only 1 of the past 14 winners (since it became 0-145) was rated below 137
- ✗ Only 1 winning favourite
- ✗ Only 2 of the past 12 winners returned at odds greater than 12-1

returning at 5-1 and 9-2 respectively, so a lot of his *'unfancied'* runners (his other four runners last year were priced at 22-1, 25-1, 66-1 and 100-1) could have been overlooked. Certainly, focus more on his shorter priced runners.

GIGGINSTOWN HOUSE STUD

BOTH Willie Mullins and Gordon Elliott have trained winners in the silks of **Gigginstown House Stud**, who have won the race four times in the past 15 years.

The trainers have provided the owner with two wins apiece and although their last winner came in 2018, they have since had placed horses, whilst Column Of Fire looked to hold every chance when falling at the final flight in 2020. The owners, renowned for buying future staying chasers, often have the right type of horse for this race and again had two runners last year. Three of their four winners were novices – the other being the twice raced *Sir des Champs* (would no longer be eligible) – so respect any horse with a similar profile.

OFFICIAL BHA RATINGS AND WEIGHTS

SINCE the upper ceiling was increased to 145 in 2012, only one of the past 14 winners was rated below 137, so that is the starting point – look upwards from there. Eight of the past 13 winners were rated in the 140s, with *Wodhooh* adding to this tally, her successful from a mark of 141. Both *Early Doors* and *Indefatigable* were able to win from a mark of 145, so the classier types are certainly now more dominant.

In terms of weight carried, all 17 winners carried 11-1 or more, whilst seven of the past 10 winners carried 11-7 or more, again suggesting that we should focus our attention on the top-end of the handicap. A dozen horses carried 11-0 or less last year, taking the tally of such runners to 0-121 over the 17 years. This clearly suggests that there is a class bias, with the higher-rated horses having too much quality for those lower-weighted/rated horses.

	Top Weight (OR)	Bottom OR	Winner OR
2025	145	126	141
2024	145	122	140
2023	145	126	138
2022	144	132	137
2021	143	132	142
2020	145	136	145
2019	145	126	145
2018	144	136	144
2017	145	135	138
2016	142	135	139
2015	144	135	135
2014	146	133	143
2013	145	131	141
2012	145	132	139
2011	140	127	134
2010	139	129	137
2009	140	128	133

COURSE FORM

FIVE of the seven British-trained winners of the race had run at Cheltenham previously, whilst *Wodhooh* added her name to the list last year, despite being Irish-trained, of course. She won a mares' handicap hurdle at the December meeting – over the exact same course-and-distance – and was then kept back with this race in mind (very much a positive pointer, in hindsight). The novices *Killultagh Vic* and *Better Days Ahead* were another pair of Irish-trained winners with course form to their name, both having contested the **Weatherbys Champion Bumper** the previous year. Whilst it is obviously more significant with British-trained contenders, *Course Form* of any nature should be taken as a positive.

CURRENT FORM

NO FEWER than 13 of the past 15 winners had recorded a top-three finish on their most recent start, with nine of those successful on their most recent start. *Banbridge*, *Iroko* and *Wodhooh* were all last-time-out winners in the past four years alone and arriving at Cheltenham in form is clearly significant. That number of last-time-out winners is also hugely important, and one which we don't necessarily see when it comes to other handicaps throughout the week. Focus on those in form.

Of those who were beaten or indeed finished out of the frame on their most recent start, several were dropping in class, with *Pause And Clause* having run in the Grade 2 Rendlesham Hurdle the time before, whilst *Galopin des Champs* had finished only sixth in the Grade 1 Tattersalls Ireland Novice Hurdle at the Dublin Racing Festival on his latest start. Respect any horse dropping in class from Graded company.

CLASS ANGLE

RATHER in-keeping with the final sentence of the previous subsection, seven previous winners were dropping in class from Graded company. Although *Iroko* and *Better Days Ahead* didn't tick this box, they had contested Grade 1s earlier in their short careers, so pay close attention to any such runners again this time around. As touched upon in the *Official BHA Ratings And Weights* subsection, class often rises to the top in the Martin Pipe and there does appear to be a gulf between the horses towards the top of the weights and those further down, with that dismal record of those carrying 11-0 or less tying in here.

NO STAMINA ISSUES

HAVING won over course-and-distance on her most recent start, *Wodhooh* certainly had *No Stamina Issues* ahead of last year's race, but even greater than that, eight of the previous 11 winners had won over a distance which was further than that of the Martin Pipe. *Better Days Ahead*, for example, was a winner over 2m7f and having those reserves of stamina is clearly advantageous. Looking through the *Roll Of Honour* and the likes of *Sir des Champs, Don Poli, Galopin des Champs, Banbridge, Iroko* and *Better Days Ahead* all went on to shine over 3m+ over fences, so it is clearly beneficial to have that abundant stamina in the locker. This race is often strongly run and there is no hiding place from the end-to-end gallop, which ensures that it is a real test over an extended 2m4f.

On a side note, three previous winners – those being *Killutagh Vic, Champagne Classic* and *Galopin des Champs* – all went on to win the Grade 1 3m novice hurdle at the Punchestown Festival on their next start, so take note if an Irish-trained novice wins and heads to that contest. 2024 winner *Better Days Ahead* also ran well in it, finishing third to Dancing City. *Banbridge* and *Iroko* both contested Aintree's Sefton Novices' Hurdle (3m) on their next start, too, so clearly those winning novices were blessed with considerable stamina and also that touch of class.

TACTICS

BACK to matters in hand and as is often the case over hurdles on the New Course, a patient ride can pay dividends. As touched upon in the previous subsection, this race is often strongly run and although we have seen a few fairly recent winners ridden a little more forward, being held-up and delivered with a late challenge can be beneficial.

MARKET FORCES

WHILST this appears to be a fiercely competitive handicap on paper, five of the past seven winners returned at 8-1 or shorter and this includes the past three winners, who returned with a starting price of 6-1, 5-1 and 9-2, respectively. There has only ever been one successful favourite – that being *Sir des Champs* – but plenty of recent winners could have been found just behind the market leader(s) and in fact, only two of the past 12 winners returned at odds greater than 12-1, and one of those was a 14-1 shot.

KEY RACES

TWO of the Gigginstown House Stud-owned winners, *Champagne Classic* and *Blow By Blow*, had run in the Grade 3 **Michael Purcell Memorial Novice Hurdle** at Thurles on their most recent start. They won it again last year with Jacob's Ladder, who bypassed Cheltenham for Aintree, and although the race takes place after the Guide has gone to print, be sure to take notice of the result.

And, domestically, during the past 13 years, a couple of winners each contested early-season handicaps over this sort of (intermediate) trip. Both *Salubrious* and *Indefatigable* ran well in the **Wasdell Group Silver Trophy Handicap Hurdle** at Chepstow, a race which was won this season by Olly Murphy's Rambo T, whilst the former went on to contest the **"Join Coral Bet £10 Get £50" Handicap Hurdle** at Newbury's Coral Gold Cup fixture. That race was won this season by French Ship, who actually fell three out in the Silver Trophy before winning at Cheltenham in October and again at Newbury.

OTHER TRAINERS TO NOTE

THE hugely impressive records of Messrs Mullins and Elliott have been covered in earlier subsections, whilst **Joseph O'Brien** has struck twice since 2019, with *Early Doors* and subsequent King George winner, *Banbridge*. Without a runner in 2025, O'Brien's impressive record stands at two winners and two placed horses from just seven runners in the Martin Pipe (since 2019) and he was also responsible for the beaten favourite in 2020, so it is clearly another handicap hurdle which his stable likes to target.

Paul Nicholls won the race twice between 2013 and 2016, but hasn't gone close since. That said, he has had just 11 runners in the race since that last winner, some 10 years ago.

And, as has been highlighted in many recent edition of the *Cheltenham Festival Betting Guide*, the record of **David Pipe** – in a race named after his father – is a disappointing one. He, too, wasn't represented (again) last year and it is now four years since his last runner in a race which he used to target with great intent to begin with (understandably so). In those early years, several 'well fancied' runners (according to the betting) came out of Pond House, but Pipe's record in the race stands at 0-23, so his runners need to be treated with a degree of caution. Again, in those earlier days, there was a suspicion that plenty of said runners were 'over-bet' with people seemingly assuming that he had targeted the race with a specific horse.

TWO UP FOR McMANUS

EARLY DOORS and last year's Grand National fourth *Iroko* have provided owner **JP McManus** with two wins in the Martin Pipe in the past seven years. The latter led home a one-two for the owner, who had four runners last year, including the third and fifth placed horses (both priced at 25-1). He was responsible for last year's disappointing beaten favourite, Kopeck de Mee, who was the subject of a pre-Festival gamble, but he has had 15 runners during those past seven renewals and it is a race which he is sure to continue to target. Interestingly, his two winners were priced at 6-1 and 5-1 respectively, so were clearly well found in the market.

DAY FOUR RACE SEVEN

Dual Gold Cup winner Galopin des Champs won the Martin Pipe in 2021

ROLL OF HONOUR

Year	Form	Winner	Age	Weight	OR	SP	Trainer	Runners	Last Race (No. of days)
2025	1	Wodhooh	5	11-5	141	9/2	G Elliott (IRE)	24	1st Cheltenham Mares' H'cap (90)
2024	F142	Better Days Ahead	6	11-7	140	5/1	G Elliott (IRE)	21	2nd Navan Nov. Hurdle (55)
2023	11	Iroko	5	11-5	138	6/1	O Greenall & J Guerriero	21	1st Wetherby H'cap Hurdle (62)
2022	111471	Banbridge	6	11-3	137	12/1	J O'Brien (IRE)	23	1st Navan Nov. hurdle (55)
2021	12P6	Galopin des Champs	5	11-9	142	8/1	W Mullins (IRE)	22	6th Gr.1 Chanelle Pharma Nov. Hurdle (40)
2020	52231	Indefatigable	7	11-9	145	25/1	P Webber	23	1st Listed Warwick Mares' Hurdle (34)
2019	52	Early Doors	6	11-10	145	5/1	J O'Brien (IRE)	24	2nd Gr.1 Christmas Hurdle (81)
2018	32161	Blow By Blow	7	11-10	144	11/1	G Elliott (IRE)	23	1st Gr.3 Thurles Nov. Hurdle (23)
2017	23213	Champagne Classic	6	11-3	138	12/1	G Elliott (IRE)	23	3rd Gr.3 Thurles Nov. Hurdle (22)
2016	235	Ibis du Rheu	5	11-7	139	14/1	P Nicholls	24	5th Gr.3 Sandown H'cap Hurdle (41)

LEADING TEN-YEAR GUIDES

Thurles Racecourse Michael Purcell Memorial Novice Hurdle 2 (*Champagne Classic* 3rd, *Blow By Blow* 1st)

OVERSEAS RACING TOURS

At Venatour 'Racing Around The World', we pride ourselves on offering a bespoke service to all of our clients, guaranteeing each and every customer an unforgettable horse racing experience with that 'personal touch'.

We are here to ensure you experience the best racing events locally and worldwide, creating memories that last a lifetime.

racingaroundtheworld.co.uk   racing@venatour.co.uk

CHELTENHAM FESTIVAL 2026 – DAY 4
Daily Tips
BY SAM TURNER

Formerly Robin Goodfellow of the Daily Mail, Sam has been a regular on Racing TV for more than two decades and now writes a daily column for Betfair.

Triumph Hurdle
PROACTIF / MACHO MAN (NRNB)

WITH four consecutive victories in the Triumph Hurdle and, thanks to Goshen's dramatic late departure in 2020, five successes in the last six renewals, there is little doubt the Willie Mullins stable is the first (and arguably last) place to look for the winner of this race.

Once again, the Closutton operation appears to have a stranglehold on the day five opener with Narciso Has strengthening his position at the head of the market courtesy of a dominant victory at the Dublin Racing Festival in the Grade 1 Spring Juvenile Hurdle.

A 4½-length defeat of stablemate and Irish debutante Selma de Vary was achieved in ruthless fashion as market rival Mange Tout, previously unbeaten over hurdles, was left toiling in third after racing a little too keenly in the second time hood.

The market had expected that the aggressively ridden Narciso Has would turn around Fairyhouse form with Mange Tout from November when they first met, granted a better level of fitness and he did that in spades, reversing a near 3-length defeat to beat his old adversary by 6 lengths.

There is little doubt he sets a very strong standard heading into Cheltenham as he boasts a very uncomplicated way of racing, hurdles superbly (RaceiQ ratings of 9.2 and 8.4 on his last two starts) and sees the trip out well so, it is understandable given he has won one of the best trials for this race, that he would be a short-priced favourite.

The only downside to his chance is the lack of a top-class time on his C.V. using the speed ratings I have called on for the past 25 years.

It could be that Narciso Has simply hasn't been challenged enough in his two Irish victories to record a big figure and that could be a perfectly viable explanation why his two wins were achieved in respectable, if unspectacular, speed figures.

He certainly appears as though there is plenty more in the tank, especially as he gave generously after the last flight at Leopardstown to stretch clear of his field.

However, at the time of writing he is a top priced 7/4 and, if I was going to play at those odds, my experience tipping in this race suggests he would ideally need a speed figure beyond 70 on the ratings I use. For the record, his three Irish figures to date are 65, 63, 64.

I reiterate, he could well be capable of leaving those numbers behind in a championship race with a bigger field allied with a strong pace and it will be intriguing to see if connections are still intent on making the running with him with the New Course less likely to play to his excellent jumping technique given they jump so few hurdles in the final mile.

Given that his trainer was prepared to run 11 horses in last year's renewal and he again, rather predictably dominates the ante-post market, there is every chance Mullins will be again mob handed so Fairyhouse scorer **Proactif** and runner-up Macho Man both interest me greatly.

There is a chance the former could be rerouted to the Supreme Novices' Hurdle so anyone taking an ante-post approach to this race could be well served by utilising the Non-Runner-No-Bet concessions that are now being introduced by a number of layers.

Proactif certainly boasts the size and scope to tackle the meeting opener but his opening Irish gambit in a very strongly run affair marked him down as a natural for a race like this.

His hurdling wasn't flawless, but it was competent and the manner with which he powered clear of the well-touted Macho Man was impressive.

The long run from the second last to the final flight should suit him ideally and he possesses all the attributes required for a Triumph Hurdle winner, not least his speed figure which was a highly commendable 71.

Macho Man, one of two horses his owners bought out of an Auteuil Conditions Hurdle at the beginning of October (the other being Warwick winner Feel Gut trained by Nicky Henderson), was rather sluggish at his hurdles and could certainly sharpen up in that sphere.

I was still impressed he managed to keep tabs on the winner and only gave way after the last when the earlier errors he accrued finally told, while he also looked to those present that the run would bring him on physically.

Needless to say, his proximity to the winner ensured that he too registered a very healthy speed rating and, with the duo stretching clear of third-home Quinta Do

Lago who boasted plenty of experience heading into the race, it looks like a strong piece of juvenile form.

As an aside, Quinta Do Lago is worth having on a shortlist for the juvenile handicap on day one, while I would also be extremely interested in the considerately ridden Munsif, a never nearer fifth at Fairyhouse, if he made the line up, given he was very decent on the level for Roger Varian.

Mares' Chase
PANIC ATTACK

THE progress made by **Panic Attack** this season has been little short of staggering.

Ruled out of last season's Plate by a setback, trainer Dan Skelton immediately set his sights on early season silverware, targeting the Paddy Power Gold Cup as her primary early season target.

Given Skelton's aim is rarely wayward with his long-range handicap ambitions, it was no real great surprise to see the daughter of Canford Cliffs expertly exploit a rating of 135 and add her name to the roll-call of famous winners of the November showpiece.

What did shock a little was the manner of the performance as she turned what appeared a competitive handicap – nine or 10 were still in contention on the home turn – into a rout as she bounded up the run in to put good distances between herself and runner-up Vincenzo and stablemate Hoe Joly Smoke in third.

If we thought Panic Attack was a one-trick pony then we were made to think again as just a fortnight later she became the first horse in 22 years to complete a Paddy Power and Coral Gold Cup (Hennessy in old money) double when she again powered away from a fiercely competitive field to thump Three Card Brag who himself had decisively put away 17 rivals at Cheltenham on his previous start.

For a mare approaching her 10th birthday, it was a remarkable performance just 14 days after winning a top-level Cheltenham handicap with authority and clearly age is just a number.

The Grand National was talked off as the ultimate aim this season and connections would have been delighted that their revitalized mare skipped round Newbury to duly win a Listed Mares' Chase in the manner her rating and odds suggested she should.

Her rating remained unchanged off the back of that 14-length success as it should have done, but the enthusiasm and exuberance she displayed for the task in hand was again notable.

There is a four-week break to the National from the final day of Cheltenham so there is every chance that her connections may roll the dice and tackle both assignments. Given that their mare has improved the thick end of a stone this season, that would appear a smart move as, last year's winner Dinoblue aside, this race may not be that blessed with huge depth.

Ante-post second favourite Spindleberry didn't enjoy the best of experiences upped in class in the Irish Gold Cup and, although her yard is famed for their restorative powers, she has yet to run at Cheltenham which leaves something of a question mark.

In contrast, Panic Attack has won two of her last four starts at Prestbury Park, she is adept at around two-and-a-half miles (2231111) and her form figures when ridden by Harry Skelton currently stand at 31211 so she could easily be in the shake up and give Dinoblue something to worry about.

Panic Attack is in the form of her life

Albert Bartlett Novices' Hurdle
THEDEVILUNO

IN MY Betfair *'Cheltenham Festival Focus'* column (shameless plug, apologies), I was very sweet on the claims of Thedeviluno for this race following his destructive display in the Grade 2 River Don Novices' Hurdle at Doncaster in January.

Admittedly, the Town Moor staying feature doesn't have a rich heritage of producing future winners of this race, but last year's fourth across the line, Yellow Car, won it before running well in this event and, of course, Stay Away Fay won the 2023 Albert Bartlett on the back of a River Don second. Maybe Paul Nolan's exciting novice can post a huge effort himself.

This year's River Don looked to have a touch of class and quality about it with the upwardly mobile Country Code fancied by your correspondent to continue his fine start over hurdles.

While Ruth Jefferson's gelding ran a fine race in defeat, he was ultimately put in his place by Thedeviluno who travelled for fun throughout the contest before powering clear after the last for a win of huge authority.

While there is little doubt, the son of Elusive Pimpernel relished sitting off a strong gallop before being produced with a well-timed challenge, that scenario could easily present itself again here and the New Course at Cheltenham should really suit a novice and rider who are willing to take their time.

Connections were reportedly disappointed their seven-year-old was beaten at Navan over 2m4f on his penultimate start, but his conqueror, Doctor Steinberg endorsed that form with a blistering performance at the Dublin Racing Festival in the snappily named Nathaniel Lacy & Partners Solicitors Hurdle.

The Doctor Dino gelding tanked through the 2m6f Grade 1 with such exuberance in the hands of Paul Townend that many in-running players questioned whether Willie Mullins' chestnut could possibly see out the trip in such exacting conditions.

While his finishing speed percentage did understandably dip below 100, Doctor Steinberg still flew the final flight before powering to an eight-length victory, a success which saw him shorten to a post-race low of 2/1 for the Albert Bartlett in some places.

I did wonder given the way he raced whether his trainer may consider coming back in trip for the Turners on day two as historically Mullins has never truly been a fan of racing his most talented novices over 3m, irrespective if their stamina looks copper-bottomed; see Final Demand.

Should connections choose to take the shorter option, Thedeviluno backers are in decent shape and I'm still happy with my ante-post position on Paul Nolan's River Don winner as his stamina at the trip is confirmed whereas Doctor Steinberg will be heading into unknown territory if he runs on Gold Cup day.

The Nolan stable has also made a bright start to 2026 with three winners from a handful of runners in January, a figure which contrasts sharply with a return of one success from 33 runners in December.

In Thedeviluno, the Wexford handler has a hurdler with an excellent technique at his obstacles (all three hurdle starts have registered in excess of 8.0 on the RaceiQ jump index) while his finishing speed percentages this season have proved that he hits the line strongly, whatever the trip.

He has already comfortably beaten the talented Skylight Hustle this season and that rival won his next two, including in Grade 1 company when arguably a little fortunate, and is a single figure price for the Turners so the selection's form is standing up to the closest scrutiny.

SHORTLISTS FOR ALL 28 RACES!

ONLY £15

THE **CHELTENHAM FESTIVAL** TEXT SERVICE

AVAILABLE TO BUY ONLINE AT
www.weatherbysshop.co.uk

t 01933 304776 | e shop@weatherbys.co.uk

CHELTENHAM FESTIVAL 2026 – DAY 4

Banker or Bust

BY RORY DELARGY

Rory is a contributor to The Irish Field and Irish Daily Star, whilst he can be seen on Paddy Power's 'The Cheltenham Countdown' show. He also co-writes the 'Punting Pointers' feature for Sporting Life.

Triumph Hurdle
NARCISO HAS

ASSESSING the Triumph Hurdle is never easy at this stage of the season with some of the top trainers having historically unveiled Cheltenham winners for the first time as late as February, or in the case of Willie Mullins last year, the middle of March. Still, the starting point has to be a look at the leading form contenders and their Timeform ratings; which gives us this:

Narciso Has	142p
Minella Study	139p
Precious Man	137p
Maestro Conti	136p
Proactif	136p
Mange Tout (f)	132
Selma de Vary (f)	129p

Narciso Has was an impressive winner of the Grade 1 juvenile at the Dublin Racing Festival, comfortably reversing earlier Graded form with Mange Tout. He also won at Leopardstown in December and has looked sharper with each run. Mange Tout was a tad disappointing at the DRF, meeting Narciso Has on 4lb better terms than when beating him at Fairyhouse but essentially looked outclassed behind the improved winner.

Narciso Has hasn't taken huge steps forward in his three runs for Mullins, but looks increasingly professional, making the running to win at Leopardstown on good and heavy ground, suggesting that he's adaptable regarding ground and he appears to have stamina to spare. This far, his jumping has looked assured and he has clearly been well schooled, while he is quite physically imposing for a youngster and promises to progress further with maturity.

Probably the most striking thing about his win at Leopardstown was that everyone connected with the horse fully expected him to win well without sounding cocky about it. The impression is that Willie Mullins, who has had many top-notch juveniles through his hands, sees something outstanding in the gelding's home demeanour.

STRENGTHS: Narciso Has is already a good jumper for one so inexperienced and has winning form on both good and heavy ground. He's attained a standard good enough to be considered for the Triumph already and the form that he's shown has come in races which have historically worked out well. He seems quite mature for his age but he retains the physical scope to keep improving and he represents the trainer who has won the last four runnings of the race and tends to have a very strong hand in the division. We are dealing with limited evidence when it comes to juvenile hurdlers, but there are no obvious flaws in Narciso Has' make-up.

WEAKNESSES: Weaknesses here are largely unknowns. We know Narciso Has is up to standard for a Triumph favourite but he's been professional rather than spectacular to date, so it's hard to know how much is left in the tank. The temptation is to suggest that there is plenty more to come, but the acid test will be when taking on all comers at Grade 1 level. He's well suited by making the running but such tactics are hard to pull off on the New Course, but that implies that he needs to make the running, which is unlikely in itself.

OPPORTUNITIES: Racing on the New Course over 2m1f will bring stamina into play and Narciso Has looks like he will stay further, so he has the opportunity to take his form up another notch in the circumstances. He seems to have the temperament to cope with the atmosphere on Gold Cup Day so that should be in his favour. He's clearly been marked out as the stable's main Triumph Hurdle horse from a strong squad and he has the chance to show the world just why he's held in such high regard when asked a bigger question.

THREATS: A first look at Cheltenham can be daunting for any horse and the atmosphere will have adrenaline flowing. If he sets off too fast – or if others do – he may not be able to do himself justice.

As the ratings show, there are plenty of unexposed potential in the Triumph while last year's winner was previously unraced over hurdles. That practice has now been banned but it means that as well as the horses who are rated within a few pounds of the favourite, those who have been entered but have yet to run remain of interest, and most of those are trained by Willie Mullins. A big-field Triumph is not the lottery that it once was, but Willie ran half the field last year and struck with an unraced 100/1 shot. The fewer he runs this year, the more you should fancy Narciso Has

VERDICT: This is a hard one to judge as the figures can hide plenty, but Narciso Has isn't just the best horse on the book, but he is the subject of the kind of confidence from Closutton that preceded wins for the likes of Faugheen and Vautour as young hurdlers. It isn't always there, of course, but the quiet confidence about Narciso Has is almost deafening.

BANKER

Gold Cup
JANGO BAIE

THE Gold Cup is Jumps Racing's Blue Riband and with 3m2½f and 22 fences to negotiate, only the bravest and the best need apply. With Galopin des Champs having seemingly lost some of his brilliance this term, the betting is very open and is currently headed by the Nicky Henderson-trained **Jango Baie**.

WINNER of the Arkle in remarkable circumstances last season, he is attempting to become the first winner of that contest to go to land the Gold Cup the following year since Alverton (1978/79). It is a pretty rare feat, although Pendil might also have done it but for being brought down when travelling best in the 1974 Gold Cup (beaten a short head in 1975). Best Mate didn't run in the Arkle but would have been favourite for the race in 2001 when Foot & Mouth claimed the Festival and then went on to win the Gold Cup 12 months later, so the double isn't a strange one by any means. There are also a few Gold Cup winners who have been placed in the Arkle, with Kicking King and War of Attrition recent examples.

Jango Baie won the Arkle through stamina, looking set to drop out when the pace lifted, but running on strongly in the straight as others faltered, and promising to be suited by a stiffer test. Since then, he's won the 1965 Chase at Ascot and was beaten barely ½ a length when fourth in the King George at Kempton when trying 3m for the first time, and it would be harsh to say that lack of stamina cost him there. That confirmed him among the elite of 3m+ chasers, but how does the overall picture look?

Fact To File	174+
Gaelic Warrior	172
Galopin des Champs	171
The Jukebox Man	167p
Banbridge	167
I Am Maximus	167
Jango Baie	166+
Spillane's Tower	166
Inothewayurthinkin	? (was 172)

We can see that Jango Baie has a little to find on ratings but he's won on both chase starts at Cheltenham, with the first of those over an extended 2m4f on the New Course. The horse who tops the ratings is not currently entered in the Gold Cup, which clouds the issue, although I'd expect to see Fact To File supplemented after his impressive Irish Gold Cup win.

STRENGTHS: Jango Baie has a perfect record over fences at Cheltenham showing his stamina on debut over 2m4½f in class 2 company and dropping back to win the Arkle over 2m despite seeing unsuited by the return to shorter.

He clearly stays 3m and is lightly raced so his prospects of getting the Gold Cup trip should be viewed positively. He is also a Grade 1 winner over hurdles on heavy ground, suggesting he's capable of coping with softer ground.

WEAKNESSES: A fourth in the King George was a fine effort but he was behind Gaelic Warrior, Banbridge and winner The Jukebox Man at Kempton, and needs to show he can progress past that trio, all of whom ran on strongly at Kempton. His jumping is far from perfect and while he avoids blunders, he tends to make one or two small errors in his races, and those can add up over the longer trip of the Gold Cup.

While his stamina for 3m on good ground has been established, stepping up another quarter mile on deeper ground and a track that tests staying power means he's far from guaranteed to relish the Gold Cup trip, and a lot will depend on the ground. His Grade 1 win in heavy ground came in the Formby Novice' Hurdle at Aintree over 2m and he was left clear there when the leader fell at the final hurdle.

While Jango Baie is capable of better, he's never been talked of in the way some of Nicky Henderson's stars have, and he strikes as the sort to make marginal gains in his second season rather than improving in leaps and bounds given he's shown precocious talent from a fairly early age. Such horses tend to peak earlier than their late-maturing counterparts, and he needs to take a step forward on the ratings to justify his position at the head of the market.

OPPORTUNITIES: The return to the New Course will suit Jango Baie, who won the Arkle despite the relative test of speed rather than because of it. Outpaced on the downhill run from the fourth last, he picked up when meeting rising ground and the longer run to the home straight on the New Course will complement his style. His stamina for the trip is unknown but his habit of racing behind the bridle is indicative of a stayer and it may be that the longer trip allows him to fully express his ability.

THREATS: Trip and ground individually are not major concerns, the Gold Cup is a very different race on soft/heavy ground than on good, and I suspect a wet spring will suit the proven stayers more than those with tactical speed. The trio who beat him at Kempton should all be as well suited by Cheltenham, although Banbridge did disappoint in last year's Gold Cup. **The Jukebox Man** ran a blinder in the Albert Bartlett and would have been a leading contender in the Broadway (Brown Advisory) but for missing the spring with a setback. In truth, I don't understand why he isn't a shorter price than Jango Baie having battled back so well at Kempton and he looks to have stamina to spare.

Fact To File has strengthened up this year and is the one to beat if supplemented, although he has looked like 3m is perhaps his limit so it will be interesting to see if he runs here or in the Ryanair which he won impressively last term. **Gaelic Warrior** is also in the Ryanair but looks like he has no stamina issues and he won the Arkle on heavy ground as a novice, so would welcome further rain. That still leaves out the last two winners of this race; both have something to prove now, but a return to form would hardly be a shock for either **Inothewayurthinkin** or **Galopin des Champs**. That is not an exhaustive list of horses with form claims by any means, and I envisage a large field given the number of horses a case can be made for.

VERDICT: The Gold Cup is an open race and a case can be made for about a dozen horses. Jango Baie is in the list, but he's going to have to progress again to be competitive, and his imperfect jumping is likely to be tested to the limit in a big field.

BUST

Jango Baie faces strong opposition in the Gold Cup

CHELTENHAM FESTIVAL 2026 – DAY 4

Daily Tips

BY JODIE STANDING

Author of Point-to-Point Recruits, Jodie excels in spotting talent at an early stage in a horse's career.

Triumph Hurdle
NARCISO HAS

SOMETIMES there is no shying away from the obvious and **Narciso Has** looks a solid banker for the Triumph Hurdle. Willie Mullins has farmed this race in recent years, winning the last four renewals, including 12 months ago with the shock 100/1 winner Poinros, who took the scalp of Lulamba on the run-in to win by a neck. Before that, it was the J P McManus-owned Majborough who landed the spoils and this year's favourite looks cut from the same mould as the now Grade 1 winning chaser.

A powerfully built individual with great size and scope, he came from France with a lofty reputation, having won his solitary start at Auteuil and made his debut in the green and gold hoops at Fairyhouse in late November. Sent off the 5/4 favourite against the race-fit Mange Tout to whom he had to concede 3lb, he travelled strongly on the heels of the leader but took a stride or two to find top gear after the second last, in which time Mange Tout quickened by and produced a better leap over the final flight before extending her advantage to 2¾ lengths at the line, with the pair putting over 9½ lengths between themselves and the third, Adrienne.

With that run under his belt, Naciso Has was a warm order to go one better in the Grade 2 juvenile hurdle at Leopardstown on Boxing Day and he didn't let his supporters down. Lobbing along with his ears pricked, he looked to find the whole exercise rather easy and sailed over his flights without barely wrapping the rubber. Kicking on after the third-last, he soared over the penultimate flight and knuckled down in impressive fashion for a shake of the reins, using his ground-eating stride to get the field on the stretch before surging clear off the home bend. Again, good at the last, he continued to pull clear on the run-in to eventually cross the line 11 lengths clear of his old foe, Adrienne.

That victory marked him down as an early favourite for the showpiece in March, a position that was cemented with his first Grade 1 success back at Leopardstown for the Dublin Racing Festival. Leading at every juncture, Narciso Has produced a blemish-free round of jumping and kicked off the home bend, lengthening rather than quickening to put daylight between himself and the chasing pack to eventually win by 4½ lengths from his stable companion Selma de Vary who was making her stable debut and came from off the pace, while a 1½ lengths behind her in third was his chief market rival and previous conqueror, Mange Tout.

Although he's now priced between 5/4 and 7/4 for the opener on the final day of the Festival, the next-best in the market is Selma de Vary, whom he has already beaten comprehensively at Leopardstown. Add to that the fact he looks tailor-made for the New Course at Cheltenham with the long run from two-out to the last providing the ideal opportunity for him to use his long-reaching stride to build up a head of steam before the kick up the hill.

Our Conor was the last horse to win this race by a double-digit margin when he came home 15 lengths to the good over Far West in 2013. The next best was Defi du Seuil in 2017, who won by 5 lengths from Mega Fortune. While Narciso Has is built in a different mould entirely to those nippy sorts, everything about his profile suggests he could deliver a similarly dominant display.

Albert Bartlett Novices' Hurdle
DOCTOR STEINBERG

THE Albert Bartlett is a stern test for any novice, examining not only their ability at the top level but also their constitution to dig deep into the stamina reserves when others are running on empty. This year's field brings together a mix of horses who have already shown their staying prowess, but there are others who look capable of elevating their level with a step up in trip after plying their trade through the winter months over shorter distances.

Doctor Steinberg is one of those untried at 3m, but his dominant display at the top table at the Dublin Racing Festival confirmed his resoluteness on stamina-sapping ground, suggesting he will have no issues stepping up in trip.

A Ballinrobe bumper winner in May would not necessarily lend itself seamlessly to this stamina test for a novice hurdler, but the Doctor Dino gelding has come on leaps and bounds since stepping up in trip and accounted for a fairly useful yardstick in Frankie John at Galway in October. He beat Denis Hogan's subsequent winner comfortably by 5½ lengths, the pair pulling 25 lengths clear of He Can't Dance in third. Travelling strongly on the heels of the leader before injecting pace into the contest on the final circuit, he edged to the front before putting his stamina to good use on the rise for home.

That was over an extended 2m5f on good to yielding ground, but he was just as effective when dropped back in distance to 2m4f on heavy ground for a Grade 2 at Navan at the start of December, this time making all before readily asserting over the last to win by just shy of 5 lengths from Thedeviluno, Kovanis and Port Authority.

That form has since taken on a solid look, with Thedeviluno accounting for the subsequently unbeaten Skylight Hustle at Gowran Park in November and later winning a strong renewal of the Grade 2 River Don Novices' Hurdle at Doncaster. The other pair were also decent winners in maiden company but have subsequently disappointed.

Crucially, Doctor Steinberg has now taken another significant step forward since those runs. Returning to Leopardstown for the Dublin Racing Festival, he stepped into Grade 1 company for the first time in the Nathaniel Lacy & Partners Solicitors Novices Hurdle over 2m6f and delivered a performance that removed any lingering doubt about his suitability for a searching stamina test.

Despite racing keenly throughout, he took up the running before the third last and immediately put the field under pressure before kicking on after the penultimate flight. With nothing able to land a blow, he stayed on strongly to the last and maintained the revs all the way to the line to win by 8 lengths from the previous Grade 2 winner Kazansky.

The six-year-old appears an uncomplicated-looking sort who usually travels a touch behind the bridle yet comes alive once given the signal to assert. His hurdling is also efficient, and even when getting into the bottom of a flight, he wastes little time in getting from one side to the other. A half-brother to five winners, including Stay Humble who won over 3m and Smuggler's Blues who scored over 3m1f, there is ample evidence to suggest the gelding will relish a further step up in trip.

With his latest Grade 1 success now underpinning his profile, he arrives at Cheltenham looking every inch a horse ready for the demands of the Albert Bartlett. The deeper the test, the more he seems to find, and his Leopardstown win strongly hints that 3m around Prestbury Park will bring about another career best.

Narciso Has wins the Spring Juvenile Hurdle

Martin Pipe Conditional Jockeys' H'cap Hurdle
FRANKIE JOHN

TRAINERS often head into the Martin Pipe mob-handed, sometimes in a bid to get out of jail if the previous 27 races haven't gone to plan. It is a race that can offer late redemption, and that was certainly the case twelve months ago with Gordon Elliott, who hit the paintwork throughout the week but had to wait for Wodhooh to beat the boys from a mark of 141 before he could finally breathe a sigh of frustrated relief.

Denis Hogan would not have the numbers to afford him the luxury of throwing a few darts at the board in the hope that one finds the bullseye, but he could still have a golden arrow in the shape of **Frankie John**, should he choose to take him to Cheltenham. The six-year-old has been asked plenty of questions already this season and has rarely taken a backward step, shaping like a horse who has both the resilience and the attitude to make his presence felt in a race of this nature.

There has been no hiding place for him since making a winning return in a bumper over 2m2f at Galway in July. He then ran a solid race in defeat following a shoddy round of jumping over the same trip on his hurdling debut at Listowel in September. From there he bumped into the subsequent Grade 1 winner Doctor Steinberg back at Galway over 2m5½f in October, making a good fist of things over the final couple of flights and keeping the winner honest on the run-in to finish 5½ lengths adrift, with a 25 length break back to the third, He Can't Dance.

A step into Grade 3 company at Navan followed in November and he once again shaped well, travelling smoothly on the bridle and still racing in a share of the lead approaching the last. An untidy leap saw him land flat-footed and lose momentum at a crucial moment, and although he stuck on willingly he was eventually beaten 7¾ lengths by Kalypso'chance, with The Big Clubman splitting the pair.

Finally his consistency was rewarded at Leopardstown's Christmas meeting, where the return to good ground suited and he dug deep to deny Jalon d'Oudairies by ½ a length over an extended 2m4f. However, he found both the quick turnaround and the step into Grade 1 company for the Ballymore Novice Hurdle at Naas just 11 days later a bridge too far, trailing home 24 lengths behind I'll Sort That after a short-lived effort around the home bend saw him weaken after the penultimate flight.

Another venture into Grade 1 company for the Nathaniel Lacy & Partners Solicitors Novice Hurdle at the Dublin Racing Festival brought the same result, this time finishing 27 lengths behind his old foe Doctor Steinberg, a combination of top-level opposition and the heavy ground both working against him. Still, it was a fair effort until the final flight as he travelled well through the race and was still in with a chance of finishing in the frame over the final obstacle but then got tired on the run-in.

Rated on a mark of 128, likely higher if he heads to these shores, he strikes me as the type who could relish the switch to handicaps, with the likelihood of contesting a big field unlikely to faze him given he has already won a 16-runner bumper at Galway. With decent form to his name, particularly on a sounder surface, he could give us a bold run for our money.

He is also a prominent racer so should not get snarled up in the hustle and bustle, and provided he gets into a rhythm with his jumping, he ought to have no problem with the trip on the New Course, especially being a half-brother to Shearer out of a half-sister to Empire Of Dirt.

With enough stamina, enough grit and enough honesty in his pedigree and his performances to suggest that, if Hogan does roll the dice, Frankie John would not be heading to Cheltenham merely to make up the numbers.

OUR ANALYSIS
DOESN'T STOP HERE!

ONLY £15

THE **AINTREE FESTIVAL** SERVICE

AVAILABLE TO BUY ONLINE AT
www.weatherbysshop.co.uk

t 01933 304776 | e shop@weatherbys.co.uk

SPRING HORSES TO FOLLOW 2026

BEL OMBRE

6yo Affinisea – Slani (Brian Boru)

Trainer
Neil Mulholland
Possible Cheltenham Target
N/A

Owner
Mrs Sarah Keys
Other Possible Spring Targets
Various Options

PERHAPS not necessarily the kind of horse you might expect to see in a list of *Spring Horses To Follow*, Bel Ombre impressed when winning on handicap debut at Taunton (2m3f, good-to-soft) during January and appeals as the type to win again, maybe more than once, before the season is out.

A horse who had caught the eye with how he moved in bumpers, the son of Affinisea was beaten 47, 22 and 27 lengths in maiden and novice company at Chepstow (twice) and Huntingdon, before hitting the target from a mark of just 98. Again, he moved stylishly throughout and could be called the winner at the top of Taunton's home straight.

Up 10lb for that victory, the six-year-old is sure to remain competitive in handicaps in the coming weeks/months and whilst he has the size to make a chaser next season, should have plenty more to offer over hurdles beforehand. Given how he moves, the better ground probably helped at Taunton and that is certainly a positive as he embarks on his spring campaign.

A full-brother to Listed bumper winner Avakate, he is the type of horse which Neil Mulholland excels with, the trainer having saddled 20 of his 44 winners this season (as at 8th February) in handicap hurdles. From a mark of 108, there should be plenty of presentable opportunities ahead.

DAVID'S WELL

7yo Getaway – Drop Of Spirit (Westerner)

Trainer
Chris Gordon
Possible Cheltenham Target
Grand Annual Handicap Chase

Owner
The Morestead Select Syndicate
Other Possible Spring Targets
Red Rum Handicap Chase

ONLY seen sparingly during the past two seasons, David's Well is developing into a rapidly-improving chaser and following wins at Haydock (2m½f, good-to-soft) and Cheltenham (2m½f, good-to-soft) during this campaign, is now unbeaten in four starts over fences.

His Haydock win was franked when the second and fourth returned to the Merseyside track to finish first and second the following month, whilst his defeat of JPR One (won the Scottish Champion Chase at Musselburgh next time) and Triple Trade (also won next time) on the New Course in December also now reads well.

Initially raised 6lb, he has since gone up another pound for collateral form, meaning that he should get into the Grand Annual from a mark of 135 and although he wouldn't have the profile of a standard winner of that race, he looks capable of making his presence felt in a good race before the season is out. Switching to the Old Course shouldn't be too much of a problem, especially if there is plenty of cut in the ground, with his two wins as a novice gained on soft.

Aintree's Red Rum would be another possible spring target for this upwardly mobile seven-year-old, who might have been forgotten about somewhat, having had another mid-season break. Usually a sound jumper, he can win again, hopefully at one of the major spring festivals.

DOCTOR STEINBERG

6yo Doctor Dino – Rosy de Cyborg (Cyborg)

Trainer
Willie Mullins
Possible Cheltenham Target
Spa (Albert Bartlett) / Baring Bingham (Turners) Novices' Hurdle

Owner
Jodmart Construction Ltd
Other Possible Spring Targets
Sefton Novices' Hurdle / Channor Real Estate Group Novice Hurdle

WILLIE MULLINS took the first two races on the rearranged second day of the Dublin Racing Festival with sons of Doctor Dino and whilst Narciso Has rightly received plenty of plaudits for his success in the Spring Juvenile Hurdle, Doctor Steinberg also impressed in winning the Golden Cygnet Novice Hurdle.

Successful just once from four starts in bumpers, he has improved over longer distances as a novice hurdler, with his early-season victory over Frankie John (finished a long way behind him at Leopardstown recently) at Galway (2m5½f, good-to-yielding) confirming that he can handle decent ground.

On testing ground, he beat Thedeviluno (winner of Doncaster's River Don Novices' Hurdle next time) in Grade 2 company at Navan (2m4f, soft-to-heavy) and bettered that with a dominant display at Leopardstown (2m6f, heavy). Out of a Cyborg (sire of Cyfor Malta, Hors La Loi III and Cyborgo) mare, he is bred to stay further and whilst he holds an entry in the Baring Bingham, the Spa (Albert Bartlett) looks the obvious target.

Versatile in terms of ground, he will likely head to Punchestown for the Channor Real Estate Group Novice Hurdle after Cheltenham, although Aintree's Sefton Novices' Hurdle is another Grade 1 option for this likeable chestnut. Yet to race beyond 2m6f, stepping up to 3m shouldn't be a problem.

DOUBLE MEASURE

5yo Goliath du Berlais – Regba (Kapgarde)

Trainer
Dan Skelton
Possible Cheltenham Target
N/A

Owner
Robert Kirkland
Other Possible Spring Targets
Various Options

ALTHOUGH he holds an entry in the Supreme Novices' Hurdle, I suspect that Double Measure will be kept to calmer waters during the concluding part of the season, but he remains very much a progressive young horse to monitor closely.

A winner at Uttoxeter on his sole start in the bumper sphere, he split two nice horses at Chepstow on hurdling debut, with the third-placed Came From Nowhere flourishing once entering handicap company, and was then badly positioned when only fourth in Haydock's Grade 2 Newton Novices' Hurdle in November.

Dropped considerably in class, he won a Huntingdon (2m, soft) maiden in a canter, successful by 11 lengths. With the second favourite departing at the first flight, the race lacked depth, but the five-year-old could hardly have won any easier. Still very much a work in progress, it wouldn't be a surprise to see him run in another ordinary novice, under a penalty, before he is given any loftier targets.

Upped 4lb (129) for his Huntingdon success, handicaps could come under consideration during the spring, with a more truly run race sure to suit this strong traveller. Being by Goliath du Berlais and out of a Kapgarde mare, he should have little trouble in getting further in time, so there ought to be plenty of opportunities for him before the season concludes.

KADASTRAL

6yo Cokoriko – Parallele (Video Rock)

Trainer
Dan Skelton
Possible Cheltenham Target
N/A

Owner
Christopher Greenall
Other Possible Spring Targets
Various Options

HAVING twice seen the rear-end of the exciting Sober Glory over hurdles, the promising Kadastral remains a horse of considerable potential and should almost certainly improve for meeting better ground in the spring.

A 12-length second to Sober Glory at Chepstow, he readily won a maiden at Newbury (2m½f, good-to-soft) before finishing 27 lengths behind Philip Hobbs & Johnson White's Supreme hopeful at the same track, where he shaped better than the bare result. Having moved up stylishly, he was brushed aside by the strong-galloping winner and was eased down in the closing stages.

The form of his bumper success – also at Newbury – from last spring now reads extremely well, with him giving 10lb and a beating to Grade 1 winner Talk The Talk (I.H.R.B. Rating of 148), with the next four home also having won over hurdles this season. That victory came on good ground, adding further weight to the theory that he will improve for reverting to a sounder surface.

Taken out of the Baring Bingham at the latest 'scratching' stage, Cheltenham is no longer an option, but from a mark of 126, he will be of significant interest once entering handicap company. He should be capable of winning another novice under a penalty before better races come under consideration and a strongly run race looks sure to suit.

KNIGHT OF ALLEN

6yo Masterstroke – Atacames (Dom Alco)

Trainer
Jane Williams
Possible Cheltenham Target
N/A

Owner
Holt, Macnabb, Robinson & Jeffrey
Other Possible Spring Targets
Various Options

JANE WILLIAMS and Ciaran Gethings have enjoyed a fine season together, with the jockey having ridden 11 of the trainer's 14 winners (as at 8th February). Stable-star Saint Segal has won twice and more recently chased home Lulamba in the Game Spirit, whilst Knight Of Allen again ran well on the same card.

Although beaten 14 lengths, he travelled well for a long way, on ground which would have been softer than ideal. Whilst he handled conditions, it probably didn't help him see out the longer trip and although that defeat all but rules out handicaps at the Cheltenham Festival, there is still a nice race to be won with him over fences.

A winner at the second attempt as a chaser, he beat Aviation (recent winner off a 2lb higher mark) in cosy fashion at Newbury (2m4f, good-to-soft), before running well in a class 2 novice chase at Cheltenham. Whilst he has operated on soft in the past, his two hurdles victories were gained on good-to-soft and good ground, suggesting spring conditions ought to suit.

If not coming too quickly, the Greatwood Gold Cup (Saturday 28th February) could be an option back at Newbury, whilst there is a 0-145 over the same course-and-distance three weeks later and he can win a handicap before the season is out. He is currently rated 127.

KOKTAIL DIVIN

6yo Masked Marvel – Divine Sainte (Saint des Saints)

Trainer
Henry de Bromhead
Possible Cheltenham Target
Broadway (Brown Advisory)
Novices' Chase

Owner
Barry Maloney
Other Possible Spring Targets
WillowWarm Gold Cup /
Manifesto Novices' Chase

MONALEE, Minella Indo and Monty's Star all finished runner-up in the Broadway Novices' Chase for owner Barry Maloney, who looks set to have another runner in the race this year, in the shape of the progressive Koktail Divin.

Runner-up to Romeo Coolio at Down Royal, he appeared to be outstayed over 3m at Punchestown before running out an impressive winner at Leopardstown (2m5½f, yielding) over Christmas. That sort of intermediate trip appears to be his optimum at this stage, but with the Golden Miller now being a novices' handicap, it seems the Broadway is his likely Festival target.

On better ground (it was testing at Punchestown) he might well stay and remains a *'lively outsider'* for the day two contest, although the fact that the distance of the Broadway has been increased this year isn't ideal. The other option would be to bypass Cheltenham with either Fairyhouse or Aintree in mind.

In fact, he could run at the Festival and still drop in distance for either the WillowWarm Gold Cup or the Manifesto. Given that there are only five days between those two races, it will be one or the other and his connections might want to avoid a re-match with Romeo Coolio. Wherever he goes, he remains a promising young horse, who appears to be improving with each run.

NARCISO HAS

4yo Doctor Dino – Chegei Has (Kahyasi)

Trainer
Willie Mullins
Possible Cheltenham Target
Triumph Hurdle

Owner
John P McManus
Other Possible Spring Targets
Champion Four-Year-Old Hurdle

A WINNER on his sole start in France (successful on testing ground at Auteuil), Narciso Has was beaten by Mange Tout at Fairyhouse on his first start for current connections, but has since improved considerably and will head to Cheltenham as a worthy market leader for the Triumph Hurdle.

Having stayed on strongly to beat the 122-rated Adrienne by a similar distance in a Grade 2 at Leopardstown's (2m, yielding) Christmas fixture (she had finished third at Fairyhouse), he showed significant improvement on his latest start, when turning the form around with Mange Tout (on worse terms) in the Spring Juvenile Hurdle (2m, heavy).

That Grade 1, staged at the Dublin Racing Festival, has been the best recent guide to Triumph success and with the longer trip (2m1f) and more expansive track sure to suit at Cheltenham, it is difficult to see that form being reversed. A strong stayer, soft ground would enhance his claims even further, but he already sets a very high standard and should be difficult to beat.

A strapping son of Doctor Dino, he will develop into a chaser in time, but in the short term, will likely head to Punchestown for the Champion Four-Year-Old Hurdle, should all go to plan in the Triumph. A top-class prospect, he boasts considerable scope for further improvement.

NEWTON TORNADO

7yo Cokoriko – New Saga (Sagamix)

Trainer
Rebecca Curtis
Possible Cheltenham Target
National Hunt Chase /
Kim Muir

Owner
Frobisher Hyde McDermott
Outhart Waters
Other Possible Spring Targets
Midlands Grand National

HAITI COULEURS featured among last year's dozen *Spring Horses To Follow* and duly provided Rebecca Curtis with a second win in the National Hunt Chase. The hope is that lightning can strike twice with the progressive Newton Tornado, who also has the option of open handicaps, as he has had four runs.

Slightly frustrating last season (finished runner-up four times), the seven-year-old has improved significantly for going chasing, despite falling four out at Cheltenham's October meeting. Up to that point, he had jumped well and handled the track, as he had done when finishing runner-up to Diva Luna in a maiden hurdle on New Year's Day last year.

Off the mark at Bangor-on-Dee (3m, heavy), he was pulled-up quickly after making a mistake at Newbury before returning to form at Doncaster (3m, soft), where he won by a commanding 6½ lengths. Up 6lb to a mark of 133, he looks capable of taking a hand in a decent race before the season is out and he threatens to improve again once faced with a stiffer test of stamina.

At his best on soft ground, the Midlands National (Saturday 14th March) might also be worth considering, in case we get a dry Festival. That seems unlikely at this stage, however, and the National Hunt Chase certainly makes most appeal. He could be a Welsh National type later in the year.

OLD PARK STAR

6yo Well Chosen – Norwich Star (Norwich)

Trainer
Nicky Henderson
Possible Cheltenham Target
Supreme Novices' Hurdle

Owner
Gordon & Su Hall
Other Possible Spring Targets
Top Novices' Hurdle

PLACED in three bumpers last season when trained by Paul Nicholls, Old Park Star has developed into a high-class novice hurdler and looks to be the leading light in the division on this side of the Irish Sea.

A strapping individual, it could well be that he was still developing, physically, last year, and he completed the hat-trick over hurdles in devastating fashion at Haydock (1m7½f, good-to-soft). Despite the sharp track, he powered clear to record a thoroughly dominant success in the Grade 2 Rossington Main Novices' Hurdle.

Earlier victories at Kempton (2m, good) and Cheltenham (2m1f, good-to-soft) had marked him down as a potential Graded class performer and the fact that he had Hurricane Pat 18 lengths away in second at Haydock just goes to show the progression which has been made (that rival had beaten him in a bumper in November 2024).

An uncomplicated son of Well Chosen who hurdles fluently and gallops strongly, he is likely to take some beating in the Supreme Novices' Hurdle. With a four-week gap between fixtures, it will be interesting to see if he then heads to Aintree, with Nicky Henderson boasting a fine record in the Top Novices' Hurdle (usually with placed horses from Cheltenham). This well-built six-year-old looks to have a huge future ahead of him and will stay further.

SCORPIO RISING

6yo Jukebox Jury – Sixofone (Tikkanen)

Trainer
Olly Murphy
Possible Cheltenham Target
N/A

Owner
Premier Plastering (UK) Limited
Other Possible Spring Targets
EBF Final /
William Hill Handicap Hurdle

THIRD in an Exeter bumper and a Ffos Las maiden hurdle last season, Scorpio Rising has thrived this term and given his physique, is another who might well have required the time to fill into his frame.

A future chaser on looks, the grey got off the mark at Perth (2m4f, soft) in the autumn, before easily defying an opening handicap mark of 113 at Lingfield (2m3½f, good-to-soft). It was his latest performance at Windsor (2m4f, soft) which really underlined him as a highly-progressive youngster, the six-year-old running out a taking winner of what appeared to be a strong novices' handicap.

The Jukebox Jury gelding defied an 8lb rise and has a further 7lb increase to contend with moving forward, but such is his rate of development, it could be that he remains ahead of the assessor. Sandown's EBF Final – for which he qualified by winning at Perth – appeals as the obvious target and although that race is always full of potential improvers (another possible contender highlighted below), he very much fits the mould.

Testing ground at Sandown would be a concern, but he has twice now won on soft and if all went well at the Esher venue, perhaps he will be considered for a trip to Aintree, where stepping up to 3m for the handicap which opens Grand National day would be an option.

STARMOUNT

6yo Mount Nelson – Sparky May (Midnight Legend)

Trainer
Ben Pauling
Possible Cheltenham Target
N/A

Owner
Dineen, King, Stokes & Wicks
Other Possible Spring Targets
Premier Kelso Novices' Hurdle /
EBF Final

BEN PAULING and Ben Jones are another duo to have enjoyed a fantastic campaign to date and one who the pairing will, no doubt, be looking forward to running again in the coming weeks is the promising Starmount, who has won twice from three starts over hurdles.

Successful at Wetherby (2m, soft) in December, he returned to the same venue to run out a 15-length winner – beating the promising Kaka's Son in the process – over course-and-distance under a penalty and under similar conditions. Sandwiched in between was a fourth place finish in the Grade 1 Formby Novices' Hurdle at Aintree, where the ground was described as being on the quick side for him and a mistake two out (usually four out) also didn't help.

The six-year-old hasn't been handed any Cheltenham entries but his upcoming options likely include the Premier Novices' Hurdle at Kelso (Saturday 28th February) – a race the stable won in 2024 with Personal Ambition – and the EBF Final (Saturday 7th March), a race in which Pauling saddled the one-two in 2024.

Aintree could become a possibility but his trainer believes that he needs soft ground, so Kelso or Sandown might offer the best opportunity for him to land a nice prize, before he is sent chasing in the autumn. He was upped 8lb for his latest Wetherby success and is currently rated 131.

BEST ODDS GUARANTEED

ON BRITISH, IRISH & SOUTH AFRICAN HORSE RACING

SCAN HERE TO FIND OUT MORE

T&Cs Apply **Be**Gamble**Aware**.org®

If you or someone you know needs help with a gambling problem, ring Gamstop on 0800 138 6518

www.hollywoodbets.co.uk

WEATHERBYS

THE ORIGINAL

GRAND NATIONAL FESTIVAL BETTING GUIDE 2026

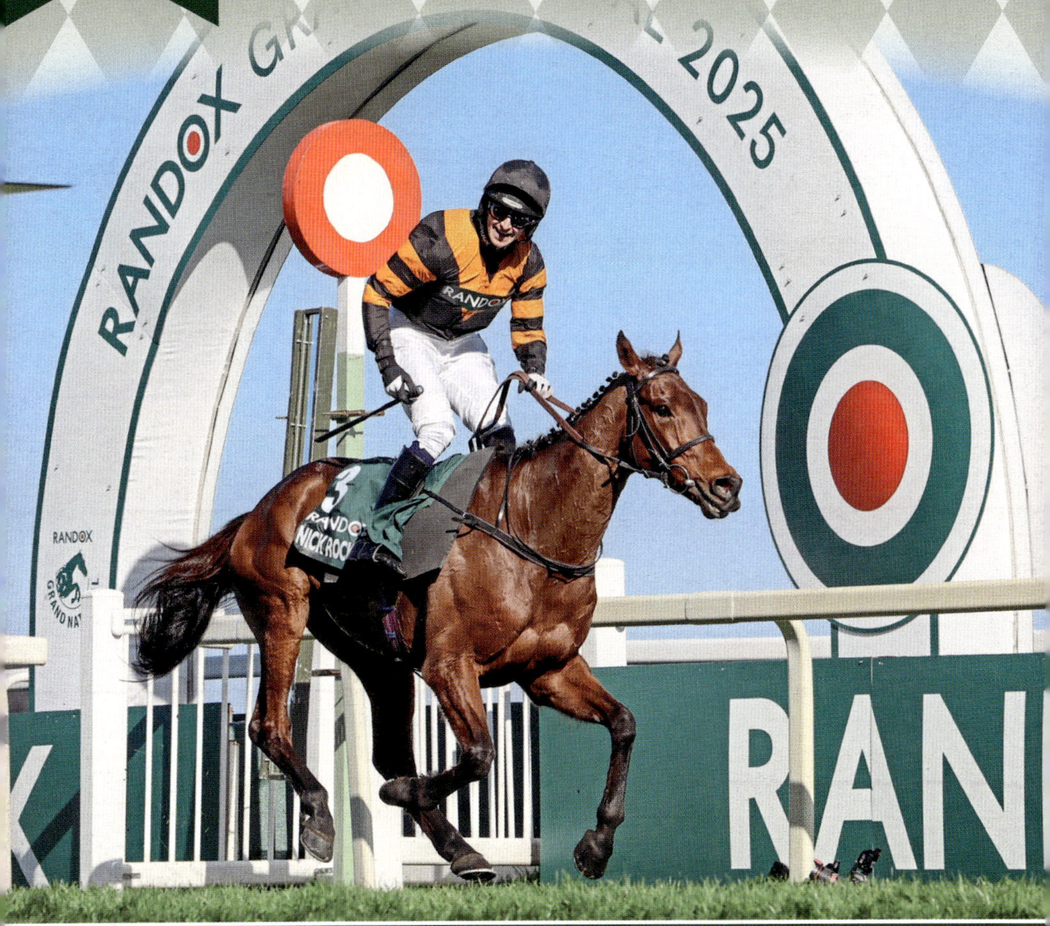

12 Big-Race Trends
PLUS AN IN-DEPTH RANDOX GRAND NATIONAL PREVIEW

IN ASSOCIATION WITH

Fresh For Aintree

WHILST the Aintree Hurdle was initially thought to be the intended spring target of the improving **Kabral du Mathan**, Dan Skelton handed the six-year-old an entry in Haydock's Rendlesham Hurdle (Saturday 14th February) on the day the Guide was being finalised for print stage. If he were to win that 3m contest, perhaps the Stayers' Hurdle will become too tempting to ignore and original plans shelved.

As things stand, he has yet to prove himself over that far, with the Relkeel Hurdle (2m4½f on Cheltenham's New Course) currently as far as he has gone. Originally, it was believed that he would head to Fontwell for the Grade 2 National Spirit Hurdle (Sunday 22nd February) before bypassing the Festival in favour of the Grade 1 over 2m4f on the opening day of the Grand National fixture.

By the time you read this, a decision will likely have been made – or certainly his target having become clearer – and Haydock will tell us, and his connections, plenty. Initially, I personally thought that the Aintree Hurdle would be just about ideal, with the son of Pastorius having plenty of natural zip, something which we associate with the hurdles course at Aintree.

It will be interesting to see which way they now head, but if sticking to Plan A, he would certainly look to be a leading contender for top honours at Aintree.

With a first trainers' title in sight, Skelton is sure to assemble a strong team for Liverpool and with Maestro Conti set to represent the stable in the Triumph Hurdle, **Precious Man** is being targeted at the Anniversary, via Kempton's Adonis Juvenile Hurdle (Saturday 21st February).

Having beaten a couple of useful sorts on his sole start in France – successful over 2m1½f on *'very soft'* ground at Auteuil – he travelled very strongly on his first start in Britain, in the Grade 2 Prestbury Juvenile Hurdle at Cheltenham in November. A serious error at the final flight didn't help, but it probably didn't make the difference between winning and losing, given that he had over-raced slightly, against a race-fit rival, on heavy ground.

Having undergone wind surgery, he returned to action at Kempton some 56 days later and ran out a comfortable winner, under a penalty. He will need to improve on this form when he returns to the Sunbury venue this month and again if he is to make an impact in the Anniversary at Aintree, but he is clearly a very speedy juvenile, who ought to be suited by the demands of both tracks, and there should be plenty more to come from this improving chestnut. It is also worth remembering that Skelton saddled Live Conti to finish runner-up in the Anniversary in 2025, on the back of just one run (in Britain) at Wetherby.

Precious Man could be Aintree bound if all goes to plan in the Adonis

The grey **Unexpected Party** – winner of the Grand Annual at Cheltenham only two years ago – could be another of Skelton's squad for Aintree. Runner-up in the same Festival contest last year, he finished just 5 lengths off Steel Ally in a graduation chase at Carlisle in November, and after being pulled-up at Kelso in December, had his attentions turned to the Hunters' Chase division from the New Year.

A winner at Taunton on 8th January, he had too much class for his eight rivals and won comfortably under jockey Heidi Palin.

Cheltenham is unlikely to come under consideration for the 11-year-old, given the distance of the race, so a trip to Aintree seems more than likely. 2m5f around the National Course should be within range, although the long run in might well stretch his stamina to the maximum. That said, he will be a fascinating runner – given his age and the fact that he was still contesting decent handicaps until recently – and Skelton has saddled the runner-up in each of the past three renewals.

Palin completed the course aboard Frere d'Armes last year when the year younger **Jet Plane** finished runner-up under Jack Andrews. She was aboard the 10-year-old for Warwick's Willoughby de Broke Open Hunters' Chase in January, a race which was won by Hazel Hill in 2019 (won the *'Foxhunters'* on his next start) and by Latenightpass in 2021 (won at Aintree the following year).

Sent off at the head of the market, the pair parted company at the twelfth fence. He had earlier been in excellent form in handicaps this season, finishing seventh in the Grand Sefton (again completing over the course), before winning off a mark of 130 at Leicester and finishing runner-up to Triple Trade in a veterans' chase at Sandown. Provided he recovers from his Warwick tumble, he could still be targeted at Aintree and with an official BHA Rating of 137, he would be another who would warrant considerable respect.

The Willoughby de Broke was won by Paul Nicholls' **Golden Son**, who was another who mainly raced over intermediate trips (up to 3m) under Rules. With that in mind, it could be that Aintree is favoured over Cheltenham for this eight-year-old, who had earlier recorded just one victory over fences. That came at Kempton, whilst he also ran well against Iroko in a novices' chase at Warwick, so flat tracks clearly suit him well.

Nicholls took the 2002 Aintree Foxhunters' with Torduff Express and he has handed Golden Son an entry in the Haydock's Walrus Hunters' Chase (Saturday 14th February), where he could clash with Unexpected Party. That race takes place over a trip marginally in excess of 2m6f, so should be within range for both and it could prove to be an informative contest.

Nigel & Willy Twiston-Davies had pencilled in a similar path – to that of Kabral du Mathan (original plan) - for their recent Windsor winner, **Potters Charm**. However, he was also handed an entry on Saturday 14th February, in Wincanton's Kingwell Hurdle, where he could meet Champion Hurdle winner Golden Ace, as well as the improving Alexei, over the minimum trip.

Potters Charm could be in line for a tilt at the Aintree Hurdle

Wherever he runs next, the Aintree Hurdle is likely to remain his primary end-of-season target, with the seven-year-old having won a Grade 1 at Aintree as a novice. Successful in last season's Formby Novices' Hurdle, he ran well behind Wodhooh at Ascot in November before looking a non-stayer in the Long Walk. Down in both trip and grade, he returned to form in the hugely prestigious (said with tongue firmly in cheek, of course) Weatherbys Cheltenham Festival Betting Guide Hurdle.

Versatile in terms of ground, he is very much one to note on the opening day of the meeting, with the Twiston-Davies stable having won the race three times this century, with Mister Morose (2000), Khyber Kim (2010) and The New One (2014).

Another who could be destined for the Aintree Hurdle is Sam Thomas' **Celtic Dino**, last seen finishing behind Sir Gino in the Christmas Hurdle. Winner of the Welsh Champion Hurdle on his reappearance, that form reads extremely well now, thanks to the subsequent exploits of both Alexei and Wilful. Stepping up in grade, he finished runner-up and one place in front of Potters Charm in the Ascot Hurdle, beaten just 2½ lengths by Wodhooh, who again advertised that form at Leopardstown over Christmas. Given plenty of time to recover from Kempton, the track at Aintree should suit (ran well in defeat in a handicap last year after being hampered early) and going back up to an intermediate trip should also help. Whilst he needs to prove himself at this level, he remains lightly-raced and will relish genuine spring ground.

Thomas' **Steel Ally** ran out a 10-length winner of the Kingmaker Novices' Chase at Warwick recently, taking his tally over fences to three from three. Winner of a graduation chase and a Grade 2 at Ascot, I had thought that the Manifesto would be an ideal target for the eight-year-old, but having given weight and a beating to two rivals in the Kingmaker, an Arkle bid seems likely. Should Thomas and owner Dai Walters opt to skip Cheltenham, 2m4f around Aintree could be perfect.

Last of three in the Kingmaker, the Manifesto could also be suitable for **Mambonumberfive**. A winner at Aintree earlier in the season, stepping up in distance would be a positive and following his disappointing run at Warwick – where he failed to get into a rhythm – Ben Pauling might just prefer to give his imposing five-year-old more time and a (likely) easier Grade 1 option. A flat track suits him well, as does decent ground, so he could easily bounce back to form in the spring, although Pauling does have No Questions Asked to consider for the same race.

Over in Ireland, **Impaire et Passe** is a likely contender to head to Aintree rather than Cheltenham, as he has done in each of the past two seasons. Winner of the Aintree Hurdle in 2024, he won last year's Manifesto Novices' Chase and could well be handed entries in both the Bowl on day one and in the Melling Chase the following day.

Impaire et Passe is becoming a standing dish at the fixture

Last seen being brought down at the Punchestown Festival, he held an entry in the Irish Gold Cup recently but after skipping the Dublin Racing Festival, could make his belated reappearance in the Red Mills Chase (Saturday 14th February) whilst the Guide is at print stage. A high-class performer on his day, the track at Liverpool clearly plays to his strengths and it would not be a huge surprise to see him win for a third successive year at the fixture.

Mullins also won the Manifesto in 2024, with Il Etait Temps, and the opening race of the fixture could be the ideal spring target for **Kappa Jy Pyke**, who has been entered in both the Arkle and the Broadway (Brown Advisory) at Cheltenham. He ran in the Baring Bingham before heading to Aintree last year, but an intermediate trip does seem to be ideal for a horse who is often overlooked. With that in mind, I would strongly consider bypassing Cheltenham with Aintree – or even the WillowWarm Gold Cup at Fairyhouse – in mind.

The six-year-old failed to perform in last year's Mersey but has won both starts over fences, despite being the stable *'second string'* on each occasion. He lowered the colours of Top Novices' Hurdle winner Salvator Mundi at Thurles, then showed a fine turn of foot to win a competitive Grade 3 at Punchestown, where the strong pace played into his hands. It might be difficult for his connections to pass up the opportunity of running at the Festival – where the Arkle would look a more likely target – but given his obvious pace, Aintree could be even more suitable.

Another who the trainer might consider sending to Liverpool is **Ballyburn**, who was beaten a nose in this season's Hatton's Grace, but was then 14 lengths behind the same rival (Teahupoo) in the Christmas Hurdle at Leopardstown, where 3m seemed to stretch his stamina. With that in mind, perhaps he is another who could be targeted at the Aintree Hurdle, which has the makings of being a very good race this year.

A three-time Grade 1 winner – twice over an intermediate trip – as a novice hurdler, things haven't exactly gone to plan since, but he remains lightly-raced and a classy performer on his day. This could be a good option for the eight-year-old and his presence would certainly add plenty to what threatens to be an excellent race.

Warren Greatrex has enjoyed a fine season to date and one who has shown plenty of improvement is **Mighty Bandit**. Bought from the Caldwell dispersal for €420,000, he failed to deliver as a juvenile hurdler and spent more than a year racing on the Flat before switching to fences at Newbury's Coral Gold Trophy fixture. Sent off at 50-1, he beat all bar Mambonumberfive (won the Wayward Lad next time) before returning to the Berkshire venue to beat Highlands Legacy and Lookaway (both won next time) off a mark of 129.

Up 5lb and meeting much softer conditions, he defied a mistake three out to follow up at Doncaster, successful by 8 lengths which resulted in another 8lb rise. Whilst the Grand Annual could be an option (he would require one more run before 23rd February to be eligible), his form strongly suggests that he is right at home on a flat, left-handed track and with that in mind, the Red Rum could be the more suitable spring target for the son of Order Of St George.

The progressive six-year-old is currently rated 142 and would certainly warrant careful consideration if heading to Liverpool.

SHORTLISTS
FOR ALL RACES!

ONLY £10

THE **AINTREE FESTIVAL** TEXT SERVICE

AVAILABLE TO BUY ONLINE AT
www.weatherbysshop.co.uk

t 01933 304776 | e shop@weatherbys.co.uk

WILLIAM HILL MANIFESTO NOVICES' CHASE
2m3f 200y (Grade 1) – Mildmay Course

OVERVIEW
INTRODUCED as a Grade 2 in 2009, the Manifesto Novices' Chase was handed Grade 1 status after just three renewals and has been the opening race of the fixture since 2015. Whilst 10 of the first 11 winners had contested either the Arkle or the now-defunct Golden Miller Novices' Chase at Cheltenham, we have seen just one winner in the past five years match this profile, with the other four arriving at Aintree having bypassed the Festival. Given the nature of Aintree's track and the fact that this meeting can be staged on spring ground, speed is essential and form over 2m – both over hurdles and fences – is a huge positive, with many a winner of this race having shown a high level of form over the minimum trip as a hurdler. Interestingly, all 16 winners were beaten on their most recent start, which is an unusual trend/statistic for a Grade 1 race.

FRESH FOR AINTREE
WITH four of the past five winners having now bypassed Cheltenham in favour of this race, we should really sit up and take note of those following a similar path, especially as the Golden Miller Novices' Chase – the Grade 1 over a similar distance – no longer takes place at the Festival. That means that Grade 1 novice chasers either have to go up (Broadway) or down (Arkle) in trip to run at Cheltenham, whereas both Aintree and Fairyhouse (WillowWarm Gold Cup) offer a Grade 1 option at an intermediate distance. Interestingly, all four *'fresh winners'* ran during February, with both *Impaire et Passe* and *Banbridge* contesting a Grade 1 at the Dublin Racing Festival, before being freshened up ahead of this fixture. Last year's first and second actually avoided Cheltenham in favour of this race, whilst *Arzal* was another such winner some 10 years ago, so pay due respect to any such runner this time around.

CHELTENHAM FESTIVAL FORM
LAST year's Arkle winner, Jango Baie, finished a close-up third, whilst *Il Etait Temps* had finished third in the **Arkle Trophy** before winning this race in 2024. Whilst he might be the only winner in the past five to have run at Cheltenham, 10 of the first 11 winners had contested either the Arkle or the Golden Miller Novices' Chase, which is obviously no longer in existence (replaced in 2025 by the returning novices' handicap chase). Given that there is no upper ceiling on the novices' handicap, it could well be that is a race which becomes a significant pointer towards this – indeed, Caldwell Potter won it last year and followed up at Aintree by winning the Grade 1 Mildmay Novices' Chase on day two – but for now, the Arkle is the key form line to note from the Cheltenham Festival.

Jango Baie was the second Arkle winner – the first being Western Warhorse – to run here, so the record of winners isn't great (0-2), although usually if an Arkle winner heads to Aintree it will be to contest the Maghull on day three. *Il Etait Temps* finished third in the Arkle before winning this race two years ago and often we will see horses stepped up in distance, on the back of a good run over the shorter trip.

On the *'Fresh v Cheltenham Form'* debate, which is an important factor at the Grand National fixture, it is worth noting that there is a four-week gap this year and that extra week of recovery time can be quite significant. The gap between the two meetings was at three weeks last year (which is more common), whereas there will now be 30 days between the Arkle and Manifesto. This is a positive when trying to rely on Cheltenham form being upheld.

TACTICS

THE past two winners have shown that a relatively patient ride can be deployed in this race, although generally speaking, it can usually pay to look towards those who like to be ridden positively over fences on the Mildmay track. Often, the Graded races will be small fields and if a good jumper can get into a nice rhythm, they will be well-positioned to fend off the closers from behind. Especially if the ground is drying, leaning towards those who like to dictate from the front – especially if it appears as though there aren't many other pace angles in the race – is certainly a positive. A good jumper who sits up with the pace can be dangerous around Aintree.

NEED FOR SPEED

AS TOUCHED upon briefly already, horses blessed with 2m speed often appear to be at an advantage in races over an intermediate trip at Aintree. The sharp nature of the track lends itself to more of a speed based horse – rather than one blessed with bags of stamina – and we see it play out in races such as the Aintree Hurdle and Melling Chase, too. It certainly seems to be a positive in the Manifesto, with plenty of winners having shown a high level of ability – over hurdles and/or fences – over the minimum trip. The likes of *Menorah* and *Impaire et Passe* were high-class hurdlers, and several others had shown strong form in novice hurdles over the minimum distance. Last year's winner, for example, had been contesting races such as the December Festival Hurdle and the Irish Champion Hurdle the previous season, whilst *Il Etait Temps* was a Grade 1 winner over both hurdles and fences over 2m/2m1f and has since, of course, gone on to prove himself a top-class performer over 2m. Respect horses with strong form over the minimum trip, be it over hurdles or fences.

GRADE 1 WINNERS

SINCE the race was upgraded in 2012, only 21 horses (including three last year) have contested the Manifesto having previously won a Grade 1 race. Six have proven successful, including the past two. In fact, the past two winners were Grade 1 winners over both hurdles and fences, so clearly held a class edge on many of their opponents.

Eight of the past 13 winners had won at either Grade 1 or Grade 2 level, so pay healthy respect to those who have already shown that they can perform to this sort of level, with those stepping up in class often found wanting.

KEY TRENDS

- ★ All 16 winners were beaten on their previous start
- ★ Grade 1 winners are 6-21 since the race was upgraded (2012)
- ★ 4 of the past 5 winners arrived at Aintree 'fresh' (having bypassed Cheltenham)
- ✓ 14 of the 16 winners were in the top-3 of the betting
- ✓ 14 of the 16 winners had run 9 times or less over hurdles (all 16 had run 11 times or less)
- ✓ 13 of the past 15 winners were rated 150+
- ✓ 12 of the past 14 winners had run 4 or 5 times over fences previously
- ✓ 11 of the 16 winners spent just one season over hurdles
- ✓ 10 of the past 11 winners had won exactly twice over fences previously
- ✓ 8 of the past 12 winners were aged 6
- ✓ 8 of the past 13 winners had already won a Grade 1 or Grade 2
- ✓ 7 of the past 13 winners ran at Aintree as a novice hurdler
- ✓ 3 of the past 7 winners wore headgear
- ✓ Willie Mullins has trained the past 2 winners
- ✓ Respect strong hurdles form (2m-2m4f)
- ✓ Respect those who like to race prominently
- ✓ Philip Hobbs-trained runners are 2-3
- ✓ Nicky Henderson-trained runners are 2-9
- ✓ Diana Whateley has twice owned the winner
- ✗ Mares are 0-6
- ✗ Paul Nicholls-trained runners are 0-17
- ✗ 5yo's are 1-9 (the other 8 all unplaced)
- ✗ Only 1 of the 16 winners was favourite
- ✗ Only 1 of the past 13 winners was aged 8
- ✗ Only 2 of the 16 winners had run just 3 times over fences previously
- ✗ Only 2 of the 16 winners were sent off at odds greater than 11-2
- ✗ Pendil Novices' Chase winners are 0-6
- ✗ Both Arkle winners to have run have been beaten

HURDLES FORM

STRONG form over hurdles is something which I have touched upon in various subsections already, but is very much a (positive) noticeable trend with winners of this race. Again, this kind of ties in with the *Need For Speed* subsection, as being competitive in top-level races over hurdles certainly requires more natural pace and that works well here.

Both *Kalashnikov* and *Il Etait Temps* had run in the **Supreme Novices' Hurdle** at Cheltenham 13 months earlier, a race in which Romeo Coolio finished third in 2025. He has developed into a high-class novice chaser this season and 2m4f around Aintree could be absolutely perfect for him. He will have the option of this race and/or Fairyhouse after Cheltenham.

Both *Captain Conan* and *Finian's Oscar* had won the **Tolworth Novices' Hurdle** the previous season and, of course, the Sandown Grade 1 was switched to Aintree three seasons ago and renamed as the **Formby Novices' Hurdle**. It was won by Jango Baie the season before last and he won the Arkle before finishing third in this race.

AINTREE FORM

WITH the Formby now taking place at Aintree, it will be interesting to see if that has a bearing on this race the following season, although it is doubtful this year, with the winner Potters Charm remaining over hurdles. Miami Magic (2nd), however, was a winner at Cheltenham on New Year's Day and looks well-suited to this sort of trip.

Form from this fixture is another obvious positive and last year's winner had won the **Aintree Hurdle** 12 months earlier, a race in which *Millers Bank* had also hit the frame, a year before winning this race.

And, no fewer than seven of the past 13 winners had run at this meeting in a novice hurdle the previous season, with both *Flying Angel* and *Finian's Oscar* running in the **Mersey Novices' Hurdle**, the latter successful. The enigmatic Regent's Stroll finished runner-up (beaten ½ a length) in the race last year, whilst Kappa Jy Pyke finished down the field for Willie Mullins and he, of course, defeated Salvator Mundi on chase debut earlier this season. Salvator Mundi won last year's Top Novices' Hurdle at this fixture, where he had too much speed for Romeo Coolio, who looked a little laboured after his Cheltenham run.

Despite the longer trip (and in contrast to the persistent pointer towards form over shorter), both *Uxizandre* and *Banbridge* ran in the **Sefton Novices' Hurdle** before dropping in distance during their novice chase campaign.

QUICKLY SENT CHASING

ALTHOUGH we have seen some high-class hurdlers win this race, the majority of winners were still sent chasing after just one season over hurdles. 11 of the 16 winners fell into this category and this tends to be a common theme among Grade 1 novice chases throughout the spring. As I often say, if you think you have a high-class chaser on your hands, send them over fences sooner rather than later and that seems to be the thinking with many a leading trainer, too.

The past two winners spent two seasons hurdling, with *Il Etait Temps* a second-season novice after failing to win as a juvenile (campaigned highly), whilst *Impaire et Passe* was campaigned as a top-class hurdler before falling just short.

LIGHTLY-RACED HURDLERS

EVEN those winners who spent an extra season over hurdles didn't have too many miles on the clock, with *Impaire et Passe* having nine runs over the smaller obstacles before switching to fences. 14 of the 16 winners had run in nine of fewer hurdle races and the other two – *Menorah* and *Clarcam* – had only run 10 and 11 times, respectively. So, don't expect to see a winner of this race to have had 15, 20 runs over hurdles for example, with those more exposed horses less likely to show improved form for switching disciplines.

CHASING EXPERIENCE

IMPAIRE ET PASSE became just the second winner of the Manifesto to have arrived at Aintree on the back of just three runs. Prior to last year, 12 of the previous 13 winners had run four or five times over fences, so having built up a good level of experience seems important. Last year's runner-up Gidleigh Park is a good example (in a negative sense) of this, with him having had just two starts over fences and in truth, he had effectively had just the one run, so in hindsight, he did well to run as well as he did. Given that we are now in April, having run four times isn't asking too much, whilst *Mad Max* is the only other winner to overcome relative inexperience, successful on his fourth start like last year's winner.

WINNING EXPERIENCE

IN TERMS of winning races over fences, 10 of the past 11 winners had won exactly twice over fences previously. Clearly a defeat earlier in the season isn't too detrimental here and it isn't a race in which you should expect to see a host of unbeaten chasers battle out the finish.

CURRENT FORM

THAT leads us on nicely to this subsection. Surprisingly for a Grade 1 race, each and every winner so far was beaten on their most recent start. As touched upon already, many of those winners ran well in defeat at the Cheltenham Festival, but even all of those who bypassed Cheltenham arrived at Aintree on the back of a defeat. The past five winners finished either second (3) or third (2) last time out, whilst four winners between 2011 and 2016 also finished second or third, so pay utmost respect to those who have run well in defeat on the latest outing.

AGE

THERE was no five-year-old representation last year and to date, *Clarcam* is the sole winner for that age group. Nine five-year-olds have run in the race and the other eight have finished unplaced. At the other end of the scale, *Mad Max* and *Wishfull Thinking* were successful at the age of eight, although there has been just one winner of that age group in the past 13 years. 11 of the past 13 winners were aged either six (8) or seven (3) so focus on that age bracket, with preference for six-year-olds.

MARKET FORCES

AGAIN, a little surprising is the fact that we have only seen one winning favourite of the Manifesto to date, that being *Captain Conan*. Although the winners in 2021 and 2022 were relatively big (in comparison to others) prices, almost all of the other winners could have been found just behind the market leader, with no fewer than 14 of the 16 winners hailing from the top three in the market. Only those two aforementioned winners returned at odds greater than 11-2, so whilst the favourite doesn't have a great record in the race, those immediately behind the market leader certainly do.

THE IRISH CHALLENGE

DURING the first 13 renewals, *Clarcam* was the sole Irish-trained winner of the Manifesto, although they have now won each of the past three renewals and perhaps, are starting to take the race more seriously.

Willie Mullins has now trained each of the past two winners and as a result, boasts the best record of any Irish trainer in the race and if he is once again in with a chance of the British trainers' title, it could well be that Mullins targets the race once again. Respect any runner from Closutton.

With no Graded race over this trip at Cheltenham, Irish trainers have the option of travelling to Aintree for the Manifesto, or targeting the Grade 1 at Fairyhouse on Easter Sunday (5th April). That race, the WillowWarm Gold Cup, has historically been the main objective for many an Irish trainer in this division.

MARES

THERE was again no representation last year, so the record of mares remains at 0-6 at this stage and whilst you might think that isn't overly disappointing, two of the six – namely La Bague Au Roi and Gin On Lime – were sent off favourite, whilst Pepite Rose was sent off at just 4-1. Despite the 7lb sex-allowance, this is clearly a difficult task for mares.

OFFICIAL BHA RATINGS

ALL 16 winners had a minimum BHA Rating of 147, with 12 of the past 15 winners rated 150+. The past three winners were either second-top or joint second-top in terms of ratings and rated between 152 and 157, so focus on those in the low-mid 150s, with *Impaire et Passe* the highest-rated winner to date. In line with the betting, those second and third in on *Official BHA Ratings* seem to have a fine record in the Manifesto.

HEADGEAR

WITH *Il Etait Temps* successful in a hood and *Impaire et Passe* successfully sporting first-time cheekpieces, it is quite noticeable that three of the past seven winners wore headgear of some sort, with *Finian's Oscar* also wearing cheekpieces. Whilst we don't see many Grade 1-winning novices falling into this category, it clearly isn't a negative in this race.

OTHER KEY RACES

INTERESTINGLY, prior to *Impaire et Passe*, the three previous Irish-trained winners had run in the **Irish Arkle** (again, highlighting form over shorter), whilst last year's winner was also in action at the DRF. Both *Clarcam* and *Banbridge* finished runner-up in the Irish Arkle, a race which was won this year by the aforementioned Romeo Coolio, who beat Kargese a neck to land a third straight Grade 1.

And, each of the past two winners contested the **Faugheen Novice Chase** at Limerick over Christmas, with *Il Etait Temps* finishing second and *Impaire et Passe* successful. It is worth noting that the distance of that race was extended slightly this season – which could impact the type of horse who is aimed at it (more of a stayer) – and it was won this season by Final Demand.

Three Manifesto winners had contested the **Lightning Novices' Chase**, although only one of late. Formerly staged at Doncaster, it now takes place at Windsor (via Lingfield) and last year's Lightning winner Gidleigh Park finished runner-up. This year's Grade 2 was won by the Ben Pauling-trained No Questions Asked.

POOR PENDIL RECORD

WHILST 2022 winner *Millers Bank* had finished runner-up in Kempton's **Pendil Novices' Chase** some 40 days before winning this race, winners of that particular Grade 2 contest have a poor record in the Manifesto. Pic d'Orhy beat *Millers Bank* before the form was reversed, whilst trainer Paul Nicholls also attempted the double with Frodon, Cyrname and again last year with Rubaud. Bags Groove and Blow Your Wad also failed at Aintree on the back of

Pendil success, so the record of winners from that race currently stands at 0-6. This race takes place after the *Cheltenham Festival Betting Guide* goes to print, but be sure to take note of the result and be cautious of the winner, if lining up here.

CONNECTIONS TO NOTE

THE disappointing run of trainer **Paul Nicholls** has been highlighted in past editions of the Guide and Rubaud took his tally to 0-17 last year. Ginny's Destiny and Stage Star are another pair who were beaten in the Manifesto for the former champion trainer in recent years, and he has yet to find the winning formula. Treat runners from Ditcheat with a degree of caution.

Aside from Willie Mullins, only two other trainers have won the Manifesto more than once, although they came back during the first five renewals. **Nicky Henderson** struck with *Mad Max* and *Captain Conan*, and although Jango Baie couldn't add to his tally last year, his runners warrant a second look.

Philip Hobbs – who now trains alongside former assistant **Johnson White** – also won the race twice, successful in back-to-back renewals with *Wishfull Thinking* and *Menorah*, who both carried the silks of leading owner **Mrs Diana Whateley**. Hobbs has only ever had three runners in the race, so boasts a fantastic strike-rate in it, whilst the Whateley horses are now mainly trained by Olly Murphy.

Willie Mullins

ROLL OF HONOUR

Year	Form	Winner	Age	Weight	OR	SP	Trainer	Runners	Last Race (No. of days)
2025	113	Impaire et Passe	7	11-7	157	9/4	W Mullins (IRE)	9	3rd Gr.1 Ladbrokes Nov. Chase (60)
2024	1213	Il Etait Temps	6	11-7	155	3/1	W Mullins (IRE)	5	3rd Gr.1 Arkle Trophy (30)
2023	1132	Banbridge	7	11-7	152	2/1	J O'Brien (IRE)	5	2nd Gr.1 Irish Arkle (68)
2022	1UU2	Millers Bank	8	11-4	147	7/1	A Hales	6	2nd Gr.2 Pendil Nov. Chase (40)
2021	1122	Protektorat	6	11-7	150	17/2	D Skelton	7	2nd Kelso Novice Chase (48)
2020	NO RACE - meeting cancelled								
2019	1122U	Kalashnikov	6	11-4	148	4/1	A Murphy	6	u.r. Gr.1 Arkle Trophy (23)
2018	132P5	Finian's Oscar	6	11-4	151	5/2	C Tizzard	6	5th Gr.1 Golden Miller Nov. Chase (28)
2017	1FP16	Flying Angel	6	11-4	150	5/1	N Twiston-Davies	6	6th Gr.1 Golden Miller Nov. Chase (21)
2016	81132	Arzal	6	11-4	151	4/1	H Whittington	8	2nd Gr.2 Doncaster Chase (68)

LEADING TEN-YEAR GUIDES

Golden Miller Novices' Chase 2 (*Flying Angel* 6th, *Finian's Oscar* 5th)
Arkle Trophy 2 (*Menorah* 3rd, *Kalashnikov* u.r.)
***Formby Novices' Hurdle (former 'Tolworth')** 2 (*Finian's Oscar* 1st, *Kalashnikov* 2nd)
***Mersey Novices' Hurdle** 2 (*Flying Angel* 3rd, *Finian's Oscar* 1st)
Irish Arkle 2 (*Banbridge* 2nd, *Il Etait Temps* 1st)
***Supreme Novices' Hurdle** 2 (*Kalashnikov* 2nd, *Il Etait Temps* 5th)
***Aintree Hurdle** 2 (*Millers Bank* 3rd, *Impaire et Passe* 1st)
Faugheen Novice Chase 2 (*Il Etait Temps* 2nd, *Impaire et Passe* 1st)

* denotes previous season

Help Make A Mission Possible

We operate one of the busiest air ambulance fleets in the UK.
Our goal: Saving lives by delivering critical care at the scene.

What we do

Serving the communities of: Gloucestershire, Herefordshire, Shropshire, Staffordshire, the West Midlands and Worcestershire.

Support us and help save lives in your area

*on average

BOODLES ANNIVERSARY 4-Y-O JUVENILE HURDLE
2m1f (Grade 1)

OVERVIEW

HANDED Grade 1 status in 2005, the Anniversary is now the only Grade 1 for juveniles staged in Britain, aside from the Triumph Hurdle. Prior to 2005, it was more difficult for horses to complete the double (as they would be penalised) but since then, five horses have managed to do so and the Triumph is often the best guide to success. French-bred juveniles have a fine record in this race and Willie Mullins has now won three of the past nine renewals, all with fillies. Nicky Henderson has won three of the past seven renewals and won it four times in all.

THE TRIUMPH HURDLE

GIVEN that it is the feature event in this division, the **Triumph Hurdle** is the obvious starting point when looking at the Anniversary. As touched upon in the *Overview*, since the race was handed Grade 1 status, five horses have managed to complete the Cheltenham-Aintree double and the other three Triumph winners to have taken their chance finished runner-up. Interestingly, last year saw just two of the *'also-rans'* from the Triumph run in the Anniversary, whereas it is usually advisable to pay utmost respect to those who ran well in the opener on Gold Cup day, with 11 of the past 20 winners having recorded a top-three finish in the Triumph.

Given that there is an extra week between Cheltenham and Aintree this year – therefore 27 days between the Triumph and the Anniversary – I would think that there is a greater chance that we will see the main protagonists head to Liverpool.

BE WARY OF THE FRED WINTER WINNER

SIX times we have now seen the winner of the **Fred Winter Juvenile Handicap Hurdle** step up in class at Aintree and all six have been beaten. Puturhandstogether was sent off 6-4 favourite last year, whilst both Sanctuaire and Band Of Outlaws suffered a similar fate (beaten favourites). Whilst the winners have a poor record here, three horses have now won the Anniversary on the back of having been beaten in the *'Fred Winter'* including *Murcia* last year. Interestingly, two of the three were well-beaten and perhaps, therefore, didn't have as hard a race as those who battled out the finish or even won the race. Whilst the form has to be given consideration – with only 4 of the past 24 winners of this race not having run at the Cheltenham Festival – it is clearly difficult for the winner to back up their winning performance in this higher grade.

OTHER KEY RACES

PREVIOUSLY another Grade 1 (downgraded a few years ago), Chepstow's **Finale Juvenile Hurdle** has also been a good guide to the Anniversary over the years. During the past 17 years, only seven winners of that contest have taken their chance at Aintree and three have proven successful. This season's Grade 2 was won by the Chester Williams-trained Tenter Le Tout.

Three of the past 11 Anniversary winners had run in the Grade 2 **Prestbury Juvenile Hurdle**, a race staged at Cheltenham's November meeting and it was won this season by Harry Derham's One Horse Town, who returned to Cheltenham in December but disappointed behind the impressive winner, Minella Study.

Three of the past seven winners had won the **Summit Juvenile Hurdle** at Doncaster en route to

Aintree, but that race was downgraded to Listed status a couple of years ago and is now staged at Aintree's December fixture. It was won this season by Lord, but in truth it bears little resemblance to the race which was won by *We Have A Dream, Monmiral* and *Knight Salute*. It remains to be seen as to whether this will have an impact moving forward. This year's race was sponsored by William Hill and staged as the **Wirral Juvenile Hurdle**.

Kempton's **Adonis Juvenile Hurdle** has proven to be a poor guide to the Triumph in recent years (was once the last key trial ahead of Cheltenham) but four Anniversary winners since 2011 ran in the Grade 2, which will have taken place shortly after the Guide was sent to print. Aintree and Kempton require a similar type of horse – both being speed-based tracks – and often form from one translates to the other.

Finally, four winners since 2009 had run and won (*Grumeti* was actually promoted to being the winner in the Stewards' Room) the **Finesse Juvenile Hurdle** at Cheltenham on trials day, the last of which being *Sir Gino*, who looked a future star when powering clear up the hill. This year's Finesse was won by Dan Skelton's *Maestro Conti*.

THE IRISH CHALLENGE

WITH Punchestown staging the Champion Four-Year-Old Hurdle shortly after, Irish challengers do have the option of staying at home during April, with Fairyhouse also hosting a Grade 2 (this year the week before Aintree). However, given the strength in depth in his stable at present, Willie Mullins (see next subsection for further details on his overall record) has won the race three times recently, meaning that five of the past 30 winners were now Irish-trained. That still isn't the strongest of records, but with four of those winners coming during the past 11 renewals, perhaps their record is on the up.

Interestingly, four of those five Irish-trained winners had contested the Grade 2 at Leopardstown's Christmas fixture, run this season as the **Changing Times Brewery Juvenile Hurdle**. *Apple's Jade* was able to complete the double, whilst this season's race was won by in impressive fashion *Narciso Has*.

MULLINS' FILLIES TO BE RESPECTED

AS TOUCHED upon in the previous subsection, trainer **Willie Mullins** boasts a fine recent record in the Anniversary, winning it three times in the past nine years. And, all three were fillies with a French background, all French-bred and all arriving in Closutton having run in France beforehand. There is a clear pattern developing here (as highlighted last year) and perhaps it is something to do with the timing between Cheltenham and Aintree, Mullins possibly feels a filly is more suitable to the quicker turnaround, rather than waiting

KEY TRENDS

- ★ 15 of the past 20 winners had won a Graded race earlier in the season
- ★ 12 of the past 17 winners started their careers by racing in France
- ★ 9 of the past 12 winners were French-bred
- ★ 3 of the past 7 winners were trained by Nicky Henderson
- ★ 3 of the past 9 winners were trained by Willie Mullins (all French-bred fillies)
- ★ Horses rated 152+ are 5-8 since 2007
- ✓ Since the race was upgraded, all 8 Triumph Hurdle winners to have run have finished 1st or 2nd (5 horses have completed the double)
- ✓ 17 of the past 20 winners had won at least twice over hurdles
- ✓ 16 of the past 20 winners were in the top-3 according to official BHA Ratings
- ✓ 14 of the past 20 winners had run 4 times or more over hurdles
- ✓ 11 of the past 20 favourites have won
- ✓ 11 of the past 20 winners finished in the first 3 of the Triumph Hurdle
- ✓ 11 of the past 18 winners were trained by Messrs Nicholls, Henderson or King
- ✓ 3 of the past 17 winners were owned by JP McManus
- ✓ Finale Juvenile Hurdle winners are 3-7 during the past 17 years
- ✓ Respect fillies (especially French-bred fillies)
- ✓ Alan King-trained runners are 4-7 since 2007
- ✓ Respect Philip Hobbs-trained runners
- ✓ Respect experienced hurdlers (6 or 7 runs)
- ✗ Only 2 of the past 20 winners had failed to win or place in Graded company
- ✗ Only 3 of the past 20 winners failed to record a top-3 finish last time out
- ✗ Only 4 of the past 24 winners failed to run at the Cheltenham Festival
- ✗ Only 4 of the past 20 winners returned at odds greater than 13-2
- ✗ Only 5 of the past 30 winners were trained in Ireland
- ✗ 'Fred Winter' winners are 0-6 since 2010
- ✗ Be wary of Joseph O'Brien-trained runners

for Punchestown. Whatever the reason, I doubt that it is coincidental and whilst any runner from his stable warrants respect, be extra vigilant when it comes to a French-imported filly.

THE FRENCH CONNECTION

THAT last comment leads us on nicely to this. This is yet another high-class juvenile contest in which both

French-bred and French-imported runners boast a fine recent record. 12 of the past 17 winners began their racing careers in France, so as with the Triumph Hurdle at Cheltenham, respect those who had a run or two in their native country before joining one of the leading British or Irish stables. Also, nine of the past 12 winners were French-bred (many ticked both boxes) and it is certainly no coincidence that such horses are ready for Grade 1s at such an early stage in their careers, them often a lot more forward in their development than Irish- or British-bred horses.

GRADED FORM

ALTHOUGH last year's winner failed to match up against this profile, 15 of the previous 19 winners had already won a Graded race over hurdles, so those with the stronger form tend to shine. This strong trend includes every winner between 2016 and 2024, with *Sir Gino* winning the Finesse Juvenile Hurdle on trials day, before being forced to miss the Triumph. Of those 15 recent winners, 14 were successful in Grade 2 company, whilst *Zenta* won a Grade 3 on her first start in Ireland. *Murcia* actually became just the second winner in the past 20 renewals who had failed to previously win, or at least place, in Graded company prior to Aintree.

OFFICIAL BHA RATINGS

RATHER in-keeping with the fact that Graded form tends to stand up, 16 of the past 20 winners hailed from the top three on *Official BHA Ratings*. Prior to last year, the previous two winners were officially top-rated and a rating in the mid-high 140s is usually the bare minimum requirement here, although *Zenta* and *Murcia* were rated 138 and 136 respectively, but of course also received that 7lb sex-allowance (more of that anon).

Since 2007, only eight juveniles have contested the Anniversary with a rating of 152 or higher and five of them were successful. The last of those was *Pentland Hills* and all five either won (4) the Triumph or finished runner-up – in the case of *Walkon* – in the Festival showpiece. Clearly, a big run at Cheltenham offers a juvenile the chance of obtaining such a lofty figure, but a record of 5-8 in noteworthy, nevertheless.

HURDLING EXPERIENCE

ALTHOUGH we have seen *Zarkandar* and *Pentland Hills* win on the back of just two previous starts (both won the Triumph after just one run) and more recently both *Zenta* and *Sir Gino* won this after just three previous runs over hurdles, experience often tells, certainly in an open year like last year, for example. Since 2014 alone, *Guitar Pete* (7 runs), *Defi du Seuil* (6), *We Have A Dream* (7), *Knight Salute* (6) and *Murcia* (7) all boasted considerable experience over hurdles. There appears to be no exact science to this but as I said, if there isn't a high-class (standout) performer in the field, perhaps experience becomes that little bit more significant and helps a horse raise their head above the crowd.

In terms of winning experience, 17 of the past 20 winners had won at least twice over hurdles previously.

CURRENT FORM

THIS was another trend on which *Murcia* fell down, as it can usually pay to have run well on your most recent start. She became just the third winner in the past 20 to arrive at Aintree on the back of finishing outside of the top-three on their most recent start, her finishing only eighth in the *'Fred Winter'* at Cheltenham, of course. The likes of *We Have A Dream, Monmiral* and *Sir Gino* arrived at Aintree on the back of a win, with all three bypassing Cheltenham, whilst we have also seen those five Triumph Hurdle winners since 2006 completing the double. Between 2005 and 2023, a further eight winners finished first or second last time out, with five of those being placed in the Triumph. Respect those who ran a big race last time out and if a horse didn't run at Cheltenham, we should be looking for a last-time-out winner.

FILLIES TO BE RESPECTED

THIS has been somewhat covered in an earlier subsection, with Willie Mullins saddling three fillies to win the race in the past nine renewals. But, *L'Unique* was another winning filly in 2013 – so that is four in the past 12 renewals – and before that, *Bilboa* struck back in 2001. Pay particular attention to French-bred fillies and those who started their careers in France, with the 7lb sex-allowance clearly a hugely significant factor in this division.

MARKET FORCES

DESPITE a seemingly disappointing run at Cheltenham, *Murcia* was still sent off second favourite at just 11-4 last year (again, possibly highlighting it as a non-vintage renewal), whilst *Sir Gino* justified favouritism in 2024 despite missing the Triumph. *Monmiral* and *Zenta* were another couple of recent successful favourites and overall, 11 of the past 20 favourites have won. We saw big-priced winners of this race in 2003 and 2004 (33s and 25s, respectively) but since then, only four of the past 20 winners returned at odds greater than 13-2, so it tends to pay to focus on the top few in the market, with *'shock'* results seemingly quite rare.

HENDERSON'S RECENT DOMINANCE

HAVING first won the race in 2008 with subsequent Champion Hurdle winner *Binocular*, who had actually finished runner-up in the Supreme Novices' Hurdle and downed that year's Triumph Hurdle winner Celestial Halo, **Nicky Henderson** has since won three of the past seven renewals, with *Pentland Hills* completing the Triumph-Anniversary double. Henderson wouldn't be a trainer to avoid Cheltenham with Aintree in mind and both *We Have A Dream* and *Sir Gino* were forced to miss the Festival rather than it being a conscious decision. Amazingly, his Triumph Hurdle winner was the biggest price of his four winners (11-4) with the other trio priced between 11-10 and 2-1. Therefore, pay even greater respect to his *'more fancied'* runners according to the market and he was without representation last year, with Lulamba set to take on his elders in the Mersey Novices' Hurdle, before eventually being declared a non-runner on the day. Despite the reversal of Hargam (beaten at 4-6) in 2015, Henderson's record in the past 10 renewals is 3-10 and his runners have to be taken very seriously.

OTHER CONNECTIONS TO NOTE

BOTH Alan King and **Paul Nicholls** have also won the race four times, Nicholls successful with *All Yours* and *Monmiral* during the past 10 renewals, with *Le Duc* and *Zarkandar* his earlier winners. Without a runner last year, he saddled Kalif du Berlais in 2024, before he returned to win the Grade 1 Maghull Novices' Chase last year, and in recent years, Nicholls has tended to aim his better juveniles at this race rather than the Triumph.

Alan King won his four Anniversary Hurdles between 2007 and 2013, and he has in fact only saddled seven runners in the race since 2007, so boasts a magnificent strike rate in it. Respect any runner from Barbury Castle, whilst two of his winners carried the silks of the **McNeill Family**, as did Kumbeshwar, runner-up in 2011.

Originally from the North West, this is likely a fixture which Max McNeill likes to target where possible.

Another trainer with a fine strike rate in the race is **Philip Hobbs** – now training alongside **Johnson White**, of course – who won the race with *Lord Brex* and *Detroit City* in the early part of this century. The stable's only winner in the past 18 renewals was *Defi du Seuil*, but runners from this yard are extremely limited and they also saddled Made In Japan and Gumball to finish runner-up, the latter in 2018.

Defi du Seuil provided owner **JP McManus** with a second Anniversary since 2008 when *Binocular* scored and *Zenta* has since made it three winners in the past 17 renewals. Ivanovich Gorbatov, Apple's Shakira, Fakir d'Oudairies, Brazil and (last year) Puturhandstogether have all finished second or third for McManus since 2016.

And, as touched upon last year, **Joseph O'Brien** is a trainer to be wary of at this stage when it comes to runners in this race. Ivanovich Gorbatov was officially trained by his father Aidan, but Joseph was reportedly influential in terms of his training regime ahead of his Triumph success, and has since seen the likes of Fakir d'Oudairies, Band Of Outlaws, Nusret, Intelotto and Puturhandstogether beaten, with four of those priced between 6-4 and 6-1. Tread carefully with runners from the O'Brien stable, especially if they are stepping up from the *'Fred Winter'*. This was highlighted last year and the fact that he was responsible for the beaten favourite further enhances the word of caution.

ROLL OF HONOUR

Year	Form	Winner	Age	Weight	OR	SP	Trainer	Runners	Last Race (No. of days)
2025	331828	Murcia	4	10-9	136	11/4	W Mullins (IRE)	13	8th Fred Winter Juv. H'cap H'dle (23)
2024	11	Sir Gino	4	11-2	145	11/10F	N Henderson	5	1st Gr.2 Finesse Juvenile H'dle (75)
2023	113	Zenta	4	10-9	138	5/4F	W Mullins (IRE)	11	3rd Gr.1 Triumph H'dle (27)
2022	111119	Knight Salute	5	11-0	138	14/1	M Harris	9	9th Gr.1 Triumph H'dle (20)
2021	111	Monmiral	4	11-0	147	10/11F	P Nicholls	6	1st Haydock Juvenile H'dle (47)
2020	NO RACE - meeting cancelled								
2019	11	Pentland Hills	4	11-0	153	11/4	N Henderson	9	1st Gr.1 Triumph H'dle (20)
2018	41111	We Have A Dream	4	11-0	145	2/1	N Henderson	10	1st Listed Scottish Triumph H'dle Trial (67)
2017	11111	Defi du Seuil	4	11-0	155	4/11F	P Hobbs	8	1st Gr.1 Triumph H'dle (20)
2016	112	Apple's Jade	4	10-7	145	3/1	W Mullins (IRE)	9	2nd Gr.1 Triumph H'dle (20)

LEADING TEN-YEAR GUIDES

Wirral Listed Juvenile Hurdle (former 'Summit') 3 (*We Have A Dream* 1st, *Monmiral* 1st, *Knight Salute* 1st)

Triumph Hurdle 5 (*Apple's Jade* 2nd, *Defi du Seuil* 1st, *Pentland Hills* 1st, *Knight Salute* 9th, *Zenta* 3rd)

Finesse Juvenile Hurdle 3 (*Grumeti* 1st, *Defi du Seuil* 1st, *Sir Gino* 1st)

Finale Juvenile Hurdle 2 (*Defi du Seuil* 1st, *We Have A Dream* 1st)

Prestbury Juvenile Hurdle 2 (*Defi du Seuil* 1st, *Knight Salute* 1st)

Changing Times Brewery Juvenile Hurdle 2 (*Apple's Jade* 1st, *Murcia* 8th)

AINTREE BOWL CHASE
3m 210y (Grade 1) – Mildmay Course

OVERVIEW
FIRST run in 1984, the Bowl – for many years run under the name/sponsorship banner of the *Martell Cup* – was handed Grade 1 status in 2010 and is the feature steeplechase among four top-level contests which take place on the opening day of the Grand National meeting. Past winners of the race include chasing greats such as *Wayward Lad* (twice), *Desert Orchid*, *Barton Bank*, *See More Business*, *Florida Pearl*, *First Gold* (twice), *Cue Card* and *Shishkin*, whilst the last pair of two-time winners – namely *Siliviniaco Conti* and *Clan des Obeaux* – were trained by Paul Nicholls, who has won the race six times since the turn of the century. Races such as the King George and, of course, the Gold Cup tend to be strong pointers towards success here, although tread carefully with those who appeared to have a tough race at Cheltenham last time out. Positive tactics are often rewarded, so look towards those who like to be ridden from the front.

GOLD CUP
RATHER surprisingly, only one of the past five winners of the Bowl contested the **Gold Cup** at Cheltenham on their previous start, with it earlier very much the starting point when assessing the race. Given that it is a Grade 1 steeplechase over an extended 3m, the feature event from the Cheltenham Festival is the obvious race for many a Bowl contender and with 26 of the 41 winners to date (26/36 read much better up to 2019) having contested the Gold Cup, it remains the key form line.

FOUR-WEEK GAP
DUE to an early April Easter in 2026, we are back to a four-week gap between Cheltenham and Aintree, meaning that there is exactly 27 days between the Gold Cup and the Bowl and this is highly significant. Often those who appeared to have had a hard race at Cheltenham struggle to back their form up at Aintree, with placed horses from the Festival failing at short odds in this race, whilst *'also-rans'* or those who departed early in the Gold Cup often come to the fore. Only three times in recent years has the runner-up from the Gold Cup gone one place better in the Bowl – those being *Exotic Dancer*, *Might Bite* and *Gerri Colombe* – and, crucially, in all three of those years there was the same *Four-Week Gap*. Therefore, statistics tell us that a horse who went close at Cheltenham is much more likely to reproduce that form this year, given the extra week of recovery time.

TACTICS
LAST year, *Gaelic Warrior* proved that a genuine hold-up performer can strike in the Bowl, but generally speaking, it pays to focus on those who like to be ridden positively. As touched upon when previewing the Manifesto Novices' Chase, a sound jumping front-runner can be difficult to pass on the Mildmay Course at Aintree and as such, those who like to go forward from flag fall are often at an advantage. Coming from behind is much more suited to the hurdles track, so despite last year's result, pay particular attention to any pace angles in the race (especially if there aren't many others in opposition) and tread carefully with those who like to come from off the pace.

ANOTHER TWO-TIME WINNER?

TO DATE, we have seen five two-time winners of the Bowl, with *Docklands Express* – successful in 1993 and 1994 – the one not covered in the *Overview*. 2024 winner *Gerri Colombe* was an absentee last year, but has since returned from injury and given that he won the Mildmay Novices' Chase in 2023, Aintree will likely once again be considered. Last year's winner is also likely to be considered for a race in which previous winners have to be respected.

PREVIOUS AINTREE FORM

IN ADDITION to the previous winners of the race, *Silviniaco Conti* finished third in 2013 before returning to win the next two renewals, whilst his stable-mate *Clan des Obeaux* was twice beaten in the race before going back-to-back. Therefore, watching last year's **Bowl Chase** is advisable and it could be that Dan Skelton's Betfair Chase winner Grey Dawning returns this year, in a bid to go one place better than in 2025.

Both *Might Bite* and *Gerri Colombe* had won the **Mildmay Novices' Chase** 12 months before winning the Bowl, whilst *Silviniaco Conti* won that race as a novice, some two years before his first victory in the Bowl. The 2024 Mildmay went the way of last year's Gold Cup winner Inothewayurthinkin, so it is clearly a breeding ground for top-level, open company success, and the 2025 renewal was won by Caldwell Potter, who beat Jordans but was sadly ruled out for the season in the autumn.

KINGS OF KEMPTON

OFTEN we see form from Kempton translate to Aintree and that is certainly the case in the Bowl. Although one is left handed (Aintree) and the other right, both are speed orientated tracks, in particular over fences, when getting into a jumping rhythm is extremely important. Rather like at Aintree, horses who get into a rhythm from the front can be dangerous around Kempton, so it is no surprise that the **King George VI Chase** has much more of an impact on this race than it does the Gold Cup. Although none of the past three winners ran at Kempton, seven of the previous eight did and extending that a little further, 14 of the past 27 winners had finished in the first four of the King George. *Silviniaco Conti* (twice), *Cue Card* and *Might Bite* have all completed the double in the past dozen years and this season's King George was won by The Jukebox Man, who came out on top in what was a memorable finish.

The previous season's **Kauto Star Novices' Chase** is another race to note, with *Tea For Two*

KEY TRENDS

- ⭐ 26 of the 41 winners had run in the Gold Cup
- ⭐ 8 of the past 14 winners had run in the King George (14 of the past 27 winners had finished in the first 4 at Kempton)
- ⭐ Paul Nicholls has won the race 6 times this century
- ⭐ The past 14 winners were beaten on their most recent start
- ⭐ Willie Mullins-trained runners are 3-7
- ✓ 12 of the past 15 winners returned at 7-2 or shorter
- ✓ 9 of the past 12 winners were in the top-2 according to Official BHA Ratings
- ✓ 9 of the past 13 winners were aged 8 or 9
- ✓ 7 of the past 10 favourites have won
- ✓ 6 of the past 13 winners wore headgear
- ✓ Horses rated 170+ are 6-13 during the past 11 renewals
- ✓ Irish-trained horses are 5-23 during the past 13 renewals (they previously had a poor record in the race)
- ✓ Respect previous form in the race
- ✓ Respect those who like to be ridden prominently
- ✗ Be wary of genuine hold-up performers
- ✗ Be wary of those who had a hard race in the Gold Cup
- ✗ Only 1 winner aged 6
- ✗ Only 1 of the past 15 winners (since the race was upgraded) hadn't already won a Grade 1
- ✗ No 11yo winner since 2005

and *Might Bite* both winning that contest in recent years. Again, dual winner *Silviniaco Conti* ran in the Kauto Star as a novice (finished runner-up) and last season's race was also won impressively by The Jukebox Man, who returned from injury to win at Haydock before that victory in the King George. He should be well suited to Aintree's Mildmay track and ran well here as a novice hurdler.

OTHER KEY RACES

AGAIN, in recent years, the first Grade 1 of the season in this division (in the UK) – the **Betfair Chase** – has been a better guide to Bowl success than Gold Cup glory, with five of the past 14 winners having contested the Haydock event. Given that *Clan des Obeaux* (ahead of his first win) is the only such winner in the past eight renewals, perhaps it is suffering a similar fate to the Gold Cup, however. This season's race wasn't staged on ground as testing as is often the case and it was won by the aforementioned Grey Dawning, under and confident and an emotional Harry Skelton.

The **Charlie Hall Chase** is also fading somewhat – even more so, in fact – with just one winner in the past decade having run at Wetherby in the early part of the season. Disappointing in this race last year, Djelo landed the Grade 2 on 1st November, beating Pic d'Orhy before dropping in trip to win a second Peterborough Chase.

Looking at the Cheltenham Festival, but away from the Gold Cup, Cue Card won the **Ryanair Chase** before he won the Bowl, albeit not during the same season, whilst First Lieutenant (actually chased home Cue Card) and Shishkin finished runner-up in the 2m5f contest, the month before winning the Bowl. Going back a little further and Our Vic completed this double in the spring of 2008, too.

And, over in Ireland, five of the past 14 winners had contested the **Savills Chase** at Leopardstown over Christmas. What A Friend and Kemboy were both successful in that Grade 1, which was won this season by Affordale Fury.

SIX ON THE BOARD FOR NICHOLLS

WITH six wins to his name, **Paul Nicholls** is the most successful trainer in the history of the Bowl. His recent dual winners Silviniaco Conti and Clan des Obeaux were preceded by See More Business, way back in 2000, and What A Friend, some 10 years later. Stage Star could finish only third for Nicholls last year, taking his tally of placed horses (2nd or 3rd) to six. He has run 23 horses in the race this century, therefore 52% of his runners have finished in the first three, which is a fantastic return for a race of this magnitude. Nicholls often likes to target Aintree these days and his runner(s) here warrant careful consideration, although with Caldwell Potter sidelined, it remains to be seen as to whether or not he will have a legitimate contender this year.

THE IRISH CHALLENGE

PRIOR to 2024, the Irish had won just four of the previous 28 renewals, in a race which tended to be dominated by the home contingent. However, Gerri Colombe and Gaelic Warrior have now provided the 'raiding party' with back-to-back wins in the Bowl, so it will be interesting to see if they begin to take the race more seriously. In fairness, Irish-trained horses have always had a decent strike rate in this race, trainers just didn't target it in great numbers, with many an Irish staying chaser given longer to recover from Cheltenham with the Punchestown Gold Cup in mind.

Interestingly, only two of the five recent Irish-trained winners of the race (since 2012) ran in the Gold Cup, and Kemboy unseated Danny Mullins at the first fence so barely had a race, meaning the 'fresh' angle certainly comes into play here. We only saw two Irish-trained runners contest the race in 2025, taking the tally during those last 13 renewals to 5-23. As I said, that is a very good strike rate and shines a much more positive light on the record of such runners.

THREE UP FOR MULLINS

HAVING first won the race in 2002 with Florida Pearl, **Willie Mullins** has added a further two Bowl victories to his name since 2019. Kemboy made all under a fine Ruby Walsh ride some seven years ago, whereas Gaelic Warrior was given a more patient/sympathetic ride by Patrick Mullins last year, when Mullins also saddled Embassy Gardens. He has now had just seven runners in the race, so three winners is a fantastic return, and both Don Poli (2nd) and Djakadam (3rd) hit the frame in the same year, so Mullins has actually only been represented in five renewals of the Bowl and has won three of them.

Interestingly, his Gold Cup winners – Al Boum Photo and Galopin des Champs – both waited for Punchestown, giving them additional recovery time (as per the previous subsection). With another British title likely to be on the line, respect any runners from Closutton this year.

Looking at the ante-post market for the Gold Cup (at the time of going to print), Mullins is responsible for Fact To File, Gaelic Warrior and Galopin des Champs, who are all prominently positioned in the betting. Add in Impaire et Passe, who is more likely to be aimed at the Melling Chase on day two, and the trainer is sure to consider one or two for Aintree.

OFFICIAL BHA RATINGS

NINE of the past dozen winners hailed from the top-two on Official BHA Ratings, with five of those winners rated in the 170s. During the past 11 renewals, only 13 horses rated 170 or higher have contested the Bowl, so pay healthy respect to any runner(s) with such a lofty rating. And, as a general guide, focus on those with the higher ratings, mid 160s and above.

MARKET FORCES

WE HAVE seen seven successful favourites in the past 10 renewals, whilst 12 of the past 15 winners returned at odds of 7-2 or shorter. Last year's winner was another well-backed second-favourite and with class often coming to the fore in the Bowl (as per the previous subsection), focus on the top end of the market, with 'shock' results – such as the 50-1 victory of Follow The Plan in 2012 – a rarity.

CURRENT FORM

THE last Bowl winner to have won on their most recent start was *What A Friend*, way back in 2010, so the past 14 winners arrived in Liverpool on the back of a defeat. Again, rather like with the Manifesto, this is a slightly surprising statistic for a Grade 1 event.

The three recent winners to have avoided the Cheltenham Festival – *Clan des Obeaux* (twice) and *Gaelic Warrior* – had run during early February, beaten in the Denman Chase in the case of the former, whilst last year's winner was beaten in the 2m1f Dublin Chase at the Dublin Racing Festival. Freshened up and stepped up markedly in distance, he became the eighth winner in the past 14 to have either finished second (5) or third (3) on their most recent start, so look towards those who hit the frame last time.

GRADE 1 WINNING FORM

SINCE the race received Grade 1 status, *Nacarat* is the only winner of the Bowl who hadn't previously won at least one Grade 1 race. On this trend alone, both Djelo and Embassy Gardens could have been ruled out immediately last year, and whilst it sounds rather obvious, focus on those with Grade 1-winning form to their name, preferably in open company over fences.

HEADGEAR

ANOTHER slightly surprising statistic for a Grade 1 race, but six of the past 13 winners wore headgear of some sort, including *Gaelic Warrior* who wore a hood last year. Interestingly, Paul Nicholls' last three winners of the race are included among that half-dozen, with four of the six winners aged either nine or 10. Often headgear is applied as a horse gets older, certainly in the case of a stayer.

Whilst it can be seen as a negative when looking at many a big race, it isn't when assessing the Bowl.

AGE

ONLY two 11-year-olds have won the Bowl this century and they came back in 2004 and 2005, respectively, with every winner since aged between seven and 10. Only two of the past 13 winners were 10-year-olds, so we are definitely starting to see a shift towards slightly *'younger'* winners, with Willie Mullins having saddled a brace of seven-year-old winners in the past six renewals.

The novice *Escartefigue* is the only successful six-year-old (his win coming back in 1998) and if the most recent results are anything to go by, we should be focusing mostly on those aged eight or nine, with nine of the past 13 winners falling into this bracket.

ROLL OF HONOUR

Year	Form	Winner	Age	Weight	OR	SP	Trainer	Runners	Last Race (No. of days)
2025	23	Gaelic Warrior	7	11-10	164	11/4	W Mullins (IRE)	7	3rd Gr.1 Dublin Chase (60)
2024	122	Gerri Colombe	8	11-10	170	9/4F	G Elliott (IRE)	7	2nd Gr.1 Cheltenham Gold Cup (27)
2023	312	Shishkin	9	11-10	173	7/4F	N Henderson	5	2nd Gr.1 Ryanair Chase (28)
2022	23	Clan des Obeaux	10	11-7	168	13/2	P Nicholls	9	3rd Gr.2 Denman Chase (54)
2021	232	Clan des Obeaux	9	11-7	169	5/2F	P Nicholls	9	2nd Gr.2 Denman Chase (46)
2020	NO RACE - meeting cancelled								
2019	11U	Kemboy	7	11-7	168	9/4F	W Mullins (IRE)	6	u.r. Gr.1 Cheltenham Gold Cup (20)
2018	112	Might Bite	9	11-7	172	4/5F	N Henderson	8	2nd Gr.1 Cheltenham Gold Cup (27)
2017	5241U	Tea For Two	8	11-7	158	10/1	N Williams	7	u.r. Gr.1 Cheltenham Gold Cup (20)
2016	4111F	Cue Card	10	11-7	176	6/5F	C Tizzard	9	fell Gr.1 Cheltenham Gold Cup (20)

LEADING TEN-YEAR GUIDES

*Kauto Star Novices' Chase 2 (*Tea For Two* 1st, *Might Bite* fell)
King George VI Chase 5 (*Cue Card* 1st, *Tea For Two* 4th, *Might Bite* 1st, *Clan des Obeaux* 3rd & 2nd)
Cheltenham Gold Cup 5 (*Cue Card* fell, *Tea For Two* u.r., *Might Bite* 1st, *Kemboy* u.r., *Gerri Colombe* 2nd)
*Aintree Bowl 2 (*Clan des Obeaux* 2nd & 1st)
Betfair Chase 2 (*Cue Card* 1st, *Clan des Obeaux* 2nd)
Savills Chase 2 (*Kemboy* 1st, *Gerri Colombe* 2nd)
Denman Chase 2 (*Clan des Obeaux* 2nd & 3rd)
*Mildmay Novices' Chase 2 (*Might Bite* 1st, *Gerri Colombe* 1st)

* denotes previous season

WILLIAM HILL AINTREE HURDLE
2m4f (Grade 1)

OVERVIEW
THE Aintree Hurdle is the only Grade 1 hurdle race staged over an intermediate distance in Britain throughout the whole season. Whilst stayers now have the option of running in the Liverpool Stayers' Hurdle on day three, it once brought together Champion Hurdle horses and three-milers, whilst we have seen several specialised *'middle-distance hurdlers'* win multiple renewals over the years, *Oscar Whisky* and *Al Eile* a couple of fairly recent examples. Form over the minimum trip is a positive, whilst mares boast an excellent recent record in the race. Genuine National Hunt greats such as *Dawn Run* and *Istabraq* feature among an illustrious list of previous winners.

MULTIPLE WINNERS
SEVEN horses have won the Aintree Hurdle more than once, the first being *Monksfield*, who dead-heated with *Night Nurse* in 1977, before winning the next two renewals in his own right. *Morley Street* – successful in four consecutive renewals in the early 90s (including when beating his full-brother Granville Again in 1993) – is the most successful horse in the history of the race, whilst *Al Eile* claimed the prize on three occasions.

Oscar Whisky is the latest dual winner of the race – successful in 2011 and 2012 – so another is due and 2m4f around Aintree looks to be just about ideal for last year's winner *Lossiemouth*. Should all go well at Cheltenham – either in the Champion Hurdle or in her bid to win a third straight Mares' Hurdle – it is likely that she will head back to Aintree to defend her crown, in an attempt to become the eighth multiple winner of the race.

PREVIOUS AINTREE FORM
GIVEN those past *Multiple Winners*, there was a time when previous form at this fixture was a huge positive. Both *Zarkandar* and *The New One* – the latter as a novice – were beaten in the **Aintree Hurdle** at the age of five before returning to win it the following year, so past renewals can be important. Last year's runner-up Wodhooh would be another likely contender for the race this time around.

Form at this fixture does seem to be less significant nowadays, however, with just one of the past 11 winners having won at the meeting previously. This record stands at nine of the past 24 winners, but it was much more prevalent a decade or more ago. Obviously, form at this fixture is not a negative, but it certainly isn't as important as once was the case.

CHAMPION HURDLE CLASS
OVERALL, 32 of the 48 winners of the Aintree Hurdle had run in the **Champion Hurdle** at Cheltenham, the most recent being *Constitution Hill*, who completed the double three years ago. Since 2016, Champion Hurdle winners are 3-3 in this race and since 1999, four of the six Champion Hurdle winners to have taken their chance have been successful. Interestingly, only two Champion Hurdle runners-up have gone one place better out of the past 19 to have tried, *Khyber Kim* doing so in 2010 and *Epatante* in 2022. Pay healthy respect to any horse who ran well in the Champion Hurdle, although treat the runner-up with a degree of caution, given the past record (likely they endured a hard race in second).

With the four-week gap between Cheltenham and Aintree in place again this year, there are 30 days between the two races.

NEED FOR SPEED

THIS kind of ties in with the previous subsection and the fact that Aintree, particularly on drying spring ground, can be a real test of speed, therefore strong form over the minimum trip should be taken very seriously. Prior to last year, three of the previous four winners were attempting 2m4f for the very first time (stepping up beyond 2m for the first time under Rules) and in fact, I will admit to having stamina reservations over *Abacadabras* and *Epatante*. Speed often wins the day at Aintree, so strong form over the minimum trip – something which the past two winners had in abundance – is a huge positive.

CHELTENHAM FORM IS KEY FOR BRITS

EACH and every British-trained winner of the race ran at the Cheltenham Festival, so the *'fresh'* angle certainly isn't something to look for with such runners. Whilst we have seen Irish-trained winners of the race bypass the Festival, skipping Cheltenham is very much seen as a negative for British-trained runners, with the only exception being *Barton* in 2001, when the Cheltenham Festival didn't take place due to the Foot And Mouth outbreak.

OTHER KEY CHELTENHAM RACES

WE HAVE seen horses drop back in distance to contest the Aintree Hurdle on the back of having run in the **Stayers' Hurdle** and although more common before the introduction of the Liverpool Stayers' Hurdle, *Oscar Whisky* was a good example, with him not an out-and-out stayer and more suited to this mid-range distance. More recently, both *L'Ami Serge* and *Supasundae* had finished down the field in the Stayers' before winning this race.

Much earlier this century, a couple of Aintree Hurdle winners – namely *Ilnamar* and *Rhinestone Cowboy* - had contested the **Coral Cup** on their most recent start, with the former successful in the Festival handicap over a similar trip. However, Grade 1 form is much more significant (more of that shortly) here and is readily preferred to handicap form.

Two of the past eight winners had contested the **Supreme Novices' Hurdle** some 13 months earlier, with *Buveur d'Air* having finished third in the Festival curtain-raiser, whilst stable-mate *Constitution Hill* completed the double.

And, away from the Festival, the race formerly known as the **Bula Hurdle**, then the International

KEY TRENDS

- ★ Every British-trained winner ran at the Cheltenham Festival
- ★ The past 13 winners (and 16 of the past 19 winners) had already won t least one Grade 1
- ★ 6 of the past 14 winners were trained by Nicky Henderson
- ★ 3 of the past 9 winners were trained by Willie Mullins
- ✓ 32 of the 48 winners ran in the Champion Hurdle
- ✓ 27 of the past 31 winners were aged 6-8
- ✓ The past 17 winners returned at 15-2 or shorter (16 of which were in the top-3 of the betting)
- ✓ 16 of the past 31 winners were trained in Ireland
- ✓ Champion Hurdle winners are 3-3 since 2016 (4-6 since 1999)
- ✓ 3 of the past 10 winners were owned by JP McManus (4 wins in total)
- ✓ 3 of the past 5 winners were running beyond 2m for the very first time (under Rules)
- ✓ Mares are 3-9 during the past 16 renewals (and 4-13 since 2006)
- ✓ Respect hold-up performers
- ✓ Respect strong form over 2m
- ✗ Only 1 of the 48 winners was older than 9 (and only 1 winning 9yo in the past 31 renewals)
- ✗ Only 1 of the past 11 winners had won at this meeting previously (was previously a strong statistic for those with form at this fixture)
- ✗ Only 2 of the past 19 Champion Hurdle seconds to have run have won
- ✗ Only 2 of the past 24 winners were sent off at double figure odds
- ✗ Only 2 of the past 35 winners were aged 5 (5yo's are 0-12 during the past 15 renewals)

before being rebranded as the **Unibet Hurdle** in recent years, has a much better record here than it does in the Champion Hurdle. As covered when looking ahead to that race, the 2m1f contest on the New Course – which now takes place on trials day rather than at the December meeting – is more about stamina than speed, so it is understandable that is has more of a positive impact over 2m4f here. Between 2010 and 2014, three winners of the *'Bula'* followed up at Aintree and this year's race was won by The New Lion, although it will be remembered for the serious injury sustained by Sir Gino.

OTHER KEY RACES IN ENGLAND

AS WE have seen when looking ahead to the Champion Hurdle, Nicky Henderson likes to start his top-class hurdlers off in the **Fighting Fifth Hurdle** at Newcastle, a race he won with both *Epatante* and *Constitution Hill* prior to them winning at Aintree. The former dead-heated in the season she won the Aintree Hurdle to be precise, and Henderson sent *Constitution Hill* back to Newcastle this season, where he memorably got no further than the second flight. Last season's leading novice The New Lion also took a crashing fall in a dramatic race, which was eventually won by last year's Champion Hurdle heroine, Golden Ace.

She then went on to chase home Sir Gino in the **Christmas Hurdle** at Kempton, with the winner returning from a year off and reverting to hurdles for the first time since winning the Fighting Fifth the previous year. Both *Epatante* and *Constitution Hill* also won the Christmas Hurdle during their respective Aintree Hurdle winning seasons and last year's winner *Lossiemouth* chased home the latter in 2024, becoming the third winner in the past four years to have run at Kempton on Boxing Day.

TACTICS

IN CONTRAST to the positivity surrounding prominently ridden horses on the chase course at Aintree, hold-up performers tend to do well in the top events over hurdles at this track. With the cross-flight omitted at the Grand National fixture (in place during the winter to ensure enough hurdles are jumped if the dreaded low sun comes into play – this was again evident on Boxing Day in the Formby Novices' Hurdle) it means that those coming from off the pace have plenty of time to make a move, following the long run from the final flight down the far side. A smooth-travelling horse, who has the speed to make up ground is often well-suited to the hurdles track at Aintree, particularly when the ground is nice. *Lossiemouth* was ridden patiently last year, only joining in three out, at the first flight up the home straight. In this scenario, a late turn of foot (that natural 2m speed) is a huge asset at Aintree.

GRADE 1 WINNING FORM

THE past 13 winners were all previous Grade 1 winners, so as touched upon briefly in an earlier subsection, form at the highest level should certainly be given priority over those stepping out of handicap company, or even those who have won Grade 2s or Grade 3s. Many a recent Aintree Hurdle winner were multiple Grade 1 winners, whilst 16 of the past 19 had won at least once, so tread carefully with those who have yet to show their class on the biggest stage.

THE IRISH CHALLENGE

FOLLOWING the victories of stable-mates *Impaire et Passe* and *Lossiemouth*, Irish-trained horses have now won six of the past 10 renewals, which followed on from five straight British-trained winners. Prior to that, the Irish had won six of the seven renewals between 2003 and 2009, whilst *Danoli* (twice), *Urubande* and *Istabraq* were winners for Ireland during the mid-late 90s. Interestingly, several of those 'earlier' Irish-trained winners arrived at Aintree having bypassed Cheltenham – something which we have not seen from British-trained winners of the race – although only *Impaire et Passe* matched this profile of the half-dozen most recent Irish-trained winners.

Having won the past two renewals, **Willie Mullins** stands on three wins in the Aintree Hurdle, having first won it with *Annie Power* some 10 years ago. With the British trainers' title likely still in the balance, it would be a shock if Mullins was not represented in this Grade 1 contest, with *Lossiemouth* again likely to be strongly considered. Given the distance of the race, it might also be the ideal spring target for Ballyburn, so he will have options.

Jessica Harrington has won the race twice in the past 10 renewals and from a much smaller pool of horses. The dual purpose trainer was successful with both *Jezki* and *Supasundae* and runners from her stable deserve plenty of respect.

And, whilst **Gordon Elliott** has yet to (officially) get his name on the board, *Abacadabras* was a winner for his Cullentra House operation whilst he was serving his infamous suspension, with Denise Foster the name on the license at the time. Elliott is often well represented by a strong team of horses at Aintree, perhaps wanting to avoid the Mullins juggernaut that turns up at Punchestown, and he has saddled a third and a second (Wodhooh last year) in the past three years.

Elliott will have options for the race this year, including last year's second and possibly Brighterdaysahead, who won the Mersey over course-and-distance a couple of years ago.

KEY IRISH RACES

THE past two winners kicked off their season in the **Hatton's Grace Hurdle** at Fairyhouse, with *Lossiemouth* completing the double. This season's race saw former Stayers' Hurdle winner Teahupoo beat Ballyburn by a nose, before confirming the form by a much greater margin in the Christmas Hurdle at

Leopardstown over 3m. *Supasundae* also began his season with a second at Fairyhouse, meaning that three of the past six winners contested the Hatton's Grace.

Over the minimum trip, the **Morgiana Hurdle** at Punchestown is the opening Grade 1 of the season in Ireland and two of the past 10 winners had contested that race, *Jezki* finishing runner-up and *Abacadabras* successful. This season's Morgiana was won by *Lossiemouth*, who started off over 2m rather than in the aforementioned Hatton's Grace.

She went on to win the **December Festival Hurdle** at Leopardstown's Christmas fixture, a race which four of the past 10 winners had contested. Interestingly, all four were beaten in that contest before proving successful at Aintree. Brighterdaysahead, who won the race the previous season, chased home *Lossiemouth*.

And, the same four horses were also beaten in the **Irish Champion Hurdle** at the Dublin Racing Festival, suggesting that they were each just below the very top-level over the minimum trip, but were able to gain further Grade 1 honours over this 2m4f trip. This year's Irish Champion Hurdle was won by Brighterdaysahead, who beat Lossiemouth by 3¼ lengths.

RESPECT MARES

LAST year's race was unusual in that four of the six runners were mares, whereas only five had taken their chance in the previous 15 renewals, with two successful. Going back to 2006, the record (prior to last year) stood at 3-9, with – as with most Grade 1s – the sex-allowance clearly being hugely advantageous when it comes to a high-class mare such as *Asian Maze*, *Annie Power* and *Epatante*. Last year, *Lossiemouth* added her name to the tally, with the record since 2006 now standing at 4-13, whilst the record for the past 16 renewals stands at 3-9 (33%).

Last year's first and second – *Lossiemouth* and Wodhooh – would once again be fascinating runners, in receipt of 7lb from the geldings.

AGE FOR CONCERN

AGE really does catch up with horses in top-level races over hurdles, certainly over shorter to intermediate trips, and it is no different in the Aintree Hurdle. Only one of the 48 winners was in double digits – that being the 10-year-old *Mister Morose* back in 2000 – whilst only one of the past 31 winners was aged nine, that being *Supasundae*. At the other end of the scale, we have seen just two five-year-old winners since *Celtic Chief* in 1988, with the last being *Solwhit* in 2009. Following the second of Wodhooh last year, the record of five-year-olds in the past 15 years stands at 0-12.

Therefore, focus on those aged between six and eight, with 27 of the past 31 winners falling into this bracket, whilst the past three winners were all aged six.

MARKET FORCES

THE past 17 winners returned at 15-2 or shorter, with 16 of those hailing from the top three in the market, so again, this isn't a race in which you should expect to see a *'shock'* result. Five favourites have won in the past 11 renewals, with four of them returning at odds-on and *Impaire et Passe* successful at Evens in 2024, whilst last year's winner was sent off the 5-4 second-favourite. Only two of the past 24 winners returned at double figure odds, so again, pay most attention to those towards the head of the market.

HENDERSON'S HALF-DOZEN

WITH *Constitution Hill* falling last year, trainer **Nicky Henderson** remains on six Aintree Hurdle wins, although he is the only British trainer to have won the race in the past decade, successful during the past eight renewals with *Buveur d'Air*, *L'Ami Serge*, *Epatante* and *Constitution Hill*. With *Oscar Whisky* providing him with back-to-back winners in 2011 and 2012, Henderson has won six of the past 14 renewals, which is a magnificent return for a race of this calibre.

It has been well documented over the years that Henderson didn't have a good record at all at Aintree during the 90s or early noughties, but that has very much changed (as the meeting has grown in stature) and his runners in this contest, in particular, warrant utmost respect.

McMANUS AT THE TREBLE

LEADING owner **JP McManus** was responsible for two of Henderson's recent winners and also saw *Jezki* carry his green and gold hooped silks to success in 2015. Having earlier won the race with *Istabraq*, McManus has won four Aintree Hurdles, but three in the past 10 is a much stronger return and he also saw his My Tent Or Yours (also Henderson-trained, incidentally) finish runner-up in both 2016 and 2017. McManus' excellent record in the Champion Hurdle has been documented in the preview for that race and it is a similar story here.

It could be that The New Lion bids to provide him with a fifth Aintree Hurdle and a fourth in the space of 11 renewals. The distance of the race (2m4f) could well prove to be his optimum, although at the time of going to print, Kabral du Mathan was reportedly being aimed at the race by Dan Skelton. With a trainers' title to secure, being doubly represented might not be a bad idea.

DAY ONE AINTREE HURDLE

The Aintree Hurdle is a target for Kabral du Mathan

ROLL OF HONOUR

Year	Form	Winner	Age	Weight	OR	SP	Trainer	Runners	Last Race (No. of days)
2025	12F1	Lossiemouth	6	11-3	160	5/4	W Mullins (IRE)	6	1st Gr.1 Mares' Hurdle (23)
2024	223	Impaire et Passe	6	11-10	160	EvsF	W Mullins (IRE)	8	3rd Gr.1 Irish Champion Hurdle (67)
2023	111	Constitution Hill	6	11-10	175	2/15F	N Henderson	6	1st Gr.1 Champion Hurdle (30)
2022	112	Epatante	8	11-0	159	2/1	N Henderson	7	2nd Gr.1 Champion Hurdle (23)
2021	2152F	Abacadabras	7	11-7	158	5/1	D Foster (IRE)	11	Fell Gr.1 Champion Hurdle (23)
2020	NO RACE – meeting cancelled								
2019	2227	Supasundae	9	11-7	161	15/2	J Harrington (IRE)	7	7th Gr.1 Stayers' Hurdle (21)
2018	12238	L'Ami Serge	8	11-7	159	5/1	N Henderson	9	8th Gr.1 Stayers' Hurdle (28)
2017	1111	Buveur d'Air	6	11-7	167	4/9F	N Henderson	6	1st Gr.1 Champion Hurdle (23)
2016	111	Annie Power	8	11-0	162	4/9F	W Mullins (IRE)	6	1st Gr.1 Champion Hurdle (23)

LEADING TEN-YEAR GUIDES

Champion Hurdle 5 (*Annie Power* 1st, *Buveur d'Air* 1st, *Abacadabras* fell, *Epatante* 2nd, *Constitution Hill* 1st)
Stayers' Hurdle 2 (*L'Ami Serge* 8th, *Supasundae* 7th)
Irish Champion Hurdle 4 (*Supasundae* 2nd, *Abacadabras* 2nd, *Impaire et Passe* 3rd, *Lossiemouth* fell)
December Festival Hurdle 3 (*Supasundae* 2nd, *Abacadabras* 5th, *Impaire et Passe* 2nd)
Christmas Hurdle 3 (*Epatante* 1st, *Constitution Hill* 1st, *Lossiemouth* 2nd)
*Supreme Novices' Hurdle 2 (*Buveur d'Air* 3rd, *Constitution Hill* 1st)
Fighting Fifth Hurdle 2 (*Epatante* DH 1st, *Constitution Hill* 1st)
Hatton's Grace Hurdle 3 (*Supasundae* 2nd, *Impaire et Passe* 2nd, *Lossiemouth* 1st)

* denotes previous season

WILLIAM HILL MILDMAY NOVICES' CHASE

3m 210y (Grade 1) – Mildmay Course

OVERVIEW

THE Mildmay is a novices' chase with a rich tradition, with the first two winners – *Bregawn* and *Burrough Hill Lad* – subsequent Gold Cup winners, whilst last year's Gold Cup winner *Inothewayurthinkin* was successful in 2024. *Native River* was another future Gold Cup winner to land this prize and 1988 Grand National winner *Rhyme 'n' Reason* was another winner during the mid-80s. *Royal Athlete* was another future National winner to land the Mildmay, a race which was handed Grade 1 status in 2014. Both Paul Nicholls and Nicky Henderson boast an excellent record in it, Nicholls winning it for a fifth time in 2025, whilst Henderson stands alone on six wins to date.

CHELTENHAM FESTIVAL FORM

RECENT results suggest that a good run at the Cheltenham is imperative, with the last dozen winners recording a first or second place finish at the Festival. That is a very strong statistic and the past two winners – *Inothewayurthinkin* and *Caldwell Potter* – were Cheltenham winners, successful in the Kim Muir and the newly-reinstated novices' handicap chase, respectively. *Holywell* – winner of the Ultima in 2014 – also showed that handicap form should not be underestimated.

Native River finished runner-up in the National Hunt Chase, when that contest was still a Grade 2 (now a novices' handicap, of course), although the obvious Cheltenham race to start with is the **Broadway Novices' Chase**, run in recent years as the **Brown Advisory Novices' Chase** (formerly the RSA). *Might Bite* completed the double some nine years ago and more recently, both *Ahoy Senor* and *Gerri Colombe* have won the Mildmay on the back of having finished runner-up on day two at the Festival.

One word of caution with regards to the Broadway is that five of the past six winners of that race to have come on to Aintree have been beaten, *Might Bite* being the exception. Take that into account, although again, the four-week gap might help this year, meaning that there are 30 days between the two races.

Four winners between 2013 and 2021 had finished either first or second in the **Golden Miller Novices' Chase**, which was run at the time as the JLT. Formerly a Grade 1, that is the race which was converted back to a novices' handicap in 2025 and was won by *Caldwell Potter*. Now run under the banner of the **Jack Richards Novices' Handicap Chase**, it will be interesting to see if it continues to have an impact here, with *Big Buck's* (back in 2008) another to have run in that race at Cheltenham – when it was originally a handicap – before scoring here.

SCILLY ISLES IS MAKING WAVES

THE record of horses stepping up in distance from the Golden Miller is surprisingly positive and it is a similar story with horses graduating from the **Scilly Isles Novices' Chase** at Sandown, with three of the past seven winners having finished first or second in the Grade 1 over 2m4f. Handstands was unable to enhance the record last year (badly hampered by a faller down the back straight) but again, the form worked out well in the spring (and beyond), with the Scilly Isles runner-up, *Jango Baie*, winning the Arkle and having since developed into a high-class chaser in open company. *Terrefort* and *Gerri Colombe* won the Scilly Isles, whilst *Lostintranslation* finished runner-up to Defi du Seuil, with the pair then going on to fill the same positions in the Golden Miller at Cheltenham.

This year's race was won by Fergal O'Brien's Sixmilebridge, who made it 3-3 over fences.

KAUTO STAR FORM

AS ALREADY touched upon when looking at the Bowl on day one, form from Kempton often stands up at Aintree and five of the six winners between 2012 and 2017 had run in the **Kauto Star Novices' Chase** on Boxing Day, with only *Dynaste* successful out of the quintet. More recently, *Ahoy Senor* was another to have been beaten in the Kempton Grade 1 before winning the Mildmay, Lucinda Russell's charge coming home in second, as he had done at Cheltenham. This season's race saw Willie Mullins' classy hurdler Kitzbuhel beat a staying on Thomas Mor and Wendigo, with Salver back in fourth.

GRADED FORM

ALTHOUGH I mentioned when looking at *Cheltenham Festival Form* that handicap form should be respected, 11 of the past 15 winners had already recorded a win in Grade 1 or Grade 2 company over fences. *Caldwell Potter* was another who failed to match this profile last year, but he had finished runner-up in the Lightning Novices' Chase over 2m and was, of course, a Grade 1-winning novice hurdler in Ireland. Pay healthy respect to those with winning Graded form over fences in the book.

PREVIOUS AINTREE FORM

THE past three winners were making their first visits to Aintree, whilst earlier winners had shown good form at this fixture over hurdles. Of the past 11 winners alone, *Holywell* had finished runner-up in the Liverpool Hurdle the previous year, *Lostintranslation* was narrowly beaten in the Mersey Novices' Hurdle 12 months earlier and *Ahoy Senor* had won the Sefton. Going back a little further and *Barton* won the Mersey in 1999 and the Aintree Hurdle in 2001, before returning to win the Mildmay in 2002. Pay healthy respect to strong, Grade 1 form over hurdles from previous National meetings.

PROVEN STAMINA?

RATHER like the Broadway at Cheltenham, it seems that proven stamina over 3m isn't essential these days, with plenty of recent winners stepping up in trip. Indeed, last year's winner had twice run over 2m before winning the novices' handicap over 2m4½f, so was having his first start over a staying trip in this event. Given that the Scilly Isles Novices' Chase is staged over an intermediate trip, it seems that a modern day winner of this race needs that bit of natural pace, something we often associate with Aintree in the spring. *Inothewayurthinkin* had obviously proven his stamina by winning the Kim Muir, but he, too, had earlier been campaigned over much shorter, so pay healthy respect to those stepping up in distance, having shaped well in Graded races over 2m4f or thereabouts.

KEY TRENDS

- ✦ The past 12 winners finished 1st or 2nd at the Cheltenham Festival
- ✦ 5 of the past 12 winners had contested the Kauto Star Novices' Chase at Kempton
- ✦ 3 of the past 8 winners were trained by Nicky Henderson (record since 2017 is 3-5)
- ✓ 28 of the past 35 winners had won over 2m7f+
- ✓ 23 of the past 25 winners had run at least 4 times over fences (13 of them had 5+ chase starts)
- ✓ The past 23 winners returned at 7-1 or shorter (15 of them at 3-1 or shorter)
- ✓ The past 22 winners were either Irish-bred (13) or French-bred (9)
- ✓ 20 of the past 25 winners had won at least twice over fences previously (10 of them had 3+ wins)
- ✓ 14 of the past 16 winners were aged 6 or 7
- ✓ 13 of the past 15 winners were in the top-2 on official BHA Ratings
- ✓ 11 of the past 15 winners had already won a Grade 1 or Grade 2 over fences
- ✓ 10 of the past 23 winners were outright favourite (plus 2 winning joint-favourites)
- ✓ 10 of the past 22 winners were trained by Nicky Henderson (5) or Paul Nicholls (5)
- ✓ 5 of the past 12 winners finished 1st or 2nd in the Golden Miller (now the novice h'cap chase)
- ✓ French-bred 5yo's are 3-8 since 2006
- ✓ Respect Grade 1 hurdle form at Aintree
- ✓ Don't underestimate handicap form from Cheltenham
- ✗ No winner this century was unbeaten over fences
- ✗ Only 1 winners this century returned at double figure odds
- ✗ Only 1 of the past 15 winners was rated below 152
- ✗ Only 1 of the past 17 winners was aged 8
- ✗ Only 2 of the past 36 winners were older than 8
- ✗ Only 2 of the past 20 winners bypassed the Cheltenham Festival
- ✗ Only 2 winners this century had 3 previous chase starts
- ✗ 5 of the past 6 Broadway (Brown Advisory) winners to have run have been beaten

Prior to last year, 28 of the previous 34 winners had still won over 2m7f+ and I am not saying that having proven stamina is a negative, simply that we are seeing a different type of winner in recent years, one who is stepping up in distance gradually.

CHASING EXPERIENCE

HAVING gained plenty of experience over fences can be a positive by the time we reach April, with 23 of the past 25 winners having run at least four times, with 13 of them having had five or more chase starts. Between 2014 and 2018, four of the five winners had run six times or more over fences, with *Terrefort* having had nine previous chase runs to his name, five coming in France. Since then, the past six winners had run four (3) or five (3) times apiece over fences, with only two winners this century – *Killyglen* and *Saphir du Rheu* – having had just three previous chase starts.

DON'T BE PUT OFF BY A DEFEAT

LAST year's winner was 2-4 over fences prior to Aintree, whilst 2024 winner *Inothewayurthinkin* only shed his maiden tag in the Kim Muir the time before. In fact, no winner this century arrived at Aintree with an unbeaten chasing record intact, so don't let a defeat earlier in the season be a concern. As touched upon in an earlier subsection, many a recent winner had run well in defeat at Cheltenham.

THE IRISH CHALLENGE

THERE have only ever been five Irish-trained winners of the Mildmay, with the first three – *Boss Doyle*, *Like-A-Butterfly* and *Quito de la Roque* – spread out between 1998 and 2011, although the two latest winners came in 2023 and 2024 respectively, so perhaps, the record of such runners is ready for an upturn in fortunes. There was a strong Irish presence last year, too, although Dancing City falling and bringing down stable-mate Quai de Bourbon left just Jordans after fence 14, with Joseph O'Brien's runner going on to chase home *Caldwell Potter*. With Punchestown staging a similar Grade 1 just three weeks later, many an Irish-trained staying novice will be given the extra recovery time. However, we know that Gordon Elliott likes to target Aintree and given his firepower in the division, Willie Mullins is likely to consider splitting his pack again this year.

With the race formerly known as the Fort Leney Novice Chase removed from the calendar this season (formerly staged at Leopardstown's Christmas fixture), the key race in Ireland over the Festive period to note is the **Faugheen Novice Chase** at Limerick. As a result of the removal of the Fort Leney, the Faugheen now takes place over 2m5f (was 2m3½f previously) and it is a race which *Gerri Colombe* won mid-season and *Inothewayurthinkin* finished third behind Gaelic Warrior and Il Etait Temps, with the latter also successful at Aintree that season (Manifesto Novices' Chase). This season's race saw Final Demand beat Gold Dancer, with their stable-mate Jimmy du Seuil disappointing back in fourth.

AGE

FIVE of the past six winners were aged seven, with *Inothewayurthinkin* being the exception, him successful at the age of six in 2024. Since 2009, 14 of the past 16 winners were aged either six (5) or seven (9), which is clearly the prime age bracket for the race, whilst three five-year-olds have proven successful since 2006. *Star de Mohaison*, *Big Buck's* (both Paul Nicholls-trained) and *Terrofort* were the trio in question and all three were French-bred. With no representation again last year, French-bred five-year-olds boast a fantastic record of 3-8 during the past 16 renewals, so respect any such youngster.

At the other end of the scale, *Barton* (successful at nine) and *Like-A-Butterfly* (successful as an 11-year-old) are the only winners over the age of eight during the past 36 renewals. There have actually only ever been three Mildmay winners over the age of eight, whilst *Might Bite* is the only winning eight-year-old in the past 17 renewals, which again suggests that we should be focusing our attention on 'younger' contenders.

BREEDING

AS TOUCHED upon in the *Age* subsection, French-bred youngsters boast a good record here. Although he wasn't five, *Caldwell Potter* became the ninth French-bred winner since 2006 when successful last year, whilst every other winner since 2003 was Irish-bred. That is common for a staying chase, whereas the record of British-bred runners isn't so inspiring, *Barton* being the last such winner in 2002. There was just one British-bred runner last year and such runners should be treated with a degree of caution.

MARKET FORCES

SINCE 2012, we have seen eight successful outright favourites, whilst *Caldwell Potter* was sent off 11-4 joint-favourite with Handstands in 2025. The past 23 winners returned at odds of 7-1 or shorter, with 15 of those winners returning at 3-1 or shorter, suggesting that 'shock' results don't really occur in the Mildmay and that we should focus our attention on the top end of the market. Indeed, since 2006, only one winner did not hail from the top-three in the betting, that being *Killyglen*, who returned the 7-1 fourth-favourite. *What's Up Boys* – who returned at 12-1 back in 2001 – is the only double figure-priced winner this century.

OFFICIAL BHA RATINGS

SUBSEQUENT Gold Cup winner *Native River* is the only winner in the past 15 renewals to be rated below 152 prior to the race, so using that as a minimum is a good starting point. Indeed, *Caldwell Potter* was rated 155 after his Cheltenham win last year, whilst recent winners such as *Lostintranslation*, *Chantry House*, *Ahoy Senor*, *Gerri Colombe* and *Inothewayurthinkin* were all rated between 157-159. The highest-rated winners during the past 10 renewals were *Saphir du Rheu* (163) and *Might Bite*, and these figures go to show the standard which is usually required to win the Mildmay.

TRAINERS TO NOTE

CALDWELL POTTER provided **Paul Nicholls** with a fifth Mildmay success, with his first four wins gained between 2006 and 2015. *Star de Mohaison*, *Big Buck's*, *Silviniaco Conti* and *Saphir du Rheu* were all aged five or six and all French-bred, whilst last year's winner was a French-bred, but aged seven.

Without a runner in each of the past four renewals, **Nicky Henderson** remains the most successful trainer in the history of the Mildmay, with the 75-year-old having won the race six times. First successful with *Sparkling Flame* back in 1991, his second win came courtesy of *Irish Hussar* in 2003, followed by *Burton Port* in 2010. More recently, *Might Bite*, *Terrefort* and *Chantry House* provided Henderson with three wins in four renewals, and he hasn't had a runner since the latter won. Henderson saddled the one-two in 2017 and has actually only had five runners during those past eight renewals. Selective in terms of his runners, any horse representing the Seven Barrows stable should be taken very seriously.

Sixmilebridge wins the Scilly Isles at Sandown

ROLL OF HONOUR

Year	Form	Winner	Age	Weight	OR	SP	Trainer	Runners	Last Race (No. of days)
2025	1321	Caldwell Potter	7	11-7	155	11/4J	P Nicholls	7	1st Golden Miller Nov. H'cap Chase (22)
2024	22391	Inothewayurthinkin	6	11-7	158	6/4F	G Cromwell (IRE)	6	1st Kim Muir H'cap Chase (29)
2023	1112	Gerri Colombe	7	11-7	159	4/6F	G Elliott (IRE)	6	2nd Gr.1 Broadway Nov. Chase (30)
2022	U1212	Ahoy Senor	7	11-4	157	4/1	L Russell	4	2nd Gr.1 Broadway Nov. Chase (23)
2021	1311	Chantry House	7	11-4	159	11/8F	N Henderson	7	1st Gr.1 Golden Miller Nov. Chase (22)
2020	NO RACE – meeting cancelled								
2019	23122	Lostintranslation	7	11-4	157	3/1	C Tizzard	6	2nd Gr.1 Golden Miller Nov. Chase (22)
2018	13112	Terrefort	5	11-4	153	3/1F	N Henderson	9	2nd Gr.1 Golden Miller Nov. Chase (29)
2017	21F11	Might Bite	8	11-4	161	8/13F	N Henderson	5	1st Gr.1 Broadway Nov. Chase (23)
2016	11332	Native River	6	11-4	149	11/2	C Tizzard	8	2nd Gr.2 National Hunt Chase (24)

LEADING TEN-YEAR GUIDES

Kauto Star Novices' Chase 3 (*Native River* 3rd, *Might Bite* fell, *Ahoy Senor* 2nd)
Golden Miller Novices' Chase 4 (*Terrefort* 2nd, *Lostintranslation* 2nd, *Chantry House* 1st, *Caldwell Potter* 1st)
Scilly Isles Novices' Chase 3 (*Terrefort* 1st, *Lostintranslation* 2nd, *Gerri Colombe* 1st)
Broadway Novices' Chase 3 (*Might Bite* 1st, *Ahoy Senor* 2nd, *Gerri Colombe* 2nd)
Faugheen Novice Chase 2 (*Gerri Colombe* 1st, *Inothewayurthinkin* 3rd)

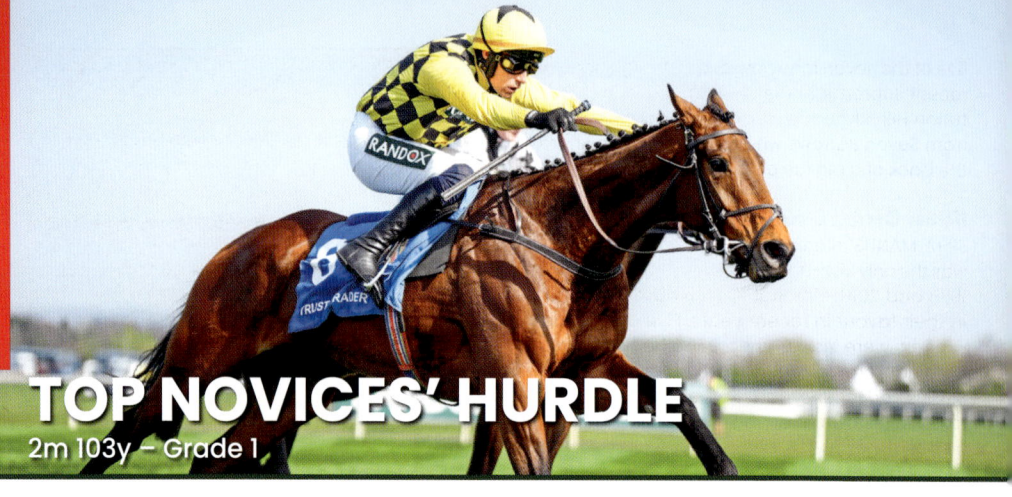

TOP NOVICES' HURDLE
2m 103y – Grade 1

OVERVIEW
ON GENUINELY good ground (like last year), the Top Novices' Hurdle can be a real test of speed and as a result, was once a race in which ex-Flat horses boasted a fine record. More recently, horses graduating from bumpers have had a much stronger record in it, whilst it often offers up an opportunity to gain compensation for a horse who runs well in the Supreme Novices' Hurdle at Cheltenham. Handed Grade 1 status in 2016, the Festival opener is usually the key form line, in a race which Nicky Henderson has won six times in the past 15 renewals. Leading owner JP McManus has won the race seven times, whilst the past two winners were trained by Willie Mullins.

SUPREME NOVICES' HURDLE
WITH 11 of the past 15 winners having contested the **Supreme Novices' Hurdle** at Cheltenham, the Festival curtain-raiser is the obvious place to start when assessing the Top Novices' Hurdle. Taking it back a little further and 16 of the past 26 winners had run in the Supreme, with the past four winners having finished second, fourth, second and fifth, respectively, in the Festival contest. 11 of those 16 winners recorded a top-four finish in the Supreme, with *Salvator Mundi* just missing out last year, he having finished fifth at Cheltenham before reversing form with the third-placed Romeo Coolio.

2024 winner *Mystical Power* finished runner-up in the Supreme on his previous start and during the past 26 renewals, seven Supreme seconds have won the Top Novices' from just eight to have run here, with only Westender failing.

Looking at the meeting as a whole and Supreme seconds boast an incredible record at Aintree. As well as the seven mentioned in the previous paragraph, Binocular went on to win the Anniversary in 2008, and both Best Mate and Spirit Son won the Mersey Novices' Hurdle on the back of finishing second at Cheltenham. Overall, 10 of the past 12 Supreme seconds to have run at Aintree have won.

That is a hugely significant trend/statistic and with an extra week of recovery time this year – meaning that there are 31 days between the two races – it is once again likely to be the key form line.

McMANUS' FANTASTIC RECENT RECORD
RATHER surprisingly, leading owner **JP McManus** wasn't represented last year, having seen his silks carried to success in the previous three renewals, thanks to *Jonbon, Inthepocket* and *Mystical Power*, who he part-owned with Mrs Susannah Ricci. McManus had won the Top Novices' way back in 1999 with *Joe Mac*, before striking with *Straw Bear, Darlan* and *My Tent Or Yours* (all four were Supreme runners-up, incidentally). All seven of his winners had run in the Cheltenham race, with six of them finishing second, and all seven were sent off as outright favourite, with their odds ranging from 4-11 to 3-1.

SIX ON THE BOARD FOR HENDERSON
WITHOUT a runner in either of the past two renewals, trainer **Nicky Henderson** has won the Top Novices' six times since 2010. Again, all six had run in the Supreme (3 of which were McManus-owned) and five of the six finished second or third, with his first winner – *General Miller* in 2010 – unseating his rider at the very first flight. Between 2010 and 2016, Henderson won

five of the seven renewals and although none of his recent Supreme winners – Altior, Shishkin or Constitution Hill – headed to Aintree, respect any runner from Seven Barrows who takes his chance here, on the back of a big run at the Festival.

IRISH CHALLENGE IS ON THE UP

JP McMANUS' aforementioned first winner *Joe Mac* was the only Irish-trained winner of the race between 1978 and 2018, although things have really turned in their favour in recent years. Five of the past six winners were Irish-trained, with the past two both coming from the **Willie Mullins** stable. Previously, Mullins had tended to save his better novice hurdlers for Punchestown, but given the strength in depth that he has in the division these days, he has been forced to split his pack somewhat. Petit Mouchoir, Aramon and El Fabiolo (the former and the latter narrowly denied) all finished second for Mullins in 2016, 2019 and 2022 respectively, before he struck for the first time with *Mystical Power*. Having run two horses in each of the past two renewals, Mullins is once again likely to be represented.

Whilst **Gordon Elliott** and **Henry de Bromhead** have each only won the race once, both trainers are inclined to send strong teams to Aintree and the former was again represented last year, with Romeo Coolio splitting the Mullins-trained pairing, to complete an Irish 1-2-3.

There have only ever been seven Irish-trained winner of the Top Novices' – the other being the Joe Crowley-trained (and ridden) *Irish Rambler* in 1977 – but five wins in the past six renewals suggests that it is no longer the negative which it once was.

MOSCOW FLYER IS A KEY IRISH POINTER

INTERESTINGLY, three of those recent winners – namely *Felix Desjy*, *Mystical Power* and *Salvator Mundi* – all won the Grade 2 **Moscow Flyer Novice Hurdle** en route to the Supreme at Cheltenham. Staged at Punchestown during January, it is a race which Willie Mullins has dominated recently and he again took this year's renewal with Sober.

BUMPER FORM

LAST year's winner had run just once in France over hurdles – chasing home Sir Gino, no less – whilst 11 of the previous 12 winners had graduated from bumpers. *Inthepocket*, who was sent straight over hurdles after winning an Irish Point, is the only exception, but as you can see, a more traditional National Hunt background is now becoming much more favourable.

Four of those recent bunch of winners had contested a Graded bumper the previous spring, with three of them having recorded a top four finish in the Grade 2 **Weatherbys nhstallions.co.uk**

KEY TRENDS

- 16 of the past 26 winners ran in the Supreme Novices' Hurdle (11 of them finished in the first 4)
- Supreme Novices' Hurdle runners-up are 7-8 during the past 26 renewals
- 6 of the past 15 winners were trained by Nicky Henderson
- ✓ 23 of the past 25 winners were aged 5 or 6
- ✓ 22 of the past 28 winners returned at single figure odds
- ✓ 11 of the past 13 winners ran in bumpers (9 of them successful at least once)
- ✓ The past 6 winners had won at least twice over hurdles
- ✓ 5 of the past 6 winners were trained in Ireland
- ✓ 5 of the past 6 winners had won a Grade 2
- ✓ 4 of the past 12 winners contested a Championship Bumper at one of the spring Festivals (3 ran in the Grade 2 at Aintree)
- ✓ 12 ex-Flat winners since 1993 (but none since 2011)
- ✓ 3 of the past 4 winners were rated between 147-149
- ✓ JP McManus has won the race 7 times (including all 3 between 2022-2024) and all 7 returned as outright favourite
- ✗ Only 1 of the past 26 winners was aged 4
- ✗ Only 2 of the past 29 winners were aged 7
- ✗ Treat Kelso's Premier Novices' Hurdle form with caution

NH Flat Race at this fixture. *Lalor* completed the double, whilst *My Tent Or Yours* finished runner-up and *Buveur d'Air* finished fourth. Last year's race was won by Green Splendour.

In general, pay healthy respect to any horse who boasts strong bumper form from last season.

OTHER KEY RACES

AWAY from the Supreme (already covered in some detail) and the Moscow Flyer (covered to a lesser degree), other races to note throughout the season include the **British EBF "National Hunt" Novices' Hurdle** from Cheltenham's December meeting. Staged over 2m1f on the New Course, it is a race which was contested by three Top Novices' winners since 2012, with *Darlan* and *Pingshou* completing the double. *Lalor* finished runner-up in a race which was won this season, in emphatic fashion, by the Nicky Henderson-trained Old Park Star, who was prominent in the ante-post market for the Supreme at the time of going to print.

Although the **William Hill Newbury Handicap Hurdle** (formerly the 'Betfair' and before that the 'Tote Gold Trophy') has a disappointing record when it comes to the Supreme, three relatively recent winners of the Top Novices' Hurdle contested it. *My Tent Or Yours* ran out a facile winner in 2013 before justifying cramped odds here, whilst *Lalor* bypassed Cheltenham after finishing unplaced at Newbury and won this on the back of a short break. *Un Sens A La Vie* (4th) was one of just two novices in this year's race.

Another race to note from Newbury is the **Play Coral "Racing Super-Series" 'National Hunt' Maiden Hurdle** from the track's Coral Gold Cup fixture. Staged on day one of the meeting, it was won previously by both *Buveur d'Air* and *Jonbon*, and Nicky Henderson again took the prize this year, with Act Of Innocence.

One race to be cautious of is the **Premier Novices' Hurdle**, a Grade 2 from Kelso which takes place after publication date. Although My Drogo was able to win that race before landing the Mersey, five fairly recent Premier winners have been beaten in the Top Novices', including Jet To Vegas last year and Personal Ambition in 2024. Admittedly, that pairing were sent off at relatively long odds, but Rouge Vif, Mount Mews (sent off 9-4 joint-favourite) and Glingerburn (sent off 7-4 favourite) were all more prominent in the market, particularly the last named pairing. Tread carefully should the Kelso winner line up once again.

And, although to a lesser degree, the **Dawn Run Mares' Novices' Hurdle** from Cheltenham is another form line to be slightly wary of. Luccia was beaten favourite in the 2023 Dawn Run before finishing third here, whilst 2016 Dawn Run winner Limini was sent off favourite to beat subsequent dual Champion Hurdle winner *Buveur d'Air*.

GRADED SUCCESS

FIVE of the past six winners had recorded a win at Graded level earlier in the season, with *Belfast Banter* the exception. He did finish runner-up in a Grade 2, whilst the other quintet had all won at that level. Aside from the trio who had won the Moscow Flyer (covered in an earlier subsection), *Jonbon* had won the now defunct Kennel Gate and the Rossington Main at Haydock, whilst *Inthepocket* had won a Grade 2 at Naas – the rerouted Navan Novice Hurdle – over 2m4f.

COURSE FORM

AS HIGHLIGHTED last year, *Course Form* doesn't come into play too much in this race – with the exception of the previous year's Grade 2 bumper – but with the **Formby Novices' Hurdle** now taking place on Boxing Day, it might not be too long before it starts to have an impact (possibly here, but certainly at the meeting as a whole). Jango Baie won the inaugural running of the Grade 1, following the switch from Sandown (formerly the 'Tolworth') and returned to run well (unlucky in running) in the 2m4f handicap hurdle on day two, whilst Miami Magic finished runner-up in last season's Formby before being sent off favourite for the Mersey. This season's Formby went the way of Idaho Sun, who stayed on strongly (with hurdles omitted) to beat Mydaddypaddy, who, at the time, sat at the top of the market for the Supreme Novices' Hurdle.

AGE

WE SAW two winning four-year-olds in the space of three years during the 90s, after which *Pierrot Lunaire* struck for that age group in 2008. However, he is now the only four-year-old winner in the past 26 years, whilst only two of the past 29 winners were aged seven. In fairness, we don't see many juveniles, or 'older' runners, so focus on those aged five and six, with that bracket providing 23 or the past 26 winners. *Mystical Power* and *Salvator Mundi* were successful five-year-olds, coming on the back of five straight six-year-old winners.

MARKET FORCES

DESPITE them hailing from the Supreme, both *Romeo Coolio* and *Salvator Mundi* were headed at the top of the market by Tripoli Flyer. Returning at 7-2, last year's winner became the 22nd during the past 28 renewals to score at single figure odds. Three favourites won in successive years between 2022 and 2024, with three favourites in a row also winning between 2012 and 2014 (all Nicky Henderson-trained).

OFFICIAL BHA RATINGS

THERE isn't too much of a pattern here – with lower-rated winners successful in 2017, 2018 and 2020 – although the past four winners were rated in the 140s. Prior to last year, the three previous winners were either top-rated or joint top-rated, with official ratings ranging between 147 and 149. Respect any horse with an *Official BHA Rating* in the high 140s. This is the kind of mark which a horse who has run well in Grade 1 company should expect, whilst any 150+ rated runners should be given even more respect.

WINNING EXPERIENCE

THE past six winners had all won at least twice over hurdles previously, with *Jonbon* the most successful, the 2022 winner having won three races before finishing runner-up to Constitution Hill in the Supreme. Prior to that, *Pingshou* had won just once and *Lalor* was a maiden when successful in 2018.

EX-FLAT WINNERS A THING OF THE PAST?

BETWEEN 1993 and 2011, a dozen ex-Flat horses won the Top Novices' Hurdle, with the track at

Aintree – especially on good, spring ground – always favouring a speed-based performer. The hurdles track at Aintree lends itself to a hold-up performer with a turn of foot, so it wasn't a surprise to see such a fine run of results. The last such winner, however, was *Topolski* some 15 years ago, and that is rather indicative of results in general in top-end novice hurdles. We see fewer high-class Flat horses switch codes these days, with many sold to race abroad.

Despite the lengthy period since an ex-Flat winner of the race, I would still give any such horse careful consideration, given the track bias.

OTHER TRAINERS TO NOTE

GOING back to the start of the century, **Philip Hobbs** – who now trains alongside former assistant, **Johnson White** – won three successive renewals with *Phardante Flyer, Ilico II* and *In Contrast*. Although it is a historical record, it is worth noting, with the stable without a runner since 2010 when Supreme winner *Menorah* finished runner-up (under a penalty, as it was still a Grade 2). With the training duo appearing to have a nice bunch of novice hurdlers this season, it could be that they are represented again this year and given their selective approach, any runner should be noted.

Old Park Star wins at Cheltenham in December

ROLL OF HONOUR

Year	Form	Winner	Age	Weight	OR	SP	Trainer	Runners	Last Race (No. of days)
2025	115	Salvator Mundi	5	11-7	142	7/2	W Mullins (IRE)	9	5th Gr.1 Supreme Nov. Hurdle (24)
2024	112	Mystical Power	5	11-7	148	11/10F	W Mullins (IRE)	6	1st Gr.2 Moscow Flyer Nov. Hurdle (58)
2023	1124	Inthepocket	6	11-7	149	3/1F	H de Bromhead (IRE)	12	4th Gr.1 Supreme Nov. Hurdle (31)
2022	1112	Jonbon	6	11-4	147	EvsF	N Henderson	9	2nd Gr.1 Supreme Nov. Hurdle (24)
2021	125621	Belfast Banter	6	11-4	135	9/1	P Fahey (Ire)	10	1st County Hurdle (21)
2020		NO RACE - meeting cancelled							
2019	75215	Felix Desjy	6	11-4	146	7/2	G Elliott (IRE)	7	5th Gr.1 Supreme Nov. Hurdle (24)
2018	2320	Lalor	6	11-4	133	14/1	K Woolacott	13	13th Gr.3 Betfair Hurdle (62)
2017	4140	Pingshou	7	11-4	133	16/1	C Tizzard	9	10th Gr.1 Supreme Nov. Hurdle (24)
2016	113	Buveur d'Air	5	11-4	152	11/4	N Henderson	11	3rd Gr.1 Supreme Nov. Hurdle (24)

LEADING TEN-YEAR GUIDES

Supreme Novices' Hurdle 7 (Buveur d'Air 3rd, Pingshou 10th, Felix Desjy 5th, Jonbon 2nd, Inthepocket 4th, Mystical Power 2nd, Salvator Mundi 5th)

EBF National Hunt Novices' Hurdle 2 (Pingshou 1st, Lalor 2nd)

*****Weatherbys nhstallions.co.uk NH Flat Race 2** (Buveur d'Air 4th, Lalor 1st)

Newbury "National Hunt" Maiden Hurdle 3 (Buveur d'Air 1st, Pingshou 4th, Jonbon 1st)

Moscow Flyer Novice Hurdle 3 (Felix Desjy 1st, Mystical Power 1st, Salvator Mundi 1st)

* denotes previous season

JCB MELLING CHASE
2m3f 200y (Grade 1) – Mildmay Course

OVERVIEW
PRIOR to the introduction of the Ryanair Chase, the Melling Chase was the sole Grade 1 steeplechase to be staged at any of the spring festivals over an intermediate trip. Similar to the Aintree Hurdle, a blend of speed and stamina is required here and we would (and still do) often seen two-milers stepping up in distance having contested the Queen Mother Champion Chase. A race which boasts a rich history, previous winners include greats such as *Remittance Man*, *Deep Sensation*, *Viking Flagship*, *Moscow Flyer*, *Master Minded* and *Sprinter Sacre*. The latter put up a devastating performance some 13 years ago, whilst his trainer, Nicky Henderson, has won the past two renewals with *Jonbon*. Form at this fixture is a huge positive.

ANOTHER MULTIPLE WINNER
LAST year, *Jonbon* became the seventh two-time winner of the Melling Chase since 1995-1996, following on from *Viking Flagship*, *Direct Route*, *Native Upmanship*, *Moscow Flyer*, *Voy Por Ustedes* and *Fakir d'Oudairies*. A course (and meeting) specialist, *Jonbon* won the Top Novices' Hurdle in 2022 and the Maghull Novices' Chase the following year, so will be bidding for five straight Aintree wins this year, as well as bidding to become the very first three-time winner of the day two feature.

Now 10, he ought to appreciate the extra half-mile come the spring and although he has the *Age* statistic to overcome (more of that shortly), he will likely make a bold bid to create Aintree history.

CHELTENHAM FESTIVAL FORM
16 OF THE past 19 winners had contested either the **Queen Mother Champion Chase** or the Ryanair on their most recent start, highlighting the importance of *Cheltenham Festival Form*. Prior to last year, we did see three successive winners bypassing Cheltenham, but that is rare and normal service was resumed last year, with *Jonbon* having finished runner-up in the Queen Mother. Prior to the introduction of the Ryanair, the Queen Mother stood out as the obvious port of call en route to Aintree, with 12 of the 14 winners between 1992 and 2005 having run in it. During that period, five horses claimed the illustrious double, something which only *Finian's Rainbow* and *Sprinter Sacre* have achieved since. They are actually the only two Queen Mother winners to have run in the Melling during the past 16 renewals, but many a winner of this had run well in the Champion Chase and that crucial extra week means that there are 30 days between the races this year.

Seven winners since 2006 had run in the **Ryanair Chase**, which is the race at Cheltenham staged over a similar (intermediate) distance. *Albertas Run* is the only one able to complete the double thus far and in fact, only one of the past nine winners came out of the Ryanair, so the Champion Chase still stands tallest in terms of Cheltenham form.

PREVIOUS AINTREE FORM
AS ALREADY touched upon in the opening subsection, *Jonbon* has become somewhat of a standing dish at this fixture, winning in each of the past four years. Whilst the multiple winners of this race clearly help the statistic, strong form from this meeting is a huge positive, with 26 of the 34 winners having won or placed in Liverpool previously.

The previous year's renewal of the **Melling Chase** is an obvious piece of form to respect, with *Politologue* and *Min* having finished runner-up the year before their respective successes and, of course, *Fakir d'Oudairies* is another very recent back-to-back winner of the race. *Jonbon* beat Protektorat last year, with the younger Matata back in third.

We will get to the record of second-season chasers in the race shortly, but given that they boast a good strike-rate in it, looking at the previous season's leading novices – and, in particular, the three Grade 1s staged at Aintree – is another positive move.

Between 2012 and 2018, five of the seven winners had run in the **Maghull Novices' Chase** 12 months earlier, with *Finian's Rainbow* and *Sprinter Sacre* both able to complete the double. *Jonbon* also won the Maghull a year before his first win in the Melling.

Both *Albertas Run* and *Don Cossack* were placed in the **Mildmay Novices' Chase** before dropping in distance to win the Melling, the latter 12 months later. Incidentally, the former was another Grand National meeting specialist, having won over hurdles at the fixture before also finishing placed in the Bowl.

And, the newest novices' chase on the Aintree roster is the **Manifesto Novices' Chase**, which is staged over the exact same course-and-distance as this race. Surprisingly, it has produced just the one winner to date, with *Pic d'Orhy* winning the Melling 12 months after pulling-up in the first race of the meeting. I suspect that, in time, it will begin to have more of an impact here, however, and would expect last year's winner Impaire et Passe (also won the Aintree Hurdle in 2024) to be strongly considered for a tilt at the Melling Chase.

SECOND-SEASON CHASERS

FOLLOWING on from the previous subsection, novice chases from the previous season are important form lines, given the positive record of second-season chasers in the Melling. Eight of the past dozen winners were second-season chasers, whilst a further two – namely *God's Own* and *Pic d'Orhy* – were successful in their first season outside of novice company, both having failed to win in their first season over fences (so spent two seasons as novices). Therefore, looking towards last season's leading novices is a good angle of attack, especially if looking away from a previous winner of the race.

Six of the past 13 winners had contested the **Arkle Trophy** at Cheltenham some 13 months earlier, with five of the half-dozen having finished second or third. *Sprinter Sacre* completed the double and although 2024 Arkle winner Gaelic Warrior didn't turn up here, it again worked out well last spring, with him winning the Bowl before following up in the Oaksey Chase at Sandown, whilst his stable-mate Il Etait Temps (3rd

KEY TRENDS

- ⭐ 26 of the 34 winners had won or placed at the Grand National meeting previously
- ⭐ 16 of the past 19 winners ran in the QMCC (9) or Ryanair (7) at Cheltenham
- ⭐ The past 8 winners were French-bred
- ⭐ Both QMCC winners to have run during the past 16 years have won
- ✓ 21 of the 34 winners contested the QMCC on their latest start
- ✓ 20 of the 25 winners this century returned at 5-1 or shorter
- ✓ 18 of the past 19 winners were aged 7-9 (8 of the past 9 winners were aged 7 or 8)
- ✓ 15 of the past 21 winners had won a Grade 1 earlier in the season
- ✓ 11 of the past 22 winners were outright favourite
- ✓ 11 of the past 27 winners were trained in Ireland (from just a 24% representation)
- ✓ 8 of the past 12 winners were second-season chasers
- ✓ 4 of the past 5 winners were owned by JP McManus
- ✓ 3 of the past 4 winners skipped the Cheltenham Festival
- ✓ Willie Mullins-trained runners are 2-7 during the past 11 renewals
- ✓ Joseph O'Brien-trained runners are 2-3
- ✗ Only 1 winning 6yo
- ✗ Only 2 of the past 23 winners had not already won at Grade 1 level
- ✗ Only 2 of the past 18 winners returned at odds greater than 8-1 (only 2 of the past 14 were priced over 11-2)
- ✗ No winner over the age of 9 since 2005

in the 2024 Arkle) won the Celebration Chase on the same card. Last year's Arkle was won by Jango Baie, who beat Only By Night, Majborough and L'Eau du Sud in a thrilling finish. The winner is likely to be aimed at the Bowl, if heading to Aintree after the Gold Cup, but those in behind should be noted.

PROVEN GRADE 1 CLASS

ONLY two of the past 23 winners had failed to win at Grade 1 level prior to winning this race. *Pic d'Orhy* was the latest, although normal service was immediately resumed, with *Jonbon* a multiple Grade 1 winner. Respect those with form at the very top level and in fact, 15 of the past 21 winners had won a Grade 1 earlier that same season, so you shouldn't need to look too far back through the form of a horse.

DAY TWO MELLING CHASE

AGE

TO DATE, there has only ever been one six-year-old winner of the race, that being *Fakir d'Oudairies* some five years ago, although in the past couple of years we have seen more four-year-olds sent chasing (during their four/five-year-old season), with it having dropped off due to the age allowance changes in the novice division. *Master Minded* was beaten in the race as a five-year-old – following his stunning display in the Queen Mother Champion Chase – and was eight by the time he won his Melling, whilst 18 of the past 19 winners were aged between seven and nine. Seven of the past nine winners were aged seven or eight, so again, if looking away from a previous winner, focus on that age bracket.

At the other end of the scale, the last double digit aged winner came 21 years ago. *Native Upmanship* (second win) and *Moscow Flyer* (twice) were successive *'older'* winners, but we haven't seen any since and in fact, there have only been four nine-year-old winners in the past 17 years. *Jonbon* is now 10 and the Age barrier is certainly something to consider with him, should he attempt to land the hat-trick.

FRENCH-BRED WINNERS

THE likes of *Voy Por Ustedes*, *Master Minded* and *Sprinter Sacre* were earlier French-Bred Winners of the race and such horses have really started to dominate of late, *Jonbon* making it eight such winners in succession. Representation continues to rise (with three of last year's four runners being French-bred) but it is still a hugely noticeable statistic and one which mirrors that of the Ryanair Chase from Cheltenham, with the intermediate trip – and having that blend of speed and stamina – often well suited to French-bred horses. The *Second-Season Chasers* angle also ties in with this (again, like the Ryanair), with the younger, up and coming chaser often being more forward if a French-bred. Pay utmost respect to those carrying the (FR) suffix.

OTHER KEY RACES

JONBON kicked off each of the past two seasons by winning Cheltenham's **Shloer Chase**, a race which *Fox Norton* also won at the beginning of the season in which he won this race. The Grade 2 is the first real opportunity for two-milers to start the campaign and it was won this term by *L'Eau du Sud*, who beat *Jonbon* by 15 lengths.

Five of the past 15 winners had contested the **Tingle Creek Chase** at Sandown in early December, *Jonbon* completing the double in each of the past two seasons. The front two from the Shloer turned up here and were both beaten behind the impressive winner, *Il Etait Temps*, who has been campaigned over the minimum trip all season, but showed he stayed this distance in the 2024 Manifesto.

Another important race in the 2m calendar is the **Clarence House Chase** at Ascot (staged over 2m1f to be precise). Whilst it is just about the key indicator towards success in the Queen Mother, it is also a significant pointer here, too, with *Jonbon* finishing second in it two years ago and winning it last year. He again won the race this year.

At the same track, the **Ascot Chase** takes place over 2m5f and is staged shortly after the Guide goes to print. Prior to the double of *Jonbon*, the previous two winners ran in that Grade 1 on their latest start, with the pair avoiding Cheltenham and heading straight to Aintree as *'fresh'* horses. Looking back a little further and *Monet's Garden, Voy Por Ustedes* and *Albertas Run* all finished first or second in the Ascot Chase (between 2007 and 2010) en route to running in the Ryanair at Cheltenham.

THE IRISH CHALLENGE

THIS is a race which, historically, the Irish have done well in, despite not having an overly strong hand in it, numerically speaking. 11 of the past 27 winners were trained in Ireland, but all from just 24% representation, with El Fabiolo the only Irish-trained runner among last year's four-strong field. The winning ratio of Irish-trained horses clearly outperforms their representation.

Willie Mullins has won the Melling twice in the past 11 renewals – with *Boston Bob* and *Min* successful – and he has only saddled seven horses during that period. *Min* finished runner-up the year before gaining his victory and with a plethora of options available to him, Mullins is sure to be represented once again. Given that he only holds an entry in the Ryanair at Cheltenham, perhaps Fact To File will be considered for the race this year, along with the likes of Il Etait Temps, Impaire et Passe and/or Majborough.

Fakir d'Oudairies provided **Joseph O'Brien** with back-to-back wins in the Melling and he has only ever had three runners in the race (all the same horse). And, although **Gordon Elliott** has won the race just once, he has had another couple hit the frame and we know that he (usually) likes to target Aintree with a strong team of horses.

KEY IRISH RACES

BOTH *Don Cossack* and *Min* won the **John Durkan Memorial Chase** at Punchestown, in the early part of their Melling-winning seasons. Now staged slightly earlier in the calendar – in order for horses to have the option of running in the Grade 1 and then again over the Festive period – it was won this season by Gaelic Warrior, who got the better of Fact To File.

And, five Irish-trained winners since 2002 had contested the **Horse & Jockey Hotel Chase** at Thurles, a race formerly known as the **Kinloch Brae**. *Native Upmanship* (twice) and *Don Cossack* were successful in the Grade 2, which is staged over a similar distance and was won this year by Appreciate It.

MARKET FORCES

FIVE of the past six winners were sent off as outright favourite and these include *Jonbon* (twice) who returned at 11-10 and 4-6, respectively. 11 of the past 22 winners were outright favourite, so the market leader boasts a 50% strike rate since 2003, with *Sprinter Sacre* the shortest-priced winner, successful at 1-3 in 2013. Generally, the other winners could have been found just behind the market leader, with only two of the past 18 winners returning at odds greater than 8-1. Therefore, don't expect to see a 'shock' result here, it rarely happens. In fact, only two of the past 14 winners had an S.P. greater than 11-2, with 20 of the 25 winners this century returning at 5-1 or shorter.

FOUR IN FIVE FOR JP

THANKS to the doubles of both *Fakir d'Oudairies* and *Jonbon*, leading owner **JP McManus** has now won four of the past five renewals. Fota Island finished runner-up in 2006 for McManus, whose form figures in the past five renewals reads 11211. McManus will have plenty of options to keep this impressive recent run going, with *Jonbon* and Fact To File likely to be seriously considered for the race, whilst Majborough is another possible. Given that team McManus now seem set on an intermediate trip for Fact To File (not entered in the QMCC or Gold Cup at Cheltenham), last year's Ryanair winner might well head to Aintree 29 days after he bids to defend his Festival crown.

TRAINERS TO NOTE

FOLLOWING the back-to-back victories of *Jonbon*, **Nicky Henderson** has usurped Paul Nicholls in becoming the most successful trainer in the history of the Melling Chase. The Lambourn veteran now stands alone on five wins in the race, with his earlier victories coming courtesy of *Remittance Man*, *Finian's Rainbow* and *Sprinter Sacre*.

Paul Nicholls has won the race four times, starting with *Fadalko* in 2001. *Master Minded*, *Politologue* and *Pic d'Orhy* have all since won for the Ditcheat maestro, with all four French-bred.

ROLL OF HONOUR

Year	Form	Winner	Age	Weight	OR	SP	Trainer	Runners	Last Race (No. of days)
2025	1112	Jonbon	9	11-10	169	4/6F	N Henderson	4	2nd Gr.1 Champion Chase (23)
2024	112	Jonbon	8	11-10	170	11/10F	N Henderson	7	2nd Gr.1 Clarence House Chase (76)
2023	1112	Pic d'Orhy	8	11-10	162	4/1	P Nicholls	7	2nd Gr.1 Ascot Chase (55)
2022	1421	Fakir d'Oudairies	7	11-7	164	10/11F	J O'Brien (IRE)	10	1st Gr.1 Ascot Chase (48)
2021	2P22	Fakir d'Oudairies	6	11-7	162	2/1F	J O'Brien (IRE)	7	2nd Gr.1 Ryanair Chase (22)
2020	NO RACE - meeting cancelled								
2019	115	Min	8	11-7	167	2/1F	W Mullins (IRE)	6	5th Gr.1 Champion Chase (23)
2018	11124	Politologue	7	11-7	161	11/1	P Nicholls	6	4th Gr.1 Champion Chase (30)
2017	1122	Fox Norton	7	11-7	166	4/1	C Tizzard	9	2nd Gr.1 Champion Chase (23)
2016	324	God's Own	8	11-10	162	10/1	T George	6	4th Gr.1 Champion Chase (23)

LEADING TEN-YEAR GUIDES

Queen Mother Champion Chase 5 (*God's Own* 4th, *Fox Norton* 2nd, *Politologue* 4th, *Min* 5th, *Jonbon* 2nd)
***Maghull Novices' Chase 4** (*God's Own* 2nd, *Fox Norton* 3rd, *Politiologue* fell, *Jonbon* 1st)
***Arkle Trophy 4** (*God's Own* 2nd, *Fox Norton* 3rd, *Fakir d'Oudairies* 2nd, *Jonbon* 2nd)
Ryanair Chase 3 (*Boston Bob* 6th, *Don Cossack* 3rd, *Fakir d'Oudairies* 2nd)
Haldon Gold Cup 2 (*God's Own* 3rd, *Politiologue* 1st)
John Durkan Chase 2 (*Min* 1st, *Fakir d'Oudairies* 4th)
Game Spirit Chase 2 (*Fox Norton* 2nd, *Politologue* 2nd)
***Melling Chase 3** (*Politologue* 2nd, *Fakir d'Oudairies* 1st, *Jonbon* 1st)
Ascot Chase 2 (*Fakir d'Oudairies* 1st, *Pic d'Orhy* 2nd)
Tingle Creek Chase 2 (*Politogue* 1st, *Jonbon* 1st)
Shloer Chase 3 (*Fox Norton* 1st, *Jonbon* 1st & 1st)
Clarence House Chase 2 (*Jonbon* 2nd & 1st)

* denotes previous season

ODDSCHECKER SEFTON NOVICES' HURDLE
3m 149y (Grade 1)

OVERVIEW

THE longest distance of the novices' hurdle staged at the fixture, the Sefton is one race in which *'fresh'* horses – those who bypassed Cheltenham – tend to have an equally strong chance of gaining Grade 1 honours, as those who contested the Albert Bartlett. In a race which can become a real test for a young horse, second-season novices (and those with experience) are certainly worth noting and the list of previous winners includes the likes of *Iris's Gift, Black Jack Ketchum, Thistlecrack* and *Champ*, whilst *Dancing City* provided the Irish with a rare win in the race in 2024.

THE 'FRESH' ANGLE

WHEN assessing any race at Aintree's Grand National fixture, it is a balancing act between focusing on Cheltenham Festival form and looking towards those who bypassed Cheltenham with Aintree in mind. The Sefton is one race in which 'fresh' horses have a good record, with *Julius des Pictons* arriving in Liverpool on the back of a 54-day break and becoming the 15th winner of the 25 this century to have avoided the Festival. That is quite a strong statistic and the fact that the race takes place over an extended 3m trip is a likely contributor; as stated in the *Overview*, this can be a test for young novices.

Therefore, at least give an equal amount of respect to any such runners, as to those who ran at Cheltenham, especially if a trainer nominated this race as a specific target earlier in the season.

CHELTENHAM FESTIVAL FORM

THOSE who have run at the Festival will invariably have the strongest form and given the similarity in distance between races, the key form line is the **Albert Bartlett Novices' Hurdle**, with seven of the past 19 winners of the Sefton having contested the race on Gold Cup day. Interestingly, however, only two of the eight Albert Bartlett winners to have run here have managed to complete the double – those being *Black Jack Ketchum* and *At Fishers Cross* – so tread carefully should the winner line up, rather like with the Mildmay Novices' Chase earlier in the day. Again, the staying test at Cheltenham probably takes a lot out of a young novice and replicating that form can prove problematic.

Since the introduction of the Albert Bartlett, only one winner of the Sefton arrived at Aintree having run in the **Baring Bingham Novices' Hurdle**, that being *Champ*, who finished runner-up in the 2m5f contest. Going back to the 90s and four winners had contested the race we currently refer to as the Turners Novices' Hurdle, although nowadays, a horse who has run well in that race will likely contest the Mersey.

One piece of form to be slightly cautious about from the Cheltenham Festival is the **Martin Pipe Conditional Jockeys' Handicap Hurdle**. A race in which novices boast a fine record, we have seen three horses beaten here following a big run in the Martin Pipe, starting with *Dallas des Pictons*, who was sent off at just 4-1 in 2019, having finished runner-up in the final race of the Festival. Since then, Festival winners *Banbridge* and *Iroko* both failed to take the step up in class in their stride, before both later developing into high-class chasers. Again, it is likely that a tough race at Cheltenham leaves more of a mark than people (and the market) might imagine.

OTHER KEY RACES

FIVE winners this century contested the Grade 2 **Prestige Novices' Hurdle** at Haydock in February, a race which was set to take place just days after the Guide went to print. *Garruth* and *Wayward Prince* were both beaten at Haydock then headed straight to Aintree, whilst *Chief Dan George* and *The Worlds End* won on Merseyside before running in the Albert Bartlett, the latter a faller when still in contention. And, back in 2003, *Iris's Gift* also won the Haydock race before running in the Stayers' Hurdle (there was no Albert Bartlett back then), then reverting to novice company to win the Sefton. Take note of the Haydock result.

Both *At Fishers Cross* and *Santini* had won the Grade 2 **Classic Novices' Hurdle** at Cheltenham on trials day. Although that race takes place over 2m4½f, it is often more of a stamina test on the New Course and a result, can have an impact here. *Thistlecrack* also ran in that race before winning the Sefton and the Tizzard stable managed to capture the prize this year, with Kripticjim.

And, going back a little further, both *Ogee* and *Beat That* were beaten in Sandown's **Winter Novices' Hurdle**. Another Grade 2 contest, it was won earlier this season by No Drama This End, who beat The Blue Room, before going on to win the Challow at Newbury.

BRITISH-BRED SUCCESS

GIVEN that representation is usually quite low (three runners last year and just one in 2024, for example), six winners from the past 21 is a fine return for British-bred runners in the Sefton, with Crest Of Fortune hitting the frame at 25-1 last year. Often such horses improve for facing a stiff test of stamina and that certainly seems to be the case here. *Santini*, the last British-bred winner of the race, was the epitome of a stamina-laden horse.

NATIONAL HUNT BACKGROUND

THE past 13 winners had a traditional *National Hunt Background*, in that they had all run in either a Point-to-Point and/or a bumper at the beginning of their careers, with 12 of the 13 successful in either/both discipline. Last year's winner was a French bumper winner (AQPS race), whereas 2024 winner *Dancing City* was an archetypal Sefton winner, in that he had won an Irish Point and won once from three starts in bumpers.

Six of the past nine winners were ex-Pointers, with *Santini* and *Ahoy Senor* British Points winners, so

KEY TRENDS

- ⭐ 21 of the 25 winners this century had won at least twice over hurdles previously
- ⭐ 19 of the past 20 winners were aged 6 or 7 (9 of the past 12 winners were aged 6)
- ⭐ The past 13 winners had run in a P2P and/or a bumper (12 were successful)
- ✓ 15 of the 25 winners this century skipped the Cheltenham Festival
- ✓ 7 of the past 10 winners were stepping up in distance
- ✓ 7 of the past 24 winners were second-season novices
- ✓ 7 of the past 19 winners had run in the Albert Bartlett Novices' Hurdle at Cheltenham
- ✓ 6 of the past 9 winners were ex-Pointers (5 had won a P2P)
- ✓ 3 of the past 11 winners were trained by Nicky Henderson
- ✓ 3 Irish-trained winners bypassed the Cheltenham Festival
- ✓ 2 of the past 5 winners were trained by Lucinda Russell
- ✓ Respect Jonjo & A J O'Neill-trained runners
- ✗ Only 1 winner this century had run in the Baring Bingham (Turners) Novices' Hurdle at Cheltenham
- ✗ Only 1 of the past 20 winners was aged 5 (5yo's are 0-27 during the past 13 renewals)
- ✗ Only 2 of the past 11 winners had won beyond 2m7f over hurdles previously
- ✗ Only 2 Albert Bartlett winners have won (from 8 to have attempted the double)
- ✗ Only 3 of the past 35 winners were Irish-trained (and only 4 winners in total)
- ✗ Irish-trained horses are 1-31 during the past 19 renewals
- ✗ Paul Nicholls-trained horses are 0-15 since 2006
- ✗ Gigginstown House Stud-owned runners are 0-14 since 2010
- ✗ Gordon Elliott-trained runners are 0-6 since 2019 (5 sent off at single figures)
- ✗ Be cautious of Martin Pipe form

pay healthy respect to form between the flags on either side of the Irish Sea.

EXPERIENCE

RATHER like the Albert Bartlett, there was a time when plenty of hurdling experience was a positive and it certainly helped *Julius des Pictons* last year, Jamie Snowden's winner having had six starts in total, including a couple of runs in France (also boasted plenty of bumper form from France). We did have a spell between 2008 and 2018 when five winners had run either two or three times before winning the Sefton, then *Ahoy Senor* defied plenty of trends to win this on just his second ever start under Rules. His victory aside, *Experience* seems to be coming back into play here with the other five winners since 2019 having raced at least four times over hurdles, with three of them having run six times previously.

Interestingly, *Julius des Pictons* became the seventh second-season novice to win this race in the past 24 renewals, something which you wouldn't expect to see too often in a Grade 1 contest. Pay attention to any such runner(s) this year.

WINNING FORM

21 OF THE past 25 winners had already won at least twice over hurdles previously, so as well as *Experience* being important, so, too, is *Winning Form*. The aforementioned *Ahoy Senor* is the only winner among the past 10 to be successful on the back of just one win, so look towards those who have shown that they know how to get their heads in front, more than once.

AGE

WE HAVE seen a quartet of five-year-olds win the Sefton overall, but none since *Saint Are* in 2011 and he is the only winner for that age group in the past 20 renewals. During the past 13 renewals, the record of five-year-olds now stands at 0-27, following on from both Moon Rocket and Holloway Queen being pulled-up last year. A real test over 3m+ is often too much for such a young horse, so tread carefully with any such runners. The other 19 winners during this latest period were all aged six (13) or seven (6), with no winner over the age of seven since *Unsinkable Boxer* back in 1998. We did see three *'older'* winners in the space of four years around that time, but we really ought to focus our attention on those aged six and seven, with six-year-olds beginning to take command (successful in nine of the past 12 renewals).

PROVEN STAMINA

WHILST having proven your stamina over this sort of trip is never a negative, plenty of recent winners of this race had been winning over intermediate trips before stepping up in distance. In fact, seven of the past 10 winners were stepping up in distance – with *Thistlecrack* having run in the 2m Imperial Cup the time before – so don't be quick to overlook those who have shown good form over shorter.

Again, although this takes some getting, the nature of Aintree's track – especially over hurdles – means a horse requires an element of natural pace to hold their position and travel within their comfort zone throughout.

Only two of the past 11 winners had previously won over a distance (under Rules) beyond 2m7f.

MARKET FORCES

THE first two winners this century returned at odds of 12-1 and 16-1 respectively, and that is kind of indicative of the Sefton, which is a race in which we do see *'bigger priced'* winners succeed. Indeed, last year's winner scored at 14-1, with *Ahoy Senor* (66s) and *Apple Away* (16s) another couple of recent examples. Certainly, don't let a big price put you off here (quite uncommon for a Grade 1 novice hurdle), with *Santini* and *Champ* the only successful favourites in the past 11 renewals. There have actually only been five winning favourites this century and there is no pattern at all, with a wide range of winners in terms of market position.

THE IRISH CHALLENGE

WITH Punchestown staging a similar contest just four weeks later, *The Irish Challenge* is often quite thin on the ground in the Sefton and as a result, *Dancing City* is the only Irish-trained winner since *Asian Maze* back in 2005. The 2024 winner had finished third in the Albert Bartlett, whilst the three previous Irish-trained winners of the race had all bypassed the Cheltenham Festival. Overall, the record of Irish-trained runners during the past 19 years stands at a disappointing 1-31.

Dancing City was the first winner for **Willie Mullins**, who had gone close in 2016 when Bellshill was narrowly denied. He saddled Argento Boy last year, who like *Dancing City*, went on to contest the Grade 1 Channor Real Estate Group Novice Hurdle (a race he won with Albert Bartlett winner, Jasmin de Vaux), so it could be that he continues to target the Sefton moving forward.

As highlighted previously, **Gigginstown House Stud** – who seem to like to target Aintree, in general – don't have a good record here and Jacob's Ladder being pulled-up took their record to 0-14 since 2010. Eight of their 14 runners were sent off at single figures, including Weapon's Amnesty, who was unable to back-up his Albert Bartlett win in 2009. Clearly, this is a race which the owners like to target, but they have yet to find the winning formula.

Jacob's Ladder was trained by **Gordon Elliott**, who ran two in the race last year. Responsible for several of the Gigginstown-owned runners in recent years, his record stands at 0-6 since 2019, with several well-fancied runners among his half-dozen. Dallas des Pictons (4-1), Absolute Notions (3-1F), Croke Park (5-1), Familiar Dreams (6-1) and Jacob's Ladder (15-2) were all sent off at single figures.

MCMANUS ON THE MARK

ALTHOUGH he is another owner who has seen an Albert Bartlett winner beaten here – that being Wichita Lineman in 2007 – his At Fishers Cross completed the double six years later and **JP McManus** won a second Sefton with Champ in 2019. Since then, both Tower Bridge and Iroko have hit the frame in McManus' green and gold silks. He has been without a runner in each of the past two renewals.

BRITISH TRAINERS TO NOTE

THIS is yet another Grade 1 contest throughout the week in which **Nicky Henderson** boasts a fine record. Henderson won the very first running of the race, with Rustle back in 1988, and has added three more Seftons to his C.V. in recent years, thanks to Beat That, Santini and Champ. Califet en Vol was unable to enhance Henderson's record in the race in 2025, but give plenty of respect of any horse who represents the Seven Barrows team this year.

Nigel Twiston-Davies – now training alongside son, **Willy**, of course – has won the race three times since 1999, although his latest victory came 10 years ago with Ballyoptic. Interestingly, his two latest winners were unbeaten over hurdles (2-2) and had been given 'light' campaigns, not having contested a Graded race.

Jonjo O'Neill – another Cheltenham-based trainer who now trains alongside his son, **A J** – won the Sefton with the well-fancied pairing of Iris's Gift and Black Jack Ketchum, before seeing his Wichita Lineman beaten by Chief Dan George in 2007. The Jackdaws Castle team don't run horses in Grade 1s for the sake of it and if one is deemed good enough to represent them here, take note, although again, their record is much more historical.

More recently, **Lucinda Russell** – yet another trainer to now hold a joint-licence, hers alongside **Michael Scudamore** – won the race in both 2021 with Ahoy Senor and again two years later, with the mare Apple Away. Subsequent Grand National winner One For Arthur represented Russell in this race as a youngster, whilst Haute Estime hit the frame at 100-1 in 2022, so it is clearly a race that the stable likes to target. Slightly surprisingly, Albert Bartlett third Derryhassen Paddy didn't run in it last year, as the yard was represented by 40-1 shot King Of Answers, who was pulled-up before three out. Given that Russell also won the Albert Bartlett with the ill-fated Brindisi Breeze and the Listed 3m novice hurdle at Perth with Giovinco in 2023, she clearly knows what is required in this division and with the stable focused on buying embryonic staying chasers, they appear to have the right type of horse to target these races.

This is a race which **Paul Nicholls** has yet to win and since 2006, his record stands at 0-15. Those 15 'losers' include nine horses who were sent off at single figure odds, with Bravemansgame (13-8F) beaten in 2021 and Stay Away Fay (4-1) is another Albert Bartlett winner who failed to follow up in 2023. This would be something to bear in mind, should No Drama This End head to Aintree after Cheltenham. If he does travel to Liverpool, he will likely have the option of running in the Mersey as well as this race.

ROLL OF HONOUR

Year	Form	Winner	Age	Weight	OR	SP	Trainer	Runners	Last Race (No. of days)
2025	2113	Julius des Pictons	6	11-8	127	14/1	J Snowden	13	3rd Listed Exeter Nov. Hdle (54)
2024	5113	Dancing City	7	11-8	150	4/1	W Mullins (IRE)	8	3rd Gr.1 Albert Bartlett Nov. Hdle (28)
2023	163211	Apple Away	6	11-1	131	16/1	L Russell	15	1st Listed Mares' Nov. Hdle (41)
2022	12241	Gelino Bello	6	11-7	138	7/2	P Nicholls	14	1st Newbury Nov. Hdle (35)
2021	21	Ahoy Senor	6	11-4	-	66/1	L Russell	12	1st Ayr Maiden Hdle (39)
2020	NO RACE - meeting cancelled								
2019	11112	Champ	7	11-4	152	9/4F	N Henderson	12	2nd Gr.1 Baring Bingham Nov. Hdle (23)
2018	113	Santini	6	11-4	150	6/4F	N Henderson	13	3rd Gr.1 Albert Bartlett Nov. Hdle (28)
2017	3111F	The Worlds End	6	11-4	149	3/1	T George	11	fell Gr.1 Albert Bartlett Nov. Hdle (21)
2016	511	Ballyoptic	6	11-4	138	9/1	N Twiston-Davies	15	1st Uttoxeter Nov. Hdle (20)

LEADING TEN-YEAR GUIDES

Albert Bartlett Novices' Hurdle 3 (The Worlds End fell, Santini 3rd, Dancing City 3rd)

TURNERS MERSEY NOVICES' HURDLE
2m4f (Grade 1)

OVERVIEW
HANDED Grade 1 status in 2014, the Mersey Novices' Hurdle was won in 2000 by subsequent three-time Gold Cup winner *Best Mate* and for a second year holds the same sponsorship (Turners) as the Baring Bingham at Cheltenham, a race which is often the best form guide to this. Gordon Elliott has now won the past four renewals and earlier winners of the race include *The West Awake, Morley Street, Cyborgo, Barton, Tidal Bay, Peddlers Cross, Spirit Son, Simonsig, Nichols Canyon* and *Yorkhill*. Rather like in the Baring Bingham, horses stepping up in distance do well here, so pay healthy respect to strong (Graded) form over shorter.

FOUR ON THE SPIN FOR ELLIOTT
FOLLOWING on from the victories of *Three Stripe Life, Irish Point* and *Brighterdaysahead*, **Gordon Elliott** made it four successive victories in the Mersey last year when *Honesty Policy* took the rise in class in his stride. Chosen Mate finished only fifth for Elliott in 2019 (his only runner between 2015-2021) before the trainer took control from 2022 onwards. Responsible for the one-two in 2024, *Honesty Policy* stayed on strongly to complete the Elliott four-timer last year and unlike his previous winners of the race, the five-year-old didn't have any earlier Graded race experience.

THE 'FRESH' ANGLE
WHILST Cheltenham Festival form can be significant (see next subsection), this is another novices' hurdle in which we have seen recent winners arriving *'fresh'* to Aintree, or on the back of a more low-key approach. Indeed, last year's winner was under the radar somewhat, with *Honesty Policy* only winning a maiden hurdle in February and running in an ordinary novice at Leopardstown during March. Five of the past eight winners bypassed Cheltenham and arrived at Aintree from elsewhere, so pay equal respect to any such runner.

Of those five recent winners, *Finian's Oscar* was forced to miss the Festival through a minor injury, whereas the other quartet skipped Cheltenham by design. Prior to *Finian's Oscar* winning in 2017, the last winner before that to avoid Cheltenham was *Bouggler* back in 2009, successful on the back of just one run over hurdles. Certainly, don't be quick to rule out those who didn't run at the Festival.

CHELTENHAM FESTIVAL FORM
WHILST *The 'Fresh' Angle* has become more significant in recent years, 16 of the past 26 winners did run at the Cheltenham Festival, where the **Baring Bingham Novices' Hurdle** – run in recent years, like this race, under the sponsorship banner of **Turners** – is the key form line. Given the similarity in distance of the two races, it shouldn't be too surprising and two fairly recent winners – namely *Black Op* and *Three Stripe Life* – had finished runner-up in that race the time before. Since 1999 when *Barton* completed the double, only four Baring Bingham winners have run in the Mersey and all four – the others being *Peddlers Cross, Simonsig* and *Yorkhill* – were all successful.

2024 winner *Brighterdaysahead* had finished runner-up to subsequent Champion Hurdle winner Golden Ace in the Dawn Run Mares' Novices' Hurdle, whilst *Lac Fontana* had won the County Hurdle on his previous start. However, aside from the Baring Bingham, the **Supreme Novices' Hurdle** is the other key form line from Cheltenham, with four winners between 2000 and 2011 stepping up in distance from the Festival opener. As touched upon in the preview to day two's Top Novices' Hurdle, runners-up from the Supreme boast a fine record at Aintree and both *Best Mate* and *Spirit Son* went one place better than their second at Cheltenham when winning this race. More recently, Ballyadam was unable to add to this tally, but pay healthy respect to any horse who runs well in either of the Grade 1s at the Festival. Of those 16 recent winners, 13 had recorded a top-four finish at Cheltenham.

STEPPING UP IN DISTANCE

GIVEN that the Supreme is staged over the minimum trip, those four winners were obviously stepping up in distance and feature among the 12 winners during the past 25 who were stepping up in trip, having contested a race over 2m-2m2f on their latest start. Five of the past eight winners fall into this category – including the past three – and again, Aintree suits a horse with natural pace, so form over shorter trips is a definite positive.

TACTICS

AS HAS already been touched upon in earlier races, horses who like to be held-up off the pace are often well suited to the hurdles track at Aintree, particularly if they have a turn of foot (i.e. form over shorter) which can be used on spring ground. *Reserve Tank* showed that a front-runner can win this race and although Regent's Stroll made a bold fist of it from the front last year, such runners are often *'sitting ducks'* for those who like to pounce late and a hold-up ride is usually more advantageous on this track. A smooth-travelling horse is what we are looking for.

GRADED NOVICE HURDLE FORM

LAST year's winner lacked any Graded form but eight of the previous nine winners had finished first or second in a Grade 1 or Grade 2 earlier in the season, with four of the eight having won at least once at either level. Recent winners with Graded form in the book include *My Drogo* (won the now defunct Kennel Gate and the Premier Kelso Novices' Hurdle, over 2m and 2m2f respectively), *Irish Point* (Grade 3 winner over the minimum trip and placed in the Royal Bond) and *Brighterdaysahead*, who had won in Listed and Grade 3 company before finishing runner-up at Cheltenham. Pay healthy respect to those with strong form in the book, especially over slightly shorter distances.

OTHER KEY RACES

AWAY from the Cheltenham Festival and both *Yorkhill* and *Finian's Oscar* won the Grade 1 Tolworth Novices' Hurdle over 2m at Sandown, a race which

KEY TRENDS

- Baring Bingham winners are 4-4 since 1999
- 11 of the past 15 winners were top- or second top-rated according to official BHA Ratings
- Horses rated 150+ are 5-9 since 2011
- Gordon Elliott has won the past 4 renewals
- 26 of the past 29 winners were aged 5 or 6
- 21 of the past 28 winners were 1st or 2nd in the betting
- 16 of the past 26 winners had run at the Cheltenham Festival (13 of them had recorded a top-4 finish)
- 14 of the past 16 winners finished 1st or 2nd last time out (this includes the past 9 winners)
- 12 of the 25 winners this century were stepping up in distance
- 11 of the past 15 winners had run 3 or 4 times over hurdles previously
- 9 of the past 15 winners had won 3 times over hurdles previously
- 8 of the past 10 winners had finished 1st or 2nd in a Grade 1 or Grade 2 novice hurdle earlier in the season (4 had won at least one)
- 6 of the past 9 winners had won a bumper and/or a P2P
- 5 of the past 16 winners were unbeaten over hurdles
- 5 of the past 8 winners bypassed Cheltenham (all 5 were last-time-out winners)
- Respect Graded form over 2m-2m2f
- Only 1 of the past 29 winners was aged 4
- Only 2 of the past 36 winners were aged 7
- Only 2 of the past 15 winners returned at odds greater than 5-1
- Only 2 of the past 11 winners had failed to win more than once over hurdles previously
- Only 4 of the past 15 winners were rated below 148
- Front-runners tend to struggle

is now, of course, staged at Aintree and under the new name of the **Formby Novices' Hurdle**. It was won this season by Idaho Sun, who finished a staying-on sixth in last year's Champion Bumper, and shapes like a longer trip will suit in time.

As touched upon in the previous subsection, *Irish Point* finished runner-up in the early-season **Royal Bond Novice Hurdle** at Fairyhouse, a race which was also won by *Nichols Canyon*. Also staged over 2m, the former Grade 1 was downgraded recently and this season's race went the way of Koktail Brut, who then disappointed behind stable-mate (both trained by Gordon Elliott, incidentally) Skylight Hustle at Leopardstown over Christmas.

Nichols Canyon also won the **Tattersalls Ireland Novice Hurdle** – registered as the **Brave Inca Novice Hurdle** – which was formerly staged over 2m2f and is now run over the minimum trip at the Dublin Racing Festival. This is often the strongest novice hurdle staged in Ireland and *Three Stripe Life* finished runner-up in it before filling the same position in the Baring Bingham at Cheltenham. This year's race went the way of Talk The Talk.

Finally, the 2m1f Listed race at Exeter – which was won by *Finian's Oscar* on his latest start and by *Spirit Son* prior to his second in the Supreme – took place shortly before the Guide went to print and was last year won by Fingle Bridge. Although he was a non-runner in this race, Regent's Stroll (2nd) went close and Sefton winner Julius des Pictons finished third, so it was a race which worked out well at Aintree. Set to be run this year as the **CopyBet Novices' Hurdle**, the race was lost with the track waterlogged.

MARKET FORCES

21 OF THE past 28 winners hailed from the top two in the betting, with that run started by *Sanmartino*, who justified odds of 8-11 back in 1997 and started a run of four successive winning favourites. More recently, nine of the past 15 winners were outright favourite, so again, this is a Grade 1 contest in which we don't really expect to see *'shock'* results. Indeed, only two of the past 15 winners returned at odds greater than 5-1 and although he lacked that Graded experience, *Honesty Policy* was sent off at just 5-1.

OFFICIAL BHA RATINGS

IN-KEEPING with the final comment of the previous subsection, and earlier subsections highlighting the importance of *Graded Novice Hurdle Form*, the higher-rated horses tend to come to the fore, with proven form usually outshining potential. It wasn't the case last year and *Honesty Policy* became just the fourth winner of those past 15 to have been rated below 148, with 11 of the previous 14 winners hailing from the top two on *Official BHA Ratings*. Since 2011, only nine horses rated 150+ have contested the Mersey and five have been successful, so focus on those rated high 140s and above, and pay particular attention to any horse who has reached a mark of 150 already.

HURDLING EXPERIENCE

GOING back to 2001, *Montalcino* won the Mersey on just his second start over hurdles, something which the aforementioned *Bouggler* managed to repeat some eight years later. Since then, however, the past 15 winners had all run a minimum of three times over hurdles, with 10 of those 15 having run three or four times previously. This is an adequate amount to expect given that we are now into April and only once in the past nine renewals has the winner had more experience, that being *Irish Point*, who had amassed five runs earlier in the season.

WINNING FORM

ONLY two of the past 11 winners had failed to win more than once over hurdles, whilst nine of the past 15 winners had recorded three wins over hurdles previously. Therefore, look towards those who know what it takes to win (more than once), whilst – as per previous subsections – pay healthy respect to placed form at Grade 1 level, particularly from the Cheltenham Festival.

THE UNBEATEN HURDLER

SINCE 1999, we have seen seven unbeaten hurdlers win this race, although after the back-to-back successes of *Yorkhill* and *Finian's Oscar*, only *My Drogo* has managed to add his name to this tally in the past seven renewals. Four of those seven were the quartet of Baring Bingham winners to have doubled up at Aintree, so pay particular attention should an unbeaten winner of that Festival contest line up here. The recent run of results, however, suggests that we shouldn't be put off by a defeat.

CURRENT FORM

THE past nine winners finished either first (6) or second (3) on their most recent outing and if we take that back to the past 16 renewals, 14 winners recorded a top-two finish last time out, with *Nichols Canyon* having finished third in the Baring Bingham. Therefore, only *Ubak* has won during this period on the back of a seemingly *'disappointing'* run (finished unplaced in the Baring Bingham). Look at those in form and if looking at horses who avoided the Festival, last time out winners are preferred.

NATIONAL HUNT BACKGROUND

RATHER like with the Supreme at Cheltenham and indeed the previous day's Top Novices' Hurdle, there was a time when ex-Flat horses had a good record here, with *Sanmartino, Montalcino, Elusive Dream* and *Bouggler* all successfully changing codes between 1997 and 2009. However, during the past 15 renewals, *Nichols Canyon* is the only ex-Flat horse to win the Mersey, with things shifting towards those with a more traditional *National Hunt Background*.

Six of the past nine winners had been successful in either – or both in the case of *Yorkhill* – a Point-to-Point or bumper, with last year's winner just missing out, as he had finished second on his sole start between the flags. *Irish Point* was a Grade 1 bumper winner in France, whilst *Three Stripe Life* and *Brighterdaysahead* were also bumper winners for Gordon Elliott.

AGE

JUVENILES running in the race are a rarity these days – although this season's leading novice chaser Lulamba was declared to run last year, until being pulled out on the day due to unsuitable ground – and although we saw three successive four-year-old winners between 1993 and 1995, the only winner of that age group during the past 29 renewals was *Bouggler*.

At the other end of the scale, *Elusive Dream* and *Black Op* are the only seven-year-old winners during the past 36 renewals, with Horaces Pearl (sent off at just 4-1 last year) the latest to try and fail. Focus on those aged five and six – who, admittedly, provide most amount of runners – with that age bracket providing 26 of the past 29 winners. Since 2010 alone, 14 of the 15 winners were aged either five (10) or six (4), with five-year-olds boasting a much stronger record in this race than they do in Cheltenham's Baring Bingham. The past three winners were all aged five.

RESPECT MARES

THERE were no mares in the field last year, but *Brighterdaysahead* struck in 2024 and Kateira (one of two runners in 2023) finished runner-up at rewarding odds. Before her, the likes of Momella, Whiteoak, Baby Shine and Utopie des Bordes all hit the frame and it seemed only a matter of time before a high-class mare would land this prize. Formerly in here for place purposes, this subsection holds more weight since the victory of *Brighterdaysahead* and in receipt of the 7lb sex allowance, mares should be respected.

OTHER TRAINERS TO NOTE

THE record of Gordon Elliott has been covered in an earlier subsection, whilst fellow leading Irish trainer **Willie Mullins** won back-to-back Merseys in 2015 and 2016 with *Nichols Canyon* and *Yorkhill*. At the time, Mullins didn't send as many horses to Aintree, but that pairing wore the silks of Andrea and Graham Wylie, based in the North East of England, which is likely part of the reason that they were aimed at this fixture. Between 2016 and 2023, Mullins only had one runner in this race but then saddled both Jimmy du Seuil and Ile Atlantique in 2024, and again saddled two last year, third-placed Funiculi Funicula and Kappa Jy Pyke.

Paul Nicholls got to within a ½ length of adding a fifth Mersey to his tally last year, with his four wins coming between 2004 and 2014. All four of Nicholls' winners were stepping up in trip, as was last year's runner-up Regent's Stroll, so look for a horse with that profile representing the former champion trainer.

Spirit Son and *Simonsig* went back-to-back for **Nicky Henderson** in 2011 and 2012 respectively, but since Utopie des Bordes finished second the following year, he hasn't troubled the judge. Lulamba was set to represent his stable last year, but with him a late non-runner, his record during the past dozen years remains at 0-9, with those Seven Barrows' *'losers'* including 2018 beaten favourite, On The Blind Side.

My Drogo is the only winner in the race for **Dan Skelton** thus far, but Three Musketeers, Captain Forez, Momella and Kateira have all hit the frame and Skelton often targets this race with a horse who bypasses the Cheltenham Festival.

With Colin Tizzard successful in both 2017 and 2019, and having saddled the runner-up in 2018 when Lostintranslation went close, it is clearly a race which the Tizzards like to target. **Joe Tizzard** is now *'officially'* in charge, of course, but I suspect that this race will be in the minds of their team, given that fairly recent run of form in it.

ROLL OF HONOUR

Year	Form	Winner	Age	Weight	OR	SP	Trainer	Runners	Last Race (No. of days)
2025	211	Honesty Policy	5	11-7	135	5/1	G Elliott (IRE)	9	1st Leopardstown Nov. Hdl (34)
2024	1112	Brighterdaysahead	5	11-0	143	6/5F	G Elliott (IRE)	8	2nd Gr.2 Dawn Run Mares' Nov. Hdle (30)
2023	12241	Irish Point	5	11-7	148	5/1	G Elliott (IRE)	14	1st Gr.3 Naas Nov. Hurdle (34)
2022	1222	Three Stripe Life	6	11-4	150	5/2F	G Elliott (IRE)	12	2nd Gr.1 Baring Bingham Nov. Hdle (24)
2021	2111	My Drogo	6	11-4	150	5/4F	D Skelton	12	1st Gr.2 Kelso Nov. Hurdle (35)
2020	NO RACE - meeting cancelled								
2019	3711	Reserve Tank	5	11-4	139	20/1	C Tizzard	9	1st Kempton Nov. Hurdle (21)
2018	4122	Black Op	7	11-4	152	3/1	T George	12	2nd Gr.1 Baring Bingham Nov. Hdle (31)
2017	111	Finian's Oscar	5	11-4	149	3/1F	C Tizzard	13	1st Listed Exeter Nov. Hurdle (55)
2016	1111	Yorkhill	6	11-4	156	30/100F	W Mullins (IRE)	6	1st Gr.1 Baring Bingham Nov. Hdle (24)

LEADING TEN-YEAR GUIDES

Baring Bingham Novices' Hurdle 3 (*Yorkhill* 1st, *Black Op* 2nd, *Three Stripe Life* 2nd)
Formby Novices' Hurdle (former 'Tolworth') 2 (*Yorkhill* 1st, *Finian's Oscar* 1st)

LIVERPOOL HURDLE
3m 149y (Grade 1)

OVERVIEW
FORMERLY staged at Ascot, the newly-named Liverpool Hurdle was switched to Aintree in 2004, when initially positioned as race one of the three-day fixture. Handed Grade 1 status in 2010, it was won for four successive years between 2009 and 2012 by the top class stayer *Big Buck's*, before the race moved to Grand National day the following year. The first running of the race (as it is now) was won by *Iris's Gift*, whilst other modern greats such as *Monet's Garden* and *Thistlecrack* feature among the list of previous winners. Previous form at this fixture is very much a positive.

MULTIPLE WINNERS
SINCE the race moved to Aintree, we have seen four horses win it more than once, with *Big Buck's* the obvious standout. Prior to the four-time winner, *Mighty Man* was successful in both 2006 and 2007, whilst more recently, *Whisper* went back-to-back in 2014 and 2015, as did *Sire du Berlais* in 2022 and 2023. *Strong Leader* was unable to add his name to the tally last year, with Olly Murphy's stable star finishing just under 3 lengths off *Hiddenvalley Lake*. He has been in consistent form this season and this will likely be his spring target once again, as he bids to become the first horse to reclaim their crown in the race. Last year's winner only reappeared on 8th February and will also likely be aimed at the race once again.

CHELTENHAM FESTIVAL FORM
INTERESTINGLY, the past two winners bypassed Cheltenham and arrived at Aintree on the back of a break of 77 and 72 days, respectively. However, since the race was moved to Aintree – and all trends are based on the past 21 runnings (and not when the race was staged at Ascot) – 16 of those previous 19 winners had run at the Cheltenham Festival.

A dozen of the 16 had run in the **Stayers' Hurdle** on their most recent start and since 2010 – when this race was upgraded, so penalties were no longer an issue – only eight Stayers' Hurdle winners have come on to Aintree and six have won. And, with four weeks between the fixtures this year (30 days between the two races), it is more likely that we will see the Stayers' winner in action in this very race.

Mighty Man twice finished placed in the Stayers' before winning this race, whilst *Blazing Bailey* finished fourth ahead of his win in 2008. Having won the Coral Cup before his first Liverpool Hurdle success in 2014, *Whisper* finished fifth in the Stayers' the following year.

Two successive winners, not so long back – *Yanworth* and *Identity Thief* – had contested the **Champion Hurdle** on their latest start, before stepping up markedly in trip. The Aintree Hurdle would have seemed a more logical target for both at the time, but both took the huge rise in distance in their stride and strong form over 2m shouldn't be underestimated here. As with the Stayers' Hurdle, those with Grade 1 form over much shorter can prove effective over a staying trip later in their careers. Such horses often hold a class edge over out-and-out stayers.

PREVIOUS AINTREE FORM
THE aforementioned *Multiple Winners* clearly aid this statistic, but this is another race in which form at

this fixture is a huge positive. Last year's winner had finished third in 2024, so *Hiddenvalley Lake* became the 15th winner (of the 21) to have recorded a top-three finish at this meeting previously. The earlier 14 had either won or finished second, so pay healthy respect to strong form at the Grand National meeting.

Mighty Man had won the **Top Novices' Hurdle** before his back-to-back wins in the race and *Strong Leader* was a fast-finishing second in the same 2m contest the year before his victory.

Over 2m4f, both *Monet's Garden* and *Blazing Bailey* had finished runner-up in the **Mersey Novices' Hurdle**, although the latter won this race two years after his second in that contest, which was last year won by Honesty Policy. He ran well in the Long Walk Hurdle on his first start out of novice company and is on course for the Stayers' Hurdle at Cheltenham at the time of writing. Given that he has had such a light campaign and that Gordon Elliott will likely prefer to keep him and Teahupoo apart after Cheltenham (with Punchestown the other option), it is highly likely that he will be considered for another trip to Liverpool.

Both *Iris's Gift* and *Thistlecrack* had won the **Sefton Novices' Hurdle**, over the exact same course-and-distance, whilst four-time winner *Big Buck's* had won the **Mildmay Novices' Chase** 12 months before his first Liverpool Hurdle success. *Solwhit* was a previous (four years earlier) **Aintree Hurdle** winner, whilst *If The Cap Fits* had run well in the Grade 2 bumper a couple of years before winning this race.

OTHER KEY RACES

IN TERMS of *Key Races* from earlier in the season, the two obvious races during the first half of the season for stayers in Britain are Newbury's **Long Distance Hurdle** and the Long Walk at Ascot. *Thistlecrack* and *Thyme Hill* are recent winners who contested both races and the Newbury race saw Impose Toi beat *Strong Leader* in November. Looking back a little further and five of the past 15 winners had won this Grade 2.

The pair went on to re-oppose in the **Long Walk Hurdle** at Ascot shortly before Christmas and the outcome was the same (level weights on this occasion), with Impose Toi gaining a first Grade 1 success. He had the aforementioned Honesty Policy (same ownership) back in third and had earlier won on reappearance here at Aintree, in handicap company. Nicky Henderson's eight-year-old also ran well in the 2m4f handicap hurdle at this meeting in 2025, finishing fourth behind Wellington Arch under joint top-weight. *Hiddenvalley Lake* finished runner-up in the Long Walk last season, so three of the past nine winners had run at Ascot.

KEY TRENDS

⭐ Stayers' Hurdle winners are 6-8 since the race became a Grade 1 (2010)

⭐ 15 of the 21 winners (since the race was moved to Aintree) had finished 1st, 2nd or 3rd at this meeting previously (14 of them had finished 1st or 2nd)

✓ 19 of the 21 winners had already won a Grade 1 or Grade 2 (15 of them had been successful in Grade 1 company)

✓ 17 of the 21 winners were aged 6-8 (14 of the past 15 winners were aged 7 or 8)

✓ 16 of the 21 winners had run at the Cheltenham Festival

✓ 15 of the 21 winners returned at 11-2 or shorter (0 of the past 4 winners, however)

✓ 15 of the 21 winners had already won over 3m

✓ 14 of the 21 winners were in the top-2 according to official BHA Ratings

✓ 9 of the 21 favourites have won

✓ 5 of the past 15 winners had won the Long Distance Hurdle at Newbury

✓ 4 of the past 7 winners were trained by Henry de Bromhead or Goron Elliott (2 wins apiece)

✓ 3 of the past 8 winners had run in the Ascot Hurdle (2m3½f)

✓ Horses rated 170+ are 6-7 since 2004

✓ Respect Grade 1 form over 2m

✓ Respect novice hurdle form from this meeting

✗ Only 2 of the 21 winners were aged 10+

✗ Only 3 of the 21 winners were rated below 155

✗ Only 5 of the 21 winners returned at odds greater than 7-1

✗ Dan Skelton-trained runners are 0-7 during the past 8 years

✗ No 5yo winner since the race was moved from Ascot to Aintree

Both *Thistlecrack* and *Strong Leader* contested the **Cleeve Hurdle** at Cheltenham on trials day, a race which is often the biggest pointer towards Festival success in the Stayers'. Both Impose Toi and *Strong Leader* finished in behind Emma Lavelle's Ma Shantou in this year's Cleeve.

And, over a shorter trip, the early-season **Ascot Hurdle** has also been a good guide in recent years, with three of the past eight winners having contested the 2m3½f event. *Yanworth* and *If The Cap Fits* completed the double, whilst *Strong Leader* finished runner-up, in a race which was won this season by the mare Wodhooh, who beat Celtic Dino. Runner-up in the Aintree Hurdle last year, that would seem a more likely target for Gordon Elliott's six-year-old.

PROVEN CLASS

19 OF THE 21 winners had already won a Grade 1 or Grade 2 contest, with 15 of the 19 having been successful at the very top level. *Whisper* (ahead of his first win) and *Strong Leader* are the only outliers, with *Hiddenvalley Lake* adding to the tally last year, by virtue of his win in the Boyne Hurdle the previous February. His narrow second in the Long Walk also proved that he was up to this level and having strong form in the book is a pre-requisite here.

OFFICIAL BHA RATINGS

LAST year's winner was rated 155 going into the race and only three of the 21 winners were rated below this, so use this figure as the benchmark/starting point. 14 of the 21 winners were either top-rated or second in that respect, so focus on the higher-rated individuals. Only seven horses rated 170+ have ever contested this race and six were successful. Such a lofty rating is quite rare for a staying hurdler, with *Iris's Gift*, *Big Buck's* (x4) and *Thistlecrack* the winners in question. Look upwards from mid/high 150s, paying greater respect to any horse rated 160 and above.

MARKET FORCES

THE past four winners returned at 16-1, 8-1, 8-1 and 12-1, respectively, which suggests that the market doesn't always reflect the chance of horses in this race. *Big Buck's* justified odds-on favouritism in each of his four years of success, whilst *Solwhit* was another winning favourite the following year. Since then, however, we have only seen three successful favourites in the past 11 renewals, and from what was once quite a predictable race – in terms of market position – (with 15 of the 21 winners returning at 11-2 or shorter) recent results suggest that has become a much more open race than the betting might suggest.

AGE

SINCE the race moved to Aintree, only *Sire du Berlais* has proven successful in double digits (twice), whilst only *Big Buck's* and *Solwhit* have scored as nine-year-olds. With no five-year-old winner of the race (since the switch from Ascot), the other 17 winners were aged between six and eight, which is very much the age bracket to focus on. There has actually only been one successful six-year-old in the past 15 renewals, so the prime age range is clearly seven or eight.

STAMINA

15 OF THE 21 winners had already registered a win of some sort over 3m, with *Hiddenvalley Lake* a Grade 3 winner over the trip as a novice. *Strong Leader* hadn't proven his stamina prior to his win, whilst recent winners *Yanworth*, *Identity Thief* and *If The Cap Fits* were all stepping up quite markedly in trip, so again, tactical speed is a positive. However, having that proven stamina in the form book is certainly a positive, especially if we get a truly-run race (wasn't the case last year).

THE IRISH CHALLENGE

BETWEEN 2004 and 2017, *Solwhit* was the only Irish-trained winner of the Liverpool Hurdle, although they have now won four of the past seven renewals, thanks to *Identity Thief*, *Sire du Berlais* (twice) and *Hiddenvalley Lake*. There has definitely been a greater Irish representation in the past couple of renewals, which suggests that it is a race which the leading Irish trainers are now beginning to target more seriously.

As for important races in the Irish calendar, *Sire du Berlais* had run in both the **Lismullen Hurdle** and Leopardstown's Christmas Hurdle in each of his winning seasons. The former – a Grade 2 staged over 2m4f at Navan in the early part of the season – was won this season by Colonel Mustard, whilst the **Christmas Hurdle** was won in impressive fashion by 2024 Stayers' Hurdle winner Teahupoo.

TWO UP FOR HDB & ELLIOTT

DURING those past seven renewals, two Irish trainers have struck twice, with **Gordon Elliott** saddling *Sire du Berlais* to back-to-back victories. He was set to be well represented last year, until pulling out Teahupoo due to the drying ground, whilst The Wallpark came home in fourth place. With Teahupoo and Honesty Policy towards the top of the ante-post market for the Stayers' Hurdle, Elliott holds a very strong hand in this division again this season and as a result, is likely to target the Liverpool Hurdle.

Henry de Bromhead saddled *Identity Thief* to win in 2018 and *Hiddenvalley Lake* provided him with a second Liverpool Hurdle success last year. As touched upon when covering earlier races, both Elliott and de Bromhead have been associated with sending strong teams to Aintree in recent years and they have been rewarded in this Grade 1. During the past decade, de Bromhead has only run his two winners, so boasts impressive form figures of 131 in this race.

McMANUS WITH THREE ON THE BOARD

LEADING owner **JP McManus** has won the race three times in the past eight renewals, thanks to *Yanworth* and *Sire du Berlais* (twice). Responsible for the runner-up in 2014 (At Fishers Cross), McManus had the one-three in 2022 when Champ finished third, whilst The Wallpark finished fourth in his silks last year. During the past 11 renewals,

McManus-owned runners have a record of 3-10, and this year he will have the option of both Impose Toi and/or Honesty Policy.

BRITISH TRAINERS TO NOTE

IN RECENT years, there hasn't been a standout in this regard, although **Alan King** is the only British trainer to have won the race with more than one horse. Successful with *Blazing Bailey* in 2008, he saddled *Yanworth* to score nine years later but hasn't had a runner since.

Paul Nicholls' four wins were all gained courtesy of *Big Buck's*, whilst both **Nicky Henderson** and **Henry Daly** have each struck twice, but *Whisper* provided the former with his two wins, and *Mighty Man* did the same for the latter.

And, although Roksana has twice finished runner-up in the race, **Dan Skelton** has yet to win this race, despite having had a runner in seven of the past eight renewals. Another trainer that likes to target Aintree, he has yet to find the required winning formula.

Ma Shantou wins the Cleeve Hurdle

ROLL OF HONOUR

Year	Form	Winner	Age	Weight	OR	SP	Trainer	Runners	Last Race (No. of days)
2025	27	Hiddenvalley Lake	8	11-10	155	12/1	H de Bromhead (IRE)	11	7th Gr.2 Galmoy Hurdle (72)
2024	0243	Strong Leader	7	11-10	150	8/1	O Murphy	10	3rd Gr.2 Cleeve Hurdle (77)
2023	55P41	Sire du Berlais	11	11-10	160	8/1	G Elliott (IRE)	10	1st Gr.1 Stayers' Hurdle (30)
2022	2P40	Sire du Berlais	10	11-7	156	16/1	G Elliott (IRE)	8	11th Pertemps Final (23)
2021	12	Thyme Hill	7	11-7	162	5/2F	P Hobbs	15	2nd Gr.1 Long Walk Hurdle (112)
2020	NO RACE - meeting cancelled								
2019	2132	If The Cap Fits	7	11-7	152	7/1	H Fry	15	2nd Gr.2 Fontwell Hurdle (41)
2018	624	Identity Thief	8	11-7	153	14/1	H de Bromhead (IRE)	10	4th Gr.1 Champion Hurdle (32)
2017	111D	Yanworth	7	11-7	163	9/4F	A King	11	disq. Gr.1 Champion Hurdle (25)
2016	21111	Thistlecrack	8	11-7	174	2/7F	C Tizzard	6	1st Gr.1 Stayers' Hurdle (23)

LEADING TEN-YEAR GUIDES

Stayers' Hurdle 2 (*Thistlecrack* 1st, *Sire du Berlais* 1st)
Long Walk Hurdle 3 (*Thistlecrack* 1st, *Thyme Hill* 2nd, *Hiddenvalley Lake* 2nd)
Long Distance Hurdle 2 (*Thistlecrack* 1st, *Thyme Hill* 1st)
Lismullen Hurdle 2 (*Sire du Berlais* 2nd & 5th)
Christmas Hurdle 2 (*Sire du Berlais* PU & PU)
Cleeve Hurdle 2 (*Thistlecrack* 1st, *Strong Leader* 3rd)
Ascot Hurdle 3 (*Yanworth* 1st, *If The Cap Fits* 1st, *Strong Leader* 2nd)
* denotes previous season

HALLGARTEN MAGHULL NOVICES' CHASE
1m7f 176y (Grade 1)

OVERVIEW
FIRST staged in 1954, the Maghull – which like the Melling Chase and Sefton Novices' Hurdle is named after a surrounding area – was handed Grade 1 status in 1995. The speed test has been won down the years by greats such as *Night Nurse, Ask Tom, Direct Route, Flagship Uberalles, Well Chief, Finian's Rainbow, Sprinter Sacre, Douvan, Shishkin* and *Jonbon*. The Arkle Trophy is often the best pointer towards success here, although *Kalif du Berlais* – who provided trainer Paul Nicholls with a record-extending eighth win in the race – bypassed the Festival in favour of this race last year.

ARKLE TROPHY
WITH the exception of 2001, when the Festival was lost due to the Foot And Mouth outbreak, every single winner of the Maghull between 1993 and 2009 had run in the **Arkle Trophy** at Cheltenham. Between 2010 and 2018, only three of the nine winners ran in the Arkle last time out, whereas four of the past six winners had contested the Arkle, which remains the key piece of form to start with, when assessing this race. Recent winners *Jonbon* and *Found A Fifty* finished runner-up at Cheltenham, whilst between 2008 and 2021, only four Arkle winners contested the Maghull and all four were successful.

The quartet in question were *Tidal Bay, Sprinter Sacre, Douvan* and *Shishkin*, whilst the only Arkle winner to have contested the race since is *Edwardstone*, beaten by *Gentleman de Mee* four years ago. Going back a little further and both *Flagship Uberalles* and *Well Chief* were another pair to complete the famous double, whilst since 1997, nine winners had finished second (7) or third (2) at Cheltenham, so pay healthy respect to any runner here who performed well in the Arkle. With the four-week gap between fixtures this year, there are 32 days between the two races.

OTHER KEY RACES
BEFORE we start to look at other novice chases staged throughout the season, looking back 13 months to the previous season's **Supreme Novices' Hurdle** is a good policy, with four of the past 13 winners having contested that race. *Douvan* and *Shishkin* were able to claim the double, whilst *Sprinter Sacre* and *Jonbon* had hit the frame in the Supreme, a race which was won last year by Kopek des Bordes, with Romeo Coolio back in third. The latter came on to Aintree and finished runner-up in the Top Novices' Hurdle and will likely be considered for a trip to Liverpool once again, where the Manifesto might prove to be a more suitable target.

Two of the past 11 winners had run in the **Henry VIII Novices' Chase** at Sandown and the opening Grade 1 of the campaign in this division was won back in December by Lulamba.

Both *Sprinter Sacre* and *Shishkin* had won the **Wayward Lad Novices' Chase** at Kempton over Christmas, a path which Nicky Henderson likes to take with his leading novice chaser when possible. He didn't run Lulamba in this season's race, however, and the Grade 2 went the way of Mambonumberfive, who ran in the Anniversary Hurdle last year.

Four of the past 14 Maghull winners had run in Warwick's **Kingmaker Novices' Chase**, as had a further four winners between 1997 and 2002. Six of those eight winners had won the Grade 2 contest which takes place in February – the most recent being *Jonbon* – and this year's race was won by Sam Thomas' Steel Ally.

Over in Ireland, both *Douvan* and *Found A Fifty* had won the **Racing Post Novice Chase** at Leopardstown's Christmas fixture and after a one year hiatus, the Grade 1 returned this season. The 2m1f contest was won by the aforementioned Romeo Coolio.

Douvan and *Found A Fifty* also returned to Leopardstown to contest the **Irish Arkle** at the Dublin Racing Festival, with the former successful in that Grade 1, too. Romeo Coolio also won this year's Irish Arkle, beating Kargese by a neck.

THE 'FRESH' ANGLE

UNTIL recently, considering horses for the Maghull who had bypassed the Festival wasn't really a consideration but *Kalif du Berlais* became the eighth such winner in the past 15 renewals, so those horses deserve due respect these days, too. Last year's winner was last seen disappointing in the Scilly Isles over 2m4f and interestingly, became Paul Nicholls' fourth winner in a row to have avoided Cheltenham (more of that anon). Several of these winners were competing at a lower level earlier in the campaign – with last year's winner successful in a couple of novice handicaps, for example – so don't be too put off by a horse seemingly *'climbing the ladder'* so to speak.

CURRENT FORM

PRIOR to last year, four of the previous *'fresh'* winners arrived at Aintree on the back of a victory. So, if looking towards a horse who skipped Cheltenham, favour those last time out winners. Including those who ran in the Arkle, 15 of the past 21 winners finished either first or second on their latest start, so arriving in form is certainly a positive. Interestingly, since 1998, five last-time-out fallers have won the Maghull, with four of those coming down in the Arkle, the last being *Ornua* in 2019.

CHASING EXPERIENCE

SINCE 2008, only two winners were able to land the Maghull on the back of three previous chase starts and the last of those came back in 2013. Seven of the past 10 winners had run exactly four times over fences previously, which is the optimum (and minimum) number. Since 2014, we have seen four winners register between five and 10 previous chase starts, so experience can be advantageous.

KEY TRENDS

- Arkle winners are 4-5 since 2008
- Henry de Bromhead-trained runners are 3-9 since 2013
- 8 of the past 25 winners were trained by Paul Nicholls
- 21 of the past 28 winners returned at odds of 7-2 or shorter
- 16 of the past 17 winners were aged 6-8 (11 of the past 13 winners were aged 6 or 7)
- 15 of the past 18 winners had run 8 times or less over hurdles
- 13 of the past 17 winners finished 1st or 2nd last time out
- 11 of the past 17 winners had won 3+ times over fences
- 11 of the past 18 winners were French-bred
- 11 of the past 14 winners were in the top 3 on official BHA Ratings (the past 5 were in the top 2)
- 8 of the past 28 winners finished 1st or 2nd in the Kingmaker Novices' Chase at Warwick
- 8 of the past 15 winners did not run at the Cheltenham Festival
- 6 of the past 12 winners were trained in Ireland (3 of them bypassed Cheltenham)
- 4 of the past 14 winners were trained by Nicky Henderson
- Willie Mullins-trained runners are 2-3 since 2016
- JP McManus owned the winner in 2022 & 2023 (3 winners in total for the owner)
- Respect flat track form
- No 9yo winner since 1973
- Only 1 5yo has won since the age allowance was removed (last year)
- Only 1 of the past 28 winners returned at odds greater than 6-1
- Only 1 of the past 27 winners was British-bred
- Only 2 of the past 26 winners finished unplaced (when completing) last time out
- Only 2 of the past 17 winners had run just 3 times over fences previously
- Only 2 of the past 17 winners had won just once over fences previously

WINNING EXPERIENCE

IN TERMS of races won over fences, only two of the past 17 winners had won just once, with 11 of those 17 having won three times or more. Therefore, look for a horse with a minimum of two chase victories to their name, whilst we have (surprisingly) seen just four *'unbeaten'* winners (unbeaten over fences that season) this century. *Well Chief* was the first of those when making it 3-3 over fences in 2004 (won the Arkle on just his second chase start), whilst the three since were also Arkle winners.

FLAT TRACK FORM

WHEN looking at the *Other Key Races* subsection, you will note that the Wayward Lad (Kempton) and Kingmaker (Warwick) take place on flat tracks and form at such venues is certainly worth noting, with other recent Maghull winners having proven successful at courses such as Doncaster and Musselburgh. The emphasis on these tracks is often on speed and accurate jumping, both important factors at Aintree.

BREEDING

11 OF THE past 18 winners were French-bred, so pay utmost respect to any such runner this year. There were just two French-bred runners last year, but they dominated the market and *Kalif du Berlais* added his name to a recent list which includes the likes of *Douvan* and *Jonbon*. If looking back a little further, 14 of the past 25 winners were French-bred and all eight of Paul Nicholls' winners ticked this box.

In contrast, only one British-bred horse has won the Maghull in the past 27 renewals, whilst German-breds have a decent record from a small pool of runners. Both *Well Chief* and *Foreman* matched this profile in the early part of the century.

AGE

BETWEEN 1954 and 1998, there was only one winning five-year-old, but we then saw four in the space of nine years, with *Flagship Uberalles*, *Armaturk*, *Le Roi Miguel* and *Twist Magic* (all Paul Nicholls-trained, incidentally) successful for that age group, in receipt of an age allowance. However, that allowance was removed the following year (2008), when Nicholls' Takeroc finished runner-up to *Tidal Bay* off level weights, and until last year, there had been no five-year-old winner of the Maghull as a level weights contest. *Kalif du Berlais*, who sadly suffered a fatal injury at Kempton in January, jumped beautifully en route to scoring and it will be interesting to see if this is a turning point. It is certainly something which Lulamba will need to overcome, if heading to Aintree after the Arkle. Mambonumberfive is another five-year-old who might be Aintree bound, for either this race or the Manifesto.

Prior to 2025, the previous 16 winners were aged between six and eight, with 11 of the past 13 winners being aged six or seven, which is the ideal age bracket (eight is a little old for a modern-day novice chaser, in truth).

QUICKLY SENT CHASING

AS WITH the earlier novice chases covered – both at Cheltenham and at Aintree – being sent chasing after just one season over hurdles is very much preferable, with 15 of the past 18 winners having raced no more than eight times over hurdles. The past five winners, for example, had run either four or five times over hurdles only, with *Kalif du Berlais* sent chasing on the back of four runs in juvenile company (one in France and three in Britain). I am a big advocate of horses being sent chasing from an early age.

OFFICIAL BHA RATINGS

PRIOR to last year, three of the previous four winners were officially top-rated, whilst the other was second best, as was *Kalif du Berlais* last year. Therefore, the past five winners hailed from the top two on *Official BHA Ratings*, with 11 of the past 14 falling into the top-three. Looking towards horses rated mid-high 150s is often a good guide, although *Sprinter Sacre*, *Douvan* and *Shishkin* were all rated in the 160s on the back of their Arkle victories.

During the past 11 renewals, we have seen just two winners rated below 151, those being *Sizing Granite* and *Diego du Charmil*.

MARKET FORCES

DO NOT expect to see a *'shock'* result here, with only one of the past 28 winners returning at odds of greater than 6-1, that being the 128-rated *Special Tiara*. He later developed into a high-class two-miler, but produced an unexpected victory at the time, scoring at 28-1. His victory aside, the winner can often be found towards the head of the market, with eight outright favourites scoring since 2004. The past six winners came from the top two in the betting and that is indicative of the Maghull, with those with stronger form often rising to the top.

TACTICS

THIS is another race on the Mildmay chase track which favours those who like to be ridden positively and the performance of *Kalif du Berlais* last year was just about perfection for this course, the five-year-old dominating a small field with an exemplary round of jumping. If a good jumper, such as him, is allowed an uncontested lead, they can prove difficult to peg back around Aintree, especially on decent ground, so pay close attention to any such runner this year.

EIGHT UP FOR NICHOLLS

AS HAS been touched upon in the *Overview* and several subsections since, trainer **Paul Nicholls** has enjoyed great success in this race, winning the Maghull on eight occasions since 1999 when *Flagship Uberalles* struck under a young Joe Tizzard. Victories with *Armaturk* and *Le Roi Miguel* soon followed and he won it with a fourth five-year-old in 2007, *Twist Magic*. *Tataniano* was Nicholls' only winner between 2008 and 2016, but he has since won it with *San Benedeto*, *Diego du Charmil* and *Kalif du Berlais*. All eight of his winners were French-bred horses, aged either five or six, and whilst his first four winners had all contested the Arkle, his latest four winners bypassed Cheltenham. 2017 winner *San Benedeto* was slightly fortuitous, in that he was left in front by the stumbling of Politologue after the final fence, the grey of course also trained in Ditcheat. Respect any runner from the Nicholls yard this year.

HENDERSON HAS FOUR ON THE BOARD

SINCE 2011, **Nicky Henderson** has recorded four wins in the Maghull, with all four having finished either first or second in the Arkle. *Sprinter Sacre* and *Shishkin* completed the double, of course, and it could be that Lulamba is considered for the race this year, with four weeks to recover from the Arkle.

THE IRISH CHALLENGE

THE Irish were out of luck last year, with Touch Me Not and Special Cadeau finishing fourth and fifth (of five) respectively, but Irish-trained horses have won six of the past 12 renewals. Three of this half-dozen bypassed Cheltenham, so don't always expect to see their leading Arkle contenders head to Liverpool, with Punchestown staging a similar contest shortly after.

Henry de Bromhead has won the race three times since 2013, successful with *Special Tiara*, *Sizing Granite* and *Ornua*. The first named pairing arrived at Aintree 'fresh' and were two of the three lowest-rated winners in the past 14 renewals, so don't be alarmed by one from this stable who is seemingly stepping up in class. The trainer excels with 2m chasers and has won the Red Rum Handicap Chase twice in the past six renewals, so pay attention to his runners at the meeting, in general.

Willie Mullins is one who often saves his top novices – both hurdlers and chasers – for Punchestown, but he won this race in 2016 with *Douvan* and in 2022 with *Gentleman de Mee*. He has actually only had three runners in this race in the past nine renewals, so boasts a fine (67%) strike rate in it.

The only other Irish trainer to win the Maghull this century is **Gordon Elliott**, successful with *Found A Fifty* two years ago. As highlighted when previewing other races, Elliott – like de Bromhead – likes to target Aintree, but has actually only had three runners in this race in the past decade, including The Game Changer who finished second in 2016.

THREE UP FOR JP

FORMER classy hurdler *Foreman* provided leading owner **JP McManus** with a first win in the Maghull some 20 years ago, and although he had to wait a long time to win it again, *Gentleman de Mee* and *Jonbon* provided him with back-to-back Maghulls in recent years. Hercule du Seuil finished only fourth (Willie Mullins' recent 'loser') two years ago, but McManus has actually only had four runners in the past 10 renewals and was without representation in seven of those. He is another with a fine recent strike rate as a result and runners in his green and gold hooped silks should be noted.

ROLL OF HONOUR

Year	Form	Winner	Age	Weight	OR	SP	Trainer	Runners	Last Race (No. of days)
2025	F114	Kalif du Berlais	5	11-7	152	15/8	P Nicholls	5	4th Gr.1 Scilly Isles Nov. Chase (63)
2024	12122	Found A Fifty	7	11-7	155	11/8F	G Elliott (IRE)	10	2nd Gr.1 Arkle Trophy (32)
2023	1112	Jonbon	7	11-7	159	2/11F	N Henderson	4	2nd Gr.1 Arkle Trophy (32)
2022	5211	Gentleman de Mee	6	11-4	158	7/2	W Mullins (IRE)	6	1st Gr.3 Flyingbolt Nov. Chase (35)
2021	1111	Shishkin	7	11-4	169	1/8F	N Henderson	5	1st Gr.1 Arkle Trophy (25)
2020	NO RACE - meeting cancelled								
2019	2122F	Ornua	8	11-4	151	3/1JF	H de Bromhead (IRE)	7	fell Gr.1 Arkle Trophy (25)
2018	132F	Diego du Charmil	6	11-4	143	5/1	P Nicholls	6	fell Ascot Nov. Chase (20)
2017	U3111	San Benedeto	6	11-4	150	4/1	P Nicholls	5	1st Ascot Nov. Chase (6)
2016	11111	Douvan	6	11-4	161	2/13F	W Mullins (IRE)	5	1st Gr.1 Arkle Trophy (25)

LEADING TEN-YEAR GUIDES

*Supreme Novices' Hurdle 3 (*Douvan* 1st, *Shishkin* 1st, *Jonbon* 2nd)
Arkle Trophy 5 (*Douvan* 1st, *Ornua* fell, *Shishkin* 1st, *Jonbon* 2nd, *Found A Fifty* 2nd)
Kingmaker Novices' Chase 2 (*Diego du Charmil* 2nd, *Jonbon* 1st)
Ascot Novices' Handicap Chase 2 (*San Benedeto* 1st, *Diego du Charmil* fell)
Racing Post Novice Chase 2 (*Douvan* 1st, *Found A Fifty* 1st)
Irish Arkle 2 (*Douvan* 1st, *Found A Fifty* 2nd)

* denotes previous season

DAY THREE GRAND NATIONAL

RANDOX GRAND NATIONAL
4m2f 74y (Premier Handicap)

OVERVIEW
THE most iconic race in the British racing calendar, the Grand National – like the Gold Cup – needs little introduction. Since the modification of the fences, the reduced distance and the increased prize money, we have continually seen stronger and better quality fields, and a different type of horse is now required to win a modern day Grand National. Younger horses have started to dominate and a bigger, old fashioned chasing type is no longer essential, with smaller, more nimble/agile jumpers able to brush through the top of the famous spruce fences. 2024 winner *I Am Maximus* is a fine example, as he wasn't always a foot-perfect jumper. Classier horses are now contesting – and winning – the National, with the front four in 2024 all previous Grade 1 winners, whilst last year's winner was successful at Grade 2 level as a novice hurdler and defied a lofty rating of 163. Again, he was chased home by a pair of Grade 1 winners, the trio rated between 163 and 167.

MULLINS GOES BACK-TO-BACK
HAVING first won the race back in 2005 with *Hedgehunter*, leading trainer **Willie Mullins** is threatening to run away with the National. He saddled the winner in 2024 and was last year responsible for the first three home, and the fifth and seventh for good measure, helping him claim another British trainers' title by the end of the month.

2024 winner *I Am Maximus* ran a gallant race in second, under top-weight and from a mark of 167, some 8lb higher than his winning mark 12 months earlier. Given the mistake he made at the last, third-placed Grangeclare West looked slightly unfortunate, but last year's result will be remembered for the fact that amateur jockey, Patrick Mullins, son of and assistant to the trainer, rode the winner on what was an unforgettable day for the family.

Mullins ran six horses last year, with Appreciate It (brought down) the only one to finish outside of the first seven. Fifth-placed Meetingofthewaters ran off 148, whereas the other five were all rated 157 or higher, which strongly suggests that the trainer is now intent on running top-class staying chasers in the race and that is surely only likely to continue.

At the time of going to print, last year's winner had yet to reappear. A non-runner in the John Durkan back in November, he does hold an entry in the Gold Cup and will need to run at least once to be eligible to defend his crown (rules state that a horse must have run in six chases, one of which being during the current campaign). With the weights not announced until after the Guide was sent to print this year, a little guesswork is required at this stage, but his current I.H.R.B. Rating is 169, so expect him to carry top-weight from that sort of mark, if he does indeed line up.

THE RISE OF THE YOUNGER HORSE
AS THE quality of runner continues to rise, *'younger'* and less exposed horses are starting to dominate the National, with the past 10 winners all aged nine or younger. *Many Clouds* started the run in 2015, with the five winners before him all double digit aged winners, three 11-year-olds successful between 2012 and 2014. It remains to be seen as to whether or not these *'older'* contenders can cope with the rising stars and the most recent set of statistics suggest not. Such horses are now likely to be vulnerable to those still on the up and capable of showing improved form,

especially with many holding a class edge (Graded performers). The first seven home last year were aged between seven and nine.

Taking it back a little further and 23 of the past 31 winners were aged between eight and 10, but the dominance of such horses is becoming even more apparent. *Noble Yeats* remains the only seven-year-old winner since *Bogskar* in 1940 and it is eight-year-olds who are starting to flourish. The past two winners were aged eight, as were *Many Clouds*, *Tiger Roll* (first win) and *Minella Times*. And, all this from a relatively small pool of runners, certainly in relation to other age groups. Pay utmost respect to a classy eight-year-old.

Back to the seven-year-olds for a moment and four took their chance last year, including beaten favourite Iroko (4th). Despite the victory of *Noble Yeats*, it clearly remains a huge ask for one so young and the consensus at this stage would be to focus on those aged eight and nine.

AINTREE EXPERIENCE

THIS was something which was much more significant, or even relevant, prior to the modification of the fences: of the past 10 winners, only *One For Arthur* and *Tiger Roll* (ahead of his second win) boasting any previous experience of the National course.

Between 2001 and 2009, seven of the nine winners had already raced over the unique fences, whereas of the past 15 winners, just three have ticked this box, the other being *Pineau de Re*. With the fences no longer as daunting, trainers seem more inclined to let their horse see them for the first time on the big day itself, rather than heading to Aintree for *'match practice'* at an earlier stage.

15 of the past 17 winners were having their first start in the race, with many of those yet to see the fences up close in any race (as per the previous paras), whilst only two of the past 41 winners had won or placed in the race previously. This is further evidence as to how difficult it can be to better a placed effort, something which Iroko will likely look to overcome this year. The theory behind the *'first start in the race'* angle is that a horse is unlikely to be as well handicapped on a second visit to Aintree, certainly not if they have been primed for that initial test, rather like in the Gold Cup, but with ratings to factor in, too.

Looking back at some of those winners who did have *Aintree Experience* on their C.V. and both *Pineau de Re* and *One For Arthur* had contested the **Becher Chase** earlier in the season. *Silver Birch* won that contest, although that victory came a couple of seasons prior to his National success. This season's race was won by Twig (beat Mr Vango a short-head), who finished 10th in last year's National.

KEY TRENDS

- ⭐ 15 of the past 17 winners were having their first start in the race
- ⭐ 23 of the past 31 winners were aged 8-10
- ⭐ The past 10 winners were aged 9 or younger
- ⭐ Willie Mullins has trained the past 2 winners (3 in total)
- ✓ Every winners this century had run at least 3 times during the current season (7 of the past 8 winners had run 3 or 4 times)
- ✓ 20 of the past 26 winners were Irish-bred
- ✓ 16 of the past 29 winners returned at 14-1 or shorter
- ✓ 15 of the past 20 winners had won over 3m1f+
- ✓ 13 of the past 26 winners were trained in Ireland (this includes 6 of the past 7 winners)
- ✓ 9 of the past 17 winners had run between 10-14 times over fences (7 of the past 10 winners had run in less than 10 chases)
- ✓ 9 of the past 14 winners finished 1st or 2nd on their latest start (6 of the past 8 winners won last time out)
- ✓ 8 of the past 10 winners were second-season chasers
- ✓ 7 of the past 15 winners finished 1st or 2nd in a bumper (6 were successful and 2 contested a Graded race in that sphere)
- ✓ 6 of the past 9 winners came out of the Irish Point-to-Point sphere
- ✓ 5 of the past 8 winners wore a tongue strap
- ✓ 5 of the past 10 winners were rated 150+
- ✓ 4 of the past 16 winners were French-bred
- ✓ 3 of the past 7 winners wore headgear
- ✓ 3 of the past 9 winners were owned by Gigginstown House Stud
- ✓ 3 of the past 15 winners were owned by JP McManus
- ✓ 2 of the past 8 winners were trained by Lucinda Russell
- ✓ 8yo's boast a fine record (from a relatively small representation)
- ✓ Respect sound jumpers (no falls to their name)
- ✓ Respect form over 3m4f+
- ✗ 0 of the past 11 winners had fallen or unseated more than once (7 had 0 Fs or Us)
- ✗ Only 1 of the past 29 winners was aged 12
- ✗ Only 2 of the past 41 winners had won or placed in the Grand National previously
- ✗ Only 2 of the past 28 winners had fallen more than twice in their career
- ✗ Only 2 of the past 16 winners were rated below 146
- ✗ Only 4 winners this century hadn't won over 3m
- ✗ Only 4 of the past 20 winners failed to record a top-4 finish last time out
- ✗ Nicky Henderson has never trained the winner

Going back to the early part of the century and back-to-back winners *Bindaree* and *Monty's Pass* had both placed in the previous year's **Topham Chase**, a race which takes place over 2m5f on day two of the Grand National meeting. It was won last year by Willie Mullins' Gentleman de Mee, a Grade 1 winner at this fixture as a novice and another example of the trainer being happy to run high-class horses on this track.

FORM AT THIS FIXTURE

AWAY from races over the National fences and eight of the past 16 winners had run at this meeting previously, either over hurdles or on the Mildmay Course. *Corach Rambler* didn't fall into this category, but had won a novices' handicap chase at the track, whilst his stable-mate *One For Arthur* is one of a couple of fairly recent winners (and some placed horses) to have contested the **Sefton Novices' Hurdle** as a youngster. Iroko added his name to the tally of placed horses last year, him having run in the Sefton at the age of five, on the back of winning the Martin Pipe at Cheltenham. Iroko returned to Aintree in 2024 to chase home last year's Gold Cup winner Inothewayurthinkin in the Mildmay Novices' Chase, so boasts a record at this fixture of 324.

2024 – A REDUCED FIELD

IN OCTOBER 2023, it was announced that from 2024, the Grand National field would reduce by six runners, from 40 to 34. Frustratingly for connections of those who missed out, there were two non-runners on the day and (presumably) as a result, reserves were included again last year. In truth, this would have made little difference in 2024, with the non-runners declared after the reserve cut-off point. All 34 faced the starter in 2025, whilst it was announced in January, that we would have 72-hour declarations for the first time this year.

The changes which were implemented in 2024 included a standing start, a reduced on-course parade, slightly smaller open ditches (fences 11 and 27) and the minimum rating for a horse taking part increasing from 125 to 130. That last point is largely irrelevant, however, with a horse rated in the 130s not contesting the National since 2015 and with the smaller field now compressing things yet further (as well as the higher quality horses heading the weights), it is unlikely to ever be a factor moving forward.

The table opposite illustrates the original bottom weight (Official BHA Rating of the 40th horse) in the 10 renewals between 2013 to 2023 (no race in 2020, of course), whilst also including the BHA Rating of the horse numbered 34. The two additional rows simply show the bottom weight from the past two years, which should give an overall feel for the figure required to now get into the National.

	Horse No 40 (OR)	Horse No 34 (OR)
2025	N/A	145
2024	N/A	146
2023	143 (OH 6lbs)	143 (OH 11b)
2022	143	145
2021	145	146
2020	No Race	
2019	142	144
2018	142	144
2017	143	145
2016	145	147
2015	139	140
2014	138	140
2013	137	131

You can clearly see that there has been a rise since 2016 and a mid-140s rating is now the minimum requirement to (likely) get a run.

WEIGHTS AND OFFICIAL BHA RATINGS

THAT previous subsection leads us on nicely to the *Weights And Official BHA Ratings* subsection. Starting with weight and between 1984 and 2004, no horse carried more than 11-stone to success in the National and that was very much a cut-off point at that time. Things have changed since, however, with *Hedgehunter* (11-1), *Don't Push It* (11-5), *Neptune Collonges* (11-6), *Many Clouds* (11-9), *Tiger Roll* (11-5 for his second victory), *I Am Maximus* (11-6) and *Nick Rockett* (11-8) all defying this statistic. Given how the race is developing, this is only likely to continue and those towards the top of the weights appear to have a class edge over those at the bottom.

The fact that both *Minella Times* (10-3) *Corach Rambler* (10-5) carried low weights from a mark of 146 just goes to show how the race has progressed. Indeed, *Minella Times* wore saddle cloth no 35, so wouldn't have even made the cut for the past two years. Last year's bottom weight, Duffle Coat, carried 10-4 from a mark of 145, whilst Kitty's Light carried 10-7 from a mark of 146 in 2024. Given the quality and Grade 1 horses at the top of the weights these days, added to the reduced fields, we could end up seeing a more compressed handicap going forward, with the bottom weights carrying those mid 10-stone amounts.

The table below illustrates the weight carried by the first four home in each of the past 10 renewals, again highlighting how far the race has come, with many more 11-stone+ figures appearing in recent renewals.

2025	11-8 / 11-12 / 11-8 / 10-11	2019	11-5 / 10-11 / 11-0 / 10-4
2024	11-6 / 11-4 / 11-6 / 11-2	2018	10-13 / 10-11 / 10-6 / 11-8
2023	10-5 / 10-6 / 11-0 / 11-11	2017	10-11 / 10-13 / 10-10 / 11-1
2022	10-10 / 11-8 / 11-9 / 11-2	2016	10-7 / 10-8 / 10-6 / 11-1
2021	10-3 / 10-9 / 10-9 / 10-13	2015	11-9 / 10-6 / 10-7 / 10-3

As you can see, the first three home last year carried big weights, with the Willie Mullins-trained trio hailing from the first four in the weights. In terms of *Official BHA Ratings*, the trio were rated between 157 and 163, whilst the first four in 2024 were rated 159, 157, 159 and 155 respectively, further heightening the belief that the better quality horses are beginning to dominate. *Many Clouds* was successful from a mark of 160 in 2015, whilst since *Don't Push It* provided AP McCoy with his National in 2010, six winners were successful from marks in the 150s. Only two of the past 16 winners were rated below 146, those being *Auroras Encore* (137) and *Pineau de Re* (143) who almost certainly wouldn't even get a run these days.

In recent additions of the Guide, I had pointed out that horses rated in the 150s were creeping into the picture in the National, with plenty placed in recent years. And, as a result, the idea of dismissing horses towards the top of the weights should really now be a thing of the past. In fact, I would actively encourage focusing on those rated 150+ and even more towards the top end of the 150s, with the bigger stables seemingly more intent on allowing top-class horses take their chance.

The table below illustrates the *Official BHA Ratings* of each of the first four home in each of the past 10 renewals.

2025	163 / 167 / 163 / 152
2024	159 / 157 / 159 / 155
2023	146 / 147 / 155 / 166
2022	147 / 159 / 160 / 153
2021	146 / 152 / 152 / 156
2019	159 / 151 / 154 / 144
2018	150 / 148 / 143 / 159
2017	148 / 150 / 147 / 152
2016	148 / 149 / 147 / 156
2015	160 / 143 / 144 / 140

STAMINA

PRIOR to 2021, there were only two winners from earlier in the century who hadn't previously won over a minimum of 3m. Since then, however, both *Minella Times* and *Noble Yeats* added their name to this tally, suggesting that it was possibly an evolving trend. *Rule The World* was a maiden over fences coming into the National and his furthest success over hurdles came over 2m4f, although he had finished second in an Irish National, suggesting that *Stamina* wasn't an issue. I am happy to admit that, personally, I was concerned about the trip for *Minella Times* and although I was proven to be wrong in that instance and good form over intermediate trips has been noticeable in recent results, having the requisite stamina is still a big positive ahead of the Grand National. Yes, the race may be slightly shorter and less demanding throughout – smaller jumps surely mean less energy is used/wasted (provided a horse jumps economically) – but the race still takes place over an extended 4m2f and as a result, form over marathon trips is still a plus.

The past three winners had all won over a minimum of 3m1½f or further, meaning that 15 of the past 20 winners had already recorded a win over at least 3m1f, with *I Am Maximus* having won the Irish National over 3m5f. Whilst we no longer need to look for out-and-out stayers, having shown ability to run over long distances is still almost essential.

CHELTENHAM FESTIVAL FORM

EIGHT of the past 18 winners had run at the Cheltenham Festival the previous month and with a four-week gap in place again this year, perhaps trainers will be more inclined to allow their Grand National hopefuls to run at the Festival. Six of the past 11 winners ticked this box, with *Noble Yeats* (9th) and *Corach Rambler* (1st) having contested the **Ultima Handicap Chase** on their previous start. *Bindaree* (7th) also ran in the Ultima before winning the National back in 2002.

In 2015, *Many Clouds* finished sixth in the **Gold Cup** ahead of his National success, whilst *Corach Rambler* also ran in the Gold Cup before attempting to defend his Aintree crown. He sadly got no further than the first fence in 2024, but I suspect that we might see more Gold Cup *'also rans'* take their chance in the National moving forward, such is the level of quality at the top of the weights these days.

Tiger Roll twice won the **Glenfarclas Chase** over the Cross-Country Course at Cheltenham before his brace of National wins, although with that race having reverted back to being a handicap ahead of last year, it remains to be seen as to whether or not we see the same calibre of horse contest it. At the time of going to print, last year's Cross-Country winner Stumptown heads the betting for a repeat success and he is one who could again be considered for Aintree, despite disappointing in 2025.

Tiger Roll had earlier won the **National Hunt Chase** as a novice, a race which the second and third from 2023 had also contested. Another former Graded race which has been converted to a handicap, it was won last year by Haiti Couleurs, who would be a fascinating runner having already collected the Irish and Welsh equivalents. He is set to run in the Gold Cup as things stand.

And, given the direction which the National is taking (classier horses entering the picture), perhaps the **Broadway Novices' Chase** – run in recent years as the **Brown Advisory Novices' Chase** – will begin to have more of an impact. *Many Clouds* ran in the Broadway 13 months before his National success, as had *Comply Or Die*, albeit two seasons before his Aintree victory. Last year's Broadway was won by Lecky Watson, who looks as though he would relish a proper test of stamina.

And, it is worth remembering that both *Don't Push It* and *Pineau du Re* had run in the **Pertemps Network Final Handicap Hurdle** as a prep for Aintree, the former finishing unplaced, whilst the latter finished third.

BOBBYJO IS ON THE RISE

WINNER of the National in 1999, *Bobbyjo* will ever be remembered for being the first of two back-to-back Irish-trained winners, who were very much family orientated successes (similar to last year). Whilst the Walsh family would strike 12 months later with *Papillon*, *Bobbyjo* represented trainer Tommy Carberry and was ridden by his son, the eccentric, but immensely talented, Paul. Four years after his success, Fairyhouse introduced the **Bobbyjo Chase** – a Grade 3 contest which is run over 3m1½f – and three Aintree winners have won that race en route. Interestingly, the three in question were all trained by Willie Mullins, with the past two winners adding to the initial success of *Hedgehunter*. It is clearly a path which Mullins likes to take with a Grand National contender and given that recent record, all eyes will be on Fairyhouse to see who he runs in February. The race is set to take place shortly after publication of the Guide.

OTHER KEY RACES

THREE of the past five winners contested the **Paddy Power Chase** at Leopardstown over Christmas, those being *Minella Times*, *Noble Yeats* and *Nick Rockett*, with the first and last-named both hitting the frame. This season's race was won by Favori de Champdou, with last year's Scottish National winner Captain Cody (Willie Mullins-trained, of course) back in seventh.

The **Irish Grand National** has always been a good guide towards future Aintree success and indeed the aforementioned pairing of *Bobbyjo* and *Papillon* finished first and second in the 1998 renewal, before they won the next two runnings of the Aintree showpiece. *Numbersixvalverde* won the Irish National a year before his Aintree win, whilst more recently *Rule The World* (2nd), *Tiger Roll* (P.U.), *I Am Maximus* (1st) and *Nick Rockett* (7th) all contested the Irish National as novices before winning at Aintree 12 months later. Last year's Fairyhouse race was won by Haiti Couleurs, who was also a novice and has since added a Welsh National to his tally.

Domestically, three of the past 13 winners had run in the **Coral Gold Cup** (formerly the *'Hennessy'*) at Newbury earlier in the season. *Many Clouds* won this race, whilst *Corach Rambler* hit the frame in it, and this season's contest was won by the improving mare, Panic Attack.

Both *Many Clouds* and *Corach Rambler* had run in the **Colin Parker Memorial Intermediate Chase** at Carlisle before Newbury, again the former successful. A nice stepping stone out of novice company, it was won this season by Resplendent Grey, who had earlier shown his staying power when winning the bet365 Gold Cup on the final day of last season. He disappointed in the Coral Gold Cup.

Those same two recent National winners had also run in the Grade 2 **Reynoldstown Novices' Chase** at Ascot the previous season. This again highlights the importance of high-class novice form and the race was won last year by The Changing Man, who came on to Aintree and finished third in the Mildmay and more recently, finished third behind Panic Attack in the Coral Gold Cup.

One For Arthur won the **Classic Chase** at Warwick on his last start before Aintree, whilst *Auroras Encore* finished fifth in the same race. *Corach Rambler* ran in the race as a novice – the year before he won the National – and it is interesting that Lucinda Russell & Michael Scudamore (Russell the trainer of two of those, of course) was set to run Myretown in the race this year. Sadly, the weather put paid to the Classic Chase for a second successive year and instead Myretown, who was sent off favourite for the Coral Gold Cup, ran in the Peter Marsh the following week. .

Looking back at the previous spring once again and back-to-back winners *Neptune Collonges* and *Auroras Encore* had run well in the **Scottish Grand National**, a race which was won last year by the aforementioned Captain Cody.

And, as well as the Bobbyjo, be sure to pay close attention to another couple of races which take place after the Guide goes to print, those being the **Grand National Trial** at Haydock (Saturday 14th February) and the **Premier Chase** (Saturday

28th February) from Kelso. Interestingly, this year's *Grand National Weights Lunch* takes place three days after the Haydock contest, so performances there will be taken into account.

CHASING EXPERIENCE
RATHER in-keeping with earlier subsections – *Rise Of The Younger Horse* and *Age* – we are seeing less-exposed horses win the National these days. Since 2015, only two of the past 10 winners had run more than 13 times over fences previously (*Tiger Roll* x2), whilst seven of the other eight winners had run 10 times or less. The past four winners had run 7, 9, 9, and 8 times respectively over fences, so *Chasing Experience* is certainly becoming less significant. In fact, rather like other handicaps throughout the season, it looks as though we should very much now be leaning towards those with fewer miles on the clock and having that greater scope to improve.

SECOND-SEASON CHASERS
AGAIN, in-keeping with the previous (and earlier) subsections, eight of those past 10 winners were second-season chasers. *Rule The World* was technically a novice, but a second-season novice, so still ticks the box and the only two exceptions to this were *Tiger Roll* (second win in the race) and *Noble Yeats*, who was a genuine novice, but had run seven times. As touched upon already, looking at last year's novices is a positive angle of attack nowadays.

ASSURED JUMPER
NONE of the past 11 winners had fallen or unseated more than once earlier in their careers and seven of them had zero falls or unseats to their name. Three of the past four winners had a blemish free scorecard going into Aintree and although it is difficult to call *I Am Maximus* an *Assured Jumper*, his form figures showed otherwise. Look for a horse with no (or minimal) letters in their form figures, with only two of the past 28 winners having fallen or unseated their rider more than twice.

JUMPING TECHNIQUE
I HAVE referred to a *'modern-day'* Grand National on various occasions and by that, I mean since the changes were made to the race. As we have seen, classier horses now contest the National and with the modifications to the fences over the years, a different type of horse is required. No longer do we need the archetypal staying chaser who jumps big and bold, time wasted in the air is precious and a low, economical jumper is now a positive. The fences can be brushed through these days, so a more nimble and agile mover is ideal. *Tiger Roll*, for example, would likely have struggled in the *'old days'* given his size, whilst French-bred horses (more on that shortly) – with a swifter *Jumping Technique* – are also the kind of horse we should be looking for. A flatter-backed technique, often referred to as a *'French way of jumping'* is definitely more favourable these days, as opposed to a horse who lingers in the air for too long.

CURRENT FORM
BETWEEN 2006 and 2016, *Comply Or Die* – successful in the Eider Chase (which also takes place after publication) – was the only last-time-out winner to score at Aintree, but more recently, six of the past eight winners won on their most recent outing. *Minella Times* finished runner-up, too, so we really should be looking towards an in-form horse and one who arrives at Aintree on the back of a positive run. There are exceptions, of course, with *Many Clouds* having a '6' next to his name, but that sixth place finish came in the Gold Cup, so it was hardly a *'poor run'*.

Of the past 20 winners, only four failed to record a top-four finish on their most recent start, so we really ought to be looking towards those horses who appear to be in a good place.

RUNS THIS SEASON
EACH and every winner this century had run a minimum of three times earlier in the campaign. Seven of the past eight winners had run three or four times earlier that season, which is possibly more realistic nowadays, with many an earlier winner having had six or seven runs. Getting miles into the legs is important during the current campaign and this would have to be a negative towards the chance of last year's winner, should he return.

BREEDING
20 OF THE past 26 winners were Irish-bred and that is to be expected, given that this is a staying steeplechase and such horses are always dominant in terms of representation.

Four of the past 16 winners were French-bred and although the representation of such horses continues to rise in many a top race, they tend to have a much smaller pool of runners in the National, so their strike rate remains most noteworthy. *I Am Maximus* might have been the first French-bred winner since 2014, but he led home a one-two for such runners and they filled the second and fourth spots last year. Often more mature, lean towards the younger French-bred runners.

POINT-TO-POINT BACKGROUND
WHILST the record of Point-to-Point graduates is surprisingly low in the Gold Cup, such horses dominate a lot of races at the Cheltenham Festival these

days and they also have a good record in the National, with *Nick Rockett* adding to the tally last year. He was a winner in that sphere, meaning six of the past nine winners started off in Points. *Rule The World*, *One For Arthur* and *Corach Rambler* were also successful, whilst *Minella Times* was a faller (never fell under Rules, incidentally) and *Noble Yeats* had finished runner-up, beaten a neck. Four of the first six home from last year were Point-to-Point winners.

BUMPER FORM

NICK ROCKETT was also successful in a bumper, with *I Am Maximus* beating Grade 1-winning novice hurdler My Drogo in a Cheltenham bumper when trained by Nicky Henderson. Five bumper winners have won in the past 11 renewals, and whilst perhaps not as significant as a *Point-to-Point Background* at this stage, such form should still be given plenty of respect. Looking back a little further and seven of the past 15 winners had finished first or second in a bumper, whilst five of them had contested a Graded race in that sphere.

THE IRISH CHALLENGE

THERE were four Irish-trained winners during the 50s, the last of which being *Mr What* in 1958 and in between his success and that of *Bobbyjo* in 1999, *L'Escargot* was the one and only Irish-trained winner of the race, during a dismal 40-year period (39 renewals, with the 1993 contest famously voided). *Bobbyjo* really started an Irish revival, however, with *Papillon* following up in 2000, whilst *Monty's Pass*, *Hedgehunter*, *Numbersixvalverde* and *Silver Birch* all won between 2003 and 2007.

That successful period was followed by another relatively *'quiet spell'* between 2008 and 2015, but since then, the Irish have been responsible for seven of the past nine winners. As with most top National Hunt races these days, Irish-trained horses are currently the dominant force and that is certainly the case again here, in a race in which they (historically) once struggled.

HEADGEAR

BEFORE 2018 and the double of the diminutive *Tiger Roll*, *Comply Or Die* was the only winner this century to wear any sort of headgear, David Pipe's winner sporting blinkers to success some 18 years ago. *Tiger Roll* wore cheek-pieces for his first National success and blinkers the following year, whilst *Noble Yeats* also wore cheek-pieces, his aid applied for the first time at Aintree. With those and hoods much more common these days, I would no longer see the *Headgear* angle as the negative that it was once perceived to be. That said, I am still not a huge fan of it being applied to younger horses, personally.

TONGUE-TIED

SUCH aids appear to be popular among winners of staying races at the Cheltenham Festival and although neither of the past two winners wore a tongue strap, five of the previous six winners did. Gordon Elliott is one trainer, in particular, who boasts a good record at the Festival with horses wearing tongue straps, so note any runner from Cullentra House with one fitted this year. *Tiger Roll* wore a tongue strap for his two wins and interestingly, only one of Elliott's five runners in 2025 had one applied (all five wore cheek-pieces).

MARKET FORCES

DURING the late 90s, *Rough Quest* and *Earth Summit* justified favouritism, whilst *Hedgehunter* was the first successful favourite this century. *Comply Or Die* and *Don't Push It* were both sent off joint-favourite, whilst more recently, *Tiger Roll* (second win) and *Corach Rambler* both justified favouritism, whilst *I Am Maximus* returned the 7-1 joint-favourite in 2024. 17 of the past 29 winners returned at 14-1 or shorter and again, since the modifications have been made to the course and restrictions put in place, the race does have a slightly more *'predictable'* feel to it. That said, we have still seen winners at 33-1 (x3), 50s and 66s since 2012, those following on from the 100-1 *'shock'* victory of *Mon Mome* in 2009.

Despite the fact that *Nick Rockett* drifted alarmingly on the day last year (returned at 33-1), five of the past seven winners returned at odds ranging from 4-1 to 11-1, suggesting that the market is starting to reflect the chance of the classier horses these days. The top two in the market from last year still managed to hit the frame, finishing fourth and second, respectively.

THREE UP FOR JP

NOT only did *Don't Push It* provide AP McCoy with his much sought after Grand National success, but he also provided leading owner (and his boss) **JP McManus** with a first win in the race. He went agonisingly close a couple of years later – when Sunnyhillboy was beaten a nose – and during the past 11 renewals, has seen a further 11 horses (including 3 last year) finish in the first five carrying his famous green and gold silks.

Often well represented, he had the first and third in 2021 when *Minella Times* was successful under Rachael Blackmore, and *I Am Maximus* provided him with a third National in 15 renewals when successful two years ago. All three of McManus' winners returned at 11-1 or shorter, so were well found in the market.

Responsible for last year's beaten favourite Iroko, McManus has seven horses entered at the initial entry stage (3rd February).

OTHER OWNERS TO NOTE
THE late Trevor Hemmings won the race three times between 2005 and 2015, those victories gained by *Hedgehunter*, *Ballabriggs* and *Many Clouds*. His famous yellow and green quartered silks are now carried by **Hemmings Racing** but they don't appear to have a suitable candidate this year.

And, more recently **Gigginstown House Stud** have also won the race three times, with *Tiger Roll* (twice) and before that, *Rule The World*. Like McManus, Ryanair supremo Michael O'Leary likes to be well represented at Aintree and although out of luck last year, Delta Work finished second for the owner in 2024. Gigginstown have seven entered this year, including Favori de Champdou and Quai de Bourbon.

OTHER TRAINERS TO NOTE
WITH Willie Mullins covered in an earlier subsection, the other leading Irish trainer to boast a similar National record is **Gordon Elliott**. His first National win came back in 2007 courtesy of *Silver Birch*, before he won back-to-back renewals with *Tiger Roll*. Responsible for the runner-up in 2024, he was also out of luck last year but is sure to have a plethora of runners once again. Elliott has entered a dozen horses for this year's race.

Lucinda Russell – who, of course, now trains alongside **Michael Scudamore** – won the race twice in the space of six years with *One For Arthur* and *Corach Rambler*, and from a much smaller pool of horses than Mullins and Elliott, for example. The Scottish operation focuses on staying chasers and as a result, the National is always likely to remain a high priority. This year, their sole entry is last year's Ultima winner, Myretown, who might struggle to get in (currently rated 142).

Another trainer to have won the race twice is **Nigel Twiston-Davies** – who is also now a joint-licence holder alongside son **Willy** – although his success is more historical, having won the race in 1998 with *Earth Summit* and in 2002 with *Bindaree*. The stable likes to target all races over the National fences and they have entered both Beauport and Top Of The Bill this year.

Finally, the race continues to elude **Nicky Henderson**, who ran both Chantry House (16th) and Hyland (P.U.) last year. Having previously trained *I Am Maximus*, the 2024 renewal was probably a tough watch for Henderson, who has won almost every other big race in the calendar. He has entered Hyland and Mister Coffey this year.

WEIGHTS ANNOUNCED
THE weights for this year's Grand National will be unveiled at St George's Hall in Liverpool on Tuesday 17th February, a week after the Guide was sent to print. Quite often this luncheon falls on the exact day we finalise the pages, so are able to confirm the weights (and ratings) of leading contenders, but that is not the case this year. They should, however, be in the public domain by the time that you read this.

ROLL OF HONOUR

Year	Form	Winner	Age	Weight	OR	SP	Trainer	Runners	Last Race (No. of days)
2025	411	Nick Rockett	8	11-8	161	33/1	W Mullins (IRE)	34	1st Gr.3 Bobbyjo Chase (42)
2024	1431	I Am Maximus	8	11-6	158	7/1JF	W Mullins (IRE)	32	1st Gr.3 Bobbyjo Chase (49)
2023	541	Corach Rambler	9	10-5	146	8/1	L Russell	39	1st Ultima H'cap Chase (32)
2022	1469P29	Noble Yeats	7	10-10	147	50/1	E Mullins (IRE)	40	9th Ultima H'cap Chase (25)
2021	122	Minella Times	8	10-3	146	11/1	H de Bromhead (IRE)	40	2nd Leopardstown H'cap Chase (62)
2020	NO RACE – meeting cancelled								
2019	411	Tiger Roll	9	11-5	159	4/1F	G Elliott (IRE)	40	1st Glenfarclas Chase (24)
2018	2P51	Tiger Roll	8	10-13	150	10/1	G Elliott (IRE)	38	1st Glenfarclas Chase (31)
2017	151	One For Arthur	8	10-11	148	14/1	L Russell	40	1st Gr.3 Warwick Chase (84)
2016	32254	Rule The World	9	10-7	148	33/1	M Morris (IRE)	39	4th Gr.3 Naas Directors Plate (34)

LEADING TEN-YEAR GUIDES

*Irish Grand National 4 (*Rule The World* 2nd, Tiger Roll p.u., *I Am Maximus* 1st, Nick Rockett 7th)
Cross Country Chase 2 (*Tiger Roll* 1st, 1st)
Paddy Power Chase 3 (*Minella Times* 2nd, Noble Yeats 9th, Nick Rockett 4th)
Ultima Handicap Chase 2 (*Noble Yeats* 9th, Corach Rambler 1st)
Coral Gold Cup 2 (*Many Clouds* 1st, Corach Rambler 4th)
Colin Parker Memorial Intermediate Chase 2 (*Many Clouds* 1st, Corach Rambler 5th)
*Reynoldstown Novices' Chase 2 (*Many Clouds* 2nd, Corach Rambler U.R.)
Bobbyjo Chase 2 (*I Am Maximus* 1st, Nick Rockett 1st)

* denotes previous season

RANDOX
Grand National Preview
BY JODIE STANDING

THERE'S always a sense of anticipation as the Grand National edges into view, and this year's renewal is no different, with a new generation of staying chasers taking on the established names who try to hold their ground. Although much has changed with the 'modern' National, the magnetism of the world's most famous steeplechase remains unchanged. Thirty-four runners, thirty fences, and 4¼ miles that tests stamina and jumping prowess in equal measure.

The fences, although more forgiving than they once were, remain a formidable test, but this is no longer a contest for the dour stayers alone. Now the National increasingly favours a classier horse, one that can travel comfortably and hold an early position, but still find depths to their stamina reserves that sometimes have never been tapped before, to get home after crossing the Melling Road for the final time.

With 78 initial entries (down by a dozen on last year), the anticipation builds for this year's race, which promises to be a compelling blend of proven Graded performers and progressive handicappers. Against that backdrop of the iconic Grandstands and the roaring flamboyant crowds, the leading contenders — some proven over these unique obstacles, others stepping into the unknown — form the most intriguing puzzle in jump racing.

As I write in early February, the ante-post favourite is the Oliver Greenall & Josh Guerriero-trained **Iroko**, who finished fourth in the race 12 months ago, beaten 7½ lengths by Nick Rockett. Then a 7-year-old running from a mark of 152, he did best of those held up towards the rear and finished off strongly, suggesting the trip held no fears.

Still a relatively young horse, he could easily find improvement despite being 5lb higher this time around. He is, though, looking in better shape than 12 months ago, having chased home the subsequent King George winner, The Jukebox Man, at Haydock on Betfair Chase day before taking the scalp of Firefox in the Howden Graduation Chase at Ascot — a race in which he fell the previous year.

Willie Mullins has 15 entries, headed by his 2024 champion **I Am Maximus**, who once again sits high in the ratings on 167 after a valiant effort under top weight last year when conditions were perhaps livelier than ideal. Despite having more miles on the clock than some, he remains only 10 and has looked better than ever this term with two excellent efforts in defeat at Leopardstown in December and February, particularly his second to Affordale Fury in the Savills Chase over Christmas. He could, though, be vulnerable to a younger pair of legs.

Last year's winner **Nick Rockett** has yet to be sighted this season, having been withdrawn from the John Durkan in November. He needs a run if he is to defend his title, with the Gold Cup or the Bobbyjo — which he won en route to Aintree last year — the obvious stepping stones. He took to the National fences with relish at the first attempt and remains the type who could follow up, though the delayed start to his campaign and the likelihood of conceding weight across the board are legitimate concerns. Officially, he is top rated on 169, 6lb higher than 12 months ago.

Grangeclare West, third in last year's renewal, is another who commands respect. He finished within 3 lengths of the winner despite a blunder at the last that halted his momentum, and the way he picked up again speaks volumes for his constitution. Without that mistake, the outcome could easily have been different. He returns in similar shape and remains the horse I marked down from last year as the most likely to repeat or better his effort.

Captain Cody already has a National to his name, having captured the Scottish version last season under an ice-cool ride from Harry Cobden, who did not move a muscle until jumping the last before quickening past Klarc Kent to win by a length. Now rated 150, 10lb higher than for that win, his season has been less straightforward, and he fell in the Thyestes at Gowran Park in January. There was encouragement, though, in his seventh behind Favori de Champdou at Leopardstown over Christmas. His engine is not in doubt, but trusting a horse over these fences who has fallen or unseated twice in eight chase starts requires a leap of faith.

Lecky Watson brings Grade 1-winning form courtesy of his Brown Advisory Novices' Chase success, achieved in strong-staying fashion. His campaign since has been less than appealing but a mark of 156 is not beyond the realms of possibility. Untried beyond 3m1f and unlikely to want soft ground, he nevertheless shapes as the type who would relish a thorough test of stamina.

Champ Kiely is worth a second look at 66/1. Although not the most straightforward, he is a Grade 1 winner over 3m1f at Punchestown, a trip he saw out strongly with the sun on his back. His season has been hit-and-miss, but there was plenty to like about how he travelled for a long way in the Irish Gold Cup at the Dublin Racing Festival, only weakening after the last with J J Slevin not being overly hard on him. He could be coming to the boil for a good spring campaign, and it would not be a shock to see him give a bold account.

Spanish Harlem also commands respect. He looked to have the Thyestes in his pocket at Gowran Park in January before a blunder at the last sent his jockey to the floor. Sixth in the Scottish National in 2024, staying on at the finish, he shapes as though this test could be right up his street and at 50/1 he could give followers plenty of fun.

Gavin Cromwell's **Now Is The Hour** was the beneficiary of Spanish Harlem's final-fence mishap in the Thyestes, staying on best from an uncompromising position to collar Better Times Ahead in the dying strides from a mark of 151. An 8lb rise to 159 demands more, but he is a strong stayer and a good run in the National Hunt Chase — his next assignment — would make odds of 33/1 a thing of the past.

Among the others from Closutton, **Appreciate It**, now 12, was brought down in last year's renewal when sent off at 28/1. He has shown good form in two runs this season, but others make stronger appeal. **Impaire Et Passe** has plenty of class but does not strike me as the type for this stamina test, while **High Class Hero** is yet to convince as a thorough stayer.

With the Mullins battalion covered, attention turns to the other challengers, beginning with Dan Skelton's **Panic Attack**, funnily enough, once trained by Mullins to win a Market Rasen bumper. It is hard to believe she is a 10-year-old, as this has been her coming-of-age season. She won the Paddy Power Gold Cup at Cheltenham by 4 lengths from Vincenzo off 135, returned just two weeks later to land the Coral Gold Cup by 6½ lengths from Three Card Brag off 139, and then added a Listed mares' chase at Newbury in January.

Her pedigree would not scream National trip, but she was not stopping at the end of 3m2f in November, and her natural, accurate jumping looks tailor-made for these fences. She is interesting, but she must find another level now rated 147, and she still needs nine to come out to even get into the race (based on ratings alone – both BHA and I.H.R.B. – with the official weights lunch set to take place shortly before publication of this year's Guide).

Rebecca Curtis has a strong contender in **Haiti Couleurs**, already a dual National winner having taken the Irish National off 141 and the Welsh National off 154. Add to that a National Hunt Chase at Cheltenham off 135 and a Pertemps qualifier off 145 on his seasonal debut, and he looks a thoroughly reliable candidate. With stamina in abundance and a prominent, bold-jumping style, he seems certain to give followers a bold show, although he is now rated 166, following his victory in Newbury's Denman Chase.

Another previous National winner in the mix is **Mr Vango**, whose chance would be enhanced by a wet spring. Sara Bradstock's 10-year-old thrives when faced with a searching test, winning two regional nationals over 3m6½f and 3m4½f before landing the Midlands National over 4m2f off 143 last season. He needs to put a poor run at Sandown behind him, but

Grangeclare West (right) ran well last year when third behind Nick Rockett

with experience over the National fences — having finished a short-head second to Twig in December — it is easy to see why he features on many shortlists. A mark of 154 will find him on a nice racing weight.

Olly Murphy's **Resplendent Grey** is another interesting contender. Although he is held on form by Panic Attack and Haiti Couleurs, he is progressing with age and shaped as though the National test would suit him, having won the bet365 Gold Cup at Sandown off 142. Having won the Colin Parker at Carlisle on his reappearance, it was disappointing to see him finish down the field in the Coral Gold Cup, but a solid run behind Protektorat in the Fleur de Lys Chase at Windsor put him back on track. The Gold Cup is his next possible assignment, although the Ultima or the Premier Chase at Kelso look more suitable. He is not without a chance if he takes to the fences, but others make stronger appeal.

Three Card Brag deserves plenty of respect and looks in better shape heading into this year's race, having finished 11th, 45 lengths behind Nick Rockett, 12 months ago. After finishing eighth in the Galway Plate from a mark of 145, the nine-year-old ran a good second to Spanish Harlem in the Kerry National over 3m before getting off the mark for only the second time over fences at Cheltenham in October, beating Backmersackme by just shy of 3 lengths from a mark of 149. He then stayed on well over 3m2f behind Panic Attack in the Coral Gold Cup from a mark of 155. Now only 1lb higher, he will likely head to the Ultima Handicap Chase, and he looks to be relaxing more through his races, giving him a better chance of staying this extreme distance. He is high on my shortlist.

Beauport was my fancy 12 months ago and ran a brave race on the sharp end, but perhaps did too much too early as he didn't get home, eventually finishing 12th, 63 lengths behind Nick Rockett. He did, though, jump the fences beautifully, and if he can harness his enthusiasm a little better, he could be more competitive late on. He is also 3lb lower on a mark of 153, and his odds of 100/1 perhaps do not give him enough respect.

Monty's Star has a pedigree packed with stamina. He has fallen just short of Grade 1 level over fences and although his effort in the Coral Gold Cup — his

Three Card Brag in winning form at Cheltenham in October

first try in a handicap — failed to inspire, there was plenty to like about how he fared in the Irish Gold Cup at the Dublin Racing Festival, where he led approaching the penultimate fence before weakening when the cream came to the top. He has plenty going for him.

Perceval Legallois fell in the race 12 months ago when sent off at 10/1 and pulled up in the Coral Gold Cup behind Panic Attack this season. There was encouragement to be gleaned from his fourth to Heart Wood at Tramore, and although he is likely to be in JP McManus' squad again, others make more appeal.

Venetia Williams has struggled for form this season but could rely on **L'Homme Presse** to put things right. A mark of 164 reflects his class, but this will be a tall order despite his excellent spin behind **Spillane's Tower** in the Cotswold Chase on Trials Day at Cheltenham. The JP McManus-owned winner could also head here and would be interesting if conditions came up soft, though his stamina for this distance is an unknown. Only eight, he has the potential to develop into a National type, and his performance in the Gold Cup, should he take his chance, is eagerly awaited.

The former King George winner **Banbridge** is yet another high-class entry with an Irish mark of 167. Joseph O'Brien's 10-year-old was denied by only a nose in his bid to defend his title at Kempton, doing his best work late on. If the ground came up good, his class could carry him a long way, but he does not strike me as the type who would improve for this distance. The yard could also be represented by **Jordans**, but his profile does not suggest he is a danger.

Grey Dawning is an interesting entry, although the Gold Cup has long been publicised as his main target this season. Dan Skelton could be tempted to roll the dice if the Trainers' Championship looks in the balance, but he's not the sort of horse who appreciates a quick turnaround.

Gordon Elliott's 11-year-old **Favori de Champdou** has steadily crept into the picture following strong-staying performances to win at Leopardstown from a mark of 140, and, more recently, a handicap over the Cross-Country fences at Cheltenham over 3m5½f from 149, forging clear up the hill despite carrying top weight. He has been around the block longer than most, but if he turns up at Aintree in the same frame of mind as his last two races, he could outrun his odds of 50/1.

Firefox is another I would not rule out in a hurry, although he could be more of a serious challenger next year rather than this. His effort to finish fourth on his first try over 3m in the Grade 1 Irish Gold Cup at the Dublin Racing Festival was decent, and a career-high rating of 154 suggests he is still improving.

Elliott's other potential challengers include **Better Days Ahead**, third behind Lecky Watson in last year's Brown Advisory, having won the Martin Pipe the previous season from a mark of 140. Rated on an Irish mark of 153, he would appreciate good ground and finished sixth in last year's Irish National behind Haiti Couleurs. I would fancy him to finish the race, but he needs to improve to win it.

Stellar Story beat The Jukebox Man by a head in the Grade 1 Albert Bartlett at the 2024 Cheltenham Festival and is bred to appreciate a searching test of stamina. An Irish mark of 153 would have him poised towards the lower end of the weights, and he is no forlorn hope at 50/1. **Croke Park**, another Grade 1 chase winner, could also carry the Gigginstown colours, but this may stretch his stamina beyond its means.

Western Fold adds further depth to Elliott's potential team, and his pedigree strongly suggests he will have no trouble with the trip. Although a novice, he has 11 chase starts under his belt, and good ground would pull him even more into the reckoning. The Brown Advisory will be his next port of call, but he has top-class handicap form having won the Galway Plate from a mark of 148. Now on 157, he is one you would rather be with than against.

Gerri Colombe needs to be respected as a top-class stayer but has been a touch disappointing this term. Perhaps this new challenge will spark him back to his best.

Another novice with an interesting profile is **Oscars Brother**. At the time of writing, he has had only five chase starts and requires one more by 24th March to qualify, but he has a rapidly progressive profile and his form continues to work out well. Moreover, JP McManus stepped in to purchase him following his success in a Grade 2 at Punchestown, where he beat the subsequent winner Koktail Divin. Following his victory in the Ten Up Novice Chase, he is now rated 151 and whilst this might not be his year, he is a horse to keep on side, wherever he turns up.

Twig has been an admirable servant for Ben Pauling and regular rider Beau Morgan, giving the team a memorable day when landing the Becher Chase in December, beating Mr Vango by a short head. Although 3lb higher now on a mark of 146, he is far from guaranteed to make the final field at around the mid-40s on the list. **Blizzard Of Oz**, **Leave Of Absence** and **Johnnywho** are three others on the same mark, with the latter two finishing second and third respectively behind Deep Cave at Ascot in December. Johnnywho had a spin over these fences when fifth in the Sefton in November, but this trip could be the making of him.

Pauling has also given an entry to the classy 155-rated **Handstands**, but he does not strike me as a type who wants this stamina test — a comment that also applies to **Ile Atlantique**, another of the Mullins battalion.

Others worth mentioning include **Jagwar**, representing the connections of Iroko. He is only seven and, while I believe he will develop into a National contender, he may need another year or two before he is mentally ready. **Intense Raffles** was a good winner of the 2024 Irish National but did not take to the fences last year and has been disappointing since. **French Dynamite** won the Munster National at Limerick in October but finished down the field in last year's Topham, while **The Real Whacker** has shaped this season as though his better days are behind him. **Gorgeous Tom** hails from the same family as the grand old servant Cappa Bleu and will relish a good-ground National. **Myretown**, **Deep Cave** and **Imperial Saint** all look likely to miss the cut, but each would have appeal if, by some miracle, they were to sneak in.

CONCLUSION:

IT'S impossible to form a strong conclusion at this stage, especially without the weights, but there are a handful of horses who appeal more than others. Top of that list is last year's third, **Grangeclare West**, who relished this test and would undoubtedly have finished closer to the winner but for that momentum-stopping error at the last. His stable companion, **Champ Kiely**, is steadily sneaking onto my radar, while **Spanish Harlem** is a little more proven in these stamina-demanding races.

Gordon Elliott looks to be assembling a strong team with **Western Fold** and **Favori de Champdou** throwing their hats into the ring. However, don't discount **Stellar Story** and **Three Card Brag** too readily, especially the latter who completed last year's race but looks a more professional challenger 12 months on and has the pedigree to relish the trip.

Among the home team, Iroko appears to have the best chance of the British-trained contenders, but **Haiti Couleurs** has all the right attributes to go close.

At the prices, **THREE CARD BRAG** is the one who makes most appeal at this early stage.

ANTE POST ADVICE:

Three Card Brag @ 50-1

Price correct at the time of going to print

PRODUCED BY

WEATHERBYS

WEATHERBYS LIMITED, Sanders Road, Wellingborough, Northants, NN8 4BX
www.bettrends.co.uk +44 (0)1933 304776
ISBN: 978-1-915899-15-6

AUTHOR Paul Ferguson

THANKS TO Rory Delargy, Donn McClean, Jess Stafford, Jodie Standing and Sam Turner. Also, to those at Hollywoodbets, Darly Jacob, Trackside and to photographers John Grossick and those at focusonracing.com (Dan Abraham).

The views, opinions and positions expressed by the authors and those providing comments are theirs alone, and do not necessarily reflect the views, opinions or positions of Weatherbys or any employee thereof. Whilst every effort has been made to ensure the accuracy of the information at the time of publication, Weatherbys will not be liable for any losses arising from its use.

The Cheltenham Festival Betting Guide went to print on Tuesday 10th February.